W9-AKX-139

Comprehensive Classroom Management

Creating Communities of Support and Solving Problems

Vern Jones

Lewis and Clark College

Louise Jones

Beaverton School District

Boston   New York   San Francisco
Mexico City   Montreal   Toronto   London   Madrid   Munich   Paris
Hong Kong   Singapore   Tokyo   Cape Town   Sydney

*To the thousands of teachers and students whose ideas and responses
to the materials in the book have enriched its content
and have been a source of professional and personal satisfaction;
and to our children, Sarah and Garrett,
who teach us so much and bring us so much happiness*

Senior Editor: Arnis E. Burvikovs
Editorial Assistant: Christine Lyons
Marketing Manager: Tara Whorf
Editorial-Production Service: Omegatype Typography, Inc.
Manufacturing Buyer: Andrew Turso
Composition and Prepress Buyer: Linda Cox
Cover Administrator: Linda Knowles
Electronic Composition: Omegatype Typography, Inc.

Library of Congress Cataloging-in-Publication Data

Jones, Vernon F.
    Comprehensive classroom management : creating communities of support
and solving problems / Vern Jones, Louise Jones. — 7th ed.
        p.   cm.
Includes bibliographical references (p.   ) and index.
    ISBN 0-205-38083-2
1. Classroom management. 2. Interaction analysis in education. 3.
Motivation in education. 4. School discipline.   I. Jones, Louise S.
II. Title.

LB3013.J66 2004
371.5'3—dc21

                                                          2003052327

Printed in the United States of America
10   9   8   7   6   5   4   3   2   1   RRD-IN   08   07   06   05   04   03

CONTENTS

PREFACE

PURPOSE

In March 1984, a ten-member Panel on the Preparation of Beginning Teachers, chaired by Ernest L. Boyer, president of the Carnegie Foundation for the Advancement of Teaching, issued a report listing three major areas of expertise needed by beginning teachers:

1. Knowledge of how to manage a classroom
2. Knowledge of subject matter
3. Understanding of their students' sociological backgrounds

Ten years later, Wang, Haertel, and Walberg (1993) conducted a sophisticated data analysis of factors influencing student learning and identified classroom management as being the most important factor. Another decade later, issues of effective classroom management were highlighted by research studies as a key to effective student learning (Shinn, Stoner, & Walker, 2002).

Research findings are supported by the beliefs held by the average U.S. citizen. Since its inception in 1969, the Annual Gallup Poll of the Public's Attitudes toward Public Education has reported student behavior and school discipline to be a leading concern among Americans.

Faced with large class sizes, increasing numbers of students who arrive at school experiencing considerable emotional stress, and classes in which students' academic and behavior skills vary widely, teachers are experiencing a heightened need for increased effectiveness in motivating and managing students. The movement toward increased inclusion of students with various disabilities and the increasing number of students whose first language is not English have increased the complexity of teaching and effectively managing classrooms. Regardless of changes that may be made in the education system, schooling in the United States will not improve significantly unless teachers develop skills in the widely varied teaching methods generally described as classroom management.

Fortunately, technology in classroom management has kept pace with the increasing demands placed on teachers. Research in classroom management has grown explosively in the past thirty years. Most teachers trained in the 1960s learned only such simple prescriptions as "don't smile until Christmas" and "don't grin until Thanksgiving." In recent years, however, thousands of articles and hundreds of thoughtful research projects have focused on student behavior and learning. The concept of school discipline, which had concentrated on dealing with inevitable student misbehavior, was replaced by the concept of classroom management, which emphasized methods of creating positive learning environments that facilitate responsible student behavior and achievement.

Our purpose is to provide the reader with specific strategies for creating positive, supportive, respectful environments that encourage all students to view themselves and learning in a positive light. Our heartfelt desire is that the book will increase each reader's ability to empower students to believe in themselves, understand the learning environment, and view the school as a place where their dignity is enhanced and where they can direct and take credit for their own learning. We agree with Mary McCaslin and Thomas Good (1992), who wrote:

> We believe that the intended modern school curriculum, which is designed to produce self-motivated, active learners, is seriously undermined by classroom management policies that encourage, if not demand, simple obedience. We advocate that a curriculum that seeks to promote problem solving and meaningful learning must be aligned with an authoritative management system that increasingly allows students to operate as self-regulated and risk-taking learners. (p. 4)

Although authors can provide research-proven methods and the theory that supports their use in schools and classrooms, we realize that the teacher is the decision maker. We strongly believe (and the best current educational research supports) that in order to create schools that will help an increasing number of students succeed in life, educators must implement many of the methods presented throughout this book. We acknowledge and respect that teachers must consider each new approach in light of their personal styles and teaching situations; we also know that the methods in this book have proven effective for thousands of teachers. Engaging in thoughtful, reflective decision making before implementing a new approach is the sign of a competent professional; failing to incorporate methods proven effective with a wide range of students is irresponsible professional behavior.

THE NEW EDITION

Comprehensive Classroom Management is divided into five parts. Part I presents an overview of the key concepts associated with classroom management and its relationship to students' basic personal and psychological needs. This overview provides a theoretical foundation for understanding and thoughtfully implementing the practical suggestions in later chapters. Part II focuses on interpersonal relationships in the classroom and on the interaction between school and home as key factors influencing students' behavior and achievement. Part III examines motivation and instruction as major variables influencing student behavior. Part IV provides numerous research-supported, practical strategies for improving classroom organization and management. Part V presents methods for working with individual students who experience ongoing or serious behavior problems.

Unlike previous editions, **this edition is written with a specific focus on individuals in teacher education programs and practicing teachers.** Each chapter includes numerous opportunities for the reader to "Pause and Consider" how the methods and concepts being presented might be incorporated into their teaching, and to share these ideas with other members of their class or faculty. Consultants, such as counselors and administrators, will find this edition presents the same practical strategies and deep understanding of classroom management.

The chapter organization is intended to help you implement that content into your classroom management process. Chapter 1 presents an overview that will help you understand the topic of classroom management. Each subsequent chapter begins with an overview of the chapter's topics and presents research to support the value of incorporating the specific methods presented throughout the chapter. This is followed by specific methods you can implement in your classroom. Each chapter includes activities to help you implement the methods and evaluate the results.

This edition of *Comprehensive Classroom Management* includes innovative methods stemming from new research and the authors' extensive work with school staff throughout the country. **Specific changes include:**

- An emphasis on creating classrooms and schools as communities of support in which students feel valued, understand the learning process, and feel personally connected to their academic work and those who share their work environment
- New strategies for working with students experiencing special needs who are included in the regular classroom
- A greater emphasis on working with a diverse student population
- An increased emphasis on conducting a functional assessment when implementing an individualized behavior change program
- New activities to help the reader examine and develop personal approaches to classroom management
- New case studies to demonstrate the implementation of the methods presented throughout the book
- A focus on the beginning teacher and questions they must answer and methods they will want to consider
- A new Complete Instructor's Manual on CD with sample test items and answers, PowerPoints™ for the text, concept maps, activities, reproducible forms, and links to useful sites
- A new Classroom Vignettes Video, free to adopters, which illustrates management issues in short clips

AUDIENCE

This book is for preservice and in-service teachers, counselors, administrators, school psychologists, and special educators. Its comprehensive and research-based presentation offers practical ideas for creating positive classroom and school climates, organizing and managing classrooms, improving instruction, dealing with classroom discipline problems, developing individualized plans for students experiencing persistent or serious behavioral problems, and developing schoolwide student management programs. These ideas enable educators in their various roles to understand the broad issues and specific skills involved in effective classroom and schoolwide student management and to work collegially in responding to unproductive student behavior.

The concepts and strategies presented in this book will assist educators who work with a wide range of students. They stem from research and have been field-tested by thousands of teachers who work with students who are African American, Hispanic, Native American, Asian, Caucasian, poor, rich, learning disabled, emotionally disturbed, and talented and gifted. Although educators who work with students at risk for school failure will find these methods essential to their students' success, those who work with students who are successful will find that implementing the ideas in this book will enrich their own and their students' educational experiences.

APPROACH

Materials used to educate teachers and administrators have too often focused on isolated aspects of effective instruction and management. To develop a realistic, workable approach to classroom management, educators have had to seek out and integrate information from literally dozens of sources—many of which have claimed to provide "the answer." This seventh edition of *Comprehensive Classroom Management* offers a thorough research-based synthesis of current knowledge in effective classroom management, instruction, and schoolwide student management. Extensive review of the research and our own experiences in classrooms highlight five major factors or skill areas involved in effective classroom management:

1. Developing a solid understanding of students' personal/psychological and learning needs;
2. Establishing positive teacher–student and peer relationships that help meet students' basic psychological needs and build a community of support within the classroom;
3. Implementing instructional methods that facilitate optimal learning by responding to the academic needs of individual students and the classroom group;
4. Using organizational and group management methods that maximize on-task student behavior; and
5. Responding effectively to inappropriate student behavior and using a wide range of counseling and behavioral methods that involve students in examining and correcting behavior that negatively affects their own learning or that of other students.

This emphasis on providing a variety of specific methods to consider does not, however, imply that teachers should implement these methods by rote. We believe that teachers should (and will) implement recommendations selectively, attending to their own teaching styles, learning goals, students' needs, and other context variables. As Brophy and Evertson (1976) stated:

> Effective teaching requires the ability to implement a very large number of diagnostic, instructional, managerial, and therapeutic skills, tailoring behavior in specific contexts and situations to the specific needs of the moment. Effective teachers not only must be able to do a large number of things; they also must be able to recognize which of the many things they know how to do applies at a given moment and be able to follow through by performing the behavior effectively. (p. 139)

We have stayed away from providing a cookbook of what to do if Johnny cheats or steals because we agree with Allen Mendler (1992), who wrote:

> It will never be possible to compile a list of all possible techniques to be used when problem behaviors occur. Formulas fail to fit all situations. It is therefore more important that educators be guided by a sound set of principles and guidelines from which they can use existing strategies or develop new ones. (p. 26)

Likewise, unlike several classroom management texts, we have not merely summarized the work of leading classroom management theorists and suggested that educators examine their own behavior in light of someone's theory. This places the emphasis on some particular model rather than asking teachers to develop their own model based on a thorough understanding of current "best accepted and promising practice" and the context in which they will be practicing their profession.

As mentioned earlier, our approach places a major emphasis on creating positive learning environments and empowering students to understand and be actively involved in classroom management and instruction. We strongly believe that a significant number of serious management problems are responses to the manner in which students are treated as human beings and the types of instructional tasks they are asked to perform.

Any writer (or reader) must be cautious about how research is used as a framework for making practical decisions. In determining the methods to be presented in this book and the research used to support and expand these methods, we have made numerous choices. These choices are based on extensive study of the available research; on personal and professional acquaintance with leading researchers and writers in the field; and on our own experiences as regular classroom teachers, special educator, public school administrator, pre- and in-service teacher trainers, psychologist, and researchers.

The methods presented in this book have been used by us and by numerous teachers whom we have taught and with whom we have worked during the past thirty-two years. The methods have been field-tested by teachers in hundreds of classrooms evenly divided among primary, intermediate, middle, and high school settings. These settings include classrooms in inner-city, rural, and suburban schools.

The first edition of this book was published nearly twenty years ago. We are delighted and rewarded by the fact that most of the current "best accepted practice" in classroom management is consistent with the model we presented then and have continued to present. The Positive Behavior Support model presented by George Sugai and his colleagues at the University of Oregon (Sugai, Horner, & Gresham, 2002) includes most of the components found in our text since its first edition in 1981. Jerome Freiberg's (1996) "Consistency Management" and Cooperative Discipline model, which has proved so successful, emphasizes creating a caring community of support; having students develop classroom norms; giving students responsibility for running the classroom and school; implementing interactive, meaningful learning experiences; and reinforcing students. Evelyn Schneider's (1996) "Educational Responsibility" involves building a community, giving students choices, and increasing student academic success. William Glasser's (1990) *The Quality School: Managing Students without Coercion*, and Curwin and Mendler's (1988) *Discipline with Dignity* focus on creating schools and responding to misbehavior in ways that enhance students' sense of personal value and efficacy. The kind of teacher behavior and learning environments Gloria Ladson-Billings (1994) speaks of in *The Dreamkeepers*, and Crystal Kuykendall (2003) writes about in *From Rage to Hope*, that help African American and Latino children succeed are similar to the methods presented in this book. Deborah Meier's (1995) work at the Central Park East Schools in New York, Anne Ratzki's (1988) work with German schools, Barbara Ries Wager's (1993) work at James P. B. Duffy School No. 12 in New York, and the schooling Linda Darling-Hammond (1997) describes in *The Right to Learn* all share much in common with the vision we have shared over the past twenty years.

We celebrate the fact that there is increasing agreement among writers, researchers, teachers, administrators, and parents regarding the factors that are associated with creating classroom and school communities that enable virtually all children to experience a community of support that enhances their academic and personal lives. We believe this book will enrich you on your journey to integrate these methods into your classroom and school.

In the twenty-first century, the topic of classroom management must include some attention to preventing the type of school violence that occurred in such places as Jonesville, Arkansas; Springfield, Oregon; and Littleton, Colorado. Although many social factors contribute to students experiencing the anger, motive, and means to kill teachers and fellow students, it is also clear that the climate of a classroom and school can do much to contribute to or reduce the factors that lead children to act violently against others. A study of teacher education programs at U.S. colleges and universities reported that most institutions were doing very little to prepare teachers to cope with the issue of school violence (Nims & Wilson, 1998). A study by the Search Institute suggests that surprisingly few students express experiencing many key "developmental assets" that are associated with reduced high-risk behaviors, including substance abuse, school failure, and violence (Benson et al., 1999).

In his book, *Lost Boys: Why Our Sons Turn to Violence and How We Can Save Them*, Garbarino (1999) presents a powerful description of the emotional damage and anger experienced by violent children and youth. Anyone who teaches in the twenty-first century will be confronted with numerous students who fit these descriptions. There are an increasing number of students who believe they will not be successful at school; who feel incompetent and powerless—often both in the academic and social realms— for most of the thirty hours a week they spend in school. This increase in children who view their world in this manner is in part because of such social factors as the continuing high rate of family breakups, poverty, prejudice, and violence in our society. Although these social factors must be thoughtfully addressed, a key question for educators becomes whether classrooms and schools can be thoughtfully, caringly, systematically, and effectively designed to provide students with alternatives to their existing perceptions. We believe they can!

This book provides the reader with numerous strategies for creating classroom and school environments in which students feel valued and empowered rather than devalued, angry, and unempowered—all factors that are the seeds of violent behavior. Recent events have provided tragic and resounding support for the authors' belief that classroom management is not about managing student behavior but rather about creating communities of support in which students' developmental and personal needs are met so learning can be enhanced, and students' need to act out their frustration and pain is lessened. In addition, this book presents best practices for responding to disruptive student behavior in ways that tend to deescalate the behavior and enable the students to feel valued and begin to develop skills for dealing with their frustration, anger, and alienation.

It is our heartfelt wish and prayer that the materials in this book will assist you and your colleagues in creating positive, nurturing environments for students from all ability levels; socioeconomic classes; ethnic groups; and with varied personal, social, developmental, and intellectual backgrounds.

ACKNOWLEDGMENTS

We wish to acknowledge the many teachers whose application of the methods presented in *Comprehensive Classroom Management* have validated their effectiveness. We thank Susan Foster, Mark Gaulke, Peter Grauff, Heather Lilley, Dean Long, Lisa Stevens, Marjorie Miller Tonole, and Terri Vann for allowing us to use student behavior change projects they completed in our graduate classes. We also thank Marty Voge for providing us with Figure 10.6. Our special appreciation goes to Cory Dunn for his sharing of the Think–Feel–Act model to problem solving and the associated case study presented here, and his work on the systems approach. We have learned a great deal from working with Cory during the past twenty years.

Many thanks to the reviewers of this edition for their helpful comments: Barbara A. Block, Florida Southern University; Kathy Piechura Couture, Stetson University; Christine Collins Hypolite, Nicholls State University; and Rosalyn Anstine Templeton, Bradley University.

Vern Jones, Ph.D., has been a junior high school teacher, a junior high school vice principal, and a district coordinator for students with emotional and behavioral disorders. He is Professor of Teacher Education and Coordinator of the Special Education Program at Lewis & Clark College in Portland, Oregon. He received his Ph.D. in Counseling Psychology from the University of Texas.

Dr. Jones's other books include, *Adolescents with Behavior Problems* (1980), *Responsible School Discipline* (1991), and *Creating Effective Programs for Students with Emotional and Behavior Disorders* (2004). He has written chapters in *Helping Teachers Manage Classrooms* (1982), *Management of Disruptive Pupil Behaviour in Schools* (1986), and *Severe Behavior Disorders of Children and Youth* (1987). He was selected by the National Association of Colleges of Teacher Education to write the chapter on classroom management for the *Handbook of Research on Teacher Education* (1996). He is currently a section editor and chapter author for the upcoming book *Handbook for Classroom Management: Research, Practice, and Contemporary Issues* (in press). Dr. Jones is coauthor of the *State of Oregon Technical Assistance Paper on the Identification and Treatment of Seriously Emotionally Disturbed Students.*

From 1986 to 1989 Dr. Jones was co-chair of the American Educational Research Association Special Interest Group on Classroom Management. Dr. Jones has served as Scholar in Residence at several universities. In 1990, he won the Burlington Northern Award as Graduate School Teacher of the Year at Lewis & Clark College. He has given keynote addresses at state conferences in more than ten states and has consulted with school districts and staff in over twenty-five states.

Louise Jones has been a teacher in grades three through six for thirty-two years. She earned her masters degree from Lewis & Clark College, where she has taught courses on classroom management. She has presented at regional and national workshops on creating positive classroom climates, and has worked with school staff to develop schoolwide student management plans.

PART one

Foundations of Comprehensive Classroom Management

Theory and practice in classroom management have improved dramatically during the past two decades. Unfortunately, practical methods presented to teachers have often been simplistic and piecemeal. Because of public and teacher concern about student behavior, new ideas have too often been quickly marketed as panaceas. Rather than helping teachers understand the issues in effective classroom management and the relationship among various strategies, much published material has presented unidimensional approaches to small aspects of classroom management.

Part I is directed toward alleviating the confusion associated with the topic of classroom management. It examines the major causes of unproductive student behavior and provides a theoretical and philosophical foundation from which to examine approaches that encourage positive student behavior and achievement and respond to disruptive behavior. Chapter 1 places the concept of classroom management in perspective by examining the extent of the problem, considering the reasons for an increase in problems associated with student behavior, describing recent trends in classroom management, defining comprehensive classroom management, and discussing the relationship between classroom management and the teacher's professional needs. Chapter 2 examines students' personal needs that must be met for them to become productively involved in the learning process. Discussions of classroom management have too often overemphasized controlling unproductive student behavior rather than creating environments that encourage productive behavior. The concepts in Chapter 2 provide a foundation for refocusing attention on preventive interventions.

After completing Part I, you should understand why discipline problems arise and the factors that can be examined and implemented in order to reduce these problems. This perspective provides a basis for employing the preventive and corrective strategies described throughout the book. Perhaps more important, this understanding provides a foundation for assisting you in analyzing your own classroom or school environment creatively and evaluating how you might implement the ideas presented in this book or create new solutions for dealing with the behavior problems that occur in your school.

CHAPTER

1

Classroom Management in Perspective

Almost all surveys of teacher effectiveness report that classroom management skills are of primary importance in determining teaching success, whether it is measured by student learning or by ratings. Thus, management skills are crucial and fundamental. A teacher who is grossly inadequate in classroom management skills is probably not going to accomplish much.

—Jere Brophy and Carolyn Evertson (1976)
Learning from Teaching

The concept of classroom management is broader than the notion of student discipline. It includes all the things teachers must do to foster student involvement and cooperation in classroom activities and to establish a productive working environment.

—Julie Sanford, Edmund Emmer, and Barbara Clements (1983)
"Improving Classroom Management"
Educational Leadership

The findings show that teachers who approach classroom management as a process of establishing and maintaining effective learning environments tend to be more successful than teachers who place more emphasis on their roles as authority figures or disciplinarians.

—Thomas L. Good and Jere Brophy (1994)
Looking in Classrooms

Classroom management can and should do more than elicit predictable obedience; indeed, it can and should be one vehicle for the enhancement of student self-understanding, self-evaluation, and the internalization of self-control.

—Mary McCaslin and Thomas L. Good (1992)
"Compliant Cognition"
Educational Researcher

> *No other topic in education receives greater attention or causes more concerns for teachers and parents and students than classroom discipline. . . . The lack of effective classroom discipline or behavior management skills is the major stumbling block to a successful career in teaching.*
>
> —Nicholas Long and William Morse (1996)
> *Conflict in the Classroom*

> *Management must be presented in an intellectual framework for understanding classroom events and consequences rather than simply as a collection of tricks and specific reactions to behavior.*
>
> —Walter Doyle (1986)

Student behavior problems have for years been a major concern of teachers, administrators, and parents. National concern about students' achievement and recent violence in schools has intensified public interest in schools and students' behavior. Although teachers face the task of educating many students whose home and community environments are disruptive, research demonstrates that teachers' skills in creating safe, supportive classrooms are a major factor influencing students' motivation, achievement, and behavior. In a meta-analysis of factors influencing student learning, classroom management was identified as the most important factor (Wang, Haertel, & Walberg, 1993). The concept of discipline, with its emphasis on dealing with inevitable misbehavior among students, has been replaced by a more comprehensive body of knowledge on how to increase students' achievement by creating classroom communities in which students' personal and academic needs are met.

EXTENT OF THE PROBLEM

PAUSE
and Consider   **1.1**

> Before reading this section, stop for a minute and write a response to the questions: "What is it about teaching that most interests and excites me, and what am I most concerned about?" Share these with colleagues or fellow students in a course you are taking. The following material provides information regarding public education and teaching concerns expressed by the general public and educators in the United States.

The issue of student behavior has been a long-standing concern of laypersons and educators. Since its inception in 1969, the annual Gallup Poll of the Public's Attitudes toward the Public Schools has found school discipline to be the public's primary educational concern on sixteen occasions. From 1986 through 1991, discipline was viewed as second to drug use as the biggest problem facing the U.S. public schools; in 1992 and 1993, concerns about student behavior ranked third behind concerns regarding school funding and drug use.

In recent years, however, public concern has returned to issues of discipline. Writing about the 1994 Gallup Poll, Elam and Rose (1995) state, "The 1994 Phi Delta Kappa/Gallup poll showed that, for the first time in the poll's history, people viewed violence and poor discipline as overwhelmingly the most serious problems in their local public schools" (p. 54). This trend continued. From 1994 through 1999 issues of discipline and violence were rated by the public as the most serious concerns facing U.S. public schools. In 2001 respondents to the Phi Delta Kappa/Gallup Poll indicated that "Lack of discipline" tied with "Lack of financial support" were the most serious problems, and that fighting, violence, and gangs in the schools ranked third. In the 2002 poll, "Lack of financial support" rated as the "biggest" problem, with "Lack of discipline" second. However, when asked to rank the seriousness of the problem, discipline was again ranked number one.

Every year the National Center for Education Statistics presents a report entitled, "Indicators of School Crime and Safety." The 2002 report indicated that, compared to other areas of students' lives, schools are relatively safe places. Nevertheless, students experience serious problems at school related to violence and substance abuse. Although disruptive student behavior at school remains a serious problem, in some areas significant reductions have occurred.

> Between 1995 and 2001, the percentage of students who reported being victims of crime at school declined from 10 percent to 6 percent. Most of this decline was due to a reduction in students being victims of theft.
>
> During the past five years, secondary principals reported a decrease in reports of physical violence, theft, student possession of weapons, and vandalism.
>
> In 2001, 8 percent of students reported being bullied at school—an increase from the 5 percent reported in 1999. Fourteen percent of sixth graders reported being bullied compared to 2 percent of twelfth grade students.
>
> The percentage of students in grades nine through twelve who reported being threatened or injured with a weapon has remained constant at approximately 8 percent since 1993.
>
> The percentage of students who reported avoiding unsafe places at school decreased from 9 percent in 1995 to 5 percent in 2001.
>
> The percentage of students in grades nine through twelve who reported having been in a physical fight at school declined from 16 percent in 1993 to 13 percent in 2001. The percentage of students who said they had been in a physical fight away from school was 20 percent.
>
> The percentage of students who reported carrying a weapon (gun, knife, club) on school property declined from 12 percent in 1993 to 6 percent in 2001.
>
> The victimization rate for nonfatal violent crimes is lower at school than away from school.
>
> Thirty-three school-aged children died of school-associated homicides in 1999.
>
> Although 47 percent of students in grades nine through twelve indicated they had at least one drink in the past month, only 5 percent reported drinking on school property during that time frame.
>
> In 2001, 29 percent of high school students reported being offered, sold, or given an illegal drug on school property. This figure has been consistent since 1993.

Although physical violence is too common in schools and boys are more likely to be victimized by it, all students, but especially girls, experience not only physical and property damage but also psychological damage. In a 1993 study entitled "Hostile Hallways," the American Association of University Women reported that within their school environment, 70 percent of girls experience harassment and more than 50 percent report experiencing unwanted sexual touching. One-third of girls report that sexual rumors are spread about them, and one-quarter state they have been cornered and molested. In the 1999 Phi Delta Kappa/Gallup Poll of the Public's Attitudes toward the Public Schools, 52 percent of the adults surveyed stated they believed student-to-student sexual harassment in the public schools was "very serious" or "somewhat serious."

Teachers support concerns expressed by students and the public. In its report, "Indicators of School Crime and Safety 2002," the National Center for Educational Statistics reported that between 1996 and 2000 teachers were victims of 321,000 non-fatal crimes per year at school, or 74 crimes per 1,000 teachers per year. This included 14,000 violent, serious crimes including rape, sexual assault, robbery, or aggravated assault. Male teachers were almost two and one-half times more likely to be victims of violent crimes than were female teachers. Teachers in urban schools were more likely to be victims of violent crimes than were teachers in suburban or rural areas. Perhaps not surprising, the Fifth Poll of Teachers' Attitudes toward the Public Schools (Langdon, 1999) showed that nearly two-thirds of teachers polled listed discipline as a very or fairly serious problem, and almost half rated fighting as very or fairly serious. In the Fourth Phi Delta Kappa Poll of Teachers' Attitudes toward Public Schools, 50 percent of teachers polled said students talking back to and disobeying teachers occurred frequently at the school where they taught, an increase of 5 percent from the 1989 poll (Langdon, 1997, p. 213). In this same poll, the following percentage of teachers stated that where they taught, the following behaviors were a problem "most of the time/fairly often."

71% schoolwork/homework assignments not completed
58% behavior disrupts class
50% talking back to or disobeying teachers
41% truancy or being absent from school

Feitler and Tokar (1992) reported that 58 percent of the 3,300 kindergarten through twelfth-grade public school teachers in their sample "ranked 'individual pupils who constantly misbehave' as the number one cause of job-related stress" (pp. 156–157). Emmer (1994) reported that many of the events that evoke negative teacher emotions are related either directly or indirectly to issues of student behavior. Interestingly, teachers express concern that if they inform parents that their child is disrupting the class, parents will be less likely to support the teacher (2000 Annual Report on School Safety). Cotton (1992) found that nearly half of classroom time involves activities other than instruction and that most of this time is consumed by discipline activities. The 2000 Annual Report on School Safety, presented by the Department of Education and the Department of Justice, reports that, "As other student behaviors (e.g., weapon carrying and physical fighting on school property) show improvement, student behavior that leads to classroom disruption is much more prevalent and has not improved over the past decade" (p. 11).

Consider a typical classroom management problem experienced by one of the author's interns. She was teaching her first class in a freshman English to a group her veteran mentor called, "a great group of kids, but the most difficult class I have experienced in 17 years of teaching." The students were very social and quite effectively ignored the intern's efforts to focus the discussion on class content. Even when some students became engaged, others continued their side conversations. Small-group work provided a higher rate of on-task behavior, but still required constant monitoring and encouragement to focus on the content. By the end of this book you will have learned multiple research-based strategies for responding to this type of situation. Indeed, we have included the strategy that finally had a positive impact on helping this lively group of first-year high school students behave in a productive manner that supported solid learning gains.

"So, other than that, how was your first day as a teacher?"

In a survey of elementary school teachers, more than 90 percent reported they needed more training in classroom management (Wolery, Werts, Caldwell, Snyder, & Lisowski, 1995). A study conducted in 2002 by the Oregon Department of Education (Dalton & Zanville, 2002) evaluated beginning teachers' reactions to their initial teaching experiences. The challenge most often cited related to classroom management, with nearly one-third of the 1,200 respondents citing this as their primary concern.

Until quite recently, the most common procedure provided to teachers for responding to disruptive student behavior was placing students' name on the board and following this by a series of checks and detentions when students continued to act irresponsibly. Not surprisingly to anyone who has worked extensively with students who exhibit ongoing behavior problems, research (Emmer & Aussiker, 1990; Nelson, 1996; Nelson, Martella, & Galand, 1998) indicates that such common responses as writing names on the board, turning over colored cards, and the associated loss of points or privileges often makes the situation only worse. Recent research suggests that, at least in their responses to disruptive student behavior, teachers may not have progressed significantly beyond this approach. Nelson and Roberts (2000) report that teachers tend to respond to disruptive student behavior with either commands or reprimands. These authors reported that, "With few exceptions, teachers' use of ultimatums, response cost, requests to leave the classroom, and ignoring remained constant" (p. 36). This research also reported that it was highly unlikely that students with ongoing behavior problems would respond positively to these teacher responses. In fact, these researchers reported that, when confronted by this type of teacher response, the behavior of students with ongoing behavior problems appeared virtually unstoppable. In a similar vein, Sugai, Horner, and Gresham (2002) note:

> When reactive management is overemphasized, and prevention is underemphasized, students with behavior problems are the most likely to (a) be excluded from school, . . . (b) drop out, . . . (c) prompt teacher requests for assistance, . . . and (d) become involved in antisocial lifestyles. . . . (p. 316)

Administrators are also required to consistently deal with issues of irresponsible student behavior at school. Between 1974 and 1998, the rate of student suspension nearly doubled from 4 to 7 percent (Justice Policy Institute, 2001). This translates into more than three million students being suspended each year. Students from certain ethnic groups are more likely to be suspended. Although they accounted for approximately 17 percent of enrolled students in 1998, African American students accounted for 31 percent of suspended students (2000 Annual Report on School Safety). African American male students account for 9 percent of the student population but 21 percent of the suspensions. Nearly identical numbers exist for student expulsions.

Schools have responded to concerns about violence in schools. In their report, "Indicators of School Crime and Safety, 2002," the National Center for Education Statistics reported that in the year 2000, 97 percent of schools reported requiring visitors to report to the office, 90 percent reported having closed campuses, 23 percent indicated they provided the daily presence of police or security personnel, 15 percent reported using surveillance devices to monitor their school, 21 percent of schools reported conducting drug sweeps, and 8 percent reported random use of metal detectors on students. In addition, 59 percent reported having developed and implemented a school violence prevention program.

Obviously, it is insufficient merely to document the severity of student behavior problems. Educators must understand why these problems arise. There are two basic reasons classroom management continues to be a major problem in U.S. schools. First, teachers are asked to instruct a wide range of students, many of whom come to school with varying degrees of emotional distress and inadequate personal skills. Second, despite significant research and the associated dramatic increase in methods for effectively motivating and managing students, many teachers have received only a limited amount of useful information about how to organize and manage classrooms in order to maximize productive student learning and behavior. The following sections examine why student behavior continues to be a major problem in U.S. schools and present a conceptual framework for understanding the steps that can be taken to significantly reduce the problem.

SOCIAL FACTORS INFLUENCING STUDENTS' BEHAVIOR

Anyone who has spent time in a faculty lounge has heard numerous statements regarding the role family and societal factors play in influencing stu-

"I can't tell you what a relief it is to relax after a year of teaching!"

dents' behaviors. The following sections examine factors outside of school that impact student behavior and require that educators possess extensive skills in creating positive school and classroom climates that prevent and respond effectively to irresponsible student behavior.

Although teachers cannot immediately or directly alter the social factors that create students' problems, understanding these factors does enable teachers to place students' failures and disruptive behaviors in perspective and to create environments that reduce rather than intensify their effects. When discussing the problem of disruptive or disturbed student behavior, teachers often ask why these problems seem to have increased during the past decade. Indeed, as education and psychology have developed an increasingly sophisticated body of knowledge, teachers have entered the classroom better trained than before. There is little question that today's teachers better understand such topics as human development and the learning process than did teachers fifteen years ago. Therefore, although unproductive student behavior is often a response to factors within schools and classrooms, it seems reasonable to assume that today's school environments are, in general, more supportive of students' needs and more conducive to learning than they were ten or twenty years ago. Consequently, although improving teachers' skills remains a major component in combating unproductive student behavior, other variables must be considered in order to develop a comprehensive understanding of the intensified problems of classroom discipline.

Divorce and subsequent single-parent households has skyrocketed in the United States in the past forty years. Only 11 percent of children born in the 1950s experienced their parents being separated or divorced; nearly 55 percent of students born in the 1990s experienced this phenomenon. In addition, one in every four children raised in the 1990s lived in a stepfamily, and it appears that, by their teens, nearly half of these children will experience a second divorce as their stepfamily breaks up. Data released in the 2001 National Vital Statistics Report indicate that these data have held constant through the beginning of the twenty-first century. Indeed, a 2001 report from the National Center for Health Statistics indicates that 43 percent of first marriages break up within fifteen years. Finally, the out-of-wedlock birthrate jumped from only 5 percent in 1960 to 18 percent in 1980 and 33.2 percent in 2000. These figures clearly indicate the extent of family breakup, disruption, and emotional turmoil experienced by students.

"He doesn't listen to a thing we say, he's very noisy, and he's always getting into trouble. I think he's ready to start school."

The report *American's Children: Key National Indicators of Well-Being, 2002* supports these concerns. The poverty rate for children was approximately 18 percent with 6 percent of children living in extreme poverty. During 2000, 8.4 million (12 percent of all children) had no health care. Since 1978, children living in conditions described as "inadequate housing" have decreased from 9 to 7 percent. In 2000, over half a million children (0.8 percent of all children) lived in a household with child hunger—a slight decrease from 1998. The percent of infants born with low birthweights (less than 5.5 pounds) increased slightly to 7.6 percent, the highest rate in more than twenty years. In 2000, the rate of young women ages fifteen to seventeen giving birth decreased to 27 per 1,000, the lowest rate since records have been kept. Between 2000 and 2001, the percentage of eighth and tenth graders who reported smoking in the past month declined (from 14 percent to 12 percent for tenth graders and 7 percent to 6 percent for eighth graders). The percentage of high school seniors who reported smoking daily decreased to 19 percent. In 2001, the rates for heavy drinking among adolescents remained unchanged from 2000, with 30 percent of twelfth graders, 25 percent of tenth graders, and 13 percent of eighth graders reported having at least five drinks in a row at least once in the previous two weeks. Similarly, the percentage of eighth, tenth, and twelfth graders reporting use of illegal drugs within the past thirty days remained stable at 26 percent for twelfth graders, 23 percent for tenth graders, and 12 percent for eighth graders.

Unfortunately, indirect abuse of children through poverty, the media, and lack of family support is, in too many cases, exacerbated by abuse. Because child abuse may involve physical, emotional, and sexual abuse and much child abuse goes unreported, it is difficult to obtain reliable estimates of abuse. However, the National Child Abuse and Neglect Data System reported that in the year 2000, over three million referrals were made concerning the welfare of over five million children, and approximately 900,000 children were found to be victims of child maltreatment. Sadly, approximately 1,200 children died of abuse or neglect in the year 2000.

Children who have been abused often believe that these experiences are normal. They need extended experiences in settings in which the rights of others are clearly respected and where people express feelings and solve problems nonviolently. Schools can assist these children to develop lifetime skills and reduce the likelihood that these students will behave violently by creating warm, supportive teacher–student and peer relationships; discussing human rights when developing school and classroom behavior standards; treating students with dignity when resolving behavior problems; and using a skill-based, problem-solving approach to student rule violations.

Given these situations, it is perhaps not surprising that during the past decade, runaways have doubled from one million to two million youth, and the number of suicides in the United States is eight times that in Japan. In addition, even homes that may look like safe, prosperous, nurturing environments often create stress for children because working parents expect children to take on major family responsibilities without adult supervision and encourage children to become involved in numerous out-of-school activities. Indeed, studies indicate that young people who commit suicide are often high achievers unable to handle the stress of fast-paced lives and high expectations for achievement in multiple tasks.

For many students, stress and violence within the home are matched by similar problems in the community. In a study of South Side Chicago elementary children, 26 percent reported having seen someone shot, and 29 percent had observed a stabbing (O'Neil, 1991).

Studies also strongly support the concept that television viewing increases aggressive student behavior (Anderson & Bushman, 2002). James Kauffman, a leader in the field of behavioral disorders noted that "high levels of television viewing, whether the shows contained much violence or not, have negative effects on children's behavior (1997, p. 284).

Substance abuse is another social factor that reduces the time, energy, and ability of students to attend to academic tasks. Student drug use illustrates the importance of considering both social and school variables as factors influencing student behavior and learning. Certainly, educators are not solely or even primarily responsible for this problem that affects them so profoundly. Conversely, schools often provide learning environments that fail to engage a large segment of students actively and meaningfully. This situation increases the likelihood that students will abuse substances during school hours and will choose substance abuse rather than involvement in school-based activities.

"I'll do my homework just as soon as something bad comes on TV."

When discussing the challenges facing school staff as they work to meet the needs of troubled children, two of the leading experts in the world, Nicholas Long and William Morse, (1996) wrote:

> Of first concern is the *significant increase* in the number of already troubled and seriously at-risk students in our schools. No letup is in sight, and there are now too many to accommodate in traditional special education. . . . Second, along with the increased numbers has come the *deeper and more profound nature* of the personal and ecological difficulties of these students. More students are deeply depressed, despairing, and suicidal; others turn defiant, angry, violent, and homicidal.
>
> Even in the best of times, special education never included all of the disturbed and disturbing students and never was designed to include those at risk. Today, these students can be half the members of a given class. (pp. xiii, xiv)

One of the authors was asked by an elementary school staff to provide a workshop on working with students who have conduct disorders. When the staff was asked to provide more specificity by describing what was meant by "conduct disorders," the staff sent the author a description of the students in one of the teacher's classes (Figure 1.1). Between 1996 and 1999, the authors asked more than 2,000 teachers to state whether they thought the profile given in Figure 1.1 was atypical. The most common

FIGURE 1.1
A Profile of a First-
Grade Class

Reprinted by
permission.

8 are in Chapter 1 (3 of which will test out as learning disabled)
1 is on a reading individual education plan
1 is an English-as-a-second-language student
3 are receiving assistance for speech problems
3 are receiving in-school counseling
2 are receiving out-of-school counseling
1 has a history of physical abuse
3 are from homes with a history of domestic violence
2 have been sexually abused
1 child lives in a shelter home
1 child is in his fourth school since kindergarten; several others in their third
2 students have been evicted from their apartments for setting fire to them

response was that primary grade teachers thought the description was quite similar to their own classes, whereas intermediate level teachers indicated that, perhaps because their students were older, had experienced more life difficulties, and received more testing at school, this was a very conservative list.

As discussed in more detail in Chapter 2, an organization called The Search Institute has developed a list of forty assets that assist students in reaching their potential. Given the data presented in this section, it is not surprising that this organization also lists five developmental deficits: (1) drinking parties, (2) being alone at home, (3) being a victim of violence, (4) overexposure to television, and (5) physical abuse. Sadly, their research indicates that "Only 15 percent of young people surveyed experienced none of these deficits. One-third of youth (32%) experienced three or more" (Benson et al., 1999, p. xiii).

Cultural diversity is another social factor influencing students' school experiences. More than one-fifth of U.S. schoolchildren come from homes in which a language other than English is spoken, and school enrollments of students with limited English proficiency is growing at 2.5 times the rate of students whose first language is English. Despite the richness of their cultural heritage, "Linguistically and culturally diverse students find themselves in a vulnerable situation on entering U.S. schools" (Garcia, 1999, p. 1). Fortunately, a wide variety of research highlights instructional strategies and school climate factors associated with successful inclusion of students whose primary language is not English. This book includes numerous strategies for providing a positive school experience for students from a wide variety of cultural backgrounds.

P A U S E
and Consider   1.2

Having read about the extent of classroom management issues and social factors that may influence student behavior, stop for a moment and write a statement about or share with a peer or small group what you found most significant about this information. Next, write or share any implications this has for issues that involve helping students make responsible decisions in a school setting.

SCHOOL FACTORS SIGNIFICANTLY INFLUENCE STUDENTS' LEARNING AND BEHAVIOR

Consider what you valued about your kindergarten through twelfth-grade school experience and what factors made school feel unsafe or caused you to feel a sense of frustration and failure. If you discuss these factors with fellow students or colleagues, it is likely you will realize most of these factors were influenced by the decisions and actions (or inactions) of educators.

Even though social factors have made the teacher's job more difficult, studies indicate that teachers and schools make a dramatic difference in the lives of many children. In her book, *Adolescents at Risk: Prevalence and Prevention,* Joy Dryfoos (1990) examined research on the causes and possible prevention and response to such serious problems as drug use, early pregnancy, school failure, and delinquency. She summed up the important role school personnel play:

"Bad day at school?"

> Many of the interventions in the other fields incorporated educational enhancement as the major program component. In fact, the prevention of delinquency appears to be embedded in the prevention of school failure. Whether delinquency prevention is actually a field in itself or whether it should be subsumed under the rubric of educational remediation is an unresolved issue. To a great degree, this may be true of prevention of substance abuse and teen pregnancy as well. The acquisition of basic skills at appropriate ages appears to be a primary component of all prevention. (pp. 236–237)

Teachers have control over many factors that significantly influence the achievement and behavior of students. Schools and teachers working with similar student populations differ dramatically in their ability to help students develop desirable behaviors and increase students' achievements. Mortimore and Sammons (1987) summarized their extensive research on factors that influence students' academic and social gains:

> In our measurement of reading progress, we found the school to be about six times more important than backgrounds (factors of age, sex, social class, and race). For written math and writing, the difference is tenfold. The analyses of speech and of the social outcomes also confirm the overriding importance of school. . . . It is the policies and processes within the control of the principal and teachers that are crucial. These factors can be changed and improved. (p. 6)

The Office of Educational Research and Improvement (OERI) publication *Review of Research on Ways to Attain Goal 6: Creating Safe, Disciplined, and Drug-Free Schools* includes a description of the role schools play in affecting student behavior.

> In the past decade, research has demonstrated that there are important school-to-school differences across secondary schools in these important student behaviors and outcomes,

differences that cannot be completely accounted for by the background of students in a school. Three dimensions of school climate appear to account for these differences:

- Goals: a strong emphasis on academic mission in the school;
- Rules and procedures: clear disciplinary standards that are firmly, fairly, and consistently enforced;
- Climate: an "ethic of caring" that guides interpersonal relationships in the school.

Each of these aspects of schools can affect outcomes independently, but when they occur in combination and are widely accepted and practiced, researchers have found that they constitute powerful and coherent school "ethos" or culture that increases the engagement of students in the academic work of schools, decreases disruptive and violent behavior in schools, and lends to increased student achievement. (Aleem & Moles, 1993, p. 12)

To make significant changes in student learning and behavior, we must seriously look at a broad range of variables in the school setting and embrace opportunities for changing our teaching behavior and how schools are structured.

Research conducted at Johns Hopkins University indicates that effective classroom management techniques in first grade can have a dramatic impact on whether students will behave violently at age thirteen. Kellam and his colleagues (Kellam, Ling, Merisca, Brown, & Ialgo, 1998) reported that highly aggressive six-year-old boys assigned to first-grade classrooms with teachers skilled in classroom management were three times less likely to be highly aggressive when they reached eighth grade than similarly aggressive boys placed in first-grade classrooms characterized by poor classroom management. These findings are consistent with experimental studies conducted in middle school classrooms by David Hawkins at the University of Washington (Hawkins, Doueck, & Lishner, 1988).

Examples of Effective Schools

All who have been involved in education as students or as professional educators have visions of the type of school in which they believe students flourish and where they would like to teach. Before reading this section, list characteristics that represent your ideal school. If possible, share your list with several colleagues or classmates. It is quite likely you will find the research indicates students behave more responsibly and are academically more successful in schools characterized by the factors you listed.

An excellent example of the positive impact of meeting students' personal needs within the school community can be found in a series of schools in Germany (Ratzki, 1988). The goal of the school change project was to reduce the failure rate on national tests and to create a larger pool of students who could be successfully employed. The changes in the schools centered around creating positive, supportive communities of support. Students were assigned to a homogeneous table group (similar to a base group) with whom they remained for at least one year. Similarly, a team of six teachers worked with eighty-five to ninety students for six years (grades five through ten). These teachers had responsibility for the students' total educational program; Ratzki wrote that they "eat with the students, counsel them on personal and academic issues, determine their class schedules, tailor their curricula, help to broaden their interests by offering special lunchtime activities, and talk with their parents" (p. 13). One of these schools is Koln-Holweide School, a large suburban school enrolling a broad spectrum of students, including nearly 25 percent whose parents are unemployed and 30 percent minority students.

> Yet only 1 percent of the school's students drop out, compared to a national West German average of 14 percent; and 60 percent of its students score sufficiently well on high school exit exams to be admitted to a four-year college, compared to a national average of only 27 percent. Moreover, the school suffers practically no truancy, hardly any teacher absenteeism, and only minor discipline problems. (Ratzki, 1988, p. 10)

In this country similar results have been obtained at Central Park East schools in New York. In writing about this school, Deborah Meier (1995) stated:

> The CPE population is roughly equivalent to a cross sampling of New York City. The majority of students are African American and Latino, most are low-income or poor, and they experience a full range of academic strengths and handicaps. . . . While some students moved and a few transferred, fewer than 5 percent of those who started with us in ninth grade dropped out along the way. And not only did the rest graduate with regular diplomas, but 90 percent went directly on to college and stayed there. These figures for 1991 have held up for each subsequent graduating class. And the graduates of 1994 outstripped their predecessors in quality of work achieved and colleges attended. (p. 16)

Deborah Meier and her colleagues built their program on a philosophy of creating a democratic community. They focused on "collaboration and mutual respect among staff, parents, students, and the larger community" (p. 22). When discussing the high school program, Meier wrote:

> We introduced two-hour interdisciplinary class periods and demanded exhibitions—projects—rather than short-answer written tests. We provided time during those two hours for presentations, seminars, group work, and independent study. We built in time for tutorials and coaching. We insisted that this was more like the real world, not less. (p. 32)

Similar results have been shown at International High School in Queens, New York. This school serves students from more than fifty countries who speak more than thirty languages and has 75 percent of its students on free or reduced lunch. Since its first graduating class in 1988, this school has had a graduation and college attendance rate of more than 90 percent.

Secondary schools and smaller schools are not alone in their ability to obtain learning gains from groups of students who have traditionally done less well. Keels Elementary School in Columbia, South Carolina, is another example of a school where positive changes have occurred (Berry, 1995). "Although fewer than half of the students entering Keels meet the state's 'readiness' standard in kindergarten, by the end of first grade over 90 percent meet state standards in reading and mathematics" (Darling-Hammond, 1997, p. 100). At Keels Elementary teachers have collaborated to implement a variety of instructional strategies including "cooperative learning in heterogeneous classes, whole language instruction and hands-on work in mathematics and science, social studies projects such as studies of the stock market. . . . Students are involved in peer teaching and in decision making about school discipline and extracurricular events" (Darling-Hammond, pp. 100, 101). Darling-Hammond suggests that the most effective schools include the following features: (1) active in-depth learning, (2) emphasis on authentic performance, (3) attention to development,

(4) appreciation for diversity, (5) opportunities for collaborative learning, (6) collective perspective across the school, (7) structures for caring, (8) support for democratic learning, (9) connections to family and community (p. 107).

There is increasing agreement among researchers (Algozzine, Audette, Ellis, Marr, & White, 2000; Freiberg, 1999; Jones, 2002; Nelson & Roberts, 2000; Sugai et al., 2001) regarding the type of school and classroom environments needed to support positive behavior among a wide range of students. These writers indicate the importance of working with students to clearly define and accept behavior expectations; developing clearly understood and educationally sound responses to rule violations, including the reteaching of expected behaviors; and developing individualized behavior support plans for students who present ongoing behaviors that violate the rights of others. In addition, several of these writers (Freiberg, 1999; Jones, 2002) highlight the importance of creating an engaging curriculum, and modifying curriculum and instruction for students who experience academic difficulties. These authors also emphasize the importance of ensuring that students experience a community of support within the school setting.

Unfortunately, much of the material written about methods that prevent students from experiencing behavior problems virtually ignores the aspect of students experiencing a sense of significance or belonging (Jones, 2002). Our experience and reading of the literature suggest that this is an essential ingredient and the foundation on which all other interventions must be built. Too often we have visited schools in which staff were working to teach prosocial skills and develop plans for recalcitrant students, but the ethos of the school was oppressive and lacked warmth and joy. Often staff in these schools continued to use punitive approaches to behavior problems, and a significant minority of students in these schools felt alienated and did not believe teachers cared about them. Unless this factor is addressed, the popularized behavioral approaches to changing student behavior will be inadequate as interventions to create safe, productive learning environments.

The media's portrayal of students' and adults' return to Columbine High School in Littleton, Colorado, presents a poignant picture of what may be missing in our approach to violent student behavior. The media focused on the rally of students and adults "taking back our school." Bands played and cheerleaders cheered. Unfortunately, the media's portrayal did not emphasize the students' and adults' commitments to ensuring that the school would become a supportive community for everyone. Perhaps some outward show of awareness that everyone needed to join together to know, care about, and embrace the diversity of each student would have had more impact and responded more effectively to a root cause of the sad events of the incident than bands and banners. One student summarized what he had learned about preventing violence when he stated, "I don't tease my friends as much as I used to. I try to be a lot nicer to everyone." A senior who was in Harris's video class said that this year, "a lot of seniors have been more open to people, even to underclassmen." (Goldstein, 1999, pp. 56, 57). The principal noted that, "I think where money needs to be spent is educating our students about tolerance, about respecting one another, about communication" (Goldstein, 1999, p. 57). The key to preventing school violence is ultimately not in guards and cameras but in students feeling cared for, competent, and valued.

CLASSROOM MANAGEMENT:
A CHANGING PERSPECTIVE

P A U S E
_____
1.3   *and Consider*

> Before reading the next section, take a moment and write a brief definition of effective classroom management. You may want to include a list of the key components you believe are involved in effective classroom management. In other words, what are the key skills demonstrated by teachers who are defined as being effective classroom managers?
>
> It is likely that your ideas were influenced by a number of factors, including family members you observed managing groups of children, leaders of community organizations you saw effectively engaging and influencing young people, and teachers creating positive learning environments. Prior to reading the next section, it might be helpful to write down specific characteristics of these individuals and also list specific strategies they used.

The materials in this section are not intended to provide you with specific skills. The skills related to the methods described in this section are presented in detail throughout the book. After reading this section you should have a better understanding of the history of classroom management; past and future trends in the field; and the multiple methods you will need to consider as you plan to develop a safe, supportive learning community.

The Counseling Approach

During the 1960s and through much of the 1970s, the emphasis in dealing with student behavior was on discipline. The little training that teachers received focused on what to do *after* students misbehaved. Because the emphasis in psychology during the late 1960s and early 1970s was on personal growth and awareness, most methods focused on understanding students' problems and helping them better understand themselves and work cooperatively with adults to develop more productive behaviors.

One of the earliest and most widely used models was William Glasser's reality therapy (1965). Glasser's model derived from the belief that young people need caring professionals willing to help them take responsibility for their behavior and develop plans aimed at altering unproductive conduct. Rudolf Dreikurs and his associates (1971) developed a somewhat more clinical model based on the belief that acting-out children made poor choices because of inappropriate notions of how to meet their basic need to be accepted. Dreikurs proposed a variety of methods for responding to children's misconduct, depending on the goal of the behavior. His model provided teachers and parents with strategies for identifying the causes of students' misbehavior, responding to misbehavior with logical consequences, and running family and classroom meetings.

Emphasis on humanistic psychology was most obvious in the models of self-concept theorists. Initially summarized by LaBenne and Green (1969) and Purkey (1970), this work focused on the relationships among positive student self-concepts, students' learning, and productive behavior. This work was extended to a more practical program for teachers by Tom Gordon (1974), whose *Teacher Effectiveness Training* provided them with techniques for responding to students' misbehavior with open communication and attempts at mutually solving problems. In the early to mid-1990s, the focus on students' needs and problem solving continued with books such as Glasser's *Quality School* (1990), Brendtro, Brokenleg, and Van Bockern's *Reclaiming Youth at Risk* (1990), Curwin and Mendler's *Discipline with Dignity* (1988), Mendler's *What Do I Do When . . . ? How to Achieve Discipline with Dignity in the Classroom* (1992), and Fay and Funk's *Teaching with Love and Logic* (1995).

In addition, an emphasis has been placed on the concepts of social skill training, and social problem solving that focus on irresponsible behaviors as skill deficits in interacting with others. A social skills approach emphasizes providing students with new skills that enable them to elicit positive responses from others and thus improve their self-esteem, enhance positive relationships with peers whose behavior is socially acceptable, and reduce the incidence of behaviors that are viewed as undesirable or unacceptable. Gresham (1998) suggests three types of social skills deficits:

> *Social skills acquisition deficits* refers to either the absence of knowledge of how to execute particular social skills or a failure to discriminate when certain social behaviors are appropriate. *Social performance deficits* represent the presence of social skills in a behavioral repertoire, but failure to perform these behaviors at acceptable levels in specific situations. *Fluency deficits* stem from a lack of exposure to sufficient models of behavior, insufficient rehearsal or practice of skills, or low rates or inconsistent delivery of reinforcement for skill performance. (p. 20)

Social problem-solving interventions are often defined as direct approaches to reducing aggressive behavior and are most often used with children and youth who display high rates of aggressive behavior. This approach emphasizes four major intervention components: (1) a focus on students' thought processes when approaching a conflict situation, (2) instruction in a specific sequence of procedures for resolving conflicts, (3) practice in using these steps, and (4) prompts, feedback, and reinforcement to assist students in understanding the utilizing the new skills (Farmer, Farmer, & Gut, 1999; Kazdin, 1991). These methods emphasize instructing students in new cognitive and behavioral skills, and they provide a blend of the traditional counseling approach with the behavioral approach.

Teacher-Effectiveness Research

While counseling approaches vied for popularity, a new emphasis on classroom management was developing during the 1970s. This new direction emphasized not what teachers did in response to student misconduct but rather how teachers prevented or contributed to students' misbehavior. This research, later labeled *teacher effectiveness*, focused attention on three sets of teacher behaviors that influence students' behavior and learning: (1) teachers' skills in organizing and managing classroom activities, (2) teachers' skills in presenting instructional material, and (3) teacher–student relationships.

Teachers' Organizational and Management Skills
A study that initially displayed the importance of teachers' organizational and management skills was reported in Jacob Kounin's 1970 book, *Discipline and Group Management*

in Classrooms. Kounin and colleagues videotaped thousands of hours in classrooms that ran smoothly with a minimum of disruptive behavior and classrooms in which students were frequently inattentive and disruptive. The videotapes were then systematically analyzed to determine what teachers in these two very different types of classrooms did differently when students misbehaved. The results showed no systematic differences. Effective classroom managers were not notably different from poor classroom managers in their ways of responding to students' misbehavior. Further analysis, however, demonstrated clear and significant differences between how effective and ineffective classroom managers behaved prior to students' misbehavior. Effective classroom managers used various teaching methods that prevented disruptive student behavior.

The Texas Teacher Effectiveness Study was a second landmark study dealing with organizing and managing behavior. In this study, reported in *Learning from Teaching* by Jere Brophy and Carolyn Evertson (1976), the researchers observed fifty-nine teachers over two years. Teachers were selected to provide two groups whose students differed consistently in performance on standardized achievement tests. Classroom observations focused on teachers' behaviors previously suggested as being related to effective teaching. The results of the study supported Kounin's findings on effective behaviors that prevented disruption and facilitated learning by creating smoothly run classrooms.

The findings of Kounin and of Brophy and Evertson were expanded by Emmer, Evertson, and Anderson (1980) in the Classroom Organization and Effective Teaching Project carried out at the Research and Development Center for Teacher Education at the University of Texas at Austin. In the first of a series of studies, these researchers observed 28 third-grade classrooms during the first several weeks of school. The research findings showed that the smooth functioning found in effective teachers' classrooms throughout the school year mostly resulted from effective planning and organization during the first few weeks of school. Effective classroom managers provided students with clear instruction in desirable classroom behavior and carefully monitored students' performance—reteaching behaviors that students had not mastered. Effective teachers also made consequences for misbehavior clear and applied these consistently. This study was followed by research in junior high school classrooms (Evertson, 1985; Evertson & Emmer, 1982a), which verified the importance that early planning and instruction in appropriate behavior have in secondary school settings.

More recently, the work in classroom and school organization and management has been expanded to include a greater focus on schoolwide approaches and the incorporation of democratic principles. Jerome Freiberg's *consistency management and cooperative discipline* emphasized a shared commitment between students and teachers to develop positive learning environments, a focus on instructional strategies, and the involvement of families (Freiberg, 1999; Freiberg, Stein, & Huang, 1995). The positive behavior support (Lewis, 2001; Sugai & Horner, 2001) approach emphasizes a schoolwide commitment to teaching behaviors that support a safe and caring school environment, reinforcing these behaviors, reteaching students who fail to consistently use these behaviors, and developing individualized plans for students who continue to make irresponsible decisions.

An approach that differs somewhat from the behavioral approaches to classroom and schoolwide student management is Forest Gathercoal's judicious discipline (Gathercoal, 2001). According to Gathercoal, an approach to student behavior is most effective when it is based on helping students understand their constitutional rights and the responsibilities stemming from living in a constitutional democracy. Students are assisted in understanding their rights but also that their behavior cannot infringe on the rights of theirs. Gathercoal's model also encourages educators to view students' poor behavior choices as opportunities to help students make amends and learn new skills.

Instructional Skills

A second area of investigation on teachers' behavior that prevents disruptive student behavior and enhances learning examines how material is presented to students. Some of the earliest work on this subject was conducted by Madeline Hunter. For more than two decades, her Instructional Theory into Practice (ITIP) program attempted to translate findings in educational psychology into practical strategies that improved instruction. Though her work emphasizes some of the skills highlighted by researchers interested in classroom organization and teacher–student relationships, her major contribution was in helping teachers understand the need to develop clear instructional goals, state these to students, provide effective direct instruction, and monitor students' progress.

This research was expanded by studies that examined the relationship between various teacher instructional patterns and students' achievement. These studies, often called *process-product research* because they examine correlations between instructional processes and student outcomes or products, were thoughtfully reviewed by Rosenshine (1983) and Good (1983).

More recently an emphasis has been placed on differentiated instruction. Differentiated instruction is supported by brain research suggesting that students learn best in settings characterized by emotional safety, appropriate levels of challenge, and active involvement in constructing meaning (Tomlinson & Kalbfleisch, 1998). Differentiated instruction emphasizes incorporating a wide range of instructional strategies and matching instruction to students' readiness, interests, and preferred ways of processing information (Tomlinson, 1999). Tomlinson provided an example of using differentiated instruction when she wrote:

> In her Algebra II class, Mrs. Wang helps students identify key concepts and skills in a given chapter. After various chapter assessments, students are encouraged to look at their own assessment results and select homework assignments and in-class miniworkshops that help them clarify areas of confusion. She encourages students to decide whether they work most effectively alone or with a partner and to make that choice when there are opportunities to do so. (p. 7)

Another field of study examines the relative merits of competitive, cooperative, and individualized instruction. This work, carried out by Roger and David Johnson of the University of Minnesota, demonstrates that cooperative learning activities are associated with many desirable learning outcomes. Students who work cooperatively on learning tasks tend to relate more positively to their peers, to view learning as more positive, and to learn more information. Additional work in cooperative team learning was carried out by Robert Slavin, who developed the teams-games-tournaments approach, and by Spencer Kagan (1989), who developed a practical book entitled *Cooperative Learning: Resources for Teachers*.

Another area of study is the variability in how students learn best and how teachers can adjust instruction to respond to students' individual learning styles. This work—carried out by Rita Dunn (Dunn & DeBello, 1999; Dunn, Theis, & Honigsfeld, 2001) has shown that when teachers allow students to study in environments modified to respond to students' varying learning preferences, students, including those with special learning needs, learn more and behave in ways that facilitate their learning and that of others. Howard Gardner's work on multiple intelligences (Gardner 1999a, 1999b; Lazear, 1999) has suggested that there are at least eight types of intelligence and that individuals respond differently to various types of content, for example, language, math, music, and so on. Gardner suggests that teachers should attempt to adapt instruction and assessment to respond in some ways to each child's individual strengths. He also suggests that teachers will be more effective in enhancing student achievement when they help students relate instructional activities to something valued in the student's world.

Recent research and practice has focused on a constructivist approach to learning in which students are actively involved in creating knowledge and meaning (Bruner, 1996; Gardner, 1999b). Modern pedagogy is focusing increasingly on the view that children should be aware of their own approach to learning. This work has included a focus on curriculum integration (Beane, 1995) real world problem solving (Nagel, 1996, 2001), and place-based education (Smith, 2002).

Increased work has also been conducted on how most effectively to assist students whose second language is English. Chapter 6 provides specific strategies and references for incorporating these areas of instruction into your teaching.

Teacher–Student Relationships

The third major research area within the teacher-effectiveness paradigm focuses on the effect teacher–student interactions have on students' achievements and behaviors. This field of study can be divided into two basic parts: (1) studies exploring the influence of the frequency and quality of teacher–student interactions on students' achievements and (2) studies emphasizing the personal, affective dimension of teacher–student relationships and their effect on students' attitudes and, to a lesser degree, achievement.

Robert Rosenthal and Leonore Jacobson's *Pygmalion in the Classroom* (1968) generated tremendous interest in the influence teacher–student relationships have on students' achievements. These authors reported that teachers' expectations for students' performance became self-fulfilling prophecies. In other words, students seem to perform as teachers expect them to. The important question became what specifically teachers do to communicate high or low expectations to students. This question was initially studied by Brophy and Good (1971, 1974) at the University of Texas. This research has been replicated and expanded (Wineburg, 1987), including examination of attribution theory and factors related to teachers' sense of control (Cooper & Good, 1983). Numerous writers have also examined how teacher–student interactions may handicap the achievement of girls. The 1992 American Association of University Women (AAUW) report *How Schools Shortchange Girls* provides an excellent summary of ways in which schools must change if they are to most effective serve one-half of the school population.

The other area of study involves the affective quality of teacher–student relationships and its effect on students' attitudes and self-concepts. This research was first widely reported in the late 1960s and early 1970s in books such as LaBenne and Green's *Educational Implications of Self-Concept Theory* (1969) and William Purkey's *Self-Concept and School Achievement* (1970). Although interpersonal relationships in the classroom were emphasized less during the mid-1970s, research and practical ideas on this subject received more attention in the early 1980s (Purkey & Novak, 1984).

Recent work has examined how teachers respond effectively to disruptive student behavior (Shores & Wheby, 1999; Walker & Sylvester, 1998). When it is necessary to redirect students who are making poor choices, these authors suggest using clear, direct, specific requests as opposed to vague demands lacking clear directives and an opportunity for compliance. In his book, *Judicious Discipline*, Gathercoal (2001) suggests that teachers examine their own behaviors to ensure that students are consistently treated with dignity.

Behavioristic Methods

As social uneasiness rose about disruptive behavior of youth, the focus of classroom discipline moved in the direction of teacher control. This increased attention to discipline was associated with the development and popularization of behavioristic methodology. Beginning in the mid-1970s, most courses aimed at helping teachers cope with disruptive student behavior focused almost exclusively on behavior modification techniques. Teachers were taught to ignore inappropriate behavior while reinforcing appropriate behavior, to write contracts with recalcitrant students, and to use time-out procedures. This emphasis on control was most systematically presented to teachers in Canter and Canter's (1976) *Assertive Discipline*. Teachers learned to state clear general behavioral expectations, quietly and consistently punish disruptive students, and provide group reinforcement for on-task behavior. Behavioral control has also been emphasized in the work of Fredric Jones (1987). Jones focuses on the teachers' effective use of body language, the use of incentive systems, and individual assistance for academic problems.

The behavioral tradition has also been characterized by change and the integration of concepts from other models. Lee Canter has expanded his initial focus on controlling student behavior by adding materials on beginning the school year, working with parents, and helping students with homework. Indeed Canter (1996) stated that although the techniques he initially recommended in *Assertive Discipline* worked well in the 1970s and 1980s, they needed to be changed for the twenty-first century. He clearly stated that, to be effective, any discipline system must be grounded in respectful, supportive teacher–student relationships.

In recent years, researchers and practitioners who emphasize the behavioral approach have increasingly focused their attention on teaching students appropriate behavior skills. Perhaps the most noted approach is termed *positive behavioral support*. This approach incorporates much of the work from earlier studies in effective classroom management. Specifically, this approach emphasizes (1) working with school staff to define, teach, and reinforce socially acceptable school behaviors; (2) providing small-group and individual instruction for appropriate behavior to students who need additional assistance; (3) developing an individualized plan to assist students who continue to make poor behavior choices based on a detailed analysis of the factors influencing a student's behavior (functional behavior assessment); and (4) creating family, school, and community partnerships to support the academic and behavioral needs of individual students (Frankland, Edmonson, & Turnbull, 2001; Lewis, 2001; Sugai, Horner, & Gresham, 2002).

As mentioned in the earlier section on the counseling approach, an increased emphasis has been placed on using behavioral technology to teach students appropriate social and problem-solving skills. Although behavioral methods continue to support practices emphasizing the reinforcement of desired behavior, the focus has shifted toward helping students monitor their own behavior and providing instruction to add new behaviors to students' repertoires.

"I've tried various forms of discipline, and I find that radio control works best."

COMPREHENSIVE CLASSROOM MANAGEMENT

Having read the previous section, take a minute and write your own definition of effective classroom management. What classroom management skills do effective teachers demonstrate? What attitudes characterize educators who are effective at helping students develop and commit to using responsible, caring behavior in classroom and school settings? It might be helpful to write down your thoughts, and, with a group of fellow students or colleagues, generate a list to share with others. Eventually, you will create an approach to classroom management that is uniquely yours. After completing this book or course, revisit your notes at this point and revise them to incorporate new ideas and understandings.

Jere Brophy (1988) provided a thoughtful, general definition of classroom management when he wrote:

> Good classroom management implies not only that the teacher has elicited the cooperation of the students in minimizing misconduct and can intervene effectively when misconduct occurs, but also that worthwhile academic activities are occurring more or less continuously and that the classroom management system as a whole (which includes, but is not limited to, the teacher's disciplinary interventions) is designed to maximize student engagement in those activities, not merely to minimize misconduct. (p. 3)

We agree with Brophy's definition and suggest that to be effectively implemented, comprehensive classroom management includes five areas of knowledge and skill.

First, *classroom management should be based on a solid understanding of current research and theory in classroom management and on students' personal and psychological needs.* The authors' experiences in teaching classroom management courses and consulting with schools suggest that, despite extensive worry about students' achievements and misbehavior, very few teachers understand why problems exist or the relationship between the problem and their own professional behaviors and the failure to meet students' personal and academic needs.

Once teachers understand students' needs and how these needs are related to behavior, the next step in developing a well-managed classroom is to ensure that students' personal needs are met in the classroom. Therefore, a second factor is that *classroom management depends on establishing positive teacher–student and peer relationships that create classrooms as communities of support.* Creating more desirable student behavior by concentrating on establishing positive, supportive classroom environments is based on a concept presented by numerous psychologists and educators: Individuals learn effectively in environments that meet their basic personal and psychological needs.

Although the creation of positive relationships in classrooms can significantly improve student behavior and achievement, research and the authors' observations increasingly support the importance of instructional excellence. Thus, the third factor in effective classroom management is that *comprehensive classroom management involves using instructional methods that facilitate optimal learning by responding to the academic needs of individual students and the classroom group.* This aspect of classroom management is based on the idea that "low motivation, negative self attitudes, and failure are largely the result of improper learning conditions. According to this learning-theory analysis, we should be able to alter a student's failure rate by changing the conditions of classroom learning and, as a consequence, increase his motivation to succeed" (Covington & Beery, 1976, pp. 12–13).

Most classrooms include twenty-five to thirty-five students. Teachers are responsible for orchestrating the movement, attention, and learning of varied students in a limited space. Therefore, regardless of how well a teacher understands students' needs, creates a positive emotional climate, and effectively provides instruction, organizational skills are critical. Consequently, the fourth factor is that *comprehensive classroom management involves using organizational and group management methods that involve students in developing and committing to behavioral standards that help create a safe, caring community and using teaching methods that facilitate clear classroom organization.* Teachers' organizational and instructional skills interact to influence students' achievements.

The creation of a positive classroom environment characterized by effective teaching and organizational skills will go a long way toward reducing behavior problems and increasing students' achievements. However, anyone who has taught or worked with children who have behavior problems is aware that some children will, at least for a time, behave inappropriately in even the most productive learning environments. Consequently, teachers need a repertoire of behavior management skills to support their instructional skills. The final factor in management is that *classroom management involves the ability to use a wide range of counseling and behavioral methods that involve students in examining and correcting their inappropriate behavior.*

Many teachers say that they do not have time to use in-depth counseling strategies; this statement is generally accurate and realistic. Teachers cannot be expected to use in-depth counseling strategies within the classroom. However, many relatively simple yet effective approaches are available for helping children examine and change their behaviors. Because teachers are increasingly faced with the task of teaching children who require special assistance, it has become necessary that teachers acquire problem-solving and behavior management techniques.

These five basic factors and their relationships to the chapter organization of this book are depicted in Figure 1.2. Even though teachers will want to examine methods associated with each factor, changes aimed at creating positive student behavior should proceed in the hierarchic order suggested in Figure 1.2. When they are faced with problems concerning students' classroom behaviors, teachers too often begin to intervene at the upper end of the hierarchy without laying a foundation by developing

Correction (Chapters 8–10)	*Factor 5* Helping students evaluate and correct unproductive behavior	Schoolwide student management programs Developing individual behavior change plans Using problem-solving methods Professional responses to disruptive student behavior	**FIGURE 1.2** Teacher Skills for Developing Comprehensive Classroom Management
Prevention (Chapters 3–7)	*Factor 4* Organization and management (Chapter 7)	Developing behavior norms and implementing methods that maximize on-task student behavior	
	Factor 3 Motivation and instruction (Chapter 6)	Incorporating teaching methods that motivate students by responding to their learning needs	
	Factor 2 Interpersonal relationships (Chapters 3–5)	Working with parents Creating positive peer relationships Establishing positive teacher–student relationships	
Theoretical Foundation (Chapters 1, 2)	*Factor 1* Developing a sound theoretical foundation	Understanding students' personal needs Understanding classroom management	

prerequisite knowledge and using preventive interventions. When they do, interventions will, at best, cause a limited, short-term improvement in students' behaviors and may create greater student resentment and alienation.

P A U S E

and Consider   **1.4**

> You have just read a section describing the key concepts and skills associated with effectively creating classroom communities in which students learn most effectively and treat others with respect. Look back at what you wrote in Pause and Consider 1.3. How does what you just read compare with what you wrote regarding a definition and key components associated with effective classroom management? You may want to write briefly about this or share your discoveries with a peer or small group.

P A U S E

and Consider   **1.5**

> Take a moment to examine Figure 1.2. Where are you most comfortable in your skills and strengths regarding comprehensive classroom management? What areas most concern you or do you view as important for professional growth?

FACTORS INFLUENCING HOW TEACHERS MANAGE THEIR CLASSROOMS

Although most key concepts in classroom management generalize quite well across settings, it is important to realize that some adjustments will need to be made to adapt concepts and strategies in light of context variables.

Students' Characteristics and Needs

One clear challenge is the number of non-White students who comprise the student population of U.S. schools and our relatively poor rate of success with many of these student groups.

> The unfortunate result is that by the eighth grade 40 percent or more of black and Hispanic students are performing one grade level or more below expected and normal achievement levels. These findings, in concert with the previously discussed high school completion and dropout data, raise important educational concerns. Clearly, as the population of nonwhite and Hispanic students increases to an estimated 70 percent of the total U.S. student population in 2026, this underachievement will be an extreme waste of intellectual potential—a loss that we cannot afford in the least. (Garcia, 1999, p. 27)

Studies indicate that high expectations, active engagement of students, thematic instruction, interactive cross-age tutoring, cooperative learning, and the incorporation of various aspects of students' cultures were important elements in effective instruction for students from diverse cultures (August & Hakuta, 1997; Freeman & Freeman, 2002; Garcia, 1999). Teachers who incorporate these methods will find that classroom management problems are dramatically reduced by instructional methods that respond sensitively to students' personal, developmental, and cultural needs. Studies also consistently support students with limited English proficiency receiving instruction in their first language during at least part of the school day (Freeman & Freeman, 2002; National Association for Education for Young Children, 1997; National Council of Teachers of English and the International Reading Association, 1996). Chapter 6 presents a wide range of strategies that have proved to be associated with higher learning gains and more positive behavior for students from diverse cultural groups.

Students' cultural backgrounds may also affect how teachers relate to students. Ballenger (1992) provides an engaging description of a North American teacher's discovery that the perspective from which she viewed behavior control and her use of language needed to be altered to effectively manage young Haitian students. Ballenger found that, when dealing with behavior problems, Haitian parents and teachers did not talk about children's feelings or individual consequences. Instead, they focused on the fact that the behavior was "bad" and that it was disappointing to significant adults in the child's life that the child would act in this manner. Ballenger (1992) noted that:

> The North American teachers characteristically are concerned with making a connection with the individual child, with articulating his or her feelings and problems. . . . The Haitian people I spoke with and observed, emphasize the group in their control talk, articulating the values and responsibilities of group membership. (p. 204)

Ballenger comments that her observations suggested that North American teachers, particularly those in the primary grades, were reluctant to firmly correct students, while Haitian teachers seemed to see this as part of strengthening teacher–student relationships. While acknowledging the fact that, "North Americans perceive Haitians as too severe, both verbally and in their use of physical punishment" (p. 206), Ballenger emphasized that creating too great a discrepancy between parental and teacher responses to misbehavior may cause serious problems because it can have a negative impact on the relationships between the teacher and the child.

Macias (1987) also described concerns regarding continuity in her study of Papago preschoolers (members of an American Indian group in Arizona). She noted:

> For many children of ethnic minority origin, the transition from home to school in early childhood appears to be a critical period of discontinuity. The way in which cultural disparities—between what has been learned at home and what school teaches—are dealt with determines to some degree the efficacy of their schooling. (p. 364)

Macias writes about the discrepancy between the Papago child's autonomy and limited restrictions at home and the rules and structures with which the child is confronted at school. She also highlights the conflict caused by the use in school of individualized reinforcement.

> Respect in the form of a deep appreciation of each child's distinctiveness is an important characteristic of Papago childrearing. But this type of respect is not dependent upon attention from adults but rather on noninterference with children's autonomy. In other words, Papagos place an emphasis on individual rights and choice rather than on the singling out of individuals from their peers or family for special recognition. In fact, Papagos generally place a negative value on calling attention to oneself, and there is a reluctance on the part of individual children to separate socially from the group. (p. 370)

One can imagine the conflicts this would cause in classrooms in which children are called on to perform and in which many of the public reinforcements are provided for individual excellence.

Macias (1987) also stated that there were numerous experiences school staff believed were valuable for the Papago children but that were incongruent with the manner in which situations would be handled in their homes. Macias described the experiences the staff at the Papago Early Childhood Head Start Program (PECHS) wanted children to have, the reason they believed these experiences were valuable for school success, the ways in which these experiences conflicted with the children's cultural values, and the strategies the teachers used to limit the negative impact of these discontinuous experiences. As Macias pointed out, it is neither possible nor desirable to replicate every approach used in a child's family or cultural setting. It is, however, important to be respectful of students' cultural values and styles, to incorporate them whenever possible, and to thoughtfully and gradually introduce new skills and behaviors.

Several years ago one of the authors was working in an elementary school located in a community in which approximately one-third of the students were Native American. Several teachers expressed annoyance when they discovered nice, shiny, "I'm #1" buttons in the waste baskets. During a faculty discussion concerning the lack of respect for school property displayed by these students, a Native American staff member informed the teachers that in her culture, students were encouraged not to outshine their friends. She noted that students from her tribe would be chastised by members of the tribe for bringing home an item indicating they had outperformed their friends and focused attention on themselves. The staff assistant had provided the teachers with an important lesson in how methods used to encourage and motivate students are more effective when they are responsive to students' cultural values.

In an ethnographic study of five student-teachers placed in schools with students from cultural backgrounds dramatically different from their own, Dana (1992) found that students reported major problems with classroom management. Her findings suggest that, rather than examine issues regarding school factors, the student-teachers attributed their difficulties to their students' backgrounds and found their efforts to implement the prepackaged technique of assertive discipline ineffective and frustrating. This highlights the problems associated with teachers being given "cookbook" approaches to classroom management.

In his year-long ethnographic study in a second-grade classroom, George Noblit (1993) recounts how his experiences challenged his White, middle-class, professorial notions of power and structure and how he came to appreciate the more structured, teacher-directed style used by an African American woman. Noblit concludes:

> I have much to learn about moral authority, but I think I now know where to focus my efforts. First, I must try to learn more from African American teachers. They may construct education and caring quite differently than my own race. (p. 37)

Noblit's initial concepts of authority in a classroom were those of someone who had never taught in a public school classroom and whose background was in organizational development rather than educational research.

Regardless of the extent to which teachers decide to adapt to the norms and parenting styles of their students' cultures or systematically assist students in learning to adapt while maintaining their cultural values, the point is that as educators we are willing to examine our own beliefs and way of working with students in light of the contextual variables existing in the classroom, school, and community.

The School Context

It is impossible to separate management from such issues as school climate, structure, decision making, and the type of professional support that is provided within the building. School variables have a significant impact on student behavior and learning. Schools in which the staff have developed a unified sense of mission and in which they work collaboratively to support one another in reaching clear goals are characterized by fewer student behavior problems (Freiberg et al., 1995; Sugai, 1997). Likewise, as discussed throughout the book, student behavior is more positive in schools where students experience a sense of belonging and support and in which instructional activities engage them in meaningful ways connected to their own lives and cultures. To establish learning environments in which students feel less alienated and isolated, an increasing number of secondary school staff are examining ways to structure the schoolday so students have longer class periods or blocked classes. This allows students to work for extended periods of time with one adult and one group of peers. The focus on student and teacher empowerment and quality of life within schools is an essential component in educators' ongoing efforts to create safer, more productive learning environments.

Our Own Personal Histories

A number of researchers have also highlighted the important role teachers' preconceptions play in teacher decision making (Brickhouse & Bodner, 1992; Kaplan, 1992). Clandinin and Connelly (1986) suggest that teachers develop practical strategies by integrating their preconceptions (personal biographies) with their interpretations of classroom situations. Studies report significant relationships between teacher personality factors and their orientation to classroom management. In a study of 156 preservice teachers, Kaplan (1992) found that "teachers' disciplinary experiences in their families of origin are predictive of the strategies they select for classroom management" (p. 263). Teachers' approaches to creating positive classroom learning environments and responding to student behavior that disrupts the learning environment is influenced by their own personal history, their personality, their experience with children, and the quality of their education regarding classroom management. Not surprisingly, therefore, teachers will vary considerably in how they approach the important tasks associated with effective classroom management.

One of the most important professional decisions you will make is how you choose to create and maintain a learning environment that is comfortable and supportive for all learners. Some educators and writers suggest that teachers should select an approach that is consistent with their own personality and matches their own preferences. Consider for a moment situations in which you seek professional help—possibly seeing a physician or dentist. Do you want the professional to choose an approach to treating you based on what makes that person most comfortable or on the most current research related to the condition that caused you to seek assistance? We have worked with many educators whose approach to classroom management involved controlling students and attempting to have the least possible contact with parents and guardians. We have worked with teachers whose classrooms were uninviting and, at times, frightening places for children. During their high school experiences one of our children was sprayed in the face with water for turning his body to be comfortable in a chair, and the other was yanked out of her seat for asking a friend a question about a computer during a study hall in the library. These methods were both defended by the educators involved as being methods with which they felt most comfortable. Certainly there is no "one correct way" to create a learning environment in which we enhance the probability that all students will experience success. However, there are strong guiding principles, methods that have proven effective, methods with sound research support, and methods that cannot be defended by other professionals.

We are not suggesting that your personal beliefs and styles should not be considered when making a decision about how to create a positive, safe, supportive learning environment. Your own values and beliefs, the ages of your students, the community in which you teach, the amount of time you have with your students, and many other factors will influence your decision. We would, however, encourage you to consider that a significant amount of research supports the five components of effective classroom management outline earlier in this chapter. If you are to be effective in creating a learning environment that supports optimal learning for a wide range of students, you will need to develop skills in each of the five areas outlined. Additionally, as a professional, you will need to ensure that the methods you select are supported by research and are deemed to be in the best interests of the students for whom you are responsible.

If you are just beginning your experience as a teacher, you are probably aware that many beginning teachers (as well as a significant number of veteran teachers) find classroom management to be the task with which they are least comfortable. First, effective classroom management requires allocating some time to creating a positive, supportive learning community. Given the emphasis on academic standards, there is increasing pressure to ignore the development of a safe community and move directly into a total focus on instruction. Although you may understand its importance, you may feel uncomfortable taking the time necessary to ensure that your students will act in ways that support a calm, positive learning environment. Second, if you are like most beginning teachers, you will find your responsibility to intervene when students act in ways that disrupt the learning environment as the most anxiety-provoking and uncomfortable aspect of your job. Most beginning teachers want to be liked by their students and are simultaneously unsure how best to intervene when students act irresponsibly. This is an aspect of teaching that requires not only knowledge and practice (a major reason we have written this text) but also experience and fine-tuning.

P A U S E

and Consider   **1.6**

At this point we suggest you stop for a minute and create a T-chart. On one side list the characteristics you believe you possess that will enhance your ability to effectively create and maintain a positive, supportive classroom environment. These may be personal characteristics, experiences with students from a wide range of socioeconomic and cultural backgrounds, experience with children, and so on. On the other side, list the concerns you have and skills you believe you will need to develop or enhance in order to more skillfully create such a learning environment. We believe this text will help you blend your strengths with new skills in a way that will prove rewarding to both you and your students. When you have finished reading this text or completed the course, we encourage you to revisit and revise this chart.

Our Beliefs Regarding the Goals of Schooling

Another key school factor influencing teachers' decisions regarding classroom management methods is the goals teachers have for their students. Although the pressures of teaching thirty-five students in a class with fewer resources than we need may have reduced the likelihood that we have asked this question recently, we will serve students best if we consistently ask ourselves, "What are my long-term goals for my students? How do I want their lives to have been impacted by the time they spent with me?" Whenever you consider what approach to use when establishing a classroom climate, motivating students, or responding to disruptive behaviors, it is influenced by your educational goals.

Perhaps one reason classroom management has historically placed such a strong emphasis on control and maximizing on-task behavior is that U.S. teachers tend to place a very heavy emphasis on academic and cognitive goals. In their comparison of teaching and teacher education in the United States and Japan, Nobuo Shimahara and Akira Sakai (1995) wrote:

> It follows that there are appreciable differences as well as similarities in what American and Japanese teachers view as the goals of education. As we have seen earlier, American classroom teachers framed them primarily in terms of cognitive achievement and academic performance. . . . In contrast, Japanese classroom teachers saw the basic goals of education much more broadly, encompassing competencies essential to the cognitive, moral, physical, social and aesthetic development of the students. (pp. 57, 58)

These writers go on to state:

> Japanese students have more opportunities than do American students for social interaction designed to improve skills in human relations, and Japanese teachers' routine responsibilities include mental, moral, aesthetic, physical, and social development. (p. 60)

There is little argument that a primary goal of public education is to provide students with skills to be happy and productive members of their societies. When considering how to best assist students in reaching this goal, we may need to ask such questions as: "What skills other than academic knowledge do we believe are necessary to reach this goal?" "What type of environment do we believe facilitates the attainment of our classroom instructional goals?"

In his book, *The Optimistic Child*, Martin Seligman (1995) wrote:

> We want more for our children than healthy bodies. We want our children to have lives filled with friendship and love and high deeds. We want them to be eager to learn and be willing to confront challenges. We want our children to be grateful for what they receive from us, but to be proud of their own accomplishments. We want them to grow up with confidence in the future, a love of adventure, a sense of justice, and courage enough to act on that sense of justice. We want them to be resilient in the face of the setbacks and failures that growing up always brings. And when the time comes, we want them to be good parents. (p. 6)

Alfie Kohn (1991) suggested that schools will best serve students and our society most productively if they focus on producing not only good learners but good people. Kohn noted that "a dozen years of schooling often do nothing to promote generosity or a commitment to the welfare of others. To the contrary, students are graduated who think that being smart means looking out for number one" (p. 498).

Kohn further suggested that schools are ideal places to nurture children's innate sense of caring and generosity of spirit. When discussing the possible argument that such a focus would involve teaching values or would detract from the families' responsibility for raising caring, honest children, Kohn wrote:

> It is sometimes said that moral concerns and social skills ought to be taught at home. I know of no one in the field of education or child development who disagrees. The problem is that such instruction—along with nurturance and warmth, someone to model altruism, opportunities to practice caring for others, and so forth—is not to be found in all homes. The school may need to provide what some children will not otherwise get. In any case, there is no conceivable danger in providing these values in both environments. Encouragement from more than one source to develop empathic relationships is a highly desirable form of redundancy. (p. 499)

Kohn suggested that teaching students in ways that facilitate caring and empathy will neither reduce their ability to function effectively in the adult world nor detract from the amount of content students will master. Indeed, he argues that both students' future success and the quality of learning will be enhanced in classroom and school environments that emphasize collaboration and caring.

In his article, "Discipline and Morality: Beyond Rules and Consequences," John Covaleskie (1992) suggested that "children must develop a sense of what it means to be a good person—what it means to choose to do the right thing, especially when circumstances are such that one is faced with the possibility of doing the wrong thing to one's own advantage, and getting away with it" (p. 174). He goes on to state that "the standard by which we should be judging 'discipline programs' in schools is that of moral responsibility: do our children learn to think, talk, and act morally? The goal is not compliance with rules, but making the choices to live a good life, an ethical life" (p. 176).

Nel Noddings (1992) responded to this issue when she wrote:

> To suppose, for example, that attention to affective needs necessarily implies less time for arithmetic is simply a mistake. Such tasks can be accomplished simultaneously, but the one is undertaken in light of the other. We do not ask how we must treat children in order to get them to learn arithmetic but, rather, what effect each instructional move we consider has on the development of good persons. Our guiding principles for teaching arithmetic, or any other subject, are derived from our primary concern for the persons whom we teach, the methods of teaching are chosen in consonance with these derived principles. An ethic of caring guides us to ask, What effect will this have on the person I teach? What effect will it have on the caring community we are trying to build? (p. 499)

An additional issue regarding the goals of schools relates to whether teachers choose a more teacher-directed, information-dissemination model of teaching or a more constructivistic, student-centered approach. Carolyn Evertson and Catherine Randolph (1995) state that "management actions communicate information to students about the kinds of knowledge and participation that are valued in a particular setting" (p. 120). If we wish students to be actively involved in constructing their own knowledge, it is likely that we will develop classroom management methods that focus more on an authoritative as opposed to an authoritarian approach, and that we will emphasize the teaching of procedures (as skills) and social skills as well as the use of problem solving to resolve conflicts.

One of the most commonly presented arguments against managing classrooms in ways that create communities of support or that focus on the student as an active learner is that it allows for less time for instruction in the "basics." Years of research seem to indicate that teachers will, of necessity, spend time dealing with issues related to student behavior. The question really becomes when and how we will spend the time. We can be proactive and spend time building a positive classroom environment in which behavioral norms are developed by, agreed on, and practiced by students and instruction is meaningful and engaging. Or, we can be reactive and spend countless minutes responding to the disruptions caused to a large degree by our decision not to spend time building a community of support. Studies (Lewis, Schaps, & Watson, 1996) suggest that a focus on building a sense of community can have many positive effects.

> At schools high in "community" . . . students show a host of positive outcomes. These include higher educational expectations and academic performance, stronger motivation to learn, greater liking for school, less absenteeism, greater social competence, fewer conduct problems, reduced drug use and delinquency, and greater commitment to democratic values. (p. 17)

Another response to the concern about "taking time away from the basics," is that the "basics" increasingly include a number of skills related to getting along with others, working collaboratively, and creating new ideas that are highly correlated with being successful in adult life. It would seem reasonable that schools provide students with skills for obtaining and maintaining employment. In their examination of national and regional studies on educational requirements needed for the job market, researchers from the Sandia National Laboratories (1993) wrote that "according to business leaders polled, the most important workplace 'skills' for future employees were not academic skills. Rather, behavioral 'skills' . . . were all listed in the 'highly critical' categories" (p. 295). It would seem that using classroom management methods that focus on teaching students to interact and collaborate more effectively may not only enhance classroom behavior but also may help students develop important life skills.

Along similar lines, in his book, *Emotional Intelligence*, Daniel Goleman (1995) suggested that how happy, fulfilled, and productive people are as adults is due only in small part to their intellectual ability as traditionally measured. He stated:

> My concern is with a key set of these "other characteristics," *emotional intelligence:* abilities such as being able to motivate oneself and persist in the face of frustrations; to control impulse and delay gratification; to regulate one's moods and keep distress from swamping the ability to think; to empathize and to hope. (p. 35)

In support of his beliefs, Goleman noted that in a follow-up study of 450 boys, results indicated that success at age forty-seven was related more to how the boys handled frustration, controlled their emotions, and got along with others than it was to intellectual ability (Felsman & Vaillant, 1987).

A second concern often expressed in response to teachers using classroom management methods that focus on developing communities of support and teaching students prosocial life skills, comes from individuals who suggest that all values are relative and, therefore, educators have no right to impose their belief systems on children. To this argument we would suggest that certain basic ethical standards exist in our society. Generally, it is considered wrong to steal from, sexually harass, or physically harm someone. Likewise, it is generally considered unacceptable to disrupt a work environment or infringe on someone's constitutional rights. Creating classrooms in which these standards are upheld seems to be educators' legal obligation rather than a reflection of their philosophy of classroom management.

All classrooms and schools operate based on some set of values or belief system. Teachers who use assertive discipline to control eighth graders who are restless because they are listening to a forty-minute lecture on content that is too abstract for their cognitive level were making a value decision based on their beliefs about learning and the developmental skills of their learners. Schools that create drug free and violence free zones are basing this on a value that students need to be protected and that students learn more effectively in safe environments. Classrooms must be built on the belief that everyone's personal and property rights and right to learn must be respected. The question is whether the beliefs and values are grounded in the best existing research regarding factors that facilitate student learning and personal growth.

PAUSE

and Consider   **1.7**

> We suggest you stop at this point and write a brief response to the following questions: What type of classroom environment do I believe enhances the kind of learning I hope my students will achieve? In addition to academic content knowledge, what skills and attitudes do I want my students to have developed or enhanced when they leave my classroom? We believe your responses to these questions will significantly influence the manner in which you choose to organize and manage your classroom. As you read this text, keep these questions in mind as you decide which classroom management skills you will incorporate in your professional repertoire.

The Importance of Personal Reflection

Because the decisions we make regarding how we build a sense of community and respond to behavior problems are heavily influenced by contextual factors, including our own personal history, it is imperative that any study of classroom management place a heavy focus on personal reflection. Stoiber (1991) conducted a study comparing technical and reflective preservice instruction in classroom management. Her findings suggest that teachers trained using a reflective-constructive approach develop more positive perceptions of themselves as problem solvers within the classroom, are able to generate more solutions to classroom management problems, take more responsibility for classroom events, and report more concern about students' feelings and attitudes than teachers provided with technical training based on the beginning school year studies.

In a similar vein, Carter (1992) recommended that teachers take advantage of opportunities to reflect on organizing concepts and principles regarding classroom management. Winitzky (1992) reported a positive correlation between the complexity of teachers' knowledge structures and their ability to thoughtfully reflect on classroom practice.

In order for you to develop organizing concepts and principles, we have included brief discussions regarding theoretical and research rationale for implementing the methods presented in the text. In order to facilitate your reflection, we have included

Pause and Consider features aimed at helping you examine how you might incorporate the methods we present. It is our fervent hope that you will find the materials in this book useful in your day-to-day work with students. Even more importantly, however, we hope the materials in the text assist you in thinking about your teaching and in developing your own, ever-changing approach to assisting students become responsible citizens both within your classroom and school and as they become adults.

SUMMARY

Teachers continue to experience persistent and often serious problems stemming from students acting in ways that disrupt the learning environment. Given the increasing number of students who will enter U.S. schools at risk for school failure, it seems likely that during the next decade teachers will continually need to upgrade their skills in motivating and managing students.

Fortunately, research in classroom management has expanded dramatically during the past twenty-five years. Teachers no longer need to depend on simplistic advice for or unidimensional answers to the complex tasks of motivating and managing students. Teachers can increasingly draw on an expanding body of methods that will enable them to create more positive, supportive classroom environments; better organize and instruct their students; and more effectively respond to the behavior of students who act irresponsibly, even in supportive, well-managed classrooms characterized by clear, meaningful instruction. The efficacy of new methods can be enhanced if teachers have a clear philosophy of classroom management and understand their own responsibilities and those of their students and the school support personnel. Finally, school systems can better assist students with serious behavior problems if all educators within the system understand the methods to be followed in responding to unproductive student behavior.

Students who create classroom management and instructional challenges are, in fact, our best staff development specialists. They let us know that even though we may be very good, we can always expand our skills. Fortunately, almost without exception, the new methods we implement to assist students who are struggling with their learning and behavior will be beneficial for all students. Effective classroom management is not a zero-sum game in that efforts to assist students in need necessarily detract from other students. When we use the methods suggested in this book, we not only enhance our ability to reach the student at risk but we simultaneously enrich the learning experience of all our students.

ACTIVITY 1.1

Developing a Theory of Management

Write a statement regarding your goals for teaching (e.g., if you are or will be teaching high school English, what are your primary goals for students for the year?).

Write a brief statement describing your current beliefs about classroom management.

Briefly describe how this approach to classroom management will facilitate your reaching the goals you described in the first section of this activity.

ACTIVITY 1.2	Write a statement regarding your beliefs about students' behaviors that includes an answer to the following questions:
Developing a Philosophy about Student Behavior Management	• What is the most common cause of student misbehavior? • When students misbehave, what type of teacher response or consequence is the most effective? Why? • As a parent or someone caring for children outside of a school setting, how do I usually respond to a behavior problem? • How do my current responses relate to those that were used with me when I was growing up? 1. After reading these statements, write a brief summary describing your general belief or philosophy about managing the behavior of children and youth. 2. As you work with the material in this book, you are encouraged to return to this summary and add comments and modifications, so that it becomes a working document for your professional examination of your classroom management methods.

RECOMMENDED READING

Baker, J. (1998). Are we missing the forest for the trees? Considering the social context of school violence. *Journal of School Psychology, 36,* 29–44.

Banks, J., & McGee Banks, C. (Eds.). (1993). *Multicultural education: Issues and perspective* (2nd ed.). Boston: Allyn & Bacon.

Beyer, L. (Ed.). (1996). *Creating democratic classrooms: The struggle to integrate theory & practice.* New York: Teachers College Press.

Bruner, J. (1996). *The culture of education.* Cambridge, MA: Harvard University Press.

Darling-Hammond, L. (1997). *The right to learn: A blueprint for creating schools that work.* San Francisco: Jossey-Bass.

Elliott, D., Hamburg, B., & Williams, K. (Eds.). (1998). *Violence in American schools: A new perspective.* Cambridge, England: Cambridge University Press.

Garbarino, J. (1999). *Lost boys: Why our sons turn violent and how we can save them.* New York: Free Press.

Garcia, E. (1999). *Student cultural diversity: Understanding and meeting the challenge* (2nd ed.). Boston: Houghton Mifflin.

Gathercoal, F. (2001). *Judicious discipline* (5th ed.). San Francisco: Caddo Gap.

Good, T., & Brophy, J. (2000). *Looking in classrooms* (8th ed.). New York: Harper & Row.

Hyman, A., & Perone, D. (1998). The other side of school violence: Educator policies and practices that may contribute to student misbehavior. *Journal of School Psychology, 30,* 7–27.

Kuykendall, C. (2003). *From rage to hope: Strategies for reclaiming Black and Hispanic students.* Bloomington, IN: National Educational Service.

Ladson-Billings, G. (2003). *The dreamkeepers: Successful teachers of African American children.* San Francisco: Jossey-Bass.

Meier, D. (1995). *The power of their ideas.* Boston: Beacon Press.

Noddings, N. (1992). *The challenge to care in schools: An alternative approach to education.* New York: Teachers College Press.

Rutter, M., Maughan, B., Montimore, P., Ouston, J., & Smith, A. (1979). *Fifteen thousand hours.* Cambridge, MA: Harvard University Press.

Sergiovanni, T. (1994). *Building community in schools.* San Francisco: Jossey-Bass.

Smith, G. (Ed.). (1993). *Public schools that work: Creating community.* New York: Routledge.

2

Understanding Students' Basic Psychological Needs

> *Teaching is difficult under the best educational conditions, and this failure to take into account the needs of students or teachers makes what is already a hard job almost impossible. Any method of teaching that ignores the needs of teachers or students is bound to fail.*
>
> —William Glasser (1990)
> *The Quality School: Managing Students Without Coercion*

> *Teachers can augment the academic self-image by identifying and developing some of the unique cultural and social strengths Black and Hispanic youth bring to the classroom. An understanding of how the social self-image can be used to bolster the academic self-image is critical.*
>
> —Crystal Kuykendall (1992)
> *From Rage to Hope: Strategies for Reclaiming Black and Hispanic Students*

Students behave appropriately and learn more effectively in environments that meet their basic personal and psychological needs. All students learn best in school settings in which they are comfortable and feel safe and accepted. Students' academic failure and misbehavior can be understood—and subsequently prevented or corrected—by examining classroom and school environments to determine which student needs are not being met.

Teachers are frequently frustrated by their inability to determine the source of disruptive student behavior that detracts from students' learning. When asked to describe why children misbehave, teachers often include in their responses such factors as poor

"Mrs. Horton, could you stop by school today?"

attitude, poor home environment, lower-than-average IQ, lack of parental support for school, and medical or emotional problems. These views suggest that teachers can merely coax or bribe these students into behaving appropriately, or remove or punish these children when misbehavior occurs. Teachers may thus absolve themselves of responsibility for students' misbehavior. In this scheme, teachers are merely reactive forces. They must put a finger in the dike when confronted with unpredictable forces over which they have little control.

Even though it is true that student behavior is influenced by factors outside the control of the school, studies on school and teacher effectiveness have demonstrated that teachers and schools have a major impact on how students behave and learn and on how they feel about themselves. Therefore, another approach to analyzing unproductive or irresponsible student behavior is to believe that almost all students can function productively in a classroom and to consider what classroom variables can positively affect student learning and behavior. Much of this book provides specific methods used by teachers to create such environments. However, professional educators must understand *why* these techniques are effective rather than merely using them as gimmicks that positively influence student behavior. Consider for a moment if you took a child with a stomachache to see a physician. How would you react if, without examining the child, the physician indicated that an appendectomy would be performed? When you asked why the physician intended to perform the operation, the doctor indicated that the previous summer he had taken a class on appendectomies, had been told the operation was helpful to all children, and had demonstrated skill in performing it. It is likely that you would seek another opinion and would perhaps even report the incident to the appropriate source. Allen Mendler (1992) placed this in perspective when he wrote:

> Most discipline programs incorrectly place their emphasis upon strategies and techniques. The latest gimmick is offered to get Johnny to behave. The problem is that there are a lot of Johnnys out there and not all respond according to how the text or technique says they should. Having worked with thousands of children and adults, I have concluded that it is fruitless to expect that any technique will work with all people who present the same symptom. . . . The competent teacher needs to get at the reasons or functions of a given maladaptive behavior to formulate a strategy likely to work. . . . When they [children] misbehave, they tell us that they need help learning a better way. They are telling us that there are basic needs not being met which are motivating the behavior. (pp. 25, 27)

Teachers are involved daily in creating the atmosphere in which children spend approximately one-fourth of their waking lives. Although this necessity obviously places considerable responsibility on the teacher, it simultaneously imparts a positive, creative dimension into teachers' professional lives. Teachers are not faced with the prospect of merely reacting to student behaviors over which they have no control. On the contrary, by creating environments that respond sensitively to students' needs, teachers can ensure that most student behavior will be positive and goal directed.

This chapter describes the basic psychological needs that must be met for students to behave in positive, productive manners. No attempt is made to present an in-depth description of any one theorist's work or to describe child and adolescent development. Rather, the chapter highlights needs that, when met within the school setting, enhance positive teacher and student behavior and thereby facilitate learning.

THEORETICAL PERSPECTIVES

One approach to understanding children's unproductive school behavior suggests that much of this behavior is a response to children not having their basic needs met within the environment in which the misbehavior occurs. This explanation has the advantage of placing the teacher in a creative, exciting position. Rather than simply reacting to uncontrollable forces, the teacher controls a wide variety of factors that influence children's behavior.

Another way to view unproductive student behavior is as a skill deficit. This model suggests that students who act aggressively on the playground lack skills to make appropriate contact with peers, to handle the inevitable frustrations and conflicts that arise, and to solve problems. Similarly, students who act out during instructional time may lack skills in understanding or organizing the work, using self-talk to handle frustration, or knowing how to obtain assistance.

This social-cognitive skill deficit model suggests that students need more than reinforcement for appropriate behavior and negative consequences for inappropriate behavior. Students need to be taught social and work skills in the same manner that they are taught reading or math skills. Indeed, it is interesting that when students have serious difficulties reading, they are referred to a specialist who works intensively with them for an extended period of time. Educators do not expect students to learn to read by being placed in time-out or otherwise isolated from classmates. Likewise, teachers seldom expect students with reading difficulties to be at grade level after only a few sessions with the reading specialist. However, when students experience difficulties with their behavior, educators often isolate them, provide little or no instruction in how to behave appropriately, and expect one or two visits to a counselor or principal to resolve the problem and ensure that the child has the skills necessary to function as effectively as his or her classmates. If we believe student behavior problems often represent skill deficits this is not realistic. Instead, educators must respond to unproductive student behavior by creating multiple opportunities for students to develop needed skills.

This chapter examines the first approach to understanding student behavior—the belief that misbehavior is a response to students' needs not being met in the learning environment. Chapter 10 presents methods for responding to behavior problems that we believe stem from student skill deficits.

Abraham Maslow (1968) suggested that for students to have energy for learning, their basic personal needs must be met. Maslow wrote:

> So far as motivational status is concerned, healthy people have sufficiently gratified their basic needs for safety, belongingness, love, respect and self-esteem so that they are motivated primarily by trends to self-actualization (defined as ongoing actualization of potentials, capacities, and talents). (p. 25)

Unfortunately, as Nicholas Long and William Morse (1996) noted:

> More students are entering public schools without the benefits of ongoing positive parental bonding and attachment. Many of these students already have been damaged emotionally by the debilitating effects of poverty, neglect, abuse, divorce, drugs, and rejection. They have not internalized a sense of trust in other adults or developed the necessary pro-social skills necessary for group instruction and personal learning. Consequently, the students have low frustration tolerance, misperceive social interactions, limited attention spans, and low self-esteem. Their social/emotional needs dominate their behavior and disrupt the learning process. (p. 239)

A number of writers have researched and written about the major needs that dominate and influence student behavior. Figure 2.1 presents the views of four researchers/theorists regarding this topic. As noted in this figure, all four theorists share the belief that for students to have their basic needs met, and thereby function effectively in the school environment, they need to experience positive relationships with others (belonging, significance, collaboration, love). Likewise, three of the writers specifically highlight students' needs for academic accomplishment (mastery, competence, content). All four writers indicated that students need some sense of choice or ability to influence their environment (independence, power, choice, power). Finally, two of the writers referred to something beyond the learner that suggests a need to share with or give to others. A third author mentioned this but did not include it in his list (Glasser, 1990).

Based on their review of the research and interviews with students, Topper, Williams, Leo, Hamilton, and Fox (1994) suggest that students themselves provide a similar list regarding their needs and wants.

What Kids Need

- Friends who care for you and you for them
- Fun and challenging things to do
- Having choices and learning how to make choices
- A chance to master skills needed to pursue a dream, for self-advocacy, and cultural interdependence
- Physical well-being
- Status and a "cool" reputation
- Unconditional love, someone who will always be your advocate
- Chance to make a difference in someone's life (Topper et al., 1994, p. 7)

Notice how similar these needs and wants are to those created by the theorists. Students want and need to have positive personal relationships characterized by mutual

FIGURE 2.1 Students' Basic Needs	Brendtro et al. (1990)	Coopersmith (1967)	Kohn (1993)	Glasser (1990)
	1. belonging 2. mastery 3. independence 4. generosity	significance competence power	collaboration content choice virtue	love fun power/freedom survival

caring and support, an opportunity to demonstrate mastery and competence, a chance to learn and use their own decision making skills and to influence their environment, and an opportunity to make a difference in the lives of others.

It is important to realize that, just as children enter school with dramatically different reading readiness, they also vary in their ability to meaningfully engage in the social life of the classroom and to be receptive to adults' attempts to provide them with significance, competence, and power. Some children have had life experiences that have led them to view relationships as less supportive and to interpret a higher range of peer and adult behaviors as negative and unsupportive. Therefore, some students require more time in a positive, supportive classroom environment in which their competence is validated and they are given choices and opportunities to express themselves openly before they can trust others, behave in a reciprocal manner, and begin to maximize their potential.

Garbarino (1999) suggests that the reason boys may express their anger and violence in school settings is that "school is still a potent setting for them, a place where what happens still matters to them—often excruciatingly so" (p. 220). School is often a place where these young people have experienced some sense of being cared for, and they may have also experienced a sense of competence. Therefore, when they feel isolated, rejected, or like failures in this last bastion of hope, their anger is intensified and the results can be disastrous. Garbarino (1999) states that:

> Having an identity in relation to peers is so important to most children and youth that even a negative definition of self is better than nothing at all. This insight is vital in understanding violent and troubled boys. They will achieve an identity, whatever the cost of doing so to themselves and their communities. Feeling like he is nobody is emotionally intolerable for a boy. (p. 227)

In discussing school programs that assist alienated students, Testerman (1996) wrote, "an adult in school who shows individualized concern for an at-risk student can have a significant positive effect on that student's attendance" (p. 364). Testerman reports a program in Lely High School in Naples, Florida, in which a group of students with a lower than 1.5 grade point average were provided with an adult advisor who met with them for at least fifteen minutes per week. When compared to a control group, students who worked with an advisor were less likely to drop out (five of twenty-nine for the experimental group compared to twelve of twenty-nine for the control group). The experimental group also had a GPA during the experiment that was almost double that of the control group.

As discussed in Chapter 1, numerous examples exist of school settings in which staff's success in meeting students' needs for significance, competence, and power enable a wide range of students to be successful. Interestingly, in its April 1996 report "How safe are the public schools?" the staff at the National Center for Education Statistics reported that school size appears to play a significant role in the amount of physical violence and weapons possession found in schools. It is likely that smaller schools are more effective in helping students meet their needs for significance, competence, and power, and that when these needs are met fewer students find it necessary to use violence to feel safe and competent. The following section provides a brief discussion of several often cited theorists who have written about the importance of students' needs.

Personal Needs Theories

Abraham Maslow

Although each theoretical conceptualization described in the previous section provides a valuable increment of insight into children's needs, Maslow's (1968) concept of basic human needs incorporates the key components of many theories in a form that allows teachers systematically to assess and respond to students' needs. Maslow has suggested that there is a hierarchy of basic human needs and that lower-level needs generally take precedence over higher-order needs. His hierarchy of needs, which has been divided in a variety of ways, includes these components:

Self-actualization
Self-respect
Belongingness and affection
Safety and security
Physiological needs

Maslow's theoretical position is that people have an innate need to be competent and accepted. Unproductive behavior is therefore not viewed as an indication of a bad child but rather as a reaction to the frustration associated with being in a situation in which one's basic needs are not being met. Maslow further suggested that these basic needs cannot be met without assistance from other people. Finally, he postulated that only when the basic needs are met can the individual become motivated by self-actualization or the need to take risks, learn, and attain one's fullest potential.

PAUSE

and Consider   **2.1**

> Stop reading for a minute and consider a student you have observed or one with whom you work who is struggling academically or behaviorally in school. Ask yourself the following questions: (1) Does this student have basic physical needs met, such as adequate diet, a consistent night of sleep appropriate for his or her age group, and so on? (2) Does this student experience a sense of safety and security at school, going to and from school, and at home? In other words, does this student ever have to worry about being physically or psychologically intimidated, harassed, or abused? (3) Does this student experience an ongoing sense of being valued and cared about by the adults and peers in his or her life? (4) Do social, cultural, academic, and personal factors allow this student to feel positive about him- or herself and to have hope for the future? Take a moment to write a brief paragraph or share with a classmate or colleague the areas in which you believe this student's basic needs may not be met.

If the answer to any of these questions is "no," Maslow's model would suggest the student lacks the foundation for obtaining maximum benefit from the academic program in which he or she is involved. The next question becomes, "How can school personnel, perhaps with collaboration from individuals in the community, work to ensure that these needs are more consistently met?" Many of the methods presented in this book focus on ways you can work with your students to ensure that these needs are met within the school environment.

Rudolf Dreikurs

Basing his work on the concepts developed by the Viennese psychiatrist Alfred Adler, Rudolf Dreikurs centered his ideas for working with children on the belief that their basic need is to be socially accepted: "We should realize that a misbehaving child is only a discouraged child trying to find his place; he is acting on the faulty logic that his misbehaviour will give him the social acceptance which he desires" (Dreikurs & Cassel, 1972, p. 32).

"It takes four cups of coffee just to get on their wavelength."

Dreikurs described four goals associated with children's misbehavior: attention getting, power, revenge, and displays of inadequacy. He suggested that "when a child is deprived of the opportunity to gain status through his useful contributions, he usually seeks proof of his status in class through getting attention" (1972, p. 34). If adults are ineffective at responding to this attention getting, Dreikurs indicated that students will seek power. If this response is thwarted by teachers' own power methods, students become deeply discouraged and seek revenge. Finally, Dreikurs suggested that "a child who has tried passive destructive forms of attention-getting in order to achieve the feeling of 'belonging' may eventually become so deeply discouraged that he gives up all hope of significance and expects only failure and defeat" (Dreikurs & Cassel, 1972, p. 39). In *Discipline without Tears* (Dreikurs & Cassel, 1972) and *Maintaining Sanity in the Classroom* (Dreikurs, Grunwald, & Pepper, 1971), Dreikurs suggested methods for assisting teachers in identifying which of the four mistaken goals the child is seeking and ways teachers can respond to children to help them return to positive involvement in the regular classroom.

Recently, Topper and colleagues (1994) offered a slightly modified list of needs met by students' challenging behaviors.

- **Attention**—the behavior serves the need to draw attention away from others and to oneself
- **Avoidance/Escape**—the behavior serves the need to end an event or activity that the student does not like, or to avoid an event
- **Control**—the behavior serves the need to control events
- **Revenge**—the behavior serves the need to punish others for something that was done to the student
- **Self-Regulation/Coping**—the behavior serves the need to regulate feelings (e.g., boredom, embarrassment, anger, fear, anxiety) or energy levels
- **Play**—the behavior serves the need to have fun (Topper et al., 1994, p. 47)

Take a few minutes to consider a student you have observed, taught, or one with whom you are otherwise familiar whose behavior has occasionally had a negative impact on his or her learning or the learning of classmates. Try to envision a specific instance in which this student behaved in such a manner. Hypothesize which of the six needs presented by Topper et al. the child's behavior may have served. Not only may this help you better understand the student's behavior but it also provides you with valuable information concerning how to assist the student in developing substitute behaviors. Write a statement about an activity you could attempt to engage this student in that would provide him or her with a better way to meet the need you believe is being met by the current behavior.

This is an important concept in working with students. All behavior is purposeful. Students are not "bad" or "disruptive"; they are simply attempting to meet their needs using behaviors that are not in their best interests or the best interests of others. Oftentimes these are behaviors that have provided them with much needed attention, a sense of control, escape from work they find difficult, a method of self-regulation, or a method for having fun. It is our role as educators to help them develop behaviors that meet these needs but that also serve them effectively throughout their lives.

William Glasser

For more than three decades, William Glasser has crusaded for increasing the sense of efficacy and power students experience. In his book *Control Theory in the Classroom*, Glasser (1986) stated, "Our behavior is always our best attempt at the time to satisfy at least five powerful forces which, because they are built into our genetic structure, are best called basic needs" (p. 14). Glasser described the five basic needs as "(1) to survive and reproduce, (2) to belong and love, (3) to *gain power*, (4) to be free, and (5) to have fun" (Glasser, 1986, p. 22; emphasis added). Glasser indicated that students will function productively only in school environments that allow them to experience a sense of control or power over their learning.

In *The Quality School: Managing Students without Coercion*, Glasser (1990) extended his ideas on enhancing students' sense of involvement and empowerment. When describing why educators see relatively high rates of off-task behavior in schools, Glasser noted:

> For workers, including students, to do quality work, they must be managed in a way that convinces them that the work they are asked to do satisfies their needs. The more it does, the harder they will work.
>
> Instead, teachers are required to stuff students with fragments of measurable knowledge as if the students had no needs—almost as if they were things. . . .
>
> Because this low-quality, standardized, fragmented approach is so unsatisfying to students (and teachers), more and more students are actively resisting and this resistance is seen as a discipline problem. (p. 22)

In order to better understand why students misbehave and the relationship between this behavior and students' needs within the school environment, the authors strongly encourage every public school educator or prospective teacher to spend an entire day every year being a student in their school. This should involve the educator either riding the bus to school or entering the school at the same time as the student and completing all activities as if he or she were a student (including lunch, physical education, recess, etc.). Having done this with more than 500 teachers, the authors are aware of how often the participants are surprised at the uncomfortable seating, the lack of breaks, and the low levels of academic involvement and positive personal contact experienced by the student they are shadowing. Activity 2.1 (on page 68) provides additional ideas for this learning activity.

Stanley Coopersmith

Another useful concept on students' needs is offered by Coopersmith (1967). In his research on the factors associated with self-esteem, Coopersmith found that in order to possess high self-esteem, individuals need to experience a sense of significance, competence, and power. *Significance* can best be defined as the sense of being valued that an individual attains from involvement in a positive two-way relationship in which both parties sincerely care about each other. *Competence* is developed by being able to perform a socially valued task as well as or better than others at one's age level. For example, winning a free-throw shooting competition involving her peers would provide a fifth grader with a sense of competence. Being able to tie her shoe or add one-digit figures would provide her with a much smaller sense of competence. Finally, *power* refers to an ability to control one's environment.

Coopersmith's research indicates that students need to experience a sense of trust and personal involvement as well as a sense of accomplishment or competence if their needs are to be met. Coopersmith also noted that in order for individuals to feel good about themselves and their environment, they must experience a sense of power or control. Students who clearly understand classroom rules and procedures and who understand what is to be learned and why it might be useful to them will experience a sense of power. Likewise, students experience a sense of power when they are allowed to choose a topic of special interest to study, provide input into how the classroom is arranged, or understand their own learning style and its relationship to their learning and teacher decision making.

As we discussed in connection with Dreikurs's theory, it is helpful to understand that these needs for significance, competence, and power exist for all of us and are appropriate, healthy needs. The real issue is finding ways for students to meet these needs in a manner that creates a positive, supportive, safe learning environment in which the student can experience success.

As you consider your own classroom or one you are observing, and as you read through this book, we strongly encourage you to keep a list of methods that facilitate significance, competence, and power for your students. The materials presented throughout this book have consistently proven to help a wide range of students improve their behavior and learning because they are based on enhancing the significance, competence, and power of each student.

P A U S E

and Consider   **2.3**

> Consider a classroom with which you are familiar. Label three columns on a sheet of paper: significance, competence, and power. List ways in which all students have an opportunity to achieve each of these in the classroom you are considering. If one of the lists is quite short or very few students have an opportunity to experience this factor, add several specific changes you might suggest for this class to improve this particular list. We believe you will benefit from sharing this list with others and perhaps adopting methods used in their classrooms to strengthen your list.

Human Development Theories

Erik Erikson

According to Erikson, there are eight stages of human psychosocial development. Each stage is characterized by a conflict in which the individual either attains a key psychosocial understanding or develops an emotional liability. Although he indicates that three stages are most likely to be experienced by school-age children, he poignantly highlights the concept that each stage builds on its predecessors. Therefore, if a child does not reach satisfactory resolution of an earlier stage such as trust, this will negatively affect the child's ability to successfully work through later developmental stages.

The first stage is infancy, in which a child develops either a sense of trust and hope or a sense of mistrust and despair. Erikson describes this first stage by noting that "the infant's first social achievement, then, is his willingness to let the mother out of sight without undue anxiety or rage, because she has become an inner certainty as well as an outer predictability" (Erikson, 1963, p. 247). Children who have been abused, abandoned, or ignored may fail to develop a sense of being able to depend on others for support. In school settings we may see children who cling to adults and constantly seek reassurance and support. Conversely, we may see children who will not engage adults or who fail to believe adults or trust them enough to risk following their lead.

The second stage is early childhood, in which children develop a sense of autonomy. If the child is given opportunities to test herself and also provided the positive, supportive structure to limit destructive behavior, she will develop a sense of self-expression with self-control. Without these opportunities children can develop a sense of shame and doubt.

The third stage Erikson describes as initiative versus guilt. Here a child has more freedom to interact with other children and practice new independence. "Initiative adds to autonomy the quality of undertaking, planning and 'attacking' a task for the sake of being active and on the move" (Erikson, 1963, p. 255). Again, support with caring structure by adults will lead to a new sense of competence, positive self-esteem, and purpose for the child, whereas lack of support or overly restrictive limits may lead to a sense of guilt and inhibition.

The fourth stage Erikson labeled "industry versus inferiority." During this stage, children must move away from playing make-believe and develop an ability to produce things. Children must learn to do something well and to develop a sense of their own competence. Erikson describes the essence of this stage:

> And while all children need their hours and days of make-believe in games, they all, sooner or later, become dissatisfied and disgruntled without a sense of being able to make things and make them well and even perfectly: it is this that I have called the sense of industry. . . . For nothing less is at stake than the development and maintenance in children of a positive identification of those who know things and know how to do things. (Erikson, 1968, pp. 123, 125)

"Actually, I don't know how to act my age. I just turned seven today!"

In Erikson's writing we can see the dual emphasis on viewing oneself as competent and on having this competence verified and expanded through meaningful contact with other people. Teachers can assist in meeting these student developmental needs by ensuring that all students (1) understand the work they are being asked to do, (2) can successfully complete the work they are given, (3) monitor and chart their progress, and (4) receive positive feedback from other people for their efforts and accomplishments. Similarly, students need to understand teachers' behavior expectations, to be allowed to practice these when necessary, and to receive assistance in and reinforcement for developing these behaviors when they are not skills the students currently possess. Many of the ideas presented in Chapters 6 through 10 will help you create a classroom setting in which this can be accomplished.

In addition to understanding theories that deal with children's needs, upper-grade elementary or middle school teachers must be aware of the unique needs of adolescents. The physical onset of adolescence is occurring at an earlier age. In addition, children are becoming more sophisticated at an earlier age because of the availability of television and of adults' tendency to encourage sophisticated behavior in children. Consequently, fifth- and especially sixth-grade teachers find themselves dealing with students who are experiencing the early stages of adolescence.

Erikson described the next developmental stage—that experienced by young adolescents—as the search for a sense of identity. During the initial phase of this stage (ages eleven to thirteen), there is a dramatic increase in self-consciousness and a lowered self-esteem. Young adolescents feel onstage, as if everyone is observing them. Elkind (1967) has labeled this the "imaginary audience." Young adolescents also view themselves and their personal problems as unique and cannot understand that other people are experiencing similar feelings. Elkind labeled this concept the "personal fable."

This means that even though secondary teachers often feel pressured to cover material and complete the curriculum, student learning and behavior can be enhanced when teachers take time to create a classroom climate in which adolescents feel comfortable with their teacher and peers and engage in cooperative learning activities that allow for supportive peer interactions. This climate serves to reduce the students' sense of self-consciousness and isolation, which releases energy for productive learning.

Young adolescents are also beginning to challenge previously accepted beliefs and values. With the gradual increase in their ability to consider abstract ideas and better understand the concepts of past and future, adolescents begin to view their world more subjectively and critically. Therefore, adolescents have a basic need to examine ideas, rules, and decisions critically. They are likely to question why they must study a topic, complete an assignment, or follow a rule that does not apply to the adults who share their environment. This often frustrating behavior increases as students move through midadolescence (ages fourteen to sixteen) and become somewhat less absorbed in egocentric, self-oriented matters and more interested in their relationship to others and in better understanding and controlling their environment. Students in grades eight through ten are often testing their new personal, physical, and cognitive skills by challenging rules or adult behavior they view as illogical or indefensible. During these early and midadolescent years, students need fair, clearly articulated structure and adults who are personally strong and flexible enough to become involved in openly discussing questions adolescents have about subject matter, teaching techniques, and school rules and procedures (Jones, 1980).

A key concept for teachers is that not only must we assist students in developing a positive resolution of the developmental stage most characteristic of their age but we must also support students who are struggling because of unsatisfactory resolution of earlier stages. The clingy third grader or the sixth grader who appears unable to work independently are examples of students who may need support in working through earlier developmental issues. In a very real sense we are providing effective reparenting for many children. While this may occur quite planfully through the efforts of a team of educators developing a special plan to assist a child, it may also happen as a natural outcome of utilizing the effective classroom management methods presented in this book.

Recent Developmental Theories

Current research has highlighted the importance of understanding the impact each child's unique biological and developmental history has on his or her behavior. In his book *Lost Boys*, a powerful study of the histories of young men who had committed violent crimes, James Garbarino (1999) wrote, "I came to understand better than ever before the power of one's story, the value of one's personal narrative in making sense of experience" (p. xi).

This point is also the centerpiece in the work of Stanley Greenspan (Greenspan, 1997; Greenspan & Wieder, 1998). Greenspan suggests that it is essential to understand that children have individual profiles concerning their developmental strengths and weaknesses and that only by developing interventions built around individual profiles can children, especially those with major developmental delays, be assisted in reaching their potential. Greenspan (1997) suggests that "In therapy, we therefore use each child's own natural intentions and feelings as his or her personal foundation of learning" (p. 16). He also emphasizes the importance of emotions as the key mediating factor in intelligence. Greenspan suggests that emotions organize experience and behavior and that to assist children, especially those struggling to master content or make connections with their world, adults must connect learning to the child's emotions and desires. This concept supports much of the discussion in Chapter 6 regarding the relationship between instruction and classroom management and in Chapters 8 and 9 regarding responding to student behavior that negatively impacts the student's learning or the learning of others.

The importance of a student's individual developmental history is further supported by Robin Karr-Morse and Meredith Wiley (1997) in their book *Ghosts from the Nursery: Tracing the Roots of Violence*. These authors discuss the critical nature of the first two years of life and the neurological and psychological damage that is caused by abandonment and lack of nurturance in a child's relationship with a primary caregiver. They cite a number of recent studies to support the concept that:

> If the synapses in this area of the brain are never built due to neglect or are destroyed by neurochemicals resulting from chronic stress, the individual may be left without the ability to connect, to trust, and ultimately to experience empathy. (p. 198)

In talking about working with boys who have histories that might lead them to be violent, Garbarino (1999) wrote, "And I came to appreciate as never before the critical importance of taking time, of being given time, and of feeling included" (p. xi). In his work with young men who had committed violent crimes, Garbarino consistently found histories of neglect and abuse. He speaks of these young men having souls that have become hidden by their need to protect themselves from further hurt. He goes on to note that one critical element in helping these boys' souls to survive is unconditional love. He notes that children are capable of and desperately need to develop new attachments with other adults. This new connection can reduce the level of depression experienced by many youth when they are not adequately cared for by their primary caregiver. Research conducted at Harvard Medical School shows dramatic increases in depression among American youth over the past thirty years (Kessler, 1998). Garbarino found that depression was a prelude to violence among young men who committed lethal crimes. In addition, he found that a sense of rejection increased a young person's risk for a high range of violent behaviors. He suggests that unless we create environments that provide these boys with surrogate adults who treat them with respect and caring, they will continue to be depressed, angry individuals who may express their feelings through acts of random violence. In addition, because rejection is so central to the depression and anger experienced by these boys, establishing peer relationships characterized by acceptance and support is also a critical factor in preventing the outburst of violent behaviors.

These recent writings support the earlier works of Bowlby (1982), Masterson (Masterson & Costello, 1980), and Nielsen (1983) regarding issues of attachment and loss. Students' abilities to care about the feelings of others and accurately read social cues are significantly influenced by early childhood experiences. This work is further supported by studies examining the early childhoods of students who are aggressive during the early school years (Dishion, French, & Patterson, 1995). Because of their developmental histories, these students enter school less secure, less able to establish relationships, and less accustomed to the structure and consistent monitoring of behavior found in the school setting. Because connections to school influence students' motivations and acceptance of school values (Goodenow & Grady, 1993), and because these students are less likely to connect to school personnel and peers, these students are less likely to accept school structures and engage in positive school behaviors. The important concept for us as teachers is that if they are to be academically and behaviorally successful, these students need to have relationships with adults and peers that are caring and supportive. Chapters 3 and 4 present specific methods for creating this type of relationship.

Early childhood is not the only developmental state recent researchers have described as having a powerful impact on students' behaviors. In her book *Reviving Ophelia: Saving the Selves of Adolescent Girls,* Mary Pipher (1994) presents a powerful argument that as they enter adolescence many girls lose the sense of empowerment, creativity, and independence that characterized their childhoods. Pipher suggests that the "conflict between their autonomous selves and their need to be feminine" (p. 21) as defined by our society creates incredible stress and a loss of self for many girls entering adolescence. Pipher points out that whereas healthy men and adults are viewed as being active, independent, and logical, healthy women are often described as "passive, dependent, and illogical" (p. 39). Pipher believes this incongruence between what girls experience as valuable during childhood and how they are expected to behave as young women during adolescence creates stress for young women and encourages them to develop a false self that is unsatisfying and confusing.

P A U S E

and Consider   **2.4**

> When you took a course in developmental psychology, it was likely you seldom stopped to consider how the knowledge you were acquiring related to how you could skillfully work with students in a classroom. Although the past section is only a brief review, it presents important human development concepts that have implications for teachers. We encourage you to pause for a moment and write two ideas from the previous section on human development theories that you believe are important to consider when working with students. For each of these ideas, write one method of teaching or working with students you believe would help support students effectively working through the development issue you listed.

Social Factors Theory

David Elkind

In *The Hurried Child,* Elkind (1981) added an interesting dimension to the topic of children's psychological needs. He stated that relationships among all individuals, but especially between children and adults, involve basic patterns of dealing with each other. He described these patterns as implicit contracts and noted that they are constantly changing. He further commented that children's needs are met when contracts change in response to changing personal and cognitive skills demonstrated by children, but that contracts must not change primarily in response to adults' needs.

Elkind described three basic contracts between adults and children: (1) responsibility–freedom, (2) achievement–support, and (3) loyalty–commitment. The responsibility–freedom contract refers to adults "sensitively monitor[ing] the child's level of intellectual, social, and emotional development in order to provide the appropriate freedoms and opportunities for the exercise of responsibility" (1981, p. 124). The achievement–support contract refers to adults expecting age-appropriate achievements and providing the necessary personal and material support to help children reach expected goals. The loyalty–commitment contract emphasizes adults' expectations that children will respond with loyalty and acceptance of adults because of the time, effort, and energy adults give. Although Elkind focused on the parent–child relationship, these contractual areas apply to all adult–child relationships.

Elkind's key concept related to contracts is that they are frequently violated by adults and that this violation causes stress for youngsters. Violation of the responsibility-freedom contract occurs when adults fail to reward responsibility with freedom. For example, when students act responsibly in making a reasonable request of a teacher or administrator and are met with disrespect, this contract has been violated. Likewise, students who have demonstrated skill in directing portions of their own learning but are not allowed to do so experience frustration and stress through violation of the responsibility–freedom contract. The achievement–support contract is violated when adults do not provide adequate support for students' achievement. The low-achieving student who receives few opportunities to respond in class, little assistance in answering questions, and less reinforcement for appropriate answers is not receiving support commensurate with desired and potential achievement. Difficulties in the loyalty–commitment contract occur when children, especially adolescents, fail to provide adults with indications of loyalty commensurate with the efforts or commitment that adults see themselves as having made. When adults respond with removal of commitment, giving up on or criticizing the student, rather than by understanding and discussing the problem, contract violation occurs. This condition is more likely to happen with low-achieving students who may not immediately repay teachers for what appear to be considerable amounts of time and effort.

Joan Lipsitz

While serving as director of the Center for Early Adolescence at the University of North Carolina at Chapel Hill, Joan Lipsitz wrote extensively on the needs of early adolescence. She noted that adults often fail to understand this age group, which leads to classroom management and instructional decisions that cause a considerable amount of the unproductive behavior that so frequently frustrates teachers who work with this age group. Lipsitz emphasized the importance of developing school environments that meet young adolescents' developmental needs. These were summarized by her colleague, Gayle Dorman (1981). These needs include:

1. The need for diversity,
2. The need for opportunities for self-exploration and self-definition,
3. The need for meaningful participation in school and community,
4. The need for positive social interaction with peers and adults,
5. The need for physical activity,
6. The need for competence and achievement,
7. The need for structure and clear limits. (p. 1)

Joan Lipsitz's thoughtful book *Successful Schools for Young Adolescents* (1984) examines four schools that have successfully met these needs.

"Oh, the stress on this job doesn't bother me. I used to teach in a junior high school."

Martin Seligman

In discussing how to assist children in developing an optimistic view of life, Seligman (1995) stated that "the basis of optimism does not lie in positive phrases or images of victory, but in the way you think about causes" (p. 52). He also noted that there are three key factors that influence how students view causes of behavior: (1) permanence, (2) pervasiveness, and (3) personalization (internal vs. external locus of control). These three factors are similar to those listed by Bernard Weiner (1979, 1990). According to Weiner, the three causes or factors to which students attribute their success or failure are (1) stability, (2) responsibility, and (3) locus. Children who believe negative situations are permanent or stable use terms such as *never, always,* and *no matter what.* Children with a more positive view of life realize that most events are temporary and use terms that suggest the influence situational events have on events in their lives. Children who experience a sense of permanence view problems as unalterable and have difficulty moving on to new opportunities and challenges. They view themselves as incompetent and unlikable in a general sense as opposed to unskilled at some task or not liked by one child or group of youngsters. Responsibility and locus relate to whether students attribute success or failure to factors within or outside of their control. Attribution research suggests that students who have an external locus of control view success as a result of luck or task difficulty (they were lucky or the work was easy), whereas students with an internal locus of control credit their own effort and ability for their successes. Likewise, when students with an external locus of control are unsuccessful, they blame factors such as teachers' failure to explain, bad luck, and lack of parental support for their failure, whereas students experiencing an internal locus of control take responsibility for their own decisions, such as failure to study, to visit the teacher, or to place their homework where they would remember it.

Developmental Assets

In recent years educators and mental health staff have begun to consider the type of experiences that serve as supports or assets for the healthy development of children and adolescents. Figure 2.2 presents a list of the forty developmental assets research at the Search Institute has found to be associated with healthy personal development. An examination of children's experiences indicates that in the United States too many young people do not experience high rates of positive assets, thus leaving them with a fragile foundation on which to build their lives. The 99,462 adolescents surveyed

External Assets

Category	Asset Name and Definition
Support	1. Family support: Family life provides high levels of love and support.
	2. Positive family communication: Young person and her or his parent(s) communicate positively, and young person is willing to seek advice and counsel from parent(s).
	3. Other adult relationships: Young person receives support from three or more nonparent adults.
	4. Caring neighborhood: Young person experiences caring neighbors.
	5. Caring school climate: School provides a caring, encouraging environment.
	6. Parent involvement in schooling: Parent(s) are actively involved in helping young person succeed in school.
Empowerment	7. Community values youth: Young person perceives that adults in the community value youth.
	8. Youth as resources: Young people are given useful roles in the community.
	9. Service to others: Young person serves in the community one hour or more per week.
	10. Safety: Young person feels safe at home, at school, and in the neighborhood.
Boundaries and expectations	11. Family boundaries: Family has clear rules and consequences and monitors the young person's whereabouts.
	12. School boundaries: School provides clear rules and consequences.
	13. Neighborhood boundaries: Neighbors take responsibility for monitoring young people's behavior.
	14. Adult role models: Parent(s) and other adults model positive, responsible behavior.
	15. Positive peer influence: Young person's best friends model responsible behavior.
	16. High expectations: Both parents and teachers encourage the young person to do well.
Constructive use of time	17. Creative activities: Young person spends three or more hours per week in lessons or practice in music, theater, or other arts.
	18. Youth programs: Young person spends three or more hours per week in sports, clubs, or organizations at school or in the community.
	19. Religious community: Young person spends one or more hours per week in activities in a religious institution.
	20. Time at home: Young person is out with friends "with nothing special to do" two or fewer nights per week.

FIGURE 2.2
Forty Developmental Assets

(continued)

Internal Assets

Category	Asset Name and Definition
Commitment to learning	21. Achievement motivation: Young person is motivated to do well in school. 22. School engagement: Young person is actively engaged in learning. 23. Homework: Young person reports doing at least one hour of homework every schoolday. 24. Bonding to school: Young person cares about her or his school. 25. Reading for pleasure: Young person reads for pleasure three or more hours per week.
Positive values	26. Caring: Young person places high value on helping other people. 27. Equality and social justice: Young person places high value on promoting equality and reducing hunger and poverty. 28. Integrity: Young person acts on convictions and stands up for his or her beliefs. 29. Honesty: Young person tells the truth even when it is not easy. 30. Responsibility: Young person accepts and takes personal responsibility. 31. Restraint: Young person believes it is important not to be sexually active and not to use alcohol or other drugs.
Social competencies	32. Planning and decision making: Young person knows how to plan ahead and make choices. 33. Interpersonal competence: Young person has empathy, sensitivity, and friendship skills. 34. Cultural competence: Young person has knowledge of and comfort with people of different cultural/racial/ethnic backgrounds. 35. Resistance skills: Young person can resist negative peer pressure and dangerous situations. 36. Peaceful conflict resolution: Young person seeks to resolve conflict nonviolently.
Positive identity	37. Personal power: Young person feels he or she has control over things that happen to him or her. 38. Self-esteem: Young person reports having a high self-esteem. 39. Sense of purpose: Young person reports that his or her life has a purpose. 40. Positive view of personal future: Young person is optimistic about his or her personal future.

FIGURE 2.2

Continued

Reprinted with permission from Search Institute, Minneapolis, MN. © Search Institute, 2002.
www.searchinstitute.org.

reported experiencing an average of only eighteen of the forty developmental assets. Almost two-thirds of the young people surveyed possessed half or fewer of the forty assets (Benson, Scales, Leffert, & Roehlkepartain, 1999, p. v).

Research conducted at the Search Institute also indicates that students are more likely to engage in positive behaviors and refrain from high-risk behaviors when they experience opportunities to develop positive personal assets in the eight major areas shown in Figure 2.2. The Search Institute staff works with school staffs and community agencies to increase the likelihood that children and adolescents will experience these assets.

In examining whether schools help students develop these assets, the Search Institute staff collected data from nearly 100,000 sixth- through twelfth-grade students in 213 communities throughout the United States. According to their findings only 25 percent of these students reported that their school had a caring climate, 29 percent stated they experienced opportunities for planning and decision making, 41 percent said they experienced high expectations, 44 percent said they thought their schools used peaceful conflict resolution methods, and 60 percent believed they experienced positive peer influences (Benson et al., 1999). Clearly, schools can improve dramatically in their efforts to enhance the extent to which students experience key developmental assets that facilitate learning and reduce high-risk behaviors.

If students are to feel capable of succeeding at school and motivated to make a reasonable effort, most theorists and researchers would agree that they need to have a sense of being able to impact outcomes that affect them and believe that things can change so that at some future date they will have a better chance to succeed. Therefore, it appears critical that we arrange classroom and school environments in ways that provide students with opportunities to develop a sense of their own competence and their ability to influence this competence (power) through meaningful contact with educators and fellow students (significance).

P A U S E
2.5 *and Consider*

Recall your own school experiences. Which of the assets listed in Figure 2.2 were enhanced by your experiences in school. Based on your own school experiences and the results reported in the previous paragraphs, select four assets you believe you, as a teacher, would have an opportunity to strengthen for your students. If you have an opportunity, join a group of classmates or colleagues and share the assets you selected. Also discuss what you might do in the classroom that would help strengthen these assets.

Brain Research

The topic of the impact of the brain on student behavior has become increasingly popular over the past decade. We believe that, to date, this research includes limited information that is beneficial for teachers in the area of classroom management. Although brain research certainly supports the importance of creating a safe learning environment, providing active instruction that meaningfully engages students, and responding calmly when students express confusion or strong emotions, it does not provide specific methods regarding such important issues in classroom management as how to develop a supportive learning environment or respond to student behavior that disrupts this environment (Sylwester, 2000). We concur with Howard Gardner's (1999b) assessment:

> To be sure, knowledge of the brain's structure and functioning might well hold interesting implications for learning and pedagogy. But the only way to know for sure whether something is possible is to try it. And should one succeed despite the predictions of neuroscience, that success becomes the determining fact. (p. 79)

Our decision for selecting materials for this book are based on whether research in classrooms have indicated that the methods have a specific, positive impact on student learning and behavior. Again, we agree with Howard Gardner (1999a):

> Indeed, in an art like teaching, the proof comes down to whether an approach works; it matters little whether the theory was correct. And, conversely, even if the theory is both correct and elegant, if it cannot be mobilized for concrete educational consequences, the theory matters not a whit to the educators. (p. 144)

It is quite likely that over the years, research in neuroscience will provide theoretical information as valuable as any found in this chapter. It is also likely that researchers will validate these theories by studying specific applications of these findings to classrooms and student learning and behavior. At this point, however, we do not believe this connection has been made in a manner that suggests emphasizing this work in a research-based book on classroom management.

STUDENTS AT RISK FOR SCHOOL FAILURE

Concern for students at risk has become a major theme in U.S. education. The term *at risk* has generally referred to students who are likely to drop out of school. The Business Advisory Commission of the Education Commission of the States (ECS) has extended this concept to include youngsters who are unlikely to make successful transitions to becoming productive adults. The authors' work with students and reading of the research suggests the following seven major areas in which students at risk experience major social or emotional skill deficits.

1. A history of poor adult–child relationships with an accompanying need for positive, supportive relationships
2. A limited sense of personal efficacy or power and the associated need to experience this by better understanding the learning process and developing a sense of personal responsibility and power
3. A tendency to focus on external factors that influence their behavior and the need to learn to accept responsibility for their behavior and to see how they can control their own learning and behavior
4. Low self-esteem, especially related to such school behaviors as achievement and peer friendships, and the need to develop and validate a positive self-esteem through positive social interactions and school success
5. A poorly developed sense of social cognition—an inability to understand others' feelings or points of view and take this into account when making decisions and the need to learn to understand others' responses and to work cooperatively with others

6. Poor problem-solving skills and the need to develop these skills as a means to enhance self-efficacy and self-esteem as well as to develop an important lifelong skill
7. Difficulties with learning caused by either limited educational experience, limited language proficiency skills, or both

Although the condition of being at risk is certainly influenced by many social factors—including poverty, racism, sexism, recent immigration, family dysfunction, substance abuse, and students' developmental backgrounds—it is also related to the quality of schooling in our society. Nearly twenty years ago the coordinator of the At-Risk Research Project of the National Center for Effective Secondary Schools highlighted this concept when he wrote:

> We have to face the fact that the condition of being at risk is partially generated by the school. The problems these kids bring to school are exacerbated by the way they're treated by the discipline system and the ways teachers interact with them. There is also a substantially detrimental effect caused by the lack of interesting and engaging experiences to which they will be able to respond. (Turnbaugh, 1986, p. 8)

According to the National Center for Educational Statistics, compared to White students, a much higher proportion of African American and Hispanic youth ages eighteen to twenty-four failed to earn a high school diploma or pass an equivalent examination. In 1999 those who had completed one of these was 91.8 percent for Whites, 83.5 percent for African Americans, and 63.4 percent for Hispanics.

Crystal Kuykendall, a prominent African American educator, noted that African American and Hispanic American (and the authors would add Native American) youth are "being 'distanced' from mainstream America. The continued underachievement and isolation of such a large and growing population is nothing short of a national tragedy" (1992, p. xii).

James Banks, a leading writer in the area of multicultural education, highlighted the problems faced by children of color when he wrote, "In the early grades, the academic achievement of students of color such as African Americans, Hispanics, and American Indians is close to parity with the achievement of White mainstream students. However, the longer these students of color remain in school, the more their achievement lags behind that of White mainstream students" (Banks & McGee Banks, 1993, p. 3).

Writers such as James Banks, Johnella Butler, Harold Dent, Geneva Gay, Crystal Kuykendall, and James Garcia have written extensively on the problems students of color confront in their attempt to achieve success in U.S. classrooms. Studies indicate that many African American, Hispanic American, and Native American students are more field dependent and group oriented than the average White student and that schools are structured as highly individualistic, competitive environments (Freeman & Freeman, 2002; Reyes, Scribner, & Scribner, 1999). According to Geneva Gay (1993), "First, the sameness of educational resources for diverse individuals and groups does not constitute comparability of quality or opportunity. Teachers, materials, and teaching environments that work well for Anglo students do not necessarily work equally well for ethnic minorities" (p. 182). Gay highlighted three reasons why students of color may fare less well than their White counterparts in traditional classrooms:

1. Most [teachers] do not know how to understand and use the school behaviors of these students, which differ from their normative expectations, as aides to teaching. Therefore, they tend to misinterpret them as deviant and treat them punitively.

2. Most curriculum designs and instructional materials are Eurocentric. . . . They are likely to be more readily meaningful and to have a greater appeal to the life experiences and aspirations of Anglo students than to those of ethnic minorities. Thus, when attempting to learn academic tasks, Anglo students do not have the additional burden of working across irrelevant instructional materials and methods.

3. A high degree of cultural congruency exists between middle-class Anglo student culture and school culture. These students do not experience much cultural discontinuity, social-code incompatibility, or need for cultural style shifting to adjust to the behavioral codes expected of them in school. (pp. 182–183)

All educators must be sensitive to the fact that their interpretations of students' behavior may be influenced by their own cultural and personal histories.

> It is this sociocultural theoretical lens, I believe, that offers us the best chance of understanding the low literacy attainment by poor and minority peoples. How can we understand why so many children do not learn what the mainstream schools think they are teaching unless we can get "inside" the learners and see the world through their eyes? If we do not try to do this, if we continue to use the mainstream experience of reality as the perspective, we fool ourselves into believing that we are looking through a window when instead we are looking into a mirror. Our explanations threaten to reflect only ourselves and our world, serving no real explanatory purpose. (Purcell-Gates, 1995, p. 6)

In her book, *The Inner World of the Immigrant Child*, Cristina Igoa (1995) considers how immigrant children often believe they cannot accept their culture of origin but they also feel unaccepted and alienated from U.S. culture. She discusses the importance of validating and supporting their culture of origin. In writing about her own experiences as an immigrant student, Igoa (1995) wrote:

> In the Philippines, we customarily greet each other with a kiss on the cheek; in America, we greet each other with a handshake or less. Each time I encountered an unexplained cultural difference such as this, I would feel awkward, confused, ashamed, or inadequate. The innumerable differences had nothing to do with language, because I was raised bilingually. I was more affected by the sense of cultural difference; the loss of cultural identify and feelings of inadequacy would well up within me as I sat in class. I felt an unexplained void, an emptiness inside. I read well. I could illustrate. But these were mere skills. What I needed was a cultural connection. I was constantly adapting to the system. I needed the system to meet me halfway, to collaborate, to include my thoughts and feelings. (p. 16)

She talks about the loneliness and sadness experienced by many immigrant children and their desperate need to be connected to someone who they believe cares and understands. Igoa makes an important point when she notes:

> In my work with immigrant children, I have become aware that each student's response and behavior in my classroom and out in the yard are a result of the complex interaction of his or her cultural background, individual nature, and length of time that student has been in the host country. (p. 17)

As with students with limited English proficiency or who are new to the U.S. culture, students with special learning and behavioral needs will benefit from our developing a better understanding of how they perceive our classroom, school, and their lives outside of school. It is important that we meet with these students, their parents and guardians, and the specialists who support them to better understand their needs and wants.

Think about a situation in which your knowledge of the activities was much less sophisticated than most of the people around you. This may have been when traveling abroad, attending an event in which you had limited background, and so on. How did you feel as you attempted to make sense of what was happening? How did those around you respond to you? What do you wish you could have done or others could have done for you? Consider that these feelings and wishes may be quite similar to the students with limited English proficiency or the students with learning disabilities in the classroom where you are teaching or observing.

Students who struggle in school are our best staff-development experts. Through their academic frustration and behavior problems they frequently inform us that while we may be doing an adequate job of teaching for some students, we need to modify our strategies for them. Interestingly, although the instructional and classroom management modifications we make in response to the demands of these students are often necessary prerequisites to their experiencing success, they also benefit virtually all other students. Many of the strategies presented in this book would be desirable but not absolutely necessary if we were teaching a senior honors class or a graduate seminar. However, when teaching a heterogeneous group of students, some of whom find the work extremely challenging or frustrating, these strategies can make the difference between an exciting, enjoyable year and a year filled with anger and frustration.

The student needs presented in this chapter, particularly the needs of students at risk, can be effectively met by teachers who choose to implement the methods presented throughout this book. This belief is supported by the fact that much of the research on effective schools and teacher effectiveness on which these methods are based was conducted in schools with many students at risk. Furthermore, in order to better respond to the needs of students at risk, the materials in this book expand on the school effectiveness research by including a greater emphasis on students' personal and social skill development as well as increasing students' motivation to learn and their sense of understanding and influencing their classroom and school environment. Specifically, the book emphasizes creating classroom and school environments that meet the following criteria:

1. Create personally supportive and engaging environments (communities of support)
2. Provide diversified instruction that meaningfully and actively engages students, enabling all students to utilize their preferred learning styles
3. Involve students in creating and learning social roles and relationships within the school context
4. Utilize problem solving and conflict management as the central theme in dealing with behavior problems
5. Teach students strategies for setting goals and monitoring their own behavior

THE ISSUES OF ORDER, CARING, AND POWER

For classrooms and schools to meet the academic and personal needs of students, schools must be safe environments characterized by a considerable degree of order.

The issue of order becomes more complex in school settings because students must function within a range of behaviors much more limited than those they would use outside of the school. Students understandably resist the expectation that, while engaged in activities that may be challenging and at times frustrating, they must remain relatively calm and respect the rights of thirty or more peers.

Envision yourself in a situation in which you were involved in a task you found somewhat demanding and you were not performing up to your expectations (for one of the authors this would be golf). If your lack of success continued, how would you respond? Now assume thirty people were present, and many of them were finding the task easy and enjoyable. Perhaps the presence of others would cause you to control your frustration. Not all young people, however, have this self-control, nor do they believe that such control in a public setting is important. In addition, even if they control themselves in the classroom setting, it is likely the frustration will be acted out on the playground, in the hallway, or on the way home from school.

Although the demands of learning increase the likelihood that students will be tempted to act in ways that disrupt the learning environment, disruptions are increased because a significant number of children enter school without their basic needs being met, and without belief systems or selected social skills that support an orderly learning environment. This reality clearly places demands on teachers.

PAUSE

and Consider   **2.7**

> Stop for a moment and jot down a list of the reasons you became a teacher or are studying to become a teacher. Share this list with several others and determine which factors you share in common.

The chances are quite good that wanting to make a difference in the lives of children, enjoying working with children or youth, and helping children develop personal skills were on this list. It is also likely that the thrill of watching children discover new knowledge was on someone's list. In Chapter 1 you were asked to list what most concerned you about teaching. For many educators this would involve some aspect of maintaining order in the classroom or responding to student behavior that disrupts the learning environment. Many beginning and veteran teachers report that, although they began teaching with a desire to create positive, supportive learning environments by collaborating with students, they soon became frustrated with student behavior that disrupted the learning environment and began using methods of authoritarian control. Many of these teachers report that they did this because they lacked both a clear philosophy and supporting strategies regarding how to develop a learning environment that supported children's emotional and social growth while simultaneously providing a safe, orderly setting that maximized student learning. The important question related to order is not whether order needs to exist but how order is established and maintained. In his book, *Constructive School Discipline*, Walter Smith (1936) wrote:

> It must be admitted, however, that the failure of the old disciplinary regime, not inaptly styled "beneficent tyranny," has left the situation somewhat chaotic. Many have discarded the authoritative type of control without developing any adequate system to take its place. . . . Discipline under the new regime cannot be made easier, but it may be made

a more vital element in moral education than it ever could under any system of autocratic domination. (pp. 8, 9)

Although Smith's statement was written sixty-eight years ago, there is an increasing body of research and literature suggesting that the issue of how order is established may be the most important factor influencing student behavior in schools. When William Wayson and Gay Su Pinnell (1982) studied high schools across the nation, they reported that "when discipline problems occur in school, they can more often be traced to dysfunctions in the interpersonal climate and organizational patterns of the school than to malfunctions in the individual" (p. 117). In her article on violence prevention in high schools, Janie Ward (1995) postulated that "solutions to violence may lie in strengthening racial identity and traditional values of caring in Black adolescents" (p. 184). In a similar vein, Pedro Noguera (1995) stated that schools that feel safe are characterized by teachers knowing and valuing students and relationships characterized by caring. Noguera (1995) wrote:

> The urban schools that I know that feel safe to those who spend their time there don't have metal detectors or armed security guards, and their principals don't carry baseball bats. What these schools do have is a strong sense of community and collective responsibility. Such schools are seen by students as sacred territory, too special to be spoiled by crime and violence, and too important to risk one's being excluded. (p. 207)

In his study on violence in high schools, Jackson Toby (1993) wrote that the first step in dealing with school violence is to "break through the anonymous, impersonal atmosphere of jumbo high schools and junior highs by creating smaller communities of learning within larger structures, where teachers and students can come to know each other well" (p. 46). This emphasis on the benefits of smaller communities is thoughtfully reviewed by Michael Klonsky (1996) in his booklet, *Small Schools: The Numbers Tell a Story.*

Discussing the importance of caring in working with students experiencing serious behavior problems, William Morse (1994) wrote:

> It is sad to note that proposals for school reform or special education inclusion seldom give attention to conditions which would facilitate the school as a setting for continuity of caring for all children. Yet caring is the experience so desperately needed especially by troubled children and those at risk. (p. 132)

Noddings (1992) wrote that "caring is the very bedrock of all successful education and that contemporary schooling can be revitalized in its light" (p. 27). Noddings also noted:

> But we rarely provide the community setting that was once available for large numbers of children. Too often, we do not even think of providing it. We think of providing specialists, computers, advanced math, and remedial reading. We could think of providing an

"I'm your teacher, Mrs. Gridley. Learn to read, write, and do arithmetic, and nobody will get hurt."

adult at each family-sized meal table. We could think of conversation, continuity, encouraging a sense of belonging. (p. 13)

As discussed throughout his book, *The Quality School: Managing Children without Coercion*, William Glasser (1990) suggests that, when schools have been successful in increasing student attendance and achievement while reducing instances of misbehavior, there is a common theme of creating student and community involvement and creating communities of caring and support. Curwin and Mendler (1988) suggested that teachers must decide whether to use the obedience model or the responsibility model of authority. In a similar vein, H. James McLaughlin (1992) wrote:

a teacher's legitimate authority has four characteristics: it derives from personal and positional relationships with students; it is both assumed and conferred; it is constrained or enabled by school and societal contexts; and it is predicated on the transformation of control by caring. (p. 4)

Bowers and Flinders (1990) have suggested that "control and caring are not opposing terms; but the form of control is transformed by the presence of caring" (p. 15).

Sergiovanni (1994) stated that one's commitment to exemplary practice serves as the basis for authority. This concept is supported by comments John Holt made in the early 1970s when he noted that all teachers needed to have authority, but that there were two types of authority. *Natural authority* is based on a teacher's natural skill in assisting students in the learning process, solving problems and modeling thoughtful, caring behavior. *Arbitrary* or *role-bound* authority is the authority granted to educators by their roles as teachers, principals, counselors, and so on. This authority is based on educators' legal right to maintain a quiet, safe environment and to facilitate the educational process. Holt suggested that students were impressed by and responded well to natural authority, whereas they often responded to arbitrary authority with confrontation and withdrawal. He suggested that the two types of authority were difficult to blend and that the more an educator used natural authority the less they would need to call on arbitrary authority. Similarly, the more we use arbitrary authority, the less students will be able to see our natural authority.

In their book, *Conflict in the Classroom*, Nicholas Long and William Morse (1996) provide a thoughtful statement about the choices teachers make when considering how to maintain a safe classroom environment:

For some educators, discipline means the power of the teacher to control the behavior of their students. . . . For other educators, discipline means an opportunity to teach students a set of values about how people can live together in a democratic society. This would include the values of honesty, fair play, the rights of others to learn, respect for property, respect of multicultural differences, and so on. Discipline is perceived as the process of helping students internalize these values and to develop self-control over their drives and feelings. (p. 238)

In his year-long ethnographic study in a second-grade classroom, George Noblit (1993) recounted his struggle to understand the relationship between caring and power. Noblit talked about his initial concern when he saw a teacher who directed much of the school day through routines and rituals. He reported that gradually he came to see how "routine and ritual established a continuity to the curriculum and instruction, and how the purposes of collective responsibility and work were continuous" (p. 35). He began to realize that it required intentionality and thoughtful planning to create a safe, orderly, caring sense of community in the classroom. In his field notes, Noblit noted a sensitive example of how the teacher used her power to ensure that the classroom was a secure place for her students.

> Outsiders came into her classroom only with her invitation. She met parents at the door and moved them out into the hall with her. I witnessed an incident in which the children were lining up near the door to the classroom to go to music class. The principal had come in to reinforce the students doing their homework, something the teachers, including Pam, had asked him to do. He asked Pam, "Have they been doing their homework?" Pam, Sharon, the children, and I knew that not all of them had. Pam looked at the kids and then back to the principal, responding, "They've done well." Taken literally, she had not answered the question asked by the principal. The principal, in kind, said to the children something to the effect of "Keep up the good work." He left, and Pam reorganized the line of students to go to music, only to have it break down into a series of children coming to her and hugging her. She had protected them. In her place they were secure—they were her students. (p. 34)

There is, however, an important issue to keep in mind when considering a classroom such as that described in the preceding quote. The teacher Noblit described built a classroom in which her caring and control protected and supported her students. Educators must be extremely careful that this type of teacher support does not become "enabling." Much as a constructivistic approach to learning emphasizes students learning to create their own meaning and learning to solve real world problems, a caring approach to classroom management means creating an environment in which students learn to solve their own problems and themselves learn how to discuss and resolve problems that occur. If the teacher takes too much responsibility for controlling the class and protecting the students, the students may be cheated out of important learning opportunities. It is interesting that in the highly successful program Jerome Freiberg has implemented in the Houston Public Schools (Freiberg, 1996; Freiberg, Stein, & Huang, 1995), students play a major role in running the classroom and have important roles in helping the school to function effectively.

We have all worked in classrooms and even schools in which student behavior is acceptable when the teacher is present but becomes hurtful and destructive when a substitute teacher, bus driver, or playground supervisor becomes involved. After our combined sixty-five years in education, it has become evident to us that a common characteristic of classrooms and schools in which this occurs is the focus on adult control through rewards and punishments. When adult power is used to influence student behavior, the behavior is likely to change dramatically when the power differential between adults and children changes. Interestingly, when discussing current methods in effective discipline, Lee Canter (1996), once perhaps the most noted advocate for a control/power method of discipline, wrote:

> There are teachers who believe that to have order, you just get tougher and tougher with kids—that you impose more rules and harsher consequences to get students' respect.
>
> But it doesn't work. . . .
>
> To be successful, a discipline plan should be built on a foundation of mutual trust and respect. That's the fundamental change in the Assertive Discipline plan for the '90s. . . . Too many kids have been let down by the adults in their lives. You have to demonstrate that you're fair, that you stick by your word, *that you care.* (p. 6)

The topic of multicultural education has provided another important forum for discussing the issue of power and control in the classroom. Sleeter (1991) wrote, "For me, and for many other advocates and theorists of multicultural education, empowerment and multicultural education are interwoven, and together suggest powerful and far-reaching school reform" (p. 2). In discussing the relationship between multicultural education, empowerment, and social change, Sleeter (1991) stated:

> The multicultural education approach, or cultural democracy, attempts to redesign classrooms and schools to model an unoppressive, equal society which is also culturally diverse. Explicitly this approach does not strongly teach social criticism and social change, but implicitly it does so in that a multicultural classroom or school implementing this approach is clearly different from the existing society. Students are empowered as individuals by achieving and receiving validation for who they are, and are empowered for social change by having lived a pluralistic model. (p. 11)

We believe that one of the most important decisions you will make as an educator involves the type of authority you will use. This decision impacts virtually every aspect of classroom instruction, management, and discipline.

PAUSE
and Consider   **2.8**

> Before moving on to the next section, take a few minutes and write a brief statement about what you believe about the issues of power, order, and caring in a classroom. Once you have completed this, join a group of classmates or colleagues and discuss your ideas.

Your views may differ from those expressed in this section. What is important is to have a solid foundation in research and theory to support your views. It is also imperative that you develop specific teaching methods that enable you to effectively implement your beliefs and goals in a manner than enhances students' dignity, academic success, and social skill development.

The Central Role of Community in Meeting Students' Needs

Closely connected to the issues of power, order, and authority is the concept of the school and classroom as a community of support. The blending of caring and order both helps meet students' personal and academic needs and is essential for teachers to meet their obligations to create safe and positive learning environments.

It is possible to create learning environments in which most students behave in ways that facilitate learning. To accomplish this we need to put students' needs at the center of school reform. Students confronted with lack of safety and support in their homes and communities are particularly impacted by the quality of community existing in their schools. Although all children will be more academically successful in a school characterized by adult caring and support, these are essential ingredients for students who live much of their lives with limited support. In his book, *Improving Schools from Within*, Roland Barth (1990) wrote:

> What needs to be improved about schools is their culture, the quality of interpersonal relationships, and the nature and quality of learning experiences.

> School improvement is an effort to determine and provide, from without and within, conditions under which adults and youngsters who inhabit schools will promote and sustain learning among themselves. By building community in schools we increase the likelihood that capacity will be tapped, conditions will become right, and the culture of the school will be improved. (p. 45)

In his book, *Building Community in Schools*, Thomas Sergiovanni (1994) stated powerfully that "if we want to rewrite the script to enable good schools to flourish, we need to rebuild community. Community building must become the heart of any school improvement effort" (p. xi). Sergiovanni further stated:

> Compliance strategies actually make things worse. Responsibility strategies are helpful but just not powerful enough. Strategies aimed at helping classrooms become democratic communities, on the other hand, can help young people reconnect with each other and with their schoolwork. Democratic communities can help students and adults come together to construct a standard for living their school lives together. And democratic communities can help students meet their needs to belong, to be active, to have control, and to experience sense and meaning in their lives. (p. 122)

Sergiovanni (1994) also suggested that "relationships in communities are characterized by the kinds of emotions—personalization, authenticity, caring, and unconditional acceptance—found in families, extended families, neighborhoods, and other social organizations" (p. xvi).

In her book, *The Good High School*, Sara Lawrence Lightfoot (1983) noted the importance of community when she wrote:

> The six portraits in this book illustrate the countless ways in which administrators, teachers, and students combine to form a community. Both adults and adolescents seem to need to feel a part of a larger network of relationships and want to feel identified with and protected by clear authority and a vivid ideological stance. (p. 347)

Pedro Noguera (1995) suggested that the most effective answer to violence in schools is not to intensify our efforts to monitor, control, and punish students but to create communities in which students feel valued. Noguera wrote:

> To address the problem of violence in schools effectively, I believe we must begin by asking ourselves why schools are vulnerable to the occurrence of violence. What is there about the structure and culture of schools that has, in recent times, increased the likelihood that acts of violence will be perpetrated within them? . . . I believe that it is in the context of fulfilling goals that have traditionally prioritized maintaining order and control over students, as opposed to creating humane environments for learning, that schools have become increasingly susceptible to violence. As an alternative approach, I will argue that schools must seek ways to create more humane learning environments, both to counter escalating violence and to transform social relationships within schools, so that those who spend their time there feel less alienated, threatened, and repressed. (p. 191)

As discussed in more detail in Part II, if we are to create meaningful changes in our schools, changes that will influence students' motivation, attendance, achievement, behavior, and futures, we will need to pay greater attention to the quality of relationships and the quality of life in schools. No educational change will have a meaningful impact if we do not simultaneously work to create more democratic, personally engaging, caring, and supportive learning environments for teachers and students. As presented throughout this book, we know that when students' needs are met within school environments, positive results occur. The issue is less the invention of methods than in the implementation of proven strategies that meet students' basic needs.

A Case Study: Meeting Students' Needs in a Middle School

Several years ago one of the authors worked with a middle school located in an area where nearly 90 percent of the students were on free or reduced lunch and were either Hispanic or Native American. When confronted with problems of student absenteeism and failure, the staff initially looked at national research on middle schools and developed a schedule and instructional strategies that they believed were best suited to the needs of middle school students. They created a block schedule in which students spent nearly half the day in a language arts, reading, and social studies block, and the other half in a science, math, and health block. In addition, to respond to problems of student tardiness and students' learning styles related to time of day, the blocks were rotated at the end of the semester. In addition, a study period was scheduled following the morning block, and students who were having difficulty with their work remained with their block teacher and an assistant while other students attended an elective. Therefore, for half the school year students had the potential for a tutorial in nearly half their academic subjects. During this time, students were guaranteed to have someone assisting them who spoke their first language.

In order to increase students' sense of significance and power, the staff created a yearly fall retreat in which approximately forty students and ten adults spent several days camping and developing a vision for the following school year. This vision was used as a theme for decorating the school, helping students set goals, and for school events. One year when the author was working at the school, the theme was "Make all the right moves." Chess figures were used to decorate the cafeteria, and students used this motto as a lead-in to short- and long-term goal setting.

In addition, the staff created a number of clubs representing activities selected by the students. The Native American club became well known regionally for their performances, and several other cultural clubs made performances and arranged special events. Students formed a recycling club that became actively involved in the community.

The faculty became concerned, however, when they noted that despite the fact that student achievement and attendance were improving dramatically, there was still a very high rate of late arrivals to school. Rather than assign detentions or use some other form of coercive discipline, the faculty met with students and parents to discuss the issue. Cultural differences regarding time were discussed. The group, therefore, decided to place the responsibility on the students to decide how important it was to be on time. The school decided to move the club program from fourth to first period. Students who arrived late were invited to study in the cafeteria but were not allowed to participate in the club for that day. Student tardies virtually disappeared. The students simply decided that the club activities were important enough to offset their lack of concern with timeliness.

METHODS FOR DISCOVERING STUDENTS' PERSONAL NEEDS

There are three basic methods for determining students' needs. First, teachers can examine what theories and associated research results say about those needs. This approach has the advantage of providing teachers with information based on a large sample of students in varied settings. Perhaps even more important, this method is relatively free from the teachers' own biases and needs. For example, the teacher who does not feel comfortable allowing students to take an active part in the learning process may, in fact, interpret student behavior as indicating that students do not want or cannot handle even a limited amount of this responsibility. Theoretical statements that have stood the test of time and data collected using sound research designs are not influenced by such individual biases and may, therefore, provide a clearer picture.

The second approach to determining students' needs within the school setting is to ask students what they need in order to feel comfortable and able to learn. An individual is the world's best expert on himself or herself. Students basically know better than anyone what factors make them comfortable, productive, and happy. It is a fact of life that students have had fewer experiences than adults and, consequently, are less knowledgeable about the relationship between behavior and its consequences. Nevertheless, students are often much more sensitive and aware than teachers acknowledge. A fourth-grade child has been involved in observing and influencing human behavior for ten years. Similarly, this child has spent ten years attempting to manipulate the environment in order to meet personal needs. Consequently, even elementary school children have considerable expertise in understanding the variables that influence their behavior. They know which environmental factors create comfort, safety, and belongingness, and which factors elicit discomfort, rejection, and the accompanying withdrawal or aggression. Given that a teacher's goal is to create environments that facilitate students' learning, it seems reasonable that teachers should systematically involve students in providing information about the learning environment.

The third method for obtaining information about students' needs is systematic observation. By carefully monitoring how children behave in various situations, teachers can learn a great deal about unmet student needs. One of the authors recently taught a child who often appeared very sluggish, unmotivated, and slow in both speech and comprehension. At times, however, the student was quite animated and aware. Before making a referral, and following an uninformative parent conference, the author began collecting data on the relationship between the student's behavior and food consumption. The student consistently seemed more animated after lunch. Data also revealed a consistent pattern between mornings when the student seemed sluggish and those when he reported having no breakfast or merely a cookie or a similarly poor breakfast. When the mother was shown these data, she reported that the child had hypoglycemia. This realization led to a discussion that culminated in the mother's agreeing to provide the necessary morning diet, and this change was followed by significant improvement in the child's behavior.

A young teacher provided another example of the benefits associated with carefully observing students' behavior as a means of assessing students' needs. When describing a student's behavior, the teacher noted that the student did not get along well with his peers and that this unmet need was very likely to be the cause of his problem. A more thorough examination of the boy's behavior, however, indicated that he had few negative peer contacts in situations such as recess or at lunch, when fights might be expected. Instead, nearly all his negative peer contacts occurred when the class was involved in seatwork. Therefore, though it was quite possible that a need for belongingness influenced the boy's behavior, a more appropriate initial intervention involved responding to his academic needs by providing him with seatwork that he could complete successfully.

ACTIVITIES FOR EXAMINING STUDENTS' PERSONAL NEEDS

This section presents several activities that can be used to examine students' personal and psychological needs within the classroom. Activity 2.1 asks you to "walk a mile in a student's shoes" in order to understand better why students may behave as they do. Activity 2.2 helps you to consider that every incident has varied perspectives. Activity 2.3 helps you better understand students' views of their classroom by directly asking them how they react to various aspects of their classroom experience. Activity 2.3 also helps you to analyze the data collected in the third activity and develop a plan of action for your classroom.

ACTIVITY 2.1 Examining Various Perspectives of a Behavior Problem	Select an incident in which a student misbehaved to such an extent that you had to send him or her to the office. Before continuing this activity, write down the punishment or consequence you would expect the student to receive for this act. On a separate sheet of paper, write a ½- to 1-page statement indicating how each of the following individuals would describe the incident leading to the referral: (1) yourself, (2) the student involved, (3) a student-centered counselor, and (4) the administrator who heard both your and the student's points of view. At the bottom of each paper, write a brief statement indicating what you think each individual would suggest as the solution or resolution to this situation. Having completed this exercise, write a statement concerning how you believe the situation should be responded to or resolved.
ACTIVITY 2.2 Discovering Students' Own Thoughts about Their Needs	Figure 2.3 presents a sample format and questions you might use when seeking information regarding how students view their school experience and whether their basic needs are being met within the school setting. Certainly, you will not want to use more than a dozen or so items at one time. With these questions as a guide, develop your own format and include questions that will help you answer important questions you have about the degree to which your students' needs are being met in your classroom and school.
ACTIVITY 2.3 Interpreting and Responding to Student Feedback	After developing and administering a student feedback form and summarizing the results, you should interpret the results and decide what changes, if any, need to be made. The following tasks and questions help facilitate this process. List the three statements students marked most frequently in the two most positive categories. For each of these statements, write one factor in the classroom that contributes to this positive student reaction. List the three statements students marked most often in the negative categories. For each of these statements, write one factor in the classroom that contributes to this negative student reaction. After completing Chapters 3 through 9, return to the activity and, following each classroom factor, list one change (including teacher's behavior) that could be made in the classroom to reduce or eliminate this factor. Complete this activity by listing three things you learned about your students' needs based on the results of the questionnaire.

Place a checkmark in the appropriate column.						

Your Thoughts about Our Class	Always	Most of the Time	Sometimes	Seldom	Never
Physiological					
1. Do you eat a good breakfast each morning?					
2. Can you see the blackboard and screen from where you are sitting?					
3. Do I talk loudly and clearly enough for you to hear?					
4. Do you have time to relax during the day?					
5. Do you have enough time to complete your assignments?					
6. Do we go slowly enough in class?					
7. Do you need a study period at the end of the day?					
8. Is the room a quiet place to work?					
Safety and Security					
9. Are your grades fair?					
10. Does each day in this class seem organized?					
11. Do you understand the school and classroom rules?					
12. Is the discipline used in this classroom fair?					
13. Can you say what you'd like to in this class?					
14. Do you feel free enough to ask me questions?					
15. Can you trust your teacher?					
16. Can you get help when you need it?					
17. Are you happy when you take your report card home?					
18. Do other students threaten you?					
19. Has anyone hurt you at school this year?					
20. Has anyone said something lately that made you feel bad?					
Love and Belonging					
21. Is the room a happy place to be?					
22. Do you think that the students in this class like you?					

(continued)

FIGURE 2.3
Student's Psychological Needs Assessment Questionnaire

Place a checkmark in the appropriate column.					
Your Thoughts about Our Class	*Always*	*Most of the Time*	*Sometimes*	*Seldom*	*Never*
23. Am I friendly and do I smile at you?					
24. Do I take time with you each day?					
25. Do I show that I like you?					
26. Do you feel that I listen to you when you have a problem?					
27. Do I praise you when you deserve it?					
28. Do other students respect your property?					
29. Do other students care about how well you do in school?					
30. Do I listen to your suggestions?					
Self-Esteem					
31. Do you feel involved in this class?					
32. Do you feel proud when you share a project with the class?					
33. Do you take part in class discussions?					
34. Do you follow the classroom rules?					
35. Do you help other students learn?					
36. Are you a good student?					
37. Do other students enjoy having you as a classmate?					
38. Are you meeting your goals this year?					
Self-Actualization					
39. Are you able to study things that interest you?					
40. Can you use what you learn in school?					
41. Do you have a chance to be creative in your schoolwork?					
42. Do you like to continue your studies at home on your own?					
43. Are you excited about what you are learning in school?					

FIGURE 2.3
Continued

Many of you who have requested written feedback from students are aware of how easy it is simply to scan the material for any positive or negative comments, feel good about having asked for feedback, and file away the material. There are two problems with this approach to responding to student feedback. First, by merely scanning the feedback, you may either fail to notice subtle but consistent feedback or overreact to several negative statements that are not representative of the feelings expressed by the majority of students. If you receive a piece of negative feedback from only one or two students, you may want to discuss the findings with the students (if students have signed their names) or to consider why a few students responded as they did. (It may simply be that the student[s] had a bad experience immediately preceding the administration of the questionnaire.) It is unlikely, however, that you would want to make a major change in the classroom, or even raise the issue with the entire class. However, if three-fourths of the class respond that they would like a change, it is important that the issue be thoughtfully examined and discussed with the class. Unless student feedback is clearly summarized and tabulated, it is easy to confuse major issues that need attention with comments from a few students that are taken too personally and blown out of proportion.

A second danger associated with merely scanning student feedback is that unless the results are shared with students and obvious responses are made to their suggestions, students begin to believe that the activity is not meaningful and that their input is not valued. Consequently, it is advisable to create a method for displaying the results so that they can be shared with students. The easiest approach is often to tally the results. Figure 2.4 provides the tallied results obtained by using the first eight questions on the student feedback form presented in Figure 2.3.

Place a checkmark in the appropriate column.					
Your Thoughts about Our Class	Always	Most of the Time	Sometimes	Seldom	Never
1. Do you eat a good breakfast each morning?	IIII	THL THL	THL I	IIII	
2. Can you see the blackboard and screen from where you are sitting?	THL THL IIII	THL I	II	II	
3. Do I talk loudly and clearly enough for you to hear?	THL THL THL III	THL II	II		
4. Do you have time to relax during the day?	III	THL IIII	THL III	II	IIII
5. Do you have enough time to complete your assignments?	THL II	THL THL I	III	II	
6. Do we go slowly enough in class?	THL	THL THL II	IIII	II	
7. Do you need a study period at the end of the day?	III	THL II	THL II	THL II	I
8. Is the room a quiet place to work?	II	THL IIII	THL IIII	II	III

FIGURE 2.4
Results of Administering a Student-Needs Questionnaire

A simple tally enables you to see where changes may be needed, as well as areas that students view as strengths. An interesting extension to tallying data is to determine a numerical average score for each item. When using a five-choice rating scale, as in Figure 2.3, a score of 5 can be assigned for each student who marked the most positive response, a score of 4 can be given for the second response, and so on. The scores can be added and then divided by the number of students completing the form in order to achieve a class score for each item. Therefore, the results shown in Figure 2.4 indicate that the class score for item 1 in Figure 2.3 is 3.6. Obtaining a class score for each item allows you to compare students' attitudes and feelings at different times throughout the school year. For example, if you responded to a low score on item 1 by teaching a unit on nutrition or sending a letter home to all parents about students' breakfasts, you could check the results of the intervention by administering the questionnaire again after several weeks and comparing the class scores on item 1 to see whether a change had taken place.

SUMMARY

Many teachers view their lack of ability to understand and effectively respond to unproductive student behavior as a major cause of job-related stress and personal frustration. Anyone who has taught has heard a colleague say in exasperation, "I just don't understand why Johnny acts that way." This chapter presented the important concept that student behavior can be understood by considering basic psychological needs students bring to the school setting. In many if not most cases when students act unproductively at school, they are responding to the fact that basic needs are not being met in the school setting. Unproductive school behavior is more frequent among students whose basic needs are not being met at home and in the community. Nevertheless, the problems outside of school are often not the major cause of the students' school difficulties, nor does their presence absolve us of our responsibility to create learning environments that meet students' basic needs.

Throughout much of the 1980s, school improvement projects focused heavily on improving the quality of instruction. During the 1990s, educators became increasingly aware of the number of students who enter school without the personal support and social skills needed to succeed. All students will experience greater success when they are educated in settings that meet their basic needs, but this factor is critical for students who enter school with many needs unmet.

RECOMMENDED READING

Banks, J., & McGee Banks, C. (Eds.). (1993). *Multicultural education: Issues and perspective*. Boston: Allyn & Bacon.

Carger, C. (1996). *Of borders and dreams: A Mexican-American experience of urban education*. New York: Teachers College Press.

Cummins, J. (1996). *Negotiating identities: Education for empowerment in a diverse society*. Ontario, CA: California Association for Bilingual Education.

Darling-Hammond, L. (1997). *The right to learn: A blueprint for creating schools that work*. San Francisco: Jossey-Bass.

Davidman, L., & Davidman, P. (1997). *Teaching with a multicultural perspective: A practical guide.* New York: Longman.

Dishion, T., French, D., & Patterson, G. (1995). The development and ecology of antisocial behavior. In D. Cicchetti & D. Cohen (Eds.), *Developmental Psychopathology, Volume 2.* New York: John Wiley.

Five, C. (1992). *Special voices.* Portsmouth, NH: Heinemann.

Freeman, Y., & Freeman, D. (2002). *Closing the achievement gap: How to reach limited-formal-schooling and long-term English learners.* Portsmouth, NH: Heinemann.

Garbarino, J. (1999). *Lost boys: Why our sons turn violent and how we can save them.* New York: Free Press.

Garcia, E. (1999). *Student cultural diversity: Understanding and meeting the challenge* (2nd ed.). Boston: Houghton Mifflin.

Gardner, H. (1999a). *Intelligence reframed: Multiple intelligences for the twenty-first century.* New York: Basic Books.

Gardner, H. (1999b). *The disciplined mind: What all students should understand.* New York: Simon & Schuster.

Garrod, A., & Larimore, C. (1997). *First person, first peoples: Native American college graduates tell their life stories.* Ithaca, NY: Cornell University Press.

Garrod, A., Ward, J., Robinson, T., & Kilkenny, R. (Eds.). (1999). *Souls looking back: Life stories of growing up black.* New York: Routledge.

Goleman, D. (1995). *Emotional intelligence.* New York: Bantam Books.

Igoa, C. (1995). *The inner world of the immigrant child.* New York: St. Martin's Press.

Karr-Morse, R., & Wiley, M. (1997). *Ghosts from the nursery: Tracing the roots of violence.* New York: The Atlantic Monthly Press.

Kauffman, J. (1997). *Characteristics of emotional and behavioral disorders of children and youth* (6th ed.). Upper Saddle River, NJ: Merrill.

Kuykendall, C. (1992). *From rage to hope: Strategies for reclaiming Black and Hispanic students.* Bloomington, IN: National Educational Service.

Lee, S. (1996). *Unraveling the "model minority" stereotype: Listening to Asian American youth.* New York: Teachers College Press.

Reyes, P., Scribner, J., & Scribner, A. (1999). *Lessons from high-performing Hispanic schools.* New York: Teachers College Press.

Sylwester, R. (2000). *A biological brain in a cultural classroom.* Thousand Oaks, CA: Corwin Press.

Creating Positive Interpersonal Relationships in the Classroom

An ounce of prevention is worth a pound of cure. This statement is the key to effective classroom management. A large percentage of classroom problems can be prevented by creating positive, safe classroom environments. Books on classroom management too often focus on techniques for modifying individual students' behavior through a system of rewards and punishments while failing to acknowledge the vital role the social atmosphere plays in influencing students' behaviors. Unfortunately, this major oversight frequently creates situations in which students are manipulated into behaving appropriately in environments that do not meet their basic psychological or academic needs. This approach is not only thoughtless and unfair to students but it also creates a situation in which the new behavior is maintained only as long as desired rewards are present. Therefore, it is easy to understand why programs based solely on behavioristic interventions have had limited success in generalizing behavior change to new environments.

Part II focuses on specific methods for preventing unproductive student behavior by creating positive interpersonal relationships in the classroom and throughout the school. These methods are important because they help create environments in which students feel happy and excited about learning. This atmosphere, in turn, tends to elicit more positive student behavior and to facilitate learning.

Educators should be aware of the dangers inherent in the completely unsubstantiated belief that time spent in creating classrooms in which students feel involved, safe, and happy could somehow be better spent in additional instructional time. As discussed in Part I, students' academic performance is enhanced when teachers take time to respond to students' personal and psychological needs. Research indicates that positive affect is associated with improved student attitudes and higher-level thinking skills. Another important reason for blending academic and personal–social skill building is that if schools' goals include preparing young people to be involved citizens, activities aimed at developing a sound base of knowledge must be balanced with skills in interpersonal relations and problem solving.

Chapter 3 examines two pivotal aspects of teacher–student relationships: (1) the personal, affective quality of these relationships and (2) how teachers communicate expectations to students. Chapter 4 focuses on the quality of peer relationships within classrooms. The chapter provides numerous activities for enhancing positive, cooperative peer relationships. Parents can do much to encourage positive student attitudes toward school, and Chapter 5 examines methods you can use to create positive, supportive relationships with parents.

CHAPTER

3

Establishing Positive Teacher–Student Relationships

Most important, students say they like classrooms where they feel they know the teacher and the other students. While students appreciate a well-organized and orderly environment, they do not like one in which the teacher is detached and treats the classroom as a whole rather than as a roomful of individuals.

—Patricia Phelan, Ann Locke Davidson,
and Hanh Thanh Cao (1992)
"Speaking Up: Students' Perspectives on School"
Phi Delta Kappan

Nowadays, to be successful in a position of authority requires an ability to connect in a caring way by inspiring hope within others and by leading one's own life in a manner that models the message.

—Allen Mendler (1992)
*What Do I Do When . . . ? How to Achieve
Discipline with Dignity in the Classroom*

If a child is to live freely and creatively and acculturate to a new social environment, then the deeper part of the child must surface. We need to help the child remove his or her mask through warmth, reverence, understanding, and listening closely.

—Cristina Igoa (1995)
The Inner World of the Immigrant Child

> *The heart of the professional ideal in teaching may well be . . . a commitment to the ethic of caring. Caring requires more than bringing state-of-the-art technical knowledge to bear in one's practice. It means doing everything possible to enhance the learning, developmental, and social needs of students as persons. The heart of caring in schools is relationships with others (teachers, parents, and students) characterized by nurturance, altruistic love, and kinshiplike connections.*
>
> —Thomas Sergiovanni (1994)
> *Building Community in Schools*

> *The most powerful restraints on violent behavior are healthy human attachments.*
>
> —Larry Brendtro and Nicholas Long (1995)
> "Breaking the Cycle of Conflict"
> *Educational Leadership*

The quality of teacher–student relationships dramatically affects whether students' personal needs are met in the classroom. Students spend nearly a quarter of their waking lives between ages six and seventeen with teachers. Because teachers are responsible for evaluating students' work and controlling the quality of life in the classroom, they are powerful adult figures in students' lives. Effective teachers understand the influence they have on students and use this influence positively.

A significant body of research indicates that academic achievement and students' behaviors are influenced by the quality of the teacher–student relationship. Students prefer teachers who are warm and friendly. More important, positive teacher–student relationships, in which teachers use the skills described in this chapter, are associated with more positive student responses to school and with increased academic achievement.

An excellent example of the importance of combining acceptance with respect for students was reported by Kleinfeld (1972) in a powerful analysis of teachers' interactions with Eskimo and Native American students who had recently moved to urban settings. Kleinfeld found that teachers who were effective with these children were able to combine showing a personal interest in the students with demands for solid academic achievement. Summarizing her findings, she stated:

> The essence of the instructional style which elicits a high level of intellectual performance from village Indian and Eskimo students is to create an extremely warm personal relationship and to actively demand a level of academic work which the student does not suspect he can attain. Village students thus interpret the teacher's demandingness not as bossiness or hostility, but rather as another expression of his personal concern, and meeting the teacher's academic standards becomes their reciprocal obligation in an intensely personal relationship. (p. 34)

Kleinfeld's work is consistent with research conducted twenty-five years later showing that successful adults who were raised in poverty point to the importance of a supportive adult who believed in and encouraged them to continue their education (Harrington & Boardman, 1997).

In a study conducted at the Center for Research on the Context of Secondary School Teaching at Stanford University, researchers examined the factors in high school environments that support positive student attitudes and learning. The study was designed to determine students' perceptions regarding factors that influence their school performance. In a review of their work, the researchers stated, "A recurring theme in students' comments is the tremendous value they place on having teachers who care. . . . In fact, the number of student references to 'wanting caring teachers' is so great that we believe it speaks to the quiet desperation and loneliness of many adolescents in today's society" (Phelan, Davidson, & Cao, 1992, p. 698).

In their extensive study of school environments that meet the needs of students at risk for school failure, Wehlage, Rutter, Smith, Lesko, and Fernandez (1989) reported the following four common impediments to students developing a sense of school community:

1. *Adjustment:* Students at risk need a more personal and supportive relationship with adults than schools typically provide.

2. *Difficulty:* "Although we found literal inability to do the work a relatively rare characteristic of at-risk students, it is the case that increased time and more intensive tutoring were required for many. . . . The educational situation students complained most about was the ubiquitous 'lecture-discussion' based on reading assignments" (p. 124).

3. *Incongruence:* This related to the lack of personal–social match between the student and the institution.

4. *Isolation:* "We found that students who had persistent conflicts with adults or who found no teacher with whom to establish a personal relationship were at risk of dropping out" (p. 131).

The authors also stated that "there are four teacher beliefs and/or values, accompanied by corresponding sets of behaviors, that together constitute a positive teacher culture facilitating membership and engagement for students" (p. 135). These beliefs are the following:

1. Teachers accept personal responsibility for student success.
2. Teachers practice an extended teacher role.
3. Teachers are persistent with students.
4. Teachers express a sense of optimism that all students can learn.

Students' statements regarding effective teachers mirror those just mentioned. "When I have asked students in interviews what makes a particular teacher 'special' and worthy of respect, the students consistently cite three characteristics: firmness, compassion, and an interesting, engaging, and challenging teaching style" (Noguera, 1995).

Interviews conducted over a three-year period with 400 inner-city middle and high school students in Philadelphia present similar results (Corbett & Wilson, 2002). These students stated that good teachers:

- Made sure that students did their work
- Controlled the classroom
- Were willing to help students whenever and however the students wanted help

- Explained assignments and content clearly
- Varied the classroom routine
- Took time to get to know the students and their circumstances (p. 18)

Clearly students believe they learn best from teachers who are committed to helping them, take time to know them personally, and provide clear and varied instruction.

We suggest that caring is much more than simply the creation of warm, interpersonal relationships. It also involves encouraging dialogue with students regarding curricular and instructional decisions, listening to students' concerns, ensuring that all students have an opportunity to experience success, and ensuring that learning is fun and interesting.

Teachers are increasingly aware of the importance of positive teacher–student relationships. Darling-Hammond (1997) found that 84 percent of teachers she interviewed stated that developing positive relationships with students and developing materials related to student needs were the most important ingredients of effective teaching.

Although students and educators seem to agree on many of the qualities of a good teacher, students too often believe teachers do not display these characteristics, and when this occurs, the results are predictable. William Glasser (1990) noted that, "By the end of the seventh grade, more than half the students believe that teachers and principals are their adversaries" (p. 29). Students often respond to this perceived sense of being devalued by misbehaving. Cusick (1994) reported that most student resistance to teacher directions occurs in classes where students report disliking their teacher. This is supported by research indicating that, "at least 50% to 60% of school children suffer from at least one occurrence of maltreatment by an educator, which leads to some stress symptoms, including aggressive responses" (Hyman & Perone, 1998, p. 20).

Although positive teacher–student relationships are an essential factor influencing the motivation, achievement, and behavior of all students, this is particularly true for students who may find school more challenging. In discussing his interviews with teachers viewed as highly effective with a culturally and linguistically diverse student population, Garcia (1999) wrote, "Each teacher spoke of the importance of strong and caring relationships among class members and particularly between the teacher and the students" (p. 276). In his book on empowering minority students, Cummins (1996) wrote, "in classroom interactions respect and affirmation are central to motivating second language learners to engage actively and enthusiastically in academic content" (p. 74).

In his book, *Lost Boys: Why Our Sons Turn Violent and How We Can Save Them*, James Garbarino (1999) states that, "It is because of the cen-

"Of course I believe that a teacher should offer a positive role model; however . . ."

tral role of shame in instigating and sustaining violence that we must communicate respect in every facet of institutional life as a precondition for transformation of troubled and violent boys" (p. 229). He argues that boys who have been emotionally damaged by parental abuse and rejection desperately need caring, supportive relationships with adults. He suggests that creating positive, long-term teacher–student relationships is an important factor in providing "remedial attachment experiences" (p. 58) that can reduce the level of depression and anger experienced by these boys. Indeed, only 35 percent of boys who have been abused become violent (Dodge, Pettit, & Bates, 1997). Garbarino (1999) suggests that a major factor influencing the fact that 65 percent of these children develop fewer violent and negative behaviors is that "with some boys, the answer seems clearly linked to a compensatory relationship" (p. 83). Students who struggle to behave appropriately need educators who continue to express warmth and caring even when they must set limits and reteach appropriate behaviors.

Many schools in which a wide range of students are succeeding have been restructured so teachers work with fewer students for longer periods of time.

> Because the schools are structured to allow teachers to care for students effectively, students develop trust, and students begin to believe that accomplishing the school's goals will be important to their later success. This faith then fuels the effort that teachers need from students to produce learning. (Darling-Hammond, 1997, p. 174)

Taken together, this research points to a need for teachers to learn and conscientiously apply skills in relating positively to their students.

THE TEACHER AS A MODEL

Young people seek models to assist them in their development of an identity. One needs only look at the sports clothing worn by teens to see how sports heroes are emulated in our society. Because of the breakup of so many U.S. families, young people are perhaps more in need of adult models than ever before. William Morse (1994) wrote:

> Deeper than management, teachers hope to change attitudes and even values in the confused and value deficient youngsters. This requires the teacher to be a model, or deeper yet a figure for identification, one who interacts and discusses with children, pointing the way to more successful ways of feeling and acting. (p. 135)

Much of children's behavior is developed by emulating the behaviors of adults who play significant roles in their lives. Research indicates that individuals are more likely to model the behaviors of people whom they view as possessing competence and control over resources, and who are major sources of control, support, and reinforcement—characteristics possessed by teachers.

Our influence as models continues throughout the school year. In many schools, student turnover is high, and the many students who transfer into a school have their initial and most influential contacts with the teacher at times other than the first days of school. Teachers frequently comment that transfer students often gravitate to a less-than-ideal group of students. If we wish to have new students accept our values, we must make a special effort to provide them with an adult model who demonstrates competence and warm care for the new student. A few minutes of extra time spent going over classroom procedures and meeting privately with the students to discuss their work and offer assistance can dramatically increase the likelihood that they will model us rather than the behavior of any potentially negative group of peers.

One fun and productive strategy for new students becoming more effectively connected to all adults in the school is a "new student greeter program." In this program students are given a coupon book in which each page lists an adult who assists students in the school. Each new student takes this coupon book around and has it signed by each adult. The adults tell students how they help students, then they give the students a small gift (e.g., a cookie from the cook, bookmark from the media specialist, and so forth). By the end of the day the new students have met virtually every key adult with whom they will come into contact and the initial interaction with this adult has been positive and informative.

Research also indicates that young people are more likely to model behavior that is exhibited by several adults. Furthermore, youngsters tend to model behaviors if they think adults benefit from the performance of these behaviors. These factors suggest the importance of creating schools in which a large percentage of adults demonstrate the skills and attitudes described in this chapter and in which teachers are reinforced by their peers and administrators for exhibiting these skills.

Before presenting specific approaches for improving teacher–student relationships, we must place this issue in a proper perspective. The quality of teacher–student relationships has great influence on the amount of productive or disruptive behavior students display in a school setting. We must be careful, however, not to confuse the importance of establishing positive teacher–student relationships with the belief that all classroom problems can be solved by love and understanding. Regardless of how concerned, positive, and fair a teacher is, students frequently misbehave in classes that are poorly organized and in which students are not provided with appropriate and interesting instructional tasks.

P A U S E
and Consider   **3.1**

> What are specific ways you act with your students that enable you to be viewed as a positive role model? We encourage you to make a list of these behaviors and to share them with several colleagues or classmates who teach students at a grade level similar to yours.

ESTABLISHING EFFECTIVE RELATIONSHIPS WITH STUDENTS

As anyone who has taught for very long realizes, students need and want positive teacher behavior to be associated with firmness, realistic limits, and competent teaching. The ability to blend warmth and caring with realistic limits is frequently a difficult task for young teachers. Unfortunately, this confusion is occasionally intensified by advice suggesting that beginning teachers should be less warm toward and more distant from their students. The main issue is not whether teachers should be less warm or friendly, but that they must simultaneously assert both their right to be treated with respect and their responsibility for ensuring that students treat each other with kindness. Warmth and concern can exist side by side with firmness. Indeed, effective teaching involves blending these vital ingredients.

Before reading any further, we recommend you stop and make two lists. First, list at least a half dozen specific situations in which you would need to firmly engage students to ensure their behavior does not violate the rights of others. Write a brief paragraph on how you feel about this aspect of teaching. Second, make a list of at least a half dozen ways you can communicate to students that you care about and are interested in them. Write a brief paragraph summarizing how you feel about his aspect of teaching. In reviewing these two paragraphs, what do they tell you about your thoughts regarding interacting with students? Does this review indicate any areas for your professional growth?

Before presenting specific communication skills that may assist you in developing open, effective relationships with students, it is important to consider the general issue of how teachers can most effectively relate to their students. In his classic book *Teacher Effectiveness Training*, Thomas Gordon (1974) wrote:

> The relationship between a teacher and a student is good when it has (1) *Openness* or *Transparency*, so each is able to risk directness and honesty with the other; (2) *Caring*, when each knows that he is valued by the other; (3) *Interdependence* (as opposed to dependency) of one on the other; (4) *Separateness*, to allow each to grow and to develop his uniqueness, creativity, and individuality; (5) *Mutual Needs Meeting*, so that neither's needs are met at the expense of the other's needs. (p. 24)

In a similar vein, Noddings (1984) wrote that moral education based on caring consists of four components: modeling, dialogue, practice, and confirmation. *Modeling* refers to how we as educators treat others—adults and children. *Dialogue* means an open-ended discussion in which the adult has not predetermined the decision. Dialogue allows students to ask why and to have input into decisions that affect them. *Practice* means that students must have opportunities to be involved in caring relationships. This may involve community-service activities, tutoring, or other occasions in which students learn to assist and encourage others. Finally, *confirmation* refers to finding opportunities to validate each student's growth toward being a caring member of the community. It also means seeking to understand why a student would make a bad choice and helping the students see that we value students and want to help them find a more acceptable and caring way to meet their need. As you read this book, you will see how many of the best-accepted practices in classroom management support Noddings's concepts of moral education based on caring.

We encourage you to put the book aside for a moment and create four columns headed by the four components described by Noddings. In each column, list five specific teacher behaviors or classroom activities you use (or would like to use) to develop each of these components of moral education based on caring.

We have often heard teachers state that students need structure and limits rather than caring. These two are not antithetical. Teachers can demonstrate respect, caring, and warmth toward students and still hold very high expectations regarding students' behaviors and academic performances.

Creating Open, Professionally Appropriate Dialogue with Students

Although the specific decisions teachers make concerning their relationships with students vary depending on their students' ages, the basic themes related to teacher–student relationships are similar across grade levels. One important question involves deciding how open and involved a teacher wishes to be with students. Teachers can select from among three general types of teacher–student relationships. Although teacher–student relationships vary on numerous dimensions, a primary factor involves the level of openness chosen. We can choose a teacher–student relationship characterized by:

1. Almost complete openness, in which we share a wide range of personal concerns and values with students
2. Openness related to our reactions to and feelings about the school environment, with limited sharing of aspects reflecting our out-of-school life
3. An almost exclusive focus on a role-bound relationship; that is, we share no personal feelings or reactions, but merely perform our instructional duties

"It's great how Mr. Watson's able to communicate with kids on their own level!"

Not surprisingly, beginning teachers often grapple with whether they should be involved in very open, personal relationships with their students. They may wonder about the extent to which they should join in with students, share students' interests, use student slang, and so on. The authors' experiences suggest that students respond best to adults who are comfortable with themselves, their values, and their personal preferences and who, when appropriate, can share these nonjudgmentally with students. Likewise, when preferences or values of a teacher differ from those of students, encouraging a two-way exchange of ideas can prove stimulating and educational to both the students and the teacher.

However, you should avoid becoming overly involved in students' interests or activities outside of school, particularly if you are a secondary teacher. Adolescents are working at developing their own identity and generally view adulthood as a positive stage in which individuals have reached desired personal and social adjustment. Consequently, adolescents are confused by adults who show intense interest in students' social activities and interests. It confuses them to see adults who appear to want to be similar to young people or a part of their peer group. If adults do not have something more interesting or valuable to offer, a major goal of adolescence—moving toward partnership in the adult community—is devalued. Students need to know that we have interesting lives apart from them and that we find life stimulating and challenging in some ways that are different from theirs. At the same time, they need us to be interested enough in them and open enough with our own values to share our ideas with them and engage them in discussions of personal as well as academic matters.

In her book, *The Good High School*, Sarah Lawrence Lightfoot (1983) provided an example of a decision a teacher made regarding how much of herself to share with her students.

> A teacher, applauded by her colleagues as one of the "stars" on the Brookline faculty, told me about the struggle she was having getting the students in her advanced writing class past their defensive, secretive posturing with one another. After trying various strategies to encourage spontaneity and expressiveness in their writing, she decided to read them a very personal letter she had written to three dear friends after the death of a fourth friend. The letter, composed in the middle of the night, was unguarded, revealing, and painful. The teacher hoped her own openness would inspire similar responses in her students. In deciding whether to use this personal piece as a pedagogical tool she struggled with herself, tried to anticipate the possible repercussions, and reflected on her motives. Was she being overly seductive by revealing so much of her person? Could she tolerate making herself so vulnerable? Would her students abuse her intentions? Would it destroy the needed separations between teacher and students? In the end, at the last minute, the teacher decided against reading the letter in class. "My gut told me it wasn't right," she said with lingering ambivalence. What is important here is not the way she resolved this educational dilemma, but the intellectual and psychological journey this teacher traveled and her perceptions of herself as a resourceful and responsible actor. (pp. 336–337)

This teacher made the decision not based on what was best for her, but what she thought was best for her students. The main point is that the teacher's knowledge of herself and her students was used to make the decision.

These issues highlight the value of establishing the second type of teacher–student relationship—one in which we share our reactions to and feelings about occurrences within the school setting and share with students limited aspects of our out-of-school life. Teachers who choose this type of relationship will often share with students occurrences involving their children, recreational activities, or cultural events they have attended. These teachers will also show considerable openness in discussing their feelings about events in the classroom.

The importance of being open enough to allow students to know us as people was highlighted for one of the authors during his experiences teaching junior high school students who had behavioral disorders. Discussions with students indicated that a number of them were involved in shoplifting from a large chain store near the school. However, these same students frequently visited a leather shop where the proprietor kept money, tools, and leather on the outer counter while he worked in a back room. When asked why they stole from the chain store but not the leather worker, the students expressed some surprise and indicated emphatically that they knew this man and they did not steal from "real people." This incident emphasized an important issue in dealing with young people. They often react negatively to and abuse people whom they view as merely roles, but they less often create problems for individuals whom they know and understand.

In addition to letting students know us as people, we can model a degree of openness to our own students' verbal expressions of concerns and feelings in our classrooms. An excellent example of effective modeling occurred several years ago when one of the authors visited the classroom of an extremely effective teacher. The eighth-grade students in his class were actively involved in a science project and the room buzzed with noise and interest. A boy called across the room to his friend, John, and requested that John throw him the scissors. John immediately obliged, and the airborne scissors narrowly missed hitting another student. Rather than shouting at John, the teacher walked over to him and put his hand on John's shoulder. He proceeded to share with John the fact that the near miss had frightened him because he cared about and felt responsible for the students in his class. He then asked John if in the future he would carry the scissors across the room. The teacher then spoke briefly with the boy who had requested the scissors and with the student who had narrowly missed being hit. At the end of the period, the teacher took time to review the importance of the classroom procedure regarding scissors and had students demonstrate the correct procedure.

After class, the teacher explained why his intervention had been so calm and personal. He stated that young adolescents are involved in so many changes that their egos are very fragile and they personalize almost everything. He went on to say that his goal was to provide the student with information in a manner that would enhance the likelihood that the student would listen. Had he yelled at the student or made an example of him in front of the class, the student probably would have responded by focusing on the teacher's mean behavior rather than by examining his own behavior. The teacher stated that by admitting to his own feeling and sharing it with the student, he had provided the student with valuable information without making him defensive.

This incident is an excellent example of a skilled teacher's ability to synthesize spontaneously a working knowledge of adolescent development with practical communication skills. The result of this synthesis was that the teacher was able to respond in a way that facilitated the student's personal growth while modeling emotional control and sensitivity to the student's feelings.

While supervising an intern, one of the authors saw another poignant example of the benefits of openness. An intern teacher consulted one of the authors regarding her problems with a high school biology class. The intern had taken over for a very dynamic and popular teacher, and the students were behaving poorly and at times even being cruel to the intern. The author suggested that the intern openly discuss her feelings with the class while also acknowledging her appreciation for the students' feelings and sense of loss. Several educators advised the intern against this, indicating that she might be opening a Pandora's box. The intern chose to have the discussion with the class and reported that students were very open in thoughtfully sharing their frustration. Indeed, one student indicated that her grade had dropped from an A to a C since the intern took over and that she was very frustrated. The intern noted that this was her first experience grading high school work and that she would be glad to meet with students to discuss their grades. Many students expressed appreciation for the intern's openness, and the intern reported that the tenor of the class changed dramatically.

As educators, we must realize that the feelings and perceptions of individuals in the classroom are important, legitimate issues of concern that affect students' motivation and achievement. If we are to be successful teaching students today, we must be willing to deal with the affective component of the classroom milieu as well as with the cognitive content. A central theme of this book is that effective classroom managers are aware of classroom processes and are willing and able to engage students in assessing and adjusting classroom procedures and instructional methods. This involves not only our own awareness and self-analysis but also involving students in open dialogue and problem solving.

Another aspect of appropriate affect with students is teachers' abilities to be comfortable with their students. Students know when we enjoy them and are comfortable with them. Likewise, they are confused and often respond negatively when working with teachers who seem uncomfortable or even fearful of them. Noguera (1995) noted that "I have generally found that teachers who lack familiarity with their students are more likely to misunderstand and fear them" (p. 202). He suggests that violence in schools is significantly influenced by teachers being uncomfortable with and even fearing their students. This leads to teachers ignoring inappropriate behavior, using oversimplified and impersonal discipline techniques, and referring students to administrators without first attempting to work with the situation.

Sarah Lawrence Lightfoot (1983) wrote that the "fearless and empathetic regard of students" (p. 342) is a key dimension of good high schools. She means that teachers understand and appreciate the developmental challenges facing their students. In addition to this understanding, teachers are not self-conscious around their students and seem to be comfortable with and enjoy students. Lightfoot wrote:

> What I am calling fearlessness in teachers should not be interpreted as careless abandon on their part. Neither is it an expression of naiveté or innocence. They feel appropriately threatened by real danger. I would not even argue that their fearlessness comes from a greater personal confidence and certainty in them. I think it reflects their intimate and deep knowledge of adolescence as a developmental period; their understanding of individual students; and the strong authority structures within which they work. I was constantly amazed by teachers' understanding, diagnosis, and quick interpretations of adolescent needs. The interpretations were rarely made explicit or clearly articulated. They seemed almost intuitive to the observer. But when I asked teachers why they had acted in a certain way or made a specific decision, they tended to have ready responses that recognized the adolescent view and perspective. Their decisions to act combined a sensitivity to the student's individual character and history and an understanding of the developmental tendencies associated with adolescence. The same behavior expressed by different students might receive very different reactions from the teacher. (p. 344)

Marva Collins (1992), the founder of Westside Preparatory School in Chicago, stated it this way:

> When I taught in a public high school for three years I always ate lunch with a different group of students whether they were in my class or not, until I got to know most of them. The teachers thought I was idiotic, but they didn't realize that it actually made it easier for me to teach, that before I could effectively discipline students, I had to earn their friendship and respect. (p. 4)

Dave Carpenter

One suspects that this educator also enjoyed her time with the students and often found it to be as intellectually stimulating and personally satisfying as her time in the faculty room.

A final example of the decision we must make about openness to student feedback occurred when a student-teacher being supervised by one of the authors was challenged by a student in his sophomore biology class. Frustrated by his inability to understand a lecture, the student stood up at the back of the class and stated loudly, "This class stinks!" Rather than sending the student to the office, the teacher responded by stating that, though he wished the student would share his frustration in a more polite manner, he was glad that he was able to state his anger rather than not come to class. The teacher proceeded to inform the student that he would like to discuss the student's concern, but that first he needed to determine whether it was shared by a majority of the class or only by a few students. The teacher's inquiry indicated that only three students shared this concern. Therefore, the teacher indicated that it made more sense for him and the three students to work together to consider how to make the class better for them. The student responded positively, and several discussions led to a positive resolution.

An interesting sidelight to this story involved the supervising teacher's reaction. This teacher strongly supported the third approach to teacher–student relationships. He stated that teachers cannot afford to be open with students or to discuss classroom instructional or behavioral matters. Instead, he believed that teachers must always be in authoritarian command of the classroom and that students must be required to do what teachers expect with no questions asked. The teacher called the author, very upset that the intern had not immediately thrown the student out of class and asked the other students whether any of them wanted to join the student in his visit to the office.

An optional manner for handling this situation within the context of the second type of teacher–student relationship was offered by a skilled middle school physical education teacher. She indicated that even though she supports the concept of teachers being open about their reactions to classroom events, she believes students can be taught that the teacher will not allow abusive language or direct confrontation of a teacher in front of a class. She believes that students should know ahead of time that when this occurs, they will be politely but firmly required to leave the class, knowing also that at a later time they will have an opportunity to discuss their concerns and behaviors with the teacher.

The different reactions chosen by the teachers in this example exemplify the decisions we must make concerning the type of openness to students' input we select. Certainly, each teacher must operate at a degree of openness that is personally comfortable. Nevertheless, the second type of openness enhances students' sense of ownership in, and impact on, the classroom environment and thus can improve classroom management and student motivation.

P A U S E

3.4   *and Consider*

Stop for a moment and consider the type of relationships you have with your students or with children or adolescents approximately the age of those you wish to teach. On a sheet of paper list at least two examples of interactions that would fall into each of the three levels of teacher–student relationship discussed in the first paragraph of this section. Consider for a moment the advantages and disadvantages of each of these three types of relationships in school settings with the age group you teach or will teach. The decisions you make about relationships with your students and the quality of these relationships may be the most significant factor in your ability to create a safe and productive learning environment in your classroom.

METHODS FOR COMMUNICATING CARING AND SUPPORT

Even though using the second type of teacher–student relationship will generally enhance the rapport teachers can establish with students, it is sometimes desirable for teachers to act more systematically in developing positive teacher–student relationships. We can express our interest and concern for students by (1) getting to know them and expressing interest in them as individuals; (2) maintaining a high rate of positive to negative statements; (3) communicating high expectations to all students; (4) giving specific, descriptive feedback; (5) listening to students; and (6) responding effectively to inappropriate or disruptive behavior.

Getting to Know Students

Teachers can enhance their ability to be invitational with their students by understanding their students and the social factors that influence their students' lives. Peregoy and Boyle (1993) suggest that teachers can ask the following questions about students who have a cultural background different from their own.

1. *Family structure:* What constitutes a family? Who among these or others live in one house? What is the hierarchy of authority?
2. *Life cycle:* What are the criteria for defining stages, periods, or transitions in life? What rites of passage are there?
3. *Roles and interpersonal relationships:* What roles are available to whom, and how are they acquired? Is education relevant to learning these roles?
4. *Discipline:* What is discipline? What counts as discipline and what does not?
5. *Time and space:* How important is punctuality? Speed in completing a task?
6. *Religion:* What restrictions are there concerning topics that should not be discussed in school?
7. *Food:* What is eaten? In what order? How often?
8. *Health and hygiene:* How are illnesses treated and by whom? What is considered to be the cause?

9. *History, traditions, holidays:* Which events and people are a source of pride for the group? To what extent does the group in the United States identify with the history and traditions of the country of origin? What holidays and celebrations are considered appropriate for observing in school? (Peregoy & Boyle, pp. 8–10, as presented in Grant, 1995)

For three years the senior author worked with a school located on a Native American reservation in Washington state. One high school teacher was particularly effective in helping his students complete high-quality assignments and do well on tests. The vast majority of his colleagues expressed extreme frustration with the lack of motivation they believed characterized their students. While one aspect of this teacher's work was clearly his utilization of many of the instructional methods described in Chapter 6, students also stated how well this teacher knew them and how much he respected their families. Further exploration led to the fact that this was the only teacher in the school who lived in the community and the only one who attended cultural events in which the majority of his students and their families were involved.

In their book on educating immigrant students, Olsen and Jaramillo (1999) noted that "understanding our English Language Learners is the key to responding effectively to their differing needs. . . . The most effective advocates know 'how to know' about their students" (p. 180). Included in their list of how to know their students is the statement "They 'know' from their hearts, from their day-to-day touching of the lives of immigrant students, from sharing their students' joys, sorrows, hopes and despair—and they use this knowledge to inform and help craft new ways of working with students" (p. 181). Similarly, in her book, *The Inner World of the Immigrant Child*, Cristina Igoa (1995) suggests the importance of addressing "the feelings of the child through the development of a close relationship and continuous dialogue between the child and the teacher" (p. 117).

Regardless of whether our backgrounds and cultural heritage are similar to our students', we will benefit from knowing more about factors that influence their lives. Teachers can ask students questions about their interests, how they spend their time, what subjects and learning activities are most interesting or difficult, and so on. For high school teachers it is important to know how many hours students work and the degree of their extracurricular activities. One of the authors worked with a high school English teacher who worked with his students in the second week of school to chart a calendar of when major tests and papers were scheduled in their other courses. He and his students then scheduled when the major work would be due in his class.

Arranging Individual Conferences with Students

Although it may not be possible to have lunch with your students, many teachers at all grade levels schedule time to meet individually with students. This can be done during your preparation period, lunch, before school, or after school. We have worked with literally hundreds of teachers who shared with us the powerful, positive impact of meeting individually with a student to discuss their work, behavior, or simply to get to know the student better. Igoa (1995) discussed the value of individual conferences with students new to the United States as a method for "validating the child's cultural history, and establishing a trusting, respectful, and warm relationship" (p. 125).

Demonstrating Interest in Students' Activities

An important way to indicate our concern for students and to enjoy our relationships with them is to take time to attend the activities in which they are involved. As a rule, parents are extremely appreciative of and impressed with teachers' attendance at student activities. Additionally, such attendance often is associated with dramatic academic or behavior improvement in the students whose activities were attended.

Eating Lunch with Students

Most teacher–student contact occurs in the presence of twenty-five to thirty other children. Unless they take the initiative by staying after school, students may never have individual private time with their teacher. One way to provide this personal time is to have lunch in the classroom with individual students. This time can be arranged by providing a sign-up sheet so that students who are interested can reserve a time to eat lunch alone with you. You and the student can use the lunch period to share personal interests. You should be willing to listen to the student's concerns about personal or school problems, but the time together should not be used as a conference in which you discuss the student's schoolwork or behavior.

Arranging Interviews

Anyone who has taught young children for several years has experienced an instance in which a student appeared surprised to see the teacher in a nonschool setting, such as the grocery store. Children often view the teacher solely as a teacher and are quite unaware of his or her interests and life outside the school setting. One approach for making you seem more real is to allow the children to interview you. You can expand this activity by having your spouse or older children visit the classroom to be interviewed by the class.

Sending Letters and Notes to Students

Beginning the school year with a personal letter from you is an effective technique for establishing rapport with students. A positive individualized letter placed on each student's desk informs each student that you are happy to have him or her in class, eager to get to know him or her, and excited about the upcoming school year. Notes given to students throughout the school year can enhance the personal relationship between you and the student. Appropriate times for expressing thoughts or providing information by notes or letters include when a student has been successful at a new or difficult task, when a student's behavior has improved, when a personal matter seems to be worrying a student, and on a student's birthday. Students also appreciate receiving a note or a get-well card along with their homework when they are sick and must miss school for several days.

Using a Suggestion Box

Students often perceive their teacher as relatively uninterested in their ideas about the classroom. Although we may view this situation as undesirable, it is to some degree an understandable response to the reality that we have primary responsibility for creating an appropriate classroom environment. One method that indicates our interest in students' ideas is to display a suggestion box and encourage students to write ideas for making the class a better place in which to learn. This approach can be expanded to include holding class meetings in which students discuss their ideas and concerns about the classroom. When classroom meetings are used, having students place agenda items on the board can replace the suggestion box. Either way, our willingness to request, accept, and respond to students' suggestions can be an effective method for improving teacher–student rapport.

"When I approved your field trip, Ms. Harris, I assumed you'd be going along with your class."

Joining in School and Community Events

Schools often organize special events such as hat days, carnivals, and bike rodeos. Similarly, communities have picnics, carnivals, and other social events. We can demonstrate our interest in students and our own enjoyment of a good time by becoming involved in these activities. Schools can also organize special events or displays that give students a chance to view teachers in a personal light and increase positive teacher–student interaction. Both authors have worked in buildings where a childhood picture of each staff member was displayed and students attempted to match the teachers with the childhood pictures. Similarly, the authors have taught in schools where a bulletin board was arranged so that teachers and students could publicly write positive statements to other students or teachers. Involvement in activities such as these helps create a positive school atmosphere, thereby significantly reducing unproductive student behavior.

Joining in Playground Games

Students enjoy having teachers participate in their playground activities. Occasionally, sharing recess time with the children is an excellent way for us to show our humanness and to demonstrate that we enjoy our students. Not only can this activity enhance teacher–student relationships but it can also provide us with an excellent form of relaxation. The physical activity and the opportunity to interact with children in a relaxed and nonacademic setting can provide a refreshing break in the school day. One way to formalize this type of teacher–student interaction is to develop several opportunities for friendly athletic competition between students and teachers.

PAUSE

and Consider   3.5

> Stop for a minute and create a list of what you or a teacher with whom you are working or observing has done to get to know the students. If you are not teaching, consider ways your own teachers learned about who you were. We encourage you to share these with colleagues or classmates. If you are keeping note cards, a journal, or some other form of record while reading this book, this would be an excellent item to place in this record

Being Aware of Issues Related to Sexual Harassment

A discussion of creating positive interactions with students would not be complete without a brief examination of issues relating to sexual harassment. Title VII of the Civil Rights Act of 1964 prohibits discrimination of the basis of sex, race, color, religion, or national origin. Courts have ruled that this act applies to educational institutions through Title IX of the Education Amendments of 1972. In August 1981, the Office for Civil Rights of the U.S. Department of Education "took another important step toward clarifying the responsibility of schools in cases of sexual harassment. The OCR issued a memorandum specifying that for institutions to be in compliance they must formulate and publish a policy opposing sexual harassment, a grievance procedure that is available to complainants, and procedures 'providing for prompt and equitable resolution of complaints' " (Yaffe, 1995, p. K-3). In Chapter 7 we examine the issue of students violating their peers' rights. Teachers, of course, must also be careful to interact with students in ways that are not uncomfortable to students and do not evoke accusations of sexual harassment.

This issue has become among the most difficult facing public schools. Whereas educators want to create communities of support in which students feel cared for and valued by adults, teachers are often simultaneously told to guard against physical contact with students. Some teachers respond by setting very clear boundaries regarding their physical contact with students. Others protect themselves by never letting students get too close. "Probably leave about this much space," said an experienced elementary teacher, as she held her hands about four feet apart. One Colorado elementary teacher who had been falsely accused and finally exonerated drew a red line across the front of his classroom and said, "Nobody crosses this line" (Yaffe, 1995, p. K-10).

We strongly believe the professionally responsible decision is to be cautious but is far from drawing a line between ourselves and our students. Certainly, teachers must be careful not to touch students in ways that make students uncomfortable. Teachers must notice when students shy away from or appear uncomfortable with touch. Additionally, teachers need to guard against situations in which students may misinterpret teacher behavior or in which the rare student may fabricate an event to obtain attention or "get back" at a teacher. One good rule of thumb is to have others around whenever you are working with a student. When working with a student during lunch or after school, find a space that is visible to others. Likewise, any time you hug a student, it is advisable for this to be in front of other students. We strongly believe that physical contact is a natural, healthy part of positive, supportive, interpersonal relationships. Teachers need to model this with their colleagues and with students. However, we live in a society in which physical contact has been sexualized by the media and in which a large number of students have experienced tragic physical and sexual interactions with adults. As professionals, we need to carefully monitor our behavior so that it heals and teaches but never offends, intimidates, or frightens our students.

The morning following the first day of school, *The Oregonian* included several articles describing the important contributions and sacrifices made by educators. One article described the work of Mary Beth Van Cleave, a principal who offered to retire but remain on the job for one year to save a teaching position. After thirty-two years as an educator, this principal gave up half her salary to help children. The article described her first day, "Van Cleave spent Tuesday doling out hugs to returning students, soothing anxious parents and helping lost students find their teachers" (*The Oregonian*, Wednesday, September 4, 1996, p. E7). The article was accompanied by a large picture of Mary Beth hugging a seven-year-old second grader as the child entered the school. In the same section is a picture of a teacher shaking hands with a student. The caption reads, "Pat Gonzales, a Madison High School English teacher, starts class by showing seventeen-year-old Jamicia Jackson the difference between a good and a bad handshake" (*The Oregonian*, Wednesday, September 4, 1996, p. E1). It appears that neither of these educators is willing to create a cold, artificial learning environment void of touch. Both, however, are handling touch in a public and professional manner to ensure safety for both their students and themselves.

While writing this book, the authors spoke with their good friend and colleague, Forrest Gathercoal, educator, attorney, and author of *Judicious Discipline*. Gathercoal shared his strong belief, based on numerous statements he has heard from teachers and on his legal background, that it is best if teachers refrain from hugging students but that handshakes, pats on the backs, and high fives generally are safe. He also noted his belief that teachers can create a positive, warm, and professional relationship without excessive touch. He noted that if a teacher is hugging children, one has to ask if this is necessary in a professional relationship and whether it meets the teacher's or student's needs. Although the authors believe that hugs, especially those initiated by elementary school students, are a healthy and natural part of adult–child relationships, we suggest that prior to making a decision regarding the type of touch you will choose to use with your students, you consider Gathercoal's argument.

PAUSE

and Consider   **3.6**

> Before moving on to the next section, stop for a minute and write down or share with a colleague your thoughts about physical contact with students. What feels comfortable and natural to you? Do your students appear to be comfortable with this? Are your decisions consistent with building, district, and community standards? Do you agree with Forrest Gathercoal's perspective or do you believe it is important to have relationships with your students that include physical touch?

Maintaining a High Ratio of Positive to Negative Statements

Children are sensitive to praise and criticism given by adults. Unfortunately, many teachers find that disruptive behavior is more noticeable and, therefore, respond to it more frequently than to on-task behavior. As indicated in Figure 3.1, frequent negative remarks by the teacher are usually accompanied by students' dislike for school. Although we often fall into the trap of believing that critical remarks will improve students' behaviors, research suggests that the opposite is true.

> In one study we took a good class and made it into a bad one for a few weeks by having the teacher no longer praise the children. When the teacher no longer praised the children, off-task behavior increased from 8.7 percent to 25.5 percent. The teacher criticized off-task behavior and did not praise on-task behavior. When the teacher was asked to increase her criticism from 5 times in 20 minutes to 16 times in 20 minutes, the children showed even more off-task behavior. Off-task behavior increased to an average of 31.2 percent, and on some days was over 50 percent. Attention to that off-task behavior increased its occurrence when no praise was given for working. Introduction of praise back into the classroom restored good working behavior. (Becker, Engelmann, & Thomas, 1975, p. 69)

An excellent example of the effect of teachers' negative or positive statements occurred several years ago in a school district in Oregon. Much to their credit, district administrators became worried about what they perceived as a negative attitude among a significant number of their young schoolchildren. The district subsequently sought the services of an outside agency to examine the situation. The consultants decided initially

	Pre 2 Weeks after Start of School (September 20–27)			Post January 22–24		
Teacher	Pos.	Neg.	Students Responding Yes to: "Do You Like School?"	Pos.	Neg.	Students Responding Yes to: "Do You Like School?"
1	.72	28	90%	.76	24	90%
2	.34	66	90%	.33	67	20%
3	.66	34	80%	.70	30	70%
4	.69	31	90%	.65	35	80%
5	.54	46	100%	.61	39	20%
6	.80	20	100%	.87	13	100%
7	.22	78	90%	.19	81	20%
8	.64	36	70%	.64	36	40%
9	.79	21	100%	.77	23	100%
10	.92	08	80%	.89	11	90%
11	.52	48	100%	.63	37	60%
12	.73	27	90%	.65	35	90%
13	.45	55	90%	.61	39	80%
14	.67	33	80%	.73	27	80%
15	.58	42	90%	.60	40	70%
16	.51	49	60%	.58	42	10%
17	.76	24	70%	.77	23	70%

FIGURE 3.1

Influence of Positive and Negative Teacher Statements on Students' Feelings about School

Source: Personal correspondence with Bud Fredericks, Teaching Research, Monmouth, OR. Reprinted by permission.

to examine the ratio of positive to negative statements made by teachers. They began their intervention by simply asking children in second-grade classrooms to answer yes or no to the question, "Do you like school?" As indicated in the fourth column of Figure 3.1, at the beginning of the school year, most students in all classes responded yes to this question. The consultants discovered, however, that, for students who experienced classrooms characterized by a low rate of positive teacher verbalizations, these positive feelings about school changed dramatically within the first fifteen weeks of school.

More specifically, in the eight classes in which teachers provided less than 65 percent positive statements, the percentage of students responding that they liked school dropped an alarming 48 percent during the fifteen weeks. In the seven classrooms in which 70 percent or more of the teachers' statements were positive, though, students' responses to the question of whether they liked school remained, on the average, exactly the same after fifteen weeks of school. These data suggest that children are much less comfortable in classroom environments characterized by a low rate of positive teacher statements.

In their book *Inviting School Success*, Purkey and Novak (1984) set forth four types of teacher behaviors toward students:

1. Intentionally disinviting
2. Unintentionally disinviting

PRINCIPAL

"I'm very sorry about your teacher. All I can tell you is that she was in a good mood when I hired her."

3. Unintentionally inviting
4. Intentionally inviting

In defining these terms, Purkey stated, "As used here, an invitation is a summary description of message—verbal and nonverbal, formal and informal—continuously transmitted to students with the intention of informing them that they are responsible, able, and valuable. Conversely, a disinvitation is intended to tell them that they are irresponsible, incapable, and worthless" (p. 3). An example of an intentionally disinviting behavior would be the teacher who, on the first day of school, privately singles out a student whose sibling had been a particular problem several years earlier and informs the child that if he is anything like his brother, this will be a very difficult year for him. Even though this teacher's statement is intentional and intended to motivate the student to behave properly, the student receives it as punitive, unfair, and disinviting. An example of an unintentionally disinviting statement was provided by a high school vice principal. He stated that the day before final exam week began, he observed a student requesting assistance from a teacher. The teacher's response, "Don't worry, you haven't got a chance of passing the test anyway," was devastating but probably unintentionally disinviting.

PAUSE
and Consider   **3.7**

> We encourage you to stop for a few minutes and write one example of each of these four types of statements based on something you have heard a staff member (including yourself) say to a student. We recommend you share these with three or four colleagues or fellow students.

Teachers make many inviting comments to students. For example, teachers often greet students at the door, state how glad they are to see a student, and respond positively to the quality of student work. Some of this inviting behavior occurs unintentionally because teachers are positive people who care about their students. On other occasions, teachers consciously consider the impact of positive invitations and intentionally invite students to be positively involved in their classes. An excellent example of intentionally invitational behavior and its relationship to teacher openness with students was shared with the authors by a high school English teacher. One day, the teacher experienced a small crisis before arriving at school. The first two periods went fairly well. However, the teacher became tired and anxious as the day went on and was concerned about teaching his unruly third-period class. At the end of the second period, one of his better junior English students asked for some assistance. The teacher stated that he was not feeling well and asked the student if he would assist the teacher.

The student was glad to help and the teacher suggested that they both stand at the door, greet the incoming students, and make a statement about what an interesting class this was going to be. The teacher reported that when the bell rang and he turned to the class, every student was seated and attentively focused on the front of the class—an unheard of reaction from these students. The teacher then noticed two sets of students who should not have been in his third-period class. They informed him that they had heard this was going to be an interesting class and had decided to attend. Two of the students had even obtained permission from their third-period teacher. The English teacher reported that after clarifying the issue of the additional students, he had one of the most rewarding instructional experiences in some time.

In addition to their value in increasing positive student attitudes, invitational interactions provide the basis for creating teacher–student relationships that facilitate the use of corrective interventions described in Chapters 8, 9, and 10. An excellent example of this concept was provided by a student-teacher one of the authors supervised. The student-teacher was working with one of the most disruptive third graders the author had encountered. Each day, the boy was involved in many instances of aggressive behavior toward peers and insubordination to adults. Because the school's assertive discipline program had only increased the student's acting-out behavior, and because the boy's parents would not allow the school to provide special education services, the principal was considering expelling the student.

The student-teacher decided to work with the student as part of her assignment in a classroom management course. In so doing, she was asked to attempt many of the methods described throughout this book and was encouraged to work consistently (and persistently) on establishing rapport with the student. The student's initial responses were extremely negative. He frequently and vividly informed the student-teacher that he hated teachers (a value reinforced by his parents) and that he wanted nothing to do with her. But the teacher persisted. She discovered that the boy's mother raised show dogs, and she watched a cable television show in which the mother's dog took second place. The student-teacher videotaped the show and discussed this event with the student. One day when a professional athlete with the same name as the boy's was traded, the teacher laminated the article in plastic and placed it on the bulletin board with a large red arrow pointing to it. The class was understandably curious, and the boy received considerable attention. Gradually, he increased his willingness to work cooperatively with the teacher. Although he would not become involved in problem solving, he did agree to a contract that was associated with considerable changes in behavior. Although the dramatic improvement in the student's behavior required behavioristic methods, these were not effective until the student was willing to work with the teacher. The improved relationship made possible other interventions that led to important changes.

An elementary school principal recently shared an outstanding example of how an administrator used invitational relationships. During a workshop presented for a state principals' association, the principal asked one of the authors if he could share something he had done based on his attending a similar workshop with the author. The principal told his colleagues that his background had caused him to be a very authoritarian person and that when he became a principal, he informed teachers that they could be guaranteed of firm support from the office. He noted that his most common intervention with students sent to his office for discipline was to intimidate and threaten the students. He proceeded to note that after attending the workshop, he carefully considered his reactions and realized that they were seldom associated with positive, long-term changes in student behavior and that he had received some negative comments from parents. He decided to try an experiment in which he selected twelve students who were experiencing ongoing behavior problems. He divided these students into three groups, and each day all three groups of four students began their day by spending approximately four minutes with him during which all four students shared a positive thing that had happened to them the previous day, one thing they were looking forward to in school that day, and anything adults at school could do to help them that day. At the end of each session, each student gave the principal his or her sign (high five, handshake, etc.) and went to class. The principal noted a dramatic improvement in these students' attendance, work completion, and on-task behavior. He shared with the audience that from that point on, he decided to alter the manner in which he worked with students.

One way the authors have thought about the establishment of positive relationships with students is as a "positive relationship bank account." Just as a person has to make deposits into a checking account to make a withdrawal, educators need to have positive interactions with students if they want students to respond positively to adult requests for effort or modified behavior. Some students come to school with many deposits already made through positive relationships with adults in their families and communities. Unfortunately, an increasing number of students have limited positive interactions with adults. If we want these students to respond positively to the requests we make (often including the difficult task of attempting what they perceive as demanding schoolwork), we have to have made deposits in the positive relationship bank account. Many of the ideas presented throughout the remainder of this chapter will help you to create these important deposits.

Communicating High Expectations

P A U S E
and Consider   **3.8**

> Before reading this section stop for a minute and think about your classes as a student. Did some students receive more attention, praise, and opportunities to respond than others? What do you think characterized those students given these favorable responses? Write a brief statement regarding any student characteristics that might make you more or less likely to positively engage a student. Are you more comfortable with boys or girls, high or low achievers, members of your ethnic group, and so on?

As educators, we must be extremely careful about our potential biases against some types of students and any tendency to expect more or less capable academic behavior from any subset of students. This section will help you understand how expectation effects can impact student learning and behavior.

How teachers communicate their expectations about how well students perform in the classroom is an important and well-documented factor in teacher–student relationships. School effectiveness research has consistently pointed to teachers' high expectations of students' performances as a key factor associated with students' achievements.

More recently research suggests that in schools where Hispanic students are successful, teachers consistently express high expectations for their students (Reyes et al., 1999). In a variety of subtle and not-so-subtle ways, we communicate to some students that they are bright, capable, and responsible, whereas other students receive the message that they are dull, incapable, and irresponsible.

Our expectations of students are influenced by a variety of factors other than actual performance or behavior. Frericks (1974) found that teachers viewing a group of students labeled low in ability described the students' behaviors more negatively than did teachers who viewed the same students but were told they were observing "regular students in a normal classroom." Spencer-Hall (1981) reported that some students nominated for a citizen-of-the-year reward had misbehavior rates as high as that of any student in the class. Teachers are obviously influenced by how students present themselves or are labeled, as well as by students' behaviors.

Unfortunately, gender and ethnicity also influence how teachers respond to students. Studies suggest that boys receive more teacher attention than do girls. For example, in preschool classrooms, boys receive more academic instruction, hugs, and teacher attention. David and Myra Sadker have conducted extensive studies that indicate that boys call out almost eight times as often as girls and teachers' responses to call outs is to listen to and comment about the boys' statements while correcting the girls for not raising their hands. In addition, teachers also appear to favor boys in terms of calling on students to volunteer (Sadker & Sadker, 1985). Studies also indicate that boys receive more praise than girls and that they are more likely to receive detailed feedback associated with their praise. Studies also suggest that boys receive particularly partial treatment in science classes (Kahle, 1990; Lee, 1991).

Students' ethnic backgrounds also appears to influence teacher expectations and treatment of students. In the 1992 *AAUW Report: How Schools Shortchange Girls*, the committee stated:

> Evidence also suggests that the attention minority students receive from teachers may be different in nature from that given to white children. In elementary school, black boys tend to have fewer interactions overall with teachers than other students and yet they are the recipients of four to ten times the amount of qualified praise ("That's good, but . . . ") as other students. Black boys tend to be perceived less favorably by their teachers and seen as less able than other students. The data are more complex for girls. Black girls have less interaction with teachers than white girls, but they attempt to initiate interaction much more often than white girls or than boys of either race. Research indicates that teachers may unconsciously rebuff these black girls, who eventually turn to peers for interaction, often becoming the class enforcer or go-between for other students. Black females also receive less reinforcement from teachers than do other students, although their academic performance is often better than boys'.
>
> In fact, when black girls do as well as white boys in school, teachers attribute their success to hard work but assume that the white boys are not working up to their full potential. This, coupled with the evidence that blacks are more often reinforced for their social behavior while whites are likely to be reinforced for their academic accomplishments, may contribute to low academic self-esteem in black girls. (pp. 70–71)

Results from classroom interaction studies indicate that teachers generally respond more favorably to students they perceive as high achievers. High achievers receive more response opportunities; are given more time to answer questions; receive more positive, nonverbal feedback such as smiles, nods, and winks; and are less likely to be ignored. Cooper and Good (1983) provided the following list of common ways in which teachers respond differently to students who are high achieving versus those who are low achieving:

1. Seating low-expectation students far from the teacher and/or seating them in a group.
2. Paying less attention to lows in academic situations (smiling less often and maintaining less eye contact).
3. Calling on lows less often to answer classroom questions or to make public demonstrations.
4. Waiting less time for lows to answer questions.
5. Not staying with lows in failure situations (i.e., providing fewer clues, asking fewer follow-up questions).
6. Criticizing lows more frequently than highs for incorrect public responses.
7. Praising lows less frequently than highs after successful public responses.
8. Praising lows more frequently than highs for marginal or inadequate public responses.
9. Providing lows with less accurate and less detailed feedback than highs.
10. Failing to provide lows with feedback about their responses as often as highs.
11. Demanding less work and effort from lows than from highs.
12. Interrupting performance of lows more frequently than highs. (p. 10)

In reviewing the research on expectation effects, Brophy (1983) cited studies suggesting that "teacher expectations do have self-fulfilling-prophecy effects on student-achievement levels, but that these effects make only a 5 to 10 percent difference, on the average" (p. 635). Brophy went on to state:

> These conclusions clearly imply that even ideal teacher education related to the topic of teacher expectations will not work miracles in our schools, but they do not imply that the topic is unimportant. Even a 5 percent difference in educational outcomes is an important difference, the more so as it is compounded across school years. Furthermore, the presentation so far has been confined to consideration of the average effect across all teachers of expectations concerning student achievement. The story becomes much more complicated, and the implications for teacher education much more obvious, when we turn attention to other kinds of expectations and to differences among teachers in predisposition to expectation effects. (p. 635)

We must realize that the concept of holding high expectations for all students does not mean that we should provide identical treatment for all students. To a considerable extent, the differential treatment students receive from teachers is a logical and often thoughtful response to individual student needs. Nevertheless, you should become aware of the potential for responding to students in ways that communicate to them that you do not expect them to complete work they are actually capable of mastering.

It is often desirable that we initiate a higher percentage of our academic contacts with students who are low achieving during individual or small-group instruction. Similarly, especially when introducing new material to younger children, we should try to maximize the percentage of correct responses so that students do not become confused by competing, inaccurate information. The critical issue is that we must become aware of ways in which we respond differently to various types of students and thoughtfully and systematically implement differential interaction patterns that support individual student and group learning. Figure 3.2 presents guidelines teachers can follow to minimize the negative effects of teacher expectations.

- *Use information from tests, cumulative folders, and other teachers very carefully.*
    Some teachers avoid reading cumulative folders for several weeks at the beginning of the year.
    Be critical and objective about the reports you hear from other teachers, especially "horror stories" told in the teachers' lounge.
- *Be flexible in your use of grouping strategies.*
    Review work of students in different groups often and experiment with new groupings.
    Use different groupings for different subjects.
    Use mixed-ability groups in cooperative exercises when all students can handle the same material.
- *Make sure all the students are challenged.*
    Avoid saying, "This is easy, I know you can do it."
    Offer a wide range of problems, and encourage all students to try a few of the harder ones for extra credit. Try to find something positive about these attempts.
- *Be especially careful about how you respond to low-achieving students during class discussions.*
    Give them prompts, clues, and time to answer.
    Give ample praise for good answers.
    Call on low achievers as often as high achievers.
- *Use materials that show a wide range of ethnic groups.*
    Check readers and library books. Is there ethnic diversity?
    Ask your librarian to find multiethnic stories, filmstrips, etc.
    If few materials are available, ask students to research and create their own, based on community or family resources.
- *Be fair in evaluation and disciplinary procedures.*
    Make sure equal offenses merit equal punishment. Find out from students in an anonymous questionnaire whether you seem to be favoring certain individuals.
    Try to grade student work without knowing the identity of the student. Ask another teacher to give you a "second opinion" from time to time.
- *Communicate to all students that you believe they can learn—and mean it.*
    Return papers that do not meet standards with specific suggestions for improvements.
    If students do not have the answers immediately, wait, probe, and then help them think through an answer.
- *Involve all students in learning tasks and in privileges.*
    Use some system for calling on or contacting students to make sure you give each student practice in reading, speaking, and answering questions.
    Keep track of who gets to do what job. Are some students always on the list while others seldom make it?
- *Monitor your nonverbal behavior.*
    Do you lean away or stand farther away from some students? Do some students get smiles when they approach your desk while others get only frowns?
    Do you avoid touching some students?
    Does your tone of voice vary with different students?

FIGURE 3.2
Guidelines for Avoiding the Negative Effects of Teacher Expectations

Source: From Anita E. Woolfolk, *Educational Psychology,* 7/e. Copyright © 1998 by Allyn & Bacon. Reprinted by permission.

As teachers, we need to be aware of the importance of communicating positive expectations to all students. Periodically, we need to (1) collect data about how we interact with students in our classes, (2) analyze the data to see if we are using primarily supportive or critical statements, (3) determine whether we are responding differently (more critically or less often) to some students, and (4) attempt to alter our patterns of interaction so that we communicate high expectations to all students. There are several activities at the end of the chapter that will assist you with this. In addition, teachers can develop creative, fun ways of ensuring that students receive equal opportunities. You can write each student's name on a tongue depressor, popsicle stick, or chip, and draw from a can to determine who will answer each question. (Remember to replace the name back into the can following each draw.) This keeps students alert and ensures that, over time, all students will receive an equal number of questions to answer.

PAUSE

and Consider   3.9

> What methods will you choose to ensure you are communicating high expectations to all students? If you have an opportunity to do so, we encourage you to complete either Activity 3.4 or 3.5 from the end of the chapter to practice monitoring whether a teacher is communicating consistently high expectations to all students. We also encourage you to make a list of methods you would like to add to your repertoire for increasing the likelihood that you will communicate high expectations to all students. It will be helpful to share these with a colleague or classmate and add them to your journal or set of note cards.

Giving Specific, Descriptive Feedback

Studies indicate that teachers are not particularly effective at providing feedback to students. When providing students with feedback about their academic performance, it is useful to ask ourselves three questions: "How much?" "To whom?" and "What type?" The answer to the first question is probably somewhat more but not too much.

Based on the results of a three-year study involving data collection in more than 100 fourth-, sixth-, and eighth-grade classrooms, Sadker and Sadker (1985) expressed concern about the quantity and quality of teachers' feedback to students. These researchers found that teachers demonstrated low rates of specific positive feedback or criticism and high rates of acceptance. "Acceptance included teacher comments that implied that student performance was correct and appropriate . . . (Examples include: 'O.K.,' 'uh-huh,' 'I see,' or simply teacher silence)" (Sadker & Sadker, 1985, p. 360). The Sadkers' main interpretation of their findings was that teacher feedback was too bland. They found that "in two-thirds of the classrooms observed, teachers never clearly indicated that a student answer was incorrect" (p. 360). Similarly, only 11 percent of teacher feedback involved praise, and in more than one-fourth of the classrooms, teachers never praised students' answers. These findings regarding the general lack of critical or specific feedback are reinforced by data reported by Goodlad (1984) indicating that 20 percent of both elementary and secondary students stated that they were neither informed nor corrected following a mistake.

The answer to the second question, "To whom should effective feedback be provided?" is closely related to the issue of expectation effects. Positive, prescriptive feedback needs to be more evenly distributed so that it is not provided only to high achievers or to students with the social skills to elicit this feedback. In fact, research indicates that positive feedback is more effective with students of lower socioeconomic status and low achievement—the students who research suggests receive the least positive feedback.

The answer to the question, "What type of feedback is most effective?" is the key question. One of the most important communication skills teachers can use is specific, clear, descriptive feedback that helps students take responsibility for their successes. Research on attribution theory indicates that students attribute their success or failure to ability, effort, luck, or difficulty of task. If students attribute their success or failure to effort, they are able to view their performance as influenced by factors within their control (an internal locus of control) and are, therefore, able to expect success in similar situations if they make the effort. However, when failure is attributed to ability, luck, or difficulty of task, students feel less control over results and begin to believe that making a concerted effort in the future will have little affect on the outcome. Praise that helps students focus on factors within their control that influenced performance allows students to develop an internal locus of control.

Unfortunately, on occasions when they are successful, low achievers tend to credit luck or the ease of a task for this success. High achievers, however, tend to credit their effort and ability for their success. Teachers can alter children's perceptions of their control over success or failure by using feedback more effectively. In an interesting study, Dweck (1975) showed that elementary students who viewed school learning as extremely hopeless could change this belief by receiving training sessions in which they were given both success and failure, and, when failing, were informed that their failure was because of lack of effort. Students who received this training responded to failure by persisting and implementing problem-solving strategies to resolve their dilemma. Schunk (1983) studied elementary students' responses to positive feedback and stated that simply providing students with statements about their effort may suggest to students that they do not have the ability to complete the task without extensive effort. It seems that the most effective feedback provides students with information revealing that they do possess the ability to achieve success and that they will need to expend effort to do the task well.

By becoming skilled in providing students with useful positive feedback, teachers can help students take credit for their successes and develop an appreciation for their ability to control the school environment in positive ways. O'Leary and O'Leary (1977) stated that to serve as an effective reinforcer, feedback (they use the term *praise*) to students must have three qualities:

1. *Contingency.* Praise must immediately follow desired behaviors rather than be applied simply as a general motivator. Anderson and colleagues (1979) found that teachers failed to use praise contingently because the rate of praise following reading turns that contained mistakes was similar to the rate following correct responses.
2. *Specificity.* Praise should describe the specific behavior being reinforced. Again, Anderson and colleagues (1979) suggested that teachers needed improvement in this area. Their data showed that teachers were specific in only 5 percent of their praise for academic work and in 40 percent of their praise for behavior.
3. *Credibility.* Praise should be appropriate for the situation and the individual. Older, high-achieving students are aware that praise is used primarily for motivation and encouragement and may find praise unnecessary and even insulting.

Perhaps the most useful information on the effective use of positive feedback to students was presented by Brophy (1981). Figure 3.3 presents Brophy's summary of research findings on the effective use of feedback (he also uses the word *praise*).

It is important to be careful how and whom we praise. Girls are more likely to believe they receive the attention they want from their teacher, and White girls are most often likely to believe this, whereas minority boys are least likely to have this experience. Teachers, especially in the elementary grades, may inadvertently be reinforcing passive behavior that is more characteristic of girls. In addition, teacher praise may have different effects on students depending on their cultural background. Students from some Native American groups may not want to be singled out for attention, and students whose families and peers distrust the educational system may find public teacher praise diminishes their status with peers (Johns & Espinoza, 1996). We should be very careful about stereotyping students' potential responses to praise. Nevertheless, we need to be aware of cultural issues related to positive teacher feedback and validate our hypotheses through discussions with students, caregivers, and community members.

PAUSE
and Consider   **3.10**

Take a few minutes and consider a situation in which you would be providing a student with verbal or written feedback regarding his or her academic work. Using Figure 3.3, select two of the factors related to effective praise and incorporate these in a statement you might make to a student. Write this statement on a sheet of paper and share it with several classmates or colleagues. Discuss each others' feedback and the helpful information this would provide the student.

Listening to Students

Listening skills are extremely important; when used effectively, they create relationships that allow students to feel significant, accepted, respected, and able to take responsibility for their own behavior. By effectively using listening skills, adults help youngsters clarify their feelings and resolve their own conflicts. Unfortunately, adults all too often provide quick answers for children rather than carefully listening in order to help the youngsters clarify the problem and then aid them in developing a solution.

According to William Glasser (1988), students' attempts to have someone listen to them is the source of nearly 95 percent of discipline problems in school. Speaking of student behavior problems in schools, Glasser wrote, "I believe that frustration of the need for power, even more than the need for belonging, is at the core of today's difficulties" (p. 40). Glasser noted that there are three levels at which students can satisfy their need for power of involvement in the school environment. First, students simply need to believe that someone whom they respect will listen to them. At the second level, someone listens and accepts the validity of the student's statement or concern. The third and highest level involves an adult's stating that the student's idea may be worth implementing.

Stop for a moment and reflect on the last several situations when a student came to you with a problem or expressed a strong emotion. What did you do? If you are like most adults, you provided a quick answer to the problem or attempted to stop the expression of emotion by providing assurances or by suggesting that the student

Effective Praise	Ineffective Praise
1. Is delivered contingently	1. Is delivered randomly or unsystematically
2. Specifies the particulars of the accomplishment	2. Is restricted to global positive reactions
3. Shows spontaneity, variety, and other signs of credibility: suggests clear attention to the student's accomplishment	3. Shows a bland uniformity that suggests a conditioned response made with minimal attention
4. Rewards attainment of specified performance criteria (which can include effort criteria)	4. Rewards mere participation without consideration of performance processes or outcomes
5. Provides information to students about their competence or the value of their accomplishment	5. Provides no information at all or gives students information about their status
6. Orients students toward better appreciation of their own task-related behavior and thinking about problem solving	6. Orients students toward comparing themselves with others and thinking about competing
7. Uses student's own prior accomplishments as the context for describing present accomplishments	7. Uses the accomplishments of peers as the context for describing students' present accomplishments
8. Is given in recognition of noteworthy effort or success at difficult (for this student) tasks	8. Is given without regard to the effort expended or the meaning of the accomplishment (for this student)
9. Attributes success to effort and ability, implying that similar successes can be expected in the future	9. Attributes success to ability alone or to external factors such as luck or (easy) task difficulty
10. Fosters endogenous attributions (students believe they expend effort on task because they enjoy it or want to develop task-relevant skills)	10. Fosters exogenous attributions (students believe they expend effort on the task for external reasons—to please the teacher, win a competition or reward, etc.)
11. Focuses students' attention on their own task-relevant behavior	11. Focuses students' attention on the teacher as an external authority figure who is manipulating them
12. Fosters appreciation of, and desirable attributions about, task-relevant behavior after the process is completed	12. Intrudes into the ongoing process distracting attention from task-related behavior

FIGURE 3.3
Guidelines for Effective Praise

Source: From "Teacher Praise: A Functional Analysis" by Jere E. Brophy, *Review of Educational Research*, *51*, p. 32. Copyright © 1981 by American Educational Research Association. Reprinted by permission.

should not be expressing the emotion. Both of these responses are commonly used because they require a minimum of time and effort and prevent adults from having to deal with a youngster's emotions. When adults consistently provide answers, however, they subtly inform students that they do not care enough really to listen to them and do not trust students' abilities to resolve their own conflicts.

Before examining the major listening skills, we must clarify an important point. There are numerous instances (perhaps even a significant majority) during a schoolday when a student is merely requesting information. If a student requests permission to leave the room or asks for clarification of directions, it is appropriate simply to provide the information. However, when students share personal problems, express confusion with their work, or display emotions, it is often most effective initially to use one or more of the listening skills discussed in this section.

The primary goal of using listening skills is to help students express their real concern, need, or want. Students often initially make general, angry statements that disguise their real concerns. A student who says "I hate this class" might be feeling frustration at his or her inability to understand the material or concern over lack of acceptance by peers. By using the methods described in the following pages, you can help the student clarify the underlying problem. Once the problem has been exposed, you must switch from merely listening to an active role in helping the student examine and solve the problem.

Empathic, Nonevaluative Listening

Empathic, nonevaluative listening involves providing the speaker with a sense that she or he has been clearly heard and that the feelings expressed are acceptable. Several major benefits can be derived from using these skills. First, students learn that their feelings are acceptable, which reduces the tension and anxiety associated with having to hide one's true feelings. This act in turn makes students feel more accepted. Second, when thoughts and feelings can be expressed openly and are received nonjudgmentally, students are much less likely to express feelings through unproductive behaviors. Acting out in the classroom, vandalism, and truancy are often indirect methods of dealing with feelings that could not be expressed openly and directly. Third, when adults listen nonevaluatively, they provide young people with an opportunity to examine and clarify feelings that are often confusing and frightening. This exchange frequently enables youngsters to understand a situation and to consider approaches to coping with a situation effectively.

One of the authors was recently given an interesting example regarding active listening. A special education director with whom the author works shared his recent conversations with a student in a high school program for students with behavioral disorders. The boy approached the director (who had been the boy's special education teacher seven years earlier) and stated in a somewhat derogatory tone that the director looked older since he had lost some of his hair. The special education director noted that rather than chastise the boy for his rudeness, he acknowledged the boy's perceptive observation, shared his own feelings about losing hair, and asked the boy how he was doing. The director reported that the boy responded calmly and asked whether people still thought he was the dumbest, most cruel student in the district. This allowed the director an opportunity to discuss the boy's behavior, his abilities, and his responsibility for his behavior. He reported that the boy was very surprised by the discussion, thanked him, and left pensively. The director indicated that had he not listened carefully to the boy, the boy would not have had an opportunity to have some important misconceptions corrected.

This is an excellent example of our need to guard against our vulnerabilities. Most of us have certain key behaviors or words from children that set us off. However, most of these stem from a belief that children should not be allowed to challenge or criticize adults. Instead, we may want to consider that the issue is *how* students challenge us. If students are unskilled in providing us with important information regarding their feelings, needs, and concerns, rather than punishing their ineffectiveness, we may want to model for them and teach them how to do this in an effective, acceptable manner.

There are two basic approaches to nonevaluative listening. First, the listener can simply acknowledge the speaker's statement by looking at him or her and making oral responses such as "M-hm," "Yes," "Uh-uh," "I see," and "I understand." This form of listening encourages the speaker to continue talking by indicating that the listener is attentive and involved. Obviously, this type of response is least effective when used in isolation; most children wish to hear more than a simple acknowledgment.

The second method for using empathic, nonevaluative listening is commonly called *paraphrasing, active listening,* or *reflecting*. In their *Learning Together and Alone,* Johnson and Johnson (1975) presented seven guidelines for using this skill.

General Guidelines for Paraphrasing

1. Restate the sender's expressed ideas and feelings in your own words rather than mimicking or parroting her exact words.
2. Preface paraphrased remarks with, "You think . . . ," "Your position is . . . ," "It seems to you that . . . ," "You feel that . . . ," and so on.
3. Avoid any indication of approval or disapproval.
4. Make your nonverbal messages congruent with your verbal paraphrasing; look attentive, interested, and open to the sender's ideas and feelings, and show that you are concentrating upon what the sender is trying to communicate.
5. State as accurately as possible what you heard the sender say and describe the feelings and attitudes involved.
6. Do not add to or subtract from the sender's message.
7. Put yourself in the sender's shoes and try to understand what it is he is feeling and what his message means. (p. 102)

Paraphrasing has the advantage of making the speaker believe he or she is being listened to while allowing the listener to be somewhat more involved than is possible when using only acknowledging responses. Furthermore, by providing a summary of the speaker's statement, the listener may help the child clarify his or her thoughts or feelings. If the paraphrased statement is not congruent with what the speaker wanted to say, the speaker has an opportunity to correct the listener's paraphrase and, thereby, clarify the initial statement.

One word of caution about the use of paraphrasing: Students may say that they do not like having someone repeat what they have just said. This response is more common in the upper elementary and secondary grades than among young children. If students frequently indicate that they view your statements as parroting their own, you will either need to reduce the amount of paraphrasing used or try to use responses that vary slightly from the student's original statement. Activity 3.7 at the end of the chapter provides several methods for helping you improve and diversify skills in empathic, nonevaluative listening.

3.11

Pause for a few minutes and think about the ways in which you listen to students. Are there times when you are accessible to students, when they believe you will really listen to them? Recall a time when listening carefully to a student provided you with information that assisted you in modifying your instruction or classroom operation in a way that helped that student (and perhaps others) have a more successful school experience. Share this situation with several colleagues or classmates.

Responding Effectively to Inappropriate or Disruptive Behavior

Consider for a moment a situation in which a student is choosing to disrupt the learning environment. Envision a situation in which a high school student is talking continuously and rather loudly to another student during large-group instruction, a middle school student refuses to move when asked to select another seat, or a primary grade student is pushing a peer in order to obtain a preferred toy. How would you respond? Chapter 8 includes many ideas for redirecting students' behaviors in order to maintain a safe, orderly classroom environment, and this section introduces some key concepts in this area of communicating with students.

When examining teachers' responses to student behavior that disrupts the learning environment, it is important to consider how teachers have presented their initial request that a student select a more responsible behavior. Walker and Sylwester (1998) discuss the differences between alpha and beta requests. Alpha requests involve the teacher providing a "clear, direct, and specific directive, without additional verbalizations, that allows reasonable time for a response, beta commands involve vague or multiple directives, given simultaneously, and accompanied by excess verbalization, and without a clear criterion or adequate opportunity for compliance" (p. 54). It is important to realize that, depending on the nature of the activity in which students are involved, primary grade teachers provide between 10 and 160 directions in any given hour (Golly, 1994). Golly (1994) reported that the first- and second-grade teachers in her study gave 59 percent alpha requests and that students complied with 88 percent of alpha requests and 76 percent of beta requests. Perhaps more important is the fact that students who have more difficulty acting responsibly in school settings are much less likely than the typical student to respond to beta directives (Wehby, Symons, & Shores, 1995). Therefore, it is imperative that teachers learn to give directions or requests calmly, clearly, and politely, in a manner that shows respect for students and encourages them to respond positively.

3.12

Stop for a minute and envision a situation in which you might have to give a student a directive to respond in a safe manner or in a manner that is less disruptive to the learning environment. Once you have a picture of this, write both an alpha and a beta statement you might make to the student. After writing this, pair up with a colleague or fellow student and say these two statements to each other. How did you feel when you received the alpha as opposed to the beta request.

In addition to the importance of sending clear requests, we have found the following methods helpful when informing a student that his or her behavior needed to change for the classroom or common area of the school be a safe, inviting place. Chapter 8 presents additional materials on responding to a variety of student behaviors that disrupt the learning environment.

1. *Deal in the present.* Information is more useful when it is shared at the earliest appropriate opportunity. Young people are very "now" oriented. It is unfair and ineffective to bring up issues after several days have elapsed. Therefore, though it may be necessary to wait until you can speak with the student alone or until the student has better control of his or her emotions, it is best to discuss important matters as soon after they occur as possible.

2. *Talk directly to students rather than about them.* Adults have a tendency to talk to parents or colleagues about students rather than talking directly to the student. The assumption seems to be that students could not understand or would be overpowered by the information. The authors' experiences strongly contradict these beliefs. Indeed, it appears that students suffer more from worrying about what has been said about them than they do from receiving skillfully presented direct feedback. By talking directly to students, we show respect for them while ensuring that they receive accurate (rather than secondhand) information about adults' feelings.

3. *Speak courteously.* Nothing does more to create positive interactions than using simple courtesy statements such as *thank you, please*, and *excuse me*. Because teachers serve as important models for students, their interactions with them should include more (certainly not less) frequent use of courtesies than do their interactions with other adults.

4. *Make eye contact and be aware of nonverbal messages.* According to an old saying, children often respond more to what adults do than to what they say. Because young people are so dependent on adults, they become adept at reading adults' nonverbal messages. It is, therefore, important that we attempt to make our nonverbal messages congruent with our verbal messages. If you are talking to a student but looking over his or her shoulder, the student will find it difficult to believe that you feel positive about her or him and are sincerely concerned. Similarly, when we shout that we are not angry with a class, the students will be more likely to listen to the tone of voice than to the words.

5. *Take responsibility for statements by using the personal pronoun* I. It is hard to underestimate the importance and value of I-messages. Students who experience consistent or serious behavior problems are often deficient in social cognition skills. Simply stated, they are not as capable as their peers of understanding and appreciating others' points of view. For example, they may not understand why a teacher is bothered by their talking out or why, despite their aggressive or rude behavior, their peers do not wish to play with them.

Just as many students learn to read before entering school, many children learn to understand others' perspectives through the use of language employed at home. Students who have not had these opportunities will, just like students who enter school unable to decode letters and sounds, need learning experiences that help them develop important social cognition skills. I-messages are one method of providing this important assistance.

In their *Discovering Your Teaching Self,* Curwin and Fuhrmann (1975) provide a succinct and sensitive statement about this skill:

PRINCIPAL'S
OFFICE →

"Geez—who would ever have figured Ms. Killebrew for a tattletale?"

Meaningful communication between people (the communication between adults and children is of special interest to us) often breaks down because one party (or both) continually tells the other what's wrong with him rather than identifying how he himself is feeling in the situation. When I tell someone what's wrong with him, I virtually take away from him all responsibility for himself. Since I know what is wrong, I also know how to "correct" it. Thus I leave him powerless and probably defensive. (p. 196)

If we say to a student, "You are being disruptive" or "You're late again!" the student is likely to feel attacked and defensive. If, however, we say, "It distracts me and I feel uncomfortable when you talk while I am talking (or when you come in late)," the student has been provided with some useful information about his or her affect on other people. Similarly, using the pronoun *we* is unfairly ganging up against a student. When confronted with statements beginning with "we feel" or "the entire class believes," the student is likely to feel attacked and defeated. Though they are flexible, children are also very sensitive and need to be confronted by one person at a time. Furthermore, because each of us is an expert on only our own feelings, it appears reasonable that each of us should share our own feelings and dispense with the pronoun *we*.

In his *Teacher Effectiveness Training* (TET), Thomas Gordon (1974) wrote that when expressing a concern about students' behavior that affects the teacher, the teacher should employ an I-message consisting of three components: (1) the personal pronoun *I*, (2) the feeling the teacher is experiencing, and (3) the affect the student's behavior is having on the teacher. We would add that an I-message also includes a polite, alpha request for the student to make a better choice. For example, a typical teacher's response to a student's interruption might be, "If you can't stop interrupting me, you can leave the room." If an I-message is used in this situation, the teacher might say, "When you interrupt me, I become concerned because I have difficulty helping the other students. Please wait until I finish helping Sam and I will be glad to help you."

Because I-messages express personal feelings and often deal with student behaviors that require change, it is best to send them privately. We should do so especially when we are dealing with adolescents. Adolescents, being particularly sensitive to peer pressure, will often respond to even the most thoughtful public criticism defensively. Because most adolescents value being treated as adults, they will usually respond positively to private expressions of our concern.

Another, less open way to send an I-message involves politely yet firmly expressing a demand using the first-person singular. Therefore, if a student began talking to another student during a teacher's presentation, the teacher might say in a nonthreatening manner, "I expect students to listen quietly while someone in this class speaks." Although this type of I-message will more likely elicit a defensive response from older students, it is a clear, straightforward way to present your expectations.

Over the past twenty years, the authors have taught this simple skill to thousands of in-service and preservice teachers and have received literally hundreds of comments from teachers on how surprised they were at the effectiveness of this strategy. The day before writing this section of the fourth edition, a young high school teacher in one of the author's classes shared with her colleagues that she had quietly sent an I-message to one of her most disruptive students. She was amazed that the student stopped by after class to apologize to her and that during the following week his behavior had dramatically improved. When asked why she thought he had apparently responded so well, she noted that he was probably used to being criticized for his behavior and he was appreciative that someone would treat him courteously. One of the activities at the end of the chapter provides you with an opportunity to practice developing and sending I-messages.

6. *Make statements rather than asking questions.* When children misbehave, they are frequently bombarded with questions. This approach leaves the child feeling intimidated and defensive. Questions such as, "Are you feeling all right?" "Would you like to leave the room for a few minutes?" or "Can I help?" can be extremely productive. However, teachers should be aware of opportunities for replacing questions with statements. Consider the different feelings a child might have on coming late to class and hearing *Where have you been?* compared to *I was concerned when you were late because we have to leave on our field trip in five minutes.* It is important to keep in mind that questions are often important tools for helping children understand and change their behavior. Asking students what they were doing or how their behavior helped them is an important component in solving problems. Questions often misdirect students from taking responsibility for their own behavior, however, while creating defensiveness. Therefore, when dealing with students' behaviors, use questions sparingly and in the context of a problem-solving approach.

EVALUATING THE QUALITY OF TEACHER–STUDENT RELATIONSHIPS

Before implementing any of the varied behaviors you can use to create positive teacher–student relationships, you should evaluate the current quality of your own interactions with students. Just as effective teaching involves both a diagnostic and a prescriptive component, any decision to alter our behavior can be helped by first assessing the students' reactions to the current behaviors. This approach enables us to focus changes in areas in which students' feedback suggests that changes may be needed in order to improve teacher–student relationships. Figures 3.4, 3.5, and 3.6 present forms that many teachers have found useful in assessing the quality of their relationships with their students.

1. Do I listen to you?			
2. Do I help you enough?			
3. Do I care about you?			
4. Do I help you feel good about learning?			
5. Do I seem happy when I teach?			
6. Do I think you can do your work?			
7. Can you share your good and bad feelings with me?			
8. Am I polite?			
9. Am I fair?			
10. Do you know what I want you to do?			
11. Do I help you understand why we are doing each activity in class?			
12. Do I call on you enough in class?			
13. Do I let you know when you have done good work?			
14. Are you excited about what I teach you?			

FIGURE 3.4
Elementary School Teacher Feedback Form

IMPLEMENTATION ACTIVITIES

ACTIVITY 3.1

Monitoring
Courteous
Remarks

1. Make a tally of the courteous remarks you make to students during a one-day period. You may want to carry a counter or a small note pad.
2. If you used fewer than twenty-five such statements (research indicates that elementary teachers have approximately 1,000 interactions with children each day and that secondary teachers have nearly 500), try to double the number the next day.
3. Briefly write (or discuss with a colleague) how it felt to increase the number of courteous statements. Did your students respond any differently the second day?

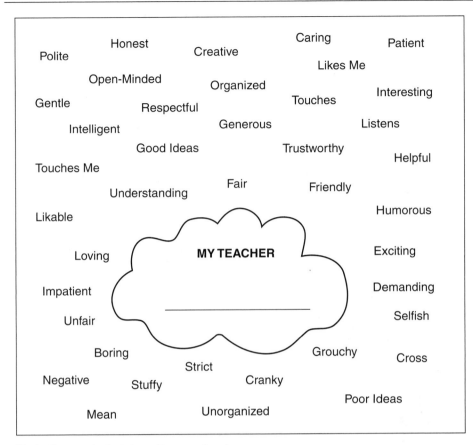

FIGURE 3.5
Teacher–Student
Relationship
Evaluation Form

Circle the words that describe your teacher.

Circle in red if the words describe your teacher most of the time.
Circle in blue if the words describe your teacher sometimes.
Circle in green if the words seldom describe your teacher.
Circle in orange if the words never describe your teacher.

ACTIVITY 3.2

Sending
I-Messages

To test your knowledge of I-messages, change each of these five statements into an I-message:

1. Late again! What's the matter with you?
2. I don't want to hear another word out of anyone.
3. No book again? How do you expect to learn anything?
4. How can you be so inconsiderate as to stand there drinking water for so long when you know other children want a drink?
5. If you get in trouble on the playground one more time, you can miss the rest of your recesses this month!

If you have difficulty with this task, consult a colleague or refer to Thomas Gordon's (1974) *Teacher Effectiveness Training.*

I believe students are knowledgeable both about how they learn best and in describing effective teaching. Therefore, I am asking you to give me some feedback on what I believe to be important aspects of my teaching. Please be serious, fair, and honest when completing this form. Also, please do not put your name on the form. Place an *X* in the column that best describes the question.

FORE!

What's the Score?	Hole in One	Birdie	Par	Bogey	Out of Bounds
1. Are the goals and objectives for each lesson clear?					
2. Do you value what you are learning in this class?					
3. Do I use different ways to teach lessons (films, projects, discussions, guest speakers, and so on)?					
4. Do you get to study subjects or ideas that interest you?					
5. Is there a good balance for you in the amount of time spent in large- and small-group activities?					
6. Do you think the skills taught in this class are useful in some other areas of your life?					
7. Do you accomplish goals you set in this class?					
8. Do tests give you information about what you have learned?					
9. Do tests help you to see what skills still need to be practiced?					
10. Do you feel pressured to finish work in this class?					
11. Are you comfortable sharing your ideas with other students in this class?					
12. Are the goals of each new assignment clear?					
13. Are you aware of how you are doing in this class?					
14. Are most of the assignments challenging but not too hard for you?					
15. Do I allow enough time for questions and discussion?					
16. Does the class allow you to express yourself creatively?					
17. Do you think the grading is fair?					
18. Do you feel you have a chance to be actively involved in learning?					

(Continued)

FIGURE 3.6
Student's Assessment of Teacher's Instructional Skills

19. The best thing about the class is . . .
20. If I were teaching this class, I would . . .
21. The way I learn best is to . . .

FIGURE 3.6
Continued

ACTIVITY 3.3

Improving Your
Positive–Negative
Ratio

1. Have a student or colleague tally the positive and negative statements you make during a minimum of two hours of instructional time. Try to include several types of lessons and do not code more than thirty minutes at a time. Especially when using students to tally remarks, it is helpful to define positive and negative statements and to provide the coder with a list of commonly used positive and negative remarks. Neutral remarks, such as statements related to instruction, or comments such as "Okay," "All right," or "Yes" should not be coded.
2. If your ratio of positive-to-negative statements was less than three to one, repeat the activity and try to focus on responding positively to productive student behavior. Following a period in which your ratio was very high, ask students to evaluate the lesson.

ACTIVITY 3.4

Monitoring Students'
Response
Opportunities

List the four highest- and four lowest-achieving students in your class. Place these students' names in the form provided in Figure 3.7. Have a colleague tally your interactions with these students during at least two half-hour periods when the class is involved in group instruction.

This activity can also be completed by presenting the observer with a seating chart and a label for each type of teacher–student interaction on which you wish to obtain data. An observer might be asked to observe several students and to tally the number of times they were asked a question, given assistance in answering a question, criticized, praised, or volunteered an answer. Figure 3.8 shows a sample of the data you might collect using this procedure.

After examining the results, respond to these statements:

Two things I learned about my interactions with these students are. . . .
Two things I will try to do differently the next time I teach a large-group lesson
    are. . . .

Student's Name	Student Volunteers Answer	Teacher Asks Student a Question	Student Response			Teacher Assists Student	Teacher Praises Student	Teacher Criticizes Student	Teacher Calls on Another Student
			Correct	Partially Correct	Incorrect				

FIGURE 3.7
Monitoring Teacher–Student Dyadic Interactions

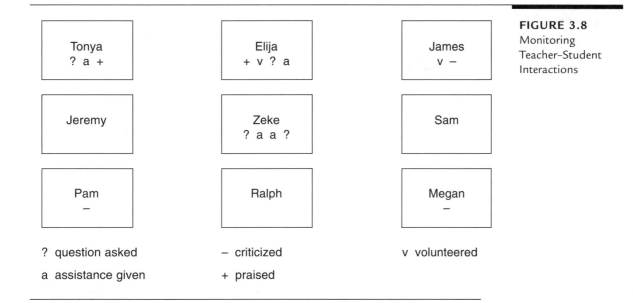

FIGURE 3.8
Monitoring
Teacher–Student
Interactions

ACTIVITY 3.5

Mapping a
Teacher's
Classroom
Movement

Draw a map of your classroom, including the location of the furniture. Ask a colleague to come into your classroom during a period of at least half an hour when the class will be involved in seatwork and you will be free to assist students. Have the observer mark your movement with a solid line during the entire observation. The observer should write a number by each place where you stop. To record the amount of time spent at each spot, have the observer place a tally mark next to the number for every fifteen seconds that you remain in that spot.

After examining the walking map, answer these questions:

1. Where did you spend the most time? Least time?
2. Were any students ignored? Were there specific reasons for not interacting with these students?
3. Did the classroom arrangement influence your movement? How?
4. What changes, if any, would you make in your walking pattern during this type of instruction?
5. What changes, if any, would you make in your classroom arrangement?

ACTIVITY 3.6

Balancing
Positive
Statements

For three days, make one inviting statement to each child in your class. In order to ensure that each child receives such a statement, make a class list and place a check by each child's name when he or she has been given an inviting statement. After completing the activity, answer these questions:

1. Were there some students whom you had to consciously remind yourself to provide with an inviting statement? If so, did these students have anything in common?
2. Did students respond any differently during the three days? If so, how?
3. Did any students make a positive comment to you about your behavior during these three days?

(Continued)

ACTIVITY 3.6

Continued

A good supplement to this activity is again to list your four highest- and lowest-achieving students. Ask a colleague, an aide, or even the principal to tally the number of positive and negative statements you make to each of these students during two half-hour instructional periods.

Student's Name	Positive Comments	Negative Comments
High achievers		
1.		
2.		
3.		
4.		
Low achievers		
1.		
2.		
3.		
4.		

After completing this activity, answer these questions:

1. What do the data indicate about how you respond to high- as opposed to low-achieving students?
2. Did you find yourself behaving differently because you were being observed? If so, what did you do differently?
3. Did any of the eight students appear to respond differently from usual while you were observed? If so, how did their behaviors change?

ACTIVITY 3.7

Practicing
Listening Skills

To examine and improve your skills in using paraphrasing, imagine that each of the following statements has just been said to you. Write two responses to each of the ten statements. In the first response, simply paraphrase the statement without mimicking the student's words. In the second response, add a feeling component.

1. Someone stole my lunch ticket!
2. This work is too hard.
3. Can we have ten extra minutes of recess?
4. Bill has had the book for two days.
5. I hate you!
6. I didn't get into trouble in music class today.
7. Nobody in the class likes me.
8. Do I have to take my report card home?
9. I never get to take the roll.
10. Mary is always picking on me.

During one schoolday, list five statements children make to you and five questions they ask you that could best be responded to by empathic, nonevaluative listening. When the list is complete, write a response to each of the ten student statements.

SUMMARY

Positive, supportive teacher–student relationships are important for all students. However, they become a critical factor influencing the behavior and achievement of students who are experiencing academic and behavioral difficulties. Although our primary role as teachers is to assist students in developing academic skills, successful teachers interact with students in ways that provide encouragement, support, and a positive learning environment for their students. The methods presented in this chapter provide a basis for creating adult–student relationships that support student learning in both the academic and social and personal domains.

RECOMMENDED READING

Bempechat, J. (1998). *Against the odds: How "at risk" children exceed expectations.* San Francisco: Jossey-Bass.

Brendtro, L., Brokenleg, M., & VanBockern, S. (1990). *Reclaiming youth at risk: Our hope for the future.* Bloomington, IN: National Educational Service.

Brophy, J. (Ed). (1998). *Advances in research on teaching: Expectations in the classroom.* Greenwich, CT: JAI Press.

Darling-Hammond, L. (1997). *The right to learn: A blueprint for creating schools that work.* San Francisco: Jossey-Bass.

Garbarino, J. (1999). *Lost boys: Why our sons turn violent and how we can save them.* New York: Free Press.

Good, T., & Brophy, J. (2000). *Looking in classrooms* (8th ed.). New York: Longman.

Kuykendall, C. (2003). *From rage to hope: Strategies for reclaiming Black and Hispanic students* (2nd ed.). Bloomington, IN: National Educational Service.

Long, N., Morse, W., & Newman, R. (1996). *Conflict in the classroom: The education of at-risk and troubled students* (5th ed.). Austin, TX: Pro-Ed.

Mendler, A. (1992). *What do I do when . . . ? How to achieve discipline with dignity in the classroom.* Bloomington, IN: National Educational Service.

Olsen, L., & Jaramillo, A. (Eds.). (1999). *Turning the tides of exclusion: A guide for educators and advocates for immigrant students.* Oakland, CA: Coast Litho.

Paley, V. (1989). *White teacher.* Cambridge, MA: Harvard University Press.

Purkey, W., & Novak, J. (1996). *Inviting school success: A self-concept approach to teaching, learning, and democratic practice.* Belmont, CA: Wadsworth.

Schmuck, R., & Schmuck, P. (2001). *Group processes in the classroom* (8th ed.). Boston: McGraw-Hill.

Creating Positive Peer Relationships

Our own research shows that classroom groups with supportive friendship patterns enhance academic learning. Our data indicate that student academic performances are conditioned by emotional contents associated with their self-concepts as peers and students, and these self-concepts are influenced, in part, by the students' friendships and influence relations with their classmates.

—Richard Schmuck and Patricia Schmuck (2001)
Group Processes in the Classroom

. . . feeling valued, cared for, and supported by others in a community is a positive motivating force that promotes attachment to the group and commitment to community norms and values. In the school context, students' sense of membership in a community promotes their attachment and commitment to school, motivation to engage in learning tasks, and valuing of learning.

—Thomas Good and Jere Brophy (2000)
Looking in Classrooms

At schools high in "community"—measured by the degree of students' agreement with statements such as "My school is like a family" and "Students really care about each other"—students show a host of positive outcomes. These include higher educational expectations and academic performance, stronger motivation to learn, greater social competence, fewer conduct problems, reduced drug use and delinquency, and greater commitment to democratic values.

—Catherine Lewis, Eric Schaps, and Marilyn Watson (1996)
Educational Leadership

Peers play an important role in determining the quality of the learning environment. With today's increased emphasis on students' achievement, teachers are often hesitant to allocate time for creating positive peer relationships in the classroom. In addition, teacher education programs seldom provide teachers with specific skills for developing positive, supportive group norms. A considerable body of research indicates, however, that time spent creating a positive peer group can eliminate much misbehavior and can provide a classroom climate that enhances students' achievement.

Peer relationships influence students' achievement in several ways. First, peer attitudes toward achievement affect students' academic aspirations and school behavior. Second, the quality of peer relationships and personal support in classrooms affects the degree to which students' personal needs are met and, subsequently, their ability to be productively involved in the learning process. Third, peer relationships can directly affect achievement through cooperative learning activities. Finally, at-risk students are more likely to feel alienated from school and have low rates of participation in school as early as third grade. It is likely that the quality of peer relationships students experience in the classroom and throughout the schoolday dramatically influence the extent to which students become involved in school.

Positive peer relationships not only enhance students' school experiences but they also provide a framework for the development of lifelong social skills and positive self-esteem. Researchers and theorists have reported that positive peer relationships are essential factors in adequate social and emotional development as well as healthy adjustment in adult life.

Anyone who has worked with groups of students has witnessed the role peers play in influencing students' behaviors. When discussing the differences between confronting an adolescent in front of the group and having a private talk with the student, teachers frequently remark that it seems as if they are dealing with two completely different students. We should not be surprised that students' feelings and behaviors are significantly influenced by their classmates. During the school year, students spend more than 1,000 hours with their classmates. Also, because most elementary school classrooms are composed of children who live near one another, friendships and conflicts that develop in the classroom often influence youngsters' lives outside the school. Peer pressure is somewhat less complex and extensive for early primary grade children whose egocentricity reduces the influence of their peers. Nevertheless, at all grade levels, the values, norms, and behaviors of the group significantly affect individual students' feelings of safety, belongingness, respect for others, and self-esteem.

In their *Group Processes in the Classroom*, Richard and Patricia Schmuck (2001) wrote of the classroom group's importance:

> The classroom clearly offers a setting in which high levels of feeling exist daily and wherein covert psychological dynamics often come into play. As students interact, and students and teachers relate, they communicate—however indirectly—their feelings about one another. Such gestures of affect influence how students view themselves, their abilities, their likability, and their general worth. Moreover, students' levels of self-esteem affect the degree to which they use their intelligence in learning academic subjects. (p. 36)

Positive peer relationships are essential factors in creating schools as communities of support. Positive, supportive communities are characterized by students showing respect for the personal and physical safety and security of their peers. As incidents such as that at Columbine High School in Littleton, Colorado, have highlighted, student alienation from peers may play a role in increasing the likelihood that students will reach the point of acting violently in school settings. "For all that is being written on the subject of violence, many of us fail to see that we won't solve the problem of violence unless we address the social ecology that supports and nurtures it" (Kauffman & Burbach, 1997, p. 321). Although boys may be more likely to respond with violence, girls are not immune to frustration and anger related to peer interactions. A study by the American Association of University Women found that 70 percent of girls reported experiencing harassment at school and more than 50 percent reported experiencing unwanted sexual touching.

We must accept the fact that a central factor affecting violence in our schools is the lack of support and caring some students experience in these settings. Students are far less likely to express violent behaviors in settings where they are nurtured, supported, and cared for by their peers. The examples of effective schools cited in Chapter 1 as well as the research on small schools (Fine & Somerville, 1998) suggest that student behavior is more civil and safe in settings in which students feel known and are part of a smaller, more intimate group. If we are to reduce school violence (including bullying and sexual harassment), we must simply pay greater attention to the manner in which we encourage or fail to encourage positive peer relationships in classrooms and schools.

UNDERSTANDING THE CLASSROOM GROUP

The classroom by nature elicits many interactions and feelings. By placing twenty-five to thirty-five individuals in a 30-by-30-foot room, schools create a highly interactive environment. Peer interaction is a natural and desirable aspect of almost all learning environments. Group instruction is used both because it is frequently more expedient and because a good education involves learning how to function as a group member. The group's influence is intensified by the competition found in most classrooms. Students compete for the highest test scores, strive to earn high grades, or run for class office. Even when we use instructional methods that deemphasize competition, students have numerous opportunities to compare their work to that of their classmates. It is understandable and perhaps unavoidable that classrooms are characterized by a fairly high level of interaction and the accompanying spontaneous interchange of feelings.

Although teachers often express concern and frustration about the negative aspects of peer pressure, the peer group can be a positive and supportive factor in the classroom. When students feel liked by their peers and when interactions are characterized by thoughtfulness and helpfulness, students experience a sense of safety and security, belongingness and affection, significance, respect for others, and power. Students are then able to concentrate more fully on learning and are willing to take greater risks in attempting to master new skills. Consequently, it is extremely important that we implement strategies that encourage the development of positive, supportive peer interactions in the classroom.

Stop for a minute and think of a class you found particularly enjoyable, perhaps one you looked forward to attending every day. Write several sentences that described the social aspects of this class. When considering and writing about this class, focus your attention on the relationships you had with other students in the class. We encourage you to share this with a colleague or several classmates. Were there common factors about which you and those with whom you shared this activity wrote?

Group Development Stages

It is beyond the scope of this book to examine group dynamics thoroughly, but it is important to realize that groups, like individuals, have needs that must be met before the group can function effectively. If the classroom group is to function in a supportive, goal-directed manner, teachers must initially set aside time for activities that enable students to know each other, develop feelings of being included, and create diverse friendship patterns. Only after these feelings have been developed can a group of students proceed to respond optimally to the learning goals of the classroom.

Like all groups, classroom groups move through a series of stages (Posthuma, 1999; Schmuck & Schmuck, 2001). The initial stage of a group involves what is often termed the *dependance stage*. At this point, group members look to the authority figure to provide structure. During this early stage, the teacher provides clarity in terms of classroom behavior standards, procedures, and academic goals. Chapter 6 and 7 provide important concepts and strategies for ensuring that this aspect of group development goes smoothly.

The second stage, which lasts for some time, is often termed the *inclusion* or *orientation stage* (Posthuma, 1999; Vernelle, 1994). During this stage, the major concern involves the issue of belonging. Students are concerned with whether they will be accepted and liked by their peers. They are also concerned about whether the adult in charge will like them and whether they are as competent as other members of the group. Notice that these issues are key factors emphasized in Chapter 3 and 6 as well as this chapter. During this stage, students may be rather passive as they "check out" the group or they may act out as another means to test the limits.

The third stage is often termed the *dissatisfaction* or *control stage*. During this stage, group members often express concern about how the group is operating and who makes key decisions in the classroom. Students have become comfortable and feel safe enough to challenge the way things are being done. This stage can be facilitated by establishing positive teacher–student relationships (Chapter 3), being clear about classroom behavior expectations (Chapter 7), clearly explaining and involving students in academic decision making (Chapter 6), and using effective problem-solving skills (Chapter 9). Our experience in classrooms clearly suggests that if strategies are used that facilitate positive resolution of the first two stages, this third stage can provide for productive dialogue and learning for students regarding democratic decision making. However, teachers who do not use the methods described in this book often find this stage continues throughout the school year.

The fourth stage has been called the *resolution* or *norming stage*. During this stage, students begin to work more collaboratively and to listen more thoughtfully to one another. This almost always involves students developing an increased sense of group unity and cohesiveness and is characterized by group members making an increasing number of positive statements about the classroom and group. Our experience suggests that when teachers use the methods discussed throughout this book, this stage is integrated with the third stage. Thus, while positive questioning and concern expressed by students continues throughout the year, limited amounts of actual dissatisfaction are expressed.

The fifth stage is often termed the *production stage*. Although there will be numerous instances in which the teacher needs to assist the group in reestablishing its cohesiveness and focus, in classrooms in which teachers use the methods described in this book, this stage usually lasts from the third or fourth week of class throughout the school year.

The sixth and final stage of group development has been labeled the *termination* or *adjournment stage*. At this point group members must place closure on their group experience and begin to say goodbye. In many classrooms this involves a sadness and sense of loss, and it is a stage teachers often fail to facilitate.

This chapter provides you with numerous activities for assisting a classroom group to productively accomplish or work through these group development stages. As you read this chapter, you may want to jot down methods or activities you wish to use to assist your students in working through these stages. Activity 4.1, at the end of the chapter, will assist you in organizing your decision making in this important area of classroom management.

The Importance of Students Working Cooperatively

The study of cooperative group work within classrooms is another area in which substantial research supports the importance of working with students to develop group skills and a sense of group cohesiveness. Students who are involved in cooperative learning activities in which they study with peers and in which their efforts produce benefits for peers as well as for themselves perform higher on standardized tests of mathematics, reading, and language and also do better on tasks involving higher-level thinking than when they study alone (Allen & Plax, 1999). Researchers at the National Center on Effective Secondary Schools at the University of Wisconsin–Madison synthesized the research on cooperative learning and students' academic success in secondary schools. With the exception of one technique (the jigsaw method), cooperative learning was found to be more successful in more than 75 percent of the studies. The authors' own work in helping teachers implement cooperative learning suggests that when teachers (1) take time to help students understand the reasons behind their decision to implement this method, (2) help students become better acquainted, and (3) assist students in developing skills for working in groups, cooperative learning is very effective in increasing motivation and learning for a wide range of students.

Good and Brophy (2000) note that cooperative learning can be an effective technique for helping students be accepted into and function effectively in the classroom. Similarly, a review of research on cooperative learning (Allen & Plax, 1999) suggests that in classrooms characterized by high rates of collaborative, cooperative learning, students are more likely to indicate they like school, the classroom, and the subject matter. Students in classrooms using cooperative peer activities are also characterized by greater group cohesiveness, more diversified friendship patterns, and greater concern for peers (Schmuck & Schmuck, 2001). Not surprisingly, when cooperative learning is used in the classroom, students have been found to be more accepting of student diversity, including greater acceptance of and sensitivity to students with special needs. In addition, students who work collaboratively tend to have a greater sense of personal responsibility for their learning.

The impact cooperative learning has on positive peer relationships and achievement provides a major incentive for you to implement at least some degree of collaborative learning. Another reason to consider the importance of creating positive peer relationships and active, collaborative learning in the classroom relates to the skills your students will need when they become workers and citizens.

Preparing Students for the Workplace and Community Life

The importance of the time when the average person lived in relative isolation and was basically self-sufficient is long past. Individuals depend on others for needed goods and services as well as for meeting emotional needs. Likewise, individuals are rediscovering the importance of coming together in order to combat social problems ranging from burglary to an energy crisis. This increased interdependence can also be seen in the move away from the Renaissance scholar toward increased specialization. In producing anything from automobiles to ideas, individuals focus on an ever more specialized aspect of their work and must cooperate with other people in order to create increasingly sophisticated products.

If schools are to prepare students for a society characterized by interdependence and cooperative effort, they must provide students with frequent and meaningful experiences in functioning cooperatively in groups. Rather than continually stressing competition and individual learning, teachers must use cooperative group work in the classroom. More than three decades ago, John Dewey emphasized that life in a classroom should mirror the processes students will face in society. He wrote too that the goal of schooling is to provide students with skills that will enable them to create a better living situation.

It is interesting that many parents share this concern for educating the whole child. In their study of schools in which Hispanic students achieved particularly well, Reyes, Scribner, and Scribner (1999) discovered that "Parents concerns were not only with how well children performed academically, but also with nurturing values of respect, honor, cooperation, good behavior, and responsibility of their children at school" (p. 37). These parents valued and were willing to support a school setting in which educators assisted their children in developing personal as well as cognitive skills.

Employers appear to agree with the values expressed by these Hispanic parents. In a report documenting the skills and behaviors identified as essential for competence in the twenty-first century workforce, the Employment and Training Administration in Washington, DC (2000), listed the skills shown in Figure 4.1. Clearly, development of the skills listed under Interpersonal for workplace competencies as well as the Personal Qualities listed for foundation skills are facilitated by students learning how to work effectively in group settings. In an interesting analysis of this data, the

FIGURE 4.1
Essential Workplace
Skills

Source: Workplace
Essential Skills,
Employment
and Training
Administration,
Office of Policy and
Research, Office of
Education Research
and Improvement
(ED): Washington,
DC (2000).

Workplace Competencies	Foundation Skills
Resources Allocates time Allocates money Allocates materials and facility resources Allocates human resources	*Basic Skills* Reading Writing Arithmetic Mathematics Listening Speaking
Information Acquires and evaluates information Organizes and maintains information Interprets and communicates information Uses computers to process information	*Thinking Skills* Creative thinking Decision making Problem solving Seeing things in the mind's eye Knowing how to learn Reasoning
Interpersonal Participates as a member of a team Teaches others Serves clients/customers Exercises leadership Negotiates to arrive at a decision Works with cultural diversity	*Personal Qualities* Responsibilities Self-esteem Social Self-management Integrity/honesty
Systems Understands systems Monitors and corrects performance Improves and designs systems	
Technology Selects technology Applies technology to task Maintains and troubleshoots technology	

Employment and Training Administration examined the degree to which entry-level employees possessed the skills desired by employers. As seen in Figure 4.2, personal quality skills and interpersonal competencies were two of the four areas in which entry-level employees were most lacking in the skills needed for employment. It seems likely that by focusing more on interpersonal and social skills, schools could do a better job of preparing students for the workplace.

As you read this chapter, you may ask whether time allocated for creating positive, supportive peer relationships in the classroom will reduce the amount of time allocated for instruction. This is an important issue. As teachers, our primary responsibility is to help students develop skills in the subject matter for which we are responsible. The evidence clearly indicates that taking time to establish a safe, supportive classroom group in which students know each other and support each other's learning will significantly enhance student learning. We can either take a small but significant amount of time to help the relationships in our classrooms run smoothly or we can risk spending extensive time and energy on responding to problems caused by students feeling isolated, unable to obtain assistance, uninvolved, and unwanted.

The activities presented throughout the remainder of the chapter can help the reader create a positive, supportive classroom environment. They can also help stu-

Competency or Skill	Needed for Entry-Level Employment	Entry-level Employees Sufficiently Possess	Difference
Thinking skills	92.8%	60.0%	32.8%
Personal quality skills	96.1	66.0	30.1
Basic skills	95.9	68.4	27.5
Interpersonal competencies	91.6	65.1	26.5
Information competencies	86.5	63.1	23.4
Technology competencies	54.5	37.8	16.7
Systems competencies	52.8	41.0	11.8
Resource competencies	60.0	53.5	6.5

FIGURE 4.2
Difference between Importance and Actual Possession of Identified Skills and Competencies

dents develop work norms and personal skills that will serve them well in their future roles as parents, spouses, friends, and workers.

During our more than sixty years in working with, supervising, and educating teachers, we have come into contact with virtually thousands of teachers, student-teachers, and interns. These valued colleagues have almost without exception testified to the benefits associated with taking some time early in the school year to help students know each other and create a sense of caring and support among peers in the classroom. A small amount of time spent during the first several weeks of school will pay tremendous dividends in terms of positive student attitudes and behavior as well as helping your students develop essential lifelong interpersonal skills.

PAUSE
and Consider

4.2

During your teaching career, you will undoubtedly encounter situations in which parents, fellow teachers, or administrators question your decision to use class time to develop a cohesive classroom group. Take a few minutes and write a brief statement you might write to a colleague describing why you allocate time in this manner. Share this with several colleagues or classmates. Their ideas may enrich your statement. Finally, we encourage you to save this statement and enhance and modify it as you continue your teaching career.

The Issue of Self-Esteem

In this chapter we have focused on the creation of positive peer relationships and the building of communities of support within the classroom rather than the development of positive self-esteem. In his book, *The Optimistic Child*, Seligman (1995) stated that the most useful and effective definition of positive self-esteem involves both the component of feeling good about oneself and the component of performing well. He suggested that too much self-esteem application in school settings has focused almost exclusively on helping students to feel good without the accompanying sense of being competent. The topic of self-esteem has long been associated with the chicken-or-the-egg debate (i.e., does self-esteem cause positive behavior changes or is self-esteem enhanced when one experiences success?). "There are, however, almost no findings showing that self-esteem causes anything at all. Rather, self-esteem is caused by the whole panoply of successes or failures in the world" (Seligman, 1995, p. 34). This, of course, does not mean that we should not utilize activities intended to assist students in acknowledging their strengths or perceiving that others have a positive reaction to these strengths. It suggests that in developing and implementing these activities, we need to be careful that they provide students with accurate and honest information. In addition, the fact that self-esteem appears to be an outcome rather than a cause of positive experiences (Baumeister, 1993) means that we need to see the building of positive interpersonal skills as important prerequisites to students having positive interaction with their peers that will, in turn, tend to increase their positive feelings about themselves. When working to enhance peer relationships, teachers can help students by emphasizing the skills students are developing as they learn to work more collaboratively, solve problems collectively and cooperatively, listen to others, and so forth.

ACQUAINTANCE ACTIVITIES

You can undoubtedly recall experiencing discomfort when walking into a party or other group setting when you knew very few individuals there. Compare this feeling with those elicited when you walk into a room filled with acquaintances and friends. People usually feel more relaxed and comfortable in discussions or other activities with people they know. Students experience similar feelings. The new student who is confronted by thirty unfamiliar faces is likely to respond either by withdrawing until the environment becomes more familiar or by acting out as a means of controlling the environment by eliciting an expected response.

Several years ago, one of the authors was contacted by a teacher who was experiencing much frustration because the students in his sophomore English class were not becoming involved in group discussions. Furthermore, the teacher said absenteeism in class was relatively high and students were not handing in the number of assignments he had expected. The teacher, a hardworking, dynamic young man, indicated that the material being read and discussed seemed to be of high interest and that he had made a special effort to relate aspects of the literature to students' lives. Students were seated in a circle and open discussion was encouraged.

While discussing this situation, I asked the teacher whether students in the class knew each other. The teacher seemed surprised by the question and indicated that because the students came from only two feeder schools and had been in his class for nearly six months, he assumed they were well acquainted. The students' behaviors suggested, however, that they felt some discomfort, and the teacher agreed to assess how well they knew one another. He was surprised to discover that only a quarter of the students in his class knew the first names of more than half of their peers. He discussed this figure with the class and explained his decision to allocate time to activities that would help students become better acquainted. Following these activities, he again collected data on attendance, percentage of assignments handed in, and students' participation in class discussions. All three variables showed changes that were statistically significant at the .01 level. These results were so striking that the teacher's English department decided to incorporate a peer-acquaintance unit into the first nine weeks of the school year.

Positive peer relationships are an important component in peer acceptance and are less likely to encourage bullying (Schwartz, Pettit, Dodge, & Bates, 2000). Friendships at school can "help children to compensate for vulnerabilities acquired through stressful experiences in the home" (Schwartz et al., 2000, p. 647) and can help children who might otherwise be victimized by peers be more accepted and successful. However, being rejected by peers tends to be associated with acting-out behavior (Laird, Jordan, Dodge, Pettit, & Bates, 2001). Students who develop a pattern of acting-out, aggressive behavior are likely to have experienced rejection from peers and not be integrated into the classroom group. Therefore, if you wish to create a classroom setting which negative peer interactions and acting-out behavior are minimized, it is essential to incorporate methods for helping students know and interact positively with each other.

The peer-acquaintance activities presented in the following section are designed to help students get better acquainted with one another so that they will feel safe and secure and will, therefore, become more actively engaged in the learning process. As students become better acquainted, the likelihood that they will interact with and be influenced by a wider range of students increases, and cliquish behavior decreases.

The Name Chain

A name chain is the most effective method for helping students learn each other's names. The following steps can make this activity run smoothly:

1. Ask the students to sit in a circle so that each one can comfortably see all the students in the group.
2. Clearly explain the reasons for being involved in the activity. You might say that one benefit of knowing everyone's name is that this increases their knowledge of the environment and thereby makes them more comfortable and more likely to become actively involved. Similarly, you may indicate that knowing other students' names will enable students to greet each other in a friendlier, more relaxed manner, which will have a tendency to make both the classroom and the school a more positive place.
3. Ask the students if they have any questions about why they are being asked to do the activity.
4. Explain to the students that each person will be asked to say his or her first name and tell the group one thing about himself or herself. They may choose to tell the group something they like to do, something interesting that happened to them recently, how they are feeling, and so on. Inform the class that they will be asked to repeat each student's name and the statement he or she has made. They will begin with the person who spoke first and stop when they have given their name and have said something about themselves. The first student may say, "I'm Bob, and I went to the beach this weekend." The next would say, "That's Bob (or you're Bob), and he (or you) went to the beach last weekend. I'm Sandy, and I enjoy backpacking." Because we are faced with the difficult task of learning a large number of names and because having an adult remember their names seems particularly important to adolescents, it is best to have you be the last person to speak. You will therefore be able to list each student's name and what they have shared with the class.
5. Have everyone take a paper and pencil and change seats. Ask the students to start with a designated individual and go clockwise around the circle, writing down each person's name. It is not necessary to have them list what each student shared.
6. Ask for a volunteer who will begin with the person designated as the starting place and slowly give the name of each person in the circle. This recital serves as an opportunity for students to check the accuracy of their list, and to learn the names of any students they might have missed. (Jones, 1980)

It is important to provide follow-up for this activity. For example, for several days following the activity, you may want to attempt to go around the class listing each student's name or ask for a volunteer to do so. We must continue to be aware of whether students are remembering names and continue to emphasize the value of knowing names. If you ask students to work in groups, you may suggest that they make sure they know each member's name before beginning the group activity. Teachers too often involve students in activities and then fail to follow up with behavior that reinforces the learning derived from and the values implied by the activity.

Know Your Classmates

Each student will need a copy of a page entitled Know Your Classmates (see Figure 4.3) and a pencil or pen. Ask students to find a person in the class who fits each description listed on the sheet and to obtain the person's signature on the line in front of the description. To encourage students to interact with numerous peers, inform them that they

---

FIGURE 4.3
Know Your
Classmates

Name _____

Collect the signatures of the appropriate persons:

_____ 1. A person whose birthday is in the same month as yours.
_____ 2. A person who has red hair.
_____ 3. A person whom you don't know very well.
_____ 4. A person who has an interesting hobby. What is it? _____
_____
_____ 5. A person with freckles.
_____ 6. A person whose favorite color is yellow.
_____ 7. A person who loves to read.
_____ 8. A person who takes gymnastic lessons.
_____ 9. A person who is left-handed.
_____ 10. A person with naturally curly hair.
_____ 11. A person who has a dog. The dog's name is _____
_____ 12. A person who belongs to a Scouting troop.
_____ 13. A person shorter than you.
_____ 14. A person taller than you.
_____ 15. A person with the same color shirt or dress as you are wearing.
_____ 16. A person who plays an instrument. What instrument? _____
_____
_____ 17. A person who traveled out of the state this summer. Where?
_____
_____ 18. A person who wants to play professional sports when he or she grows up. Which one? _____
_____ 19. A person with more than four children in the family. How many? _____
_____ 20. A person who plays soccer.
_____ 21. A person with braces on his or her teeth.
_____ 22. A person who rides horseback.

cannot have the same person sign their sheets more than twice. The descriptions can be adapted to fit the specific interests of children at different ages and in different settings.

Bingo

For upper elementary and middle school, on the first day of class have each student complete a brief self-information sheet. You may ask them about things they did this summer, special interests, pets, hobbies, and so on. Take this information and place one interesting piece of information about each student in each square of a bingo grid. The next day each class member is given a bingo card and the students are asked to walk around the room and obtain the signature of the person who is associated with each square. This can be continued until someone has obtained a signature for each square, has a signature on each square in two rows, or a designated period of time has elapsed.

Interviews

Interviews are an excellent means for students to become better acquainted with each other. This activity often fosters new friendships and feelings of self-importance. Lack of information about others is often a major barrier to establishing new friendships. When children do not know their peers, they tend to make assumptions and develop unrealistic fears or unfounded biases. As students interview each other, they learn new and exciting information about their peers. This knowledge, in turn, promotes diversified friendship patterns in the classroom.

We can use interviews in the classroom in many ways. One method involves introducing the interviewing process by having students list ten questions that would help them know a classmate better. Following are examples of questions that might be asked by nine year olds:

1. What is your favorite color?
2. What is your favorite sport to play? To watch?
3. What are you proudest of?
4. Do you have any pets? If so, what are their names?
5. What is your favorite professional team in football? Basketball? Baseball?
6. What kinds of foods do you like to eat?
7. If you could go anyplace on a vacation, where would you go? Why?
8. Do you take any lessons?
9. Do you have any hobbies?
10. Do you like your first name? If not, what would you change it to?

Write these questions on the chalkboard and tell the students each to choose a person whom they do not know very well and, using the ten questions as a guide, learn as much as they can about their partner. After ten minutes, ask each pair to separate but stay within viewing distance and draw their partners. These portraits are later shared and displayed. The next step consists of the pairs drawing a map of how to walk to each other's homes (used only for students old enough to understand the streets in their neighborhood). The final step is for each student to share the information about their partner with the rest of the class. Because you are a group member, you should participate in this activity.

Another approach to interviewing also begins by developing a list of questions students might ask each other. These questions are written on the board and referred to as students interview each other in pairs. After these questions have been asked, each pair of students joins with another pair. The four children share the new information they have learned about their partners. After a few minutes, ask the class to reconvene and request each person to share five things about his or her partner with the class.

A third interviewing technique has a student sit in a place of honor at the front of the classroom. The student is asked questions by the other class members. Students enjoy being in the limelight and often state that this is their favorite approach to interviewing.

A final interviewing approach has several students serve as reporters. They interview their peers and obtain such information as where students were born; the number of members in their families; a student's favorite television show, food, color, or animal; a special hobby or pet; any unusual places they have visited; and students' future goals. The teacher tabulates the information and either duplicates it and gives it to each student or makes a large chart in the hall for other classes to read.

The results of these interviewing activities can often be seen in new friendships and more open communication in the classroom. This atmosphere in turn makes the classroom a safer and more relaxed learning environment for students.

Guess Who?

An acquaintance activity used by a number of secondary teachers gives students an opportunity to discover how well they know their peers. The steps for setting up this activity are as follows:

1. Briefly describe the activity to the students and elicit their willingness to take part in the activity.
2. Ask students to write brief (two- or three-line) statements about themselves, which can include facts about their personal histories, family, hobbies, and so forth.
3. Collect all the autobiographical statements.
4. Ask each student to take out paper and pencil. Read each description and ask the students (you, too, should be involved) to write the name of the student they believe wrote the description.
5. After all the descriptions have been read, reread them and ask the authors to identify themselves. Ask the students to indicate on the list whether they made the correct choice. On completing the task, you may ask students to indicate the number of their peers whom they correctly identified. These results can be used to initiate a discussion about the degree to which class members have become acquainted.
6. An interesting alternative to this activity is to have students write brief statements that include one false statement about themselves. Then give the class the student's name and personal description and ask them to decide which statement is false. This activity can be performed by the entire group or can be developed as a contest between two groups.
7. A second variation of this activity is to have students write poems or riddles about themselves. These poems are put into a box. Each student draws a poem from the box and reads it aloud to the class. Based on the information in the

poem, the class tries to identify the author of the poem. As a follow-up, students could draw self-portraits that could be placed on a bulletin board with their poems below them.

Who Are We?

In this activity, students are given a 5-by-7-inch index card and asked to complete the following information.

1. Write your student ID number on the top line of the card
2. On the same side of the card make three columns
3. Label the first column "interests" and list three interests you have
4. Label the second column "journeys" and list three journeys you have made
5. Label the third column "facts" and list three facts about yourself others in the class might not know
6. On the blank side of the card, create a collage containing images that represent you, your interests, things you like, things you do, and things you want to do.

These are then hung where students can see them. During warm-ups or as part of group activity students are asked to guess who is represented by each card.

Having students know and feel supported by their peers is valuable at all grade levels, but it may be particularly critical as young people move through early adolescence. Students in grades six through eight are experiencing rapid cognitive and physical changes. This is a time of heightened self-consciousness and decreased self-esteem. Consequently, students learn much more effectively in environments in which teacher–student and peer relationships are characterized by warmth, support, and stability. Schools for young adolescents should not only use a wide range of acquaintance activities but should also be organized so that students spend a sizable portion of the schoolday with students and teachers whom they know. Lipsitz (1984) described successful schools for young adolescents:

> The groups of students are small enough that, as the teachers and paraprofessionals in the schools say, they know the students' moods and do not make the interpersonal mistakes that would be unavoidable in large, more impersonal settings. The students are secure in being known, and staff members are relaxed because of their deep familiarity with the students and their confidence in dealing with them. . . . The schools have adopted policies that strengthen and stabilize peer groupings by extending the time students remain together, both during the day and also over a period of several years. . . . Antisocial behavior that results from the randomness and brevity of student groupings in most secondary schools is substantially reduced in these schools. (p. 182)

T-Shirt

One of the senior author's favorite acquaintance activities is providing students with an 8½-by-11-inch sheet of paper with the outline of a T-shirt drawn on it. Students are asked to design a T-shirt they could wear to school that would help others know them better. For middle and high school students, the author usually indicates that the T-shirt should include materials the students could show the principal and their grandmothers. Students are told they can draw, sketch, write, or make displays—however they are most comfortable. Colored pencils are provided. When students have completed their designs, they share these in groups of four. After these groups have shared, students can form new groups of four.

Concentric Circles

Students are given sheets of paper with three concentric circles. They are asked to interview someone and to place interests, personal characteristics, and so forth that both partners share in the center area and to select one of the outer spaces and place those that are unique to them in that space. Students are then asked to switch partners, to share what they wrote in their space with their new partner, and to find additional overlapping interests. This usually continues for four rotations. The class is then asked to share areas in which they were pleased or surprised to find someone with a similar interest and to report any topic they alone listed. The class then checks to see if anyone in the class had listed that area.

Blue Ribbon Kid

This activity is appropriate in an elementary school classroom or middle school block class. On Friday a child's name is drawn and this student is given a piece of white butcher paper. The child takes this home and has a parent, guardian, or friend trace an outline of the student's body on the paper. The "paper doll" is cut out, colored in an outfit the student selects and brought back to school on Monday. During the weekend, the child is asked to collect artifacts that represent her or him (a table is available on which students place these items). On Monday, the student hangs the paper person on the bulletin board and the class gathers to listen to the child describe the artifacts she or he has brought. These often include pictures of family members and pets, and pictures cut from magazines that depict the student's interests. Throughout the week the class writes positive statements about the student and places these on the paper doll. On Friday, the child takes all the materials home and a new student is selected. It is important that the teacher is also part of the process of being selected and writing positive statements.

Shoe Box or Paper Bag

Students are given a shoe box covered with butcher paper or a paper bag. One approach is to provide the students with a lesson on drawing portraits and have them draw and paint self-portraits on the lids of their shoe boxes. The students take their boxes or bags home and place in them five items they select to represent them. Students are asked to be sure these items are appropriate for sharing at school—they might include pictures of their families, a golfball indicating they like to play golf, a soccer shoe, and so on. Each day during the following several weeks a few students share their items. If you have had students draw portraits, the boxes are kept in the room and shared with the parents at back-to-school night.

Incorporating Acquaintance Activities into Course Content

Especially in secondary school classrooms where mastery of content and preparing for state and national assessments within a limited time frame have, in many school settings, become central goals, whenever possible it is beneficial to integrate acquaintance activities into the content. We know a high school social studies teacher who has students develop a time line of significant events in their lives and bring artifacts that help others better understand each student. He connects this to classroom work emphasizing the use of time lines and artifacts within the context of history. We also know several high school English teachers who begin the year with Sandra Cisneros's (1991) short novel, *The House on Mango Street,* about a young girl growing up in a Latino neighborhood in Chicago. Early in the book the girl talks about her name, and the teachers use this as an opportunity for students to write about and share factors related to their names.

If you are interested in incorporating additional acquaintance activities into your lesson plans, you can find numerous resources. Especially useful are Borba's *Esteem Builders* (1989); Canfield and Siccone's *One Hundred Ways to Develop Student Self-Esteem and Responsibility* (1992); Gibbs's *Tribes: A New Way of Learning and Being Together* (2000); and Duval's *Building Character and Community in the Classroom* (1997).

PAUSE
4.3 *and Consider*

As a teacher you will make important decisions regarding the amount of time and types of activities you use to create a community of support in your classroom. Take a few minutes and write down the acquaintance activities you currently believe you would implement during the first three weeks of the school year. Highlight your favorite activity. Next, meet with a group of three or four colleagues or classmates who teach students at a grade level similar to the one you are teaching or observing and share your favorite activity. This should provide you with a wonderful array of activities for helping students become better acquainted.

ACTIVITIES FOR ESTABLISHING A COHESIVE, SUPPORTIVE GROUP

Group cohesiveness refers to the extent to which a group experiences a sense of identity, oneness, and esprit de corps. Cohesive groups are characterized by warm, friendly interactions among all members rather than by positive interchanges limited to small cliques within the group. Cohesive groups provide settings in which students feel safe, experience a sense of belonging, and view themselves as being liked and respected by others. Research (Lewis & St. John, 1974; Schmuck, 1966) indicates that students who are accepted by their classmates have more positive attitudes toward school and are more likely to achieve closer to their potential than are students who feel rejected and isolated. These findings are supported by other research (Combs & Taylor, 1952) that indicates that students perform less effectively when they feel threatened by the environment.

> Cohesiveness is correlated with the productivity of a group, provided the norms are supportive of production. Cohesive groups are more goal-directed than noncohesive groups, and as long as the goals of the individuals are in line with productivity, cohesiveness is a facilitating factor. Classroom groups which have strong goals have satisfied students. Moreover, students who know what is expected of them and who are involved and close to their peers in pursuing educational goals are more satisfied than students in classrooms that are disorganized and fragmented. (Schmuck & Schmuck, 1974, p. 31)

Group cohesiveness and a positive group identity do not develop simply because students spend time together. Rather, positive feelings about being a group member are developed by making the group seem attractive, distinguishing it from other groups, involving the group in cooperative enterprises, and helping students view themselves as important components in the group. The activities described in this section are designed to accomplish these goals. The activities are most effective when used in association with acquaintance activities and with activities for creating diverse liking patterns.

Activities aimed at creating a cohesive classroom group will be most effective when introduced at the beginning of the school year. One important reason for developing group cohesion early in the school year is that cohesive groups are desirable only if the group's norms support your learning goals. If you can begin the year by establishing a positive group feeling while creating norms that support academic achievement and productive behavior, the school year will be pleasant and productive.

Activities for Elementary School Classrooms

Ways of Having a Happy Classroom

Focusing on the positive qualities of a classroom sets a tone for the entire year. In the fall, ask students to list things they can do to make the classroom a happy place to be. Students can be encouraged to describe ways of positively interacting with each other, ideas for having fun in the classroom, and so on. The students' ideas can be written on a large sheet of paper and posted in the classroom. Every month, students can be asked whether they are acting in accordance with the ideas expressed on the chart and they can evaluate each item to see if it is still applicable. New ideas may be added at any time.

Group Contributions

To establish a cohesive classroom, it is important that students focus on their contributions to the group. This theme can be enhanced by creating a display of student contributions. Give each child paper, pencil, and crayons and ask him or her to draw a self-portrait. After these have been completed, ask students to think about what contribution they can make to the group. After you have led a short discussion to clarify the concept and provide students with ideas, give them a strip of paper and tell them to write down their contributions. Collect the pictures and contributions and mount them on a bulletin board for all to see. This is an excellent way of reinforcing the facts that everyone can contribute to the classroom and that the classroom will be a better place if all contribute some of their special talents.

Classroom Arrangements

Developing a comfortable classroom environment can enhance students' motivation and provide opportunities for increasing their sense of competence and power. It is desirable to involve students in decisions about the classroom arrangement whenever possible. Give them a basic floor plan of the room, including all built-ins. Then ask them to sketch in the desks and any other movable furniture in ways they think will facilitate smooth classroom operation. The arrangements can be displayed and the students and you can choose the floor plan with which all would be most comfortable. By giving students responsibility for a room arrangement, we indicate our respect for their judgment and they gain a sense of significance, competence, and power.

Students can also be active in decorating the room. They can be encouraged to take part in designing bulletin-board displays and determining the types of plants they would like in the room. Increased student involvement in organizing and decorating the room is almost always associated with an intensified group feeling, higher motivation, and reduced vandalism.

Class Spirit

At the beginning of the school year, most students are excited and motivated. Teachers can take advantage of this excitement by establishing a class spirit that creates a bond among the students. Many activities throughout the year can revolve around this class spirit.

To create a class spirit, teacher and students discuss the kinds of group identity they would like to develop and formulate a list. The list might include a class animal, name, flower, insect, song, flag, color, cheer, game, cartoon character, sport, bird, and poem. Suggestions are welcomed, and eventually students vote to determine their choices in each category. When the class spirit is completed, it is displayed proudly in a prominent place in the room.

It is very important to reinforce this activity by using parts of the class spirit whenever possible throughout the year. For example, when sending a newsletter to parents, we might draw several of the class symbols on the letter and copy the newsletter onto paper that is the class color. Similarly, giving the class cheer before special sporting events or singing the class song at the close of each week enhances class spirit.

Class History

An effective activity that helps mold students into a cohesive group is the development of a class history or class yearbook. When approached with this idea in the fall, students are always overwhelmingly in favor of making a class history.

Four to six students are chosen either by the teacher or by their peers to write the history, and all students are encouraged to contribute ideas. Every month, the history writers meet and decide what events, assemblies, new lessons, and so on they wish to incorporate into their class history. The historians then divide the writing assignments. At the end of the year, students have a collection of the year's events. In addition to these events, the class history can include poems written by students, a student directory of addresses and phone numbers, an autograph page, a page about students' thoughts on the year, and a letter written to the students by the teacher. The class history helps create a sense of group purposefulness and commitment and is a memorable treasure for each student.

Photo Album

Whenever a special event occurs, capture the moment in a photograph. Students can become actively involved by learning to use a camera. Pictures taken by students can be accompanied by written statements and put on the bulletin board until replaced by a picture and description of a new event. The old material can then be placed in the class photo album and some of the written material can be incorporated into the class history.

The photo album can be shown to parents during scheduled conferences or when a parent drops by the school. Parents enjoy seeing pictures of their children involved in special school activities. This sharing enhances parents' interest in their children's school experiences and increases parental support for the teacher and the school. When a particularly good picture of a child is obtained, the teacher can make a copy and send it to the parents along with a short note. Parents appreciate this thoughtful gesture, and their increased interest in their child's classroom experience helps their child develop a sense of pride and commitment.

When there are a few moments left in a day, it is enjoyable to recall several of the special events by looking at the pictures in the class photo album. This is an effective means of reinforcing a sense of identity and creating positive feelings about the class.

Opening and Closing Questions

Students arrive at school with many different feelings and needs. Some students may arrive in irritable moods resulting from an argument with a younger brother or lack of a proper breakfast. Another student's favorite goldfish may have died, while another child may be happy because it is his birthday. It is often hard for students to make the transition from home to school. Therefore, it is important that students be given a few minutes at the beginning of each day to share any events that are significant to them.

Students are asked to meet in a circle. The teacher then asks whether any person needs or wants to share anything. One student who has just broken her foot may need someone to carry her lunch tray, whereas another student whose dog just died may need some care and understanding. Teachers also have days when they are tired or not feeling well and, therefore, would like the students to be particularly quiet and helpful during the day. When students are treated kindly and their needs are accepted and respected, they will respond to your needs and desires.

For students who are less comfortable sharing their needs in a group, an optional activity is to have them write down their needs and place them in a box or bag. You can check several times during the day to see whether any child has put a need in the box.

The end of the schoolday can be an important time to establish closure on any issues that occurred during the day. Questions such as "What did you learn today?" "How do you feel about the day?" or "What did you like and dislike about today?" often evoke serious discussion. It is advisable to allow at least ten minutes for this session. Taking time at the end of each day encourages students to examine what they have accomplished and also helps to ensure that the day will end on a positive note.

Special Days

Assigning special days allows students to have some influence over their environment while enhancing a sense of group identity. Special days might include a day on which everyone wears the same color, a day for wearing favorite buttons, a day for dressing as students did during the 1950s, a day when everyone wears his or her favorite hat, and so on. You can add to the special day by relating various subjects to the day's theme. Math problems to solve batting averages could be included on uniform day, music of famous singers during the rock'n'roll era might be discussed and listened to during music class on 1950s day, or students might read stories involving hats on hat day.

My School Bulletin Board

Creating a cohesive group is very important, but it is often useful to expand this concept beyond the classroom. One way to do so is to have students make a hall display or decorate a bulletin board with the theme "What I Like about My School." Use pictures, essays, or a collage. This activity enhances school spirit and focuses on the positive aspects of a school. This concept can be extended to include a large hall mural with the same theme to which each class contributes their ideas about why they like their school.

Service Projects

Students can build a sense of community by solving a common problem or sharing in assisting others. One of the first experiments in group dynamics, the classic Sherif experiment conducted in 1958, showed that groups of students who were in conflict could become unified when they experienced a common need to solve a problem. Similarly, a classroom group who mentors a group of younger students, works to beautify the school, or assists in solving a problem or providing assistance in the community will almost always develop a closer bond.

Activities for Secondary Classrooms

Because secondary school students spend considerably less time in one classroom group, most secondary teachers choose to incorporate fewer activities for enhancing group cohesiveness. Instead, they tend to support several structured, group-cohesiveness activities with instructional activities, such as cooperative learning and peer editing, that emphasize creating positive peer relationships and active involvement in the learning process. The authors have found several activities and processes particularly valuable in helping secondary students develop skills in functioning as supportive group members.

Five Square

The five-square activity involves students cooperating to reach a goal, followed by systematically discussing the behaviors that facilitated or blocked the group's efforts. As described in Figure 4.4, students are placed in groups of five, and each group is given the task of passing puzzle pieces until each group member has an equal-sized square in front of him or her. Tell students that groups who complete their task can quietly observe groups still at work. Finally, if one or more groups has difficulty completing the task, members of these groups can raise a hand, signaling that they would like to be replaced by a student from a group that has completed the task. This student then joins the group still working and continues to follow the rules. The addition of a new member who has seen the correct pattern will usually facilitate quick task completion.

When all groups have completed the task, you can involve students in discussing the groups' functioning. On a chalkboard or butcher paper, make columns labeled "Behaviors That Facilitated Task Completion" and "Behaviors That Hindered the Group." Then ask students, without mentioning names, to describe behaviors that helped their group complete their task. Next, students can list behaviors that blocked their group. Then lead a discussion on group behavior. Interestingly, this activity may also highlight additional factors related to establishing effective learning environments. For example, when using the activity recently, a student in one of the author's classes indicated that he had experienced considerable anxiety when other students began watching his group. This comment led to a productive discussion on the advantages and disadvantages of anxiety in learning and a further discussion on how anxiety could be limited in the class.

FIGURE 4.4

The Five-Square Game

Preparation of Puzzle

A puzzle set consists of five envelopes containing pieces of stiff paper cut into patterns that will form six-inch squares, as shown in the diagram. Cut the squares into parts and lightly pencil the letters *a* through *j* as shown below. Then mark the envelopes *A* through *E* and distribute the pieces thus:

> Envelope A—j, h, e
> B—a, a, a, c
> C—a, i
> D—d, f
> E—g, b, f, a

Erase from the pieces the lowercase letters and write instead the envelope letters *A* through *E*, so that the pieces can easily be returned for reuse.

Several combinations of the pieces will form one or two squares, but only one combination will form five squares.

Instructions for Students

Each person should have an envelope containing pieces for forming squares. At the signal, the task of the group is to form five squares of equal size. The task is not complete until everyone has before him or her a perfect square and all the squares are of the same size. These are the rules: (1) No member may speak, (2) no member may signal in any way that he or she wants a card, and (3) members may give cards to others.

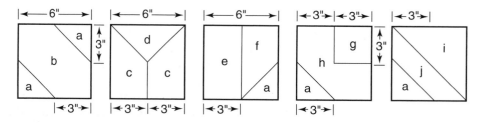

Even though this activity requires most of a class period, the authors and dozens of secondary teachers with whom the authors have worked have found that the benefits in terms of students' understanding how groups operate and appreciating the value of involving everyone in group activities far outweigh the time cost.

Group Contributions

A teacher of junior writing and American literature recently shared a technique for incorporating group cohesiveness activities. During the first week of school, she has the class brainstorm ways in which individuals contribute to the class as a whole. These are listed on the chalkboard and may include such statements as:

> Adding humor
> Listening carefully and quietly

Making perceptive observations
Contributing personal experiences
Bringing the group back to the topic being discussed
Asking someone to clarify a point
Summarizing
Asking questions
Helping people get along

This material is used to stimulate a discussion about how there are many ways of contributing to a class and how students will differ in their contributions. About a week later, pass out slips of paper with the name of a student on each slip. Each student in the class receives one slip and is asked to write one positive comment about a contribution the student listed on the slip has made to the class. The slips are handed in, and students volunteer to read several of them.

Tower Building

Divide the class into groups of four or five. Give each group a deck of cards and some tape (you may also use straws and paper clips). Students are told they have ten minutes to build the highest tower. As with the five-square activity, after teams have completed the activity, ask each team (beginning with the winning team and going in order to the team with the lowest tower) to describe one factor that facilitated their work. Place these on butcher paper. Next, reverse the process and have each team, beginning with the team who built the lowest structure, list one thing that occurred in their group that blocked the group's effectiveness. Finally, have the class discuss and summarize what they have learned about group functioning and how this can apply to their work in the class.

Paraphrasing Passport

An important component to creating a sense of cohesiveness is for all members of the group to be involved in academic learning. In many classrooms a relatively small number of students provide a majority of the answers. In addition, while students are speaking, other students are frequently considering what they want to say rather than thoughtfully listening to what their peers are saying. One method for helping students listen effectively to their peers is to periodically implement the procedure we call "paraphrasing passport." In this procedure, prior to providing a response, an individual must first paraphrase the statement made by the previous speaker. We have found this significantly increases the degree to which students respectfully listen to their peers.

Discussion Tokens and Discussion Records

Two additional methods we and teachers with whom we have worked have found effective in increasing the number of students actively involved in class discussions are "discussion tokens" and "discussion records." Discussion tokens involve providing students with a designated number of cards or tokens. These tokens have the student's name on them and are handed in each time the student speaks during a class discussion. One students have used their tokens, they must wait until other students have used at least one of their tokens before being reissued tokens. We have found this to be effective both during small- and large-group discussions. A somewhat different method used to obtain the same goal of increased participation of a wider range of students involves keeping a record of who speaks during class discussions. One method of accomplishing this is to assign a student as record-keeper. The record-keeper simply tallies who speaks and how often. In some cases we have created a coding sheet in which the record-keeper records information such as whether the student asked a question, made a short comment, reinforced someone's work, or provided an extensive answer. A powerful and fun activity for highlighting who is involved in discussions begins with having the students sit in a circle during the discussion. The teacher begins the discussion holding a ball of yarn and when she has made a comment, holds onto one end of the yarn and rolls the ball to the next speaker. After responding, that speaker also holds onto the yarn and rolls the ball to another speaker. This continues for the duration of the discussion. At the end the class can make observations about the pattern of involvement.

Group Decision Making

Group cohesiveness may also be enhanced by involving students in shared decision making about classroom organizational factors or problems. As discussed in Chapter 7, students can cooperatively develop classroom rules and procedures. As discussed in Chapter 9, teachers can work with students to resolve problems that arise. Recently, a friend reported that he had been working with his junior English class to resolve the problem of student papers being late. The teacher stated that more than half his class worked part time and several teachers were requiring that major projects be due on the same day. The teacher and his students collected data on due dates for each student's assignments and developed a series of due dates that was approved by all students in the class.

"I've brought along a jury of my peers."

Using Base Groups

In his book, *Building Community in Schools*, Thomas Sergiovanni (1994) discussed the importance of creating some form of "primary-group network of relationships" (p. 127) within school settings. Similarly, in his book, *The Quality School*, William Glasser (1990) suggested that, after elementary school, more than half of all students are not friends with students doing well in school. Given the lack of community experienced by many youth today and the fact that these youth are often seeking this sense of community in gangs, it seems critical that schools consider ways to create positive, supportive peer groups in the classroom.

One method the authors have found particularly helpful is the formation of base groups. As defined here, a *base group* is a group of four students who support each other for either a term or a year. Like a cooperative group, a base group is heterogeneous with regard to gender and ethnicity, as well as how successful students are with the course content. Since the base group will stay together for an extended period of time, many teachers have found that it is worth the time to allow students some input into the makeup of their group. This can be done by asking students to list three or four students they would like to have in their group and perhaps one student with whom they would prefer not to work. Although developing groups takes longer when this information is used, the groups initially function much more smoothly and it appears well worth the initial investment.

The group is not intended to be a cooperative group that works together on specific course projects. Instead, the group meets several times a week for five to fifteen minutes to check on everyone's content mastery and progress. If someone is absent, a member of the base group collects assignments and is prepared to assist the absent student. If a student is absent for several days, a member of the base group might call and tell the student that she is missed and ask if any help is needed. If a member of the base group is having difficulty with content, the group can help tutor the student. This may take place during a lengthened base group session or at times arranged by the students. If a student fails to respond to this assistance or is failing to make a good effort in class, the base group can ask for the teacher's assistance.

Base groups can also be used to check homework assignments, to ensure that everyone has adequate notes or materials prior to a test or major assignment, and even to provide study groups for tests or daily assignments. At the very least, the base group provides a setting in which at least three members of the class are concerned about each student's learning. This helps create a sense of each student being known and valued in the class—a key prerequisite to learning for many students.

Prior to using base groups, it is important that the teacher first clearly outline the group's roles and assist the students in getting to know each other. Second, the teacher must initially provide some structure for the base groups. For example, members of a base group can be asked to go over each student's assignment sheet or to examine each student's goal sheet or portfolio to ensure that everyone understands the work or is making adequate progress. Base groups are particularly valuable for field-dependent learners and students new to a class, but they help all students learn to work as a team and to develop empathy and communication skills.

P A U S E

4.4 *and Consider*

Pause for a moment and make a list of activities you could use to increase your students' sense of group cohesiveness. Highlight your favorite activity. Next, meet with a group of three or four colleagues or classmates who teach students at a grade level similar to the one you are teaching or observing and share your favorite activity. If there are several groups completing this task, share your group's favorite activity with the larger group.

ACTIVITIES FOR ENHANCING DIVERSE LIKING PATTERNS

You have undoubtedly been involved in groups in which everyone was comfortable with and enjoyed every group member. Whether it was an extended family, school staff, religious group, or group of close friends, you probably looked forward to being with this group and found that the group supported personal and intellectual growth. Compare this experience with working in a group characterized by cliques and numerous isolated individuals. Anyone who has been unfortunate enough to work in such a group knows that it is much less supportive of creativity, risk taking, and productivity.

Students are similar to adults in that they are happier and more productive in environments that provide warmth and friendship. The Lewis and St. John (1974) study discussed earlier in this chapter indicated that the presence of high-achieving students was not in itself enough to increase achievement among lower-achieving students. In addition to being exposed to norms that supported academic achievement, the lower-achieving students needed to be accepted as friends by their classmates. When students believe they are liked by their peers, they experience a sense of significance, belonging, safety, and respect of others. Unless these basic personal needs are met, students will have less energy to expend in learning.

The activities described in this section increase the likelihood that all children in the classroom will be liked and accepted by their peers. Though it is important to use several of these activities early in the school year, we should reinforce positive peer interactions by using activities such as these throughout the school year.

As with the activities connected with helping students become better acquainted and building group cohesiveness, elementary and middle school teachers will be most likely to use the specific activities described in this section. Because teachers in kindergarten through eighth grade work with groups of students longer, it is appropriate that they spend more time involving students in activities encouraging positive peer relationships and improved self-esteem. Secondary teachers will find that by incorporating the methods described in the previous section, student friendships will become more widespread and cliquishness will be reduced. These results are more likely to occur if elementary and middle school teachers have used activities such as those found on the following pages.

Good Deeds Tree

To build on the theme of helping others, a large paper tree or branch is placed on the bulletin board. Students are asked to pay special attention to the nice things people say and do. Whenever they see something nice being done, students write down what happened on a leaf made of green paper and pin it to the tree. The result is a tree full of leaves and a room filled with happy children.

Variations of this activity can be created by using pumpkins in a pumpkin patch at Halloween or shamrocks in a field near St. Patrick's Day. When working with children who cannot write their responses, set aside several times a day to ask children to list nice things they have seen or heard. Write these on the appropriate paper and allow the children to pin them on the bulletin board.

Wanted Posters

Another activity that helps create an environment of warmth and friendship is construction of Wanted posters. Students are given a piece of parchment paper. An adult burns the edge of the paper to make it look like a poster from the old West. Students print the word WANTED on the paper. Next, a student mounts a picture of himself in the center and writes the phrase FOR A FRIEND BECAUSE . . . underneath the picture. Around the picture each student writes words describing the qualities that make her or him a good friend. A piece of tagboard or brown construction paper can be used as a backing or support. A discussion about friendship and an opportunity to share the posters should follow this activity.

Warm Fuzzies

People enjoy receiving compliments. Everyone likes to receive positive attention and recognition in the form of a warm smile, physical touch, or kind word. Unfortunately, children often receive more criticism and frowns than compliments and smiles. In response to this situation, Claude Steiner (1977) wrote a children's book entitled *The Original Warm Fuzzy Tale*. This delightful story can be read to students of all ages. After reading the story, you can lead a discussion that helps students clearly understand the concepts of warm fuzzies and cold pricklies and how they make people feel. Following this discussion, students will often initiate the idea of giving warm fuzzies to each other.

One approach to helping children learn to be more positive with their classmates is to make warm fuzzies. Warm fuzzies can be made by wrapping yarn around one's fingers several times. The wrapped yarn is then tied in the middle and the ends are cut off. The ends are then fluffed up and a warm fuzzy has been created. After students have made a warm fuzzy, they are asked to think of a reason they deserve a warm fuzzy. Students are encouraged to share their reasons. Each student then keeps his first fuzzy. The class should continue making fuzzies until each child has between five and ten fuzzies. To conclude this activity, students can be asked to give a fuzzy to a friend. When giving a fuzzy, students are asked to tell the reason it is being given. Even though the teacher may choose to set time aside daily to hand out fuzzies, students should also be encouraged to give a fuzzy whenever they wish.

Another way to give warm fuzzies is to have a Fuzzy Box where students place positive notes about their peers (students often choose to attach a warm fuzzy to their note). These notes can be read aloud during the last few minutes of the day. Students enjoy receiving compliments in front of their peers.

Valentine Booklets

Another activity that encourages sharing positive feelings is creating Valentine booklets. Give each child a Valentine's Day booklet with their name on it cut in the shape of a heart. The front and rear covers are red hearts, and the inside pages are white hearts. There should be as many white heart pages as there are members in the class (including the teacher). A booklet is created by punching each heart and attaching the pages with string.

Students sit in a circle with their Valentine booklets on their laps. Ask the children to pass their books to the person on their right. Students then write a nice phrase about the person whose booklet they receive. When you or the timekeeper see that each child has finished writing, speak the phrase "Pass to the right" again. This activity continues until the students all have their own booklets again. It takes about one hour to complete, but the results are worth the time spent. Students enjoy this activity and are often seen reading through their booklets when they need a lift.

This activity can be used in association with a variety of special days. Shamrock books can be used on St. Patrick's Day, and the words *I am lucky to know Scott because*... written on the outside. Similarly, booklets can be developed around the theme of being thankful at Thanksgiving, and special qualities each student possesses that will help that student succeed can be used as a theme on a holiday celebrating the birthday of a famous person.

Secret-Pal Books

Positive communication is vital in a classroom. The secret-pal book activity is a strategy for increasing positive communication. On Monday, each child draws the name of another student. During the week, the students observe the nice things that they see their secret pals doing and write these in their secret-pal books. These books can be made of colored construction paper covers and plain white pages. Students can be encouraged to decorate the books by drawing pictures, writing positive adjectives that describe their secret pal, or writing a word that begins with each letter of the child's name (e.g., Brian: B = brave, R = responsible, I = interesting, A = athletic, N = neat). On Friday, students reveal their secret pals and present them with their books. Students enjoy this activity very much and always look forward to finding out who their new secret pal will be.

A daily variation in the week-long secret-pal books involves having children write their own names on a "secret-pal smiley face." These faces are placed in a basket and each child draws one, making sure that it is not his or her own name. Throughout the day, each child watches the secret pal and writes down two or three friendly or helpful things the child observes the secret pal doing. At the end of the day, the secret pals are revealed and the smiley faces may be taken home.

I-Booklet

Each child cuts eight capital *I* letters out of colored construction paper. The students use the first *I* to decorate a cover using their names in colored cutout pieces of construction paper. On the first page of the book, the children focus on their names by writing them in as many unusual ways as possible. On the second page, the students illustrate favorite things, such as food, toys, colors, friends, television shows, and so on. On the third page, the students draw pictures of things they like to experience with each of their five senses. On page 4, ask students to think about the seasons and what they enjoy doing on the weekends during the various seasons. They can either cut out pictures or draw favorite activities for each season. The next page is devoted to pictures of their families, their houses, special friends, pets, and something special their family enjoys doing, such as camping. On the sixth page of the book, the *I* is divided into black and white, representing night and day. Students draw several things they do during the day and several things they do in the evening. Page 7 focuses on facts about the students, such as age, height, address, brothers and sisters, or pets. On the last page, students write poems about themselves, list positive words that describe them, or write stories about themselves. When all the *I* pages are completed, they can be assembled to form an I-booklet. These booklets should be shared with other classmates. Unlimited topics can be chosen to form these booklets, and topics should be adjusted according to grade level. For primary students, you could have a laminated person in jeans but without hair or eye color. Each week a student's name is drawn and the child colors in his eyes and hair on the laminated figure. The chosen child adds patches to the jeans with titles such as height, weight, favorite color, favorite food, phone number, address, or friends, and fills in the patch with the designated information.

Positive Bombardment

Positive self-concepts are sustained and strengthened in an atmosphere of trust and security. When this type of environment has been established, a positive bombardment can be effectively used. This activity can be implemented in a variety of ways. One technique is to have a child seated on a stool in a circle. The students take turns sharing reasons they like or respect the person being bombarded. Once students have become familiar with this activity and have learned how to give specific, positive feedback, the positive bombardments can take place in small groups. Students can now assume greater responsibility for the activity, and more children can become involved in a shorter time.

Another alternative is to choose a theme such as *I felt really happy when you . . .* or *You really are a friend because . . .* and have students complete the phrase as they talk to the person being bombarded. Positive bombardments can also be used as an ending to class discussions or class meetings. For example, children can be asked to make one nice statement to the person seated on either side of them.

Student Directory

Almost all students have special interests and abilities about which they feel confident. When students feel comfortable in the classroom, they will often be excited about sharing their expertise with their peers. The creation of a student directory is an activity designed to help students identify their strengths and encourage them to use each other as resources.

Students are asked to identify the activities or skills they believe they perform effectively enough to teach another child. These topics should not be limited to school subjects. They may include skills such as basketball dribbling, downhill skiing, working with dogs, model rocketry, borrowing in subtraction, organizing desks, writing a report, or calligraphy. These lists are collected, tabulated, and placed in alphabetical order with the name(s) of the student(s) listed after each skill. The student directory is typed up and each student receives a copy. A directory is also placed in the front of the room for use by the students. The directory can be a valuable tool for a child who needs assistance with a topic. Students will often use this directory as a way to improve their skills by asking an expert to help them.

The "I Can" Can

The "I can" activity provides students with a visible means of becoming aware of their successes and achievements. Give all children a soup or coffee can and ask them to decorate the cans in some way that represents themselves, such as favorite color, activities, or hobbies. Next, students write the words *I CAN* on their can. Each time students master a new skill, they write the mastered skill on a piece of paper, roll it up like a scroll, tie it with ribbon, and place it in their cans. Periodically, the students should take their cans home and share their successes with their parents.

Social Skills Training Programs

Another increasingly popular approach to creating positive peer relationships and integrating isolated or aggressive children into their peer group involves implementing social skills and problem-solving training activities with the entire class. In its simplest form, social skills training can be accomplished by instructing students in many of the skills described in Chapters 3, 4, and 9 of this book. For example, we could instruct children in sending I-messages and warm fuzzies. Students could practice these skills as a group and be encouraged to use them frequently in their daily classroom interactions. Similarly, we can teach students active listening (Chapter 3) and problem-solving skills (Chapter 9).

There are several advantages to using social skills training in the classroom or other school-group setting. First, youngsters generally find a group setting more attractive than individual work. Second, a group makes better use of the teacher's or counselor's time. Third, the group provides diverse models and an opportunity for students to receive feedback from peers. Fourth, the group provides an opportunity for students to teach each other, thus facilitating development of their own social competence.

The recommended readings at the end of the chapter include several excellent resources for group social skill training. As discussed in Chapter 10, it is important to realize, however, that some students will require individual social skill training in response to very specific problems they are experiencing.

SCHOOL CLIMATE

Improving the classroom climate by systematically monitoring and improving the quality of teacher–student and peer relationships will do much to create positive student behavior and increased achievement. Students' and teachers' attitudes and behaviors are also affected, however, by the quality of life in the school at large.

The importance of classroom and school climate was emphasized by John Goodlad (1984). He and his colleagues studied thirty-eight schools in seven regions across the country. The study involved interviews with all thirty-eight principals, 1,350 teachers, 8,624 parents, and 17,163 students, as well as intensive observations in 1,016 classrooms. Analyzing the results of this study, Goodlad reported that schools differed very little in the type of instruction found within classes. He reported, though, that differences in student achievement were found. Goodlad (1983b) summarized these findings.

> I have used the adjectives, "healthy," "satisfying," and "renewing" to describe schools in our sample that pay more than average attention to the quality of interactions among those inhabiting the school and to the physical and social context in which those interactions occur. . . . Schools differed in their ability to create an academic ambience, but the differences appear to be more related to school and classroom climate factors than to methods of teaching per se. (p. 555)

More specifically, Wayson and Pinnell (1982) cited a variety of studies to support their contention that "eight features of schools have a strong relationship to the quality of discipline" (p. 118).

1. Patterns of communication, problem solving, and decision making
2. Patterns of authority and status
3. Procedures for developing and implementing rules
4. Student belongingness
5. Relationships with parents and community forces
6. Processes for dealing with personal problems
7. Curriculum and instructional practices
8. The physical environment (p. 118)

In their study of twelve London high schools, reported in *Fifteen Thousand Hours*, Rutter, Maughan, Mortimer, Ouston, and Smith (1979) reported that a variety of schoolwide factors differentiated schools with positive student behavior and high achievement from schools facing serious problems in these areas. Factors within the school's control that significantly influenced students' behavior and performance included the degree to which teachers emphasized academic achievement; teachers' organizational, instructional, and classroom management skills; high teacher expectations about students' performance; teachers' willingness to see students about problems at any time; an emphasis on rewards rather than punishments; teachers' involvement in decision making and the associated consistency in teachers' expectations and behavior; and students' involvement in positions of responsibility within the school. Rutter and his associates concluded that "the pattern of findings suggested that not only were pupils influenced by the way they were dealt with as individuals, but also there was a group influence resulting from the ethos of the school as a social institution" (p. 205).

The factors described by Wayson, Pinnell, and Rutter and his colleagues have also been reported in three books whose authors conducted ecological analyses of effective secondary schools. Joan Lipsitz's (1984) analysis of four high-quality middle schools reported in *Successful Schools for Young Adolescents*; Sarah Lawrence Lightfoot's (1983) study of six high schools, *The Good High School*; and Wehlage, Rutter, Smith, Lesko, and Fernandez's (1989) *Reducing the Risk: Schools as Communities of Support*, a study of secondary school programs successful for serving high at-risk youth, offer thoughtful portraits of secondary schools that are serving youths well.

More recently, numerous authors have pointed to the importance of increasing student achievement and reducing violence by creating school environments characterized by students' believing they are known and liked by their teachers and peers (Jones, 2002; Noddings, 1992; Noguera, 1995; Schmuck & Schmuck, 2001). Recent work points to the benefits of smaller schools (Duke & Trautvetter, 2001; Keller, 2000; Lee & Loeb, 2000; Wasley et al., 2000). In her book, *The Right to Learn*, Linda Darling-Hammond (1997) highlights the importance of supportive interpersonal relationships in creating environments that enhance student motivation and learning. When students are involved in smaller school settings in which they are actively engaged as meaningful participants in both the classroom and school setting, schools become settings in which a wider range of students experience success and fewer students experience the anger and frustration that underlie violent behavior.

The important point is that teachers should work together to consider not only how their classroom management and instruction influence students' behaviors and achievements but also how the school environment can be altered to encourage positive student attitudes. This can prove to be an exciting, cooperative project that effectively and creatively uses teachers' creativity and concern for students. The authors have taught in and worked with schools in which a committee consisting of students and teachers was established to generate ideas for improving school climate. Figure 4.5 offers some examples of positive school climate activities initiated by these committees.

Issues Related to Peer Harassment and Bullying

Juvonen and Graham (2001) define peer harassment as:

> victimization that entails face-to-face confrontation (e.g., physical aggression, verbal abuse, nonverbal gesturing) or social manipulation through a third party (e.g., social ostracism, spreading of rumors). The crucial element that distinguishes peer harassment from other types of negative encounters, such as conflict, is that there is an imbalance of power between perpetrator and target. (p. xiii)

FIGURE 4.5
Activities for Creating a Positive School Climate

1. Take pictures of students (including those with a history of school problems) involved in positive behavior. Enlarge these and post them in the hallway.
2. Hold assemblies at least each quarter to reinforce positive student accomplishments. Emphasize improvement as well as standard excellent achievement.
3. Involve students in beautifying the school. Plant flowers around the outside of the school.
4. Provide a space in the hallway where teachers can post positive comments about students and students can write positive statements about their teachers.
5. Create an award (a stuffed turtle or giraffe works nicely) to be presented each week to the staff member who stuck his or her neck out to help students. The recipient initially can be selected by the school climate committee with subsequent selection made by the previous recipient.
6. Involve students and staff in a fund-raising activity, such as a jog-a-thon, with proceeds going to a local charity or other worthy cause.
7. Rather than have an attendance officer call absent students, have an adult with whom the student relates well call.
8. Involve the entire school in a day-long evaluation of the school, with ideas generated to resolve problems and make the school even better.
9. Set aside some time each day or week when everyone in the school stops what they are doing and reads quietly.
10. At the end of each day, have everyone in the school write on a 3-by-5 inch card one positive experience they had that day.
11. Release teachers to spend a day experiencing the same schedule as a student who is having an unsuccessful school experience. Have the teachers report to the faculty what they saw, how they felt, and any suggestions they have for making the school a better place for that student to learn.
12. Encourage the school staff to write notes to their colleagues whenever they observe a colleague involved in an especially helpful or thoughtful interaction with a student or staff member.

The term *bullying* is often used interchangeably with the term *peer harassment.*

Bullying is a serious problem in many schools. Barone (1997) reports that whereas teachers in the schools he sampled believed approximately 16 percent of students were victims of bullying, nearly 60 percent of students reported they had been bullied. This general lack of awareness by staff was reported in a Canadian study in which researchers observed bullying on the playground (Craig & Pepler, 1996). These researchers reported that duty teachers on the playground were aware of only 17 percent of bullying events and responded to only 23 percent of bullying they observed. Thus, teachers responded to only 3.9 percent of actual bullying events.

Implementing the types of peer relationship activities described throughout this chapter will often help to reduce negative peer interactions, including bullying. Another approach to preventing bullying in a school setting is to implement schoolwide programs aimed at helping students develop empathy for their peers and improved skills in interacting with others. There are a number of programs available to assist students in this area. The authors have worked to reduce bullying with numerous schools, and one of the authors teaches in an elementary school that has implemented the Second Step Violence Prevention Program. The program is "organized around three areas of social-emotional competency: empathy, impulse control, and anger management" (Frey, Hirschstein, & Guzzo, 2000). Research (Grossman et al., 1997) involving observations in classroom and on playgrounds suggests this program reduces students' aggressive behaviors and increases socially desirable behaviors. The Second Step Violence Prevention Program is available for grades preschool/kindergarten, grades one through three, grades four and five, and grades six through eight.

The authors have also worked with school staff who have been impressed with the positive effects of a program called Peace Builders. This program is designed for students in kindergarten through fifth grade and includes sections entitled praise people, give up put-downs, seek wise people, notice and speak up about hurts, and right wrongs. This program incorporates a school pledge; a school song; and language emphasizing positive, peaceful behavior that is taught to students. The curriculum is provided in both English and Spanish.

An excellent curriculum for preventing harassment and bullying has been developed by the staff at the Linn-Benton-Lincoln Education Service District in Albany, Oregon. This curriculum, entitled, Harassment Prevention Curriculum: Empowerment and Skill-Building for Student Safety can be obtained by writing this organization at 905 Fourth Avenue SE, Albany, Oregon, 97321-3199. Another curriculum the authors believe is effective is PATHS: the Promoting Alternative THinking Strategies program (Kusche & Greenberg, 2000). This program provides programs for both kindergarten and grades one through six focused on increasing students' emotional competency. If you are interested in a thorough examination of current programs, Greenberg, Domitrovich, and Bumbarger (2001) have provided an excellent review of research related to programs for improving students' social skills and mental health.

Bullying is also influenced by the manner in which adults and students respond to this type of behavior. In Chapter 8, we discuss approaches for responding to bullying behavior in ways that both protect and support the victim and provide effective skill development for the student involved in bullying behavior.

ACTIVITIES FOR EXAMINING PEER RELATIONSHIPS IN THE CLASSROOM

There are three basic methods of determining the degree to which children in the class are accepted by and feel involved in the classroom group. One method is the sociometric test for determining which students are most frequently chosen by other students as desired work or play partners. To collect these data, students can be asked to list (younger children may tell you their choices) the two students in the classroom with whom they would like to eat lunch, work on a school project, or do some other activity.

Students can also be asked to list three students they like best and three students they know least well in the classroom. You may also wish to add questions such as who the students would most like to work with in a group in order to examine the difference between students being liked versus those valued as colleagues. By creating a matrix with the student listed on the vertical rows and vertical columns for tabulating the number of times each student was listed as well liked, not well known, or desired as a group member, you will develop a sense of who are the well-liked versus the isolated students.

A second method for examining the group dynamics in a classroom is to create a sociogram by actually recording the instance in which students interact with each other in the classroom. One method for accomplishing this involves simply creating a classroom map and drawing arrows indicating when one student makes contact with another student. These arrows can show direction (who initiated the contact) as well as the positive or negative nature of the contact (a plus or minus sign written near the arrow). This can provide an accurate picture of the general types of interactions taking place in your classroom and which students are most likely to be receiving and sending positive or negative interactions. A sociogram can also be developed by observing a class for a time and recording every instance in which a child has a positive or negative interaction with another child. This method has the advantage of providing an indication of the actual interaction patterns in a classroom.

The third method for determining students' feelings about their position in the classroom group as well as their general feelings about the group is to develop a questionnaire that allows them to report their feelings about the group. The advantage of this approach is that it can provide more detailed information than is available through a sociometric test or observation. The main problem with this approach is that students must experience fairly high degree of trust before they will accurately report the information. Even during the initial stages of group development, however, this approach will often reveal useful information. Figure 4.6 is an example of a questionnaire that can be used at several grade levels.

Once you have discovered the dynamics in the classroom, the next step is to implement activities that create more positive peer relationships and group norms. As discussed in this chapter, there are several methods for developing positive peer relationships in the classroom. You can begin the school year by helping students become better acquainted with their peers. This endeavor can be accompanied by activities that create a class spirit and positive group identity. Throughout the year, support these activities by involving students in other activities aimed at building friendships. You can also enhance positive peer relationships by implementing instructional strategies such as peer tutoring and cooperative learning, which reinforce the value of supportive peer interactions. Finally, use problem-solving approaches focused on helping peers resolve their own conflicts.

Please answer these questions as carefully as you can.

FIGURE 4.6
Group
Assessment
Questionnaire

1. Do you like being in this class? _____ _____
   Yes No
   Why? _____

2. Would you say that you are a leader or a follower in this class?
   (Circle your answer in red)   Leader   Follower

3. Would you rather be the opposite of the answer that you gave in question 2?
   (Circle your answer in green)   Yes   No   Maybe

4. Do you listen to people in our class?
   (Circle your answer in yellow)   Usually   Sometimes   Seldom

5. Do other children listen to you when you are talking? _____ _____
   Yes No

6. Are you comfortable helping people in this class?

   _____ _____ _____
   Yes No Sometimes

7. Are you comfortable asking for help from class members?

   _____ _____ _____
   Yes No Sometimes

8. Name three things that you contribute to our group.
   a.
   b.
   c.

   HELP?!!

9. Name two things you would like to contribute to our group.
   a.
   b.

10. How do you feel about the students in your class?
    _____ I like all the students.
    (Check in blue) _____ I like most of the students.
    _____ I like only a few students.

11. Do the students like you?
    _____ Most of the students like me.
    (Check in orange) _____ Some of the students like me.
    _____ I don't think the students like me very much.

12. Do you have friends to sit with at lunch? _____ _____
    Yes No

(continued)

FIGURE 4.6
Continued

13. When you are at recess, do members of this class let you play with them?

　　　　　　　　　　　　　　　　　 _____　 _____　 _____
　　　　　　　　　　　　　　　　　　Yes　　　No　　Sometimes

14. If you could change one thing about the people in this class, what would you change? _____

Thank you for filling out this questionnaire.

SUMMARY

Prior to the recent focus on cooperative learning, the quality of peer relationships was perhaps the most underestimated factor influencing student behavior and achievement. The emphasis on achievement test scores and the associated concern with covering content led even some teachers who valued and were comfortable with their role in creating positive peer relationships to view time spent on building positive, supportive peer relationships as a luxury they could not afford. Many lessons learned in school programs for at-risk children and youth during the late 1960s and 1970s were apparently forgotten with the focus on on-task behavior, direct instruction, and achievement test scores.

Fortunately, recent research on cooperative learning has again provided an impetus for teachers to consider the creation of positive peer relationships as an important variable influencing student behavior and learning. Hopefully, today teachers are increasingly provided with information about the importance of selecting a range of methods for creating classroom environments supportive of high student achievement. The recent concern about at-risk students should help ensure that a greater emphasis is placed on meeting students' personal needs both as a critically important goal in itself and as a prerequisite to higher achievement.

ACTIVITY 4.1

Implementing Peer
Relationship
Activities

On a sheet of paper create columns or areas with the following headings: (1) helping students become acquainted; (2) creating a cohesive, supportive group; and (3) creating diverse liking patterns. Notice that these goals relate to the second and fourth stages of group formation discussed in this chapter. For each heading write at least three activities you can use to accomplish the goal. We strongly encourage you to share these with other teachers working with students in the same grade level. After you have selected three activities you would like to implement, write these into your long-term lesson plans. This will help you to determine how you want to space these activities and how they support one another. Keep in mind that you will want to include several of these in the first week of school. However, do not overwhelm students with these, and do not ignore academic procedures and content during the first week. Also, it is important to include activities from these groups periodically throughout the year, especially when new students join the class.

RECOMMENDED READING

Allen T., & Plax, T. (1999). Group communications in the formal educational context. In F. R. Lawrence (Ed.), *The handbook of group communication theory and research* (pp. 493–515). Thousand Oaks, CA: Sage.

Borba, M. (1989). *Esteem builders; A K–8 curriculum for improving student achievement, behavior and school climate.* Rolling Hills Estates, CA: Jalmer.

Canfield, J., & Siccone, F. (1992). *One hundred ways to develop student self-esteem and responsibility.* Boston: Allyn & Bacon.

Duke, D., & Trautvetter, S. (2001). *Reducing the negative effects of large schools.* Washington, DC: National Clearing House of Educational Facilities.

Duval, R. (1997). *Building character and community in the classroom.* Cypress, CA: Creative Teaching Press.

Foyle, H., Lyman, L., & Thies, S. (1991). *Cooperative learning in early childhood education.* Washington, DC: National Education Association.

Freeman, S. (1997). *Character education: Teaching values for life.* New York: McGraw-Hill.

Gibbs, J. (2000). *Tribes: A new way of learning and being together.* Sausalito, CA: Center Source

Good, T., & Brophy, J. (2000). *Looking in classrooms* (8th ed.). New York: Longman.

Huggins, P. (1990). *Helping kids handle anger: Teaching self-control.* Longmont, CO: Sopris West.

Huggins, P., Moen, L., & Manion, D. (1993). *Teaching friendship skills: Primary version.* Longmont, CO: Sopris West.

Johnson, D., & Johnson, R. (1994). *Learning together and alone: Cooperative, competitive, and individualistic learning* (4th ed.). Boston: Allyn & Bacon.

Johnson, D., Johnson, R., & Holubec, E. (1993). *Cooperation in the classroom.* Edina, MN: Interaction Book Company.

Johnson, D., Johnson, R., & Holubec, E. (1994). *The new circles of learning: cooperation in the classroom and school.* Alexandria, VA: Association for Supervision and Curriculum Development.

Johnson, R. (1993). *Reaching out.* Boston: Allyn & Bacon.

Kerr, R. (1997). *Positively: Learning to manage negative emotions.* Portland, ME: J. Weston Walch.

Lipson, G. (1997). *Self-esteem, K–3: Concepts for activities discussions and insights.* Carthage, IL: Teaching & Learning.

Mecca, J. (2001). *Character education book of plays: Elementary level.* Nashville, TN: Incentive Publications.

Mecca, J. (2001). *Character education book of plays: Middle grade level.* Nashville, TN: Incentive Publications.

Mumper, M. (2000). *Teaching kids to care and cooperate.* New York: Scholastic.

Pincus, D. (1990). *Feeling good about yourself.* Carthage, IL: Good Apple.

Purkey, W., & Novak, J. (1996). *Inviting school success: A self-concept approach to teaching, learning, and democratic practice* (3rd ed.). Belmont, CA: Wadsworth.

Schmidt, F., Friedman, A. (1990). *Fighting fair: Dr. Martin Luther King, Jr. for kids.* Miami, FL: Grace Contrino Abrams Peace Education Foundation, P.O. Box 191153, Miami Beach FL 33119.

Schmuck, R. & Schmuck, P. (2001). *Group processes in the classroom* (8th ed.). Boston: McGraw-Hill.

Schwartz, L. (2001). *Taking steps towards tolerance and compassion: Creative projects to help kids make a difference.* New York: Learning Works.

Wasley, P., Fine, M., Gladden, M., Holland, N., King, S., Mosak, E., & Powell, L. (2000). *Small schools: Great strides.* New York: Bank Street College of Education.

Whittington, R., Crites, L., Moran, G., Kreidman, N., & Beck, B. (1989). *Peace begins with me: A non-violent values curriculum for K–6th grade students.* Honolulu, HI: Family Peace Center.

Peer Harassment/Bullying

Fried, S., & Fried, P. (1996). *Bullies and victims: Helping your child through the schoolyard battlefield.* New York: M. Evans & Co.

Juvonen, J., & Graham, S. (2001). *Peer harassment in school: The plight of the vulnerable and victimized.* New York: Guilford Press.

Kusche, C., & Greenberg, M. (2000). *PATHS: Promoting alternative thinking strategies: A comprehensive curriculum for preventing bullying and increasing critical-thinking skills in grades K–6.* South Deerfield, MA: Channing Bete Company.

McNamara, B., & McNamara, F. (1997). *Keys to dealing with bullies.* Hauppauge, NY: Barrons.

Olweus, D., & Limber, S. (1999). The bullying prevention program. In D. Elliott (Series Ed.), *Blueprints for violence prevention.* Boulder CO: Center for the Study and Prevention of Violence, Institute of Behavioral Science, University of Colorado.

Ross, D. (1996). *Childhood bullying and teasing: What school personnel, other professionals and parents can do.* Alexandria, VA: American Counseling Association.

Sullivan, K. (1998). *Peacebuilders action guide.* P.O. Box 12158, Tucson, AZ 85732: Heartsprings, Inc.

———. (2000). *The anti-bullying handbook.* Auckland, New Zealand, Oxford University Press.

———. (2000). *Second step to success: A violence-prevention curriculum.* 2203 Airport Way South, Suite 500, Seattle, WA 98134; (206) 343-1223.

———. (2001). Harassment prevention curriculum: Empowerment and skill-building for student safety; can be obtained by writing this organization at 905 Fourth Avenue SE, Albany, OR 97321-3199.

CHAPTER

Working with Parents

Research has shown that parents and family are critical factors in children's education, particularly for those who are at risk of dropping out of school. Numerous studies demonstrate that the influence and support given by the family may directly affect the behavior of children in school, their grades, and the probability that they will finish high school.

—Paul Haley and Karen Berry (1988)
Home and School as Partners

What are optimal conditions for a parent-teacher conference? A quiet corner, protection from interruptions and a teacher who listens. The words exchanged during the conference may be forgotten, but the mood of the meeting will linger on. It will decide the subsequent attitudes and actions of the parents.

—Haim Ginott (1972)
Teacher and Child

The way schools care about children is reflected in the way schools care about the children's families.

—Joyce Epstein (1995)
Phi Delta Kappan

Parents and guardians are the most important and influential adults in students' lives. Even at the secondary level, parents' attitudes toward school dramatically affect students' feelings and behaviors. Parent involvement clearly impacts students' learning (Christenson & Sheridan, 2001). In a survey of students and teachers (Binns, Steinberg, & Amorosi, 1997), 87 percent of students who earned primarily A's and B's indicated their parents were available to assist them with homework as compared to 24 percent of students who earned grades lower than C's. Similarly, 84 percent of students who earned A's and B's compared to 27 percent of students who earned lower than C's reported their parents encouraged them to pursue their dreams. This is consistent with the findings that teachers cite lack of parental support as the major factor preventing students from completing homework. Based on the National Longitudinal Study conducted by the National Center for Education Statistics, "parental involvement in school activities had a consistent effect on all three measures of school failure, even after holding constant the student's sex, race-ethnicity, and socioeconomic status. . . . The frequency of discussions between the parent and the child about school-related concerns also had a consistent impact on whether or not the student dropped out. Students were particularly at risk if their parents never talked to them about these matters" (Kaufman, Bradby, & Owings, 1992, p. 22).

Although it was conducted many years ago, a study by Williams and associates (1987) indicated that teachers who developed strong home–school connections were more satisfied with their work and were more likely to remain in the profession. Not surprising, given the positive impact parental involvement has on students' behavior and achievements, teachers and administrators are aware of the value of teachers working effectively with their students' parents or guardians. Williams (1992) reported that 87 percent of teachers and 92 percent of the principals believed teachers needed more training in working effectively with families.

Anyone working in schools today realizes that, for many students, the primary support person outside of school and the primary caregiver may not be a biological parent. Therefore, in this chapter, we interchangeably use the terms *parent*, *guardian*, *primary caregiver*, and *family* to represent the adults in the community who provide this support.

Although a teacher's primary role is to work with students, teachers find that, for several reasons, an important and rewarding role includes their work with parents. First, children's attitudes about school are influenced by their parents (Epstein, Coates, Salinas, Sanders, and Simon, 1997). When parents feel good about their children's teacher and school, the youngsters are more likely to receive encouragement and reinforcement for desirable school behavior. Second, adults who are legally responsible for a student should be kept informed about the student's behavior and academic performance. Third, parents and guardians can be valuable resources for teachers. They can volunteer time to tutor students, assist teachers by keyboarding or copying materials, or share their expertise on special topics with students. Finally, in a limited number of instances, the rewards and punishments available in school are not powerful enough to elicit desirable behavior from youngsters. When this occurs, school personnel need to involve parents in developing a behavior change program for the students.

Even though teachers can derive numerous benefits from interacting with parents, many teachers indicate that parent contacts are a difficult and relatively undesirable aspect of teaching. Teachers' discomfort in working with parents is based on several factors. First, parent contacts are often time consuming and energy draining. When teachers have worked with students for seven hours and had approximately 1,000 interchanges, it is understandably difficult to be enthusiastic about additional school-related interactions. By the end of the day, teachers are usually tired and face several hours of marking papers and planning. Time spent contacting parents means that a larger amount of this work must be completed at home in the evening. Teachers also find parent contacts difficult because parents are aware that they pay for their children's education and they therefore believe they should be able to monitor teachers' performance. This situation is intensified because the teaching profession has never been viewed with the awe or respect bestowed on such professions as medicine or law. Perhaps because all parents have been students, they believe themselves knowledgeable about what their youngsters need in order to function effectively in school. These factors cause many teachers to be somewhat intimidated by parents and, therefore, to minimize their parent contacts.

These factors increase the likelihood that contacts with parents will be seen as a necessary task rather than an enjoyable sidelight. Teachers can, however, develop attitudes and skills that will make parent contacts much more enjoyable and productive. This chapter provides methods for making positive contacts with parents throughout the school year, implementing effective parent conferences, and handling parent confrontations.

As with most classroom management methods, each of us must decide how much time and effort we wish to invest in working with parents. Elementary school teachers are expected to maintain frequent contact with parents, and children at this age generally respond well to parents' encouragement. At the middle and high school level, most teachers work with between 80 and 200 students and thus will choose to implement only a few of the ideas presented in this chapter.

The authors and most secondary teachers with whom we have worked have found that the benefits of teacher–parent communication can be obtained with a reasonable amount of contact and by using methods that are pleasant and not overly time consuming. As students move into the upper middle school and high school grades, they can and should become more responsible for their own behavior, and parent contacts can become primarily informational in nature. Nevertheless, parents of students at every grade level should be informed when students are experiencing serious or persistent problems.

KEEPING PARENTS INFORMED

Importance of Early Contacts

Obtaining parental support is facilitated by familiarizing parents with the teacher's instructional goals and classroom methods as soon as possible. Parents are no different from children or teachers. They are more likely to feel positive about and support issues they clearly understand and have had an opportunity to discuss. Parents who perceive themselves as being treated warmly and respectfully by us and who are familiar with our instructional goals and classroom management procedures are much more likely to encourage student achievement and support us if problems arise.

By introducing parents to the curriculum and major classroom procedures early in the year, we are also able to work with the parents before any worries about their child's achievement or behavior make contacts less positive. A major reason for teachers' concerns about parental contacts is that, except for parent–teacher conferences, most teacher–parent contacts focus on negative student behavior. When our initial interaction with the parents is positive, we are more likely to feel comfortable contacting the parents as soon as their involvement appears necessary. Relationships based on infrequent interactions are seldom as warm and comfortable as those in which contacts are more frequent. Therefore, if we wish to feel comfortable in our contacts with parents, we must instigate relatively frequent, positive contacts with them. Contacts with parents are an excellent example of the idea that an ounce of prevention is worth a pound of cure. Several suggestions are offered here for initiating such contacts.

Methods for Obtaining Parental Support

There are many approaches to developing parental support for student achievement and positive classroom behaviors. The ideas presented here are among those that the authors and teachers with whom the authors have worked have found particularly useful. You are encouraged to modify these methods creatively in order to develop an approach best suited to your situation.

An Introductory Letter

Perhaps the easiest approach for making the initial contact is to send a letter to each student's parent(s). Because the letter will include information that you will want to present personally to students, it is best to send the letter so that it arrives one or two days after school begins. In the letter, you can introduce yourself, state your interest in developing positive teacher–parent contacts, and invite the parents to attend a back-to-school night or a similar event in which you and they have an opportunity to meet and discuss the school year. Figure 5.1 is an example of an introductory letter. We strongly encourage you to provide any materials sent home in as many of the languages spoken by parents in your classroom as possible.

The Initial Meeting

It is very important to try to meet parents as soon as possible. The most expedient approach to meeting between 30 and 150 parents seems to be to provide an evening when parents are invited to visit their child's classroom(s) and discuss the teacher's approach to instruction and

"Wilson sometimes has a little difficulty handling parent conferences."

FIGURE 5.1
Introductory Letter
to Parents

(Date)

Dear Parents,

   With school under way, I'd like to take a moment of your time to welcome you and introduce myself. My name is Mrs. Louise Jones and I have taught in the Beaverton School District for 32 years. I completed my undergraduate work at Oregon State University and received my master's degree from Lewis and Clark College.

   I am very interested in making this a successful and happy school year for your child. To ensure this success, we must keep the lines of communication open. I respect the fact that you know your child very well, and so when either you or your child feel worried, please contact me. Likewise, if there is an activity or project that you enjoy, please let me know. I am available at school until 4:00 P.M. each day. I will be contacting you throughout the year about projects, upcoming events, the nice things I see your child doing, and problems, if any arise.

   In a few weeks our school will have its annual back-to-school night. At that time I will discuss in detail the academic program, my discipline procedures, grading, and my goals and expectations for this year. There will also be a display of books and materials that your child will be using during the year. I encourage you to attend this special evening because it will give you an opportunity to understand the fourth-grade program and to become better acquainted with the room and materials that your child will be using throughout the coming year.

Sincerely,
Mrs. Louise Jones

classroom management. It is helpful if the school supports this concept by arranging a formal back-to-school night. If this opportunity is not available, though, it is worth the effort to arrange such an event for ourselves and any colleagues who may be interested. It is sometimes necessary to arrange an alternative meeting time for parents who are unable to attend or uncomfortable attending an evening session. Information about the times that are most convenient for parents can be obtained by requesting this information in the initial letter sent to parents.

   Prior to the initial meeting with parents, it is important for elementary teachers to make a telephone contact in which something positive about the child is reported, and to obtain the parents' commitment to attend the parent orientation meeting. This telephone contact also breaks the ice and sets the stage for future telephone conversations.

   First impressions are extremely important—especially when a relationship involves sporadic and somewhat role-bound interactions—and it is imperative to do everything possible to create a positive initial meeting. In addition to the obvious factors of being well groomed and personable, the teacher should be well organized and the classroom should look interesting and include a personal touch. Parents are very impressed by competence. You may start the meeting on a positive note by placing an outline of the evening's topics on the board. Figure 5.2 provides an example of an

I. Introducing the Teacher
   A. College training and degrees earned.
   B. Professional experience:
      1. length of teaching experience
      2. type of classroom—open vs. self-contained

II. Social and Personal Expectations for Students during the Year
   A. Students will develop responsibility:
      1. for themselves
      2. for their property
      3. for their assignments
   B. Students will learn to respect their peers' successes and weaknesses.
   C. Students will develop a feeling of pride for their accomplishments.
   D. Emphasis will be placed on maintaining and improving self-concept:
      1. focus on the positive at school
      2. encourage parents to reinforce positive behavior at home
   E. Students will learn to work harmoniously in groups: emphasis on sharing.
   F. Emphasis will be placed on teaching students the skill to communicate openly with each other and adults.

III. Academic Curriculum and Goals
   A. Students will be successful in developing a variety of new skills.
   B. Discuss the concept of a successful learner.
   C. A short discussion on the major topics covered in each academic subject:
      1. reading
      2. math
      3. language arts
      4. handwriting
      5. spelling
      6. social studies
      7. science
      8. physical education
      9. music
     10. library

IV. Emphasis Will Be Placed on Organizational Skills
   A. Notebooks will be organized by subjects and returned papers will be filed under the proper heading.
   B. Desks will remain neat and orderly.

V. Grading System
   A. Students' grades are determined by the marks: O—outstanding; S—satisfactory; N—needs improvement.
   B. Report cards are given four times a year.
   C. Conferences are held in the fall and spring quarters.

VI. Students Will Have Homework under These Conditions:
   A. To reinforce a weak skill area.
   B. To reinforce a new concept: short practice on the multiplication factor or weekly spelling word list.
   C. When students have failed to use their academic time wisely in school.
   D. Students are encouraged to read for a few minutes each night.
   E. Discuss Weekly Planner.
   F. Friday Envelopes.

FIGURE 5.2
Outline for Parent
Orientation Meeting

(continued)

FIGURE 5.2
Continued

   VII. Discipline Procedure
         A. Parents will be contacted when necessary.
  VIII. Teachers' Comments on the Student's Study Habits So Far This Year
    IX. Miscellaneous Comments
         A. Mark all clothing with the student's full name.
         B. Keep emergency card current.
         C. Please send a note when your child has been ill, is riding a different bus
             home, or is leaving before the end of the school day.
     X. Your Child's Success Is a Collaborative Team Effort.

---

outline for a parent orientation meeting. This outline can be accompanied by a folder
for each parent, including:

1. A description of the curriculum for the grade level
2. An introductory letter about yourself that includes professional background and
   a philosophy of education
3. A class schedule
4. A handout describing the emotional and social characteristics of a child at the
   grade level
5. A list of special projects that may require some parental assistance
6. A statement of your classroom-management procedures
7. Materials students will be reading throughout the year
8. A parent resource form eliciting information about what parents can offer to
   the class

By providing parents with written information, you indicate that the information is important. A folder also creates ready-made notes and thus increases the likelihood that parents will learn and recall the information presented.

You can also facilitate a positive meeting by providing a personal touch; obviously, there are many ways to do this. One activity for elementary teachers is to have each student make a silhouette of his or her head or a life-size outline of his or her body. The silhouette can be placed on the desk, or the outline can be seated in the child's chair. The parent(s) can then be asked to find their child's seat. Students can also write a note to their parent(s) to indicate several things they would like their parent(s) to see in the classroom.

During the parent orientation, your approach to classroom management can be discussed. Parents can be provided with copies of the classroom rules, and you can discuss how both minor problems and consistent behavior problems will be handled. For example, you may wish to describe the problem-solving approach that will be used, and discuss behavior contracts. You should also make a clear statement on when parents will be contacted about students' behaviors.

Similarly, you should clearly outline the instructional methods that will be used to help the students. Discuss the class schedule and indicate the types of instruction that will be used in teaching each topic. Discuss the types of homework students will be assigned and describe how parents can best respond to the homework. You may want to state that should students ever be confused and overly concerned about a particular homework assignment, the students or parents are welcome to e-mail or call you at home for assistance. Experience indicates that although parents appreciate and are impressed by this offer, teachers receive very few evening phone calls about assignments.

"We don't have school tomorrow. It's time for parent/teacher confrontations."

When discussing academic work, you may want to describe the various special services, such as reading or gifted programs, that are available for providing students with individualized instruction outside the classroom. Similarly, you should discuss how individual differences are attended to in the classroom. Along these lines, it is helpful to outline the grading system that will be used and to discuss such issues as whether grades will reflect improvement or performance measured against some external standard. You may also want to describe any special instructional methods, such as peer tutoring, individual goal setting, or group projects. Finally, parents can be informed that they will receive letters announcing any special projects or assignments that may require that they provide their children with some assistance. By clarifying the academic program and informing parents when and how they will be involved in helping their children, teachers begin to create an accepting, supportive parent response.

You should also inform parents that they can expect to receive telephone calls and notes when their children make a special effort, show improvement, or do something new or especially interesting. Similarly, the parents should be informed that they will also be notified when problems arise so that they are aware of what is happening. Teachers can make this process easier and more comfortable for themselves and parents by obtaining information concerning the most convenient time to contact each parent. Indicate that although you accept the responsibility for providing an exciting educational experience and helping the students to learn social skills and responsibility, the most effective approach to motivating student learning and dealing with any problems that arise is for the home and school to work together effectively.

For parents who may have difficulty attending meetings at school, consider holding the conferences in a site more comfortable or convenient for the parents. For example, conferences might be held at a meeting room in an apartment complex housing a number of students. In addition, some families find using e-mail a more convenient method for obtaining information. Family members can be provided with information or encouraged to communicate with the teacher using e-mail.

We also encourage you to ask parents for their communication preference and try to incorporate this into your pattern of communicating with them. For example, some parents or guardians cannot be contacted at work, others may wish to be contacted primarily by e-mail or to meet personally at school.

Follow-Up

Do not wait too long before reinforcing the ideas presented in the orientation meeting. You may do so by arranging to involve parents in an instructional activity within a week or two following the meeting. The involvement may include an assignment in which parents are asked to help their children obtain information. You might ask the students to develop a family tree or to interview their parents for a career day. Another follow-up activity involves sending positive notes to parents about improvements or achievements their children have made in the specific areas discussed during the orientation meeting.

An additional aspect of follow-up is contacting parents who did not attend an orientation session. One approach is to send the parents their folder along with a letter stating that they were missed and inviting them to schedule a time to visit the classroom and discuss the material in the folder. It is helpful to call parents who do not respond and ask them whether they had any questions about the material they received. Although such contacts do require additional time, they are worth the effort because they create a foundation for increased parental support.

Since many families have VCRs, one way to provide all families access to the information in your initial meeting with parents is to videotape the session. If you have a number of families who have interested caregivers with limited English proficiency, you might consider having the text of the presentation translated and dubbed in with their first language.

Continuing Teacher–Parent Communication

All parents care about their children, and virtually all parents want their children to be successful at school (Epstein & Sanders, 1998). Therefore, it is important to keep parents continually informed about their children's progress in your class.

Teachers should also contact parents when a child consistently begins to act out in class, falls behind in schoolwork and may need special assistance, or needs to complete some work at home. As in any relationship, it is better to deal with problems when they first arise than to wait until a crisis has occurred. Parents are justified in their annoyance when they attend a conference and discover that their child has been behind for six or eight weeks. Although it is true that some parents are less able to provide assistance in working with their child, it is important to hold positive expectations. It is surprising how often parents with reputations for lack of concern or for ineptness in helping their child can respond productively when contacted early and treated thoughtfully. There is an important distinction between teachers' constantly calling parents for support and calling parents to provide them with information. Parents have a right to expect teachers to handle minor problems and seek professional assistance in coping with major problems. Parents should be informed, however, when minor problems such as incomplete assignments or failure to bring supplies become frequent occurrences. Similarly, parents should be informed when major behavior or academic problems arise.

WEEKLY PLANNER.   Especially in elementary school, parents appreciate having weekly contact regarding students' work. A weekly planner can help to accomplish this. On Monday, students are given a Weekly Planner (see Figure 5.3), which is placed in the front of their three-ring notebooks. The teacher discusses the planner with the class,

FIGURE 5.3
Weekly Planner

SUBJECT	MONDAY	TUESDAY	WEDNESDAY	THURSDAY
Weekly Planner	NAME		WEEK OF October 19–23rd	
1 Reading	Maniac Magee Chapters 37–38 • Vocabulary concentration • Homework. "Heroic Feats" Write two paragraphs about a hero.	Maniac Magee Chapters 39–40 Maniac's Map	Maniac Magee Chapters 41–42 "Good Leadership activity."	Maniac Magee Chapters 43–45 Webbing of Characters + their traits
2 Spelling	Spelling Lesson ai and ay words page 27	Spelling Workbook pages 28–30 Watch the directions on page 30!	Practice Studying your words and "Other Word Forms"	Spelling test and workbooks due today.
3 Math	Calculator Investigations Digit Possibilities Everyday Counts	Secret Rule using the function key Calculator Calculators Skill Power p.54	"Challenge 500" Arithmetivists p27 Everyday counts	Pattern magic What's My number?
4 Science Social Studies	Mapping Skills pages 6–10 (United States & Its Neighbors) questions 1–4 page 10. pages11–13 (Read)	Mapping Skills Review directions and hemispheres. (map activity)	D.A.R.E	Time for Kids Current events worksheet
5 Writing Language Arts	"The Great ——— Robbery" Writing traits • organization • voice Prewriting	Do rough draft of "The Great ——— Robbery."	Continue rough draft Revise Edit	Write 2nd draft, peer edit on Friday.

* Book Fair Tu–Fri. 8:30–4:30 Wednesday evening until 8:00 pm

Reminder: Mapping project due next Tuesday, October 27th

explaining what the students will be doing throughout the week. Each day students highlight any work not completed. The students are expected to take the notebook and planner home each evening. Parents are told about this at back-to-school night, through a videotape about the classroom, or in a phone call. The planner may also include a reminder to parents about upcoming school or class events and information about long-term assignments or projects.

FRIDAY ENVELOPES.   On Friday students are given a Friday Envelope filled with the work they have completed that week, which has been responded to by their teacher, as well as school announcements. The students share the envelope with their parents and bring the envelope back the following Monday signed by their parents. Space is provided for the parents to write comments or ask for a phone call.

ADDITIONAL METHODS.   Another method of communicating with parents is to send informational letters about upcoming areas of study, field trips, long-term projects their children will be asked to complete, or newsletters about class happenings. Parents appreciate receiving information regularly, and a bimonthly or monthly letter seems most appropriate.

Another approach is to have students make personalized stationery during the first weeks of school. They can design their own patterns and decorate their stationery using felt pens, charcoal, paint, or any other art medium. Teachers can use this stationery to send positive notes home about the student. It is best if elementary teachers send positive notes home at least twice a term. Most teachers find it helpful to record when notes were sent as well as the content of the notes. In this way, you can send notes to all students and focus on different positive events each time a note is sent.

Phone calls are another method for contacting parents. Teachers who call each child's parent(s) at least once before scheduling the initial conference and at least once a term thereafter find that parent–teacher contacts are more relaxed and enjoyable. Teachers often shy away from parents who have reputations for being difficult. These, however, are the parents whom we should make the most effort to know. Parents appreciate knowing that their child's teacher cares enough to make a phone call, and the most critical parents will frequently become supporters of the teacher who takes time to call. When making phone calls, always begin and end the conversation with a positive statement about the child. Also ask the parents how the child is reacting to school and whether the parents have any information that might assist you in making the school experience more productive for the child. Like children, parents respond more positively when given a sense of competence and power.

Parents can also be contacted informally when you attend extracurricular activities in which their children are involved. This strategy is particularly effective with the parents of students who are doing poorly in school. On a number of occasions, the authors have made concerted efforts to attend athletic performances of students involved in persistent school misbehavior and have found that when the parents saw concrete evidence of the authors' concern for their children, they became much more involved in encouraging the students to behave responsibly in school.

A final method for keeping parents informed is to ask them to serve as volunteers in the classroom. Parents are more likely to support us if they understand and feel a part of what goes on at school. Many parents of students with behavior problems had negative experiences when they were in school. Consequently, they respond negatively to and are often intimidated by teachers. Involving these parents in a positive manner in the classroom can do a great deal to alleviate these negative feelings. Parent volunteers who are treated with respect by teachers almost always become strong supporters of the teacher. As anyone who has worked with parent volunteers knows, the teacher will initially need to spend time discussing the volunteer's role and helping volunteers understand and respond consistently to our instructional and discipline style. It is important to recognize situations in which a parent's style of interacting with children may contradict the teacher's methods. In such cases, perhaps the volunteer's efforts can be channeled into support activities that involve minimal contact with students.

P A U S E

5.1   *and Consider*

Take a few minutes and write down the methods you have found most effective for communicating with parents. If you are currently student teaching or observing in a classroom, ask the teacher with whom you are working, and, if possible, other teachers in the building, to share the methods they have found most effective. Once you have a list of specific methods, join a group of peers or classmates and share these methods.

PARENT CONFERENCES

For most teachers, parent conferences are a required form of parent contact. Parent conferences can play a vital role in eliciting parents' support for us and can help us work with students who are experiencing difficulties. Unfortunately, a poorly organized or otherwise negative conference can create or intensify parental dissatisfaction. This dissatisfaction will frequently be reflected in students' behaviors. Furthermore, coping with parental criticism diverts valuable teacher time and energy. Therefore, parent conferences have a real influence on classroom discipline.

By thoughtfully preparing for a conference and implementing a well-organized conference, we can reduce our own anxiety about conferring with parents while increasing the likelihood that parents will leave the conference feeling positive about and supportive of us. This section offers suggestions for improving skills in conferring with parents.

Preparing for a Conference

Because teacher, parent, and student all care about the outcome of a teacher–parent conference, it is important to consider how best to prepare each of these individuals for the conference. A conference will be more comfortable and productive when each person involved (the student is integrally involved even if not present) is prepared for the conference.

Preparing Students

The first steps in preparing students are to discuss the goals of conferences and to allow children to ask questions and express their concerns. Students need to know why their parents are being given a report and what will happen at the conference. The next step is to provide students with an opportunity to evaluate their own work. Because the primary goal of periodic teacher–parent conferences is to clarify and communicate students' accomplishments, it is logical that students should be involved in this process. Providing students with an opportunity to evaluate their own work also reduces their anxiety about the type of information their parents will be receiving. Self-evaluation provides children with a sense of significance, competence, and power.

There are several approaches to involving students in self-evaluation. The most specific and valuable method is to allow students to fill out a report card on themselves. The easiest and most effective method of developing a self-evaluation report card is to ask students to rate themselves on the same items on which the district or school requires you to rate them. Figure 5.4 is an example of such a form. Once the student has completed a self-evaluation form (younger children or students who have difficulty with reading will require assistance in completing a form), you can schedule time to discuss the results individually with each student. Inform the students that this conference will allow them to discuss with the teacher any discrepancies between their evaluations. It is extremely important to discuss these differences. Student resentment and hostility are often the outcomes of a conference in which parents are given negative information about a student before this information has been systematically discussed with the student. The implications for classroom management are obvious and dramatic. Students will treat their teacher and peers with greater kindness and respect when they believe they have been treated fairly.

Another method that can be incorporated with a self-evaluation report card is to have students examine their behavior and academic achievements compared with their stated goals. If students have been involved in writing goals for the grading period, they can be asked to write a short statement about the degree to which they have met these goals. This procedure not only places their learning and subsequent grade in perspective but it also reinforces the concept of students' responsibility for their own learning.

Preparing Parents

There are two basic methods for preparing parents for a teacher–parent conference. First, as discussed earlier, you should already have had several positive contacts with the parents. These contacts ideally include a back-to-school night, a phone call, and several notes home on their child's progress. Second, about one week before the conference, you should send the parents a note reminding them of the conference and providing them with an agenda for the conference. Figure 5.5 provides an example of such a note and outline.

Name _____

FIGURE 5.4
Self-Evaluation
Report Card

Reading

1. Approximately how many pages of outside reading have you done this term?
   _____
2. Have you reached your personal goal for outside reading?
   _____
3. Have you kept up your daily assignments in your literature book or reading text?
   _____
4. What grade do you deserve in reading?
   grade: _____   effort: _____

   reason: _____

Math

1. Have you worked hard to get all your assignments done on time?
   _____
2. Are there any of the multiplication tables that you are not sure of?
   _____ If so, which ones? _____
3. Are there any areas of math that you are not clear about or need more help in?
   _____
4. What grade do you deserve this term in math?
   grade: _____   effort: _____

   reason: _____

Spelling

1. Have you studied your list words each week? _____
2. Have you been completing your workbook assignments each week on time?
   _____
3. Do you think you remember the words that you learn to spell each week?
   _____
4. How well do you spell your words in your writing and on daily assignments?
   superior   very good   fair   poor   (Circle one)
5. What grade should you receive for spelling this term?
   grade: _____   effort: _____

   reason: _____

Cursive Writing

1. What do you need to work on? _____
2. What grade do you feel you have earned this term in cursive writing?
   grade: _____   effort: _____

   reason: _____

Science, Social Studies, and Art

What grade would you give yourself in each of these areas for this term?
Please give a reason for each grade.

Science: grade: _____   effort: _____
reason _____

(continued)

FIGURE 5.4
Continued

Social Studies: grade: _____   effort: _____
Reason _____

Art: grade: _____   effort: _____
Reason _____

What areas are you doing well in at school? _____

What do you need to work on? _____

In what ways do you feel you have grown personally this term?
_____

Please evaluate your study habits and personal growth, using these ratings.

     + = outstanding growth
     = = okay or satisfactory growth
     ✔ = need to improve in this area

Put the appropriate mark on each line below.

Study Habits

_____ Following directions
_____ Completing assignments on time
_____ Working well in (your) a group
_____ Working well alone
_____ Listening well to whoever is speaking
_____ Showing neatness in your work and desk
_____ Assuming responsibility for your work

Personal Growth Areas

_____ Considering other people's feelings
_____ Following school rules in a positive way
_____ Taking care of your personal belongings
_____ Controlling your own behavior
_____ Being able to accept responsibility for your own actions
_____ Being able to get along well with others

Is there anything that you would like to share with me about yourself or your work?
_____

Is there anything you would like me to write on your report card or share with your parents? _____

Do you have any comments about my teaching this term? _____
_____
_____

Other comments that might be helpful for me to know? _____
_____

Thank you for your help!

FIGURE 5.5
Agenda for a
Parent Conference

Dear Mr. and Mrs. Smith:

I am looking forward to our conference on Wednesday, November 6, at 3:30 P.M. In order to help us use the time most effectively, I will try to follow the agenda listed below. I hope that this list will cover all areas you would like to discuss. If you have any special questions, it might be helpful to jot them down prior to the conference.

Conference Agenda

1. Share positive personal qualities about the student.
2. Read student's self-evaluation.
3. Discuss the report card and examine samples of the student's work.
4. Discuss the student's behavior and peer relations.
5. Parent/guardian questions or concerns.
6. Summarize the conference by discussing the student's strengths and areas that need improvement.

Sincerely,

Mrs. Johnson
Third-Grade Teacher

Teacher Preparation

Teachers are responsible for providing the parent(s) with clearly presented information in the context of a positive, comfortable interaction. There are three basic steps in accomplishing this goal: First, as discussed in the preceding paragraphs, we should adequately prepare the student and parent(s) for the conference. Second, we should acquire and clearly organize important information about the student. Third, we should create a comfortable, relaxed environment.

Parents are impressed with data. Data indicate that we have invested time and energy in preparing for a conference. Data also testify directly to our professional competence. By focusing on specific data, we quickly move ourselves out of the parents' conception of teachers as professional babysitters and into the category of skilled professional educators. Data also have the obvious advantage of objectifying a discussion. The presence of data greatly diminishes the likelihood that a conference will turn into a debate over whether a student's grade is fair or whether a student's behavior really warrants concern.

Data also provide protection for the teacher by furnishing a record of a student's academic progress and behavior as well as of our attempts to make thoughtful interventions aimed at improving skills and behaviors. The availability of data prevents us from being accused of exaggerating a problem, picking on a student, or not having attempted to solve the problem ourselves. Regardless of how competent we may be, lack of specific information significantly undermines our position when working with parents. Consequently, well-organized data are a necessary component of any parent conference and are especially important when a conference focuses on dealing with inappropriate student behavior or poor student achievement. The four major types of data that are useful in a parent conference are:

1. Data on the students' and parents' feelings about the class
2. Data on the students' behavior and the results of attempts to improve the behavior
3. Data on the students' academic work
4. Data on conferences with colleagues and specialists aimed at developing a solution to any matter that is a problem

It is helpful to acquire information about how the parents perceive the school year is progressing for their child. By requesting this information, we acknowledge the importance of the parents' concerns and ideas. Information about the parents' perceptions of their child's reactions to school and the parents' own wishes can also enable us to be better prepared for the conference. Figures 5.6 and 5.7 provide examples of a cover letter and parent questionnaire used by intermediate grade teachers.

Specific data on a student's behavior will be necessary only when conferring with parents whose child is having serious behavior problems. In such cases, the parents should be presented with specific data on the child's behavior and our approaches to helping the child improve the behavior.

Because the school's primary function is to provide each student with basic academic skills, the teacher–parent conference should heavily emphasize informing parents about their child's academic progress. You should prepare for each conference by providing a folder that includes samples of the student's work in each major subject. The folder should include specific examples that will help the parents understand any areas in which the student is having particular difficulties.

If the data on the student's academic progress indicate that the student is not functioning well, be prepared to provide the parents with examples of ways in which the student's academic program has been adjusted in order to meet the student's special needs. If you have worked with specialists in developing an individualized program, it is helpful to provide information about these conferences. This can be done by using a standard form to record the results of such conferences. Figure 5.8 is an example of a form you can use for this purpose.

FIGURE 5.6
Cover Letter
to Preconference
Parent
Questionnaire

Dear Parents,

In order to make your parent conference valuable for your child and you, I would like to have as much information as possible for the conference. You can help me by responding to the questions on the attached sheet. If there are any questions that you do not care to answer, please feel free to leave them blank. I would very much appreciate your returning this questionnaire to me at least one day before the conference. If that is not possible, please bring it to the conference with you.

I appreciate the time you are taking to help make this a rewarding conference for all of us.

I look forward to seeing you next week.

Ms. Wilson

Please complete this questionnaire and return it as soon as possible. Thank you.

FIGURE 5.7
Preconference
Parent
Questionnaire

Name: _____

1. My child's general attitude toward school this year is _____
   _____

2. My child expresses most interest in school in _____
   _____

3. My child's greatest concern in school seems to be _____
   _____

4. Some things my child does very well are (these do not have to pertain to school)
   a. _____   d. _____
   b. _____   e. _____
   c. _____   f. _____

5. An area I would like to see my child work especially hard in is _____
   _____

6. Please list some positive qualities that you child has so that we can discuss good qualities at school (such as trustworthy, patient, understanding, punctual) _____
   _____

7. Something I have wondered about this year is _____
   _____

8. Some things that seem difficult for my child are (not necessarily school work: example, doing small tasks with fingers) _____
   _____

9. Something my child would like to do in school is _____
   _____

10. Several subjects that my child seems to enjoy are (include interests and hobbies) _____
    _____

11. I would appreciate any suggestions or comments you have that would help me work more effectively with your child. _____
    _____
    _____
    _____

Thank you for taking time to complete this questionnaire.

There are several advantages to presenting this type of data. Data concerning professional consultation reflect the teacher's concern and resourcefulness. Furthermore, they indicate to the parents that their child's problem is not simply a personality conflict with a teacher or the result of an incompetent teacher's having difficulty teaching their slightly energetic student. Another advantage to having consulted with specialists is that this procedure should present the parents with clearer and more thorough data. Especially in the area of academic difficulties, classroom teachers often have limited skills in diagnosing the specific factors that may be causing a student's problems. By

FIGURE 5.8

Teacher–Specialist Conference Form

Source: From Vernon F. Jones, *Adolescents with Behavior Problems: Strategies for Teaching, Counseling, and Parent Involvement,* p. 274. Copyright © 1980 by Allyn & Bacon. Reprinted with permission.

Consultant's Name _____   Date _____

Consultant's Position or Role _____

Reasons for holding the conference:

Goals for the conference:

Information obtained:

Decision(s) reached:

Additional comments:

consulting specialists, not only can the teacher provide the parents with more detailed information but the teacher can also simultaneously acquire information that can assist in developing a more appropriate academic program for the student.

We have found it helpful to summarize how the student is doing by, prior to the conference, having both the student and the teacher complete a conference summary form similar to the one shown in Figure 5.9. The student begins by describing two areas in which the student believes he or she is doing well at school, and one area in which the student would like to improve. The teacher then completes this form, discusses it with the student, and takes it to the parent conference. At the beginning of the conference the completed form is shared with the parent(s) or guardian(s). At the end of the conference, the parent or guardian completes the third section and takes it home to share with the student.

It is helpful to provide parents with a conference summary. This review can focus the conference and can also serve as a reminder because teachers often hold several consecutive conferences. The parent should be given the summary sheet at the end of the conference. Figure 5.10 is an example of an elementary school conference summary form.

Once we have prepared students and parents and have collected and developed the important data, the final preparation involves creating a comfortable conference setting. If possible, the conference should be held at a round table so that neither party

Two Stars and a Wish
for Fall Conference 2003

FIGURE 5.9
Conference
Summary Form

By each star write something positive about this student (behavior or learning).
By the wish write one hope for this student in fifth grade.

Student's Option	Teacher's Option	Parents' Option
★	★	★
★	★	★
WISH	WISH	WISH

Signature_____   Signature_____   Signature_____
　　　　　Student　　　　　　　　　　*Teacher*　　　　　　　　　　*Parents*

is in a dominant position. The atmosphere can be made more relaxed by placing some flowers on the table and having cookies and coffee available. The agenda should be placed on the board or on a large sheet of butcher paper as a reminder for both parties. Parents also appreciate knowing what topics and skills have been covered during the term. A piece of paper listing these skills can be placed next to the agenda for reference during the conference. Pencil and paper should be provided so the parents can take notes during the conference.

Providing an Effective Conference

If you have prepared effectively, the actual conference will usually be quite easy and comfortable. After greeting the parent(s) warmly and chatting for a moment about any positive topic, begin the conference by sharing several positive personal qualities the child displays at school. Encourage the parent(s) to discuss any aspects of the student's behavior they have enjoyed or been particularly pleased with recently. The next step is to ask the parent(s) to read the student's self-evaluation report card and any other material the student has written about his or her progress during the term. Students often

FIGURE 5.10
Parent Conference
Summary Form

Student's Name: _____

Academic Achievement

Reading
Doing well in: _____
Needs to work on: _____

Math
Average of math scores: _____   _____
                                    tests   daily work
Strong areas: _____
Needs to improve on: _____

Writing
Strength: _____
Continue to focus on: _____

Other subjects: _____
_____

Behavior and Personal Characteristics

Positive personal qualities that I see in your child: _____
_____

Improvement needed in: _____
_____
_____

Comments about how your child is relating to his or her classmates: _____
_____

Final Comments

You could help at home by: _____
_____
_____
_____

Any additional comments: _____
_____
_____
_____

are so critical of their own work that this is an interesting and sensitive preparation for any critical comments that you may need to make. Once they have read their child's own critical evaluation, parents are less likely to question your statements about areas in which their child needs improvement.

Many parents are concerned about their child's report card, so the next step is usually to discuss the actual report card and examine specific examples of the student's work.

When doing so, initially focus on positive aspects of the student's work. Parents respond well to the sandwich theory of feedback, in which critical comments are sandwiched between positive comments about their child. Another strategy is to introduce an area that needs improvement with the statement, "I would like to encourage your child to. . . ." By focusing on the positive, you can minimize parental defensiveness and criticism.

Once academic matters have been discussed, focus on the student's behavior and peer relationships. It is important to discuss positive aspects of the student's behavior as well as aspects that require improvement. Also, if the student has experienced serious behavior problems, provide the parents with specific data on the student's behavior and efforts to assist the student in changing behavior. During this portion of the conference, it may be appropriate to invite the principal or any other specialists to join in the discussion.

After you have discussed the student's academic progress and behavior, the parents should be encouraged to ask questions and make comments. If the parents do not have any questions, you can help them focus on their thoughts and concerns by referring to any pertinent items on the preconference parent questionnaire (Figure 5.7).

Conclude the conference by summarizing the student's academic and behavior strengths and goals. Goals for improvement can be written down (Figure 5.11), and you can discuss any ways in which the parents can assist the child at home. These should be listed on the conference summary form (Figure 5.10). Discuss any follow-up contacts that appear desirable based on the information discussed during the conference, and express sincere appreciation for the parents' efforts and input.

PAUSE

5.2   *and Consider*

> Create a list of methods you could use at your grade level for preparing parents, students, and yourself for conferences with parents or guardians. If you are currently student teaching or observing in a classroom, ask the teacher with whom you are working, and if possible, other teachers in the building, to share the methods they have found most effective. Once you have a list of specific methods, join a group of peers or classmates and share these methods.

In our work with graduate students completing a year-long teaching internship in a secondary school site, we have consistently been impressed with the powerful positive impact on student learning and behavior when interns work closely with parents. We realize that because our interns begin teaching only one class and never teach more than three classes, they have more time to work collaboratively with families than do teachers who work with five classes and 180 or more students. Nevertheless, these interns consistently find that time spent engaging parents, guardians, and other adult support persons has a dramatic impact on students—many of whose behavior was causing serious concern for the intern and negatively impacting the learning environment.

Introductory Letters

Teachers can provide parents with a wide range of information by sending home a form letter describing selected aspects of learning goals, instructional methods, and classroom procedures. A letter might include a course syllabus or similar list of topics to be

FIGURE 5.11
Plan for
Improvement

PLAN FOR IMPROVEMENT

STUDENT'S NAME: _____

TEACHER'S NAME: _____

PARENT'S NAME: _____

DATE: _____

AREA TO BE IMPROVED: _____

_____

THE TEACHER WILL: _____

_____

THE STUDENT WILL: _____

_____

THE PARENT WILL: _____

_____

LONG-RANGE GOAL: _____

_____

covered and specific skills the students will learn. Teachers may also comment on the specific teaching methods that will be used during the course. For example, if you use group work or projects, you might describe the activities in which students will be involved as well as the educational rationale for using these methods. Teachers may also comment on grading procedures, decisions on when to inform parents about lack of student progress, and methods that will be used in responding to disruptive student behavior. This material should be prefaced by suggesting that such behavior is not anticipated, because the combination of interesting and effective instruction and the commitment to assist students will make it unlikely that these methods will prove necessary.

Introductory Phone Call

Although a letter requires much less time than a telephone call, there are times when the benefits of the personal contact offset the time required. One of the senior author's students, who was an intern in a secondary social studies class in an inner-city school, expressed concern to his mentor that student behavior was disrespectful to himself and other students. This contrasted with the generally polite behavior students displayed when the mentor was teaching. Despite discussions with the class and several individual students, a number of students continued to act in ways that created a rather unproductive learning environment. Because the intern had taken over complete teaching responsibility for this class only about a week earlier, the mentor suggested the intern call every parent or guardian over the weekend and introduce himself. The mentor also suggested the intern make some positive comment about each student and indicate to the parents or guardians that he would be keeping them apprised of their student's progress. The intern acknowledged being somewhat anxious about completing this task, but spent several hours during the weekend contacting each family. He indicated he spoke with members from 60 percent of the families, left messages for another 25 percent, and was unsuccessful at contacting 15 percent of the families. Despite speaking a second language common in the school where he was working, the intern noted that several of his conversations were with individuals who appeared not to speak English or Spanish.

The intern reported his amazement at the change he experienced in his students' behavior. First, he noted that nearly a quarter of his students greeted him at the door and made a positive comment regarding the fact that he had spoken with their parent or guardian over the weekend. Second, he noticed a dramatic increase in students' respectful responses to his requests and instructional direction. When the intern's mentor, a twenty-year veteran teacher, shared this series of events with a group of twenty other veteran mentors, it was impressive how many of them reported having had a similar experience.

Newsletters

A newsletter is an expedient way to keep large numbers of parents informed. Because most secondary teachers have three separate preparations, each for a different course, a newsletter sent every three weeks for each class requires a teacher to write one newsletter each week. The newsletter can involve less than a page, describing subjects currently being taught, projects due, films being shown, and so on. You can also use this opportunity to jot a personal note on newsletters to parents whose child is experiencing noteworthy success or problems.

Progress Reports

Many schools require that teachers notify parents at midterm of each nine-week period if their children are earning lower than a *C* grade. You can readily develop your own form for immediately contacting parents whose children are beginning to experience academic or behavioral problems. Because this form should be sent when students are just beginning to experience a problem, you should summarize the steps you will be taking to help the students.

Ongoing Communicating with Families

When the son of the authors was a sophomore in high school, he experienced considerable harassment, and during one semester he skipped a number of classes. It was not until final grades were sent home that the authors became aware of this situation and the impact it had on their son's grades as well as his self-esteem. We believe it is imperative for school staff to communicate with parents or guardians whenever a student is making dramatic progress or experiencing significant problems. Although this requires effort for teachers who work with 180 or more students, as indicated by the response from students when the intern called all of their homes, very positive benefits often occur when parents or guardians are contacted. The authors themselves, and hundreds of interns and teachers with whom they have worked, have reported significant improvement in students' academic work and behavior following contact with parents or guardians. In addition, failure to make these contacts sends a message to students and the community that school staff do not care or are not comfortable interacting with members of the community. This can have a devastating result in terms of student achievement and behavior, just as frequent and supportive contact with families can have a dramatically positive impact on achievement and behavior (Reyes et al., 1999; Roderick, 2001).

DEALING EFFECTIVELY WITH PARENTS' CRITICISMS AND CONFRONTATIONS

Anyone who has taught for several years has had to deal with an angry or critical parent. Many teachers state that, along with classroom discipline, this type of confrontation is perhaps the least desirable aspect of teaching. Although there is no foolproof method for dealing with an angry parent, there are several strategies that can be used to cope with such situations in an effective, professional manner.

1. Meet with the parent or guardian in a setting in which you are physically safe and able to obtain assistance. If you have reason to believe the guest may become confrontational, schedule the meeting to include an administrator or counselor.

2. Greet the parent in a pleasant manner. It is more difficult for parents to remain critical and aggressive if you seem glad to see them.

3. Use active listening to defuse the parent's emotions. Becoming defensive or initially arguing with the parent will usually only intensify the parent's emotions. By using phrases such as "I appreciate your concern" or "I can see that you are really concerned about this," you can help the parent feel understood. This tactic will gradually enable the parent to calm down and replace angry or frightened feelings with more positive and productive feelings.

4. Look genuinely interested and listen carefully. This attitude also helps the parent feel accepted and will gradually reduce negative or intense feelings.

5. Present a calm, professional manner. Stand erect, look at the parents, and remain calm. Just as students respond more effectively to teachers who remain calm and in charge during a crisis (Brophy & Evertson, 1976; Kounin, 1970), parents need the structure provided by a calm response.

6. Ask the parents what they wish to accomplish. One method of structuring a confrontation conference is by questioning the parents: "I appreciate your concern. What would you like to accomplish with our discussion today?" This approach helps focus the parents' energy and moves the conference away from a gripe session into a potentially productive problem-solving conference.

7. Set a time limit if necessary. If your time is limited, it is important to inform the parent. Do so by stating, "I have twenty minutes before I have to be back with my class. Let's see how far we can get in solving the problem in that time. If we need more time, I will be glad to schedule a conference as soon as possible."

8. Ask the parent whether the student is aware of the problem. Because the student is the most important person involved, it is important to clarify how he or she feels about the issue being raised by the parent. This question also slows the parent down and creates a more productive focus for the conference. Furthermore, the question helps introduce the issue of the student's responsibility for any problem that may exist.

9. Be honest. When confronted by parents, it is easy to understate the seriousness of a problem or to accept too much responsibility for a problem that is largely something the child must work on. Maintain your professional integrity and set the stage for future conferences by initially presenting an honest and clear statement of the problem.

10. Emphasize specific data. Data are simultaneously one of your best professional tools and your best defense. If a parent angrily states that his daughter did well in math last year but is having difficulty this year, the most logical and effective approach is to examine data on the student's math skills.

11. Tell the parent specifically what will be done to deal with the problem. Parents have a right to know what the teacher will do to alleviate a difficulty. Furthermore, critical parents can often become strong supporters if they learn that they will be listened to, shown data, and presented with a plan. If the parents' worry was not justified, the plan may involve a follow-up conference to examine the results of the current program. If, however, the parents highlighted an area that required attention, developing a plan shows respect for the parents' concern and competence on your part.

While writing the current edition of this book, an intern working with one of the authors experienced a situation in which a student's aunt became upset because the student was required to work with the teacher and administrator regarding her physical and verbal abuse of peers. The aunt had a history of being verbally abusive to teachers, but was also a strong advocate for her niece and had worked cooperatively with the intern during the first several months of school. One morning after the student's mother had been contacted concerning the student's bullying of a peer, the aunt came to the classroom and insisted on speaking with the intern. The intern agreed to meet, asked her mentor to take over the classroom, and proceeded to a small room adjacent to the main school office to meet with the aunt. The intern entered the narrow, windowless room first, seated herself near the far wall, and was followed by the aunt who shut the door and pushed her chair against the door. The aunt proceeded to shout at the intern, verbally threatened her physical safety, and on one occasion stood up and moved toward her. Fortunately, the intern had been involved in deescalation methods. She listened to and paraphrased the aunt's anger, and suggested the aunt might want to report this to the principal and discuss it with her. The aunt was pleased to have an opportunity to tell someone in authority how badly her niece had been treated, and allowed the teacher to exit the room with her to schedule an appointment with the principal.

This incident highlights the importance of teachers having a plan for working with angry parents or guardians and, particularly, the importance of being aware of the first point made in this section—not meeting with a potentially angry parent or guardian in a setting in which support is not available.

PAUSE
and Consider   5.3

> We encourage you to work with three or four colleagues or classmates and select a situation in which you have been, or can imagine being, confronted by an upset parent. Discuss the situation and then do some role-playing. Have one member of the group act the part of the parent and another the teacher. Following the role-play, have the other members of the group provide feedback. If the feedback is substantial, you may want to repeat the role-play with another student acting as the teacher.

PLACING SCHOOL–HOME INTERACTION IN PERSPECTIVE

A chapter on teacher–student contacts is not complete without clarifying the parameters of school–home contacts. As mentioned throughout this chapter, when teachers take a proactive approach by providing early positive and informative contacts with parents, teacher–parent interactions can be a positive, enjoyable aspect of a teacher's job. Similarly, when teachers develop skills for calmly and professionally responding to parents' concerns, even potentially negative interactions with parents can become less stressful and can serve to initiate greater parent understanding and support.

Unfortunately, the high rate of divorce, substance abuse, poverty, family mobility, and two working parents have all created a society in which an increasing number of students live in homes where the caregivers lack the preparation, emotional stability, time, and support to provide effective support for their children's efforts in school. This means that many students come to school anxious or upset about situations that have occurred at home.

Our responsibility as teachers is to use methods such as those described throughout this book that create positive, caring, supportive, well-structured environments for all students. As discussed in Chapter 10, teachers are also responsible for obtaining the help of other teachers and school support personnel in developing special methods for working with students who experience ongoing problems. This is the extent of our responsibilities as teachers. Teachers are not mental health specialists and cannot be expected to provide parent training or to help parents obtain resources for resolving family problems.

Even though teachers' responsibilities in working with parents are limited, school staffs can provide varied assistance to parents. Schools are the one societal institution with which all children and parents come into contact. School personnel thus are often the first to become aware of problems, and parents may be more likely to seek assistance from schools than from social service agencies. Schools can provide an important service to parents and children by offering limited direct services and by referring families to other community resources. School counselors are an obvious source of direct services to parents and children. Unless these services are available, some of the most needy children will be hampered by emotional problems that will seriously limit their obtaining essential learning.

Another type of assistance to families includes classes on parenting skills. Many schools offer parents periodic seminars or classes on methods of effective parenting. Because virtually all parents have some contact with their child's school, and because, for most parents, the stigma of attending a session at their child's school is less than that of attending a mental health clinic class, the schools are an important resource for providing parenting skills. The authors have provided numerous parent training sessions and classes and have consistently found parents to be appreciative and pleased with the applicability of their new skills.

Schools can provide another important support service for parents and families in turmoil. Many schools have begun to contract a social worker or other social service professional to serve as a liaison between the home, family, and community for children who are experiencing ongoing school problems in association with serious home problems. Mental health agencies employ systems and language different from those used by school personnel; therefore, someone familiar with these systems can use these resources more effectively. A school–community liaison can serve as a resource for educators and parents and can help obtain much-needed community services for children and their families. Even though schools are not responsible for resolving all problems faced by the students they help educate, they do have an obligation to identify and provide effective referrals for children experiencing stress and trauma that are affecting their ability to benefit from the educational environment.

As seen in Figure 5.12, Joyce Epstein, a leader in researching and developing school/family/community support, has outlined six areas in which school staff can involve families. Families need support in helping their children develop positive social skills. Research indicates that providing parents with support in parenting, job training, and mental health or substance abuse counseling can have a positive effect on reducing violence in children (Yoshikawa, 1994).

Reporting child abuse is a special issue in home–school relationships. An educator's responsibility for reporting child abuse is an example of the coordination of school and community resources to help children and their families. To help abused children, states have enacted legislation that requires educators to report child abuse. In Oregon, educators are required to report suspected physical abuse, neglect, mental or emotional abuse, sexual abuse, and sexual exploitation. Oregon law also provides the professional who makes the report with safeguards against legal prosecution, as in the following:

Type 1 Parenting	Type 2 Communicating	Type 3 Volunteering	Type 4 Learning at Home	Type 5 Decision Making	Type 6 Collaborating with Community
Help all families establish home environments to support children as students.	Design effective forms of school-to-home and home-to-school communications about school programs and children's progress.	Recruit and organize parent help and support.	Provide information and ideas to families about how to help students at home with homework and other curriculum-related activities, decisions, and planning.	Include parents in school decisions, developing parent leaders and representatives.	Identify and integrate resources and services from the community to strengthen school programs, family practices, and student learning and development.
Sample Practices	**Sample Practices**	**Sample Practices**	**Sample Practices**	**Sample Practices**	**Sample Practices**
Suggestions for home conditions that support learning at each grade level. Workshops, videotapes, computerized phone messages on parenting and child rearing at each age and grade level. Parent education and other courses or training for parents (e.g., GED, college credit, family literacy). Family support programs to assist families with health, nutrition, and other services. Home visits at transition points to preschool, elementary, middle, and high school. Neighborhood meetings to help families understand schools and to help schools understand families.	Conferences with every parent at least once a year, with follow-ups as needed. Language translators to assist families as needed. Weekly or monthly folders of student work sent home for review and comments. Parent/student pickup of report card, with conferences on improving grades. Regular schedule of useful notices, memos, phone calls, newsletters, and other communications. Clear information on choosing schools or courses, programs, and activities within schools. Clear information on all school policies, programs, reforms, and transitions.	School and classroom volunteer program to help teachers, administrators, students, and other parents. Parent room or family center for volunteer work, meetings, resources for families. Annual postcard survey to identify all available talents, times, and locations of volunteers. Class parent, telephone tree, or other structures to provide all families with needed information. Parent patrols or other activities to aid safety and operation of school programs.	Information for families on skills required for students in all subjects at each grade. Information on homework policies and how to monitor and discuss schoolwork at home. Information on how to assist students to improve skills on various class and school assessments. Regular schedule of homework that requires students to discuss and interact with families on what they are learning in class. Calendars with activities for parents and students at home. Family math, science, and reading activities at school. Summer learning packets or activities. Family participation in setting student goals each year and in planning for college or work.	Active PTA/PTO or other parent organizations, advisory councils, or committees (e.g., curriculum, safety, personnel) for parent leadership and participation. Independent advocacy groups to lobby and work for school reform and improvements. District-level councils and committees for family and community involvement. Information on school or local elections for school representatives. Networks to link all families with parent representatives.	Information for students and families on community health, cultural, recreational, social support, and other programs or services. Information on community activities that link to learning skills and talents, including summer programs for students. Service integration through partnerships involving school; civic, counseling, cultural, health, recreation, and other agencies and organizations; and businesses. Service to the community by students, families, and schools (e.g., recycling, art, music, drama, and other activities for seniors or others). Participation of alumni in school programs for students.

FIGURE 5.12

Epstein's Framework of Six Types of Involvement and Sample Practices

Source: Epstein, J. L. (1995). School/family/community partnerships: Caring for the children we share. *Phi Delta Kappan, 76*, 701–712. Reprinted by permission.

418.762—Immunity of Persons Making Reports in Good Faith.

Anyone participating in good faith in the making of a report pursuant to ORS 418.750 to 418.760 and who has reasonable grounds for the making thereof, shall have immunity from any liability, civil or criminal, that might otherwise be incurred or imposed with respect to the making or content of such report. Any such participant shall have the same immunity with respect to participating in any judicial proceeding resulting from such report.

All teachers and administrators should become familiar with the child abuse laws in their states and the reporting and follow-up procedures used by their districts. Many districts have developed working relationships with community children's service agencies responsible for handling reported child abuse to ensure that proper follow-up is provided and to coordinate efforts to help the child cope with the temporary emotional stress often associated with this type of report.

ADDITIONAL METHODS FOR POSITIVELY ENGAGING PARENTS OF SECOND-LANGUAGE LEARNERS

Studies suggest that teachers may perceive the role of families and the involvement families may have in students' educational experiences differently from family members and guardians. In their study of schools in which Hispanic students achieved extremely well, Reyes and colleagues (1999) discovered that teachers viewed family involvement as attending school events, participating in meetings, and serving as volunteers. Family members, however, viewed the most important involvement as, "checking homework assignments, reading and listening to children read, obtaining tutorial assistance, providing nurturance, instilling cultural values, talking with children, and sending them to school well fed, clean, and rested" (Reyes et al., 1999, p. 37). It is not surprising, therefore, that staff in schools in which Hispanic students were most successful focused more effectively on directly involving families in their children's education within the home environment. Similarly, based on an examination of forty-two projects, Chavkin and Gonzales (1995) reported the following strategies to be effective in fostering family involvement: (1) providing reception areas with bilingual staff, (2) communication in Spanish, and (3) visiting with family members at sites away from school.

Research suggests that schools in which Hispanic students do particularly well are characterized by the warmth of the staff and the personal relationships staff develop with families (Reyes et al., 1999). These authors found that it was important whenever staff met formally or informally with family members to acknowledge the student's accomplishments. These authors stressed the following characteristics of schools for Hispanic students to perform well:

1. Build on cultural values of Hispanic parents
2. Stress personal contact with parents
3. Foster communication with parents
4. Create a warm environment for parents
5. Facilitate structural accommodations for parent involvement

PAUSE

and Consider   **5.4**

> If you work in a school with specialists who serve students whose second language is English, meet with one or more of the specialists and discuss methods they have learned that provide assistance for family members of English as a second language (ESL) students. Join a group of four colleagues or classmates and share the methods you have found.

ASSESSING PARENT CONTACTS

Awareness is almost always the first step in changing one's behavior. Before deciding whether to take the time and risks involved in trying new behaviors, most people choose to examine their present behavior. Activity 5.1 provides you with an opportunity to examine your current parent contacts. It also offers several ideas for systematically improving these contacts.

ACTIVITY 5.1

Assessing and
Improving
Parent Contacts

Assessing Your Parent Contacts

To assess the current level of your contact with parents, answer these questions:

1. How many informational letters have you sent out to every parent so far this year? _____

2. What percentage of your students' parents have received a positive phone call about their child's work or behavior? _____

3. What percentage of your students' parents have received a positive note about their child's work or behavior? _____

4. How many students in your class are experiencing what you would define as significant academic or behavior problems? _____

5. How many parents of these students have you talked to about the problem and your approach to dealing with it? _____

6. How many parents have served as volunteers in your classroom this year? _____

7. How many hours a week is a parent present in your classroom? _____

Improving Your Parent Contacts

1. Send an informational letter to your students' parents. After two weeks, evaluate this effort by answering these questions:
   a. How many parents made a positive comment about the letter? _____
   b. How many students said something positive about the letter? _____
   c. List two advantages to sending the letter:
      (1)_____
      (2)_____
   d. List any disadvantages associated with sending the letter.
2. Over a two-week period, send a positive note home with each child in your class. After two weeks, evaluate this effort by answering these questions:

ACTIVITY 5.1

Continued

a. How many parents made a positive comment about the note? _____
b. How many students said something about the note? _____
c. List two advantages to sending the note:
   (1)_____
   (2)_____
d. List any disadvantage associated with sending the note.

IMPLEMENTING AND ASSESSING NEW METHODS

Having examined a variety of methods for preparing and implementing parent conferences, the next step is to select specific methods you believe will make your next set of conferences more productive and enjoyable. Activity 5.2 will assist you in assessing methods you decide to implement. If you are somewhat tentative about a new method, you might wish to use it with several parents with whom you are most comfortable.

ACTIVITY 5.2

Implementing and Assessing New Methods

Select one method for improving student, parent, and teacher preparation for your next conference. Write these on a sheet of paper and make a specific statement about how you will implement each method. Next, select one method from the section on implementing an effective conference.

During your next series of parent conferences, implement each of the methods you have selected. After the conferences are completed, evaluate the new methods by completing these statements for each new approach:

The most beneficial aspect of this new approach was . . .
Another advantage was that . . .
Parents' responses to this approach were . . .
Students' responses were . . .
One difficulty with this new approach was . . .
I felt more comfortable when using this method because . . .

SUMMARY

Teachers often underestimate the power parents give to teachers. The authors are acutely aware of the value of parent–teacher contacts. Like virtually all parents, the authors are deeply concerned about their children's progress in handling new social and academic expectations. Teachers provide parents with input concerning how intelligent and skilled their children are and how well they are getting along with others. These are extremely important facts to almost all parents. Indeed, the defensiveness you may experience when working with parents of children who are struggling in school is in large part because of the importance parents place on the information you are giving them and the difficulty they have accepting negative information about their children.

Because information about their children's school progress is so important to parents, it is necessary that this information be shared on a regular basis. As teachers, we can establish more positive, supportive teacher–parent relationships when we initially inform parents about the curriculum, instruction, and classroom management to which their children will be exposed. This needs to be followed by periodic updates about classroom activities and student progress. In addition, any time a student begins to have an academic or behavioral problem, we should contact the parents as soon as it appears that the matter cannot be quickly and smoothly resolved between us and the student.

Teacher–parent contacts can be time consuming and, like all aspects of our profession, require practice before we become comfortable and adept at them. They can, however, be among the most rewarding aspects of our teaching experiences and can have a significant impact on the most important and rewarding aspect of our job—seeing improvement in the quality of student behavior and learning.

RECOMMENDED READING

Chavkin, N. (Ed.). (1993). *Families and schools in a pluralistic society.* Albany, NY: State University of New York.

Christenson, S., & Sheridan, S. (2001). *Schools and families: Creating essential connections for learning.* New York: Guilford Press.

Dietz, M. (Ed.). (1997). *School, family, and community: Techniques and models for successful collaboration.* Gaithersburg, MD: Aspen.

Dodd, A., & Konzal, J. (1999). *Making our high schools better: How parents and teachers can work together.* New York: St. Martin's Press.

Epstein, J., Coates, L., Salinas, K., Sanders, M., & Simon, B. (1997). *School, family, and community partnerships: Your handbook for action.* Thousand Oaks, CA: Sage.

Hoover-Dempsey, K., & Sandler, H. (1995). Parental involvement in children's education: Why does it make a difference? *Teachers College Record, 97,* 310–331.

Johnson, V. (1996). *Family center guidebook.* Baltimore: Center on Families, Communities, Schools and Children's Learning, Johns Hopkins University.

Kidalgo, N., Bright, J., Siu, S., Swap, S., & Epstein, J. (1995). Research on families, schools, and communities: A multicultural perspective. In J. Banks (Ed.), *Handbook of research on multicultural education* (pp. 498–524). New York: Macmillan.

Martin, J. (1992). *The schoolhome: Rethinking schools for changing families.* Cambridge, MA: Harvard University Press.

McLoughlin, C. (1987). *Parent–teacher conferencing.* Springfield, IL: Charles C. Thomas.

Procidano, M., & Fisher, C. (Eds.). (1992). *Contemporary families: A handbook for school professionals.* New York: Teachers College Press.

Reyes, P., Scribner, J., & Scribner, A. (1999). *Lessons from high-performing Hispanic schools.* New York: Teachers College Press.

Roderick, T. (2001). *A school of our own: Parents, power, and community at the East Harlem block schools.* New York: Teachers College Press.

Sartain, H. (1989). *Nonachieving students at risk: School, family and community intervention.* Washington, DC: National Education Association.

Swap, S. (1993). *Developing home–school partnerships: From concepts to practice.* New York: Teachers College Press.

Turnbull, A., & Turnbull, H. (1996). *Families, professionals, and exceptionality: A special partnership.* Upper Saddle River, NJ: Merrill.

U.S. Department of Education. (1994). *Strong families, strong schools: Building community partnerships for learning.* Washington, DC: U.S. Department of Education.

U.S. Department of Education. (1997). *Achieving the goals: Goal 8, parental involvement and participation.* Washington, DC: U.S. Department of Education.

U.S. Office of Educational Research and Improvement. (1997). *A guide to community programs to prevent youth violence for parents/about parents.* Washington, DC: U.S. Department of Education.

Webster-Stratton, C., & Herbert, M. (1994). *Troubled families—problem children: Working with parents: A collaborative process.* New York: Wiley.

Villa, R., & Thousand, J. (2000). *Restructuring for caring and effective education.* Baltimore, MD: Brookes.

PART three

Increasing Student Motivation and Learning by Implementing Instructional Methods That Meet Students' Academic Needs

Effective classroom management is closely related to effective classroom instruction. When students fail to attend school or classes or when they act out or fail to be productively engaged in classroom activities, teachers must carefully examine whether the curricular content and instructional methods are actively and meaningfully engaging students at an appropriate level of difficulty and in ways that respect their cultural heritage and relate to their own lives. Part III presents current theory and practice on student motivation and effective instruction. Chapter 6 begins with a brief examination of current research on motivation to learn and indicates the relationship between this research and classroom practice. The chapter continues with a discussion of and practical suggestions for implementing a variety of instructional methods proven effective in increasing student motivation and learning. This chapter responds to the large body of data indicating that many students find schools confusing, boring places in which to learn. Clearly, students' misbehavior, violent behavior, and leaving school is related to the degree to which they believe the academic content and the manner in which it is presented treats them with respect and engages their need for competence. In Chapter 6, methods are presented that will enable you to increase the degree to which you actively engage and show respect for your students by clarifying instruction, increasing meaningful student involvement in the learning process, and using teaching methods that respond to individual students' needs.

Enhancing Students' Motivation to Learn

This important work of several decades ago, as well as much of what has since been in the forefront of educational thought, stresses the importance of teachers finding ways to make subject matter relevant to students, to involve students in setting their own goals, to vary the ways of learning to use approaches that employ all of the senses, and to be sure that there are opportunities for relating the knowledge to experiences or actually using it.

—John I. Goodlad (1984)
A Place Called School: Prospects for the Future

Good instruction is now known by researchers to be the first line of defense in behavior management. That is, a good instructional program prevents many behavior problems from arising. . . .

—James Kauffman (1997)
Characteristics of Emotional and Behavioral Disorders of Children and Youth

If school is not inviting, if the tasks are not clear, interesting, and at an appropriate level, how can we expect pupils to be on task? Adverse student reactions should be expected when classes are dull, teaching is uninspired, and failure is built in. Their oppositional behavior is a sign of personal health and integrity.

—William Morse (1987)
Teaching Exceptional Children

Numerous leaders in the field of classroom management highlight the relationship between desirable student behavior and effective instructional strategies. Effectively planned, well-paced, relevant, and interesting instruction is a key aspect of effective classroom management.

Students spend a sizable part of their lives in school. For schools to be positive, supportive communities in which students feel respected and valued, instructional methods and content must meet students' academic needs. Students' unproductive behavior and failure can often be traced to failure to create an educational environment conducive to learning. Educators have also begun to appreciate that students vary in the type of classroom structure and instruction that best facilitate their learning. Understanding the instructional needs of an individual child or group of children provides teachers with information essential for creating a positive learning environment.

Teachers currently face the dilemma of personally and meaningfully engaging students while simultaneously responding to state-mandated assessment requirements that often emphasize highly focused, standardized testing. We believe that state learning goals can be incorporated into lessons that meet students' needs as described in this chapter. Effective teaching that builds a sense of community and shows respect for students and their interests can occur while teachers help students master content that has been determined to be essential.

KEY ISSUES IN STUDENT MOTIVATION TO LEARN

Although meeting students' personal needs (as discussed in Chapter 2) provides a foundation for creating environments supportive of personal growth and learning, closely related and equally important needs exist within environments that are specifically designed to help children acquire academic knowledge. Many students meet their personal needs by successfully completing classroom activities and assignments. Other students find school to be an anxiety-producing, frustrating setting and look elsewhere for the significance, competence, and power they so desperately need. Understanding the research on motivation and its relationship to student academic needs enables teachers to implement instruction that results in virtually all students' obtaining feelings of worth within the school setting.

When frustrated by students' failure to pay attention, complete assignments, or attend class, teachers often blame family and community factors for students' lack of motivation to learn. Our own experiences and reading of the research suggests another explanation. The authors have never met a student who was unmotivated to learn. The authors have met many students who were unmotivated in certain settings but highly motivated in others, that is, students who were motivated when their learning needs were met but appeared unmotivated when they were not. Consider how you would feel if you were placed in a third-year, second-semester medical school program and told that your future success would be influenced by how you performed. Most people would search for ways to withdraw from or deny the value of this anxiety-provoking, stressful situation. More concretely, consider how you respond in a college course, in-service workshop, or meeting in which the content seems irrelevant or boring or when you are not asked to be actively involved. In our more than sixty years of attending faculty meetings, we have seen numerous examples of teacher behavior that looked similar to the behavior of the students sent to the senior author's office when he was a junior high school vice principal.

Like many other writers, the authors' view of motivation incorporates the expectation × value theory (Feather, 1982). This model suggests that the extent to which people become actively and productively involved in an activity is based on (1) whether they believe they can be successful at the task and (2) the degree to which they value the rewards associated with successful task completion. The authors add a third variable—

climate, or the quality of relationships within the task setting during the time the people are engaged in the task. Thus, the formula becomes:

motivation = expectation × value × climate

Because it is described as a multiplicative function, this model suggests that students will not be motivated unless all three components are present—that is, they (1) expect they can accomplish a task, (2) find value in the task, and (3) complete the task in an environment supportive of their basic personal needs.

It is important to note that this formula involves multiplication rather than addition signs, indicating that the components are related in a nonlinear fashion. For example, students might expect they can complete the work and enjoy the climate of the classroom, but have virtually no motivation because they do not believe the work is interesting or valuable. Similarly, students who want to accomplish a task and are working in an emotionally supportive environment will soon lose motivation if the work is simply too difficult to accomplish with any degree of success. This formula is supported by research indicating that teachers who are most effective with students whose second language is English but who have lived in the United States for a number of years, "devote considerable time helping their students learn to value school and to begin to see themselves as successful learners" (Freeman & Freeman, 2002, p. 10).

PAUSE
6.1 *and Consider*

Consider a recent learning experience you found stimulating or beneficial. On a sheet of paper create three columns or sections labeled expectation, value, and climate. In each section write a brief statement describing how the learning experience met each of these criteria for motivating your learning.

If a similar vein, if you are currently teaching or observing in a classroom, try to recall a situation in which a student you and others viewed as rather unmotivated to perform in school was productively involved in the learning process. Can you list the events that allowed this student to expect he or she could be successful at that task, value the work, and feel comfortable working in the setting?

The second concept that organizes the authors' thinking about motivation is Eccles and Wigfield's (1985) idea that three types of value may be associated with a task: (1) intrinsic value—the simple interest or enjoyment associated with engaging in a task; (2) attainment value—the value of obtaining achievement, notoriety, or influence through accomplishing a task; and (3) utility value—the benefits to one's career or other personal goals associated with performing a task successfully. This threefold concept suggests that teachers need to ensure that at least one type of value is present if students are to be motivated by the task.

In the authors' experiences, this concern about valuing learning is disproportionately expressed by teachers working in multicultural classrooms. In their article, "A Framework for Culturally Responsive Teaching," Raymond Wlodkowski and Margery Ginsberg (1995) "propose a model of culturally responsive teaching based on theories of intrinsic motivation. This model is respectful of different cultures and is capable of creating a common culture that all students can accept." These authors stated that the model is based on creating a learning environment that includes the following conditions:

1. Establishing inclusion—creating a learning atmosphere in which students and teachers feel respected by and connected to one another
2. Developing attitude—creating a favorable disposition toward the learning experience through personal relevance and choice
3. Enhancing meaning—creating challenging, thoughtful learning experiences that include student perspectives and values
4. Engendering competence—creating an understanding that students are effective in learning something they value (p. 19)

Perhaps the area in which teachers express the most concern is in the area of value or goals. Many teachers state that their students simply do not value learning, or at least not learning the content presented in their class. In his book, *Motivating Humans*, Martin Ford (1992) points out that although it is desirable for students to have multiple reasons for being involved in academic activities, for some students, educators may need to be creative to find one reason for students to become productively engaged in an activity.

> For example, by providing opportunities for self-determination or peer interaction, it may be possible to facilitate meaningful engagement in low-achieving students who generally focus more on fun and friendships than on learning and self-improvement. . . . Similarly, by organizing tasks so that they require teamwork and accountability to the group, students and workers who might be unenthusiastic about the substance of a task . . . will nevertheless have other reasons to commit themselves to good performance on the task . . . In short, although high achievement may require motivational patterns strengthened by the union of multiple goals . . . one may be able to ensure at least adequate levels of performance by designing classroom and work contexts so that everyone can find at least one good reason to invest themselves in contextually appropriate activities. . . . (p. 102)

As with personal needs, the understanding and response to students' academic needs is a central factor determining whether we as educators can create communities in which learning is viewed as desirable. The remainder of this chapter presents strategies for understanding and responding to students' academic needs that will allow us to build such communities.

STUDENTS' ACADEMIC NEEDS

Figure 6.1 provides a list of student academic needs that, when met, enhance student motivation and achievement. The list is based on the authors' own categorization of research and has been validated and expanded by lists generated by more than 1,000 teachers.

Support for these academic needs is found in the work of Eugene Garcia (1999). Based on his own research and an extensive review of existing work, Garcia presents a number of teacher characteristics and instructional methods associated with high achievement for students from diverse cultural backgrounds. These teacher behaviors include (1) focusing instruction to some degree on what has meaning to students; (2) using a thematic approach to instruction; (3) incorporating active learning, including a workshop approach to literacy; (4) implementing cooperative/collaborative learning activities; (5) communicating high teacher expectations for achievement of all students; (6) developing warm, caring relationships with students that often extend beyond the

1. Understand and value the learning goals.
2. Understand the learning process.
3. Be actively involved in the learning process.
4. Have learning goals relate to their own interests and set learning goals.
5. Experience success.
6. Receive realistic and immediate feedback that enhances self-efficacy.
7. Receive appropriate rewards for performance gains.
8. See learning modeled by adults as an exciting and rewarding activity.
9. Experience a safe, well-organized learning environment.
10. Have time to integrate learning.
11. Have positive contact with peers.
12. Receive instruction matched to their learning style and strengths.
13. Be involved in self-evaluating one's learning and effort.
14. Have instruction be sensitive to the needs of second-language learners.

FIGURE 6.1
Students'
Academic Needs

schoolday—including teachers learning about the students and their culture; (7) integrating aspects of all students' cultures into instructional activities; (8) creating opportunities for cross-age tutoring; and (9) incorporating specific instructional techniques for students with limited English proficiency. The approaches presented in this chapter are consistent with and provide specific methods for incorporating all of these methods into your instructional approach.

The methods presented in this chapter are also consistent with those recommended for the inclusion of students with special needs (Mastropieri & Scruggs, 2000; Salend, 1998). Mastropieri and Scruggs (2000) state that in order to be successful with students needing modifications in their class work, it is essential that the work is at an appropriate level of difficulty, the tasks are meaningful, and student success is based on improvement and obtaining goals rather than on comparison to fellow students. The methods presented throughout this chapter will assist you in creating lessons that meet these criteria.

The remainder of the chapter examines specific ways in which teachers can effectively meet these key academic needs and in so doing increase student motivation, learning, and productive behavior.

Academic Need 1: Understand and Value the Learning Goals

Walter Doyle (1983) wrote that "the quality of the time students spend engaged in academic work depends on the tasks they are expected to accomplish and the extent to which students understand what they are doing. It is essential, therefore, that direct instruction include explicit attention to meaning and not simply focus on engagement as an end in itself" (p. 189). Unfortunately, many students do not really understand why they are involved in a learning activity. They study to obtain good grades, please their parents or teacher, or avoid punishment. In summarizing the findings of a study on student engagement in academic tasks, Brophy (1986b) stated:

> Analysis of the teachers' presentations of assignments to the students suggested that teacher failure to call attention to the purposes and meanings of these assignments was a major reason for the students' low quality of engagement in them. Most presentations

included procedural directions or special hints (Pay attention to the underlined words), but only 5 percent explicitly described the purpose of the assignment in terms of the content being taught. (p. 11)

Fortunately, research suggests that teachers can quite rapidly learn to give students specific explanations concerning the purpose of instructional activities. Results indicate that students taught by these teachers demonstrate significantly greater understanding of and appreciation for the purpose of the instruction (Roehler, Duffy, & Meloth, 1987).

The authors have worked with several colleagues who have permanently written on their whiteboards the words:

- Objective(s)
- Reason(s)
- Activity(ies)
- Assessment

They begin almost every lesson by writing a statement providing responses to these terms as they apply to the upcoming lesson. This not only provides students with an opportunity to examine and discuss the learning goals but also helps students to understand the learning process.

In your own teaching, we strongly encourage you to work with students to develop and understand why learning objectives are important. Just as personal self-esteem is based on significance, competence and power, one of the foundations of academic self-esteem and motivation is student empowerment through understanding.

PAUSE
and Consider   **6.2**

We encourage you to keep a learning log of classrooms in which you are a student, observer, or teacher. Whenever a lesson is presented to a whole class, small group, or individual student, record what was said to help the student understand and value the learning goals. What percentage of the lessons or task introductions were associated with a clear statement regarding the reason for mastering the content? Were students involved in discussing and presenting their ideas regarding the benefits of mastering the learning goals? Did a pattern exist between involving students in this type of understanding and student motivation, engagement, and mastery?

Academic Need 2: Understand the Learning Process

In order to help students better understand the learning process, the authors have found it helpful to assist students in developing six key concepts related to learning.

Develop a Functional Definition of Learning
First, it is important to begin the school year by having students develop a functional definition of learning. The vast majority of students believe that effective learning means doing better than many of their classmates on homework assignments, in-class assessments, and standardized tests. Unfortunately, in every class and every school, 25 percent of the students are in the bottom quartile on any of these tasks (statistically, they must be). If teachers continue to allow students to define learning as the process of "winning,"

we will continue to have a significant percentage of students acting out and dropping out in response to their perceived failure.

One of the authors begins every school year by having students describe what an effective learner "looks like" and "sounds like." After students have generated this list, the class works to create several definitions of an effective learner. These might include that an effective learner makes a good effort and asks for help if needed, and makes progress towards meaningful goals. Figure 6.2 presents the responses generated by students in a fourth- and fifth-grade blended classroom taught by one of the authors during a recent school year. Once students have determined the characteristics of an effective learner, these standards can be used as criteria against which students can assess

"You were supposed to find the hypotenuse."

their own behavior. This allows students to redefine learning as being something concrete and obtainable rather than the elusive attempt to "be one of the best." It also creates a healthy set of behavioral norms for students.

Understand Basic Concepts of Motivation

A second approach to helping students understand the learning process involves teaching them the basic concepts of motivation described in this chapter. We believe students benefit from knowing that their motivation and behavior in a classroom will be influenced by their confidence in their ability to complete the work (expectation), the degree to which they find value in the work (value), and the quality of peer and teacher–student relationships in the classroom (climate). Although we have found many teachers reluctant

---

Looks Like

Eyes focused on speaker
Concentrates on their work
Is well organized
Cooperates with others
Follows classroom rules and procedures
Sets goals
Stays calm when having a problem
Uses time wisely
Learns from mistakes
Shares materials
Does not give up

Sounds Like

Gives encouragement
Uses appropriate voice level
Asks questions
Asks for help when needed
Shares their ideas with others
Comments are on-task
Is courteous to others
Uses problem solving

FIGURE 6.2
A Successful Learner

A successful learner is someone who works hard, cooperates with others, takes risks, sets goals, makes a good effort and asks for help if needed, doesn't give up, and learns from his or her mistakes.

to share this with students, our experiences indicate that teachers who share this with their students and use it as a basis for discussing student motivation are significantly more successful at obtaining high-achievement gains and supportive student behavior.

> Pause for a moment and consider what you have done or observed that helped students understand that learning is a process involving skills at which they can all be successful. You may not have your students define an effective learner, but it will be important to help them dispel the notion that effective learners are only those who find learning easy, score well on tests, or receive high grade averages. Discuss with several colleagues or classmates what you might do to help students in your class develop a healthy, functional definition of being an effective student/learner.

Appreciate and Use One's Special Abilities

A third method for enhancing students' understanding of the learning process involves teaching students Howard Gardner's concept that there are a number of types of special abilities and that students vary regarding which of these are strengths for them. Although various lists of special abilities have been presented and Gardner has considered expanding his list (Gardner, 1999a), we have found the most useful to be Gardner's original areas of intelligence or special abilities: (1) verbal/linguistic, (2) logical/mathematical, (3) visual/spatial, (4) musical/rhythmic, (5) bodily/kinesthetic, (6) interpersonal, (7) intrapersonal, and (8) naturalistic.

We have found it very helpful for students to understand that we all have areas of particular strength and areas we find more difficult to master. This is particularly important for students whose greatest areas of skills are not those most readily associated with academic content mastery, that is, verbal/linguistic and logical/mathematical. Virtually all these students possess wonderful skills. By introducing them to the concept of multiple intelligences (or, we prefer, "varied strengths") students can begin to understand that everyone has different areas of strength and limitations. When introducing this concept to students, the senior author tells the story of when he was in fifth grade and drew what he thought was the finest picture he had ever produced. When the teacher called the only two men in the building (the principal and the sixth-grade teacher/basketball coach) into the classroom to look at his piece, the author was devastated when they all began laughing so hard they nearly cried. The author did not draw again until he was seated with his five-year-old daughter at an evening parent event in her preschool. The teachers asked the parents to draw with their children and the author replicated the drawing he had produced twenty-six years earlier. The teacher walked past the author, put her hand on his shoulder and said, "What a thoughtful father to draw a picture just like a five-year-old." The author has not drawn a picture since that time. The author shares that should he decide to improve his art skills and enjoy drawing, he would need to work somewhat longer and more diligently than some of his students. Nevertheless, he could enjoy drawing and improve his skills. Students can be encouraged to examine and celebrate their own skills by creating a graph indicating how strong they believe they are in each of the eight areas previously listed. Students can then set goals for improvement in each area and determine methods for reaching these goals. Figure 6.3 presents an example of one such graph developed by a fifth-grade student in one of our classrooms.

A number of books are available to assist teachers in helping students understand the concept of multiple intelligences. The one we have found most useful is *Multiple Intelligences: Helping Kids Discover the Many Ways to Be Smart* (Huggins, Manion, Shakarian & Moen, 1997).

A section later in the chapter examines how you can incorporate multiple intelligence work into your classroom. At this point, it is helpful to consider how you want to help students appreciate that they all have areas in which they have special abilities and that you will provide them with opportunities to use these abilities in the classroom.

Learn about Your Learning Style
Fourth, it is important that students understand that individuals differ in their preferred approach to learning. Students can learn that everyone has different strengths and limitations regarding how they process information and how they prefer to learn. A positive, productive learning environment is one in which individuals accept and respond to these differences by creating opportunities for all students to use their preferences and strengths. As discussed later in this chapter, a wide range of methods exist to assist students in understanding and using their unique learning styles to strengthen their abilities as learners.

Understand a Taxonomy of Learning
Before examining how to incorporate methods for teaching students about various levels of learning, it is important to consider why this concept is important. The teaching

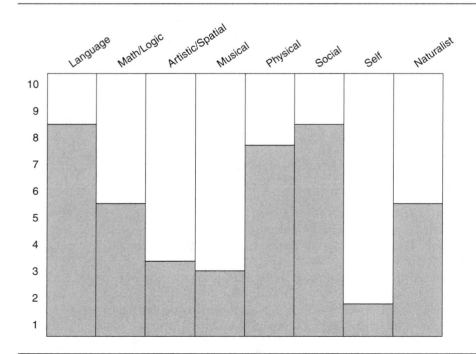

FIGURE 6.3
Take a Guess about Your Seven Intelligences

of factual material is certainly one function of the public schools. Schools serve society by transmitting information and providing children with basic skills in reading, writing, and arithmetic. The acquisition of basic factual information and skills is, especially in the primary grades, an important component of a child's learning. In a society characterized by rapid changes in technology and information processing, the acquisition of facts is increasingly a means to an end rather than an end in itself. Schools must begin early to help children use their basic skills for more analytic and creative purposes. Basic skills are important prerequisites to higher-level cognitive functioning. Especially at the secondary level, though, curriculum and instructional techniques used with students who possess basic skills too often focus on memorization and low-level cognitive skills.

When asked which values might best be taught by public schools, respondents to the 1999 Phi Delta Kappa/Gallup Poll of the Public's Attitudes toward the Public Schools listed patriotism (90 percent), moral courage (90 percent), caring for friends and family (93 percent), acceptance of people of different races and ethnic backgrounds (93 percent), democracy (93 percent), and honesty (97 percent). In addition, when asked in which area "local public schools should give the main emphasis," 46 percent of the respondents listed "ability to take responsibility," 39 percent listed "academic skills," and 13 percent listed "ability of students to work with others" as their top choice. Apparently adults in this society believe there is more to schooling than facts.

Levels of Instruction

The *facts* level involves providing students with basic information. When developing a unit on ecology, information on the chemicals that are associated with pollution, what causes pollution, and the effects various pollutants have on the human body would be included. This level is similar to the *knowledge* level described by Bloom (1956).

The *concepts* level focuses on the relationships among facts and examines major themes associated with facts. An ecology unit might examine the concept of people's relationships to their environments, the benefits and costs associated with progress, or responsibility to future generations. This level incorporates what Bloom describes as *comprehension* and *analysis*.

The *generalizations* level provides students with an opportunity to use the information they have obtained and the concepts they have developed to solve problems or interpret situations. In the context of an ecology unit, students might be asked to write legislative proposals dealing with ecology or to develop a model city. The educational objectives associated with these activities are similar to those Bloom labels *application*, *synthesis*, and *evaluation*.

At the final level is *personal application*. Here, students are asked to relate their learning to their own beliefs, feelings, and behaviors. In an ecology unit, students might be asked to discuss their own behavior regarding such topics as litter, recycling, or water usage. This level relates to the learning objectives in the affective domain described by Krathwohl, Bloom, and Masia (1964). Because it is at this level that students relate learning directly to their own lives, teachers should, whenever possible, incorporate this level into their instruction. No other level has greater potential for stimulating students' interest and increasing on-task behavior. The relationship between these four levels and Bloom's taxonomy is shown in Figure 6.4.

Teaching More Than Facts	*Bloom's Taxonomy*
Facts	Knowledge
Concepts	Comprehension Analysis
Generalizations	Application Synthesis Evaluation
Personal application	Affective domain

FIGURE 6.4
Comparison of Bloom's Taxonomy of Educational Objectives and Teaching More Than Facts

It is obvious that older students will be better able to become involved in instruction associated with higher levels. Nevertheless, primary teachers should attempt to help children develop simple concepts, think creatively about generalizations and applications, and, most important, view learning as something that relates to their own lives. Failure to incorporate higher levels indicates to children that learning is merely the acquisition of often unrelated facts. When this failure occurs, it is more difficult for teachers in subsequent grades to introduce higher levels of instruction.

An Example

An example of a lesson used by one of the authors in a fourth-grade class can help to clarify how each level can be incorporated into an instructional unit. The example, involving a unit on the Northwest Indians, begins with students learning numerous *facts* about the lives and history of these Native Americans. Individual student interests are accommodated by having each student choose a topic of special interest, obtain relevant material, and make a presentation to the class. As students learn about the beliefs Native Americans held and how their lives have changed over the years, discussions take place on *concepts* such as prejudice, progress, and might makes right. In this lesson, instruction at the *generalization* level takes two forms. First, students are asked to discuss such topics as what legislators could do to assist the Native Americans, how society should handle such current problems as salmon-fishing rights, and whether Native Americans should live their own lifestyle separately or be integrated into society. Second, students design and perform a *potlatch*. This performance involves creating costumes, learning authentic songs and dances, making dried food, and decorating the room.

One of the authors and a colleague have also developed a method for incorporating the *personal application* level by providing students with an intense personal experience related to this unit. The activity has one class move out of the classroom on the pretext that the other class needs the room to complete some useful research. The displaced class is placed in a corner in the hall behind a chalkboard. When students become uncomfortable and complain, it is suggested that they petition the principal to change the situation. The principal's refusal almost inevitably provokes anger associated with a sense of impotence. Once students have been allowed to experience these feelings, they return to their classroom and are assisted in sharing their feelings with the class that displaced them. The teachers then help the students draw the analogy between their experience and that of Native Americans. The activity ends by the two classes having a small party to reduce any negative feelings that may have been created by the experience.

It is likely that students will remember this activity and the basic concept taught. Although this example provides a rather dramatic approach to incorporating students' feelings into a lesson, there are numerous less time consuming approaches. Figure 6.5 outlines a high school unit that incorporates all four levels.

We encourage you to incorporate this information into your planning and to discuss with your students the various types of learning you are assisting them in developing. We have found it most helpful initially to teach a brief lesson on the levels of learning, and to follow this by initially beginning each lesson with a discussion of the level(s) of learning associated with the goals selected for the lesson. Although this approach is used by fewer teachers than most methods presented in this chapter, our experience suggests that student motivation and learning is enhanced when students understand the various types of learning outcomes.

PAUSE

and Consider   **6.4**

> You may find it helpful to examine a series of lessons or a unit you are teaching or observing someone teach. List several learning goals associated with each of the four levels discussed in this section. If virtually all of the goals are at a factual level, are there some students for whom this is not an engaging curriculum? If one or more levels are not being addressed, is there some way the curriculum could be modified slightly so as to incorporate these other levels? We encourage you to work with a colleague or classmate to take a lesson you will be teaching and see if you can create an outline similar to that found in Figure 6.5.

Learn How to Study Effectively

Many students lack skills for effectively learning new information. Interventions aimed at assisting students in developing improved learning strategies can be placed into three categories: (1) *cognitive interventions,* including skills for accomplishing specific tasks, such as underlining, highlighting, using a mnemonic, outlining, summarizing, and so on; (2) *metacognitive interventions,* including planning and monitoring one's use of strategies and determining when specific strategies are best used; and (3) *affective interventions* emphasizing attribution and attitudes (Hattie, Biggs, & Purdie, 1996). When the authors' daughter was in eighth grade, we realized she did not know how to read a novel differently from a history textbook. We taught our daughter to read textbook-like materials by looking at the headings and subheadings to determine what content was being covered in the chapter or section she was reading. Next, we suggested that she read the material and highlight what she believed to be the key content. As she completed each section, we taught her to write or say what she had learned from the section and how this related to the previous section or other material she was learning. We taught her to summarize by creating some form of visual schema or diagram to highlight her learning. Finally, we suggested that she write down questions she had regarding the material

Factual Level

Activities

1. Read the play aloud, with students taking parts and the teacher reading the more difficult parts and explaining as the students progress through the play.
2. Discuss what happens in each act, using a guide sheet.
3. Introduce students to the structure of a Shakespearean tragedy.
4. Introduce major themes and elements of a Shakespearean tragedy.
5. Give quizzes after the completion of each act and at the end of the play.

Concept Level

Activities

1. Relate the plot of *Romeo and Juliet* to movies the students have seen or books they have read. (A shortened version of *West Side Story* might be taught at the end of this unit in which character-by-character and scene comparisons are done.)
2. Discuss the problems Romeo and Juliet had in communicating with their parents. (Relate to Romeo's tragic flaw—impetuousness.)
3. Discuss the effects of hate and prejudice.
4. Discuss the concept of fate.
5. Introduce students to Elizabethan concepts relevant to a greater understanding of the play.
6. Point out universality of themes, characters, and situations to show their relevance to students.
7. By reading the play in class students will study it as a literary work and dramatic performance but they also will be viewing the Franco Zepherelli version of *Romeo and Juliet* to analyze his interpretation.
8. Discuss the plot complication of Juliet's impending marriage to Paris.

Generalization Level

Activities

1. Relate the specific problem of Romeo and Juliet to adolescents today.
2. Discuss alternatives to the outcome of Romeo and Juliet.
3. Discuss examples of hate and prejudice today.
4. Help students realize that reading Shakespeare's plays, like reading any great works of literature, is both a demanding and a rewarding experience.
5. Do environmental situations influence prejudice? Would there be more prejudice against gays in a small rural town or San Francisco?
6. Give examples of prejudice against nationalities, beliefs, appearances, and values.

Personal Application Level

Activities

1. What could Romeo and Juliet have done differently?
2. Do you think their death justifies the ending of the feud? (Do the means justify the end?)
3. Are Juliet's parents hypocrites?
4. How do you view the nurse's relationship to Juliet and did she betray Juliet?
5. Has the friar done the right thing for Romeo and Juliet?
6. What prejudices do you think you have?
7. How did you arrive at those prejudices? Did anyone or any situation influence you?
8. What can you and society do to help eliminate or reduce prejudice?

FIGURE 6.5
Teaching More Than Facts: A Lesson Design for Teaching *Romeo and Juliet*

and develop a plan for having these questions answered. This included our teaching her how to schedule time with a teacher and ways to ask teachers questions. The process we taught our daughter and have subsequently taught our son and many students is similar to the SCROL method developed by Grant (1993) in which students are asked to (1) Survey, (2) Connect, (3) Read, (4) Outline, and (5) Look Back; and the SQ3R method of Scan, Question, Read, Reflect, Review.

When reading a novel or other text without headings, we taught her to use a highlighter to mark key facts or concepts she thought the author was attempting to develop. We then suggested she again create some form of visual outline. Because she learns very well through interpersonal interaction, we then suggested she call or speak with someone in her class to discuss the material and the key concepts involved.

Students often have difficulty grouping or organizing material that is not in printed form. Learners construct knowledge as they build cognitive maps for organizing and interpreting new information. Effective teachers help students make such maps by drawing connections among different concepts and between new ideas and learners' prior experiences. There are several ways to help students organize their learning. First, we can provide students with a graphic organizer that provides students with an overview of key concepts and how they relate to one another. Crank and Bulgren (1993) suggest that there are three major types of graphic organizers: (1) central and hierarchical, (2) directional, and (3) comparative. Central and hierarchical indicate how a key concept is divided into components. In central organizers, the topics are shown as radiating from a central theme, whereas in hierarchical organizers key items have supporting information below them. A web is an example of a central organizer, and an outline using a format with Roman numerals, upper-case letters, numbers, and so on would be an example of a hierarchical organizer. Directional organizers show information in a time frame or cause-and-effect sequence. Comparative organizers show how two concepts compare and contrast.

We have worked with students who find spontaneous writing very difficult but who, once they create a central organizer, are freed to write rapidly and creatively. Many students simply need assistance and training in how to organize material so it is more readily accessible for retention or creative use.

Research is generally supportive of teaching learning skills, although these interventions are more effective under specific conditions. Most importantly, similar to the teaching of social skills discussed in Chapter 10, learning skills are most effectively taught when they focus on specific learning situations and attend to the practice and generalization of these skills.

Rather than present learning skills as a sequential curriculum, it is more effective to determine specific skills students may need to learn material within the upcoming days, and to provide them with strategies for more effectively learning the material. If this learning is to generalize to other classroom settings, students will need assistance in using their new techniques and understanding that it was the use of these methods, rather than your assistance, ease of task, or luck that enabled them to effectively master the content.

Study skills materials are available that provide teachers with a variety of strategies. Anita Archer and Mary Gleason (1989, 1994) have developed two programs: Skills for School Success (for grades three through six), and Advanced Skills for School Success (for middle school and high school). These programs provide a rich array of strategies for assisting students in mastering a wide range of learning goals.

Before continuing, consider a lesson or content you are currently teaching or observing someone teach. Are some students struggling to master or understand this content? Is it possible that part of their difficulty stems from their lack of skill in knowing how to study the material? Carefully observe several students who appear to be having difficulty mastering the content and consider how you might assist them in thinking about and studying the material. List one or more specific strategies you might assist them in using. Share this with at least one colleague.

General Methods for Demystifying Learning

There are a multitude of methods for ensuring that the learning process becomes less mysterious and better understood by students. Figure 6.6 provides a list of twenty-six ways to demystify the learning process by helping students develop a

1. Work with students to clearly and explicitly define learning.
2. Celebrate students' successes based on this definition.
3. Write and verbally explain the goals and objectives for each lesson and why these have been chosen.
4. Relate learning to students' own lives and interests.
5. Teach students a taxonomy of learning.
6. Teach students some basic concepts about student motivation.
7. Explain to students why you chose each instructional method to reach your stated goal.
8. Have students establish learning goals.
9. Use "experts" from the community to evaluate student performance, and demonstrate and discuss its value.
10. Teach students about learning styles.
11. Teach students about types of special abilities (Howard Gardner's concepts).
12. Teach students about learning disabilities (differences) and how students can work with these differences.
13. Use peer tutoring and teach students how to be tutors.
14. Teach students key instructional methods being used by a large number of staff, and involve students in providing teachers with feedback on how these are being implemented.
15. Involve students in teaching small lessons to the class so they can learn to appreciate the skills involved in effective teaching and the prerequisites for effective learning.
16. Have students provide ongoing feedback to the teacher regarding how the teacher is using effective instructional and management methods.
17. Explain to students your philosophy of assessment.
18. Be very specific in clarifying when assessment will occur, how it will be used, what to study, and how to study.
19. Have students monitor their own learning gains and grades.
20. Have students develop test questions.
21. Provide alternative methods for assessing students' knowledge.
22. Involve students in assessing their own effort in reaching learning goals.
23. Teach students a variety of study skills.
24. Provide students assistance in how to study specific types of materials.
25. Involve students in developing classroom rules and procedures.
26. Involve students in assessing how well they are following the rules and procedures.

FIGURE 6.6
Methods for
Demystifying the
Learning Process

clear understanding of what learning is and why curriculum and instructional decisions are made.

P A U S E

and Consider   **6.6**

> At this point, we encourage you to complete Activity 6.1 at the end of the chapter. This activity will help you make decisions regarding the methods you would like to incorporate to assist your students in better understanding the learning process.

Academic Need 3: Be Actively Involved in the Learning Process

Consider situations in which you were motivated to accomplish a task and found enjoyment in the work. It is likely that many of these tasks involved your active participation in the learning process. Although we cannot always meet this student academic need, student motivation and achievement will be enhanced by actively involving them in the learning process.

Although it is likely that almost all learners benefit from instructional activities that actively engage them, a number of writers have indicated that students of color respond more effectively to an instructional style that permits active student involvement. Kuykendall (1992) wrote that "educators who are serious about enhancing the achievement and motivation of Black and Hispanic youth must be willing to use a variety of activities to stimulate interest and facilitate student growth. . . . Black and Hispanic youth are likely to respond favorably to think-pair-share activities, lively group discussions, cooperative learning, group projects, and telling of stories about personal experience" (p. 39). Writers such as Banks and Banks (1993), Hale-Benson (1986), Kuykendall (1992), and Shade (1989) have noted that African American, Hispanic, and Native American students tend to be field-dependent learners who need to be more actively involved in the learning process.

It is useful for teachers to examine their daily and weekly schedules to determine the type of instructional activities in which they are engaging students. This might include the approximate percentage of time students are involved in teacher-directed activities, independent work, and cooperative group activities. This might be further broken down into active versus passive learning. For example, a week might be depicted as follows:

	Passive	**Active**
Teacher-directed	20%	15%
Independent work	30%	0%
Cooperative work	0%	35%

This would suggest a blend of activities as well as a balance of passive and active learning. Of course, even the more passive learning, such as listening to a lecture or reading, will be more likely to emotionally engage students if it is related to their interests and lives.

"In arithmetic, we're studying 'guzintas'—three guzinta nine three times, two guzinta four two times. . . ."

Academic Need 4: Have Learning Goals Relate to Students' Interests and Have Students Set Learning Goals

Several years ago one of the authors was supervising a student-teacher who had left a career in engineering to become a teacher. The student-teacher was taking over a high school physics class and asked the author to visit one of the first classes he would be teaching. During the class students were quite talkative and became increasingly inattentive as the class progressed. Several critical, disgruntled comments could be heard as the bell rang and the students left the class. The student-teacher, a mature and rather confident individual, was devastated. He slumped into a chair and emotionally told the author he apparently did not have what it took to be an effective teacher, that the class period had been painful, and he did not want to face another group of students.

The mentor teacher (a talented teacher with many years experience) overheard the conversation and assured the student-teacher that with some minor tinkering, the lesson could be a real success. He asked the student-teacher if he would be willing to teach the same lesson to a physics class two periods later with the caveat that the mentor would have five minutes to introduce the class. The mentor assured the student-teacher that he had a great deal to offer the students, and that his lesson needed only a little fine-tuning to be outstanding. The student-teacher reluctantly agreed to teach the lesson again.

When the classroom filled, the mentor teacher began the lesson by asking how many of the students had, at the beginning of the year, listed understanding flight as an interest and learning goal for the class. Most students raised their hands, and the teacher reinforced this response by providing the data that had been generated during the first week of class. He then informed the class that the next two weeks would be spent on some difficult material that, by itself, had little meaning. He noted, however, that when combined with one additional skill, this material would allow them to figure trajectories and other factors associated with flight. He then asked how many of the students were interested in delving into this difficult but important material. All the students in the class raised their hands. The mentor then informed the class that aerospace engineering was not his strength, but that the student-teacher who would be teaching them his unit had this very background and the students were in for a real treat working with him. With this introduction, the student-teacher took center stage and presented a lesson identical to that which one hour earlier had been met with student apathy, frustration, and disruptive behavior. This time students were attentive and frequently raised their hands to ask clarifying questions. When the class ended, approximately half of the students clapped to show their appreciation of the lesson. The student-teacher walked to the door, and as students left, a number of them thanked him for the lesson. In debriefing the lesson, the mentor reminded the student-teacher of the importance of connecting content to students' interests. He noted that this was not always possible, but when he was able to do it, the results were usually dramatic.

In reviewing research on effective instruction for students whose second language is English, Reyes and his colleagues noted, "But perhaps the most powerful finding pertaining directly to classroom learning was the incorporation of students' interests and experiences . . ." (Reyes et al., 1999, p. 14).

In their book, *Women's Ways of Knowing*, Belenky, Clinchy, Goldberger, and Tarule (1986) indicated that women benefit from learning environments that emphasize quality personal relationships and that value the learner's voice. Women seem to be more motivated and effective when they are able to relate material to their own lives, use their own experiences as valid contexts for interpreting and expanding information, and work collaboratively with others. This work has been expanded by others (Butler, 1993; Tetreault, 1993) who argue for a more personal and less competitive learning environment.

As teachers, we are making a major mistake and creating many problems for ourselves when we fail to provide productive outlets for students' interests. We can increase their motivation and learning by using a wide range of strategies that directly incorporate students' interests into the curriculum. The following methods suggest various approaches to incorporating students' interests.

Methods

1. *Early in the school year, have students build a list of things they would like to learn about in each major curriculum area to which they will be exposed.* This activity provides you with valuable information and stimulates students' interest by showing that some of their learning will relate directly to their interests. You may choose to create a unit on one or more topics that received widespread interest. Topics of interest can also be incorporated into the regular school curriculum. Finally, you may integrate these interests into several of the other strategies presented in this section.

2. *When introducing a unit, have the students list questions they have about the topics that will be covered.* In addition to providing you with useful information, this activity creates for the students an association (often lacking) between their interests and the material they are asked to learn.

3. *Teach students how to order films on topics that interest them.* Students can watch these films during study times when they have completed their work, in place of recess, or when you structure time for exploring individual interests. If a film is of particular interest because it relates to a topic being examined by the entire class or because many students share an interest, it can be shown to the entire class.

4. *Teach students how to invite guest speakers (including parents) to discuss a topic of interest to students.* You will, of course, always want to confirm younger students' contacts, but they can learn to take major responsibility for obtaining interesting guests.

5. *Create a unit on biographies.* Students can be asked to choose a person about whom they would like to know more and acquire information about this person. Each student can then dress up like the person they have researched and make a presentation to the class as that person.

6. *Allow individual students to choose special topics they would like to study.* When presenting a unit, have students choose different aspects of the topic and report their findings to the class.

7. *Create opportunities for structured sharing.* Each day of the week can be designated as a time for sharing what students have read or accomplished in a particular area. Monday might be set aside for sharing written compositions, Tuesday for newspaper articles, Wednesday for something positive students did for someone else, and so on.

8. *Have students develop special-interest days or weeks.* Students can decide on a topic they would like to study. All subject matter for the day (or week) can be related to this topic. If they selected whales, lessons in math, reading, creative writing, science, and social studies could be constructed around whales.

9. *When involving students in creative writing, do not always assign topics.* At times, allow students to write stories related to experiences that have been meaningful to them.

10. *Use learning logs.* In their learning logs, students write in their own words what they are learning, what it means to them, and how it relates to their own life.

11. *Begin a unit by having students write what they already know about the topic.* In addition to providing diagnostic information, you can use these data to involve students who have special interest and knowledge in instructing small groups or the entire class.

12. *Allow students to develop their own spelling list.* Teachers who use this approach often find that students who have previously learned very few spelling words make dramatic gains and select words more difficult than those they had been misspelling.

13. *Develop future plans.* Many students will be more motivated when we can make important connection between their own lives and classroom content. Future plans involve students in writing about what they want to do when they grow up (e.g., when they are twenty-five years old). This includes not only the job they would like to have but also what they would do with their leisure time, their roles in a family and community group, and so on. As students study various content areas, they are asked to discuss how what they are learning will help them enjoy these activities or perform adult tasks more successfully. This assessment and discussion can be incorporated on a weekly basis in secondary school base groups and in middle school advisory sessions, and on a daily basis in elementary school classrooms.

P A U S E

6.7   *and Consider*

Put the book aside for a moment and create a list of methods you have used or observed a teacher use to connect learning objectives and activities to students' interests. Share this list with a group of three or four colleagues or classmates and add some of their ideas to your list.

Utilizing Thematic Units

Several authors (Beane, 1997; Cummins, 1996; Garcia, 1999) suggest that in classrooms that more effectively served students with limited English proficiency, academic content is arranged around thematic units. In many instances students collaborated with teachers to select the themes.

One of the authors has been using this approach for more than thirty years. Working in a state that has adopted rigorous standardized testing to assess student learning, she has not abandoned this technique. Instead, much more care is taken to ensure that the academic skills learned as students become proficient are aligned with the state requirements. This creates a win–win situation for students. While remaining excited about and actively involved in meaningful learning, students continue to develop skills that will indicate to some decision makers that they have mastered key content and may progress to a higher grade. Figure 6.7 presents an outline of a thematic unit organized around the Iditarod dogsled race in Alaska. References at the end of the chapter list books to further explore integrated curriculum as a method for enhancing students' motivation to learn.

Place-Based Education

Another way to create thematic units involves what has been termed *place-based education* (Smith, 2002). The key concept in place-based education is that students are actively involved in learning experiences that involve and provide benefit to the communities in

FIGURE 6.7
Iditarod Thematic
Unit

I. Reading
  A. Iditarod vocabulary . . . word search
  B. Literature novels: *Woodsong, Stone Fox, Kiana's Iditarod, Julie of the Wolves*
  C. Short stories
  D. "IditaRead" reading race
II. Social Studies
  A. Serum Run of 1925
  B. History of the Iditarod
  C. Study of Alaska
  D. Map the route
  E. Geography of Alaska
  F. Directions during the race
  G. A typical day on the trail
  H. Native peoples and cultures of Alaska
III. Math
  A. Compute the distance of the race
  B. Examine distances between checkpoints using mean, median, and mode
  C. Math problem of the day
  D. Iditarod logic problems
  E. Compare prices for groceries in Alaska with those in your own state
  F. Iditarod problem solving
IV. Writing/Language Arts
  A. Write to a musher
  B. Follow a musher and write newspaper articles
  C. Daily oral language using sentences about the race
  D. Keep a diary as if you were a musher on the trail
  E. Write a congratulatory letter to a musher for finishing the race
  F. Write a poem about some aspect of the race
V. Science
  A. Create a weather center for weather reports during the race
  B. Graph temperatures at checkpoints in Alaska
  C. Invite a rescue official to talk about hypothermia
  D. Study glaciers and volcanoes and create a model of one
  E. Study an arctic animal and write a report
  F. Pretend you are an architect. Design a home for northern Alaska. How would you guard against permafrost?
  G. Draw an ecosystem that survives and adapts to the Arctic climate
  H. Study the Aurora Borealis
  I. Bring a veterinarian to talk about treatment of the dogs
  J. Study the equipment needed for the race; plan to pack a sled by drawing what is needed.
VI. Art
  A. Create a watercolor of the Aurora Borealis
  B. Design a poster for this year's Iditarod race
  C. Build a model of a musher's sled
  D. Design a picture of what clothes a musher must have on the trail
  E. Create dream catchers
  F. Make a native story mask
VII. Music
  A. Learn songs from the trail
  B. Create a song about the Iditarod using familiar tunes
  C. Listen to and make native musical instruments

which they live. Smith (2002) suggests that there are five types of place-based education: (1) cultural studies, (2) nature studies, (3) real world problem solving, (4) internships and entrepreneurial opportunities, and (5) induction into community processes. Individual teachers working with their students can quite readily accomplish the first three of these. In cultural studies projects students study and write about their communities and members in the community. Nature studies may involve the study of an issue related to conservation or an endangered species. Real world problem solving involves students in selecting a problem in their community and solving this problem. Nancy Nagel (1996) provides numerous examples of this process being effectively implemented, including work by interns in a master's degree teaching license program. Examples include students cleaning up and refurbishing their playground in an area racked by vandalism and graffiti, and students solving a water runoff problem based on the destruction of a stand of trees at their school. Results of each type of placed-based education program show marked improvement in

"That class ought to come with a warning: 'May cause drowsiness.'"

students' positive behavior and academic achievement. It is exciting to see students and entire classes that had been defined as classroom management problems be viewed as responsible citizens when they are given the opportunity to serve as responsible citizens.

PAUSE

6.8   *and Consider*

Before continuing on with the chapter, take a minute to consider a unit you will be teaching within the next several months. If you are observing in a classroom, consider a unit the teacher will be teaching. Write a brief statement about how you might involve students in relating this curriculum to their lives, perhaps by developing a thematic unit around a topic the students select or developing the content within the context of a real-world problem-solving activity. Share your idea with two or three colleagues or classmates and have them provide you with feedback and suggestions.

Involving Students in Academic Goal Setting

Individual goal setting is perhaps the most effective method for enabling students to experience a sense of understanding and controlling their own learning while incorporating their own interests. This method also has potential for helping students select learning activities that are congruent with their learning style. Teachers need to help students develop goals that are both realistic and directed at improving skill deficits revealed by diagnostic testing and observation, but students' involvement in establishing goals and recording progress can also significantly enhance their motivation and reduce acting-out or withdrawal behavior.

An academic goal statement or contract should include (1) what material the student plans to learn, (2) what activities the student will engage in to develop these skills, (3) the degree of proficiency the student will reach, and (4) how the student will demonstrate that the learning has occurred. Several approaches may be used when implementing academic goals. Each student can be involved in working toward one or more academic goals associated with a personal skill deficit or interest. This emphasis on goals can be expanded to incorporate term-length goal statements. Because most schools provide an academic report to parents (and, hopefully, to students) following a nine-week term, students can be aided in setting several academic goals on a term basis. Nine weeks will be too long for primary children, but most intermediate grade and secondary students find nine-week goal setting provides a sense of direction and commitment. At the beginning of each term, you and the student can examine the student's current performance level and the material the student will study during the term. The student can be helped to write several goals for the term, perhaps stating that by the end of the term she or he will be able to solve two-place multiplication problems with 80 percent accuracy. It is obviously important that you help each student choose goals that are attainable but that will require some additional effort by the child. Although children are motivated to achieve goals that require some real effort, they are also frequently intimidated by goals that seem impossible to reach. Furthermore, continued failure tends to reduce students' achievement orientation and self-concept. Figure 6.8 is an example of a form an elementary or middle school teacher could use to help students commit themselves to specific academic goals.

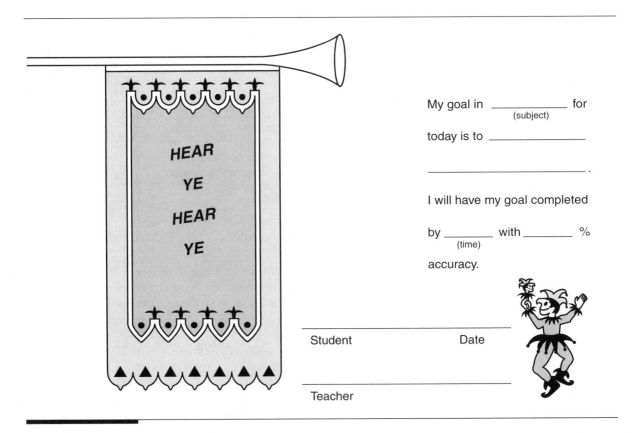

FIGURE 6.8
Goal-Setting Form

Another approach to employing academic goal setting involves designing assignments that allow students to choose the type of work they will complete, and, if appropriate, the grade they will earn for completing the designated amount of work. The most common format for using this method involves listing assignments for earning each grade and having students sign a contract indicating which assignments they plan to complete. This approach is particularly effective when you wish to involve all students in an assignment on which lower-achieving students might experience considerable difficulty with more complex aspects of the assignment. A contractual approach enables each student to choose an appropriate level of difficulty, and you can ensure that the basic concepts are learned by incorporating them within the lowest acceptable level. Students respond positively to this approach because it is a clear statement of what they will learn and what they must accomplish.

The benefits of this approach were highlighted in a study involving adolescents with behavior problems (Maher, 1987). In this study, forty-nine high school students identified under special education classification as behavior disordered were placed in mainstream classes. Half the students and their mainstream teachers were involved in jointly setting academic goals and specifying the instructional methods that would be used to reach these goals. The remaining students were placed with teachers who were required to set instructional goals but who did not work with students in setting these goals or discussing instructional methods. Results indicated that students involved in goal setting and a discussion of instructional methods learned more, felt more positive about school, and felt that this approach would be useful with other students who have behavior problems. Teachers involved in the experimental group used a greater diversity of instructional methods, were positive about the approach, and stated that they could incorporate the approach within their normal planning.

Academic Need 5: Experience Success

No one enjoys being in a setting in which he or she consistently fails.

P A U S E

6.9   *and Consider*

Consider for a minute a situation in which you lacked the skills others around you possessed. Perhaps you were one of the last to be chosen for playground games or your artwork was met with giggles and stares of disbelief. How did you feel in these situations? Write a brief statement about a situation in which this happened to you. What was your reaction?

If you are like most people, you avoided getting yourself in these situations and, when required to be there, you found ways to reduce your involvement in the activities or to leave the setting entirely. To a large degree, this behavior was influenced by the need to view oneself as competent. Success experiences are instrumental in developing feelings of self-worth and confidence in attempting new activities. "It is through achievement that academic self-confidence grows, and increased confidence in turn promotes achievement through inspiring further learning. In short, confidence and competence must increase together for either to prosper. When they do not grow apace, students are likely to suffer" (Covington & Beery, 1976, p. 5).

Teacher effectiveness research suggests that students' learning is increased when they experience high rates of success in completing tasks. When the teacher is available to monitor and assist students, success rates of 70 to 80 percent are desirable. When students are expected to work on their own, success rates of 95 to 100 percent are desirable. Studies suggest that when students are given inappropriate tasks, the tasks are much more likely to be too difficult than too easy. Following successful experiences, individuals tend to raise their expectations and set higher goals, whereas failure is met with lowered aspirations. Success or failure also influences individuals' self-evaluations. Studies also indicate that praising students' work produces greater performance gains than does criticism and that the positive effects in self-rating and performance tend to spread to areas related to those in which praise was provided for success experience.

Students who have a history of school failure and are concerned about future failure are at a distinct disadvantage. Students who are anxious about their performances divide their attention between the material being taught and their concerns about failure, or being criticized or embarrassed. These students are involved in a downward spiral; they miss considerable amounts of information because of their anxiety. The power associated with preventing feelings of humiliation and incompetence is supported by the fact that many students choose a teacher's frustration and criticism about their behavior rather than risk another academic failure. Students who experience a low rate of school success are more likely to have an external locus of control. Students who believe that their past failures were caused by lack of ability are less likely to anticipate future success and are therefore less likely to exert effort. In extreme cases, this can lead to learned helplessness, in which the students feel that nothing that they do matters.

One of the authors recently worked with a talented high school teacher in a district serving approximately 85 percent Chapter I students. In order to increase student motivation, the teacher incorporated four key methods. First, he used peer-relationship activities to help create a more cohesive group. Second, he established base groups so students had peer invitations and accountability. Third, he expanded his use of cooperative learning. Fourth, he used the goal setting and monitoring form seen in Figure 6.9. He discovered that students were particularly unskilled at specifying strategies they could use to complete their work. The form provided an impetus to work with students on their planning skills and for students to hold themselves and their peers accountable. He reported that student work completion and attendance increased dramatically and that many students commented on the chance to set their own goals and evaluate their progress.

Modifying Instruction and Assessment

Students need to know that we will modify classroom work so they can experience success. Several years ago the authors' daughter who reads

"Of course it's wrong. That's why I go to school."

Subject	Homework Assignment	Due Day/Date	Study Strategy (Where-When-How)	Target Grade	Date Completed	Strategy Grade	Grade

The study strategy that I found most helpful this week was: _____

FIGURE 6.9
Homework Plan

rather slowly was told by her teacher that he loved to read and hoped all his students would enjoy the extensive reading they would be completing during their eighth-grade year. He also informed them that students who had difficulty completing their reading were welcome to read like he does (using books on tape or having someone read to them)—because he is blind. This kind of creativity, compassion, and flexibility provides all students with the opportunity to feel competent and empowered in the classroom.

You will have access to many books, workshops and assistance from specialists regarding how to modify instruction. Because student success is such an essential factor related to creating positive learning communities in which students behave in ways that benefit themselves and others, we offer several ideas that have proved helpful in our thinking about how to modify instruction.

Because all good instruction begins with knowing your students and planning, Figure 6.10 presents a list of planning questions you may want to consider in order to facilitate your modification of materials for students who will need some special assistance.

Once you have determined the type of assistance a student may need, you will find many methods available for assisting students in having successful learning experiences. One approach we have found very helpful involves a model developed by Cole et al. (2000a) that provides a conceptual framework for adapting curriculum and instruction to enhance teachers' skills and to increase options for adapting across the curriculum. The components of this model were developed by teachers at the elementary, middle, and high school levels. The process begins with the selection of the subject, lesson, curricular goal, and instructional plan for most learners. The next step is to identify the learners who will need adaptations to the curriculum or instructional plan. Based on the curricular goal and instructional plan, educators can use the nine types (see Figure 6.11) to determine which adaptations will be the most appropriate for the individual child's needs. In this model, educators examine pupils' needs, interests, and abilities, and the delivery of instruction as possible adaptations. Figure 6.12 shows how the process is applied. Although there are numerous ways to modify instructional factors, Figure 6.13 presents a list we have found helpful.

P A U S E

and Consider   **6.10**

> Regardless of whether you are currently teaching, student teaching, or observing, we encourage you to complete Activity 6.3 at the end of the chapter. You may wish to do this activity with several colleagues or classmates. This will allow you to practice and/or reinforce modifying instruction and assessment to assist a student who is struggling with some aspect of the classroom content. This practice of "leveling the playing field" is an essential component of effective classroom management.

Another strategy we have found extremely helpful in implementing the idea that all students can succeed is a success contract (Figure 6.14). This contract is a formal, collaboratively designed agreement between the teacher and student to clarify what both parties will do to ensure the student's success. The authors have worked with more than 100 teachers who have reported dramatic results with this format.

I. Content

1. What are the content requirements of the curriculum?
2. Which objectives are most essential?
3. Which students require a functional curriculum and need parallel instruction (same basic content but on a less taxing conceptual level)?
4. What alternative materials are available (including audiovisual materials)?
5. What rubrics will be used to measure student performance?
6. What role will students play in suggesting activities or the unit?
7. Will this material motivate students who are not usually interested in school?

II. Student Concerns

1. Which students can effectively learn the material with little adaptation?
2. Which students require basic instruction on only the essential components?
3. Which students require alternative reading materials or taped readings, but can handle the concepts intellectually?
4. Which students can master the objectives and will require more depth or breadth in their study?
5. What behaviors will the students engage in during the unit activities?
6. Will personal assistance or natural supports be necessary for any students?

III. Instructional Methods

1. Which instructional approaches are going to be most effective with the content?
2. Where will group activities fit into the plan?
3. Which students will benefit from peer tutoring or being a peer tutor?
4. How will the room arrangement affect the instructional plan?
5. How will groupings be determined?
6. What purpose will groupings serve?
7. How will student interest be sparked in introducing the unit?
8. Will students have an opportunity to interact?
9. What role will the teacher play during instruction (direct teaching, tutoring, facilitating, observing, etc.)?
10. What behaviors will the student engage in during the unit activities?
11. How will IEP goals and objectives be met through the planned activities?
12. How will student progress be monitored and evaluated (daily, weekly, for the unit)?
13. How will outcome expectations be communicated to the students?

FIGURE 6.10
Preplanning Questions

Source: From Dianne Bradley, Margaret King-Sears, & Diane Tessier-Switlick, *Teaching Students in Inclusive Settings*, p. 231. Copyright © 1997 by Allyn & Bacon. Reprinted by permission.

Academic Need 6: Receive Realistic and Immediate Feedback That Enhances Self-Efficacy

Closely associated with the need for success experiences is the need to receive immediate and specific feedback. Because students care about being successful, it is important that they receive feedback clearly designating the extent to which they have succeeded at a task. Studies suggest that students' achievements are enhanced by providing them with information about their current level of performance followed by specific learning tasks aimed at mastering the material.

In fact, students most concerned about failing are most in need of immediate feedback; without it, they tend to judge their performance as unacceptable.

FIGURE 6.11
Nine Types of
Adaptations

Source: From Cole,
S., Horvath, B.,
Chapman, C.,
Deschenes, C.,
Ebeling, D. G., &
Sprague, J. (2000).
*Adapting curriculum
and instruction in
inclusive classrooms:
Staff development kit,*
2nd ed.
Bloomington, IN:
Indiana Institute on
Disability and
Community.
Reprinted by
permission.

Input
The instructional strategies used to facilitate student learning.
For example:
Use of videos, computer programs, field trips, and visual aids to support active learning.

Output
The ways learners can demonstrate understanding and knowledge.
For example:
To demonstrate understanding, students write a song, tell a story, design a poster or brochure, perform an experiment.

Size
The length or portion of an assignment, demonstration or performance learners are expected to complete.
For example:
Reduce the length of report to be written or spoken, reduce the number of references needed, reduce the number of problems to be solved.

Time
The flexible time needed for student learning.
For example:
Individualize a timeline for project completion, allow more time for test taking.

Difficulty
The varied skill levels, conceptual levels and processes involved in learning.
For example:
Provide calculators, tier the assignment so the outcome is the same but with varying degrees of concreteness and complexity.

Level of Support
The amount of assistance to the learner.
For example:
Students work in cooperative groups, or with peer buddies, mentors, cross-age tutors or paraeducators.

Degree of Participation
The extent to which the learner is actively involved in the tasks.
For example:
In a student written, directed, and acted play, a student may play a part that has more physical action rather than numerous lines to memorize.

Modified Goals
The adapted outcome expectations within the context of a general education curriculum.
For example:
In a written language activity, a student may focus more on writing some letters and copying words rather than composing whole sentences or paragraphs.

Substitute Curriculum
The significantly differentiated instruction and materials to meet a learner's identified goals.
For example:
In a foreign language class, a student may develop a play or script that uses both authentic language and cultural knowledge of a designated time period, rather than reading paragraphs or directions.

Supportive comments, accompanied by statements about specific strengths and weaknesses in students' work, are more effective in improving students' performances than are either grades or brief positive comments. Butler and Nisan (1986) compared student responses to papers with either substantive comments and no grade or grades with no comments. Students who received comments more fre-

1. Select the subject area (and grade level) to be taught:

   math   science   history   literature   business   P.E.   fine arts   health

   Grade level: _____

2. Select the lesson topic to be taught (on one day): _____

3. Briefly identify the *curricular* goal for most learners: By the end of this class, students will know _____

   _____

4. Briefly identify the *instructional* goals: As a teacher, I will _____

   _____

   _____

5. Now use nine types of adaptations as a means of thinking about ways you could adapt what or how you teach to accommodate this learner in the classroom for this lesson.

Input	Output	Time
Difficulty	Level of Support	Size
Degree of Participation	Modified Goals	Substitute Curriculum

FIGURE 6.12

Creating Ways to Adapt Familiar Lessons— Secondary

Source: From Cole, S., Horvath, B., Chapman, C., Deschenes, C., Ebeling, D. G., & Sprague, J. (2000). *Adapting curriculum and instruction in inclusive classrooms: Staff development kit,* 2nd ed. Bloomington, IN: Indiana Institute on Disability and Community. Reprinted by permission.

quently stated that they (1) found the task more interesting, (2) worked on the task because they were interested in the material, and (3) attributed their success on the task to their interest and effort.

The quality of feedback is important because it affects students' perceptions of themselves as learners. Stipek (1988) stressed the importance of students receiving feedback that helps them see their progress: "Unless students actually perceive themselves to be making progress in acquiring skills or new knowledge, they will not feel efficacious, even if they are rewarded for their efforts and even if their performance is better than others'" (p. 94).

Not all feedback is effective in improving students' performances. Studies show that hostile or extensive criticism creates negative attitudes and lowers achievement, creativity, and classroom control. Praise is often overused and is not a powerful reinforcer for many children. Praise can be an effective form of feedback when it provides students with specific information about the quality of their work and the effort made to complete the work. However, praise is often misused. Teachers frequently praise incorrect answers, and this false praise is more often given to lower-achieving students.

Rosenholtz and Simpson (1984) examined classroom variables that affect how students view their abilities. They categorize classrooms as unidimensional (creating a sense that ability is a stable characteristic and in which students know who has and does not have ability) and multidimensional (in which ability is not nearly as stratified). In

FIGURE 6.13

Instructional
Adjustments for
Students with
Special Academic
Needs in a Regular
Classroom

Time—Adjust work time by

1. Giving a longer time to complete assignments.
2. Allowing the student to work at reading and writing assignments for short periods of time, perhaps only 10 or 15 minutes depending on student's ability to concentrate, followed by other types of activities for short periods of time.
3. Setting up a specific schedule for the students so that they know what to expect.
4. Alternating quiet and active time, having short periods of each.
5. Reading the test, if necessary.

Learning Environment—Adjust the learning setting by

1. Permitting students to do their work in a quiet, uncrowded corner of the room, or in some school area they choose; however, do not isolate them against their will.
2. Placing the student close to the teacher for more immediate help when needed.
3. Placing the student next to another student who can help when needed.
4. Separating the student from students who are most likely to be distracting.
5. Letting the student choose a quiet area of the room to work.
6. Formulating a small work group of three or four students, hold all members of the group responsible for making certain that each group member completes assignments successfully.
7. Providing a peer helper who can assist by (a) making certain the student understands directions or assignments; (b) reading important directions and essential materials to the student; (c) drilling the student orally on key material; (d) summarizing orally important textbook passages; (e) writing down answers to tests and assignments for the student; (f) working with the student on joint assignments; and (g) editing the student's work, making suggestions for improvements.

Content—Adjust type, difficulty, amount, or sequence of material by

1. Giving a lesser amount of work.
2. Breaking assignments down into short tasks.
3. Giving only one (or a few) question at a time during testing.
4. Including in assignments only material that is absolutely necessary.
5. Highlighting or underlining textbook passages that contain key facts or concepts.
6. Using markers to tell students where to start or stop an assignment.
7. Providing specific questions to guide their reading.
8. Establishing academic goals and strategies for reaching the goals.
9. Making certain students' desks are free from unnecessary material.
10. Picking up work as soon as it is completed.
11. Giving immediate feedback on tasks or work completed.
12. Having on hand alternate and supplementary materials.
13. Giving students several alternatives in both obtaining and reporting information—tapes, interviews, reading, experiences, projects, and so forth.
14. Having frequent (even if short) one-to-one conferences with students.
15. Helping students to restate what they are responsible for.
16. Helping students assess their progress toward completion of work.
17. Eliminating unnecessary words on tests.
18. Capitalize and underline words such as *always, never, not on test;* avoid negatively stated questions, especially in true–false questions.

Organization—Organizational notebook

FIGURE 6.13
Continued

Many students, especially students with learning disabilities, frequently have difficulty with tasks involving organization of time and materials. Success for these students may be facilitated by teaching such skills as notebook organization. Both the teacher and students may then have a system to assure that such activities as homework assignments have been copied accurately. Include the following.

1. Three-ring binder to hold all materials.
2. Paper calendar—attach the current month on the inside cover of the notebook for assignment due dates.
3. Plastic pouch for pencils, erasers, pens, cards, file cards, and so on.
4. Folder with pockets for each class to hold assignments and study guides.
5. Spiral notebook.
6. Copy of SQ3R (Scan, Question, Read, Reflect, Review) study technique taped to inside back cover.

The organization notebook has proven effective for both elementary and secondary students.

Success Contract

FIGURE 6.14
Success Contract

I, _____, have decided that I want to pass Mr. Jones's class. Mr. Jones cares about my being successful and has agreed to provide the following assistance:

a. _____
b. _____
c. _____

What I will need to do in order to take advantage of these opportunities is:

a. _____
b. _____
c. _____

Mr. Jones and I will examine my progress and share it with my parent(s)/guardian and _____ on _____.
    (Support person)   (Date)

I will know I have succeeded when _____
_____

Signed

_____   _____   _____
   (Student)   (Teacher)   (Support Person)

---

unidimensional classrooms, feedback is provided in such a way that students can easily compare their work with others. For example, charts indicating the level of student performance are placed on the walls, and exemplary work and the names of students whose work is missing or needs redoing are prominently displayed. Rosenholtz and Simpson suggest that to encourage students to see ability as a trait or factor that is flexible and related to effort, teachers should make feedback and evaluation a more private matter.

Effective feedback provides students with important benchmarks. It enables students to understand where they are in relation to achieving goals, the amount of progress they have made toward a goal, and what they need to do to continue or improve on their progress. Effective feedback also communicates that the teacher believes the student can reach predetermined goals, that the student's effort is a major factor influencing the outcome, and that how a student's progress compares to that of other students is not a major factor.

P A U S E

and Consider   **6.11**

> Pause for a moment and consider how you, or a teacher with whom you are working, provide feedback to the students. Does the manner in which student work is responded to and displayed create a sense that student effort and improvement are valued, or that excellent performance is the most important factor? We encourage you to form groups of three or four and discuss ways teachers at the grade level and subject matter you are teaching or observing use feedback to encourage all students. You may want to share your small-group results with a larger group and develop several key concepts and a number of methods that encourage and empower students.

Academic Need 7: Receive Appropriate Rewards for Performance Gains

"Rewards are one proven way to motivate students to put forth effort, especially when the rewards are offered in advance as incentives for striving to reach specified levels of performance" (Good & Brophy, 1994, p. 225). When considering the value of rewards for performance gains, however, educators need to consider several important problems associated with the use of rewards. First, numerous studies indicate that external rewards can reduce intrinsic interest in a task. Children who receive a reward for participating in an activity may show less interest in the activity. Therefore, rewards should be used only when other attempts, such as altering the approach to presenting the material, individual goal setting, and other motivational and instructional strategies, have failed.

Although we generally agree with Kohn's (1993) concerns about rewards expressed in his book, *Punishment by Rewards*, the negative effects of extrinsic rewards appear to be greatest when students already value the work, when giving the reward distracts the students from their work, or when some other form of goal conflict is operating. If, however, the individual has virtually no motivation for engaging in an activity, providing a reward (especially if the reward is related to a student's goals, was negotiated with the student, or otherwise enhances the person's sense of efficacy and personal control) can be used to enhance motivation to learn. One way for rewards to be effectively integrated into your school or classroom is to view rewards as one aspect of a celebration. It is important to celebrate group and individual successes at the smallest possible unit (i.e., within the supportive classroom rather than at an all-school event). The authors will never forget their daughter's reaction on her last day of what she felt had been a successful sixth-grade year. She returned home following the school awards ceremony and announced in an uncharacteristically despondent manner that she must have had a terrible year because she sat for nearly two hours while awards were presented and never heard her name.

Academic Need 8: See Learning Modeled by Adults as an Exciting and Rewarding Activity

As mentioned in Chapter 3, teachers possess many characteristics that make their behavior likely to be modeled. Therefore, teachers should carefully consider how they model an interest in and excitement about learning. Research suggests that teachers who are more effective in enhancing students' motivation to learn show an interest in and excitement about learning and model task-related thinking and problem solving. When students observe you in the classroom, are they seeing someone who appears sincerely and enthusiastically interested in what they are doing and teaching? Many secondary teachers we know work with their students, sharing their poetry, outlines, and thoughts about social events, scientific work, and so on. Although we must be careful to not overshadow our students or provide ideas they should be generating, we will be more effective when they observe us actively and enthusiastically engaged in the learning process.

Academic Need 9: Experience a Safe, Well-Organized Learning Environment

Given the number of students who come from home environments characterized by a lack of support, safety, and consistency, it is imperative that teachers develop clear expectations about student behavior and academic performance. These expectations should include the statement that the teacher will fulfill his or her responsibility to ensure that other students will not interfere with a student's right to feel safe, supported, and able to work in a calm learning environment. Students also need to understand how the classroom will operate, how problems will be resolved, and how they will be involved in influencing classroom structures—including curricular and instructional decisions. The skilled teacher balances the value of structure in creating a safe, clearly understood classroom environment with the costs associated with too much teacher dominance or control. Chapter 7 presents methods for creating well-structured classrooms. Chapters 8 through 10 offer methods for increasing classroom order and safety by helping students modify their unproductive behavior.

"But I didn't mean to be disruptive . . . it just seemed to me that such a serious subject cried out for some comic relief."

Academic Need 10: Have Time to Integrate Learning

Students need time during the schoolday to slow down and integrate what they have learned. All too often, students are rushed from one activity to another, with no time allotted for summarizing the learning that has taken place in each activity. When this hurry occurs, students begin to feel confused and often experience a sense of failure because they frequently have not understood what it was they were supposed to have learned from the preceding activity. As teachers, we are often lulled into believing that everyone has understood because several of our students who learn quickly indicate that the material has been learned and understood. Students learn at varying rates, however, and in different ways, and it is important to slow down and provide all students with an opportunity to organize the new ideas that have been presented. Effective teachers develop specific instructional activities designed to help students summarize new learning and relate this new knowledge to previous and future learning and the students' own lives.

During the past decade, many elementary, middle, and secondary schools have moved toward scheduling lessons and classes for extended blocks of time so teachers have greater flexibility in incorporating interactive, interdisciplinary instruction and students have more time to explore and integrate new learning.

Academic Need 11: Have Positive Contact with Peers

As discussed in Chapter 2 and expanded on in Chapter 4, having support from peers is a major factor influencing students' motivation to learn. The increased use of activities to help students know their peers, develop a sense of being part of a group, and develop improved group skills are essential aspects to motivating all students to learn.

Academic Need 12: Receive Instruction Responsive to Students' Learning Styles and Special Abilities

Teachers can increase students' motivation and success by responding effectively to students' learning styles. Students differ in their approaches to learning. Every student has a cognitive or learning style that represents the general approach the student takes to learning and organizing material. Teachers too often examine students' failures by considering personal and social problems rather than focusing on the child's special interests or learning styles to determine the best approach to providing instruction. Teachers who use the same instructional methods with every student or who use a limited range of instructional activities will create a situation in which some students become frustrated, experience failure, and respond by misbehaving.

The authors had this concept personally highlighted. Our daughter, a vibrant, sensitive young woman with marvelous ego strength, experienced a terrible year in tenth grade. Although she studied nearly five hours a night, she earned only a C+ grade average, experienced health problems caused by tension, and seemed to find almost no joy in learning. During her college years, she was excited about learning, relaxed, and had an A– average. What was the difference? Teachers whose style of teaching matches her way of learning! She is a dynamic, interpersonal learner who values relationships and warm, personal interaction in the classroom. When these factors are present she quickly masters concepts and finds herself effortlessly putting time and energy into learning. Perhaps more than ever we understand that students' attitudes and behaviors are influenced by the instructional strategies and type of learning atmosphere they experience in the classroom.

Applying Learning Style Research

Applied learning style work falls into two general approaches. Some writers emphasize the importance of adjusting environmental factors including the student's preferred modality (e.g., visual, kinesthetic, or auditory), time of day the student prefers to learn, and so on. Other writers focus on how students prefer to work with information (e.g., they may want to relate it to their own lives, analyze it, or create something from it).

Extensive research by Rita Dunn and her colleagues provides support for the environmental emphasis (Dunn, Thies, & Honigsfeld, 2001). Dunn's research has demonstrated that a variety of elements differentially affect individuals' learning. Figure 6.15, a chart designed by Kenneth and Rita Dunn, demonstrates these variables or elements. Dunn (2001) reports various studies demonstrating that allowing students to work in classroom settings in which environmental, physical, and sociological factors were similar to those preferred by the student dramatically enhances student learning.

For example, studies (Dunn, 2001) suggest that many students learn material more effectively and score higher on tests when allowed to sit on comfortable materials rather than at standard desks and when allowed to work in noisy environments, and that some students, especially elementary children, learn more effectively and are less fidgity in lowered rather than in bright lights. In one study, half of all seventh-grade students in one junior high school learned more effectively when allowed to move about during learning activities. Student learning can also be enhanced by allowing students to eat when they need to, study material at a time of day best suited to their learning preference, and learn through modalities they prefer.

Adjusting Environmental Factors to Meet Students' Learning Needs

Research (Dunn, 1989) indicates that most students are significantly affected by approximately six of the factors that influence students' learning. By adjusting the classroom environment and some instructional methods, teachers can easily create a learning environment more conducive to many students' unique learning needs. The following methods have been implemented by the authors and by many teachers with whom they work.

Methods

1. *When presenting material, use visual displays, such as writing on the overhead projector, to assist students who are visual learners.* Dunn (1983) stated that approximately 40 percent of students learn more effectively when they can read or see something. Interestingly, Price (1980) suggested that most children are not good visual learners until they reach third or fourth grade.

2. *Allow students to select where they will sit.* Students vary in the amount of light, sound, and heat they prefer and may, in fact, self-select seats that provide more productive learning environments for them. Teachers often comment, especially during

FIGURE 6.15
Diagnosing
Learning Styles

Source: Rita Dunn,
School of Education
and Human
Services, St. John's
University.
Reprinted by
permission.

ELEMENTS

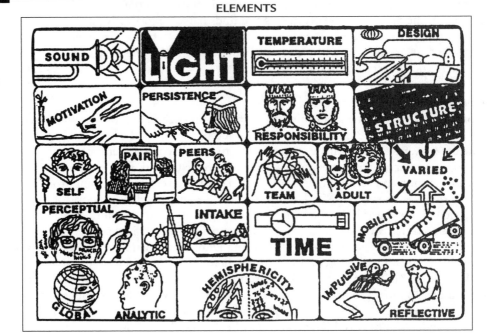

junior high school, that some students may abuse this privilege. The authors have found that they seldom do so if they are taught the concept of learning styles and if classroom procedures, such as allowing students to select their own seats, are presented as part of a procedure to make learning more personalized and effective for all students.

3. *Permit students to choose where they wish to study.* Some students work most effectively at a table, others in a soft chair, and others seated at a traditional school desk. The authors have taught children who worked best when they could move around the room and do their work on clipboards.

4. *Be sensitive to individual students' needs to block out sound or visual distractions.* Teachers can discuss differences in learning style with the class, and allow students to select a quiet study carrel. Also, observe students to see whether they appear easily distracted during seatwork. Teachers frequently move easily distracted students nearer to the teacher's desk; however, because this is often the busiest place in the classroom, this move may aggravate the problem by creating more distractions for the student.

5. *Make healthy snacks available to students or allow them to bring their own.* Because many students fail to eat an adequate breakfast, midmorning is a key time for allowing them to have a snack. Teachers who try this tactic generally find that initially all students take a cracker, carrot, or celery stick. Soon, however, only students who are hungry or who work best when they can eat will choose to eat.

6. *Provide opportunities for students to select whether they will work alone, in pairs, or with a small group.* Students can work with peers to complete assignments, study for tests, work on long-term projects, or critique each other's work.

7. *Provide adequate structure for both short-term and long-range assignments.* Students learn more effectively when seatwork is preceded by substantial direct instruction. Likewise, students need the structure provided by periodic conferences with the teacher or an assignment checklist and timetable for longer assignments.

8. *Give students instruction in study skills.* Both reflective and impulsive learners can benefit from learning to organize material prior to writing a formal paper. Some students organize material best using an outline format. More right hemisphere–oriented students may prefer to organize by mapping—a process of making connections in nonlinear fashion. Likewise, visual and kinesthetic learners profit from learning how to take notes.

9. *Employ individual goal setting, self-monitoring, and contracts.* These devices can assist students who require structure and concrete evidence to enhance motivation.

10. *Realize that some students require more frequent breaks than do others.* Teach students how to take short breaks without disrupting the class.

11. *Consider that students doing poorly in a subject might perform better if that subject were taught at a different time of day.* It is somewhat difficult to make this adjustment, but dramatic results can be obtained by switching a student's basic-skill lesson from morning to afternoon. Secondary school schedules that rotate the periods at which classes are taught allow students to study all subjects at a time when they work best.

12. *Increase the length of time you wait before calling on a student to answer a question.* This added time assists more reflective learners. Again, it is important to explain and teach this procedure to the class before implementing it.

13. *Develop learning centers that incorporate a variety of learning modalities.* Learning centers can be created that allow students to learn visually, auditorially, and kinesthetically. Learning centers also enable students to make decisions concerning light, sound, and design preferences, whether to work independently or with other students, and to select activities that allow them to deal with the material supportive of their own cognitive learning style preference.

P A U S E

6.12   *and Consider*

> Pause for a few minutes and consider a student who is struggling academically and behaviorally in a class you are teaching or observing. Write a list of ways you might adjust the learning environment to help this student more closely match his or her learning style to the environment. Share this with a group of two or three colleagues or classmates and provide each other with feedback and ideas.

Incorporating a Variety of Instructional Techniques

A second approach to accommodating various student learning styles has focused on training teachers to use a wide range of instructional methods when presenting information to students. Learning style proponents suggest that there are distinct styles of learning and that individuals generally have a preferred learning style. Teachers can facilitate learning by implementing varied instructional approaches that respond to the learning styles of all learners.

Bernice McCarthy (1987) stated that students' learning styles can be described by four categories. Rather than emphasizing the importance of determining each student's preferred category, McCarthy encouraged teachers to develop lesson plans that include learning activities that systematically respond to all four student learning styles. In each unit, this approach provides some instruction matched to each student's preferred approach to learning, but it also requires that students experience and hopefully develop further skills in the other three styles of learning.

Figure 6.16 presents a description of the four types of learners described by McCarthy and the role the teacher can serve to assist each type of learner. Figure 6.17 provides a sample unit plan that offers activities for each of the four quadrants of learning styles as well as for right- and left-brain–dominated learners.

Innovative Learner	Analytic Learner	Common-Sense Learner	Dynamic Learner
The Learner	*The Learner*	*The Learner*	*The Learner*
Seeks meaning	Wants to know the	Needs to know how	Needs to use the
Wants reasons for	facts	things work	self-discovery
learning new material	Perceives information	Seeks usability	method
Needs to be	abstractly and	Enjoys solving	Takes risks
personally involved	processes it	problems	Is flexible
in the learning	reflectively	Desires hands-on	Relishes change
process	Can create concepts	experiences	Seeks action
Desires to work with	and build models	Wants ideas to be	Follows through with
people	Enjoys collecting data	practical	plans
Is highly imaginative	Needs to know what	Needs to know how	Enjoys the
Has good divergent	the experts think	things that they are	trial-and-error
thinking skills	Values sequential	asked to do will help	method
Perceives information	thinking	in real life	Receives information
concretely and		Likes to practice ideas	concretely and
processes it	───────────────	Perceives information	processes it actively
reflectively	*The Teacher*	abstractly and	
	Provides information	processes it actively	───────────────
───────────────	by direct instruction		*The Teacher*
The Teacher	Sees knowledge as	───────────────	Is a resource
Is a motivator	increasing	*The Teacher*	Becomes an evaluator
Uses the discussion	comprehension	Becomes a coach	Serves as a facilitator
approach		Models	Encourages a variety
Incorporates a great		Involves the student	of learning
deal of		Gives immediate	approaches
teacher–student		feedback	

FIGURE 6.16
Learning Styles

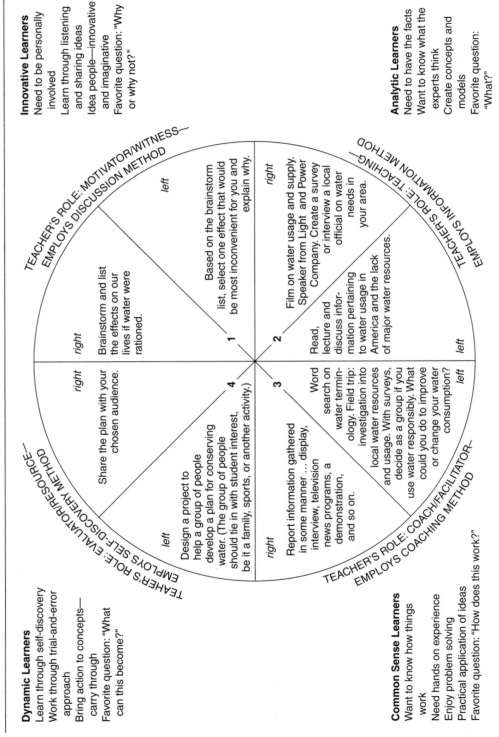

Innovative Learners
Need to be personally involved
Learn through listening and sharing ideas
Idea people—innovative and imaginative
Favorite question: "Why or why not?"

Analytic Learners
Need to have the facts
Want to know what the experts think
Create concepts and models
Favorite question: "What?"

Dynamic Learners
Learn through self-discovery
Work through trial-and-error approach
Bring action to concepts— carry through
Favorite question: "What can this become?"

Common Sense Learners
Want to know how things work
Need hands on experience
Enjoy problem solving
Practical application of ideas
Favorite question: "How does this work?"

TEACHER'S ROLE: MOTIVATOR/WITNESS— EMPLOYS DISCUSSION METHOD

TEACHER'S ROLE: EVALUATOR/RESOURCE— EMPLOYS SELF-DISCOVERY METHOD

TEACHER'S ROLE: TEACHING/ EMPLOYS INFORMATION METHOD

TEACHER'S ROLE: COACH/FACILITATOR— EMPLOYS COACHING METHOD

left
Based on the brainstorm list, select one effect that would be most inconvenient for you and explain why.

right
Brainstorm and list the effects on our lives if water were rationed.

1

right
Film on water usage and supply. Speaker from Light and Power Company. Create a survey or interview a local official on water needs in your area.

2

left
Read, lecture and discuss information pertaining to water usage in America and the lack of major water resources.

right
Share the plan with your chosen audience.

4

left
Design a project to help a group of people develop a plan for conserving water. (The group of people should tie in with student interest, be it a family, sports, or another activity.)

3

right
Report information gathered in some manner ... display, interview, television news programs, a demonstration, and so on.

Word search on water terminology. Field trip: investigation into local water resources and usage. With surveys, decide as a group if you use water responsibly. What could you do to improve or change your water consumption?

left

FIGURE 6.17

Sample Activities for a Unit on Water Supply

Source: McCarthy, Bernice, *The 4-MAT System.* Barrington, IL: Excel, Inc., 1980. Reprinted by permission.

There are several important points in applying McCarthy's model. First, there is no new material taught in association with instructional activities in the first quadrant (innovative learners). Instructional activities in this quadrant are used to discover what students know and how they feel about the area to be studied. The intent of activities in this quadrant is to engage students by relating the concepts to be studied to students' lives and interests. Second, each quadrant has a section identified as left and right. This refers to whether the instructional activities connect more clearly to the left side of the brain with its logical, sequential emphasis, or the right side with a more nonlinear, personal, interactive focus. Third, it is not always possible or desirable to follow the sequence like a mathematical formula. For example, in the second quadrant, it is suggested that some form of interactive, experiential instructional activity (right brain) would come first. This is not always possible. A film, speaker, field trip, and so on might not be available prior to the time when it is necessary for students to read content, or hear a lecture, and so on (quadrant 2, left). Fourth, it is perhaps obvious that lessons will often move from the second to the third quadrant and back. For example, after students have experienced an instructional activity in quadrant 2, we may want to assess what they learned by having them complete either a quadrant 3 right or left activity. We might then return to an instructional activity in quadrant 2. Fifth, whereas it might be desirable to have every unit end with a personalized, quadrant 4 set of activities, this is not always possible given the demands of high-stakes standardized testing. We might need to end a unit with a quadrant 3 right activity that actively engages students in creatively demonstrating their understanding and ability to work with the content.

P A U S E
and Consider   6.13

> We encourage you to complete Activity 6.4 at the end of the chapter. This will allow you to experiment with McCarthy's approach to unit planning as a method for ensuring that all students have instruction closely matched to their preferred way of learning.

Howard Gardner's Work on Multiple Intelligences

When examining Howard Gardner's work it is important to realize that he has suggested that the concept of multiple intelligence is not a goal in itself but rather a way to assist students in reaching important goals selected by them and the adults with whom they work (Gardner, 1999a). He argues that in order to help students learn and develop critical understandings, it is important to know the student and to incorporate the student's strengths into how we encourage the student to work with materials to develop new understandings and how we assess whether the student has, indeed, understood and can use the new information and understandings. Gardner noted that the most important contribution multiple intelligence theory makes to education is that it "stimulates teachers and students to be imaginative in selecting curricula, deciding how the curricula are to be taught or 'delivered,' and determining how student knowledge is to be demonstrated" (Gardner, 1999a, p. 152).

Gardner has suggested that there exist at least eight forms of intelligence or methods for understanding and learning. Figure 6.18 presents an overview of these eight types of intelligence. Gardner points out that most of us possess each of these intelligences but in different amounts. Sadly, when schools focus primarily on verbal/linguistic and logical/mathematical intelligences, we limit the motivation, achievement, and self-esteem of many students whose gifts are ignored and underutilized. Instead, he suggests we can serve all students more effectively when we create classroom environments that allow students to learn and demonstrate their knowledge using multiple forms of intelligence.

Many of the ideas presented in this chapter support a multiple intelligences approach to teaching and learning. In their book, *Teaching and Learning through Multiple Intelligences*, Campbell, Campbell, and Dickerson (1999) provide both a summary of what has been learned by numerous schools involved in implementing multiple intelligence concepts into their work with children and numerous practical ideas for incorporating the eight multiple intelligences. They suggest that the lessons learned by staff involved in implementing multiple intelligences into their work, "fall into five broad areas: (1) how we perceive students, (2) how we teach, (3) how we organize curriculum, (4) how we assess, and (5) how we develop as educators" (p. 340). Our own experiences incorporating multiple intelligence concepts into our work support this finding. When

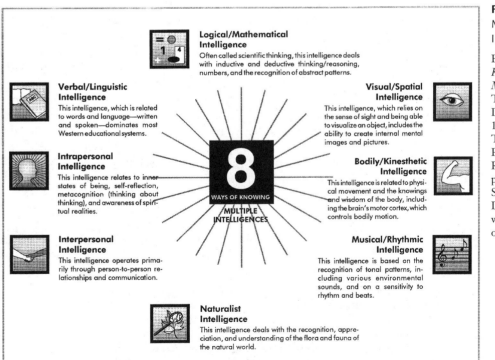

FIGURE 6.18
Multiple Intelligences

From *Eight Ways of Knowing: Teaching for Multiple Intelligences*, Third Edition, by David Lazear. © 1991, 1999 by SkyLight Training and Publishing, Inc. Reprinted by permission of SkyLight Professional Development, www.skylight.edu.com or (800) 348-4474.

we accept this concept, we realize that all students have strengths and much to offer to their classmates and the learning environment. As discussed earlier in the chapter, especially at the elementary and middle school levels where students spend considerable time with one group of students, we have found it helpful to have students assess their own special abilities and share these with the class. This helps students appreciate and respect one another's strengths and helps individuals understand and value their own special skills.

According to Campbell and colleagues, "the eight intelligences become an organizing tool for educators to determine how many windows exist into the content they teach" (1999, p. 341). As indicated by the ideas presented in this chapter on incorporating students' interests, the McCarthy approach, and real world problem solving, curriculum and instruction can be developed to allow students to use a wide variety of intelligences in understanding content and solving problems.

We have been consistently impressed with how much learning and creativity students can demonstrate when allowed to do so using multiple intelligences. A teacher in one of our in-service graduate classes shared the following story. He was teaching a sophomore history class and several weeks into the class noticed a student who was seldom involved in the class drawing cartoons during a class discussion. The teacher met privately with the student to discuss this behavior and was informed that this is how the student took notes—he drew a chronological cartoon of events and concepts being discussed. The student showed the teacher several of his daily cartoons and they indeed appeared to display a fine understanding of the content. The teacher expressed surprise that the student had failed the first quiz. The student informed the teacher that he was not a good writer and did not explain things well in writing. The teacher asked the student if he would be interested in using his cartoons as the class notes and having a presentation of his cartoons to the class serve as a test. The teacher suggested this might serve as a good review for the students—especially those with strong visual/spatial abilities. The student agreed. The teacher reported that, despite the fact that his school attendance was problematic, the student did not miss a day of his class the remainder of the semester. In addition, the teacher indicated the student began to take a more active role in the class and earned a B+ for the course. Although the teacher continued to encourage the student to value and strengthen his writing skills, he honored the student's special abilities and everyone was rewarded by the student's performance.

P A U S E
and Consider   **6.14**

We encourage you to take a few minutes or become involved in an activity with a group of your classmates or colleagues in which you consider ways in which you currently incorporate multiple intelligence concepts into your teaching and how you might more systematically implement this concept. You might form a group of four and share the methods you currently use that have proven beneficial to your students. Next, you might take a unit you will teaching and examine ways that the curriculum, instruction, and assessment might be modified to incorporate opportunities for students to use their special abilities.

Academic Need 13: Be Involved in Self-Evaluating One's Learning and Effort

Involving students in self-evaluation provides students with opportunities to understand their academic performance better and to experience a sense of personal responsibility. When students evaluate and record their own work, they are more likely to develop an internal locus of control and view their progress as based on their own efforts. Similarly, self-evaluation enables students to acknowledge areas that need improvement.

Students are impressed with displays of data, especially when the data deal with their own performances. Data provide immediate, concrete reinforcement for learning. Students often fail to associate their seemingly herculean efforts with actual increased knowledge or changes in behavior. Data make the learning or behavior change a concrete experience, which alone often provides more reinforcement than any free time or praise from the teacher. Surprisingly, the benefits associated with monitoring progress may be particularly great for students who are progressing slowly. These students often view themselves as making no progress or actually falling behind (as indeed they may be when the basis for comparison is their peers' work). Providing these students with specific data that demonstrate their progress is perhaps the most effective and honest motivational strategy.

Figure 6.19 presents an example of collecting and displaying data related to students' academic progress. This system was developed by a teacher who taught a fourth-grade class in which many students were doing very poorly on their weekly spelling tests. A significant number of students reported disinterest in studying the materials and a large number expressed that they were simply poor spellers. The teacher had attended a workshop conducted by one of the authors and had heard about the benefits of having students establish personal learning goals and keep records.

The teacher maintained her procedure of having students take a weekly pretest and posttest (students of varying abilities had different words and sometimes different numbers of words to learn). The students recorded their pretest scores by coloring in the weekly chart to indicate the number spelled correctly (four in the example). Based on their score, each student selected a goal for the number of words they would spell correctly on the posttest. This goal was indicated by drawing a line above that number on the weekly chart. Thus, in the example in Figure 6.19 the student selected eight as her first weekly goal. On a separate chart, students recorded the number of words they learned each week and the cumulative total for the year. It is quite possible that some of the less-skilled spellers would learn more words because they may have missed more on their pretest yet done well on their posttest.

Finally, the students listed the strategy they would use for learning spelling words for the upcoming week. When the teacher began using this approach, she indicated her surprise at how limited students were in their strategies, and how few of the students connected the use of learning strategies to successful learning. She assisted the students by having the class brainstorm strategies they could use and allowing students to select one of these or develop a new strategy for the week. She also had the students rate daily their use of the strategy on a 0 to 2 scale, with 0 indicating they forgot to use the strategy, 1 meaning they used it a little but not as they had planned, and 2 indicating they had used it as planned. At the end of the week, students who met their goals would stand up, tell the class the strategy they used, and read their scores

PRETEST	4	PRETEST _____	PRETEST _____	PRETEST _____
GOAL	8	GOAL _____	GOAL _____	GOAL _____
POSTTEST	9	POSTTEST _____	POSTTEST _____	POSTTEST _____
LEARNED	5	LEARNED _____	LEARNED _____	LEARNED _____

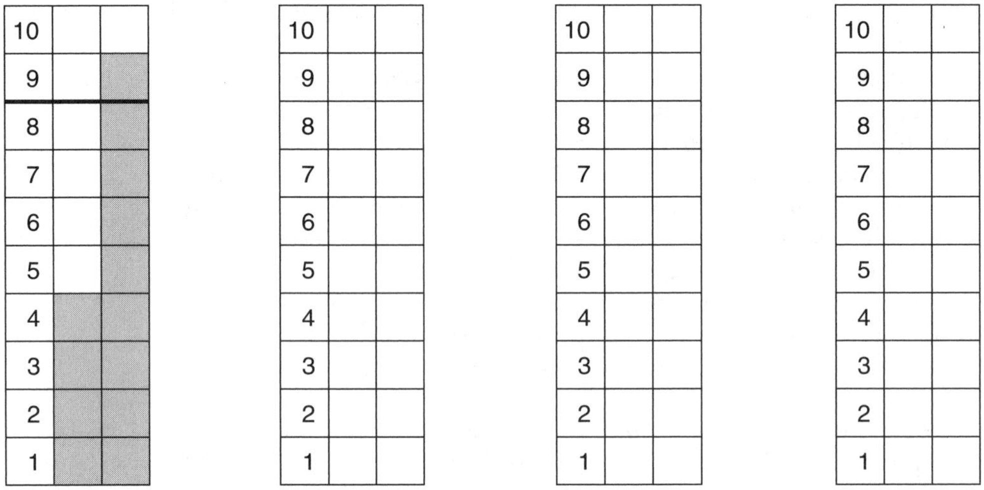

10		
9		
8		
7		
6		
5		
4		
3		
2		
1		

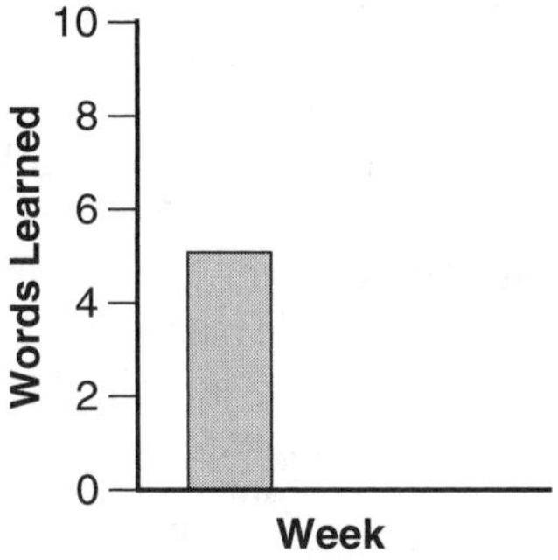

10		
9		
8		
7		
6		
5		
4		
3		
2		
1		

10		
9		
8		
7		
6		
5		
4		
3		
2		
1		

10		
9		
8		
7		
6		
5		
4		
3		
2		
1		

Words Learned

Week

My strategy for this week is _____

_____

How well did I use my strategy?   **Rating Scale**

Mon.   Tues.   Wed.   Thurs.   0   1   2

FIGURE 6.19
Spelling Goals and Strategies

for strategy use. This facilitated students' development of an internal locus of control by helping them learn the relationship between strategy use and achievement.

The teacher reported dramatic improvement in students' learning new spelling words as well as students' attitudes about learning new words. The teacher presented this information to her colleagues. She showed her fellow teachers the portfolios of two students who, prior to her implementing this and goal setting in reading, writing, and math, had completed almost no work. The students' work, following the teacher's introduction of goal setting, selecting learning strategies, and self-recording, showed dramatic progress. The following year several of her colleagues implemented these methods with similar results. Not surprisingly, they also observed dramatic improvements in the behavior and work of students who had been experiencing limited academic success following the introduction of these methods.

P A U S E
6.15   *and Consider*

> Stop for a moment and consider a situation in which several of your students or students in a classroom where you are observing are struggling to master the material and perhaps feeling rather defeated. Write a brief statement describing a method you could use to help them collect data on the progress they are making and highlight the effective learning strategies they are using. We encourage you to share this with two or three colleagues or classmates.

Academic Need 14: Have Instruction Be Sensitive to the Needs of Second-Language Learners

Have you ever been in a situation where you needed to understand the directions and they were being given in a language you did not understand? Many of us who have traveled overseas and have limited proficiency in the language(s) spoken where we traveled have had such an experience. Although this experience engenders feelings of boredom or mild frustration if the content of the situation is nonessential—such as watching a play—feelings of anxiety, anger, and distress arise if it is important that we understand what is being said, such as from where the train will be departing or how to find lodging.

Imagine the feelings experienced by many students who desperately want to succeed and be accepted in our classrooms but who do not understand what is being said or happening. Not only are these students often confused and anxious but they must also be exhausted and feel less than capable at the end of most schooldays. Given the fact that we want them to feel exhilarated and competent, what strategies can we use to assist these students?

Although there are no easy answers to this question, and entire books have been written on assisting students with limited English proficiency (see references at the end of this chapter), there are a number of strategies teachers can use in their day-to-day instruction. Figure 6.20 presents a list of these. Studies (Cummins, 1996; Garcia, 1999) also suggest that second-language learners benefit from classrooms in which individual seatwork and large-group instruction is deemphasized. Instead, teachers work with small groups of students or move around the room assisting small groups of students. This allows opportunities for students to see modeling of several students and seek affirmation regarding classroom events and academic content.

FIGURE 6.20

Methods for
Presenting
Information Orally
to Students with
Limited English
Proficiency

1. Speak clearly and carefully pronounce key words.
2. Face the students when you speak.
3. Repeat, clarify, paraphrase: Use simple subject–verb–object sentences.
4. Use gestures, intonation, and other nonverbal aspects of communication.
5. Use pictures, objects, graphs, maps, and charts both for presenting material and assessing mastery.
6. Use hands-on activities, mime, and pointing.
7. Preteach vocabulary—keep important words on the board or chart paper; use graphic organizers when possible.
8. Give and request examples of abstract and difficult concepts.
9. Check frequently for understanding.
10. Have students share in pairs—often with students who speak the same language.
11. Use peer tutoring and cross-age tutoring.
12. Provide preteaching whenever possible.
13. Allow students to use their first language.
14. Provide an outline for the lesson.
15. Review material frequently.
16. Provide samples of final projects.

In discussing their findings regarding effective schools and classrooms for Hispanic students, Reyes and colleagues (1999) reported that teachers who were more effective in facilitating learning among Hispanic students employed active learning methods, such as cooperative learning, and peer and cross-age tutoring. These teachers used thematic units to provide meaning and context for students' learning, and they drew on students' experiences and were able to scaffold instruction to build on students' English proficiency.

Many, if not most, of the methods we have chosen as the most consistently related to positive student behavior and learning are also those recommended by individuals who research and teach about how to create productive learning environments for students whose first language is not English. Yvonne and David Freeman (2002) provide a thoughtful summary of how teachers can be more effective in developing lessons that involve ESL students.

1. *Joint productive activities.* Students are encouraged to work with each other, the teacher, and parents to reach their instructional goals and objectives.
2. *Language development.* Teachers provide students with opportunities to use conversational and academic language appropriately in a variety of settings, adjusting the language to students' experience with English and providing first-language support.
3. *Contextualization.* Teachers draw upon students' backgrounds and cultures and bring in guests who can foster respect for multicultural perspectives.
4. *Challenging activities.* Teachers plan for and implement activities that encourage academic concept development by drawing on cultural funds of knowledge and using culturally appropriate approaches to teaching.
5. *Instructional conversations.* Teachers organize their classrooms to ensure that conversation between the teacher and peers develops academic concepts and language.
6. *Diverse entry points.* In all content areas and in all interactive activities, the teacher is sensitive to the students' needs, interests, talents, and understandings and is able to use that information to extend students' learnings. (Freeman & Freeman, 2002, p. 57)

By using the methods discussed in this chapter, you will facilitate the learning of many students whose first language is not English or whose cultural background is not white European American. We encourage you, however, to go further than this. We suggest that you interview several of your students with cultural backgrounds different from your own and ask them what classroom factors facilitate their learning. We encourage you to ask them what they want to learn, how they want to learn, and to describe their educational goals. Based on this, your reading of this chapter, and your discussion with colleagues or classmates, what changes could you implement in your classroom to enhance the learning of students whose first language is not English or whose cultural background is not European American?

TWO ADDITIONAL METHODS FOR ENHANCING STUDENTS' MOTIVATION TO LEARN: COOPERATIVE LEARNING AND PEER TUTORING

Cooperative Learning

Cooperative learning is perhaps the most popular and effective method for meeting students' varied learning styles and actively involving students in the learning process. A 1998 survey of elementary teachers indicated that 93 percent of the teachers surveyed used cooperative learning in their classrooms (Antil, Jenkins, Wayne, & Vadasy, 1998). The majority of these teachers indicated cooperative learning methods enhanced students' progress toward both academic and social learning goals. Reviews of the literature indicate a wide variety of advantages associated with cooperative learning (Good & Brophy, 2000; McCaslin & Good, 1996). Many teachers have students work in groups but fail to incorporate methods proven to increase the success of student learning within cooperative groups. The following section provides materials we have found most important in effectively implementing cooperative learning in the classroom.

Teachers interested in implementing cooperative learning can choose from a wide variety of methods. Cooperative learning methods, however, generally fall into three types or approaches: (1) simple structure, (2) process, and (3) extended structure.

Simple Structure Activities

Simple structures refer to activities teachers can use periodically to stimulate discussion and review materials. In his book *Cooperative Learning: Resources for Teachers*, Kagan (1989) presented a number of simple structure activities that can be used in any subject matter. Roundtable is one activity in which the teacher asks a question that has numerous possible answers—such as to list all the possible causes of the Civil War or all the common denominators for 24 and 42. Students then make a list on one sheet of paper, with each student adding one answer and passing the paper to the left. Numbered Heads Together is another activity. Students are again asked a question and placed in small groups to develop an answer. Each student in the group is assigned a number. The students work until the teacher signals them to stop. The teacher then calls out a number and all students assigned that number raise their hands. These students are the groups' representatives and can be called on to present the groups' answers.

Another simple structure activity called Stars is used to review material and prepare students for a quiz or test. After the teacher has presented the material, study groups of three or four students of mixed abilities are assigned. Each group is asked to develop five questions related to the material being studied and to provide the correct answer for each question. Each member of the group makes a copy of this material. The next task (usually occurring the following day) involves creating quiz groups consisting of students from different study groups. In the quiz group one person at a time reads a question from his or her list and the other students write down the answer they think is correct. The person who reads the question then provides the correct answer and the person to the right asks the next question. This process continues until each person has read all the questions prepared by the study group. The questions are then collected and the teacher prepares a test from these questions.

Teachers interested in developing simple structure cooperative activities can find excellent ideas in *Cooperative Learning: Resources for Teachers* by Spencer Kagan (available by writing Resources for Teachers, Suite 201, 27402 Camini Capistrano, Laguna Niguel, CA 92677) and in Johnson and Johnson's (1985) *Cooperative Learning: Warm-Ups, Grouping Strategies and Group Activities.*

Process Approach

David and Roger Johnson have conducted numerous research studies and written extensively on cooperative learning. Their approach highlights a *process*, or series of steps, teachers can apply to implement cooperative learning with any subject matter. The Johnsons have stated that there are five basic elements of this process (Johnson, Johnson, & Holubec, 1993):

1. *Positive interdependence.* This element involves structuring goals and activities so that students must be concerned about the performance of all members of the group. This can be accomplished through such methods as providing only one copy of the material (materials interdependence), assigning each group member a role (role interdependence), making success dependent on all members' reaching a specified goal (goal interdependence), assigning the same grade or reward to each group member (reward interdependence), or providing each member only a portion of the information necessary to complete the task (resource interdependence). The key is that the group members know that they are in it together and that they sink or swim together.

2. *Individual accountability.* This means that every student is accountable for mastering the material. This can be accomplished through the traditional means of having each student take a quiz or otherwise demonstrate competence, or by indicating to students that any group member can be asked to demonstrate mastery of the content by being called to the overhead or by being called on in some other way.

3. *Face-to-face interaction.* Students are arranged in such a manner that they are knee to knee and eye to eye and are involved in actively sharing and discussing the content.

4. *Teaching collaborative skills.* To function effectively in groups, students must learn how to work cooperatively in a small group. Figure 6.21 lists specific group skills the authors have found important to teach students. Figure 6.22 presents the steps Johnson and Johnson (1994) have outlined for teaching students cooperative skills.

1. State the assignment.
2. State the group process goal(s).
3. Call attention to the time limit.
4. Assign group roles (if used).
5. Proceed with the assignment.
6. Summarize the activity.
7. Evaluate the group process skills.

FIGURE 6.21
Group Collaborative Skills

1. Do students believe the skill is needed and useful?
2. Do students understand what the skill is, what the behaviors are, what the sequence of behaviors is, and how it looks when it is all put together?
3. Have students had an opportunity to practice the skill?
4. Have students received feedback that is immediate, descriptive, and specific?
5. Have students persevered in practicing the skill?
6. Have students had the opportunity to use the skill successfully?
7. Have students used the skill frequently enough so that they have integrated the skill into their natural behavior?
8. Do the classroom norms support the use of the skill?

FIGURE 6.22
Helping Students Develop Collaborative Skills

5. *Processing group skills.* Once students have been introduced to cooperative group skills, it is necessary to monitor and reinforce these skills consistently. This task will initially be accomplished by the teacher, but it can be transferred to students as they develop proficiency in the skills. When initially teaching and monitoring group skills, it is best to focus on one or two skills at a time. As students become more familiar with group skills, they can be monitored on three to five skills at a time. Figure 6.23 provides an example of a form the authors have found helpful for monitoring group skills.

Figure 6.24 presents the steps Johnson, Johnson, and Johnson-Holubec (1993) suggested for teachers who are interested in incorporating cooperative learning into their classrooms. Teachers interested in incorporating the Johnsons' approach to cooperative learning into their classrooms can find a variety of materials available and can also attend well-designed workshops to develop the needed experience and skills. The materials the authors have found most helpful are *Learning Together and Alone, Circles of Learning, Cooperation in the Classroom*, and *Cooperative Learning: Warm-Ups, Grouping Strategies and Group Activities.* (These materials can be ordered through Interaction Book Company, 7208 Cornelia Drive, Edina, MN 55435. Additional information can be obtained through the Cooperative Learning Center, the University of Minnesota, 612-624-7031.)

Extended Structure Approach

Robert Slavin and his colleagues at Johns Hopkins University have produced several approaches and a variety of methods that combine cooperation and competition with a game or tournament activity. These methods are referred to as Student Team Learning. The most popular are Teams Games Tournament and Student Teams–Achievement Division.

Tally the number of times student demonstrates a skill.

	Group One				Group Two		
Skill	*Bob*	*Nancy*	*Tariq*		*Rolando*	*Marissa*	*Beryl*
Contributes ideas							
Encourages others							
Listens							
Participates							
Checks for understanding							
Organizes the task							

FIGURE 6.23
Teacher Observation Sheet

FIGURE 6.24
The Teacher's Role in Cooperation Learning

Source: From *Cooperation in the Classroom* (pp. 2:28–2:29) by D. Johnson, R. Johnson, and E. Holubec, 1993. Edina, MN: Interaction Book Company. Reprinted by permission.

Make Pre-Instructional Decisions

Specify Academic and Social Skill Objectives. Every lesson has both (a) academic and (b) interpersonal and small group skills objectives.

Decide on Group Size. Learning groups should be small (groups of two or three students, four at the most).

Decide on Group Composition (Assign Students to Groups). Assign students to groups randomly or select groups yourself. Usually you will wish to maximize the heterogeneity in each group.

Assign Roles. Structure student-student interaction by assigning roles such as Reader, Recorder, Encourager of Participation, and Checker for Understanding.

Arrange the Room. Group members should be "knee to knee and eye to eye" but arranged so they all can see you at the front of the room.

Plan Materials. Arrange materials to give a "sink or swim together" message. Give only one paper to the group or give each member part of the material to be learned.

Explain Task and Cooperative Structure

Explain the Academic Task. Explain the task, the objectives of the lesson, the concepts and principles students need to know to complete the assignment, and the procedures they are to follow.

FIGURE 6.24
Continued

Explain the Criteria for Success. Student work should be evaluated on a criteria-referenced basis. Make clear your criteria for evaluating students' work.

Structure Positive Interdependence. Students must believe that they "sink or swim together." Always establish mutual goals (students are responsible for own learning and the learning of all other group members). Supplement goal interdependence with celebration/reward, resource, role, and identity interdependence.

Structure Intergroup Cooperation. Have groups check with and help other groups. Extend the benefits of cooperation to the whole class.

Structure Individual Accountability. Each student must feel responsible for doing his or her fair share of the work. Ways to ensure accountability are frequent oral quizzing of group members picked at random, individual tests, and assigning a member the role of Checker for Understanding.

Specify Expected Behaviors. The more specific you are about the behaviors you want to see in the groups, the more likely students will do them. Social skills may be classified as **forming** (staying with the group, using quiet voices), **functioning** (contributing, encouraging others to participate), **formulating** (summarizing, elaborating), and **fermenting** (criticizing ideas, asking for justification). Regularly teach the interpersonal and small group skills you wish to see used in the learning groups.

Monitor and Intervene

Arrange Face-to-Face Promotive Interaction. Conduct the lesson in ways that ensure that students promote each other's success face-to-face.

Monitor Students' Behavior. This is the fun part! While students are working, you circulate to see whether they understand the assignment and the material, give immediate feedback and reinforcement, and praise good use of group skills. Collect observation data on each group and student.

Intervene to Improve Taskwork and Teamwork. Provide **task assistance** (clarify, reteach) if students do not understand the assignment. Provide **teamwork assistance** if students are having difficulties in working together productively.

Provide Closure. To enhance student learning have students summarize the major points in the lesson or review important facts.

Evaluate and Process

Evaluate Student Learning. Assess and evaluate the quality and quantity of student learning. Involve students in the assessment process.

Process Group Functioning. Ensure each student receives feedback, analyzes the data on group functioning, sets an improvement goal, and participates in a team celebration. Have groups routinely list three things they did well in working together and one thing they will do better tomorrow. Summarize as a whole class. Have groups celebrate their success and hard work.

Teams Games Tournament (TGT) includes four steps. First, the teacher presents material to the whole class. Second, students study together in heterogeneous groups of four or five to master content and prepare for a tournament at the end of the week. Third, students are assigned to tables comprising three students of similar ability and from different teams. The three students compete at academic games (usually questions on cards or paper prepared by the teacher) to demonstrate mastery of material covered that week. By answering questions, students earn points for their team. Fourth, the points earned by team members at their various tables are totaled to determine the team's weekly score. These scores are often published in a weekly newsletter as a means of providing students with recognition for their efforts. In addition, depending on individual performance in the weekly tournament, the teacher may rearrange the groups to ensure that all groups have an opportunity to experience success.

Student Teams–Achievement Division (STAD) is a modified form of TGT. In this approach, weekly individual quizzes replace the tournaments, but points are still totaled for the group and recognition is provided for group scores. STAD has become increasingly popular because it is easier to implement than TGT. Also, because it does not include face-to-face competition, it is less competitive; this is important for some students. (Information on the use of these methods can be obtained by writing The Johns Hopkins Team Learning Project, Center for Research on Elementary and Middle Schools, The Johns Hopkins University, 3505 N. Charles Street, Baltimore, MD 21218.)

Summary of Cooperative Learning

In general, research seems to indicate that cooperative learning activities that include some form of competition and group rewards are more effective than those that depend on the benefits of students' working together. However, the benefits of cooperative learning are considerable even when these variables are not a major focus of the activity. Given the problems associated with competition and rewards, teachers are encouraged to focus as much as possible on the benefits of improved learning for all students, to help individual students and the class keep records of learning gains, and to emphasize the joy in assisting one another. Also, teachers should emphasize social and activity reinforcement and minimize the use of concrete, tangible rewards for achievement gains.

It is also important to realize that none of the authors or trainers involved in cooperative learning believes it should replace teacher-directed instruction. Even though cooperative learning can be used to generate ideas or can serve as a pretest to determine students' knowledge, students need to learn material from teachers and in many cases do not have the skill to develop new information or a new concept. Therefore, cooperative learning is most effective when it is used to practice or work on the application of material first introduced by a teacher. As noted earlier in this chapter, cooperative learning can be used in the context of different learning activities intended to meet the needs of students with varying learning styles. Cooperative learning is a technique that supports and enhances a number of instructional decisions, but it is not intended to be an end in itself. Nevertheless, the benefits of using cooperative learning are considerable, and we encourage readers not currently using this method to consider incorporating it into their instructional repertoire. Good and Brophy (1987) effectively summarized the value of cooperative learning:

> Achievement effects appear to be positive for all types of students, although there are some indications that black and Hispanic students gain even more from cooperative learning arrangements than Anglo students do. Effects on outcomes other than achievement are even more impressive. Cooperative learning arrangements promote friendship choices and prosocial patterns of interaction among students who differ in achievement, sex, race,

or ethnicity, and they promote the acceptance of mainstreamed handicapped students by their nonhandicapped classmates. Cooperative methods also frequently have positive effects, and rarely have negative effects, on affective outcomes such as self-esteem, academic self-confidence, liking for the class, liking and feeling liked by classmates, and various measures of empathy and social cooperation. (p. 416)

When implementing cooperative learning, teachers should realize that having students work in groups, even when the teacher has structured the activity to encourage positive interdependence and individual accountability, will not ensure a productive learning environment. As with any other activity (see Chapter 7), teachers need to instruct students in the classroom procedures to be followed when involved in cooperative learning activities, such as the following:

1. Do the students clearly understand their task and the associated learning goals?
2. Do the students understand why you have chosen to use group work to facilitate their learning the content?
3. Do the students find intrinsic, achievement, or utility value in the material?
4. Do the students possess the skills necessary to complete the task; that is, do they know how to use the materials, and can at least several students in each group read any written material associated with the task?
5. Are all materials readily available, and has a procedure been established so they can be easily obtained?
6. Do the students know how much time they have to complete the task?
7. Do the students know what they should do if they require assistance?
8. Do the students know what to do if they finish early or what options are available if they cannot complete the task in the allotted time?
9. Have you established a method for gaining the students' attention should it be necessary to add an instruction, clarify a problem, or ask the groups to stop their work?
10. Do the students know the behaviors that will be expected of them while they work in the group?

P A U S E
6.17 *and Consider*

This section has provided a considerable number of methods you might add to your teaching repertoire. Take a few minutes to review this section. Next, make a list of three specific changes or additions you would like to make to enhance the quality of cooperative group work in your classroom or the classroom you are observing. Share this list with a small group of colleagues or classmates. If you have an opportunity to implement these changes, share the results with this same small group.

Peer Tutoring

A number of benefits can be derived from implementing peer tutoring in a classroom. First, tutoring fosters the concept that asking for and offering help are positive behaviors. This act encourages cooperation and concern for peers and thereby creates a more supportive, safe learning environment. Second, the opportunity to instruct another child can provide a student with a sense of competence and personal worth. Third, in assisting another student, the student frequently learns the material more thoroughly. The combination of increased understanding and the act of instructing another student frequently makes a student a more excited and confident learner. Finally, peer tutoring helps the teacher monitor and individualize instruction. By allowing students to serve as resources for other students, the teacher increases the availability of individual attention, thereby reducing students' frustrations and accompanying acting-out behaviors.

Although peer tutoring has many benefits, it can become a frustrating and counterproductive activity if students are not provided with skills in how to assist each other. Therefore, it is important that if you plan to implement peer tutoring, you provide your students with instruction in how to assist another student. Do so by listing and discussing the dos and don'ts of helping someone with the work. You can then model appropriate behavior and then allow students to practice this behavior and receive feedback. If the equipment is available, students can be videotaped while assisting other students, and the tape can be viewed and discussed. An exciting aspect of providing students with instruction in how to teach another student is that this activity helps them better understand the learning process.

There are numerous approaches to implementing peer tutoring. Students can be provided with green and red 8½-inch square cards attached to their desks so that they can be displayed in front of the desk. Students who need help during seatwork can display a red card, and students who understand this material and are willing to assist other students can display a green card. This procedure can be particularly helpful when you are busy working with a small group and are not available to assist students. A similar approach involves listing on the board the names of students who are able to assist their peers on a project.

Assigning individual students to work with a student who needs assistance is another common approach to peer tutoring. This activity may involve students in the same class or students from higher grades. Another method involves arranging students' desks in groups of four and informing students that they may assist their peers as long as they follow previously learned procedures for effective teaching.

One of the authors observed a young teacher presenting an art lesson to a group of eighth-grade students. The teacher was working with a particularly difficult class; the class included several students the school had characterized as having behavior problems, as well as a boy who was very withdrawn and who had emotional problems. The teacher indicated that she was somewhat concerned about the day's lesson because she had a very limited background in the material she was presenting. She also said that the last period of the day on a particularly nice spring day was not the ideal time to be teaching eighth graders a concept as difficult as depth perception. With this introduction, the author was prepared to observe chaos and to have numerous opportunities for observing the teacher's skills in dealing with behavior problems.

The teacher began the lesson by briefly reviewing the material she had presented on the previous day. She appeared comfortable responding to a variety of students' questions. On one occasion, a student pointed out a major flaw in something she had presented. The teacher indicated that she did not see his point and asked the student if he would be willing to come up to the board and clarify his point for both her and the class. The student did so, and the class responded politely to his brief instruction.

After perhaps ten minutes of instruction, the teacher indicated that the students should continue working on their assignments. She commented that some students were finding the tasks more difficult than others and suggested that when they had a problem, they find another student to help them. As students began working on their projects, the teacher circulated around the room answering students' questions and reinforcing students' work. It soon became apparent, however, that she could not possibly answer all the questions that were being fired at her. Her interventions then changed from direct work with students to serving as a clearing center for resources available within the classroom. As she moved around the room, she made comments such as, "Why don't you ask John? He does a good job with two-point perspective." "It might help, Bill, if you could explain to Maria why you. . . ." "I really appreciate your helping, Sue. You did a really good job of teaching because you helped him to discover the answer for himself."

The author was impressed with the extremely high percentage of on-task behavior displayed by the students. In addition, the teacher's role as facilitator freed her to spend much time with her most severely disturbed student. Because she had structured students' responses to be positive and supportive, students' interactions throughout the class period were extremely positive. In addition to assisting each other, students frequently showed their work to their peers and almost always received either compliments or constructive suggestions.

In examining the dynamics of this class period, it is interesting to recall Postman and Weingartner's (1969) statement that teachers should perhaps teach subjects outside of their area of academic preparation. When teaching subjects they understand extremely well, teachers often do all the teaching while the students are forced into the role of passive learner. However, when teachers are learning the material or are somewhat unsure of the content, it may be easier to allow students to become involved as colearners and team teachers. It may appear that material is being covered more slowly (and perhaps more noisily) when using this format, but the theoretical considerations and research results presented earlier in this section point to many advantages associated with this form of instruction.

An increasingly popular approach to peer tutoring involves creating support groups outside the classroom for students who have the ability to complete their work but who have experienced serious and persistent achievement problems. Sullivan (1988) reported the results of a special study groups program for middle school students whose ability levels indicated that they could pass their courses but who were failing one or more courses. Students were involved in weekly study skills meetings with the vice principal, met with their group to work on assignments several times a week, and received a progress report every Friday. Results indicated that 50 percent of the total number of grades received by students in the study skills groups went up at least one grade, and only 10 percent of the grades went down. Results for a control group showed that only 14 percent of the grades went up.

EXAMPLE OF ENHANCING MOTIVATION AND STUDENT SUCCESS

We want to close this chapter by providing an example of how a teacher used the methods presented thus far in the book to assist a student who was failing in her class. We encourage you to implement the methods presented in this book to assist both individual students and entire classes of students. Although we appreciate the demands of working with 35 elementary school students, 150 middle school students, or 225 secondary school students every day, we also believe these methods can make your work more enjoyable and effective, and that they can be used to enhance student motivation and learning in a wide variety of settings.

This case study, taken verbatim from a project completed by a high school English teacher as part of her work in a graduate education course, typifies how you can incorporate ideas found throughout this book to help individual students reach their potential. The authors chose this example because:

1. It was carried out and written by a teacher who deals with 140 students each day.
2. The teacher developed and carried out the project with no assistance.
3. The teacher had just completed a course using this text as the major sourcebook.

> At first I didn't take much notice of Bill in my freshman and sophomore-level writing class. He's one of those quiet, unobtrusive students, the kind you love to use in a seating chart as a barrier between the class clown and a social butterfly. Rarely, if ever, did he call attention to himself. He never raised his hand to volunteer an answer, and when called on, would struggle so to come up with an appropriate response that I would too frequently— to avoid his obvious embarrassment—cut short his efforts and recognize one of the hands waving excitedly around him. He is never late to class; he has never asked for a hall pass; he never questions directions or instructions for an assignment; he seldom visits in class with his neighbors; he always appears to listen attentively to lectures. Therefore, next to the 140 other students who come to me daily with varying levels of ability and enthusiasm for "creative writing," Bill, at first, didn't demand a lot of my attention.
>
> A couple of weeks into the term, however, I began to notice that in fact Bill was becoming a problem of the subtler type; he was not doing his assignments. In fact, his pattern of behavior seemed suspiciously close to what has been categorized as "failure syndrome"— a feeling of defeatism and helplessness resulting from repeated failure. Therefore, after three weeks of inconsistent, below-class-average performance, I decided to investigate Bill's history as a student in our district.
>
> I discovered that in his elementary years he was apparently a pleasure to his teachers. Their comments on his conduct and citizenship grades suggested he was a model of exemplary behavior, and his academic marks were "satisfactory" or better. In junior high school, however, his grades began to slip, notably, those earned in English dropped to a "D" average throughout his seventh and eighth grades. As a result, his junior high English teachers recommended that he be placed in Sentences (our low-level remedial-writing class) during the first term of his freshman year in high school. Let there be no doubt that, as well-intentioned as this program may be, a stigma is attached to this placement as surely as if these students wore a badge that proclaimed their lack of proficiency and their below-average performance. At any rate, in Sentences he earned a term grade of "C minus" and was promoted the next year to Paragraphs. That is where our paths crossed.
>
> Next, I checked into Bill's current C.A.T. scores. The grade-level score for overall comprehension for his age group is 9.7; Bill's score was 7.7—two years below grade level. On the Gates Reading Test he had scored 8.3 on comprehension; the grade-level score is 9.3. He scored about a year below grade level, no small consideration in a class such as writing, which is a complex activity requiring mature, advanced mental operations. Therefore, his scores indicated that many of the writing tasks I required of him were quite possibly beyond his level of competence.
>
> I wondered about his other classes. So I sent a Progress Report form to his other teachers to determine how successful he was in his other courses. The results were that in classes requiring incremental, concrete, mechanical exercises he was doing above-average work. But in the majority of his classes—those requiring more abstract, complex cogni-

tive processes—his grades were below average. Unfortunately, the beginning of a pattern seemed to be developing that, without intervention, sooner or later would probably lead to resignation on his part.

Glasser's theory indicated what my first move should be: provide a caring atmosphere. I decided to make a point of casually noticing him, smiling and saying hello as he entered the classroom daily. I routinely do this to my students at random, and so this notice didn't cause him to be unduly curious. But each day I made sure I spoke to him until it became a habit for both of us. The next step he provided. He received the "Outstanding Athlete of the Week" award, for which I, of course, complimented him and placed his newspaper picture on a bulletin board in my room where "Class Heroes" who have received such an honor get recognition of some sort. On seeing his picture in this spot and receiving accolades from his classmates, I believe his chest size must have expanded three inches.

While he was feeling more comfortable and "invited" in the classroom, he seemed to be gaining confidence in himself, which was reflected in his assignments. (And was I also—albeit unconsciously—giving him more credit as a struggling student who deserved the benefit of the doubt?) I used as many opportunities as possible to reaffirm these signs of success—praised his improved writing, included a well-written narrative paper (on soccer, naturally) as a class model for effective writing. As research on attribution theory suggests, low-achieving students need to be reminded that their success is due to their efforts. A "Happy-Gram" sent home mentioning specifically his particularly good narrative paragraph, followed two weeks later by his "Goal Completion Award," seemed to be the turning points that altered his downward slide in my class.

During this intervention I made some academic changes as well as the social ones. First, I allowed more flexibility in the topics I assigned for writing projects so that Bill (and the other students) had more options to choose from. The more interested he was in a topic, the more knowledgeable he was about it, and the more motivated he became to write. I also began to assess his learning style—both by analyzing the type of assignments he did well on and by conversations with him when I asked for feedback. As a result, after giving directions for an assignment, I used my "roaming" time for private contact with him to clarify his understanding and review his independent work, making solicited suggestions so that I could spot misunderstandings and frustrations and offer follow-up assistance. I also began to use a different approach to grading his writing. Martin and Lauridsen (1974) suggest in *Developing Student Discipline and Motivation* that students need to be graded on an individual basis. Consequently, I allowed him to compete against himself and not his more academically mature classmates, so that his continuous progress merited praise. Then, because he was growing in confidence and self-esteem, the next step seemed to be to try the suggestions of Johnson and Johnson (1987) and allow Bill to work in a group. Their research suggests that successfully orchestrated group work increases confidence in one's ability. And so I arranged for Bill to participate in a peer editing group in which he was both academically and socially compatible. In this setting, a feeling of interdependence grew between him and members of the group, fostering sociability, responsibility, and self-esteem.

Meanwhile, research by Jones (1980) suggests that students should share the responsibility in behavior modification by some type of self-monitoring. Therefore, it became Bill's responsibility to keep personal records on a weekly Progress Report form I filled out. He also continued to keep a class notebook in which he copied daily assignments from the board and kept them in front of his notebook as a type of table of contents. The completed assignment then, after it was graded and returned, was kept chronologically in his notebook and a check mark was made on the assignment page. As a back-up reminder, in case an assignment did not get turned in by the deadline, we agreed that a "Homework Alert" notice was to be sent home, signed by his parent, and returned to me within two days. If the card was not returned within the time limit, Bill was aware I would be calling home to discuss the situation with his parent. This back-up strategy was never necessary, however. In fact, during the past five weeks, Bill has missed only one assignment (because of a late soccer game and a long bus ride home).

A statement by Jere Brophy (1982) summarizes my intervention best:

> For example, in dealing with failure-syndrome students who have essentially given up attempts to cope with classroom demands, effective teachers refuse to cave in by reducing task demands and treating these students as if they are really unable to succeed in the classroom. Instead, they approach such students with a mixture of sympathy, encouragement, and demands. These teachers reassure the students that they do have ability and that work given will not be too difficult for them. Then, the teachers help them to get started when they are discouraged or need some support, reinforce their progress, and perhaps offer contracts providing rewards for accomplishments and allowing opportunities for students to set goals. In general, the emphasis is on encouragement and help rather than prodding through threat of punishment. Failure-syndrome students are not merely *told* that they can succeed, but *shown* convincingly that they can, and helped to do so. (p. 23)

These suggestions seemed to have worked in providing more realistic expectations, building self-confidence, and in creating a more comfortable classroom in which Bill could become the student he can be.

IMPLEMENTATION ACTIVITIES

In addition to the Pause and Consider activities throughout this chapter, the following activities are offered to assist you in incorporating the materials presented in this chapter into your teaching repertoire.

ACTIVITY 6.1	For each of the fourteen student academic needs listed in Figure 6.1, list two ways in which you currently meet the need within the classroom. Be specific. For example: I use interest centers to respond to students' needs to follow their own interests. If you are not currently teaching, select a classroom that you have observed recently.
Evaluating a Classroom Environment in Light of Students' Academic Needs	Next, list two specific ways in which you could alter your teaching methods in order to meet these needs more effectively.

ACTIVITY 6.2	Turn to Figure 6.6. Circle the number in front of each method on this list that you currently incorporate into your teaching. Next, place a box around any method that sounds interesting and you believe would assist the students you teach. Finally, place an X through the number before any method you believe would not be appropriate or effective with your students. After completing this task, meet with a group of four or five colleagues. Have those who circled an item share how it works in their classrooms. Make sure that anyone who has a box around an item is provided with ideas on how they might incorporate that item into their classroom.
Selecting Methods to Demystify the Learning Process	

Select a student who is having difficulty mastering some skill you are helping students learn. Complete Figure 6.12 and fill in at least five of the areas in which you could make a modification to assist this student in being more successful. Next, select and implement two of these methods. Then, write a brief response to the following questions:

> Did the student experience greater success following the modifications?
> Did the student's behavior change in any way as he or she was working on this material?
> Have you noticed any difference in the student's attitude or behavior since you implemented the modifications?

Finally, we encourage you to interview the student and discuss how he or she felt about the work completed.

Select a unit you will be teaching or observing sometime within the next month. If you are student teaching or observing in a classroom, you may want to ask the teacher with whom you are working to assist you in selecting a unit. Form a group of three with two other teachers or students who are teaching a similar grade level or subject matter. Begin by selecting one of your units and create at least one activity for that unit that could be placed in each of the eight sections of the McCarthy unit planning format presented in Figure 6.17. Next, if you are involved in a university class and other groups are involved in this activity, obtain some feedback (and present them with a gift) by discussing your unit and instructional activities with another group of three who are working with or observing students in a similar grade level or for similar subject matter. Incorporate into your plan any feedback they may give you. If possible, teach this unit and ask yourself the following questions.

1. Were there some students who became more involved in various aspects of the unit?
2. Were there some students who were more involved and behaved more responsibly than previously?
3. How did students in general respond to the instruction provided in this unit?

If you are having problems with the behavior of a student or group of students, it is important to consider instructional factors that may be causing the problem. First, write the name of the student or students who are creating the most difficulty for you in class. Next, complete the form in Figure 6.25 for each student you have listed. After carefully examining your responses, answer these questions:

> One reason this student(s) may be acting out in my class is. . . .
> This activity made me realize that. . . .
> In order to help this student(s) behave more appropriately in this class, I will need to. . . .
> Two specific things I will change in this class or with this specific student are. . . .

FIGURE 6.25
Analyzing the
Classroom
Environment

Source: From
*Developing Student
Discipline and
Motivation* by Reed
Martin and David
Lauridsen.
Copyright © 1974
by Research Press,
Champaign, IL
61820. Reprinted by
permission.

As you present your next lesson or assignment in an area in which a student or group of students has had trouble, notice:

	Almost Always	Sometimes	Almost Never
1. Is the subject area one in which the student has always failed?			
2. Can the student read at whatever level the material is presented?			
3. Is the assignment clear enough so the student knows exactly what is expected?			
4. Is the task at a level of difficulty that is challenging but which offers a chance of successful completion for the individual (rather than for the class average)?			
5. Is the material presented in a manner which seems to interest the student: written, lecture, audiovisual, programmed workbook, independent work, group assignments, etc? Is the material content of interest?			
6. Is enough time allowed to get into the assignment and develop an interest and complete the task satisfactorily?			
7. Will the student be graded on an individual basis so that successful completion will get a good grade?			
8. Is there a pleasant consequence that you know appeals to the student (possibly chosen by the student) that will follow successful completion of the task?			
9. Is there some motivating consequence to at least complete part of the assignment, even if the student cannot complete all of it?			
10. Do you give the student another chance to do the assignment correctly and to improve the grade?			
11. Do you give more attention to the student when he tries a task than you do when he refuses to try?			

SUMMARY

For many years, research, theory, and in-service education in the area of classroom management and school discipline ignored the relationship between student behavior and students' attitudes toward learning. Classroom management often focused on how to increase on-task behavior with relatively little attention paid to whether the curriculum and instructional methods motivated students to learn. Fortunately, educators have become increasingly aware of the relationship between motivation and behavior. This chapter examines the key factors that influence the degree to which students are motivated to learn and will become positively engaged in instructional activities. When these factors are ignored, teachers find themselves spending much time attempting to control student behavior. When these student needs are met, however, a greater portion of students' classroom behaviors become directed toward completing learning tasks.

RECOMMENDED READING

Teaching Students in Multicultural Classrooms

August, D., & Hakuta, K. (1997). *Improving schooling for language-minority children: A research agenda.* Washington, DC: National Research Council.

Bielow, B., Christenson, L., Karp, S., Miner, B., & Peterson, B. (1994). *Rethinking our classrooms: Teaching for equity and justice* (Vol. 1). Milwaukee, WI: Rethinking Schools.

Bigelow, B., Harvey, B., Karp, S., & Miller, L. (2001). *Rethinking our classrooms: Teaching for equity and justice* (Vol. 2). Milwaukee, WI: Rethinking Schools.

Boyer, J., & Baptiste, P. (1996). *Transforming the curriculum for multicultural understanding.* San Francisco: Caddo Gap Press.

Cummins, J. (1996). *Negotiating identities: Educators for empowerment in a diverse society.* Ontario, CA: California Association for Bilingual Education.

Faltis, C., & Hudleson, S. (1997). *Bilingual education in elementary and secondary school communities: Toward understanding and caring.* Boston: Allyn & Bacon.

Fashola, O., Slavin, R., Calderon, M., & Duran, R. (1997). *Effective programs for Latino students in elementary and middle schools (Report No. 11).* Baltimore: Center for Research on the Education of Students Placed at Risk.

Freeman, D., & Freeman, Y. (2001). *Between worlds: Access to second language acquisition.* Portsmouth, NH: Heinemann.

Freeman, Y., & Freeman, D. (2002). *Closing the achievement gap: How to reach limited-formal-schooling and long-term English learners.* Portsmouth, NH: Heinemann.

Garcia, E. (1999). *Student cultural diversity: Understanding and meeting the challenge* (2nd ed.). Boston: Houghton Mifflin.

Garcia, E., & McLaughlin, B. (Eds.). (1995). *Meeting the challenge of linguistic and cultural diversity in early childhood education.* New York: Teachers College Press.

Gersten, R., & Jimenez, R. (1994). A delicate balance: Enhancing literature instruction for students of English as a second language. *The Reading Teacher, 47,* 439–449.

Hamayan, E. (1994). Language development of low-literacy students. In F. Genesee (Ed.), *Educating second language children: The whole child, the whole curriculum, the whole community* (pp. 278–300). New York: Cambridge University Press.

McLeod, B. (1996). *School reform and student diversity: Exemplary schooling for language minority students.* Washington, DC: Institute for the Study of Language and Education, George Washington University.

Nicholson-Nelson, K. (1998). *Developing students' multiple intelligences: Hundreds of practical ideas easily integrated.* New York: Scholastic.

Reyes, P., Scribner, J., & Scribner, A. (Eds.). (1999). *Lessons from high-performing Hispanic schools: Creating learning communities.* New York: Teachers College Press.

Thomas, W., & Collier, V. (1997). School effectiveness for language minority students. Washington, DC: National Clearinghouse of Bilingual Education.

Valdez, G. (2001). *Learning and not learning English: Latino students in American schools.* New York: Teachers College Press.

Walqui, A. (2000). *Strategies for success: Engaging immigrant students in secondary schools.* ERIC Report EDO-FLO-00-03. Washington, DC: Center for Applied Linguistic.

Meeting the Needs of Students in Inclusive Classrooms

Bradley, D., King-Sears, M., & Tessier-Switlick, D. (1997). *Teaching students in inclusive settings.* Boston: Allyn & Bacon.

Janney, R., & Snell, M. (1999). *Modifying schoolwork.* Pacific Grove, CA: Brooks/Cole.

Kame'enui, E., Carnine, D., Dixon, R., Simmons, D., & Coyne, M. (2002). *Effective teaching strategies that accommodate diverse learners* (2nd ed.). Upper Saddle River, NJ: Merrill Prentice Hall.

Mastropieri, M., & Scruggs, T. (2000). *The inclusive classroom: Strategies for effective instruction.* Upper Saddle River, NJ: Merrill.

Salend, S. (1998). *Effective mainstreaming: Creating inclusive classrooms.* Upper Saddle River, NJ: Merrill.

Tomlinson, C. (1999). *The differentiated classroom: Responding to the needs of all learners.* Alexandria, VA: Association for Supervision and Curriculum Development.

Vaughn, S., Bos, C., & Schumm, J. (1997). *Teaching mainstreamed, diverse, and at-risk students.* Boston: Allyn & Bacon.

Integrated Curriculum

Beane, J. (1997). *Curriculum integration: Designing the core of democratic education.* New York: Teachers College Press.

Nagel, N. (1996). *Learning through real world problem solving: The power of integrative teaching.* Thousand Oaks, CA: Corwin Press.

Pate, E., Homestead, E., & McGinnis, K. (1997). *Making integrated curriculum work.* New York: Teachers College Press.

Stevenson, C., & Carr, J. (1993). *Integrated studies in the middle grades: Dancing through walls.* New York: Teachers College Press.

Smith, G. (2002). Place-based education: Learning where we are. *Phi Delta Kappan, 83,* 584–594.

Learning Styles

Belenky, M., Clinchy, B., Goldberger, N., & Tarule, J. (1986). *Women's ways of knowing: Development of self, body and mind.* New York: Basic Books.

Dunn, R., Thies, A., & Honigsfeld, A. (2001). *Synthesis of the Dunn and Dunn learning-style model research: Analysis from a neuropsychological perspective.* Jamaica, NY: St. John's University School of Education and Human Services.

McCarthy, B. (1987). *The 4-MAT system: Teaching to learning styles with right/left mode techniques.* Barrington, IL: Excel.

McCarthy, B., & Leflar, S. (1983). *4-MAT in action: Creative lesson plans for teaching to learning styles with right/left mode techniques.* Barrington, IL: Excel.

McCarthy, B., Leflar, S., & McNamara, M. (1987). *The 4-MAT workbook: Guided practice in 4-MAT lesson and unit planning.* Barrington, IL: Excel.

Multiple Intelligences

Campbell, L., Campbell, B., & Dickerson, D. (1999). *Teaching and learning through multiple intelligences* (2nd ed.). Boston: Allyn & Bacon.

Gardner, H. (1993). *Multiple intelligence: The theory into practice.* New York: Basic Books.

Gardner, H. (1999). *The disciplined mind: What all students should understand.* New York: Simon & Schuster.

Gardner, H. (1999). *Intelligence reframed: Multiple intelligences for the twenty-first century.* New York: Basic Books.

Huggins, P. (1993). *The assist program: Multiple intelligence lessons.* Longmont, CO: Sopris West.

Lazear, D. (1999). *Eight ways of knowing: Teaching for multiple intelligences* (3rd ed.). Arlington Heights, IL: SkyLight Training and Publishing, Inc.

Cooperative Learning Materials

Abrami, P., Chambers, B., Poulsen, C., DeSimone, C., d'Apollonia, S., & Howden, J. (1995). *Classroom connections: Understanding and using cooperative learning.* New York: Harcourt Brace.

Andrini, B. (1991). *Cooperative learning and mathematics: A multistructural approach.* San Juan Capistrano, CA: Resources for Teachers.

Bernstein, B. (1993). *Cooperative learning in math: Skill-oriented activities that encourage working together.* Carthage, IL: Good Apple.

Breeden, T., & Mosley, J. (1992). *The cooperative learning companion: Ideas, activities, and aids for middle grades.* Nashville, TN: Incentive Publication.

Cantlon, T. (1991). *The first four weeks of cooperative learning: Activities and materials.* Portland, OR: Prestige.

Cantlon, T. (1991). *Structuring the classroom successfully for cooperative team learning.* Portland, OR: Prestige.

Johnson, D., & Johnson, R. (1993). *Cooperation in the classroom.* Edina, MN: Interaction Book.

Johnson, D., Johnson, R., Bartlett, J., & Johnson, L. (1988). *Our cooperative classroom.* Edina, MN: Interaction Book.

Johnson, D., Johnson, R., & Johnson-Holubec, E. (1986). *Circles of learning: Cooperation in the classroom.* Edina, MN: Interaction Book.

Johnson, R., & Johnson, D. (1985). *Cooperative learning: Warm-ups, grouping strategies and group activities.* Edina, MN: Interaction Book.

Johnson, R., & Johnson, D. (Eds.). (1984). *Structuring cooperative learning: Lesson plans for teachers.* Edina, MN: Interaction Book.

Kagan, S. (1987). *Cooperative learning: Resources for teachers.* Laguna Niguel, CA: Author.

Stone, J. (1991). *Cooperative learning and language arts: A multistructural approach.* San Juan Capistrano, CA: Resources for Teachers.

PART four

Minimizing Disruptive Behavior and Increasing Learning by Effective Classroom Organization and Management

I n his chapter on classroom organization and management in the third edition of *Handbook of Research on Teaching*, Walter Doyle (1986) wrote, "Broadly speaking, classroom teaching has two major task structures organized around the problems of (a) learning and (b) order. Learning is served by the instructional function. . . . Order is served by the managerial function, that is, by organizing classroom groups, establishing rules and procedures, reacting to misbehavior, monitoring and pacing classroom events, and the like" (p. 395). In their synthesis of forty classroom management studies, Evertson and Harris (1992) noted that effective classroom management included the dual functions of planning well-organized, engaging lessons and ensuring on-task student behavior by teaching students classroom procedures to facilitate smooth implementation of lessons and making management decisions that enhanced on-task behaviors. In the previous chapter, we examined some important findings on instructional methods that teachers can use to increase the likelihood that students will be motivated by learning tasks and will benefit from instruction. Part IV focuses on the second major task associated with classroom teaching.

Studies indicate that the amount of time students are engaged in instructional activities varies from less than 50 percent in some classes to more than 90 percent in others. This section helps you increase the time students spend actively engaged in learning. More effective teachers use their management time wisely and thereby enhance the time available for instruction and monitoring student work. In a study of eight secondary schools, Stallings and Mohlman (1981) found that effective teachers spent less than 15 percent of their time organizing and managing their classes. Teachers who effectively use the time needed to organize and manage classrooms can minimize the time required for these important functions.

The first part of Chapter 7 presents the methods effective teachers use at the beginning of the school year. The text emphasizes strategies for developing general rules and ensuring that all students learn such key classroom procedures as what to do during the first few minutes of class, how to request assistance with seatwork, when it is appropriate to talk, and how to request permission to leave the room.

The second major section in Chapter 7 describes strategies that effective teachers use when presenting material to students and monitoring students' seatwork. Researchers have demonstrated that use of these strategies is associated with high rates of on-task student behavior and great academic achievement.

CHAPTER

7

Developing Standards for Classroom Behavior

Although the rules and procedures used by effective classroom managers vary from teacher to teacher, we do not find effectively managed classrooms operating without them.

—Edmund Emmer, Carolyn Evertson, Julie Sanford, Barbara
Clements, and Murray Worsham (1981)
Organizing and Managing the Junior High School Classroom

Until students are allowed to have and begin to feel a proprietary interest in school and classroom rules, classroom control and a good learning environment will always be at risk.

—Forrest Gathercoal (2001)
Judicious Discipline

The most effective approaches to school-based prevention of anti-social behavior are proactive and instructive—*planning ways to avoid failure and coercive struggles regarding both academic and social behavior and actively teaching students more adaptive, competent ways of behaving.*

—James Kauffman (2001)
*Characteristics of Emotional and Behavioral
Disorders of Children and Youth*

Teaching is a demanding, fast-paced job. Each day, the typical elementary school teacher has more than 1,000 teacher–student interactions and teaches six subjects. Secondary teachers often teach 150 or more students with only four minutes between classes. Those demanding working conditions can cause confusion and frustration and limit students' learning time. Research indicates that effective teachers take time early in the school year to develop classroom rules and procedures that help their classrooms run smoothly and minimize disruptions, and thus maximize students' learning time.

Extensive research clearly indicates the benefits of helping students understand and accept school and classroom behavior standards. In schools where classroom and schoolwide behavior expectations are taught, practiced, and retaught when students fail to follow these clear guidelines, there is a significant reduction in classroom disruptions and office referrals for behaviors that violate the rights of others.

Although this book emphasizes practical methods, we believe it is important for you, as a professional, to understand the research that supports recommendations we make and methods you will implement. The initial research related to beginning the school year by creating behavior standards within the classroom occurred at the Research and Development Center for Teacher Education at the University of Texas at Austin (Emmer, Evertson, & Anderson, 1980; Evertson & Emmer, 1982a.) This research clearly indicates that effective classroom managers at both the elementary and junior high school levels spend time teaching students classroom rules and procedures. Emmer and colleagues (1981) described *rules* as "written rules which are either posted in the classroom, given to students on ditto or other copy, or copied by students into their notebooks" (pp. 18, 19). *Procedures* were defined as, "Procedures, like rules, are expectations for behavior. They usually apply to a *specific* activity, and they usually are directed at accomplishing, rather than forbidding some behavior" (p. 19). Effective teachers do more than post rules or present procedures. Teachers work with students to ensure that they understand and can demonstrate rules and procedures. This is an important point. Students' behaviors need to be approached in a manner similar to academic skills. Teachers spend considerable time during the first few weeks of school assessing students' knowledge, reviewing material, and reteaching academic skills students have forgotten. Similarly, when effective teachers first introduce important academic material, they attempt to provide clear instruction, carefully monitor students' progress, and provide immediate corrective feedback if a student or group of students is having difficulty with the material. In the same manner, teachers must begin the school year by teaching the classroom rules and procedures, carefully monitoring students' behaviors, informing students of mistakes, and reteaching rules or procedures that students are frequently failing to follow.

The initial studies involving teacher behavior at the beginning of the school year were correlational; teachers whose students made greater achievement gains were observed establishing rules and procedures, and carefully monitoring student work. Following these discoveries, however, several studies were conducted to determine whether teachers trained in the materials in this chapter were more effective in increasing student on-task behavior and learning than were teachers who did not receive this training and implement these new teacher behaviors. Results from these studies (Evertson, 1985; Evertson, Emmer, Sanford, & Clements, 1983) clearly demonstrate that providing training in these methods can lead to changes in teacher behaviors that are associated with improved student behavior.

More recently work by Jerome Freiberg at the University of Houston (Freiberg, 1999; Freiberg et al., 1995), Ron Nelson at Arizona State University (Nelson, 1996; Nelson, Martella, & Galand, 1998), and the Positive Behavioral Support work by George Sugai at the University of Oregon and Tim Lewis at the University of Nebraska (Lewis, 2001; Sugai, Horner, & Gresham, 2002) have reinforced the importance of teaching desired behavior and establishing agreed-on behavior standards. Recent proponents of the benefits of studying the human brain in order to develop and validate best practices in teaching also provide support for the benefits of classroom structures. Robert Sylwester (2000) suggests that biology supports the concept of a classroom being an independent organism that requires students be provided with initial structure and support and then to gradually become more independent and autonomous.

Several words of caution are offered before discussing approaches to establishing productive classroom rules and procedures. Rules and procedures should be developed in conjunction with teaching strategies that help students meet their personal and academic needs. Unfortunately, students are sometimes expected to behave in compliance with rules and procedures even though the learning environment does not respond sensitively to their needs and interests. When this condition is found in a classroom, it is understandable that students' behaviors begin to oppose the classroom rules. The educational exchange must function effectively in both directions. Students can be expected to support rules and procedures that enhance learning only if the learning process is respectful of students and their needs.

As discussed throughout this chapter and the remainder of the book, there are two primary reasons educators must establish and monitor behavior standards. First, student learning is dramatically related to the creation of a safe climate in which everyone is treated with dignity. Second, students benefit from learning about their rights as citizens and seeing that these rights and their dignity are upheld and fostered in the school environment.

This chapter is about working with students to create behavioral norms that help create safety and security within the learning environment. It is also about teachers monitoring their own behaviors in ways that facilitate clarity and continuity of instructional activities in classrooms. Safety, security, clarity, and continuity need not suggest control of students. Indeed, without these factors, a classroom can quickly become a setting in which students are not free to be spontaneous, take risks, learn from their mistakes, or become actively involved in the learning process. As educators, we need to ensure that structure is always a means to an end, rather than an end in itself. Additionally, we need to involve students in developing the guidelines that facilitate a safe, supportive environment. The creation of needed structure can be an important aspect of community building.

Another concept that can help you thoughtfully develop classroom rules is the fact that rules should not be designed to catch children misbehaving so that they can be punished. Instead, rules should provide guidelines or benchmarks that help children examine their behaviors, considering its effect on themselves and others. Consequently, behavior that violates accepted rules should be dealt with by discussing the matter with the child. When dealing with unproductive behavior, teachers must help children examine both their motivations and the consequences of their actions. Overemphasis on punishment often obscures the issue of motivation and attitude and simultaneously limits the child's attention to the immediate negative consequences of the behavior. This pressure tends to limit thoughtful consideration of either the effect the behavior has on others or the long-term consequences associated with continuing the behavior. In a real sense, a punishment orientation reinforces a low level of moral development and does not help children develop a higher, more socially valuable level of morality.

DEVELOPING GENERAL BEHAVIOR STANDARDS OR RULES

We have some concern about using the term *rules*. The term suggests a compliance orientation to classroom management, whereas, as presented throughout this book, we believe that the goals of education and the needs of students are better served by working with students to create a sense of shared community. Therefore, it might be more effective to replace the word *rules* with words such as *behavior standards* or *norms*. Because we believe the process is far more important than the terminology, and because the term *rules* is used by many schools and better understood by younger children, throughout this chapter we variously use terms such as *rules*, *behavior standards*, *norms*, and *behavior expectations* to describe the agreements teachers and students make regarding the types of behaviors that help make a classroom a safe community of support.

Several factors increase the likelihood that students will accept and consistently follow classroom rules. First, students need to be involved in developing the behavior standards that apply in the classroom. Second, rules need to be clearly stated. Students have difficulty responding to glittering generalities such as "behave appropriately." Third, although it is important to state behavior expectations clearly, it is just as important to develop as few as possible. Fourth, students must clearly indicate their acceptance of the behavior standards agreed on by the classroom group. Fifth, because behavior standards established in the school setting may conflict with those children experience outside of school, it is important that student behavior be monitored and frequently discussed to ensure that it is consistent with the classroom standards. Finally, students will be more likely to behave in accordance with rules if they know that the rules are accepted by significant others, such as their parents and peers.

The specific methods presented in the remainder of this chapter apply most directly to elementary school classrooms or other relatively small, self-contained settings, such as a special education class or a small alternative school. The basic ideas, however, describe the essential ingredients in establishing classroom rules and responsibilities. Whenever significant variations are needed for secondary classrooms, they are included.

PAUSE
and Consider   **7.1**

> Pause for a moment and think about situations you have experienced with large numbers of people. Were you ever frustrated when individuals pushed in front of you, cut you off in a car, or otherwise failed to demonstrate thoughtful, civil behavior? At these times did you consider that the environment would have felt safer and healthier had all individuals followed guidelines that helped everyone meet their needs? Write a short statement regarding what you believe about benefits and costs of having behavior standards within a group setting. Discuss this with a group of colleagues or classmates.

Discussing the Value of Rules/Behavior Standards

The first step in developing classroom rules is to discuss with students why it is important to develop standards that all members of the class agree to follow. You may want to introduce or stimulate the discussion by asking students why adults have rules such as obeying traffic signals, paying taxes, and not crowding in lines. Throughout this discussion, reinforce the concept that the classroom group and the school are a society, and, like larger societal groups, it will function more effectively when people agree to behavior standards that help to ensure a safe, caring environment. Help students understand how rules benefit people who must work together. This topic places the focus clearly on the advantages each child derives from class members' accepting those standards. For example, students may state that rules are important because if everyone did whatever they wanted, the classroom might become too disruptive for effective studying.

"And then, of course, there's the possibility of being just the slightest bit too organized."

In his book, *Judicious Discipline*, Forrest Gathercoal (2001) discusses the value of helping students understand their constitutional rights and the fact that rules exist to ensure that no one has these rights denied. In addition to teaching students about their constitutional rights, Gathercoal introduces students to the concept that a person's constitutional rights do not include the right to violate the rights of others. This concept, which Gathercoal calls *compelling state interests*, states that students are denied their individual rights when their actions seriously affect the welfare of others. Gathercoal notes that students cannot violate the following rights of the majority:

1. Health and safety
2. Property loss or damage
3. Legitimate educational purpose
4. Serious disruption of the educational process

Health and safety deals with the fact that students do not have the right to act in a manner that infringes on the physical or psychological health or safety of others. Therefore, a student does not have the right to engage in harassment, bullying, fighting, or running in the halls because these behaviors violate the health and safety rights of others. This compelling state interest is the basis for U.S. laws regarding sexual harassment and protection against racial bias. *Property loss and damage* refers to the fact that all students and staff have the right to work in an environment where their property is not stolen or damaged. No student can successfully argue that their right to freedom of expression allows them to damage property, for example, writing graffiti on the walls. *Legitimate educational purpose* gives teachers the right to select instructional

"Maybe next time you'll listen when I tell you not to lean back in your chair, Jimmy."

materials, assess student learning, ask that students be on time, and so on. Finally, *serious disruption of the learning environment* means that although students may express their disagreement or frustration in a calm manner, they may not express themselves in a style that seriously disrupts the learning environment. Thus, although students have freedom of speech and due process rights, they must practice these rights in a manner that does not seriously disrupt the educational environment.

Gathercoal described a major advantage of developing behavior standards based on constitutional law rather than teacher or school values.

A shared knowledge of constitutional principles allows objectivity because educators themselves are not personally identified with the rules. When personal biases are used as the basis for rules and decisions, educators are more likely to interpret rule violations as violations against them personally. This often leads to an adversarial relationship. On the other hand, educators are far more successful with misbehaving students when those students feel they are working together with someone trying to help them understand and find ways to live within society's reasonable expectations. (Gathercoal, 1996 personal correspondence)

Likewise, students and parents are more likely to accept the necessity for behavioral standards when they understand that these standards are derived not from the teacher's biases but from constitutional and case law. Most teachers have had a parent tell their child that in order to defend her- or himself or to retaliate, it is acceptable to hit another student. Although physical violence may be permitted in their homes, these parents and students need to know that this conduct may be a violation of basic human rights and will not be allowed to occur in a school setting.

Students' statements on why it is important to develop classroom rules can be written on the chalkboard or a large piece of butcher paper. The latter approach is more advantageous because the list is easier to save for later discussion should the group have difficulty in following its rules.

Developing a List

The next step in developing functional behavior standards for the classroom is to have the students list all standards they believe are important. Students may be asked to describe "the way we want to act in our classroom so it is a good place for everyone to learn." During this stage, encourage the students to state standards in a positive manner. If a student states, "Don't talk while others are talking," help the student rephrase this as: "Listen quietly while another person is talking." Similarly, "Students should not steal from each other, the teacher, or the school" could be restated as, "If anyone needs something, he or she will ask to borrow it." Once the students and you have completed the list of standards or rules, help them cross out any that do not apply and combine as many as possible.

Forest Gathercoal (2001) recommends having students develop a rule to cover each of the compelling state interest rights that must be protected. Figure 7.1 presents a list of rules students might develop to ensure that students' rights are protected. When developing such a list with young children, teachers can increase students' understanding by discussing, role-playing, and initially displaying (pictorially or in writing) several specific behavioral examples of following and violating each rule. Activity 7.1 (at the end of the chapter) offers you an opportunity to practice developing classroom rules that would be appropriate and effective with the students with whom you work.

Secondary teachers may not want to develop a separate list for five or six classes. Some teachers prefer to present their own behavior expectations and ask students in each class to discuss and edit them. The teacher could then combine the various classes' editorial comments and present the edited version to all classes the next day. Some teachers present their own rules and ask each class if they believe one or two additional rules might help their class.

Because high school students may have often experienced the process of establishing classroom norms, in many cases this process can be shortened dramatically for these older students. We work with several secondary teachers who have their students generate a list of participant behaviors that must exist in order to have a productive learning environment. These are consolidated and summarized into a list entitled, "behaviors to which we commit in order to have a productive learning environment." The key is that students understand why these standards must exist and that students have a role in discussing these behavior expectations.

Another method we have found helpful in assisting students understand and establish behavior norms is ending the year by having each student in the class write a letter to students who will be enrolled the following year regarding behaviors that helped make everyone's learning experience productive. The following year each student receives a letter from one of the students who attended the class the previous year. We know secondary teachers who use this letter as the basis for developing a set of standards

---

Health and safety

Treat each other politely and kindly

Property loss and damage

Treat school and personal property respectfully

Legitimate educational purpose

Follow reasonable teacher requests
Be prepared for class
Make a good effort and ask for help if you need it

Serious disruption of the educational process

Solve problems nonviolently

FIGURE 7.1

Classroom Rules Consistent with Ensuring Students' "Compelling State Interests"

to which the group would like to adhere. In elementary school, we work with teachers who have the new students write letters back to the older students asking them for additional clarification or advice regarding behaviors that will facilitate their successes.

Gathercoal (2001) presents another very useful concept when he notes that all behavior needs to be evaluated by examining time, place, and manner. Most behavior is appropriate at some time, in some place, and if done in a particular manner. For example, talking with peers during cooperative learning is desirable behavior, whereas talking during the test that follows is usually inappropriate (time). Boxing is an Olympic sport but is at no time appropriate in a classroom or hallway setting (place). Likewise, although it is appropriate to politely request clarification regarding a teacher's particular instructional decision, it is not appropriate to stand up in the back of the room and announce, "This material stinks!" (manner).

Many students believe numerous adult decisions are not only arbitrary but also are actually intended to frustrate and demean the students. When students learn that adults are not stating that student behaviors are "bad" but rather that they must stand the test of time, place, and manner, students often have a much different reaction to limits teachers set in a school environment. When he was a junior high school vice principal, the senior author not infrequently happened on two students in an embrace in a school hallway. He found it much more effective so say, "Please consider time and place" rather than confronting them with the fact that adults did not want them embracing. Almost all students accept redirection when it makes sense to them and can be stated in a manner that treats them with dignity.

Getting a Commitment

When the final list of rules has been developed, you can lead a discussion to clarify each rule and ask students to indicate whether they can accept the behavior standard. During this important stage, several students may state that they do not believe they can abide by a particular rule. You can then ask the students whether the rule seems to be one that does not help people or whether they agree that it is a good rule but do not believe they can consistently act in accordance with it. If they express the latter, you can explain that they are not expected to be able to act perfectly all the time. Just as they will learn how to solve new math problems and read more efficiently, they will also learn how to behave in ways that are more effective. The initial question is not whether the students can already solve all their math problems or consistently behave appropriately, but whether they believe that these skills are helpful to them and if they will attempt to improve these skills. If the students state that a rule is not acceptable, you can help them clarify why they believe it to be undesirable. In most cases, students will quickly acknowledge the basic value of the rule. If one or more students persist in stating that a rule is unacceptable, however, you have the option of deleting the rule or asking to postpone further discussion of the item until you have had an opportunity to discuss it with the small group of students who disagree.

A number of teachers have their students take the list of rules home (usually with an accompanying statement about how the teacher will handle persistent rule violations) for parents to sign and return. This strategy is particularly useful when working with intermediate and middle school students or a group of students who a teacher expects may have difficulty consistently demonstrating responsible behavior. The fact that everyone responsible for the students' behaviors understands the rules and consequences can have a positive effect on their behaviors and can minimize the confusion and tension associated with instances when parents must be contacted about a student's inappropriate behavior.

When sending a list of rules and consequences home, it is important to include a general philosophy statement about your classroom management and instruction. This lets you present the issue of rules in a positive manner that indicates their relationship to effective instruction and student learning. For example, your statement might begin:

> As an educator, I believe all students can learn, demonstrate concern for others, and choose to act responsibly in the classroom. My goals as a teacher are to help all students learn to the best of their capabilities and to assist students to work effectively with others. My goal is to create a classroom environment that encourages mutual respect and cooperation and that provides opportunities for students to make choices regarding their behavior. In order to create a positive and productive learning environment in which all students can achieve and learn to take responsibility for themselves, I have worked with the students to create a list of rules and procedures that will guide our behaviors. Because I know you share my deep concern for the quality of your child's learning, I would appreciate your discussing the attached material with your child, signing it, and returning it to me by _____ . I look forward to working with your child and to communicating with you concerning his or her progress, special achievements, and any concerns that may arise.

The authors work with a talented secondary teacher who developed with her ninth-grade students the student and teacher expectations shown in Figure 7.2. In addition to having the students and their parents or guardians acknowledge their understanding of these guidelines by signing them, the teacher created a quiz to determine whether all students understood the expectations. Figure 7.3 presents the quiz the teacher presented in association with the expectations listed in Figure 7.2. Many high school teachers believe it is not necessary to involve high school students in this manner. Many high school students view themselves as responsible and may resent methods that remind them of elementary or middle school activities. When working in a high school setting, be sensitive when developing behavior standards as this process may be frustrating to older students. We have found that the best policy is to discuss the matter with other teachers and students prior to determining how to work with students to develop classroom behavior expectations.

Monitoring and Reviewing Classroom Rules

Once students have developed reasonable rules and agreed to behave in accordance with them, the next step is to help them recognize and monitor their behavior. One approach helpful with primary age children is to have them take turns acting out the rules. Each child can be asked to role-play both the appropriate and inappropriate behavior, and you can ask their peers to raise their hands whenever the student is behaving appropriately and place their hands in their laps when the student is behaving inappropriately. This activity is helpful in ensuring that every child clearly understands the rules.

Especially in elementary school classrooms, it is important to review the rules frequently for several weeks. A good approach is to review them every day for the first week, three times a week during the second week, and once a week thereafter. It is also

FIGURE 7.2
Classroom
Expectations

Source: Based on
materials developed
by mentor teacher
Mary Holmes and
intern Barbara
Dowdell Brown.

Class Expectations
Mrs. Brown
English Department

Student Expectations

1. Treat others politely and with respect
2. Treat your school and personal property with respect
3. Follow teacher requests
4. Be prepared for class
   • Attend regularly and on time (ready to learn when music stops)
   • Have paper, pen, notebook, text, or other required materials
   • Take responsibility for any missed work
   • Turn in assignments on time
5. Make a good effort at your work and request help when you need it
   • Complete all your work *to the best of your abilities*
   • Seek out teacher assistance during Academic Support

Teacher Expectations

1. Create a fair and safe classroom atmosphere where students will feel free to share their ideas and ask questions
2. Maintain an environment conducive to learning (limited distractions)
3. Discover and work toward improving individual students' strengths
4. Be available to students before and after school for extra help
5. Work toward making learning not only interesting but also meaningful beyond the classroom

I have read the course expectations and syllabus.

Student signature _____ Date _____

Parent signature _____ Date _____

helpful to have the rules displayed in a prominent place in the classroom. During the first week, discuss them briefly at the beginning of each day, and end the day by having the class evaluate their behavior and consider whether improvement in any area is needed. If the entire class consistently displays appropriate behavior or shows considerable improvement over the previous day, you may want to send a positive note or award home with each student. Significant individual improvements can be similarly rewarded. After the first month of school, there are several occasions on which the rules should be brought to the class's attention. First, it is a good idea to review these rules every two weeks to determine whether they are still meaningful and whether any rules need to be added or deleted.

Classroom rules also need to be reviewed with each new student who enters the class. Many students who transfer during the school year come from highly mobile families. Some of these students have often had a pattern of difficulties in school. It is important that these students get off to a good start, which can be facilitated by their

Name: _____

FIGURE 7.3

Classroom
Expectations Quiz

Expectations/Rules Quiz

Class Expectations
Mrs. _____
English Department

Source: Based on
materials developed by
mentor teacher Mary
Holmes and intern
Barbara Dowdell
Brown.

Student Expectations

1. Treat others _____ly and with _____
2. Treat your _____ and _____ _____ with respect
3. Follow _____ _____
4. Be _____ for _____
   • Attend regularly and   _____ _____
     (ready to ____ ____ ____ ____ _____)
   • Have _____, _____, _____,
     _____, or other required materials
   • Take responsiblity for _____ _____ work
   • Turn in _____ on _____
5. Make a good effort at your work and _____ _____
   when you need it
   • _____ all your _____ *to the best of your abilities*
   • Seek out _____ _____ during Academic Support

knowing the expectations for classroom behavior. A student who has been demonstrating responsible behavior can be assigned to help new students learn classroom rules and procedures.

Rules should also be discussed when a student or the teacher indicates that violation of one or more of the rules is detracting from learning or is infringing on a student's rights. Recently, a secondary school intern teacher met with one of the authors to express concern about a sophomore class he viewed as very difficult to manage. The intern noted that students talked incessantly while peers were answering questions and that there was a very high rate of put-downs. The intern, who had been skeptical of some of the materials presented in this book, decided that things were going so badly that he had nothing to lose by taking several class periods to discuss the problem with the students and attempt to establish some expectations and procedures for the class. The teacher discussed his concern with the class and allowed them to brainstorm a set of expectations they thought would be realistic. Students edited these as a whole class and signed an agreement to attempt to follow their new expectations. The teacher then asked students to give input on what should occur if students chose to violate these expectations. Students developed the procedures they believed the teacher should follow. The next day, the intern presented a typed copy of the decisions to students and everyone signed it. The expectations and procedures for responding to violations were posted on the wall. The intern commented that he simply could not believe the difference in the class. Indeed, he shared with his colleagues that on the following day, when two of his most disruptive students started to talk out, he simply nodded toward the posted lists and the students apologized and returned to their work.

PAUSE
and Consider 7.2

Consider a class you are currently teaching, one you have observed, or one in which you are working. Write a brief statement regarding how behavior standards were developed during the first week of class. Based on what you have just read, what modifications might you make in developing these standards? Share this writing with at least two other colleagues or classmates.

CLASSROOM PROCEDURES

As mentioned earlier in this chapter, research indicates that effective teachers not only work with students to develop general behavior standards (rules) but also teach the procedures they expect students to follow during specific classroom and school activities. This research also provides specific information on the types of classroom activities for which effective teachers develop procedures. In their research in elementary classrooms, Evertson and Emmer (1982b) found five general areas in which effective teachers taught students how to act:

1. Students' use of classroom space and facilities
2. Students' behavior in areas outside the classroom, such as the bathroom, lunchroom, drinking fountain, and playgrounds
3. Procedures to follow during whole-class activities, such as whether to raise a hand to speak, where to turn in work, and how to get help during seatwork
4. Procedures during small-group work
5. Additional procedures, such as how to behave at the beginning and end of the schoolday, and when a visitor arrives

Effective Procedures

Figure 7.4 outlines the major classroom activities for which elementary teachers who are particularly effective managers develop and teach procedures. For junior high school classrooms, researchers found four key areas in which effective teachers developed procedures:

1. Beginning the class
2. Whole-class activities
3. Procedures related to academic accountability
4. Other activities, such as the end of the class period, interruptions in the class, and fire drills

Figure 7.5 outlines the major classroom activities for which secondary teachers who effectively manage their classrooms develop and teach specific procedures. Figure 7.6

FIGURE 7.4
Elementary
Classroom
Procedures

I. *Room Areas*
   A. Student desks, tables, storage areas
   B. Learning centers, stations
   C. Shared materials
   D. Teacher's desk, storage
   E. Fountain, sink, bathroom, pencil sharpener
II. *School Areas*
   A. Bathroom, fountain, office, library
   B. Lining up
   C. Playground
   D. Lunchroom
III. *Whole-Class Activities/Seatwork*
   A. Student participation
   B. Signals for student attention
   C. Talk among students
   D. Making assignments
   E. Passing out books, supplies
   F. Turning in work
   G. Handing back assignments
   H. Make-up work
   I. Out-of-seat policies
   J. Activities after work is finished
IV. *Small-Group Activities*
   A. Student movement into and out of group
   B. Bringing materials to groups
   C. Expected behavior of students in group
   D. Expected behavior of students out of group
V. *Other Procedures*
   A. Beginning of schoolday
   B. End of schoolday
   C. Student conduct during delays, interruptions
   D. Fire drills
   E. Housekeeping and student helpers

outlines the areas in which effective classroom managers teach specific procedures related to student accountability for academic work. Appendix A presents a list of specific procedures that might be developed in an elementary school.

An example from junior high school can clarify the concept of procedures. Most junior high school students have only four or five minutes between classes. Therefore, they usually enter the classroom excited or agitated, having had little time to review what they learned in their previous class or to get mentally prepared for the coming class. The teacher discussed this problem with the students in his class and worked with them to develop procedures for making a smooth transition when entering the classroom. First, the class and the teacher listed warm-up activities for the first four minutes of class. These activities, which changed every month, included:

1. An instructional warm-up activity
2. Sharing something they had learned in school during the past day

FIGURE 7.5
Secondary
Classroom
Procedures

I. *Beginning Class*
   A. Roll call, absentees
   B. Tardy students
   C. Behavior during PA
   D. Academic warm-ups or getting ready routines
   E. Distributing materials
II. *Instructional Activities*
   A. Teacher–student contacts
   B. Student movement in the room
   C. Signal for student attention
   D. Headings for papers
   E. Student talk during seatwork
   F. Activities to do when work is done
III. *Ending Class*
   A. Putting away supplies, equipment
   B. Organizing materials for next class
   C. Dismissing class
IV. *Other Procedures*
   A. Student rules about teacher's desk
   B. Fire drills
   C. Lunch procedures
   D. Bathroom, water fountains
   E. Lockers

"Bill missed rehearsal."

3. A relaxation activity
4. Listening to music selected by the teacher
5. Listening to music selected by the students
6. A "brain teaser" activity

Students daily selected the transition activity, each activity being used once each week. The teacher also developed a procedure for tardy students to report to class, a procedure for taking roll, and a signal for gaining the students' attention at the end of the transition activity. Similar procedures were developed for summarizing the day's lesson and leaving the classroom.

Procedures can also include involving students in running the classroom. For years one of the authors,

I. *Work Requirements*
   A. Heading papers
   B. Use of pen or pencil
   C. Writing on back of paper
   D. Neatness, legibility
   E. Incomplete papers
   F. Late work
   G. Missed work
   H. Due dates
   I. Make-up work
II. *Communicating Assignments*
   A. Posting assignments
   B. Requirements/grading criteria for assignments
   C. Instructional groups
   D. Provisions for absentees
   E. Long-term assignments
III. *Monitoring Student Work*
   A. In-class oral participation
   B. Completion of in-class assignments
   C. Completion of homework assignments
   D. Completion of stages of long-term assignments
IV. *Checking Assignments in Class*
   A. Students' exchanging papers
   B. Marking and grading papers
   C. Turning in papers
V. *Grading Procedures*
   A. Determining report card grades
   B. Recording grades
   C. Grading stages of long-term assignments
   D. Extra credit
VI. *Academic Feedback*
   A. Rewards and incentives
   B. Posting student work
   C. Communication with parents
   D. Students' records of their grades

FIGURE 7.6
Accountability Procedures

like many teachers, has had her students decide on classroom jobs students could accomplish in order for the classroom to run more smoothly. In addition to such traditional classroom jobs as line leader, caring for pets, running errands, and so forth, students can learn to take responsibility for such tasks as starting the school day and assisting substitute teachers. Not only does this create a greater sense of significance, competence, and power for students but it can also dramatically assist the teacher by having students take responsibility for tasks that may take considerable time away from a teacher's availability for students. Students may need to receive some training to effectively carry out the requirements of their jobs. This can take place during lunch or recess times.

P A U S E

and Consider   **7.3**

Consider a class you are currently teaching, one you have observed, or one in which you are working. Create a list of ten procedures you believe are among the most important for facilitating a smooth, calm flow in your classroom. You may want to refer to Figures 7.4 through 7.6 for ideas regarding the areas in which procedures exist in your classroom. Join with three or four colleagues and share your procedures. We are virtually certain you will find an appreciative audience and obtain several wonderful ideas for creating a more productive learning environment. In addition, you may want to complete Activity 7.2 at the end of the chapter. It will help you further clarify areas in which you may want to develop classroom procedures.

Teaching and Monitoring Classroom Procedures

A procedure is best taught by:

1. Discussing the need for the procedure
2. Possibly soliciting student ideas
3. Having students practice the procedure until it is performed correctly
4. Reinforcing the correct behavior

When introducing the procedure of developing a signal to obtain students' attention, you might work with the class to develop the signal, set a goal (everyone facing the teacher and quiet within five seconds), use the procedure while students are engaged in an activity, and reinforce them when they respond within the determined time limit. For a procedure such as lining up, you might elicit ideas for behaviors students display when lining up, practice lining up, and reinforce the class when they line up in the desired manner.

Classroom procedures must be carefully monitored during their initial acquisition. Early in the school year, teachers should respond to almost every violation of a rule or procedure. When you notice that the class or an individual student is not correctly following a procedure, the best approach is to ask the student to state the correct procedure and then to demonstrate it. If a class lines up poorly after having once demonstrated the correct procedure, you should politely comment that you know the class can line up more effectively and ask them to return to their seats so that they can practice the procedure. You might then ask students to describe the behaviors associated with lining up correctly. The class could then be asked to demonstrate their skill and be reinforced for their improved effort. Effectively teaching procedures to students is similar to good athletic coaching. The skilled coach first demonstrates the new procedure—often having the athlete perform the maneuver in slow motion. The athlete is then asked to perform the task and receives feedback on the performance, sometimes in the form of videotape replay. The coach has the athlete practice until the feat is performed satisfactorily. Later, perhaps under game conditions, if the athlete performs the task incorrectly, the coach reteaches it in a subsequent practice session. Figure 7.7 lists a number of interesting and fun methods for teaching classroom rules and procedures to students.

1. *Puppet Plays:* Use puppets to role-play responsible behaviors. Have students discuss what was appropriate. Have students identify what behaviors were not appropriate, what rules relate to the behaviors, and what behaviors should have happened instead.
2. *Storytime:* In September, read books to students that teach lessons on following rules and procedures and the rewards from self-discipline.
3. *Posters:* Have students make good behavior, good study habit, safety rules, etc. posters for the classroom, school hallways, cafeteria, and so on. Hang them where appropriate to remind students of your expectations.
4. *Letters:* Teach how to write friendly letters. Have students write letters to playground aides, bus drivers, cooks, custodians, the principal, etc., regarding the rules and their plans to be self-disciplined in the area of interest to whom the letter is written.
5. *Oops, I Goofed!:* Conduct a class discussion on student experiences when they broke a rule. Have students share a personal experience when they goofed in their behavior. Have students share what they should have done instead. Focus in on the idea that we all make mistakes and it is OK if you learn from the mistake and don't repeat it.
6. *Create a Play:* Have students write and produce a play on rules and procedures. Have students present the play to other classes in the school.
7. *School in Relation to Community Rules:* Have students share how school rules and the reasons for following them relate to community rules and their responsibilities as citizens.
8. *Rule Unscramble:* Have your class/school rules stated in phrases. Mix up the words in the phrase. Have students put the words in correct order so they make sense. Or mix up the letters of the words in a rule and have students put the letters of each word back in order so rules make sense.
9. *Rule Bingo:* Make bingo cards with classroom/school rules listed in each square. Have a student or the teacher act out the rule. Students cover the square if they have the rule listed that is being acted out.
10. *Wrong Way:* Have students role-play the wrong way to behave or the wrong way to follow procedures. Videotape the role-playing and have the whole group review and discuss not only what was done wrong but also how to do it the right way.
11. *Hug or Handshake:* When the teacher or students "catch" others following the rules, ask them if they want a hug or handshake and reward them with their wish.
12. *Contract for Success:* Have students write a letter to their parents listing the rules for the class and their plan for successful behavior and self-discipline for the school year. Have students take the letter home and review it with their parents. All persons sign the Contract for Success. Student returns the contract to school the next day.
13. *Picture Signals:* Have pictures as signals for each classroom rule. For example, ears for the rule "We listen politely" or chair for "Sit correctly in your chair." Then use the pictures to signal students if they are not following the rule. The picture signals allow silent management rather than having to stop teaching to tell students what they are doing wrong.
14. *Rules in the Sack:* Write rules on cards and put them into a paper sack. Have a student draw out a rule from the sack and explain it to the rest of the class.

(Continued)

FIGURE 7.7
Creative Ways to Teach Rules and Routines

Source: Deborah Johnson, Lidgerwood Elementary School, Spokane, Washington. Reprinted by permission.

FIGURE 7.7
Continued

15. *Hidden Rules:* Fold paper. On the inside write the class rule. On the outside of the folded paper give clues to the rule. Students read clues and guess the rule. They open the folded paper to see if they are correct. This also works well for a bulletin board display.

16. *Numbered Rules:* Give each classroom rule a number. When a student is following a rule correctly, ask students to hold up the number of fingers which related to the rule being followed. Or when teaching rules, give clues for a specific rule and students hold up the correct number of fingers for the correct numbered rule.

17. *Discrimination:* Develop a list of correct and incorrect behaviors relating to the rules and routines of the classroom and school. Have students read through the list and separate the correct from the incorrect, thus making two lists from the one. Use this discrimination activity during a reading class.

18. *Wheel of Fortune:* Play *Wheel of Fortune* where rules are the puzzles to be solved. Students guess letters of the puzzle and try to guess the rule in the puzzle.

19. *Awards:* Design certificates or bookmarker awards for classroom rules. Give students the awards when their behaviors reflect appropriate behaviors in relation to the specific rule.

20. *Picture Posters:* Have students bring pictures of themselves to school. Use student pictures on posters to highlight a school rule. "The following students believe it is important to respect all teachers." Show their pictures listing their names and grades. Post the posters throughout the school. Use positive peer pressure for pride in school.

One of the authors found that her classroom was becoming quite noisy during an afternoon study period. Despite several clear I-messages from the teacher as well as several students, the classroom continued to be unproductively loud during this time. Consequently, at the beginning of the study period the next day, the teacher asked the class to discuss the procedure of maintaining a noise level that was conducive to studying. The class decided that they often became too loud and agreed to reduce their noise level. The teacher decided to provide clear instruction and a visual to assist her fourth- and fifth-grade students in developing skill in appropriate voice levels. Because she taught in a forested area with fire danger signs, she decided the students would enjoy and understand using an information sign color-coded identical to those used to inform campers of the extent of fire danger. Figure 7.8 presents the sign. For several days, prior to each activity the teacher placed the pointer on the area pointing at the appropriate voice level and briefly discussed how this would help students learn more effectively. If students began to speak too loudly for the activity, the teacher simply pointed to the sign. After several days the sign was used somewhat randomly and eventually was taken down. The students had enjoyed the sign and had learned an important procedure.

Although it is obvious to any veteran teacher that there were other factors involved—including the teacher's respect for her students and her attempt to actively engage them in the learning material—the teacher herself noted that she believed the key variable was her actively involving students in solving the problem and committing to their decisions.

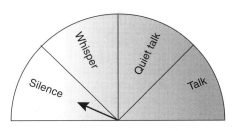

FIGURE 7.8
Voice Level Meter

CREATIVE EXAMPLES OF TEACHING RULES AND PROCEDURES

Case Study: Dealing with the Dilemma of Gum Chewing

In his thoughtful book *Judicious Discipline*, Forrest Gathercoal presents a marvelous true story about how one administrator handled the issue of gum chewing. Gathercoal (2001) wrote:

> Instead of using gum rules and punishments as a means of teaching obedience, for example, why not approach the matter as an educator would—teach students how to use gum properly. . . . [Students] are far more likely to develop good character and become accountable for their behavior when they are respected as student/citizens capable of learning personal responsibility.
>
> I remember an anecdote an elementary principal shared with me about his experience with "the gum problem." He had been a teacher in his building before being appointed principal and was familiar with the problems they had with gum damage. The custodian was constantly complaining about the wrappers on the floor and gum under the furniture. The punishments for chewing gum were harsh, but the problem continued.
>
> When he became an administrator, one of his first acts was to revise some of the rules. One change in particular reversed the ban on gum chewing. His new plan suggested that the faculty spend some time during the first day of class teaching students how to use gum properly. Teachers instructed their classes in the appropriate way to chew gum, how to wrap it in paper when out of their mouths, where to discard the gum, and how to care for the empty wrapper.

"I always expect her to say 'heel.'"

Curious about the effect of this educational approach, a few weeks into the school year the principal asked the custodian if there was a problem with gum in the building. The custodian replied that he was surprised by the fact there was no gum anywhere around school, not even the wrappers on the floor. "I don't know what you did," he said, "but you are the toughest principal we ever had here."

Another three weeks passed. The conversation again surfaced and still no evidence of gum damage was found. "You really are tough," the principal was told. "What did you do?" The principal explained that the old rules were replaced by a more positive educational approach to teaching responsibility. The custodian listened in disbelief and, without a word, walked away shaking his head. (pp. 80, 81)

P A U S E

and Consider   **7.4**

In the classroom in which you are teaching or observing, there are undoubtedly some times when student behavior and the classroom flow detract from valuable instructional time. Take a few minutes to describe a situation in the classroom in which this is the case. Next, try to determine a procedure that would allow the class to flow more smoothly. Share this with several colleagues or classmates. We believe you will discover that, when classroom management problems exist, one of the first and most important things you will learn is to examine and modify classroom procedures.

Case Study: Developmental Recess

A number of years ago, one of the authors was asked to assist an elementary school staff in solving the problems of repeated referrals for playground misbehavior. The staff was concerned that their responses to continued misbehavior were not severe enough and wondered if they needed a more progressive approach to disciplining the repeat offenders. The author took two approaches to assisting the staff with their concern. First, the staff involved in playground supervision, along with the schoolwide student management committee, examined data to determine the type and frequency of misbehavior leading to a referral. This was done to determine whether there were key procedures (such as how to use a particular piece of equipment or how to play a game) that needed to be taught or retaught.

Following this, the committee was asked to consider how they were defining discipline. When confronted with continued behavior problems, it is more effective to consider what procedures or skills need to be taught to the students involved. Based on the belief that many behavior problems can be dealt with by providing students with new skills (see social skills training in Chapter 10 for further information), the author assisted the staff in establishing a developmental recess. Developmental recess removes students who have had a designated number of behavior problems on the playground and provides them with an opportunity to learn and practice the procedures for successful participation. After demonstrating acceptable behavior for a designated number of days in the developmental recess, the student may return to the normal recess activities. Physical education teachers, parent volunteers, instructional assistants, and principals have staffed this activity.

One of the authors recently worked with a staff who implemented a developmental lunch in which they provided students who had difficulty using acceptable cafeteria manners with an opportunity to learn and practice these behaviors. Figure 7.9 presents an outline of a developmental recess procedure developed by a state director of special education.

The Concept

FIGURE 7.9
Developmental
Recess

Developmental recess is one technique for helping children learn the specific skills they need to behave successfully while at recess. Because successful recess experience requires skills important to success in many other areas of life, developmental recess is viewed by many as an important component of comprehensive school curriculum.

If a child is having difficulty behaving appropriately during recess, it is very likely that the child has social skill or other playground skill deficits. Although appropriate consequences for irresponsible choices can be valuable teaching tools, the application of negative consequences as a stand-alone intervention does little to remediate playground skill deficits. When a child has difficulty reading, schools teach specific reading skills. The child is not placed in time-out with the hope that reading will be better in the future. When a child has difficulty with playground behavior, it is just as essential that appropriate replacement behaviors be taught and rehearsed.

This concept may be used with activities and situations other than recess. Such structured teaching of prosocial skills may be of value in relation to cafeteria behavior, school assembly behavior, and so on.

Sample Developmental Recess Model

Developmental recess is a relatively new concept, and a number of developmental recess models are being developed. All derive from the basic concept of teaching prosocial replacement behaviors. One model gaining popularity in a number of Oregon schools involves the following:

1. Teaching prosocial skills in small groups just prior to recess
2. Monitoring student choices during recess
3. Positive debriefing with those students immediately following recess

The following specific steps may be useful to those implementing this model for the first time:

1. Identify two school adults who are skilled and willing to work with students who have behavior difficulties at recess. One of these adults might be a school counselor, school psychologist, behavior consultant, child development specialist, and so on. The other could be a classroom teacher, administrator, playground assistant, and so on.
2. Identify a small group of students who could benefit from involvement in developmental recess.
3. Inform parents of the purpose and nature of developmental recess and obtain written authorization from parents to include the selected children in the group.

(Continued)

FIGURE 7.9
Continued

4. Assess the selected students to determine skill deficits and gather appropriate instructional materials needed for teaching prosocial skills. Assessment strategies could include the use of behavior rating scales, student self-report instruments, direct observation, and the like.

5. Schedule developmental recess in consultation with the classroom teachers of the selected students. It is recommended that students participate in developmental recess at least three or four times per week for four to six weeks. Many schools have developmental recess occur during recess.

6. As children demonstrate appropriate behavior during developmental recess (usually for three to five consecutive days), they return to the regular recess.

7. For several days following their return, students check with the developmental recess facilitator prior to recess to discuss their goals and after recess to evaluate their behavior. As students experience success, they can report less frequently.

Case Study: Teaching Students to Respect Physical Space

One of the authors recently worked with a staff whose elementary students were frequently involved in inappropriate (violent or sexual) touch. A staff committee developed a plan for teaching students about individuals' personal space. In a large assembly followed by work in classrooms, students were shown (by a flashlight hanging over a student in a darkened room) that everyone has some physical space. Students were then asked to use yarn to circle themselves with the physical space they needed in various situations. This was then used during classtime and recess for several days. The staff reported that students quickly learned the procedure of not invading another person's physical space and that inappropriate touch on the playground, although still present, occurred at a much lower rate.

Case Study: Teaching Students Hallway Behavior in a Middle School

One of the authors recently worked with a staff who was concerned about student behavior in the hallways. Some teachers were concerned that students were not punished enough when caught being unsafe in the halls, and other teachers pointed to the lack of staff consistency in responding to inappropriate student hallway behavior. The author asked the staff to discuss where the problems occurred. It soon became obvious that students were having problems in two specific areas of the building. Someone suggested that the staff involve the students in examining the problem and determining a solution. The staff and students developed a series of traffic signs (such as "yield right," "merge left," etc.) that were placed in the necessary areas. Students were then given instruction in how to move in the congested areas. Results indicated that referrals for student misconduct in hallways decreased dramatically once the procedures were collaboratively developed and effectively taught.

Changing Teachers' Procedures

Although most attention is focused on teaching students to follow selected school and classroom procedures, student behavior can often be more quickly and dramatically improved by altering the procedures adults follow. For example, one of the authors recently worked with an elementary school staff that expressed concern about student behavior both at the end of recess and in the hallways. After considerable discussion about how to teach students to behave more responsibly in these settings, one of the teachers noted that if teachers would develop the procedure of meeting their students outside at the end of recess and walking their students to physical education, music, and lunch, there would be much less chaos and many happier students. The teachers discovered that although it took approximately four minutes more each day to follow this procedure, they were saving at least five times that much instructional time because of the decrease in disruptive student behavior during and following transition times.

In a similar vein, one of the authors worked with a school staff that was concerned about how rudely students responded to adults. Again, the staff was engaged in very positive discussions about how to teach students improved communication skills. After implementing this social skills training, however, the staff remained frustrated by the level of rude responses. With some outside assistance, the staff began to realize that a significant amount of this rudeness, or failure to respond positively to adult statements, occurred when adults were correcting students. The staff discovered that when, instead of criticizing or correcting students, they validated the students' feelings and asked students how else they could respond, the amount of negative student behavior was dramatically reduced.

A final example comes from a high school program with a student experiencing serious behavioral and emotional problems. The student had received numerous office referrals and several suspensions for his aggressive responses to adults. As part of his treatment plan, the special education teacher worked with the boy and his teachers to determine ways the teachers could provide correction in a manner the boy perceived as more respectful and less confrontational. When the teachers began using this new procedure, the student's aggressive responses to adults were almost eliminated. As in the previous example, although it was important to teach new procedures to the student, it was equally important to alter the teachers' procedures for responding to inappropriate student behavior.

Teaching Rules and Procedures to New Students

When new students enter the classroom, it is imperative they understand how the classroom operates. There are a variety of methods for accomplishing this. Most teachers simply assign a student to discuss classroom behavior standards and key procedures with a new student. In an elementary school this may be a class job. The new student may spend a recess and lunch period with the mentor learning about key classroom expectations. In a secondary school several students may volunteer for a two-week or monthly role of teaching new students about the classroom. In both cases, this is facilitated by having the materials in writing or having the teacher or class develop a videotape describing these materials. The teacher may also design a quiz about classroom operation and ask all new students to earn 100 percent on this quiz.

When the new student has limited English proficiency, if at all possible, someone who speaks the student's language should work with the student to help the student understand how the classroom operates. In some cases schools and classroom teachers have developed videotapes in several languages to explain these procedures. Additionally, some schools have volunteers who work with new families and students to provide an orientation to the school in the family's first language.

AN OUTLINE FOR BEGINNING THE SCHOOL YEAR

The most effective way to create a safe, positive setting in which students are motivated to learn will vary with grade level, subject matter, and teacher style. However, there are some key ingredients to creating a positive learning environment. This section offers suggestions for beginning the school year in elementary, middle school, and high school classrooms.

Elementary Classrooms

Figure 7.10 presents the outline of training workshops developed by Carolyn Evertson and her colleagues (1983) to assist teachers in improving their skills in effectively

FIGURE 7.10
Major Components Presented in Beginning-of-Year Treatment

Source: C. Evertson, E. Emmer, J. Sanford, and B. Clements. "Improving Classroom Management: An Experiment in Elementary School Classrooms," *Elementary School Journal, 84* (1983): 173–180. Copyright © 1983 by The University of Chicago.

1. *Readying the classroom.* Be certain your classroom space and materials are ready for the beginning of the year.
2. *Planning rules and procedures.* Think about what procedures students must follow to function effectively in your classroom and in the school environment: decide what behaviors are acceptable or unacceptable; develop a list of procedures and rules.
3. *Consequences.* Decide ahead of time consequences for appropriate and inappropriate behavior in your classroom, and communicate them to your students; follow through consistently.
4. *Teaching rules and procedures.* Teach students rules and procedures systematically; include in your lesson plans for the beginning of school sequences for teaching rules and procedures, when and how they will be taught, and when practice and review will occur.
5. *Beginning-of-school activities.* Develop activities for the first few days of school that will involve students readily and maintain a whole-group focus.
6. *Strategies for potential problems.* Plan strategies to deal with potential problems that could upset your classroom organization and management.
7. *Monitoring.* Monitor student behavior closely.
8. *Stopping inappropriate behavior.* Handle inappropriate and disruptive behavior promptly and consistently.
9. *Organizing instruction.* Organize instruction to provide learning activities at suitable levels for all students in your class.
10. *Student accountability.* Develop procedures that keep the children responsible for their work.
11. *Instructional clarity.* Be clear when you present information and give directions to your students.

beginning the school year. Our work supports this pioneering work in beginning the school year. We have also found several additional activities that help create a positive learning community. Figure 7.11 is an outline taken from a fifth-grade classroom taught by one of the authors.

Secondary Classrooms

Figure 7.12 presents the outline of training workshops developed by Carolyn Evertson (1985) to assist teachers in improving their skills in effectively beginning the school year. Although our work supports her pioneering efforts, we have found that the following provides a solid outline for creating a positive, cohesive community of learners in which students are motivated to learn and experience a sense of safety and personal investment in the learning process.

> *Provide a cognitive map (outline) for the year.* Describe to students the general outline of the course, content they will be working with, instructional and assessment methods you will use, and so on.
>
> *Define learning.* Using the approach discussed in Chapter 6, have students work collaboratively to develop a list of characteristics they agree are found in a successful learner and create a definition of an effective learner.
>
> *Ask students what they want to learn and what types of instructional activities best facilitate their learning.* Have students individually write about what they want to

---

First-Day Schedule

Place on the students' desks: nametags, class name word search, sacks, letter from the teacher to the student

Teacher introduces self

Take attendance using name chain

Learn the school pledge

Practice assembly procedures

Attend all-school assembly

Overview of the year's curriculum

Snack from the bags placed on the student's desk (also in bag is a bookmark, pencil, sticker, and piece of candy)

Students write letters to the teacher telling about themselves, their families, summer highlights, and something they want to learn this year

Packets go home

Practice closure procedure

Practice bus procedure

Second-Day Schedule

Mystery student warm-up

Practice morning procedures

Bingo acquaintance activity

Introduce key classroom procedures

Snack and stretch break

Music class

Paint portraits on shoe box

Practice lunch procedures

Lunch and recess

Read aloud

Successful learner activity

Group contributions activity

Recess

Organize notebooks

Closure

Bus dismissal

FIGURE 7.11
Beginning the School Year in an Elementary Classroom

FIGURE 7.12
Outline of
Workshop Content
for Secondary
Teachers in the
Experimental Group

Source: Carolyn M.
Evertson, "Training
Teachers in
Classroom
Management: An
Experimental Study
in Secondary School
Classrooms," *Journal
of Educational
Research*, 79(1): 54,
1985. Reprinted with
permission of the
Helen Dwight Reid
Educational Foun-
dation. Published by
Heldref Publications,
1319 Eighteenth St.,
NW, Washington,
DC 20036-1802.
Copyright © 1985.

I. *Planning* (before school starts)
  A. Use of space (readying the classroom)
  B. Rules for general behavior
  C. Rules and procedures for specific areas
    1. Student use of classroom space and facilities
    2. Student uses of out-of-class areas
    3. Student participation during whole-class activities/seatwork
    4. Student participation in daily routines
    5. Student participation during small-group activities
  D. Consequences/incentives for appropriate/inappropriate behavior
  E. Activities for the first day of school
II. *Presenting Rules, Procedures, and Expectations* (beginning of school)
  A. Teaching rules and procedures
    1. Explanation   3. Feedback
    2. Rehearsal   4. Reteaching
  B. Teaching academic content
  C. Communicating concepts and directions clearly
III. *Maintaining the System* (throughout the year)
  A. Monitoring for behavioral and academic compliance
  B. Acknowledging appropriate behavior
  C. Stopping inappropriate behavior
  D. Consistent use of consequences/incentives
  E. Adjusting instruction for individual students/groups
  F. Keeping students accountable for work
  G. Coping with special problems

learn in the class. Are there special interests or knowledge they have related to the class? Ask students to describe the instructional and assessment methods that seem to work best for them and perhaps give examples of these from previous classes they have taken.

Be inviting and help students know you. Be positive and excited about your teaching. Learn students' names and something about each student. Make a positive contact with each student during the first two weeks of school. Keep your ratio of positive to negative statements at least four to one.

Allow students to interview you. Let students learn about you as a person as well as your beliefs as an educator.

Help students to become better acquainted. Involve students in at least three activities (see Chapter 4) designed to help students know each other's names and learn something about each other.

Teach judicious discipline concepts and establish behavioral norms. Inform students that one role you have is to ensure that the constitutional rights of all students will be protected in the classroom and that no class member (including the teacher) can behave in a manner that violates the rights of others. With this background, either have students develop a list of behavioral norms that ensures that all four compelling state interests are met or provide students with a list and have a discussion that may lead to modifications of this list. Have all students sign this list, indicating their understanding of it and their commitment to respect the rights of all members of the class.

Teach key behavioral procedures. Determine the key procedures you wish to teach. Teach these as they are needed in the classroom. Whenever a problem occurs, ask yourself what procedure you and your students could develop that would eliminate this problem.

Develop an approach for how you and students will respond when someone's rights are violated. Present your approach to responding to violations of classroom behavioral expectations. Allow students' input into this process. Once agreement has been reached, print this, have all students sign it, and provide a copy of this to your administrator.

Carefully monitor students' work and homework and provide reteaching opportunities early. Early in the first marking period provide opportunities for students to present their learning in several ways—tests, projects, writing, and so on. Meet with students who have difficulty presenting a mastery of the material and discuss ways to modify the presentation of materials as well as the assessment of learning.

Involve students in assessing their own efforts and learning. Have students describe their own efforts in mastering the content. Have them list what is working for them, any assistance they might need, and methods they might use to improve their work. A success contract (Chapter 6) might be helpful.

Involve students in assessing your teaching and their feelings about the class. Have students provide you with feedback regarding the class (Chapter 3). Share this feedback with students and work with them to make some modifications in the class.

With the apparently ever-increasing focus on student achievement on standardized tests, even many elementary and middle school teachers express concern about spending a good portion of the first week of class building a community of support and establishing clear behavior guidelines. As stated at the beginning of this chapter, our experiences and extensive research over the past twenty-five years have supported the benefits to student achievement when teachers take the time to thoughtfully develop a safe supportive environment.

P A U S E

7.5   *and Consider*

Consider a class you are currently teaching, one you have observed, or one in which you are working. As well as you can remember, draft an outline of the first five days this class met during the current school year. If you did not teach or observe at the beginning of this year, move immediately to the next part of this activity. Next, create an outline for how you would like to organize the first five days of your next school year. Do not include specific academic activities, but do indicate when these will occur. Once again, we encourage you to join with a group of colleagues or classmates to share your ideas and learn from each other.

CLASSROOM MANAGEMENT SKILLS THAT HELP MAXIMIZE ON-TASK BEHAVIOR

The importance of teachers using the skills described in this section was emphasized by Kounin's (1970) research on classroom discipline. Kounin began his study by collecting several thousand hours of videotapes, both from classrooms of teachers who were acknowledged to be extremely effective in managing their classes and from classrooms of teachers who had serious, continuing management problems. Kounin expected to find significant differences in how teachers from these two groups handled discipline problems that occurred in their classrooms. Surprisingly, the results indicated that the successful teachers responded to control problems in much the same manner as did the teachers whose classrooms were often disorderly.

Based on these findings, Kounin reexamined the tapes, seeking any real differences between the teaching methods of teachers who were successful and those who experienced major management problems. He discovered that the differences lay in the successful teachers' ability to prevent discipline problems. These teachers used many types of management skills to ensure that students were consistently and actively engaged in instructional activities. Successful teachers were better prepared and organized and moved smoothly from one activity to another. These teachers also maintained students' involvement in instructional activities by initially stimulating the students' interests and effectively holding their attention throughout the lesson. Similarly, successful teachers used seatwork that was individualized and interesting. Kounin also discovered that the more effective teachers had greater classroom awareness, constantly scanning the classroom so that they were aware of potential problems and could deal with these before any real difficulties arose. These teachers anticipated students' needs, organized their classrooms to minimize restlessness and boredom, and effectively coped with the multiple and often overlapping demands associated with teaching.

In research conducted to further investigate Kounin's (1970) findings, Brophy and Evertson (1976) found that the same teacher behaviors that reduce classroom disruption are also associated with increased student learning. In describing the findings of the two-year Teacher Effectiveness Project, which examined the relationship between various teacher behaviors and gains in students' learning, Brophy and Evertson (1976) stated, "Our data strongly support the findings of Kounin (1970). . . . That is, the key to successful classroom management is prevention of problems before they start, not knowing how to deal with problems after they have begun" (p. 127). Brophy and Evertson also wrote, "Of the process behaviors measured through classroom observation in our study, the

"How do you do it, Angela?"

group that had the strongest and most consistent relationships with student learning gains dealt with the classroom management skills of the teachers. By 'classroom management,' we mean planning and conducting activities in an orderly fashion; keeping students actively engaged in lessons and seatwork activities; and minimizing disruptions and discipline problems" (p. 51).

The research on academic learning time (ALT) further supports the idea that teachers should incorporate teaching methods that increase on-task student behavior. "If 50 minutes of reading instruction per day is allocated to a student who pays attention about one-third of the time, and only one-fourth of the student's reading time is a high level of success, the student will experience only about four minutes of ALT-engaged reading time at a high success level" (Berliner, 1984, p. 62). Classes vary dramatically in the percentage of time students are engaged in instructional tasks, with rates ranging from consistently less than 50 percent to 90 percent (Fisher et al., 1978). Rosenshine (1983) summarized specific teacher behaviors found to be associated with students' achievement gains and included many of the skills presented in this section.

The section is organized around the ten general instructional management skills listed in Figure 7.13. It is critical to understand how to use the methods in this chapter. They are not offered as gimmicks for increasing students' time on-task or your control. Instead, they are methods that can assist you in helping students better understand their schoolwork and enhance the quality of learning time. Neither are these methods offered as a cookbook of behaviors to be routinely followed. Like the neophyte cook, the beginning teacher may choose to implement many of these methods. Much as cooks alter and discard recipes depending on the outcomes, skilled teachers season standard methods with their own experiences and action research. Teachers constantly need to monitor their own behaviors and their relationships to students' learning in order to develop teaching methods that are maximally effective in the classrooms. In addition to the ideas and activities presented in this book, you will find Good and Brophy's (2000) *Looking in Classrooms* particularly useful in helping monitor and adjust classroom organization and management behavior.

Giving Clear Instructions

A key step in presenting a lesson is to provide clear instructions for the activities in which students will be engaged. A significant amount of disruptive student behavior stems from students not knowing how they are to proceed or what they are to do when

1. Giving clear instructions
2. Beginning a lesson
3. Maintaining attention
4. Pacing
5. Using seatwork effectively
6. Summarizing
7. Providing useful feedback and evaluation
8. Making smooth transitions
9. Dealing with common classroom disruptions
10. Planning for early childhood settings

FIGURE 7.13
Instructional Management Skills That Facilitate On-Task Behavior and Academic Achievement

they require assistance or complete their work. Students are often poorly prepared for seatwork assignments.

Methods

1. *Give precise directions.* Instructions should include statements about (a) what students will be doing, (b) why they are doing it, (c) how they can obtain assistance, (d) what to do with completed work, and (e) what to do when they finish. It is also helpful to indicate how much time they will be spending on the task. This direction may include a statement about when the work can be completed if it cannot be finished within the designated time limits.

2. *Describe the desired quality of the work.* This can increase students' sense of accountability and decrease their anxiety.

3. *After giving instructions, have students paraphrase the directions, state any problems that might occur to them, and make a commitment.*

4. *Positively accept students' questions about directions.*

5. *Place directions where they can be seen and referred to by students.*

6. *Have students write out instructions before beginning an activity.*

7. *When students seem to be having difficulty following directions, consider breaking tasks down into smaller segments.*

8. *Give directions immediately prior to the activity they describe.*

9. *Model the correct behavior. If students have been asked to raise their hands before answering, you can raise your hand while asking the question.*

10. *Hand out worksheets or outlines before taking a field trip.*

11. *Create a space for placing all assignments so students who are absent or forget to write down an assignment can independently access this information.* This can be supported by having several students designated each week to provide additional information for students who are unclear about the materials found in the assignments folder.

Beginning a Lesson

Teachers frequently have difficulty in attracting students' attention and getting a lesson started. The reason is at least partly that students often attempt to postpone the beginning of a lesson by socializing or moving about the room. Students quite accurately realize that the best time for buying time is before the lesson begins.

Methods

1. *Select and teach a cue for getting students' attention.* Students benefit from having a consistent cue indicating that it is time to focus their attention. They hear standard phrases such as, "Okay, we are ready to begin" so often that these statements are often ineffective for eliciting attention. One of the authors has her class select a new cue each month. Students enjoy being involved and choose catchy phrases. During a recent year, students chose "Boo" for October, "Gobble Gobble" for November, and "Ho Ho Ho" for December. While teaching a summer institute on classroom management, the value of using a catchy phrase was demonstrated by recording the time it took forty teachers to pay attention quietly following the phrase "May I please have your attention?" The average time for five such requests was nearly two minutes (in each instance, students were involved in group work). The class was presented with this figure and asked to develop a less common phrase. They chose "Rain Rain Go Away." This phrase was practiced until the class could attend within ten seconds. Follow-up data gathered during the next two weeks showed that the group never took more than ten seconds to become completely quiet.

2. *Do not begin until everyone is paying attention.*

3. *Begin the lesson by removing distractions.*

4. *Clearly describe the goals, activities, and evaluation procedures associated with the lesson being presented.*

5. *Stimulate interest by relating the lesson to the students' lives or a previous lesson.*

6. *Start with a highly motivating activity in order to make the students' initial contact with the subject matter as positive as possible.* One of the authors begins a unit on the Lewis and Clark expedition by dressing up as Meriwether Lewis and collaborating with a colleague to present a skit summarizing the lives of these two noteworthy explorers.

"First, you have to get their attention."

7. *Distribute an outline, definitions, or study guide to help students organize their thoughts and focus their attention.*

8. *Challenge students to minimize their transition time.* Children enjoy games and are impressed by data. Draw on this knowledge by presenting students with data indicating the amount of time it requires them to settle down and asking them to try to reduce this time. There are six basic steps to implementing this approach. First, collect baseline data (see Chapter 10) and record them on a large and easy-to-read chart. Second, the data should be discussed with the students and their assistance requested. Third, help the students choose an appropriate and reasonable goal. Fourth, define exactly what you mean by being ready for class. Fifth, the class must develop a system for collecting and recording data. Finally, it may be necessary to determine a reward for reaching the stated goal.

Maintaining Attention

The amount of time students spend involved in instruction is significantly related to their achievement. Many teachers state that one of the most frustrating tasks associated with teaching is maintaining students' attention during group instruction. Although children and young adolescents do in fact have a somewhat shorter attention span than do adults, their ability to attend quietly to an interesting television program or video game suggests that the skilled teacher can stimulate more consistent attention to task than is seen in most classrooms.

Methods

1. *Arrange the classroom to facilitate the instructional activity you have selected.* When a lesson involves the teacher as the center of attention, students should be seated so that everyone is facing the teacher. This arrangement can be accomplished using rows, a circle, or a U-shape. When students are seated in small groups, request that all students face you before beginning a lesson. Similarly, if you wish students to talk to each other, desks must be arranged in a circle, square, or U-shape so that students can comfortably see and hear each speaker. Teachers who use a variety of instructional activities should consider teaching students a procedure for quickly and quietly moving desks. With a small amount of instruction, students in all grades can learn to rearrange desks in approximately one minute.

2. *Employ a seating arrangement that does not discriminate against some students.* Teachers tend to place higher-achieving students nearer the teacher and provide them with more contact. Research suggests that when low-ability students were moved to the front of the room, their achievements improved more than that of low-ability students who remained at the back of the room. Interestingly, the high-achieving students' achievements did not suffer when they were moved farther from the teacher. Similarly, students' involvement is more evenly distributed when high- and low-achieving students are interspersed throughout the room. Teachers can increase on-task student responses by adjusting seating arrangements and moving around the room so that all students become actively involved in meaningful classroom interaction.

3. *Use random selection in calling on students.* This can be accomplished by placing students' names on popsicle sticks, in a hat, and so on, and simply drawing names to determine who will be called on.

One danger in involving students randomly is that you are less likely to receive an immediate correct answer to every question. Studies indicate that, especially in the primary grades, student achievement is enhanced when teachers provide information, ask focused questions, and receive correct answers from students. Therefore, you should carefully consider when to involve lower-achieving students. For example, these students might be called on when they raise their hands during skill-acquisition lessons and might be encouraged to become actively involved during lessons that involve personal issues or opinions.

4. *Ask the question before calling on a student.* When teachers select the student before asking the question, other students may become less interested in the question. By asking the question, looking around the room, and providing students with an opportunity to consider the question, you create greater interest and anticipation, thereby, increasing attending behavior. Also take this opportunity to reinforce the procedure of students raising their hands to answer questions (e.g., "Raise your hand if you can answer this question," or "John, you have your hand raised. What is the answer?").

5. *Wait at least five seconds before answering a question or calling on another student.* Most teachers are surprised to learn that research indicates that, on the average, teachers wait only one second for a student to respond before answering a question themselves or calling on another student. Consider, however, the process students must go through when asked a question. First, they must hear the question and decide whether they understand it. Second, they must search for the information. Third, they must consider whether their response will be accepted. Fourth, they must decide whether they will receive reinforcement or rebuke for their response (in some situations a correct response will be reinforced by the teacher but punished by peers). This process may occur very rapidly for bright students, but most students require considerably longer than one second to complete it.

1. Length of students' responses increases
2. Number of unsolicited but appropriate answers increases
3. Failure to obtain a response decreases
4. Children's confidence increases
5. Teacher-centered teaching decreases
6. Students' questions increase
7. Lower-achieving students contribute more
8. Students' proposals increase
9. Students give more evidence to support their answers
10. The variety of students' responses increases

FIGURE 7.14
Advantages of Increasing Teachers' Wait Time

Rowe (1986) reported that when teachers increase their waiting time, a variety of positive things occur. Figure 7.14 summarizes her findings. In a review of studies involving wait time, Tobin (1987) found that when average teacher wait time was greater than three seconds, teacher and student discourse changed and higher cognitive level achievement occurred at all grade levels.

6. *Ask students to respond to their classmates' answers.*

7. *Do not consistently repeat students' answers.* Many teachers parrot nearly every answer provided by a student. This practice is intended to ensure that all students hear the correct answer. But it also teaches students that (a) they do not need to speak loudly because the teacher is the only one who needs to hear their answer, (b) they do not need to listen to their peers because the teacher will repeat the answer, and (c) the teacher is the source of all learning in the classroom. All these negative side effects reduce students' motivation, involvement, and attention.

8. *Model listening skills by paying close attention when students speak.*

9. *Be animated.* In his classic work on classroom discipline, Kounin (1970) wrote, "Teachers who maintain a group focus by engaging in behaviors that keep children alert and on their toes are more successful in inducing work involvement and preventing deviancy than are teachers who do not" (p. 123). Studies indicate that not only do students like enthusiastic teachers but also that teacher enthusiasm facilitates student achievement. Demonstrate enthusiasm and animation by moving around the room, varying your voice level, using interested facial expressions, and maintaining a high energy level.

10. *Reinforce students' efforts and maintain a high ratio of positive to negative verbal statements.*

11. *Vary instructional media and methods.*

12. *Create anticipation.* Create a sense of interest by making statements such as, "This is a tough one" or "I'm not sure we've talked about this but maybe someone can answer it."

13. *Ask questions that relate to students' own lives.*

14. *Provide work of appropriate difficulty.* Students' misbehavior is often a response to work that is either too easy or too difficult. Students prefer work that is moderately difficult over tasks that are too easy. When work is too difficult, though, students become discouraged. Failure also causes students to lower their expectations of their own performances.

Research suggests that when the teacher is available to provide assistance (as during monitored seatwork or recitation), students should be able to answer 70 to 80 percent of questions correctly. When students must work independently (as on independent seatwork or homework), students should be able to answer 95 percent correctly (Brophy, 1982; Fisher et al., 1980). Seatwork must not only allow for these high success rates but must also be different enough from previous work to challenge students.

Similarly, teacher questions to students should also elicit a relatively high rate of correct responses. Brophy (1986a) states that approximately three-fourths of teachers' questions should elicit correct responses and the remainder should elicit some form of incorrect or incomplete answer rather than failure to respond. Success rates can be expected to be lower when new material is being introduced but higher during reviews. Brophy noted, "Consistently low success rates (below about 65 percent), however, suggest that the teacher is 'teaching over the students' heads' or has not prepared them effectively for the questions" (p. 9).

15. *Provide variability and interest in seatwork.* Seatwork can be made more interesting by developing units that relate to current events, such as sports or students' other interests (animals, entertainment figures, etc.), or by creating seatwork that is based on some form of board game. Students can also be involved in working cooperatively with peers or presented with a competitive situation.

16. *When presenting difficult material, clearly acknowledge this fact, set a time limit for the presentation, and describe the type of follow-up activities that will clarify the lesson.*

Pacing

Methods

1. *Develop awareness of your own teaching tempo.* Students' behaviors and performances are affected by their teacher's tempo. We can learn to generate interest and enthusiasm effectively or to create a calming effect by adjusting our own personal pace in the classroom. The best method for examining your own pace is to videotape yourself during large-group instruction. As you watch the replay, ask yourself questions such as Did I talk too fast? Was I animated? Did I repeat myself too often? and Would I enjoy listening to my own presentations?

2. *Watch for nonverbal cues indicating that students are becoming confused, bored, or restless.*

3. *Divide activities into short segments.* The use of films as instructional aids helps demonstrate this strategy. Teachers almost always allow a film to run all the way to the end before discussing its content. There are, however, several advantages to stopping the film at important points and discussing the ideas being presented. First, major points of information can be highlighted. Second, this procedure allows students to assimilate smaller amounts of information at a time. Many students simply cannot process the material offered in a half-hour film. Third, this method differentiates viewing a film at school from watching a movie or viewing television. Students can begin to learn that movies shown in school are meant to convey specific information and ideas rather than simply to entertain.

4. *Provide structured short breaks during lessons that last longer than thirty minutes.*

5. *Vary the style as well as the content of instruction.* Students often become restless when faced with extended instructional periods using only one type of instruction. If students have completed a large-group discussion in social studies, it is best not to move directly to a large-group science presentation. Teachers with good classroom management skills learn to move smoothly among a variety of instructional approaches.

6. *Do not bury students in paperwork.*

Using Seatwork Effectively

Research in hundreds of elementary school classrooms shows that students spend more than half their time working privately at seatwork. Data from some of the classes of the Beginning Teacher Evaluation Study (Fisher et al., 1978) also show that in some classes students make nearly 100 percent errors during 14 percent of the time they are involved in seatwork.

"Miss Marpole, I need to talk to you about your seating arrangement."

Methods

1. *Make seatwork diagnostic and prescriptive.* Seatwork should be designed to provide students with meaningful practice while enabling teacher and student to assess the student's progress. Therefore, seatwork should be checked by the teacher or student, recorded and filed by the student, monitored by the teacher, and discussed in periodic teacher–student conferences.

2. *Develop a specific procedure for obtaining assistance.*

3. *Establish clear procedures about what to do when seatwork is completed.*

4. *Add interest to seatwork.* Include cartoons, puzzles, or personalized questions on worksheets.

5. *Work through the first several seatwork problems with the students.* All students will then understand the procedure to be followed and will be able to ask questions if they do not understand the work.

6. *Monitor students' seatwork and make needed adjustments.* While observing a student-teacher in a fifth-grade class, one of the authors noted that students in the class completed seatwork at varying rates, and the teacher's failure to adjust seatwork or provide optional learning activities meant that many students were free to wander and disrupt the class. To bring out this point for the teacher, the author coded at five-minute intervals the number of students who had completed one-quarter, half, three-quarters, or all their work. The results (Figure 7.15) clearly indicate the inappropriateness of giving all students the same seatwork task. In addition to monitoring the time required to complete seatwork, monitor the percentage of students who complete their work with at least 75 percent accuracy (a higher percentage should be selected if you are not available to monitor the seatwork). This information, as well as a group average score, should be recorded as a basis for determining future seatwork assignments for individual students or the class as a whole.

FIGURE 7.15
Number of
Students Who Had
Completed Various
Amounts of
Seatwork at Five-
Minute Intervals

	Percentage of Work Complete			
	0–25%	*26–50%*	*51–75%*	*76–100%*
5 minutes	11	12	8	2
10 minutes	6	10	10	7
15 minutes	4	6	13	10
20 minutes	3	4	7	9

7. *Monitor seatwork by moving around the room systematically.*

8. *Spend considerable time in presentation and discussion before assigning seatwork.*

9. *Keep contacts with individual students relatively short.* Longer contacts minimize your ability to scan the room or to provide assistance to all students.

10. *Have students work together during seatwork.* Students can jointly develop solutions or cooperatively prepare for group competition.

Summarizing

Many children view the schoolday as a series of tasks to be completed and do not understand what they have learned or how the learning relates to specific learning goals or their own lives. When combined with clearly stated goals and useful feedback, the methods presented in this section provide students with a sense of accomplishment and meaning in their school experience.

Methods

1. *At the end of a lesson or a schoolday, ask students to state or write in a journal one thing they learned during the day.*

2. *Have students play the role of a reporter and summarize what has been learned.*

3. *Have students create a skit to act out what they have learned.*

4. *Ask students to create learning displays.* Students can develop a collage, outline, newspaper article, and so on to display their learning. They might write an article reporting on how plants grow. Students could also draw a chart that demonstrates this process.

5. *Encourage students to present their learning to others.*

6. *Display students' work.*

7. *Provide frequent review sessions.*

8. *Use tests as tools for summarizing learning.*

Providing Useful Feedback and Evaluation

Collecting an analyzing feedback regarding student learning significantly influences student motivation, learning, and behavior (Stiggins, 2001). The methods presented next reinforce these purposes and offer practical ideas for effectively using evaluation in the classroom.

Methods

1. *Help students view evaluation as part of the learning process.*

2. *Tell students the criteria by which they will be evaluated.* When working with specific skills, students should know what they are to learn and what level of performance is acceptable. Similarly, when they are assigned projects they should be informed about the specific goals for the lesson, and, if their work will be evaluated, what specific criteria will be used.

3. *Relate feedback directly to individual or teacher goals.*

4. *Record data so that students can monitor their progress.*

5. *Provide immediate and specific feedback.* Students' learning is enhanced when they are provided with specific positive and negative information about their performances. Generalized feedback, such as a grade or comments like "Good" or "Nice work," do not tend to improve students' performances on subsequent tests.

6. *Provide honest feedback.* It is important to focus on students' successes, but students' performances are not aided by feedback that is inaccurately positive. Students resent feedback they perceive as fake. Furthermore, providing students with too much praise for work that does not meet acceptable standards only confuses them and reduces their motivation and performance.

7. *Ask students to list factors that contributed to their successes.*

8. *Deemphasize comparisons between students and their peers.*

9. *Deemphasize grades as feedback on students' work.* Instead, provide information on specific skills the student has demonstrated as well as skills the student may want to improve. While helping the student to set goals for improvement, emphasize the good decisions and important learning and improvement the student has made.

10. *Provide students with clear information regarding their progress.* This is especially helpful in high school where grades impact students' futures. This feedback should provide students with accurate, ongoing data concerning their grades.

Making Smooth Transitions

A surprisingly large amount of classroom time is spent in transition from one activity to another. The approximately thirty major transitions each day in elementary classrooms account for nearly 15 percent of classroom time (Rosenshine, 1980).

Methods

1. *Arrange the classroom for efficient movement.*

2. *Create and post a daily schedule and discuss any changes in schedule each morning prior to beginning the class.*

3. *Have material ready for the next lesson.*

4. *Do not relinquish students' attention until you have given clear instructions for the following activity.*

5. *Do not do tasks that can be done by students.*

6. *Move around the room and attend to individual needs.*

7. *Provide students with simple, step-by-step directions.*

8. *Remind students of key procedures associated with the upcoming lesson.*

9. *Use group competition to stimulate more orderly transitions.* We can involve the class in attempting to reduce the amount of time required to make a transition.

10. *Develop transition activities.* Students often find it difficult to make the transition from home to school or from lunch or physical education back to a quieter setting. Smooth transitions can be facilitated by implementing structured activities that help students make these transitions. Ask them to begin the schoolday by writing in their journals or by discussing the daily schedule. Transitions from active periods, such as lunch, into quieter learning activities can be facilitated by transition activities, such as reading to the students or leading students in deep muscle relaxation. When these activities are used consistently, students not only find safety and comfort in this structure but also learn how to monitor transitions for themselves. Materials in the Recommended Reading at the end of this chapter provide a wide range of fun, brainteaser activities that can be added to academic content warm-ups to assist you in transitions into the beginning of class.

11. *Use teacher-directed instruction as a transition at the end of the class session.* Especially in grades six through nine, students have difficulty handling lack of structure at the end of a class period. This can be minimized by bringing students back together for teacher-directed summary time prior to releasing students to their next class. You may want to help students highlight main points from the work they have been doing, remind students of homework or test dates, have students write in their journals or log books their assignments and plans for completing them, and so on.

Dealing with Common Classroom Disruptions

Use a procedure for responding to student tardies that allows you to (1) keep accurate records, (2) limit classroom disruptions, and (3) provide educational consequences when students continue their behavior. We have found it most effective to have students sign in when they are tardy. Each day simply have a sheet for students to sign in, indicate whether their tardiness is excused or unexcused, and if excused, to attach (have a paper clip attached to the sheet) their excused slip. Although it may be necessary to check this for accuracy, it places the responsibility on students and limits classroom disruptions. Should a student have more tardies than you or your school policy allow, the consequence will be most effective (and deemed more fair and respectful by the student and his advocates) if it involves the student meeting with you or writing a statement regarding the problem and the solution. Should this tardiness continue after she or he has committed to an approach for being on time, having the student write this statement to a parent or guardian or in your presence calling the parent or guardian may increase the accountability.

For students who must return to their locker, use a procedure that follows the same requirements as that used for a tardy. You may have hall passes prepared for students to complete, and inform students that should they arrive back after the class starts, it will count as an unexcused tardy to be recorded on the sheet. Many trips to the locker can be prevented by having students (perhaps by base groups—see Chapter 6) borrow or share needed materials from their colleagues.

Develop a homework procedure that enhances student learning, helps students learn responsibility, yet shows respect for personal situations. Our combined sixty years of teaching experience has taught us that, if given the opportunity, some students will turn in a vast majority of their work late. This is not fair to you because it inevitably means marking large amounts of work near the end of the grading period. Additionally, failure to provide students with immediate feedback on their work—especially on work that is used as the foundation for future learning, is an educationally unsound practice that reduces student learning. Therefore, it is important to develop a procedure that assists students in turning in work on time. We have found the following methods helpful.

- Provide students with a clear statement about your late paper/homework policy. This might include taking a designated percentage off for each day homework is late, accepting only a certain number of late assignments during a grading period, and accepting no work that is more than one week late.
- Allow students to have one or two assignments they do not have to turn in during a marking period. For example, you might give each student two coupons for daily homework that does not have to be submitted. This makes sense given the number of events in a student's life that might make it nearly impossible for homework to be completed on a given day.
- Use your base groups and other methods, such as having students write down assignments, and strategies for completing them.
- Ensure that work is within the ability of all students.
- Ensure that all students have someone they can call or e-mail if they become confused by their homework.

Planning for Early Childhood Settings

Early childhood settings provide a somewhat unique set of challenges for maximizing on-task behaviors. Wolery, Bailey, and Sugai (1998) described four environmental categories a teacher can assess when considering factors that may be influencing children's behaviors in a preschool:

1. Instructional dimension (e.g., are materials and activities too easy or difficult, or have they been used too repetitively so children have tired of them?)
2. Physical dimension (e.g., are sound, light, and movement factors influencing student behavior?)
3. Social dimension (e.g., are there too many students in one area? Is student behavior being influenced by the manner in which adults are responding to students?)
4. Environmental changes (e.g., are transitions or interruptions to the environment influencing student behavior?)

In their book, *Early Violence Prevention: Tools for Teachers of Young Children*, Slaby, Roedell, Arezzo, and Hendrix (1995) present seven points for arranging a classroom to increase positive student behavior:

1. Create classrooms with sufficient space in those activity centers that are likely to encourage social interaction.
2. Design classrooms with distinct walkways and play spaces to eliminate accidental physical contact with people and objects.
3. Design an environment where children can help themselves and others with material preparation and activities, freeing teachers for positive guidance roles.

4. Provide extra guidance during unstructured times and when children are playing in activity areas where aggression is likely.
5. Plan activities in which children can practice cooperating, sharing, and helping, including assigning classroom helper roles.
6. Support a positive classroom atmosphere through pleasant interactions, neat storage, and attractive decorations.
7. Eliminate the frustration of abrupt transitions, excessive waiting, or sitting for long periods of time. (p. 31)

Classroom design and the type of activities presented to students can significantly affect the amount and type of negative peer interactions in a classroom. Young children are more likely to engage in negative peer interactions in play areas involving blocks, dramatic play, and woodworking centers, which are by their nature characterized by interactive play. It is important to balance the amount of structure needed to ensure positive, safe student behavior while providing enough opportunity for independent play that fosters social skill development and an internal locus of control. Our own work with early childhood and primary grade classrooms suggests a number of additional classroom organization and management issues teachers may wish to consider.

1. When setting up learning centers, try to keep quiet area activities together and have active areas in close proximity to each other but as removed from quiet activity areas as possible.
2. Use dividers, tables, or something else to separate different classroom areas. Eliminate large, open areas, which may give children too little sense of structure and encourage more outdoor-type behaviors.
3. Limit the number of children using one area by strategies such as having tickets for each area, carpet squares to indicate the number of students that may use an area, having a number and a corresponding picture of this number of children playing in the area, or placing a limited number of chairs in an area.
4. Arrange materials so students have access to them in a manner the teacher deems desirable. For example, in a preschool setting the teacher may want to arrange some materials so students will need to use language to request the materials. Other materials that can be used for cooperative play may be placed near each other to encourage this type of play.
5. Consider the order in which you introduce materials to students. For example, reading to children after recess has been shown to reduce behavior problems. Similarly, having students listen to stories, having quiet music playing, or having children do calm art activities such as finger painting can be a good transition into circle time or some other more interactive and group-oriented activity.
6. Structure transition times. Have a set signal for transitions. Singing a particular song, playing a musical instrument, or using a rainstick are examples of effective, calm transition signals. It is also important to provide students with cues prior to transition. For example, the teacher can indicate when five minutes and one minute remain prior to terminating the activity. Transitions can also be smoothed by engaging students in games and songs as they make the transition. The teacher might read a story, play finger puppets, or have a story on tape as students line up and wait for their peers. A thoughtful approach to assessing your preschool environment can be found in the Preschool Assessment of the Classroom Environment Scale (PACE) (Dunst, McWilliams, & Holbert, 1986).

P A U S E

7.6

and Consider

It is quite likely as you read this section, you took notes and considered changes in the way you operate your classroom or a classroom you are observing. At this point, however, we encourage you to take out several sheets of paper and create headings to match each of the general areas listed in this section, for example, Giving clear instructions, Beginning a lesson, and so on. Next, under each heading, write (or use the numbers associated with the method) any methods you currently use or have been observing that you believe assist you, or a teacher whose classroom you are observing, ineffectively accomplishing this task. Next, under each heading, list methods from the text or from your observations you believe could be added to help you accomplish these important tasks. Finally, we hope you have an opportunity to share these with a group of peers who are involved in teaching or observing a classroom at a similar grade level. Our many experiences in having teachers and future teachers participate in this activity suggest it will provide you with many very helpful strategies that will enhance student motivation, positive classroom behavior, and learning.

ACTIVITIES FOR IMPLEMENTING AND ASSESSING NEW METHODS

A major problem associated with reading a long list of methods is the tendency to acknowledge their value but not slow down long enough to implement any one method systematically. You may feel stimulated or overwhelmed by the many methods presented in the previous section. Unfortunately, neither of these feelings has a direct, positive effect on students' behaviors. To improve student learning and behavior, you must take time to use several of these methods thoughtfully in the classroom.

The activities in this section give you an opportunity to work with several of the major skills presented in this chapter. The value of these activities can be enhanced if you discuss them with a colleague. The activities may suggest changes you wish to incorporate in your classroom. If you make changes, keep a record of them. One week after implementing the change(s), take time to write about and share with a colleague the results of these changes.

ACTIVITY 7.1

Selecting Your Classroom Rules

List five classroom rules you would choose for your class. When you are satisfied with the rules, discuss them with a colleague who teaches or has recently taught at your grade level.

ACTIVITY 7.2

Deciding on Your Key Classroom Procedures

For this activity, refer to Figures 7.4 and 7.6 if you are an elementary teacher and Figures 7.5 and 7.6 if you are a middle school or high school teacher. For each area in which effective teachers teach classroom procedures, list a procedure you would feel comfortable using in your classroom. Following is an example of this activity.

(continued)

General Area	Needed Procedures	Specific Procedure
Beginning the class	1. Getting students' attention 2. Entering the class 3. Obtaining materials 4. What to do if tardy 5. Where to put slips that need signing 6. 7.	Students determine a signal
Whole-class activities	1. How to leave the room 2. What to do when work is completed 3. Voice level 4. How to get help on an assignment 5. Using the pencil sharpener 6. When students can leave their seats 7. 8. 9.	Sign your name, destination, and the time you leave and return
Student assignments	1. How to find work missed while absent 2. How late work will be handled 3. Heading papers 4. Where to hand in work 5. Credit for late work 6. 7.	Refer to the notebook on the back table
Other activities	1. Dismissing 2. Public address system and announcements 3. Fire drill 4. Guest entering the class 5. 6. 7.	Everyone must be seated and quiet

Evaluate your use of various methods of developing classroom rules and procedures by completing the following form. If you are not currently teaching, respond by recalling a classroom in which you previously taught or observed.

	Yes	Somewhat	No
1. Do clear classroom rules apply in your class?			
2. Are the rules listed in the form of positive statements?			
3. Are there six or fewer rules?			
4. Can every student list these rules from memory?			
5. Are the rules clearly displayed in your room?			
6. Are students involved in developing the rules?			

7. Does each student make a clear commitment to follow these rules?
8. Do you discuss these rules frequently when they are first developed?
9. Do you review the rules every three weeks?
10. Do students clearly understand your approach to handling rule violations?
11. Do you teach students the important procedures related to classroom activities?
12. Do you teach students the major procedures related to behaviors outside the classroom?
13. When students fail to follow a procedure, do you immediately reteach the procedure?
14. Does every parent know the classroom rules that apply in your class?
15. Does every parent know your methods of handling discipline problems?

Carefully examine your responses to the preceding questions and then complete the following statements:

> I learned that. . . .
> I am pleased that I. . . .

Three approaches I will implement in order to develop more productive classroom rules and procedures are:

1.
2.
3.

I will also consider the possibility that next year I could. . . .

This activity will be most effective if it can be completed with three or four colleagues.

First, select four of the ten areas from Figure 7.13 (e.g., giving clear instruction, beginning a lesson, and so on) in which you are particularly interested in improving your skills.

Second, for each of these four areas do the following:

1. Circle the number of each of the strategies you currently use in your classroom or which you believe you are prepared to use.
2. Place a box around the number of all the strategies you would be interested in using but which you would need some assistance or practice in developing.
3. Place an X through the number preceding each of the strategies you believe do not fit your teaching style or which, given the age of your students or your teaching methods, would be inappropriate in your classroom.

Third, as a group, select three of the ten major areas listed in Figure 7.13. This can be developed by finding out how many people in your group chose that area and selecting topics several of you chose.

Fourth, for each of the three topics on which your group chose to focus, go down the numbers, and any time a person has a box around the number in front of a strategy, have other members of the group (perhaps someone with the strategy circled) share with you how they implement this strategy in their classroom or how they have seen it implemented.

SUMMARY

Teachers whose students have higher rates of on-task behavior spend time early in the school year developing and teaching classroom rules and procedures. This provides students with a much needed sense of structure and security. More effective classroom managers also view their roles less as disciplining students and more as reteaching appropriate behaviors when students have difficulty demonstrating these behaviors. Simply stated, the teaching of appropriate behavior has become an additional curriculum in schools.

Even prior to the research on beginning the school year, the research on classroom management had focused on the noninstructional aspects of teacher behavior that prevented disruptive student behavior. Jacob Kounin discovered that what differentiated effective from less effective classroom managers was what these teachers did before, not after, students became involved in unproductive behavior. Even though we now know that this is only one aspect of effective classroom management, you will find that by using a variety of the methods presented here, you can create a more smoothly run, efficient classroom in which student behavior is significantly more goal directed.

RECOMMENDED READING

Emmer, E., Evertson, C., Sanford, J., Clements, B., & Worsham, M. (2000). *Classroom management for secondary teachers.* Englewood Cliffs, NJ: Prentice-Hall.

Evertson, C., Emmer, E., Clements, B., Sanford, J., & Worsham, M. (2000). *Classroom management for elementary teachers.* Englewood Cliffs, NJ: Prentice-Hall.

Evertson, C., & Harris, A. (1999). Support for managing learning-centered classrooms: The classroom organization and management program. In J. Frieberg (Ed.), *Beyond behaviorism: Changing the classroom management paradigm* (pp. 59–74). Boston: Allyn & Bacon.

Freiberg, J. (Ed.). (1999.) *Beyond behaviorism: Changing the classroom management paradigm.* Boston: Allyn & Bacon.

Gathercoal, F. (2001.) *Judicious discipline.* San Francisco, CA: Gaddo Gap Press.

Good, T., & Brophy, J. (2000). *Looking in classrooms* (7th ed.). New York: Harper & Row.

Landau, B. (Ed.). (1999). *Practicing judicious discipline: An educator's guide to a democratic classroom.* San Francisco, CA: Gaddo Gap Press.

Lewis, T. (2001). Building infrastucture to enhance schoolwide systems of positive behavioral support: Essential features of technical assistance. *Beyond Behavior, 11,* 10–12.

Nelson, J. (1996). Designing schools to meet the needs of students who exhibit disruptive behaviors. *Journal of Emotional and Behavioral Disorders, 4,* 147–161.

Nelson, J., Martella, R., & Galand, B. (1998). The effects of teaching school expectations and establishing a consistent consequence on formal office disciplinary actions. *Journal of Emotional and Behavioral Disorders, 6,* 153–161.

Sugai, G. & Horner, R. (1999). Discipline and behavioral support: Preferred processes and practices. *Preventing School Failure, 43,* 6–13.

Sugai, G., Horner, R., & Gresham, F. (2002). Behaviorally effective school environments. In M. R. Shinn, G. Stoner, & H. M. Walker (Eds.). *Interventions for academic and behavioral problems: Preventative and remedial approaches* (pp. 315–350). Silver Springs, MD: National Association of School Psychologists.

PART five

When Prevention Is Not Enough: Methods for Altering Unproductive Student Behavior

When sensitively and consistently used, the methods presented in Parts II, III, and IV can result in increased student achievement and the elimination of a significant amount of disruptive student behavior. A few students, however, will cause major or consistent behavior problems despite our efforts to create positive, supportive, well-organized, and stimulating learning environments. Furthermore, the pressures and inevitable frustrations of learning and working in a relatively small area with thirty or so classmates create a situation in which some students will occasionally misbehave and require assistance in controlling and improving their behavior.

Part V presents many types of intervention strategies that teachers, counselors, child development specialists, and administrators can use to help students choose to act responsibly. When examining and implementing these strategies, educators should keep in mind that these methods will be more effective when used in conjunction with the methods discussed in the previous chapters. In fact, the authors believe that adults harm youngsters by implementing behavior control strategies to ensure that young people act passively and positively in environments that do not meet their basic psychological and academic needs.

Several key concepts underlie the materials presented in Chapters 8, 9, and 10. First, teachers will be most effective in their efforts to help students develop new skills and demonstrate responsible behavior when everyone in the school understands their responsibility and works cooperatively. As discussed in Chapter 1, the term *systems approach* is used to describe this coordination of efforts.

Second, all interventions made in response to student behavior problems should be educational in nature. As educators, we will be most effective in assisting students if we view irresponsible student behavior as based on the dual factors of student responses to skill deficits and an environment in which their personal and academic needs are not being met. Therefore, once we have made every attempt to adjust the environment, the next step is to assist students in developing new skills.

Third, a hierarchy exists for responding to irresponsible, unproductive student behavior. It is most beneficial to students if we first implement interventions emphasizing the creation of positive learning environments followed by interventions that focus primarily on student involvement and responsibility for resolving problems. Methods that depend on external reinforcers or that place outside restrictions on students' behaviors are used as a last resort.

Fourth, underlying the behavior change interventions presented in Part V is the belief that students should be actively involved in all attempts to alter their behavior. Students should be involved in solving problems, helped to collect and understand data about their own behavior, and be instrumental in developing contracts aimed at altering their behavior. Finally, although it is neither feasible nor desirable to have students present during all discussions of their behavior, they should be included in many such discussions and should always be aware of the problems being discussed and the programs being implemented.

Chapters 3, 4, 6, and 7 have provided methods for meeting students' needs by creating positive, supportive, safe classroom settings in which students' academic needs are met. Part V presents methods for responding to students who experience behavior problems despite our best efforts to incorporate the materials presented in these earlier chapters. Chapter 8 offers an overview of how to conceptualize and respond to student behavior that disrupts the learning environment. Chapter 9 presents methods for incorporating problem solving and conflict resolution into your approach for creating a supportive classroom community in which students learn nonviolent methods for resolving problems; Chapter 10 examines methods for developing individual behavior change plans for students who experience serious and ongoing behavior problems.

Throughout these chapters, our focus is on interventions that enhance students' dignity and teach them new skills. Violent student behavior will only be exacerbated by interventions emphasizing rules and punishments. In its report on how to handle adolescents' aggressive, violent behavior, the Panel on High Risk Youth of the National Research Council (1993) clearly stated that punitive approaches were unsuccessful in creating positive behavior changes. They noted that these methods only bred resentment and desire for revenge and increased the pattern of violence. Instead, students must be helped to realize that they are cared for and valued. They must also realize that when they choose to violate the rights of others, they will be asked to take responsibility for their behavior. They will, however, be asked to work with other students and staff to examine what factors in the environment may need to change for the classroom and school to feel like a personally and psychologically safe place. They will also be given assistance in developing more acceptable ways to express their pain, confusion, and frustration. Discipline will always answer three questions: (1) What needs to be changed here to make the classroom and school a better place? (2) What needs to be done here to repair any physical or personal damage done by the student? and (3) What needs to be learned here so the student has other ways of presenting legitimate concerns without violating the rights of others? When adult responses to student behavior problems emphasize these three questions, students will generally accept discipline and will not view adults as arbitrary and uncaring.

Responding to Violations of Rules and Procedures

Teachers and administrators must move away from the appearance of a teacher-imposed, "hard-line" method to an educational approach emphasizing our skills and abilities as professional educators.

—Forrest Gathercoal (2001)
Judicious Discipline

For some educators, discipline means the power of the teacher to control the behavior of their students. . . . For other educators, discipline means an opportunity to teach students a set of values about how people can live together in a democratic society. . . . Discipline is perceived as the process of helping students internalize these values and to develop self-control over their drives and feelings.

—Nicholas Long and William Morse (1996)
Conflict in the Classroom

Whether teaching classes to preservice teachers or presenting workshops to veteran educators, the question we are asked most frequently and with the greatest passion is, "What do I do when students act in ways that violate the rights of others?" Most educators entered the field with an excitement about helping students learn and find the matter of responding to irresponsible and disruptive student behavior to be one of the most demanding and least rewarding aspects of teaching.

We encourage you to view this matter differently. First, although academic skills are extremely important to students, so are skills in making positive, productive choices regarding their behavior. One of the most important skills and greatest gifts we can give students is how to effectively and productively behave in a group setting. Second, modeling for students skills in responding to behavior that is a concern to us and teaching students how to act responsibly can be a highly rewarding part of teaching. Therefore, when considering the question, "What can I do when students behave in ways that violate the rights of others?" you might reframe the question as, "How can I most effectively model productive responses to irresponsible behavior so I can teach my students these important skills?"

PAUSE

and Consider   **8.1**

Before reading further, pause for a moment and consider your goals when responding to student behavior that violates the rights of others by disrupting the learning environment. Write a brief statement regarding what you hope to accomplish in responding to this behavior. We encourage you to share these with several peers. As you read about and practice the methods presented in this chapter, consider how they can help you accomplish these goals.

APPROPRIATE AND EFFECTIVE RESPONSES TO IRRESPONSIBLE STUDENT BEHAVIOR: LOGICAL, INSTRUCTIONAL CONSEQUENCES, OR PUNISHMENT?

Although teachers respond to incorrect academic behavior with prompts, cues, and instructional interventions, they tend to respond to student disruptions in ways that emphasize critical, punitive responses. This is understandable because, compared to academic errors, mistakes in demonstrating responsible behavior have a greater impact on teachers' abilities to do their jobs and thus evoke stronger emotions. These punitive responses are, however, generally ineffective in either bringing about the desired student behavior or teaching students alternative methods for responding (Nelson & Roberts, 2000).

A number of factors make it imperative that educators learn effective methods for responding to student behavior that negatively affects the learning environment. First, student learning is significantly affected by the creation of safe, calm environments in which disruptions to the learning environment are minimized. Second, teachers are faced with an increasing number of students who demonstrate disruptive behavior. Even the average prekindergarten classroom has an average of three children who display disruptive behavior (Gordon, Henry, Mashburn, & Ponder, 2001). Third, students' abilities to respond cooperatively to adult requests are an essential skill associated with school success (Rimm-Kaufman, Pinata, & Cox, 2000). Finally, students who continue to display difficulty in responding to adult requests are likely to continue to have serious behavior difficulties (Walker, Colvin, & Ramsey, 1995). Therefore, adults who can effectively respond to disruptive student behavior in ways that model effective skills and help students respond positively are providing students with important lifelong skills that may significantly impact their ability to remain in school and be successful learners.

Figure 8.1 presents a comparison of two ways to view problematic student behavior. School personnel have too often viewed inappropriate behavior as an attitude rather than as a skill issue and have responded using the sequence suggested on the right side of Figure 8.1. We believe that current research and theory clearly support viewing and responding to student behavior problems using the paradigm suggested on the left side of Figure 8.1. By treating behavior problems similarly to academic problems, teachers are allowed to use their considerable expertise in analyzing environments and assisting students in developing alternative strategies.

Interestingly, studies indicate that teachers who are willing to use a more personal, instructional approach to working with inappropriate student behavior are rated

It is a common practice among educators to approach academic problems differently from social problems. Essentially, instructional principles are used to remediate academic problems, whereas negative consequences typically are used to manage social problems. The differences are summarized here.

Kind of Error	Procedures for Academic Problem	Procedures for Social Problem
Infrequent	Assume student is trying to make correct response.	Assume student is not trying to make correct response.
	Assume error was accidental.	Assume error was deliberate.
	Provide assistance (model-lead-test).	Provide negative consequence.
	Provide more practice.	Practice not required.
	Assume student has learned skill and will perform correctly in future.	Assume student will make right choice and behave in future.
Frequent (chronic)	Assume student has learned the wrong way.	Assume student refuses to cooperate.
	Assume student has been taught (inadvertently) the wrong way.	Assume student knows what is right and has been told often.
	Diagnose the problem.	Provide more negative consequences.
	Identify misrule or determine more effective manner in which to present the material.	Withdraw student from normal context.
	Adjust presentation. Focus on rule. Provide feedback. Provide practice and review.	Maintain student removal from normal context.
	Assume student has been taught skill and will perform correctly in future.	Assume student has "learned" lesson and will behave in future.

FIGURE 8.1
A Comparison of Approaches to Academic and Social Problems

Source: Reprinted by permission from Geoffrey Colvin.

ROOM 210
INSCHOOL SUSPENSION

more highly by their principals (Brophy & McCaslin, 1992). In addition, Agne, Greenwood, and Miller (1994) reported that teachers selected as Teacher of the Year were significantly more likely than a matched group of colleagues to view their role in responding to student behavior problems as an interpersonal, skill-based issue rather than a control issue. This suggests that administrators and others who assess teacher performance support teacher decision making that emphasizes helping students become more effective self-managers and responsible citizens. Administrators may increasingly appreciate the benefits of having discipline methods be congruent with instructional methods. If instruction emphasizes becoming active learners and effective problem solvers, it seems logical that responses to inappropriate student behavior would have similar goals.

In their book, *A Positive Approach to Understanding and Addressing Challenging Behaviors*, Karen Topper and her colleagues (Topper et al., 1994) noted that teachers who implement a democratic teaching style using logical consequences are guided by the following principles:

- The dignity of those involved is their first consideration.
- The consequences should make sense and be logically connected to the student's behavior.
- The consequence teaches the student what to do the next time a similar situation occurs.
- Teachers respond only to the present situation, not a buildup of past events.
- Teachers are respectful and follow through.
- The consequences permit choice and stress accountability for both students and teachers.

Before presenting a variety of methods for responding to student behavior that disrupts the learning environment, it is important for you to consider the general procedure you will implement in your classroom for responding to irresponsible behavior. Therefore, the next section of the chapter helps you examine and develop a classroom discipline procedure. This will be followed by several sections on responding to disruptive behavior ranging from mild disruptions to violent behavior.

A CLASSROOM PROCEDURE FOR RESPONDING TO DISRUPTIVE BEHAVIOR

Recall from Chapter 7 the importance of creating classroom procedures to enhance a smooth flow of academic work in the classroom. Perhaps the single most important procedure you develop is how you will respond when students act in a manner that disrupts the learning environment and violates the rights of others.

Consider for a moment your own classroom or a classroom in which you are working or observing. Take a moment to write a brief statement regarding what adults in the classroom do when students act irresponsibly and disrupt the learning environment. Specifically, focus on any sequence or procedure you use rather than on an individual strategy such as moving closer to the student.

After writing your statement, assess your approach by completing the quiz found in Figure 8.2. Tally your score to make a sum. We encourage you to share the results with several colleagues or classmates and discuss the components of your classroom system that score high on this quiz and those that may need modification.

If you score high on this quiz, you have a system that is professionally defensible and should, if used along with the other methods in this book, be associated with students' developing positive feelings about school and responsible behavior. Figure 8.3 offers an additional series of questions for you to consider when examining how you and your colleagues respond to student behavior that violates the rights of others and limits the effectiveness of the learning environment.

In the mid-1990s, Lee Canter developed a system he titled "Assertive Discipline." In its initial form, this program emphasized informing students of the classroom rules and responding to rule violations by placing the student's name on the chalkboard. Any additional violation that day was met with a check placed after the student's name. Each check meant a designated time taken away from recess or lunch, and a designated number of checks (usually five) led to the student being removed from the classroom. More recently, some teachers have changed this method to having each student's name on a

Create a picture in your mind of your classroom management system—how you respond when students fail to follow the reasonable rules and procedures you have worked with them to develop, learn, and practice. Although it will be very subjective, score your system on the following criteria with 5 being outstanding and 0 being low.

_____ **Clear** (if you interviewed ten students, they would all be able to describe the system very much the way you described it)

_____ **Sequential** (rather than an immediately harsh or disruptive response, you use a series of responses that gradually increases in severity)

_____ **Dignifying** (the responses enhance or maintain students' sense of dignity or self-esteem)

_____ **Educational** (the responses in your system provide cues that help the students focus on positive behaviors or learn alternative behaviors)

_____ **Environmental Analysis** (when a problem occurs, you ask the question, "What classroom factors might be eliciting this behavior, and what might I change to decrease the likelihood this behavior will occur?")

FIGURE 8.2
Classroom Management Quiz

"I never use it, but I've found it to be a great deterrent."

bulletin board adjacent to a cardholder. Color-coded cards are placed in the cardholder to indicate whether the student is behaving responsibly (green for responsible, yellow for warning, and red to indicate a punishment is forthcoming). Studies suggest these types of responses are ineffective (Emmer & Aussiker, 1987; Nelson, 1996; Nelson, Martella, & Galand, 1998), and Lee Canter has suggested his initial model not be used in classrooms (Canter, 1996). One reason these methods have been shown to be ineffective is that although they score a strong 5 on the first two criteria listed in Figure 8.2, they score a 0 on the last three. While a batting average of .400 will likely earn one a spot in the Baseball Hall of Fame, a classroom management plan in the twenty-first century that scores .400 not only will be ineffective but also may elicit considerable parent criticism.

When developing a professionally responsible, effective plan for responding to unproductive student behavior, there are several important factors to consider.

FIGURE 8.3
Key Concepts
in Discipline

1. Do I view conflicts as a natural, neutral part of my life as a teacher?
2. Do I use conflict resolution and skill building to alter students' behavior, or do I use power-oriented methods of influence?
3. When students misbehave, do I teach them the correct procedure for meeting their needs?
4. Do I have a strategy for ensuring invitations, especially to those students who struggle behaviorally or academically in our class?
5. Do I teach students how conflicts will be resolved in our classroom?
6. When a student's behavior necessitates removal from the classroom, do I, the student, and the person to whom the student is referred all acknowledge that we care about the student and simply need to have a more effective forum for resolving the conflict that led to the student's misbehavior?
7. Are all my responses to student behavior problems oriented around providing new skills for the student and modifying the classroom environment so the student can more readily meet his or her needs and act responsibly?
8. Prior to students returning to a setting from which they were removed, is there an opportunity for the parties involved in the "dispute" to briefly discuss any plan that has been devised?
9. When students have continued or serious behavior problems, are limits set in a clearly structured form agreed to by all parties?
10. When students have continued or serious behavior problems, is there a procedure in our school for a team to meet and work with the students to develop a plan to assist the students?

1. Students must be clearly aware of the rules and procedures and the consequences for violating them.
2. Students must be given clear, polite cues indicating that continuation of a behavior will evoke the specified consequences.
3. It is important to be as consistent as possible in employing consequences.
4. Students should be informed that they are choosing the consequence.
5. The consequence should be educational in nature.

Figure 8.4 outlines a procedure for responding to a rule or procedure violation that the authors have used as teachers and have taught to hundreds of teachers. This method involves first using a signal to help students become aware of their behaviors. If the student does not see this action or fails to respond to it, say the student's name and politely request that the student follow the classroom rules. If the unacceptable behavior continues, inform the student that should this behavior continue, she or he will be choosing to take time to develop a solution to the problem. Ideally, this work will occur in the classroom, where the student can benefit from instruction and also realize that the problem can be resolved among those involved. Students who have adequate writing skills may be provided with an area in which to work and materials necessary for them to complete a problem-solving form.

It is essential that students clearly understand each step in this sequential process. This can be accomplished by role-playing each step in Figure 8.4 and then asking a student to violate a classroom rule (such as talking to a neighbor while you are talking). You then ask the student to stop the inappropriate behavior when you employ a designated step. This procedure can be continued until several students are involved in responding to each of the first three steps. You can then instruct the students in writing solutions and plans. Each student writes a plan; you check these and subsequently discuss them with the class.

Several years ago during a graduate seminar, one of the authors commented that it was probably not necessary to teach the problem-solving step to students in college preparatory courses for juniors and seniors. A seminar participant who had been in a course one of the authors taught five years earlier disagreed with this statement. He said that he role-played the procedures with all his juniors and seniors in chemistry

Step	Procedure	Example
1.	Nonverbal cue	Raised index finger, proximity.
2.	Verbal cue	"John, please follow our classroom rules."
3.	Indicate choice student is making	"John, if you continue to talk while I am talking, you will be choosing to develop a plan."
4.	Student moves to a designated area in the room to develop a plan	"John, you have chosen to take time to develop a plan."
5.	Student is required to go somewhere else to develop a plan	"John, I really wish we could solve this here. If we cannot, you will need to see Mrs. Johnson to develop your plan."

FIGURE 8.4

Steps in Responding to Students' Violations of Rules and Procedures

and physics. He noted that students and parents frequently commented on the value of this process. This teacher was convinced that despite needing to use the fourth step only about a dozen times each year, it was a vital aspect of an effective classroom management program.

It is essential to understand that this is not a sequence for which you keep a record, place names on a clipboard, or otherwise turn into a legalistic format. This is simply a pattern for responding to behaviors that disrupt the rights of others. Indeed, it is not dissimilar to how we might respond at a dining room table or faculty meeting. We might try to catch the attention of the person who is behaving in a manner that is making someone feel bad or causing the environment to be less positive. Next, we might make a brief statement to the person. Finally, we might suggest that the person display the behavior somewhere else. More than once the senior author has been given such cues when watching a sporting event on television while eating dinner with the family or when chatting during a faculty meeting. These are natural and appropriate cues adults give each other, and they are dignifying and effective with students.

In his work on schoolwide student management procedures, Ron Nelson has presented the idea of think time, in which students leave the room to problem solve (Nelson, 1996; Nelson, Martella, & Galand, 1998). This approach is similar to the fifth step here and is a thoughtful approach for using discipline responses as a method for helping students develop new skills.

One question often asked by teachers is whether it is desirable to have students complete a problem-solving form when they have reached the point of needing quiet time to consider their behavior. A written form has the advantage of providing a record regarding the students' assessments of their behaviors and a new plan of action. It also has the advantage of providing the students with something to do while away from the group. The disadvantage of written forms is that many students who struggle to behave responsibly also struggle with academic work. Students may view completing a written form as a punishment that highlights their skill deficits. When this occurs, students often respond with frustration and anger at being asked to complete a form. Our experience in working with literally hundreds of school staff on this issue has shown it is best to provide the student with the option of completing a form in writing or merely thinking through it.

Figure 8.5 is an example of a problem-solving form that a primary grade teacher might use. Figure 8.6 provides a form for an upper-elementary or secondary classroom. Once a student has completed the form, it is placed in a designated spot or shown to the teacher; the student then returns to her or his seat. It is, of course, important to have a brief discussion with the student about the responses on the form. This can be done near the end of class or at the beginning of the next class period. It is particularly important that students feel invited back to the class and that they realize that even though you could not accept the behavior that necessitated the problem solving, you care about them, respect their ability to be responsible for their behavior, and are glad they have rejoined the class. The next chapter provides an extended discussion and examples of how to implement problem solving in the classroom and presents methods for incorporating problem solving into a schoolwide student management plan.

As with all methods suggested in this book, you should carefully consider its applicability to your own teaching setting and should critically assess results when you use the new method. Should you choose to implement the preceding method for re-

Name _____ Date _____

FIGURE 8.5
Primary Grade
Problem-Solving
Form

In order to be my best self, I need to work on:

☐ Following directions of school adults.

☐ Caring for and sharing school property.

☐ Treating everyone with respect.

☐ Acting in a safe manner.

☐ Doing my personal best.

What happened: _____
_____

Why this is a problem: _____
_____

I will work at being responsible by: _____
_____

This is what I look like being responsible!

```


```

Child Signature _____

Teacher Signature _____

Parent Signature _____

sponding to rule violations, it is critical to ensure that it is not used in a manner unduly emphasizing disruptive behavior. Studies show that teachers often attend more frequently to disruptive than to on-task behavior, and that this action tends to increase off-task student behavior. Therefore, when implementing this method, attend to desired student behavior frequently and monitor behavior to assess whether the new approach was indeed associated with an increase in on-task behavior.

FIGURE 8.6
Problem-Solving
Form

Choose to Be Responsible

Name _____ Date _____

Rules we agreed on:

1. Speak politely to others.
2. Treat each other kindly.
3. Follow teacher requests.
4. Be prepared for class.
5. Make a good effort at your work and request help if you need it.
6. Obey all school rules.

Please answer the following questions:

1. What rule did you violate? _____
   _____

2. What did you do that violated this rule? _____
   _____

3. What problem did this cause for you, your teacher, or classmates? _____
   _____

4. What plan can you develop that will help you be more responsible and follow this classroom rule? _____
   _____

5. How can the teacher or other students help you? _____
   _____

I, _____, will try my best to follow the plan I have written and to follow all the other rules and procedures in our classroom that we created to make the classroom a good place to learn.

Should a student refuse to go to the designated area or to complete the form, the teacher needs to express a belief that the problem can be resolved and that the teacher sincerely wishes the student to remain. For example, you might say, "Sam, I'm sure we can work this out, and I would like to have you remain in the class. If you will start developing a plan, I'll come over as soon as I can, and I'm sure we can work this out together." If the student continues to be defiant, the teacher needs to indicate that the student is making a choice. For example, you might say, "Sam, if you choose not to work this out here, you are choosing to do it in the office. I care about you and I would like to have you remain here."

The Role of Reinforcement in a Classroom Procedure for Enhancing Responsible Student Behavior

Another question we are often asked is, "It is wrong to use reinforcement to encourage students to behave responsibly?" Teachers often note that they have heard or read that students should not be reinforced for making positive behavior choices because this will create a dependence on external factors and minimize students developing an internal sense of responsibility. Certainly, our goal as educators is to help students learn to make positive choices because these choices help them and others to feel good and learn effectively. The reality is that virtually everyone has much of their behavior impacted by outcomes other than good will. Many people drive more safely when they see a police car. Few teachers would work if they were not paid, and few consultants travel around the country making presentations for free. To some degree people expect and enjoy receiving rewards for their work. This is particularly important when the work is difficult or involves risk—a situation that exists for many students whose behavior at school creates problems for others. Most of us enjoy celebrations when we perform well. One need only watch the behavior of a team who has won a championship to know that individuals are expected to celebrate after making substantial progress or reaching an important goal. Finally, many younger students have been socialized to receive some reinforcement for their efforts. Although we may wish to gradually help them depend less on extrinsic rewards, this may need to be done gradually. Just as a student does not learn to read or multiply in one day or even one year, learning to value responsible behavior for its own sake is a gradual process.

Therefore, we acknowledge that there will be situations in which it is helpful to provide students with various forms of reinforcement when they show effort and excellence in behaving responsibly. For example, while writing the seventh edition of this book, the senior author received a call from a veteran teacher who had been a student many years ago. The teacher had taught in an inner-city school, left the profession to raise a family, and recently returned to teaching in another inner-city school with many students who were struggling academically. She called because she had classroom management concerns. She was frustrated with her students, raised her voice frequently, and believed her classroom was less safe and organized than she thought was good for her or her students. She shared that after rereading an earlier edition of the authors' book, she had begun to reestablish a positive learning environment. She had held classroom meetings to determine students' concerns, had the students create and sign a set of behavior expectations, and began to use problem solving. She expressed concern, however, that she had also begun reinforcing students for behaving responsibly. She noted that she stamped students' cards when the students made behavior choices that supported a positive, caring learning environment, and that the stamps could be exchanged for school supplies and other items students valued. She asked the author whether this was damaging to the students because it emphasized external controls.

The author's response was to help her acknowledge the good work she was doing and the importance of creating a safe, well-organized learning environment that facilitated student learning. The author also shared his belief that students need to be reinforced for doing well and he made several suggestions. First, the author encouraged her to always pair the giving of the stamp with some form of verbal statement that helped the student understand how his or her behavior was helping the student and others learn. The goal is to associate the token reinforcement (the stamp) with social reinforcement so that the social reinforcement gradually replaces the need for the more concrete external reinforcement. Another important goal is to have the social reinforcement provide information that helps the student understand why the behavior is valuable in itself. Second, the author encouraged her to begin to have social reinforcers replace the material reinforcement she was providing. Therefore, when students made good decisions (perhaps initially demonstrated by earning a designated number of

"As a student teacher, the first thing you must learn is how to make your kids behave for you. My own successful disciplinary formula is based on understanding, firmness, determination, and all the bribery I can afford."

stamps), the teacher could call home and inform the parent or guardian how responsibly their child was acting and how this was leading to success. The principal, counselor, or other significant adults could also be involved in providing specific social reinforcement by speaking with students, having lunch with students, and calling home. In all cases, an emphasis would be on helping the student understand how his or her behavior was leading the student to success and happiness.

The point we are making here is that, like any reading or math program, a program for reinforcing student behavior is a means to an end. The goal is for students to develop skills and take responsibility for their behaviors and successes. The manner in which we do this should be influenced by the unique needs of the students, the best available research, and the skillful use of this information by a professional educator.

Why Focus on Problem Solving Rather Than Punishment?

No discussion of a classroom management system would be complete without a brief response to the issue of problem solving versus punishment. Over the years one of the most frequently asked questions when we have conducted workshops for veteran teachers is, "Where is the punishment?"

First, we would return to the earlier discussion regarding the comparison between academic and behavior errors. We strongly believe that educators' responses to both types of errors need to assume that the student needs support and assistance in developing new skills. Second, in addition to failing to emphasize skill development, a focus on punishment appears to inhibit learning. Students in classrooms in which teachers are judged as more punitive tend to express less value in learning, be more aggressive, and learn less. Third, research suggests that punishment is not an effective method for changing student behavior. Emmer and Aussiker (1987) examined the literature on the results of research evaluations associated with four approaches to discipline—teacher effectiveness training, reality therapy, assertive discipline, and Adlerian-based approaches. They also contacted 120 school districts in the United States and Canada to obtain evaluation studies about these programs. Their findings indicated that the most punitive-oriented approach (assertive discipline) was the least effective.

Similar findings concerning the impact of punitive responses to student misbehavior were reported thirty years ago by Becker, Engelmann, and Thomas (1975).

These researchers found that when teachers were asked to increase their use of punitive control methods of responding to disruptive student behavior, misbehavior in the classes actually increased from 9 to 31 percent of student behavior.

Fourth, punishment allows the student to project blame rather than to accept responsibility for the behavior. Punishment tends to create a situation in which the student becomes angry or blames the individuals responsible for the punishment rather than examining personal responsibility for the problem. Glasser (1988) stated that 95 percent of all student discipline problems in schools are caused by students' lack of power and that misbehavior is an attempt to gain some sense of power. Punitive responses to student misbehavior detract from rather than enhance students' sense of power and efficacy and often lead to withdrawal or actively destructive and confrontational responses.

Fifth, using such activities as writing sentences, assigning additional homework, and lowering a student's grade as punishment may create a negative attitude regarding these activities. Activities and settings in which one is involved when receiving punishment tend to become aversive. Teachers do not want this connection made with homework or writing.

Englander (1986) stated that even though responding to student misbehavior with punishment is both common and natural, it is nonetheless impractical. Based on his extensive background in the field and his thorough review of the research, he summarized his assessment of punishment: "If punishment works it does so only under very precise and complicated conditions, much too complicated for us to consistently use in classrooms. The controls that one must utilize to optimize the effectiveness of punishment are not possible in day-to-day operations either within families or schools" (pp. 40–41).

P A U S E

8.3   *and Consider*

You have now read our thoughts about creating a classroom procedure for responding to student behavior that disrupts the learning environment. Perhaps you have also visited several Web sites on the issue and discussed with your peers the procedures that exist in their classrooms. At this point we recommend you put the book aside and draft an outline of the procedure you would like to use for responding to disruptive behavior in your classroom. We encourage you to write your thoughts out in enough detail that you could teach it to your students, post it in your classroom, and, if you are in an elementary or middle school, possibly communicate it to your students' caregivers. Once you have developed this procedure, we encourage you to share it with several colleagues and obtain their feedback.

TIPS FOR RESPONDING TO MINOR DISRUPTIONS

Misbehavior often occurs because students find acting out to be more interesting than a boring lesson or a better option than another failure experience. Similarly, unproductive student behavior often occurs because students do not understand a task, are not involved in the learning activity, or are unable to obtain assistance when it is needed.

Therefore, most minor discipline problems can be alleviated by implementing the instructional methods discussed in Part III of this book or incorporating the procedures discussed in Chapter 7. Nevertheless, when students are required to work for approximately six hours a day in a 30-by-30-foot area with thirty peers, minor problems will inevitably occur. A major factor in effective classroom management is teachers' abilities to deal with minor disruptions before they become major problems.

Whenever possible, it is more effective if the teacher handles instances of noncompliance and verbal aggression. When teachers immediately refer students to a counselor or administrator for situations in which students challenge a teacher or student, the teachers are indicating that they do not possess the *natural authority* to handle these situations in the classroom. Most educators would prefer that developing skills for handling such situations were not part of teaching. Similarly, most teachers would also prefer to teach bright, highly motivated students who arrive at school with their personal needs met. Unfortunately, teaching in the twenty-first century requires that educators be able to handle a wide range of student behavioral challenges and a broad band of academic challenges.

The authors have asked thousands of teachers to recall their childhood and youth and to describe the manner in which they were responded to when they misbehaved. Not surprisingly, the vast majority of educators describe confrontational methods, such as threats, physical punishment, and loss of privileges. A very small percentage list calm dialogue, problem solving, or conflict resolution. Therefore, when confronted with a student who is noncompliant or who challenges their authority, most educators have at least some inclination to use some form of confrontational approach. Unfortunately, this type of response usually serves only to escalate the student's emotions, and the student either becomes more aggressive or, for younger children, becomes frightened and withdrawn.

We might like to believe that harsh discipline that diminishes students' self-worth and fails to provide appropriate modeling for students occurs seldom and primarily in settings in which teachers are overtaxed and working with a significant percentage of students whose behaviors violate general school norms. Interestingly, the authors' own children experienced several incidents of unacceptable discipline during their high school careers. As a freshman, the authors' son was squirted in the face with a spray bottle when he was seated slightly sideways in his rather small chair. When she was a junior and class president, our daughter was yanked out of her chair in a library for quietly discussing an assignment with a study partner. Although our children responded by simply informing the teachers that they did not appreciate the behavior and reporting it to an administrator, not all students respond this way.

In his book, *Lost Boys*, Garbarino (1999) discusses key concepts in working with students who are potentially violent. He states that "adults dealing with these kids should avoid power assertion whenever possible to reduce the experience of threat and thus maintain the youth in an emotionally engaged and nonaggressive state" (p. 220). Based on his extensive studies of violent youth, Garbarino also noted the importance of developing supportive, calm relationships in which the children understand the adult is in charge and will protect them while at the same time is caring and fair in relationships with students. Not surprisingly, studies suggest that teachers who respond in a calm, positive manner to student behavior problems have fewer problems with student misbehavior (Roy, 1998; Tomal, 1998).

The following sections present ideas for responding to student misbehavior in a manner that will generally have a positive effect on students' behaviors and feelings about school.

General Methods for Responding to Disruptive Behavior

1. *Arrange seating patterns so that you can see and easily move to be near all students.* Try to arrange the classroom so you can see all students and can move comfortably about the classroom. If you create a time to work for an extended period with a small group, try to arrange their backs to the class with you facing the class.

2. *Scan the class frequently in order to notice and respond to potential problems or minor disruptions.* One of the most difficult tasks for beginning teachers to learn is how to attend to more than one thing at a time. Teachers frequently become so engrossed in working with a group or an individual student that they fail to notice potential problems stemming from a frustrated student or a minor argument. Although it is important to attend to the student(s) being taught, teachers must learn to frequently scan the room.

3. *The disruptive influence of the teacher's intervention should not be greater than the disruption it is intended to reduce.* Teachers often create more disruptions with their attempts to discipline students than the students are causing themselves. Whenever possible, ignore such minor disruptions as a dropped book or overuse of a pencil sharpener. If an individual student continually creates minor disruptions, this problem can be dealt with effectively by discussing the issue privately with the student. If many class members are involved in low-key disruptive behavior, the behavior can be discussed during a class meeting.

4. *An inappropriately angry teacher response creates tension and increases disobedience and disruptive behavior.* Both Kounin (1970) and Brophy and Evertson (1976) found evidence of a "negative ripple effect" associated with harsh teacher criticism. Rather than improving student behavior, students tend to become more anxious and disruptive in classes characterized by overly harsh discipline. Therefore, although firmness can have a positive effect on classroom behavior, it should be associated with teacher warmth, politeness, and explanations.

5. *A positive ripple effect is associated with a calm and immediate response to a problem.* When teachers react calmly and quickly to a student's disruptive behavior, other students respond by improving their own behavior.

6. *When misbehavior occurs, the first step is to make contact quietly with the student.* This can be done with a glance, by moving close to the student, by touching the student on the shoulder, or by asking the student for an on-task response. When asking the student to respond, always ask a question the student can answer. If the student has obviously not been listening to the discussion,

"Cheer up. Not everyone gets the hang of class control the first time."

you will embarrass the student by asking, "Sam, what do you think about Tom's answer?" Asking Sam a new question, however, or paraphrasing Tom's statement and asking Sam for his opinion can productively reintegrate Sam into the mainstream of the classroom activity. Another approach to making a positive initial contact with the student is to praise a positive behavior that competes with the negative behavior. Rather than criticize a student's off-task behavior, praise the student the moment she or he begins to work on the assignment or focus on the class discussion.

7. *Remind students of the classroom rule or procedure they are not demonstrating.* Rather than yelling, "Chris, stop bothering Mary while she is working!" simply walk over to Chris and ask quietly, "Chris, do you know which rule you are not following?" You could also point to the chart you developed regarding what it looks like and sounds like to be an effective student and ask the student to please use these skills. Similarly, if an entire class is becoming disruptive or lining up without having cleared their desks, ask the class to describe their behavior and mention any classroom procedures that are being neglected.

8. *When one or two students are being extremely disruptive, it is best to focus the other students' attention on their tasks and then talk privately with the disruptive students.* You might say, "Would you all please help me by working quietly on your spelling sentences while I help Tom and Bob solve their problems?" By handling the situation calmly and positively, you indicate your competence, which in turn will have a calming effect on the other students.

9. *Provide students with choices.* When responding to students who are upset, it is often helpful to provide them with choices. This responds to students' needs for competence and power and helps to reduce their perception that someone is trying to control them or is going to do something to them. For example, if a student appears unready to leave an area, instead of saying, "I'll give you ten more seconds to leave this area or you will be in even more trouble!" we might say, "Looks like you're pretty upset right now. Would you rather wait in my room or the counseling office to chat about this and work out a solution?"

During a recent workshop conducted by the senior author, a Nebraska teacher shared how she had used her new skills on giving choices while working with her son who had been having difficulty with arguments and accompanying temper tantrums when asked to run errands with his mother. Instead of bribing or threatening him, she attempted sending an I-message—her need to go, her desire to have him with her—and asking him what would make the trip more enjoyable. The boy indicated that he was hungry and would like a snack for the ride.

"If the class doesn't stop talking, you're all staying after school. Pass it on."

The mother asked him what he thought would be a healthy snack that would be neat enough for the car. The boy responded that he thought an apple would be healthy and not too messy. The mother then asked him if there was anything else that would make the trip more pleasant, and he said he would like to bring a new play figure his father had recently purchased for him. The mother said the boy was delighted at his involvement in the decisions and that, unlike many of their recent excursions, they had a very enjoyable time together.

10. *Remind the student of the positive consequences associated with behaving in a prosocial manner.* For example, you might say, "If you ask in a positive way, he might let you play with the blocks," or, "If you can wait in line without bumping anyone, we'll get out to recess sooner and have more time to play."

11. *Reinforce behavior of students close by who are behaving in a desired manner.* For example, you could say, "Juan, it really helps me teach the lesson when you sit quietly and look at the overhead. Thank you."

12. *See if the student needs some assistance, acknowledge this, and provide the assistance.* For example, if a student is acting out and you notice she is having difficulty because she cannot draw a straight line, you could provide the student with a ruler. This type of quick environmental analysis can go a long way toward reducing behavior problems. This can be supplemented by a comment such as, "When you have the right equipment, you really do well, Luanna. Next time you have trouble, try to think about what would help you, so you can solve the problem rather than getting upset."

13. *Ignore the behavior.* Ignoring is best only for behaviors that cause only limited interference with your ability to teach or students' abilities to learn. Although this strategy can be effective for minor behaviors, it also suggests you are not aware of the misbehavior or that you do not care about the behavior. In addition, the behavior may be reinforced by attention from other students. It is best to ignore only minor misbehavior and to associate this ignoring with praise for appropriate behavior.

14. *Use a signal to indicate you would like the behavior to stop.* This might involve pointing to the classroom rules or your list of what it looks like and sounds like to be an effective student, or simply a surprised or confused look—to indicate you're surprised to see such a helpful student disrupting the class. We suggest that you do not use the evil eye or dirty look many teachers have been taught. We would hope this is not what is used by colleagues at a faculty meeting or family members at a holiday meal. Likewise, it is not a behavior that enhances students' self-esteem and is not a desirable classroom intervention.

15. *Use proximity control.* Simply move closer to a student who is misbehaving. This can ideally be done as you continue to teach.

16. *Place a small note (sticky notes work well) on the student's desk.* This might involve an invitation to talk with you when the lesson is over, a statement that you will soon be switching to an activity the student particularly enjoys, or a strategy the student might use to solve the problem.

17. *Call on the student or involve him by using his name in a story or question.* Sometimes mild inappropriate behavior is a sign of boredom or lack of engagement. Simply providing a brief engagement can reconnect the student with the lesson.

18. *Increase interest by using humor or connecting the lesson to some topic in which the student may be particularly interested.* For example, if the lesson involves division, you might relate it to how athletes' batting averages or shooting percentages are calculated. Similarly, a lesson on passing a law might be spiced up by commenting on impending legislation related to limiting teenage drivers' rights.

P A U S E

and Consider   **8.4**

> Take a few minutes and write down a situation in which you had to engage a student to help him or her act more responsibly. For this specific situation, select two or three of the interventions listed on the previous pages. Ask a peer to role-play the behavior you have written while you implement the method(s) you have selected. How did this feel? Ask the other person to describe how he or she felt when you responded. Based on these two bits of information, do you believe the intervention was effective? If so, why? If not, how could you modify your response?

RESPONDING TO DEFIANT BEHAVIOR

Perhaps the most demanding situation adults face in working with children is responding to defiant behavior. Many adults in U.S. society have been raised in homes in which challenging an adult was not acceptable. Therefore, a common adult response to virtually any student challenge is to use power to gain control. This often results in the adult yelling at the child, threatening, putting a name on the board, removing the child from the room, or even grabbing the child. Although removal may ultimately be necessary, there are a series of steps we can take prior to or along with removal. The importance of learning these methods was recently highlighted when one of the authors was asked by a major school district to address all district staff on the topic of responding to student confrontation. The request was based on the alarming number of teachers who had been involved in violent behavior toward children.

Prepare Students for Situations That May Be Difficult

Prepare yourself and your students for situations that might lead to conflicts. As discussed in Chapter 7, this means teaching key procedures for handling new or demanding situations such as group work, test taking, playground confrontations, and the like. As it relates to communication, it means teaching students and ourselves a model for effectively dealing with our feelings. Figure 8.7 presents a model called the Ladder of Success. The authors have found it effective in providing a basic language and schema for responding to feelings in school settings. The model, which is supported by a series of twelve lessons, graphically indicates that when problems occur, we all have the choice of going up the ladder and responding in a positive way that follows school rules and would be acceptable on most jobs or down the ladder and violating school rules and jeopardizing our ability to maintain a job.

In Figure 8.7, the third step above the problem entitled "Deal directly" is followed by a rectangular window, behind which is located the wheel found at the bottom of Figure 8.7. Students turn this wheel so that various solutions for dealing

FIGURE 8.7
Ladder of
Success:
Problem-Solving
Skills and
Problem-Solving
Wheel

Source: Sharon
Haugen, *Ladder
of Success: Problem-
Solving Skills.*
Reprinted with
permission.
© 1991, 1993
Sharon Haugen.

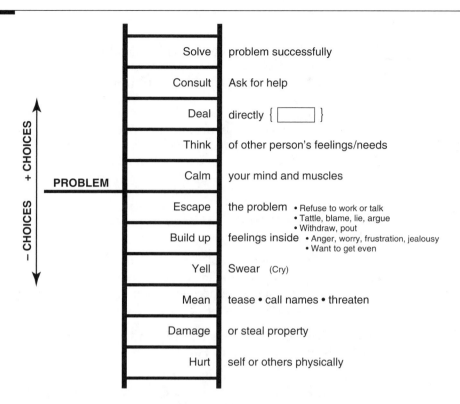

+ CHOICES

− CHOICES

PROBLEM

Solve	problem successfully
Consult	Ask for help
Deal	directly { ☐ }
Think	of other person's feelings/needs
Calm	your mind and muscles
Escape	the problem • Refuse to work or talk • Tattle, blame, lie, argue • Withdraw, pout
Build up	feelings inside • Anger, worry, frustration, jealousy • Want to get even
Yell	Swear (Cry)
Mean	tease • call names • threaten
Damage	or steal property
Hurt	self or others physically

Try two of these strategies when you have a problem

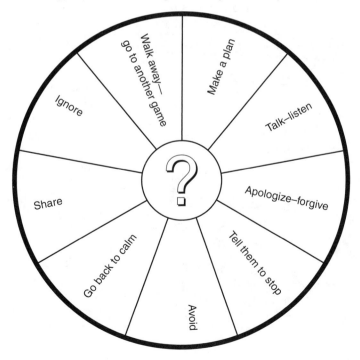

Walk away— go to another game

Make a plan

Ignore

Talk–listen

?

Apologize–forgive

Share

Go back to calm

Tell them to stop

Avoid

For intimidation or fighting, tell an adult right away.

directly with the problem show through the window. It is important that staff use active instructional techniques to teach students how to use these methods. For example, students may be taught how to effectively send an "I-message" or walk away. The key is that students are provided with specific skills to support a nonviolent approach to dealing with their feelings. Several other programs have similar circles or wheels that present students options for solving conflicts. One we have used many times is included in the program, *Kelso's Choice: Conflict Management for Children* (O'Neill & Glass, 1994). This program uses a frog named Kelso to engage students in considering productive methods for responding to their frustration or anger.

Build a Positive Relationship Bank Account with Known Power Strugglers

This involves being intentionally inviting and using many of the methods described in Chapter 3. As noted earlier, students are far less likely to respond violently in the presence of adults whom they respect and whom they believe care about them.

Ensure That Your Requests Have Been Made Clearly, Politely, and Firmly

As discussed in Chapter 3, Walker and Sylvester (1998) distinguish between requests teachers make that are clear and direct (alpha requests) and those that are rambling and vague (beta requests). While our experiences support the need for clarity and conciseness when presenting requests to students, we believe the nonverbal cues and degree of courtesy associated wth teacher requests are significant factors in determining how students respond. We believe a key ingredient is that the student feel respected and not attacked when receiving directives. For example, when asking a student to stop talking and return to his seat, a teacher might shout, "Jeremiah, get back in your seat right now!" While this is clear and concise, it is rather rude and combative. Instead, a teacher might say firmly, "Jeremiah, please return to your seat and raise your hand if you would like me to come over and assist you."

There are obviously many ways to make requests that are clear, polite, and specific. Rhodes, Jenson, and Reavis (1993) present the "precision request." This involves the teacher initially stating, "Please" followed by the request. If the student fails to comply, the teacher says, "I need you

"Johnny! Please exercise your right to remain silent."

to" followed by the request. If the student does not comply, the teacher provides the student with a choice to comply or experience a mild negative consequence. The teacher might say, "Either you may choose to move to the quiet area or you are choosing to spend time at recess working on a problem-solving plan."

When cuing students regarding their behavior, it is more effective to use the word "reminder" or to refer to the agreed-on classroom rules rather than to use the word "warning." Our experience suggests that students find the term *warning* as somewhat aggressive and may take it as a challenge, in turn creating a springboard to further confrontation. Using polite language and reminding students about behavior norms or procedures to which they agreed are much less likely to evoke strong negative emotions than is giving them a warning.

Similarly, it is generally more effective to request that a student initiate an action rather than terminate an action. For example, when a student is wandering around the room agitated by an inability to complete a task, we might ask the student to check with a study partner as opposed to telling the student to stop wandering and sit down.

P A U S E
8.5   *and Consider*

Recall a situation in which a student you teach or were observing refused to follow a reasonable teacher request. If you cannot recall a situation, create a scenario in which a student fails to do as you request. Write two teacher statements: (1) the statement made to the student that was responded to with noncompliance, or a statement you might make to a student in the scenario you considered that might be met with noncompliance; and (2) a statement using the ideas previously discussed that might be met with compliance. We encourage you to share these with several colleagues or fellow students. If possible, role-play several of these scenarios so you become comfortable giving requests that are responded to positively by your students.

Model Self-Control

Self-control requires us to guard against our vulnerabilities and be smarter than a fish. Like the wily trout who knows better than to strike at every imitation lure, we must be careful not to become snared by students' attempts to gain control or negative attention by making inappropriate comments.

It is important to remain calm when responding to defiant student behavior. When we become anxious or angry, this creates a lack of structure and security that may intensify a student's emotional distress. In addition, our heightened emotional state may remind the student of other situations in which adults became aggressive, and this may increase the student's emotional stress. Finally, when we become angry or critical, students may blame our behavior and not assume responsibility for themselves. In order to remain calm, you may wish to take several deep breaths, tell yourself that you have the skill to work with this child, and tell yourself that if your efforts are not effective, others in the school will be glad to assist you.

Respond Thoughtfully and with Purpose to Deescalate the Behavior

Responding thoughtfully requires being aware of such early warning signs as the student stopping work, refusing to talk, looking angry or upset, making comments under their breath, looking anxious or depressed, or disengaging from the group by turning away or looking distracted. When a student shows one of these signs or initially confronts you with statements such as, "This stuff is boring!" "Who wants to learn this?" "You don't care about me!" and so on, you have several options:

1. Expand on the active-listening technique, and *identify the feelings* the student may be experiencing. For example, you might say, "It sounds like you're frustrated with how easy the work is" or "I would be angry too if I thought I was asked to do something I didn't think had been explained very well."
2. *Send an I-message* to let the student know the behavior is creating discomfort for you. This will work especially well if you have placed some deposits in your positive relationship bank account. An I-message can also include a clear, positive statement about your expectations. For example, you might say, "Reggie, I expect all students to make only positive comments to their classmates."
3. *Offer assistance.* You might say, "It looks like I didn't explain that so you could understand. Would you like me to go over that again?" or "It sounds like you're frustrated with the assignment. Let's see if we can work it out so it is more interesting to you."
4. *Provide options.* You might say, "If Melinda is bothering you, it might be better to work at the science center for a while" or "Can you use one of the strategies we agreed to use when we studied the Ladder of Success?"
5. *Predict a positive choice and its consequence.* For example, you might say, "I think if you tried two problems and then asked your partner for help, you would know what to ask for and you'd get help before you became too frustrated."
6. *State the expectation in a positive manner.* If a student spoke out of turn, you might say, "Keith, remember our agreement that during class discussions students will talk only when called on so it is easier for everyone to understand each other."
7. *Review available options and consequences, and give the student space and time to make a choice.* For example, you might say, "Jeremy, remember our procedure for sharing ideas. I will call on you soon when your hand is raised, but if you talk out, we'll need to do some practice during recess."
8. Sometimes it is best to just *walk away* and give the student space. Although this is usually not desirable in cases where a major confrontation has taken place, it

can be used occasionally when a student seems agitated and you know it is likely the student will settle down if given some space.

9. Ultimately, you may have to *clarify that the student must make a choice*. If a student continues to disrupt a discussion, you could say, "Celeste, I'd like you to stay because we have some interesting things planned, but you need to choose either to follow our procedure for talking during discussions or to go to the problem-solving center until we can solve this."

10. Give the student an errand to run or in some other way structure a brief break for the student.

11. As discussed in Chapter 10, for students who display a pattern of becoming frustrated or angry, it may help them to develop a menu of strategies from which they can select when confronted with a frustrating situation. Figure 8.8 presents a model the authors have used extensively in helping teachers develop skill in responding calmly and with purpose to deescalate students who are becoming agitated.

These are all up-the-ladder responses that help maintain the student's dignity while still indicating the teacher's expectation that all students follow the agreed-on behavior standards. Experience clearly indicates that teachers who use these responses have a very low number of situations where student misbehavior escalates to where it must be dealt with as a serious behavior problem.

Phase I: Validating/Clarifying

Validate the underlying feeling: "It's okay to be frustrated with someone, but how else can you express that in our class?"

Help them understand the impact the behavior has on others: Send an I-message: "When you yell at someone, I get concerned because I care about this class being a safe place to study."

Help them understand that the behavior violates someone's compelling state interest or classroom rule: "When you yell at someone like that, which one of our classroom rules are you violating?"

Phase II: Choices/Options—Educative Function

"What would be a better way you could tell her you're frustrated?"

"What would be a better choice right now?"

"Would you like to take a few minutes in our quiet area, or would you rather do your relaxation at your desk?"

"If you continue to violate her rights, you would be choosing to work this problem out with the principal."

Phase III: An Invitation

"I'm sure we can work this out."

"You've been making good choices lately so I know we can come up with a way to solve this."

"I really want you to stay here and solve the problem because we would miss you if you left."

FIGURE 8.8
Deescalation Sequence

PAUSE
and Consider **8.6**

> Consider a situation in which a student is expressing a strong emotion and needs assistance in managing this emotion. Take a minute to write a brief statement about what the student is doing and saying. Next, using the sequence in Figure 8.8, write a statement you might make to the student. When you have finished, share this with several colleagues or fellow students. Once again, we strongly suggest you role-play several scenarios in order to further develop this type of intervention.

Handling Violent Student Behavior

Unfortunately, as discussed in Chapter 1, teachers are increasingly being asked to respond to rather violent student behavior. When this type of behavior occurs, you need to make a firm yet polite statement that you expect the behavior to stop. You might say, "I understand that you two are angry, but we have other ways to solve problems in this school." Jim Fay and David Funk (1995) discuss the importance of teachers staying calm when responding to student behavior problems. They stated that "one of the most common ways teachers allow students to displace their responsibility is by giving them a high emotional overlay to react to" (p. 78). They noted that a major disadvantage to teachers responding too emotionally is that "the attention of children is easily captivated by emotion. When the teacher displays anger, the child gets caught up in the anger . . . the child is so busy thinking about the adult's anger, there is little thought about the mistake or new plan of behavior" (p. 36).

Unfortunately, there will be situations in which the teacher arrives after the escalation has occurred, in which the teacher has a limited relationship with the student, or in which the student is simply not willing or able to back down or to be calm. Because these situations occur with increasing frequency, it is important for teachers to have procedures for protecting themselves and their students from violent behavior.

At this point it is helpful for the teacher to use several strategies. First, it is important to send someone for assistance. Assistance may be needed to protect others from the student's behavior. It is also helpful to have adults who can witness the teacher's interventions so they are not misinterpreted and inaccurately reported by the student (e.g., "She swore at me" or "She hit me" when the teacher had remained calm and had only raised her arm to protect herself from the student). Many schools have developed a procedure for notifying the office when a student becomes physically aggressive with another student or a staff member. Some schools have students take a red card with the name of the class or common area on the back and carry it to the office. This alerts those in the office that they need to immediately interrupt their work and attend to the student. This is often used to report emergencies on the playground or to indicate a fight is taking place. In any event, it is best for the teacher, instructional assistant, or other adult to remain with the injured or aggressive student and provide assistance.

Second, "Teachers should guard against the use of punitive, confrontational and deprecatory methods because these have been shown to increase the possibility of violent reactions from students" (Murdick & Gartin, 1993). The teacher can continue to acknowledge a student's right to have strong feelings, offer assistance, inform the student of the consequences should the behavior continue, and state that the teacher does not want the student to choose these consequences. For example, you might say, "I know you are angry, but we can work this out. Would you like me to meet with the two of you?" You could add, "You know that if you throw punches in this school, you will be suspended and will have to return with your parents. I really would like you to be able to stay at school today." If two students are involved, it is usually most effective to speak directly to the student you know best and to personalize your statement. You might say, "Jeremy, I really want you to be involved in our debate tomorrow, and I hope you'll solve this peacefully so you can be in our class tomorrow."

Third, it is important for the teacher to use nonverbal cues that are nonthreatening and nonconfrontational. Teachers need to talk in a calm, gentle, yet firm voice. Teachers will be more effective standing in an open position with their hands to their side and in plain view of the students. Students need to be given adequate space so they do not feel the teacher is infringing on their space or forcing a confrontation.

Fourth, it is often a good idea to ask other students to leave the scene. This is particularly likely to happen when other students are observing and encouraging a fight. It may also be helpful when a student has become overly distraught in a classroom and will not respond calmly to a teacher's attempts at deescalation. Asking the other students to go to the library or some other designated space can take away the audience effect and allow the student to respond to the teacher in a more reasonable manner. In schools in which violence has been common, it may be helpful to practice with students how you would like them to respond in the event that any violence occurs in the classroom. This may involve leaving the room without getting too close or speaking to the angry student(s).

While waiting for assistance, continue to talk to the students. You might say, "I have sent someone to get an administrator, and I hope we can solve this before we have to involve someone else. I know you're both angry, but at this school we can solve problems without violence." Increasingly, school districts are deciding to refer serious offenses to the police by filing criminal charges. If your district has such a policy, you might also remind students of this (e.g., "If this fight continues, the police will be contacted. I don't want you two to get criminal charges when we can solve this here at school").

In many instances, school staffs are being trained in safe physical restraint skills such as those provided by the Crisis Prevention Institute. Schools often develop a terminology such as *code blue* to indicate that assistance is needed. When this occurs, the trained staff move to the crisis area and use deescalatory skills to calm the students. If students are unable to respond to skillful deescalation, this staff may be required to assist students from the setting.

In their thoughtful book, *Techniques for Managing Verbally and Physically Aggressive Students*, Johns and Carr (1995, pp. 55–61) offer the following tips for dealing with aggressive behavior:

1. An ounce of prevention is worth a pound of cure.
2. Teacher tension can often agitate crisis behavior.
3. Always remain calm.
4. Lower your voice.
5. Slow your rate of speech.

6. Arrange the environment to minimize risk.
7. Give the student space.
8. Be aware of your body stance.
9. Dress in a manner that minimizes risk of injury.
10. Remind misbehaving students of the consequence of their behavior.
11. Allow verbal venting.
12. Ignore irrelevant comments: Redirect the student back to the problem at hand.
13. Provide choices.
14. Set limits.
15. Use physical restraint techniques as a last resort.
16. Once the student is calm, use the incident to teach alternative appropriate ways to deal with aggression.

One of the authors recently had a discussion with a highly regarded elementary school principal concerning the issue of breaking up fights. This principal, who works in a school with a high Chapter I student population, informed the author that she has a policy in her building that the staff will not restrain students except in an absolute emergency. Therefore, students are told that if they are fighting, they will be firmly asked to stop. If the fight continues, other students are removed from the area (or window blinds are closed) to eliminate the audience factor. While the principal or designated adult continues to encourage the students to stop their fight, the police and the students' parents are called. The principal believes students need to know that, unless it is necessary to protect students' physical safety, educators will not physically restrain them. She further believes physical restraint by educators is a violent act that compromises the positive, supportive perception students in her building need to have of adults in their school. She reported that during the past year there had only been four instances in which police had to be called, and that incidents of violent student behavior had been reduced dramatically.

PAUSE
and Consider   **8.7**

> Although you may never encounter a situation in which you are confronted by violent student behavior, it is important to be prepared for the possibility. We encourage you to meet with the building principal or vice principal to discuss any policies or procedures they have for responding to violent student behavior. We suggest you take careful notes and encourage you to share your findings with colleagues or classmates.

Using Time-Out

Time-out is one of the most controversial interventions used to assist children in dealing with their behavior. Within a behavioral paradigm, time-out is the removal of reinforcement that may be contributing to the inappropriate behavior. Therefore, if a teacher believes a student is acting out for peer or teacher attention, the student may be placed in time-out to eliminate these reinforcers for a period of time. Within a cognitive behavioral approach, time-out provides an opportunity for children to calm down so they may benefit from some form of problem solving or opportunity to practice behaviors to use when again confronted with a frustrating situation. Additionally, time-out can provide an opportunity for students to share their perceptions regarding the incident that led to time-out and to negotiate for changes in the classroom environment that will allow them to experience a greater sense of significance, competence, and power.

It is important to keep in mind that there is usually a continuum to the use of time-out. For years, one of the authors has assisted teachers in instructing students in a sequence of methods for taking some quiet time to calm themselves. Initially, students are asked to "take two" (i.e., to

"Quiet time not working out, Ms. Jones?"

take several minutes to stop their work and relax at their desks). If students continue to disrupt or are unable to calm themselves after several brief opportunities at their desks, it is helpful to have a place in the classroom where students can go to work out a plan (see Chapter 9). On those rare occasions where this fails, students are asked to complete their problem solving in another area of the building (usually another classroom, but possibly a *problem-solving* or *solution room* staffed by a paraprofessional). When this procedure is taught to students and they understand that this is not a punishment but a way for them to gain control and solve the problem, and when students know that throughout the sequence they will be treated with dignity, very few students in any setting require interventions beyond the solution room. It is critical that students understand and role-play this process so they know how this process will be used.

School staff should strongly consider eliminating the use of the term *time-out* and replacing it with *resolution* or *problem-solving time*. If a student were having academic difficulties, we would be considered unprofessional and quite possibly liable for a lawsuit if we placed him or her in a time-out setting to improve work. Instead, we would be expected to provide support and alternative instructional strategies. Extrapolating this to students who experience behavior problems, best practice suggests we would assist the students in developing new skills. The use of the term *time-out* suggests we are isolating the student but not replacing ineffective ways of responding with new skills. Therefore, we represent ourselves and our work more professionally when we use terms that describe the intended purpose and the actual procedures we are using in our work with students.

METHODS FOR SOLVING MAJOR AND CONTINUING STUDENT BEHAVIOR PROBLEMS

The previous methods are designed as responses for individual incidents of disruptive classroom behavior. Educators are also increasingly faced with students who continue to experience academic failure or disrupt the classroom despite the use of professionally responsible responses. When this occurs, several options are available to the teacher:

1. Examine the classroom environment to determine what factors may be causing the undesirable behavior and what, if any, adjustments can be made to increase the likelihood that the student will behave productively in the classroom.

2. Meet with the student to discuss the problem and attempt to generate a solution.
3. Contact the parents and inform them of the problem and of the attempts being made to improve the student's behavior.
4. Implement some form of behavioral intervention to help the student improve behavior.
5. Refer the student to the office for consequences associated with the schoolwide student management program.
6. Refer the case to a team whose responsibility is to (1) examine the student's needs, strengths, and behavior problems; (2) review previous methods used to assist the student; and (3) work with the student and significant others to design an individual behavior change plan aimed at modifying the learning environment to better meet the student's needs and provide the student with new skills to assist in benefiting from the positive learning environment. Figure 8.9 presents an outline of these procedures.

The remainder of the book presents methods for responding to ongoing and increasingly serious student behavior problems. Chapter 9 examines how to incorporate problem solving into your classroom management plan, and Chapter 10 examines how to conduct a functional behavioral assessment and develop an individual behavior change plan.

ACTIVITY FOR ASSESSING YOUR SKILLS IN RESPONDING TO ESCALATING STUDENT BEHAVIOR

ACTIVITY 8.1	Select two colleagues who teach or are planning to teach students similar in age to those with whom you work or want to work. Have one person agree to be an upset student, one person a teacher, and the third person an observer. Role-play a classroom situation (perhaps assisting students in groups or with individual work) in which the student becomes upset and confronts the teacher (possibly criticizing the assignment or refusing to complete assigned work). After the role-play, have the person who played the teacher discuss how she or he felt when confronted, why the response(s) given were selected, and how the interchange was perceived. Next, have the student discuss how the teacher's response was perceived. Finally, have the observer discuss the response to the intervention.
Responding to Confrontation	

Switch roles and try this several more times. You may find it productive to videotape the role-plays and play examples back to the class or faculty.

SUMMARY

Teachers who are effective classroom managers develop and teach clear methods for responding to unproductive student behavior that emphasize helping students take responsibility for their own behaviors and learn alternative ways for handling frus-

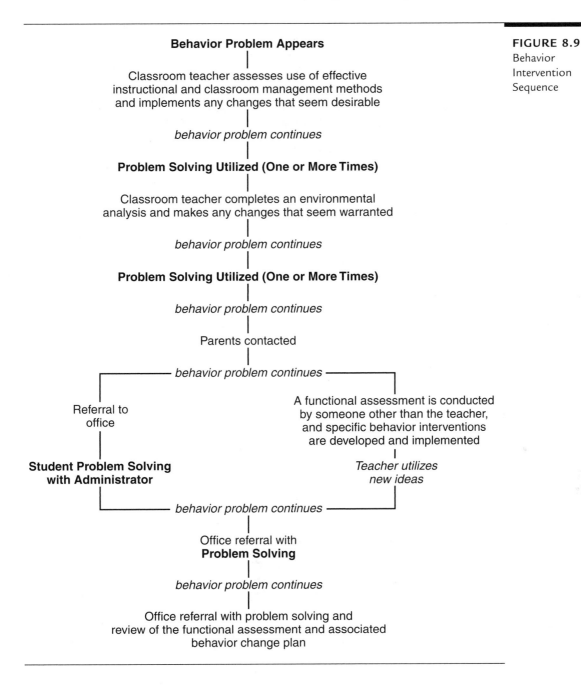

FIGURE 8.9
Behavior
Intervention
Sequence

trating situations. As teachers are asked to work with greater numbers of students who come to school with negative emotional states and poor problem-solving skills, we will need to become more skilled at implementing the methods presented in this and the following chapters.

RECOMMENDED READING

Fay, J., & Funk, D. (1995). *Teaching with love and logic.* Golden, CO: The Love and Logic Press.

Kauffman, J., Hallahan, D., Mostert, M., Trent, S., & Nuttycomb, D. (1993). *Managing classroom behavior.* Boston: Allyn & Bacon.

Long, W., & Morse, W. (1996). *Conflict in the classroom: The education of at-risk and troubled students.* Austin, TX: Pro-Ed.

Mendler, A. (1992). *What do I do when . . . ? How to achieve discipline with dignity in the classroom.* Bloomington, IN: National Educational Service.

Murdick, N., & Gartin, B. (1993). How to handle students exhibiting violent behavior. *The Clearing House, 66,* 278–280.

Noguera, P. (1995). Preventing and producing violence: A critical analysis of responses to school violence. *Harvard Educational Review, 65,* 189–212.

Walker, H., Colvin, G., & Ramsey, E. (1995). *Antisocial behavior in school: Strategies and best practices.* Pacific Grove, CA: Brooks/Cole.

Walker, H., & Walker, J. (1991). *Coping with noncompliance in the classroom: A positive approach for teachers.* Austin, TX: Pro-Ed.

Using Problem Solving to Resolve Behavior Problems

Philosophically, there is little question about the desirability of extending autonomy and freedom of choice to everyone; the problem is determining when and how much. The ability to act independently and make wise and appropriate choices is learned just like any other facet of behavior. . . . A child needs not only experience but the right kind of experience. And he needs a wise guide who can steer him clear of danger and who encourages, prompts, and reinforces behavior that is adaptive and successful.

—Garth Blackham and Adolf Silberman (1975)
Modification of Child and Adolescent Behavior

People take time. Dealing with discipline takes time. Children are not fax machines or credit cards. When they misbehave, they tell us that they need help learning a better way. They are telling us that there are basic needs not being met which are motivating the behavior.

—Allen N. Mendler (1992)
What Do I Do When . . . ? How to Achieve Discipline with Dignity in the Classroom

Part of what is learned in dialogue is interpersonal reasoning— the capacity to communicate, share decision making, arrive at compromises, and support each other in solving everyday problems. The school presently puts tremendous emphasis on logical-mathematical reasoning but almost none on interpersonal reasoning. . . . Interpersonal reasoning is necessary in caring that involves associates and members of the community as well as intimate others.

—Nel Noddings (1992)
*The Challenge to Care in Schools:
An Alternative Approach to Education*

*The benefits gained from learning how to manage conflict con-
structively far outweighs the costs of learning time lost by students being
upset and angry. From a cost-analysis perspective, one of the soundest in-
vestments educators and students can make in classroom and school productivity is teaching students how to manage conflict constructively.*

—David and Roger Johnson (1991)
Teaching Students to Be Peacemakers

Regardless of how effectively we create positive learning environments and implement varied instructional methods, some disruptive student behavior is almost inevitable. At all grade levels, students' developmental needs conflict with an
environment that requires large groups of students to engage in learning new skills
for an extended time. Skilled teachers prevent most disruptions by using methods of
classroom management and instruction that encourage positive interpersonal relationships and academic success. They also, however, possess a repertoire of methods
for helping students responsibly solve minor conflicts that arise. Whereas several
methods for responding effectively to unproductive student behavior were presented
in the previous chapter, this chapter examines the essential classroom management
skill of conducting problem-solving conferences with students.

It is interesting that teachers, especially in secondary schools, so often struggle
with the concepts in this chapter. Although they frequently applaud such curricular
changes as the National Council of Teachers of Mathematics' curriculum revisions
with their focus on applied mathematics and problem solving, or the use of senior
projects, service projects, and portfolios, there seems to be a hesitancy to use conflict resolution with an angry student or to hold a class meeting to solve a problem
presented by several frustrated students. Given the skills employers believe are
needed by their employees, and the obvious and almost desperate need in our society to teach people to solve conflicts nonviolently, it is surprising that secondary
schools place so little emphasis on using problem-solving skills to resolve student
behavior problems. Indeed, in a society in which more than three million parents
themselves report physically abusing their children—and this does not include
spanking or slapping (Lewin, 1995)—it would seem absolutely essential that we
model and teach nonviolent, nonhurtful ways of responding to frustration and working to create environments that are orderly, safe, and respectful for all involved.

The ultimate goals of implementing methods to reduce unproductive or disruptive
student behavior are (1) to increase the achievement of both the individual student and
his or her classmates and (2) to help youngsters develop positive social skills. The fact
that schools group thirty or more students for instruction creates a situation in which
some minor conflicts are likely to occur. Unfortunately, many teachers lack training
and skill in helping students solve their problems. Teacher training programs have frequently failed to provide teachers with either prerequisite communication skills or

specific methods for involving students in solving problems. Consequently, teachers all too often find themselves resorting to the authoritarian models they experienced as students. This point was brought home recently when a young teacher told one of the authors, "My voice is one octave lower than it was at the beginning of the year. I really hate myself for yelling at the students, but I don't know what else to do."

Regardless of the approach we take, working with students whose behavior is disruptive requires time and energy. Research indicates that teachers spend considerable time attempting to control acting-out students. This process can be physically and emotionally exhausting. Teachers will be more effective if they spend less energy attending to and trying to control disruptive behavior and considerably more energy implementing the methods described in Parts II, III, and IV. When disruptions occur in spite of our using effective interpersonal, organizational, and instructional strategies, we should focus our energies on involving students in examining their behavior and developing mutually agreed on methods for changing the behavior.

Whenever confronted with the decision to use an authoritarian or problem-solving approach to discipline, one of the authors is reminded of a comment made by a veteran junior high school teacher. When talking to a group of young teachers about the teaching profession, the teacher stated that it was impossible to be a teacher and not go home tired every night. The teacher said, however, that there were two ways to go home tired. The first was to leave the school building and sigh with relief that another day was over and the students had been kept in line relatively well. He stated that this feeling usually stemmed from teachers' taking an authoritarian, power-oriented approach to discipline; this type of teacher frequently spent evenings worrying about whether the students would behave the next day and what could be done if they did not. The second type of fatigue, he stated, was based on using a problem-solving approach to discipline. He described it as caused by having interacted openly with students all day. Because he experienced the latter type of fatigue, he almost always felt good about his work and generally looked forward to seeing the children the next day. Allen Mendler (1992) placed the concept of discipline in a social context when he noted:

> What we must realize is that, while obedience models of discipline always had a down side, in today's world they simply no longer work. The only kids who behave as a result of "obedience" methods are those who have "respect" or fear authority. And most of them will stop obeying unless they feel respected by those in authority. . . . Nowadays to be successful in a position of authority requires an ability to connect in a caring way by inspiring hope within others and by leading one's own life in a manner that models the message. (p. xl)

A basic assumption that teachers must accept before using a problem-solving approach is that they can reduce their authoritarian control and replace it with natural authority. Natural authority is the logical and readily accepted leadership associated with obvious competence, interest, and concern.

Veteran teachers often ask why students today fail to respond to authoritarian methods of discipline when these methods worked years ago when the teachers were students. The authors believe this is largely because of the way students view authority. First, students today are much more aware of their own rights. The idea that children should be seen and not heard is much less common than it used to be. Second, the way children see authoritarian adult behavior implemented in their homes is different today than it was for the typical student twenty years ago. The authors themselves and many teachers with whom the authors have spoken were raised in very authoritarian homes that were also highly stable, loving, supportive environments. Authoritarian control was, therefore, associated with stability and support. Unfortunately, many students today see authoritarian discipline associated with physical and psychological abuse and abandonment. Therefore, when confronted with authoritarian methods of student management, rather than comply, these students experience fear, anxiety, anger, and rebellion. This is exacerbated by the fact that they correctly believe that the authoritarian methods used by school personnel will not be as physically or psychologically damaging as those experienced at home.

There are three basic situations in which teachers must make decisions regarding the type of authority they will use: (1) in responding to student concerns about issues of curriculum, instruction, and matters of classroom operation; (2) in efforts to alter persistent problems concerning student behavior and learning; and (3) in attempts to stop disruptive or inappropriate student behavior. In all three situations, natural authority will be more effective because students are more likely to accept it. In addition, natural authority allows the teacher to serve as a role model for students, an increasingly important factor because schools are responsible for working with many youngsters who have not been exposed to effective adult role models. Arbitrary, authoritarian, role-bound authority should never be used in the first two situations. In serious instances of aggressive student behavior toward another student, however, a teacher may need to assert authoritarian control if methods based on natural authority fail. As discussed in the previous chapter, however, the teacher should continue to talk to the student in a manner that indicates a focus on caring for the student and the teacher's desire to be involved in problem-solving activities.

An important point to consider when deciding whether to give up authoritarian control is that this approach becomes noticeably less effective as students become older. Authoritarian control can be effectively used in the primary grades (although the effects on children are often destructive), but it is less effective with older students, who are beginning to enter a developmental stage whose main task is developing an individual identity and sense of independence.

As suggested by the teacher who discussed the two ways in which teachers can go home tired, giving up authoritarian control can have benefits for teachers as well as students. As teachers begin to involve students in solving classroom problems, the teacher's role changes from that of an all-knowing, totally responsible adult to that of an effective facilitator. Although teachers cannot abdicate their ultimate responsibility, they can create classroom settings in which they do not have to be constantly and totally in charge of every decision. The difficulty of maintaining an authoritarian role and the number of teachers who continue to accept it are two reasons for continuing high teacher turnover.

A year after taking a course given by the authors, a teacher with more than thirty years' experience suggested that when presenting the material in this book, the authors should tell the readers that the ideas in the book are as beneficial to teachers as they are to students. This teacher indicated that she had just completed the best teaching year of her career because of her decision to *work with* the students rather than to constantly attempt to *control* them.

There are several advantages to initially using fewer teacher-directed, behavioristic interventions. First, though some young people will, in fact, respond only to very structured, controlling interventions, others will respond surprisingly well to effective problem-solving approaches presented in a safe, caring environment characterized by effective teaching. Because it is impossible to determine which students will respond to less control-oriented methods, it is always desirable to try these first. Second, students know when they are being singled out from their peers. Students view adults as powerful and knowledgeable, and so they internalize much of what adults' words and actions say about them. Consequently, when adults use behavioristic methods for controlling a student's behavior, students may learn that they are different from and less capable than their peers. Although this situation is sometimes inevitable, its influence can be reduced by initially employing problem-solving interventions with all students. Students who perceive that a more behavioristic intervention is a response to their inability to respond to a problem-solving approach will understand more clearly why they are being provided with a structured program than will students who are initially confronted with such a program. Third, by providing acting-out students with an introduction to problem-solving approaches, educators increase the likelihood that the youngster who must be temporarily removed or controlled by a structured behavioristic program will be more knowledgeable about and able to adjust to less controlled methods when these become appropriate. Fourth, because they are quite effective in controlling behavior, behavioristic methods are often used by teachers without first examining such important variables as the quality of teacher–student and peer relationships or the instructional materials and techniques being used in the classroom. Therefore, behavioristic approaches are sometimes used to manipulate pupils into behaving passively in environments that are not meeting their basic needs. Because problem-solving approaches give students an opportunity to discuss the environment, they are an important environmental analysis/functional assessment tool and are definitely a precursor to behavioristic interventions. Fifth, many children enter school highly stressed by events occurring outside of school. For example:

> A newly enrolled third grader became wild and disrespectful, resulting in almost daily removal from the class. It was several weeks before the staff discovered that he and his siblings had been abandoned by their mother shortly after they moved to a deserted farm. Fearful of being separated, the children told no one and continued riding the bus to school each day. (Brendtro & Long, 1995, p. 54)

The authors have worked with hundreds of students whose school behaviors are partially a result of environmental factors—including those at school—that are causing the student anxiety and pain. If we are to effectively assist students in resolving their behavior problems, we must have as clear an understanding as possible of the factors influencing the behaviors. "Those who simply punish are often the last to discover what is causing a child's life to fall apart" (Brendtro & Long, 1995, p. 54). Those who use problem solving, however, are more likely to assist the child in explaining their perception of the problem and thereby opening doors for creative solutions to the problem.

Finally, there appears to be growing evidence that punitive methods, while at times necessary, serve only to aggravate students' sense of anger and alienation and also increase violent behavior (Reiss & Ross, 1994). Furthermore, studies suggest that schoolwide management methods that focus on problem solving (Nelson, 1996) and reteaching (Sugai, Horner, & Gresham, 2002) are the most effective in creating positive, safe school environments.

Problem solving has an additional distinct advantage over methods emphasizing immediate teacher control. Problem-solving methods help to enhance a wide range of social, interpersonal, and cognitive skills important to personal success and happiness.

As you know from reading this text, we strongly believe the manner in which educators respond to irresponsible student behavior should help students to learn new skills. Figure 9.1 presents a list of skills or abilities enhanced by involving students in a problem-solving process.

P A U S E

and Consider   **9.1**

> Take a few moments to consider the types of discipline you received in your home and school. When was the discipline most helpful to you? What types of responses to your behavior that concerned others did you find the most respectful? What responses did you find the most educational?

P A U S E

and Consider   **9.2**

> Discuss with a group of colleagues or fellow students the type of discipline used in the classrooms or schools where they work. Is the approach to discipline they describe characterized by natural or arbitrary authority? Regardless of your findings, discuss with your colleagues why you believe this approach to discipline exists in the setting where you are working or observing.

PLACING PROBLEM SOLVING IN CONTEXT

When considering when and how to implement problem solving, teachers must answer three important questions: (1) What do I want to accomplish in responding to inappropriate student behavior? (2) Where does problem solving fit into my classroom management plan? and (3) How does problem solving relate to other corrective behavior management interventions I or other school staff may choose to employ? In an-

---

FIGURE 9.1
Skills Enhanced through Problem Solving

Source: Behavior Management: Application for Teachers, 3e, by Zirpoli/Melloy, © 2001. Reprinted by permission of Pearson Education, Inc., Upper Saddle River, NJ.

1. *Alternative solution thinking.* The ability to generate different options or potential solutions to a problem
2. *Consequential thinking.* The ability to consider consequences that a behavior might lead to, which goes beyond the consideration of alternatives to the consideration of the consequences of potential solutions
3. *Causal thinking.* The ability to relate one event to another over time with regard to why a particular event happened or will happen
4. *Interpersonal sensitivity.* The ability to perceive that an interpersonal problem exists
5. *Means–ends thinking.* The step-by-step planning done in order to reach a given goal; means–ends thinking involves insight, forethought, and the ability to consider alternative goals
6. *Perspective taking.* The ability of the individual to recognize and take into account the fact that different people have different motives and may take different actions

swering the first question, most teachers state that in addition to wanting to maintain a positive, supportive learning environment, they want to teach students to be responsible for their own behavior and they want students to develop prosocial skills. By involving students in examining their own behavior and developing alternative responses, problem solving allows students to accept greater responsibility for their behavior and develop important citizenship skills.

As discussed in Chapter 8, it is increasingly recommended that problem solving be used several times when a student continues to act unproductively in the classroom despite the teacher's best efforts to create a positive, well-structured learning environment. Problem solving may involve the teacher taking time to meet with the student and verbally problem solve. Additionally, effective schoolwide student management programs also involve the student in problem solving when a persistent or serious misbehavior has led to an out-of-class or office referral.

Even teachers skilled in involving students in solving their own problems find that some students have major skill deficits or personality disorders that prevent them from responding to interventions requiring the establishment of a trusting relationship and an ability to evaluate one's behavior in light of its effect on others. Problem solving is the intervention teachers should use following or in conjunction with attempts to alter the classroom environment in order to create a positive, supportive learning environment. However, teachers may also need to incorporate other individualized intervention methods when problem solving does not have the desired results. In addition, teachers cannot be effective in helping students with serious behavior problems unless the school incorporates a variety of methods to provide assistance and support to teachers.

A MODEL FOR SOLVING PROBLEMS WITH INDIVIDUAL STUDENTS

As presented in this chapter, there are several types of problem solving. The most commonly used approach to problem solving is some form of William Glasser's "Reality Therapy." Though Glasser provided several step-by-step approaches to problem solving, the method found by the authors to be most effective involves these seven steps: (1) be warm and personal and be willing to get emotionally involved; (2) deal with specific, current behavior; (3) help the youngster make a value judgment about her or his behavior; (4) work out a plan for changing the behavior; (5) get a commitment from the student to carry out the plan; (6) follow up by checking to see how the plan is working; (7) do not punish the student by being negative or sarcastic, and do not accept excuses if the inappropriate behavior continues. Figure 9.2 outlines Glasser's seven steps as modified by the authors. This approach is directed by the teacher and assists the teacher and student in quickly resolving problems related to academics or behavior.

Several writers have developed methods for helping students resolve problems and take responsibility for their own behavior. In his *Teacher Effectiveness Training*, Tom Gordon (1974) offered a six-step approach to problem solving. Frank Maple's (1977) *Shared Decision Making* describes a variety of skills needed to resolve problems effectively. Curwin and Mendler's (1988) book, *Discipline with Dignity*, and Mendler's (1992) follow-up book, *What Do I Do When . . . ? How to Achieve Discipline with Dignity*

FIGURE 9.2
Problem-Solving
Method

Step 1:   Establish a warm, personal relationship with the student.
    (Develop a "positive relationship bank account" with the student.)

Step 2:   Deal with the present behavior.
    "What happened?"
    (Develop a time line/functional assessment.)
    "What did you do?"
    (Help students take responsibility for their role in the problem. Help them develop an internal locus of control.)

Step 3:   Make a value judgment.
    "Is it helping you?"
    (Help students consider their own behavior and underlying assumptions.)
    "Is it helping others?"
    (Enhance student's social cognition.)
    "Is it against a rule/Does it violate a compelling state interest?"
    (Help students understand their own and others' rights and responsibilities within the community.)

Step 4:   Work out a plan.
    "What can you do differently?"
    (Social skill training)
    "What do you need me to do?"
    (Empowerment/functional assessment)
    "What do you need other students to do?"
    (Empowerment/functional assessment)

Step 5:   Make a commitment.
    "Are you going to do this?"
    (Enhance student's accountability/responsibility.)

Step 6:   Follow up.
    "I'll check later and see how the plan has worked."
    (Supportive/caring environment)

Step 7:   No put-downs, but do not accept excuses.
    "If the plan didn't work, let's analyze why and develop a new plan."
    (High expectations and persistence in working with students)

---

in the Classroom, provide good information on helping students develop an ability to solve their own problems. Jim Fay's book *Teaching with Love and Logic* (Fay & Funk, 1995) and his workshops on discipline with love and logic provide another good opportunity for teachers to examine this practice as, of course, do workshops offered through the Glasser Institute. More recently, research by Ron Nelson (Nelson, 1996; Nelson, Crabtree, Marchand-Martella, & Martella, 1998) has demonstrated that the use of "Think Time"—a problem-solving approach built into the schoolwide student management plan—has been associated with significant reductions in student behavior problems and referrals.

Professionals who work with students experiencing serious emotional and behavioral problems may use a form of problem solving known as life space crisis intervention. This model, initially developed by Fritz Redl and later modified for school settings by William Morse, Nicholas Long, and others (Long & Morse, 1996), involves a more in-depth examination of the problem event. This includes determining whether the event represents a pattern of dysfunctional thinking or perceiving and providing the student with insight into the pattern as well as alternative ways of responding.

Finally, many schools now use conflict resolution as an approach to assist individuals resolve conflicts. This process differs from problem-solving methods because it involves a third party in facilitating a dialogue to assist two parties resolve a conflict. This chapter provides a detailed examination of Glasser's approach and a discussion of conflict resolution. If you are interested in exploring the life space crisis intervention model, we encourage you to examine the references at the end of this chapter.

Glasser's Seven Steps to Effective Problem Solving

Many teachers find the issue of dealing unsuccessfully with persistent student behavior problems to be one of the most frustrating and time-consuming aspects of teaching. Though most teachers are well trained in subject matter methods, many are untrained or uncomfortable with the role of problem solver and classroom manager. Furthermore, with the increased emphasis on achievement test scores, some teachers feel anxious about time spent solving problems. We are, however, confronted daily with individual problems that must be resolved in order for students to benefit from our instruction. Therefore, we need to develop skills in solving problems in a positive and rapid manner. Recently, a teacher in Lincoln, Nebraska, shared a concept she had found helpful in her thinking about working with behavior problems in her classroom. She noted that she believed that although teachers were not responsible for counseling students, teachers were increasingly responsible for doing what they do best—teaching students a wide variety of behaviors as well as academic skills. She noted that defining her responses as teaching new behaviors had given her a new perspective and enthusiasm for working with students experiencing behavior problems.

Advantages of Glasser's Method

Four factors make Glasser's model extremely useful for school personnel. First, the problem solving can be accomplished in a short time. Most conflicts can be resolved in less than five minutes, and frequently a solution can be developed in only a minute or two. Therefore, though it is often desirable to remove the student from the group so that the discussion can take place privately, you do not need to become involved in a lengthy discussion that diverts your attention from other instructional or supervisory duties. Second, because the model employs a step-by-step procedure, it is easy to learn. Furthermore, if a problem-solving session does not go well, you can analyze each step and discover what needs to be improved to make the session more effective.

Third, by actively involving the student in the problem-solving process, the model responds to a variety of students' needs. Rather than establishing a teacher-versus-student debate or a situation in which you manipulate the student by offering rewards for changed behavior, the student is meaningfully involved in examining his or her behavior and developing a plan for changing the behavior. Finally, because the model focuses on specific, observable behavior, data can be collected and the student is accountable for the results. The focus on observable behavior also enables you and the student realistically to analyze the effectiveness of the plan. To become competent at using Glasser's approach, you need to understand each step and then frequently use the approach with students.

Step One

The first step is presented in Chapter 3. If you employ the communication skills and other strategies for improving teacher–student relationships described in Chapter 3, students will sense that you care and will almost always be willing to work with you to examine and attempt to change their behavior.

Step Two

The second step is to ask the student to describe the behavior. Awareness of actions is an important component in any behavior change program. Indeed, a simple increase in children's awareness of their behavior is often accompanied by major changes in their behavior. You can help students describe their behavior by asking questions such as, "What did you do that upset Sally?" The emphasis should be placed on specific, observable behavior. If a student states that he was bad or didn't obey you, help the child specify what request he did not obey and what he said or did when rejecting the request.

Students will sometimes respond to your question about what they did by saying, "Nothing" or "I don't know." You then have several options. First, you may respond by stating, "John, I'm not trying to blame you or get you in trouble. What I want to do is help you solve the problem, and I need to know what you did so I understand what happened." When you focus on the problem rather than threaten the student or focus on the punishment, students are often willing to discuss their behavior.

Second, students may balk at describing what they did because in the past admitting what they did was associated with strong punishments. We have increasingly found it helpful to begin by asking the student, "What happened?" This allows the student to provide his or her perspective and give us a context for the behavior. Although it also allows them to attempt to justify irresponsible behavior, we have found that when allowed to provide a brief context, students are more willing to describe their behaviors and thus their responsibility for any problem. Another approach is to ask students if they would be willing to hear what you observed or, if you were not present, to have someone else share what was observed. It is important that this option be presented positively and not as a threat. When confronted with this option, students will normally discuss their behavior. A teacher recently solved this problem by asking students, "If I had a video camera taping what happened, what would I have seen?" She says that students find this nonthreatening because while they describe their own behavior, they are allowed to describe the entire event as they perceived it.

If a student does not respond positively to any of these options, it usually means he or she is quite emotional and may need time to calm down and think about the problem. You can deal with this situation by saying, "John, it seems you don't feel comfortable talking about the problem right now. Why don't we talk about it during recess." Providing the student with time to relax often facilitates a positive resolution of the problem.

Teachers often note that they doubt whether students will honestly tell them what happened. If you have a sibling within several years of your age, consider for a moment several situations in which you did something you knew was not acceptable in your home but that no one could prove you had done. If you are like most people, there were several occasions in which your parent(s) asked you whether you had done the act and you said, "No," knowing that this would make your parents either become detectives (which they were too busy to do) or punish an innocent person. The number of times you used this strategy was quite likely related to the severity of punishments used in your home. Like most people raised in fairly large families with strict punishments, most students who have persistent behavior problems become political experts in knowing how to avoid punishment. If you want students to be willing to problem solve with you, you must make it clear that discipline does not mean being punished or hurt but rather it means being asked to take responsibility for one's behavior and to learn new methods for solving problems.

Step Three

Once the student has described the behavior, you should help the student determine whether the behavior is desirable. Students will not make meaningful, lasting changes in a behavior unless they decide that the behavior should be altered. When directing a program for seventh- and eighth-grade students who exhibited serious behavior problems, one of the authors was surprised when a number of the students stated that when they changed their behavior to earn the rewards offered by a contract, they thought they were being bribed and earned the rewards only to play the system. The students resented not being involved in assessing their behavior. Consequently, behavior changes occurred only as long as the staff could devise adequate rewards or punishments. Based on this information, subsequent behavior change interventions used more dialogue and a less unilateral approach to solving problems. Research results indicate that this approach was more successful.

Glasser suggests that, when helping youngsters make a value judgment about their behavior, you ask them: "Is the behavior helping you? Is it helping me? Is it helping the other students?" When children are involved in obviously unproductive behaviors, they will almost always answer *no* to these questions. If they answer *yes*, you can ask, "How is it helping you?" or "How is it helping the others?" Finally, if the student insists that the behavior is helping him and his peers, you can describe how the behavior is causing problems for you or others in the school, that it violates a school rule, or that it infringes on the rights of others (compelling state interests). If you have established a positive relationship with the student, this will often provide the impetus for the student to acknowledge that the behavior needs to be changed.

Another approach to helping youngsters make a value judgment is to have them list the advantages and disadvantages or payoffs and costs of their behavior. When working with older students, we can ask them to put the payoffs and costs in writing. Figure 9.3 provides a form that can be used to facilitate this process. Because this procedure requires more time than simply problem solving, it is most often used by counselors, coaches, or when teachers have time to meet for an extended time with a student. We know many middle school teachers who use this to assist students in their advisory or block classes in considering the implications of their behavior.

If a student continues to state that an unproductive behavior is helping her and that she wishes to continue the behavior, it is likely that she is feeling backed into a corner or is testing your resolve. It is usually best to postpone the discussion for a short time. If a student continues to insist that an unproductive behavior is acceptable, you

FIGURE 9.3
Payoff–Cost Model of
Behavioral Counseling

Source: From Vernon
F. Jones, *Adolescents
with Behavior Problems:
Strategies for Teaching,
Counseling, and Parent
Involvement*, p. 200.
Copyright © 1980 by
Allyn & Bacon.
Reprinted with
permission.

	Short Term	Long Term
Payoffs		
Costs		

may need to confront the student with the logical consequences of the behavior. We should be very careful not to rush to this point without exhausting all possible approaches to helping the student decide to alter the behavior. If it is necessary to use this intervention, however, it should be discussed in a matter-of-fact, nonthreatening manner, and you should clearly explain to the student why the behavior must be altered. You might say, "I am sorry that you do not see the behavior as harmful. It is my job, though, to make sure that our classroom is a safe, comfortable place. Therefore, if you do not choose to be responsible for your behavior, I must take responsibility." If the student continues to insist that the behavior does not need to change, you should inform the student of the specific consequences that will occur if the behavior continues.

Step Four
After the student has decided that the behavior really does need to be changed, the next step is to help him develop a workable plan for making the change. Start by asking the student a question such as, "What do you think you can do so that you can study without bothering other students?" or "What kind of plan or strategy could you use so that you don't disrupt learning during music class?" Do not accept a superficial plan such as the statement, "I won't do it again" or "I'll try harder." You might be relieved to hear these promises, but they do not provide the student with a specific approach for dealing more effectively with the situation. Consequently, you can respond to promises by saying, "I'm glad that you are going to try not to do it. That will certainly help. But what else can you do? What can you do when you start to get frustrated with your work?"

Students are refreshingly creative at devising useful plans/strategies for solving their own problems. Nevertheless, students sometimes state that they cannot think of a solution. Your first response should be to encourage them to think about the situation and report back to you at a designated time. Students have frequently become so accustomed to having adults provide answers that at first they are confused by having the burden placed on them. When given time to think about the situation, though, they often devise thoughtful plans. If the student is unable to develop a workable plan, you can offer several ideas for the student to consider. Offer several suggestions so that the student will make the final decision. This involvement in choosing the solution increases the likelihood that the student will accept and follow through on the plan.

With elementary and middle school students, it is helpful to teach several lessons on developing plans or strategies for responding to various situations in which problems frequently arise. The class can be asked to describe common situations in which students become engaged in inappropriate behavior and then list alternative behaviors for dealing with the situation. These can be posted in the classroom, and students can refer to them if they violate a school rule and become involved in problem solving. Especially when working with younger students, it can be helpful to ask them to evaluate their plan against such basic criteria as whether it is safe, fair, and kind. Will it work, and how will it make others feel?

Plans should initially be relatively simple and unstructured, such as a student's decision to work with another student in order to stay on task and complete her work. Plans may, however, involve a somewhat more structured approach. In fact, when less structured solutions have failed, many of the procedures described in this chapter can serve as methods for implementing a plan to help a child alter her behavior. For example, students might be involved in writing a formal contract or self-monitoring their behavior.

Step Five

The next step is to ensure that both you and the student clearly understand the plan and to ask the student to make a commitment to the plan. You can say, "All right, that seems like a good plan. Now, just to be sure that we both understand it, what are you going to do when you become frustrated with your work?" After the student describes the plan, you can paraphrase the student's decision and acknowledge your role in the plan. You might say, "Okay, whenever you get frustrated you're going to raise your hand. If I'm busy and can't help you, you're going to quietly walk over and ask Sally for help. Then, it is my responsibility to come over and check your work as soon as I get a chance." Although it is often adequate simply to obtain an oral agreement, it is sometimes helpful to put the plan in writing. This is especially valuable when students are first introduced to problem solving or when the final plan is developed in the form of a contract in which both parties agree to behave in a specified manner.

Once the plan has been clarified, the student should make a commitment to try the plan. This *compact* can be accomplished by asking, "Do you believe this is a good plan? Will you give it a try?" Although this step is often part of the final negotiation of a plan, it is important to elicit a clear commitment to the plan.

Step Six

The sixth and seventh steps involve follow-up. In devising a workable solution to a problem, it is necessary to designate a time when the two parties will meet to discuss how the plan is working. Step six provides you with an opportunity to reinforce the student's efforts and to discuss any problems that might arise. If the plan involves a behavior that occurs frequently throughout the day, you should meet briefly with the student on the same day as the plan is made. Furthermore, if you see the student successfully implementing the plan, praise the student for her efforts. If the plan involves a behavior that occurs only occasionally—as during the student's music class—you can agree to meet the student as soon as possible following the class. Follow-up sessions need not take long. You can simply ask, "How did your plan work?" If the plan worked well, express your pleasure and ask the student how she felt about the results. If it would reinforce the student, you may choose to provide additional follow-up by asking the principal to praise the student or by sending a positive note home with the student.

Step Seven

The final step in Glasser's plan deals with what to do if a plan does not work. First, do not be critical or sarcastic or punish the student. A major assumption underlying the use of a problem-solving approach is that in a positive, supportive environment students will want to be responsible and behave appropriately. Therefore, the student's inability to carry out a plan should not be punished. At the same time, you should not accept excuses. Students often defend their failure to change their behavior by blaming other people. Rather than allowing the student to describe what other people did that caused his failure to follow his plan, you should begin another problem-solving conference. Because the student will already have examined the behavior and made a decision to change it, the first three steps will usually take only a minute or two to complete. The conference should then focus on asking the student to consider why the plan did not work and helping him develop another plan. If the behavior is one that is harmful to other students, such as pushing children on the playground, you may need to inform the student of the consequences that will be incurred should the behavior continue. Although the emphasis should always be on devising a plan rather than on punishing the student, situations in which it is necessary to incorporate a punishment into a plan do occur.

Examples

The following examples of first an upper elementary and then a middle school teacher using Glasser's model with a student indicate how effective communication skills can be combined with Glasser's step-by-step procedure to create a positive resolution to a problem.

Example 1: Upper Elementary School

STEP 1.   TEACHER: Darby, can I talk to you by my desk for a little bit?

DARBY: Okay.

STEP 2.   TEACHER: After we corrected math today, I went over everyone's paper. Can you tell me what I found on your paper?

DARBY: I didn't get finished.

STEP 3.   TEACHER: That's right. Is it helping you to not get your work done on time?

DARBY: I guess not.

TEACHER: What happens when you don't have your work ready?

DARBY: Jon doesn't have a paper to correct.

TEACHER: Yes, can you think of any other things that happen?

DARBY: I'll get a bad grade and have to do my work again.

TEACHER: Okay, and does it make it even harder for you to have to complete this assignment and then begin working on the one for tomorrow?

DARBY: Yeah.

TEACHER: Well, Darby, would you like to start having your work done on time so that you don't get behind and so that you can feel good about giving Jon a completed paper to correct?

DARBY: Yeah.

STEP 4.   TEACHER: All right. Can you think of a plan that can help you get your work done on time?

DARBY: No—I'll just try to get it done.

TEACHER: Well, that's super to hear, but can you think of a specific plan for getting this work completed?

DARBY: Oh, I guess I could do it after I get home from school, before my mom gets home from the beauty shop each night. But I like to play, too.

TEACHER: Well, let's plan it out. What time does your mother get home?

DARBY: 5:30.

TEACHER: And what time do you get home from school?

DARBY: 3:15.

TEACHER: Now, do you think you can play for a while . . .

DARBY: Oh, I know. I'll play until 4:30 and then do my work from 4:30 to 5:30!

STEP 5.   TEACHER: Darby, that sounds like a great idea! I'm sure that most days you won't even need a whole hour to finish your work, especially when you get into such a good habit! And won't it be nice to be all done when your mother gets home! How long do you think you could make this plan work?

DARBY: Forever!

TEACHER: Wow!! I'm excited, too, but let's try it for a few days and talk about how it works for you.

DARBY: Okay. I will do it tonight and tomorrow night.

TEACHER: Great! Then Jon and I can expect to see completed assignments on Thursday and Friday!

Thursday

STEP 6.   DARBY: It worked! I played, got my math done in thirty minutes (it was easy!), and was watching TV when Mom got home. Boy, was she surprised when I showed her my work!

TEACHER: Darby, I knew you could do it! It sounds like you feel good about your plan, and I'm excited because you feel good and it will help you learn your math.

Example 2: Middle School

STEP 1.   TEACHER: Horace, may I please speak with you for a few minutes?

HORACE: Okay.

STEP 2.   TEACHER: What did you do that upset Larry?

HORACE: I didn't do anything.

TEACHER: Horace, I'm not trying to blame you or get you in trouble. What I want to do is try to help you solve the problem. But before we can solve it, I need to know what you did so that I understand what happened.

HORACE: Well, I pushed Larry's books off his desk and onto the floor, and his papers got all messed up.

STEP 3.   TEACHER: Thank you for being honest with me. It sounds like you are really making an attempt to try to figure this problem out. Is this helping you or Larry in any way?

HORACE: No, but he marked in ink on my assignment sheet that I was just about to hand in, and he ruined it. And so, now I have to do it all over again.

STEP 4.   TEACHER: I will talk to Larry about this problem after we get finished dealing with your part of the problem. What kind of plan do you think you could work out so that you won't retaliate against someone the next time something like this happens to you?

HORACE: I won't do it again.

TEACHER: I'm glad that you are going to try to not do it again. That will certainly help. But what else can we do?

HORACE: I don't know.

TEACHER: Well, how about if I make a few suggestions and you pick one of my plans to try to work with?

HORACE: Well, okay.

TEACHER: How about sending that person an I-message telling them how you feel. Like, "It upsets me when you ruin my homework and I have to do it over again." Or you could just get up and move away from that person, showing them that you don't appreciate what they've done. Do you like either one of these plans, Horace?

HORACE: Well, because we've worked on I-messages and you want us to work out our own problems, I will try an I-message next time.

STEP 5.   TEACHER: Great; now, just to be sure we both understand, what are you going to do the next time somebody bothers you and your work?

HORACE: Send that person an I-message.

TEACHER: Good; I'll check back with you in a couple of days to see how your plan is working.

A couple of days later

STEP 6.   HORACE: It worked!! Gary ripped one of my papers yesterday, and I sent him an I-message, and he actually apologized to me. I couldn't believe it.

TEACHER: I'm proud of you for working out your plan. I can see by your reaction that you are happy with your results.

Now that you have been introduced to the steps in problem solving with students and have read two examples, it is important that you practice this approach. We have found several practice methods most effective. First, we encourage you to write a dialogue in which you implement the seven steps in helping a child solve a real or potential problem. This dialogue would look like the ones you just read in that it would include your statements and those of the student. When you have completed this, we encourage you to have a colleague or classmate read your dialogue and give you feedback on how effectively you incorporated the seven steps and how you might fine-tune your use of this problem-solving model. Second, we encourage you to role-play situations with your colleagues or classmates. When doing this, it may be helpful to have a third party observe your dialogue and be the first to provide you with some feedback—the person playing the student will also have some helpful tips. Finally, we encourage you to use this method with students in your school and to discuss the results with others.

Implementing Problem Solving in the Classroom

As discussed in Chapter 8, problem solving will be most effective when it is an integral part of a teacher's classroom management plan. You must decide for yourself how this method will be incorporated into your plan. Some teachers choose to focus almost exclusively on a written form of problem solving. Other teachers prefer to have students go to a problem-solving area, think about the problem, generate a plan, and share the plan verbally when time permits. Many teachers use a combination of these methods in which written responses are the consequence for continued rule violation and verbal problem solving is used in response to behaviors that have occurred only one or two times. As mentioned earlier, several studies have shown that, when combined with teaching students classroom and school behavior expectations, the use of problem solving can have a positive effect on student behavior (Nelson, 1996; Nelson, Martella, & Galand, 1998). Our own work has shown this combination is associated with reductions of between 30 and 50 percent in office referrals and suspensions.

As with any procedure used in the classroom, it will be dramatically more effective and efficient if students are taught how to use the procedure. The following ten activities are those the authors and many teachers with whom the authors work use in teaching a problem-solving method to students:

1. Provide the students with a handout and write the steps on the overhead.
2. Discuss each step and provide an example.
3. Role-play several situations in which a student misbehaves and the teacher uses this method for assisting the student in taking responsibility for her behavior.
4. Lead a discussion following each role-play.
5. Have the students practice by taking the role of both student and teacher and role-playing several situations.

6. Process these interactions.
7. Provide the class with an example of a violation of a classroom rule and have each student write a problem-solving plan.
8. Have students share and assist the class in evaluating and, if necessary, modifying several plans.
9. Explain how the problem-solving process relates to the classroom management plan and the difference between verbal and written plans.
10. Quiz students on the steps in the sequence and the classroom management plan.

When implementing Glasser's approach, it is important not to skip any of the seven steps listed in Figure 9.2. The authors often see teachers working with a student to develop a plan when the student has yet to make a value statement about his behavior. Regardless of the student's age or the nature of the problem, it is critical that the adult involved use each step and proceed in the order presented. The authors have used this method with their own children beginning at age two, with students at every age and grade from four-year-olds to high school seniors, and with students ranging from talented and gifted to incarcerated delinquents. The authors firmly believe that it is a central factor in creating positive learning environments and helping students learn personal responsibility. The teacher who uses Glasser's approach will find that student attitudes about the teacher and school in general will improve and that students will learn to take more responsibility for their behavior.

INCORPORATING PROBLEM SOLVING INTO A SCHOOLWIDE STUDENT MANAGEMENT PLAN

If you are a beginning teacher or just beginning to implement a problem-solving approach into your classroom management plan, you are probably wondering what you do when a student does not respond to your effectively using a problem-solving approach. The next chapter is dedicated to providing you with individualized behavior change methods teachers have found effective in helping students who require more than a caring environment, engaging instruction, and problem solving to assist them in developing and choosing to use positive, socially accepted behaviors in a school setting. This section describes how school staff support teachers by providing opportunities outside the classroom for students use problem solving to develop new behavior skills.

Before examining methods for incorporating problem solving into methods used to assist teachers when their work with students does not help the student make responsible choices, it is important to consider what currently exists in many schools. In an analysis of office referrals, Sugai, Kameenui, and Colvin (1993) reported that more than 90 percent of school disciplinary responses involved merely negative consequences. Likewise, studies suggest that at least in middle schools, there is often little relationship between the behaviors for which students are referred and the consequences they receive (Skiba, Peterson, & Williams, 1997). It is, therefore, not surprising that a majority of students express anger or relief at being given a consequence by school personnel (Costenbader & Markson, 1998).

Given both the high cost of destructive behavior by students who become angry at school personnel and the importance of creating situations where all students feel valued and aware that adults can separate the student from the behavior, we must begin to conceptualize our responses to disruptive student behavior in new ways. It is imperative that discipline be used to (1) assist students in knowing they are cared for, (2) help students understand that they have violated the rights of others (and thereby enhance their understanding of others' feelings), and (3) provide students with new skills for coping with their frustration. Interestingly, studies suggest that students who had been suspended listed numerous interventions they felt would help them more than the suspension, including, "a desire to learn alternatives to the behaviors that resulted in their suspension" (Costenbader & Markson, 1998, p. 76).

School staff who are effective in creating safe, positive learning environments find ways to incorporate problem solving into their schoolwide student management plan. All teachers at some time need assistance from other teachers, counselors, and administrators in assisting students in learning and choosing responsible behaviors. This is most effective when it is a clear, consistent procedure that is used by all those who work with students and communicated to students and parents.

"Remember what you told us: 'If you can't say something nice, don't say anything at all.'"

One of the most common supports for teachers is to have another area in the building where students can go and problem solve if they are not able to successfully complete this task in their classrooms. In many elementary schools this involves a "buddy class," in which two classrooms are paired so that students who need to take a break and problem solve somewhere else have a specified place to go. Most often this involves classrooms at different age levels, which helps to reduce student embarrassment by being viewed as having a problem by their age-mates. It also reduces the effect of the student playing to the audience of same-age peers. In a number of schools where the authors have worked and consulted, a problem-solving room has been established and is staffed by an instructional assistant. This allows students to work directly with an adult trained in problem solving without having a classroom disrupted.

School staff vary on how this problem-solving time is handled. In many cases, the student takes a minimum amount of time (often ten minutes) to calm down and reflect on what happened. They may then signal their readiness to return to the classroom. On their return, they are expected to problem solve with the teacher as soon as it is convenient within the flow of classroom activities. In other cases, while in the "buddy classroom" students are asked to complete a problem-solving form such as the ones found in Figures 8.5 and 8.6. When this has been successfully completed, they return with this form to their classroom. In other schools, the student completes a shorter problem-solving form in which they simply write how they plan to respond more effectively should this event occur again and how they can come to resolution of the current problem. They take this written statement back to the referring teacher. The key concepts are that students have a way to take a break from the setting in which

"Mr. Johnson certainly makes no attempt to make this any easier."

the problem is occurring and they have an opportunity to consider and eventually discuss with an adult how they can more effectively respond in the future.

In cases where students are not able to move to another setting or when their behavior continues to be disruptive in that setting, it is necessary to involve another educator, such as an administrator or counselor. Again, school staff committed to a problem-solving approach use this as an opportunity to have another person help students understand their behavior and develop new skills. Therefore, the counselor or administrator would problem solve with the student and find an opportunity to meet briefly with the student and teacher to reintegrate the student into the classroom.

School staff must also decide at what point parents or guardians are informed of the student's difficulty in making responsible choices. In most schools where the authors have worked and consulted, the staff set a designated number of problem-solving sessions, after which the parents are informed. For example, parents will be informed when a student has more than three problem-solving events requiring leaving the classroom in any six-week period. Although it is important for students and families to know that school staff will be responsible for helping students develop more responsible behavior, it is also imperative that families know when their children are having difficulty making responsible choices at school. Instances that result in the student needing to work with a counselor or administrator usually require a contact with guardians.

PAUSE
and Consider   **9.4**

If you are observing, student teaching, or interning in a classroom, we recommend you meet with the teacher with whom you are working and separately with the principal or vice principal to discuss the procedures in your school for responding to students who are unable to quietly resolve their problems within your classroom. Write a summary of this and be prepared to share and critique it with a group of at least two other students in your program. This should allow you to understand the procedures you will be expected to follow in your classroom and also to obtain some excellent ideas from other school settings.

Using Problem Solving on the Playground and in Other Common Areas

In elementary school settings, many of the behaviors with which students need assistance occur in common areas, such as the playground, cafeteria, hallways, and restrooms. School staff who use a problem-solving approach to responding to irresponsible student behavior incorporate this approach in all school settings. First, these staff effectively teach all students the behaviors they expect students to display in the common areas. They also find ways to celebrate when students make responsible choices by demonstrating these behaviors. When students make poor choices, these staff work with students to understand why the behavior was a problem and to develop alternative skills.

For example, many schools with whom the authors have worked set aside an area on the playground for students to move to when they are making poor choices. The staff on duty can cue a student to take time to calm down and problem solve. The student then moves to the designated area and remains there until he or she signals the staff member and is ready to share the plan. The student then joins the staff member (who continues to monitor the playground) and shares the plan. If the staff member believes the plan is productive, the staff member or the student writes it on a form indicating the date, time, event, and plan, and the student returns to the playground. As with problem solving in the classroom, when, within a prescribed period of time, students are in-

"If I had this to do over, when she asked, 'Do you boys want to go see the principal?' I would not say, 'Been there, done that.'"

volved in a designated number of instances requiring problem solving in common areas, the parents or guardians are contacted. Similarly, if the student cannot calm down or refuses to go to the problem-solving area, he or she is referred to another educator—usually a counselor or the principal.

The key to using a problem-solving approach is that throughout the school students are held accountable for their behavior in a manner that emphasizes treating students with dignity and helping them develop new skills. The more broadly this approach is implemented, the more effective it will be.

METHODS FOR SOLVING PROBLEMS BETWEEN STUDENTS

Teachers too seldom allow students to work out their own solutions to conflicts involving two or more students. By the third or fourth grade, most children have considerable experience in resolving interpersonal conflicts. Furthermore, students' disagreements are often short-lived. It is not unusual to see younger children who were fighting one minute playing happily together several minutes later. Indeed, adults' attempts to involve children in extensive problem solving about peer conflicts often tend to extend, compound, and intensify the problem. Similarly, when adults provide strong punishment for peer conflicts, they may inadvertently intensify the conflict. Rather than being forgotten, conflicts may linger on as students recall the punishment they received.

Excessive teacher involvement in resolving peer conflicts also suggests that students are unable to resolve their own conflicts. By reinforcing the concept that teachers alone possess the knowledge and skill for solving problems, we inadvertently encourage students to be more dependent. This situation affects both teachers and students negatively. Students are prevented from developing a sense of industry, competence, and power. This interference negatively affects their self-esteem, and students will often find less productive means of demonstrating their power. The effect on teachers is less pronounced but nevertheless notable. Teachers who attempt to solve every minor problem are often inundated with student concerns. This flood not only drains energy but also detracts from the teacher's ability to assist children with their academic tasks.

Given the disadvantages associated with teachers' too frequently or rapidly intervening in peer conflicts, it is useful to examine how to increase students' involvement in this process. The first factor to consider before encouraging students to solve their own conflicts is the degree to which students in the classroom know and like one another. If you have employed a variety of peer-relationship activities, such as those presented in Chapter 4, and if you have implemented cooperative learning, students will be much more likely to work together to solve their own problems. If students are highly competitive, however, or have not been assisted in establishing a positive peer culture, they will normally be much less effective in solving their own problems. Similarly, even when positive peer relations have been established, you should be careful about having two students resolve a conflict if one student has considerably more power or prestige than the other. Unless the more powerful student is very sensitive and willing to use her power to help facilitate a positive solution, the situation may be characterized by negative manipulation. When there is good reason to question the students' ability to obtain a positive resolution, it may be best for you to serve as a third-party facilitator during the discussion.

The actual process of involving students in solving their own conflicts is quite simple. The first step is to discuss the procedure with the class. You can introduce the topic by asking students how they think problems are solved most effectively. When working with older students, you may wish to incorporate a brief discussion of the ways in which nations or individuals in the larger society resolve differences of opinion. The purpose of a discussion is to increase students' involvement in the process while making the point that disagreements are usually most effectively solved by direct communication between the parties. Even when a third party is involved, this person's role is merely to facilitate a productive dialogue between the disagreeing parties. Once the students have discussed this issue, you should inform them that whenever a student comes to you with a problem or you are required to intervene temporarily in an angry interchange between students, they will be asked to set a time to meet to resolve their differences.

It is important to provide adequate structure for these student meetings. You should designate an area of the room where such meetings will take place. The authors know a teacher who tapes two lines on the floor so that students will discuss their differences while remaining far enough apart so that physical contact is discouraged. You may also wish to designate a time when conflict-resolution conferences will take place. Students can be informed that these will occur during recess periods, lunch breaks, or after school. You can also provide students with a worksheet that helps them structure their meeting and clearly report their solution. Figure 9.4 is a form that has been used with children in grades four through eight. Finally, you can help students develop the skills necessary for productive conflict resolution. Students can be taught to use I-messages and active listening. You can also model an effective conflict resolution and can involve the class in role-playing several typical conflicts. This skill building takes very little time, is an enjoyable activity for students, and significantly increases the percentage of conflict-resolution meetings that result in two happy students and a positive solution.

**WORKING
TOGETHER**
to
Solve
Problems

FIGURE 9.4
Problem-Solving
Form

1. What happened that caused the other person to become upset?

Before	*During*	*After*
_____	_____	_____
_____	_____	_____
_____	_____	_____
_____	_____	_____

2. Did the behaviors described above violate a school or classroom rule?

   _____   _____   If so, which one? _____
   no   yes

   _____

3. Did the behaviors help you to positively resolve the problem?

   _____   _____
   no   yes

4. What agreement or plan can you create to resolve the problem? Complete the sentence.

   We have decided that we will _____

   _____

   _____

5. What plan can you develop for preventing future problems? Complete the sentence.

   The next time one of us does something that bothers the other, we will

   _____

   _____

_____	_____	_____
Student 1 signature	Student 2 signature	Date

During the past decade, much progress was made toward implementing peer conflict resolution in the schools. This progress stemmed from the work in the area of community mediation. Finding the courts glutted with cases, lawyers and concerned citizens established community mediation programs to reduce court cases dealing with minor neighborhood disputes. Today, there are more than 400 dispute-resolution programs in existence. Concern about world peace is another factor that stimulated interest in student conflict resolution. Organizations such as Educators for Social Responsibility and programs such as Brooklyn community school district 15's Model Peace Education Program have extended the concept of world peace to conflict resolution in schools.

Many school districts have begun implementing conflict manager programs. In the spring of 1987, the Chicago school district introduced a curriculum on dispute resolution in all of its high schools. The six-week unit includes a focus on interpersonal as well as global conflict resolution. The Conflict Manager Program developed by the Community Board Center in San Francisco is another widely used program. It provides students with sixteen hours of training in communications and problem-solving skills. Students then serve as mediators in their schools. In elementary school buildings, student mediators wear bright conflict manager T-shirts to designate their role.

The authors' son was a conflict manager at his elementary school. The program used a model developed by the Classroom Law Project associated with the Lewis and Clark College Northwestern School of Law in Portland, Oregon. Figure 9.5 shows the

---

FIGURE 9.5
Elementary School Conflict Management Process: Steps for Problem Solving

Source: Classroom Law Project, 6318 S. W. Corbett, Portland, OR 97201. Reprinted with permission.

1. Introduce yourselves: "Hi, my name is _____. I'm a conflict manager and this is my partner _____."
2. Ask the parties: "Do you want to solve the problem with us or with a teacher?" If necessary, move to a quiet place to solve problem.
3. Explain to the parties: "First you have to agree to four rules:
   a. Agree to solve the problem.
   b. No name calling.
   c. Do not interrupt.
   d. Tell the truth."
4. Conflict Manager #1 asks Person #1: "What happened? How do you feel?"
   Conflict Manager #1 repeats what Person #1 said, using active listening: "So, what you're saying is . . ."
5. Conflict Manager #2 asks Person #2: "What happened? How do you feel?"
   Conflict Manager #2 repeats what Person #2 said, using active listening: "So, what you're saying is . . ."
6. Ask Person #1: "Do you have a solution?"
   Ask Person #2: "Do you agree with the solution?"
   If no: "Do you have another solution?" and so on until disputants have reached a solution agreeable to both of them.
7. Have disputants tell each other what they have just agreed to: "So will you tell each other what you've just agreed to?"
8. Congratulate them both: "Thank you for working so hard to solve your problem. Congratulations."
9. Fill out Conflict Manager Report Form.

sequence of interventions elementary students are taught to use when responding to peer conflicts, and Figure 9.6 provides a list of ways to nonviolently resolve a conflict. Figure 9.7 provides an outline on conflict management used in training middle school and high school conflict managers. Additional materials on conflict management are provided at the end of this chapter.

A useful model for helping teachers resolve peer conflicts with students is the think–feel–act model, introduced by Cory Dunn, coordinator of Regional Behavior Supports in Linn, Benton, and Lincoln Counties, Oregon. Figure 9.8 illustrates this method. In implementing this approach, the teacher's role is to allow students to take turns stating their account of what happened, how they felt, and what they believe needs to be done. After each statement, the other student paraphrases the statement so each person experiences a sense of having been heard and understands the other student's point of view. This process will be much easier to implement if students have been taught and practiced the method prior to its implementation.

The following dialogue in which the think–feel–act model was used occurred on the playground following an incident in which a small third grader who had emotional problems was accidentally hit in the face with a ball and had his glasses knocked off. When teaching students to use this method, and whenever convenient when using it with students, it is useful to draw the arrows (as seen in Figure 9.8) to indicate who is speaking and to demonstrate that each student has had an opportunity to speak and be heard.

Teacher Facilitating a Student Problem

PETER: (Crying) He hit me with the ball and broke my glasses.

TEACHER: (Puts arm around Peter) I'm sorry you're hurt. That must have been a surprise to have that ball fly over and hit you. Let's talk to Bill and see what

---

Share
　　WE CAN BOTH DO IT

Take Turns
　　WE CAN DO IT YOUR WAY THIS TIME, MY WAY NEXT

Compromise
　　GIVE UP SOME—GET SOME

Chance
　　FLIP A COIN

Outside Help
　　LET'S ASK A TEAMMATE, CLASSMATE, TEACHER

Postpone
　　LATER—WHEN WE COOL DOWN

Avoid
　　AGREE TO DISAGREE—WITH RESPECT

Humor
　　IS THIS IMPORTANT TO JOE'S TURTLE?

FIGURE 9.6
Eight Modes of Conflict Resolution

Source: Classroom Law Project, 6318 S. W. Corbett, Portland, OR 97201. Reprinted with permission.

FIGURE 9.7
Secondary
Mediation Process

Source: Classroom
Law Project, 6318
S. W. Corbett,
Portland, OR
97201. Reprinted
with permission.

Mediation is a method of conflict resolution that stresses compromise and agreement between two parties rather than one party winning and the other losing. It also gives an opportunity to the parties to come to their own solution to a problem rather than having someone impose a solution on them.

I. INTRODUCTORY PHASE

Purpose: Explain Ground Rules and Procedures
Introduce yourself as a mediator and explain that your role is to help the parties in conflict come to a workable solution that resolves their conflict. Each person will have an opportunity to tell his/her side of the story and to address issues raised by the other party. Explain that you are not here to judge guilt or innocence or to find fault. Emphasize that everything said during the session will be confidential.

   Ask them to agree to ground rules:

1. Don't interrupt
2. No name calling
3. Agree to work towards a solution together
4. Respect each other
5. Remain seated during session
6. Keep everything said during session confidential

Note: Be sure that you have agreement from all parties that they will follow ground rules before you proceed.

II. IDENTIFY THE PROBLEM AND ISSUES

Purpose: Parties Tell What Happened
   Mediator #1 asks first party what happened and how they feel. Mediator paraphrases what the first party said.
   Mediator #2 asks second party what happened and how they feel.
   Mediator #2 paraphrases what the second party said.
   Mediators ask any clarification questions necessary to get additional information about the conflict.

III. UNDERSTANDING THE PROBLEM

Purpose: Parties Talk to Each Other
   Ask parties to paraphrase the other's position and how they feel.
   Ask parties to tell each other what they could do differently to avoid this conflict in future.

IV. SOLUTION SEARCH

Purpose: Parties Brainstorm Solutions
   Mediator #1 asks one party if s/he has a solution to the problem.
   If yes, then mediator asks other party if s/he agrees with that solution.
   If no agreement, other mediator asks other party if s/he has another solution.
      If yes, ask other party if s/he agrees.
   Continue searching for a solution going back and forth between parties until they find a solution to which both parties can agree.
   Ask parties to repeat to each other what they have just agreed to.

V. AGREEMENT

Purpose: Confirm and Write Agreement

Ask parties to sign written agreement specifically articulating what each party will or will not do.

If mediators think follow-up will be needed to ensure that agreement is completed, set up another meeting time to get back together to check in to see how things are going.

VI. FOLLOW-UP

Purpose: To Change Agreement or to Check In to See How It's Going

VII. DEPARTURE

Purpose: End the Mediation Session

If possible, have parties shake hands. Thank them for working so hard to solve their problem and tell them they are free to contact you if problems occur or just to let you know how it's going.

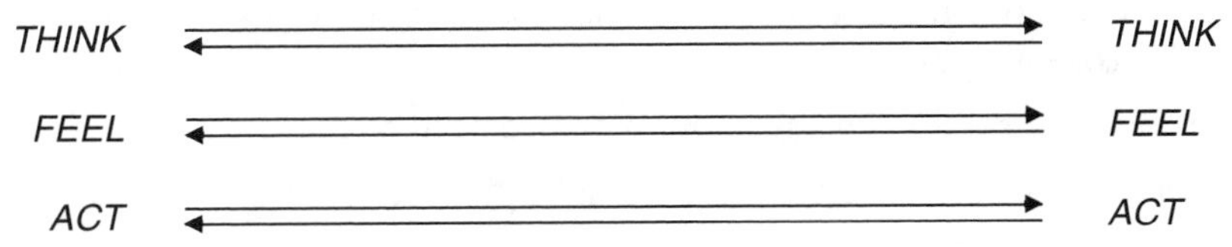

FIGURE 9.7
Continued

FIGURE 9.8
Think–Feel–Act
Method of
Conflict
Resolution

happened. Bill, would you please come here for a minute? (Bill leaves his game and joins the teacher and Peter.) Peter, can you tell Bill what happened?

PETER: You threw a ball and broke my glasses.

TEACHER: Bill, what did Peter tell you he thinks happened?

BILL: I didn't break his glasses. He's just being . . .

TEACHER: (Interrupts Bill) Remember our method for problem solving, Bill. What I need you to do is tell us what you heard Peter say.

BILL: He said I threw a ball and it hit him in the face and broke his glasses.

TEACHER: Thank you, Bill. I appreciate your being responsible and helping us by using the problem-solving method. Now, Bill, would you please tell Peter what you thought happened?

BILL: We were playing catch with the football and John threw it over my head and it hit Peter. I jumped as high as I could to catch it, but it was too high.

TEACHER: Peter, can you tell us what Bill just said?

PETER: He said he didn't hit me with the ball.

TEACHER: What did he say happened?

PETER: He said John threw it over his head and he tried to catch it.

TEACHER: Peter, that was a very good job of stating what Bill said. Now, Peter, can you tell me how you are feeling?

PETER: I'm sad that my glasses are broke and I'm mad that someone broke them.

TEACHER: Bill, can you state back to us how Peter is feeling?

BILL: He's feeling mad and sad because his glasses are broken.

TEACHER: Thank you, Bill. Now, can you tell Peter how you are feeling?

BILL: I don't know.

TEACHER: Well, are you happy, sad, angry?

BILL: I guess I'm sad that his glasses got broken, but I didn't do it.

TEACHER: Peter, can you tell us how Bill said he is feeling?

PETER: He said he is feeling sad but that it's my fault the glasses are broken.

TEACHER: You're right that he said he was sad that your glasses were broken, but he didn't say it was your fault; he said that he did not break them. Okay, Peter, can you tell us what you think we need to do to solve this problem?

PETER: Yes, somebody has to buy me new glasses. My mom will kill me if I come home with broke glasses.

TEACHER: Bill, what did Peter say about what we need to do?

BILL: He said I have to buy him new glasses, but I didn't even break them.

TEACHER: Well, he said someone ought to pay for new glasses. I will take care of checking on the glasses. Bill, what do you think will help to solve this problem?

BILL: Well, I think John and me could apologize and I think we could be more careful about where we throw the ball. But Peter needs to be more careful about where he stands.

TEACHER: Peter, what did Bill just say?

PETER: He said him and John would apologize and be more careful.

TEACHER: Anything else?

PETER: Yah, he said I should look where I stand.

TEACHER: Peter, does that sound like a fair solution to the problem?

PETER: Yah, as long as someone pays for my glasses.

TEACHER: Bill, do you think we've solved the problem?

BILL: Yah.

TEACHER: Okay, boys, why don't you shake hands and then Bill will go over and get John so they can apologize to you, Peter.

The boys shook hands and Bill walked over to explain the situation to John. At this point, Peter took his glasses and started to bend them. In doing this, he realized that he had flexible stems and the stem popped back into place.

PETER: Hey look, they're not busted. They just got bent.

TEACHER: That's great, Peter. I'm really glad. Let's tell Bill and John that when they come over.

Even though using this method takes some time, it is very effective. Not only does this approach allow students to feel heard and help them develop problem-solving skills but it also helps students understand others' points of view and develop skill in identifying their feelings. As mentioned earlier in this chapter, all interventions in response to behavior problems should be educational in nature. This approach helps students develop a number of skills in which most students with behavior problems are deficient.

P A U S E
9.5   *and Consider*

Write a brief statement regarding how you would like to use conflict management with your students. Be specific. Describe the types of student behaviors with which you would use this approach, what approach you would use, how you could incorporate this into your teaching day and classroom management approach. Share and discuss this statement with several colleagues or classmates who teach at a similar grade level.

P A U S E
9.6   *and Consider*

If you decided you would like to implement a conflict resolution approach into your work with students, write a dialogue that provides an example of the approach you would like to use. Share this with a colleague or classmate and obtain feedback. Next, join two colleagues or classmates and actually role-play a situation in which you use the model to assist two students in resolving a conflict.

Dealing with Situations in Which a Student Has Been Victimized

In their book *Early Violence Prevention: Tools for Teachers of Young Children*, Slaby, Roedell, Arezzo, and Henrix (1995) note that when a child is aggressive toward another child, it is important for the adult to provide support for the victim and ensure that reinforcement for the aggressor is minimized. They suggest having the teacher assist the victim in assertively stating his rights to the aggressor. The teacher might say to the victim, "No one is allowed to hurt you for any reason; you can tell him to stop kicking" (p. 70). By telling this to the victim, the teacher is clarifying the rules and also providing the victim with a tool for asserting himself appropriately. This also does not provide attention to the aggressor.

These authors note that, in order to prevent inadvertently reinforcing the offender's behavior by providing immediate teacher attention, it is best to wait before working with this child to teach alternative skills. Ideally, sometime within the next hour, the teacher or other adult will work with the aggressor to examine alternative behaviors for meeting the needs he attempted to meet using the aggressive behavior. It is important that the other children in the room see the teacher supporting the victim and not providing undue attention to the aggressor. If the teacher does work immediately with the aggressor, it is helpful for the other children to see and even overhear the teacher instruct the child in using new skills. For example, the teacher might say, "I understand that you wanted to use the engine. In this class no one can hurt anyone or take anything from someone. If you wanted to play with it, how could you have asked Rolando if you could share it with him or use it?"

Likewise, the teacher may want to assist the victim in developing skills for responding assertively when another child is being aggressive. This may involve sending a firm I-message or telling the aggressor he needs to see an adult for a conflict-resolution meeting. It will often be helpful to teach such skills to all students as part of the procedures for solving conflicts nonaggressively.

When considering how to respond to disruptive behavior, it is important to keep in mind the importance of reinforcing the appropriate behavior. For example, if a child has quite consistently attempted to join a game by grabbing the ball or is dominating play, and instead asks to join and takes a more moderate role in the activity, it is important to catch the student being effective, label this skill, and point out the positive consequences associated with this new behavior. It is important not only to label the positive consequences for the child but also for other children and the teacher. Therefore, the teacher might state, "I enjoyed watching you play and have fun today. The other children seemed to like having you play with them and enjoyed the way you took turns with them."

Bullying is a common problem in many schools today. The references at the end of this chapter provide resources for preventing and responding to this issue within your school. Kauffman (1997) described the following features of effective programs:

- A school climate characterized by a warm, positive, supportive school atmosphere in which adults set clear and firm limits on unacceptable behavior
- Nonhostile, nonphysical sanctions applied immediately and consistently to violation of behavioral expectations.
- Continuous monitoring and surveillance of student activities in and around the school
- Adult mediation of student interactions and assumption of authority to stop bullying when it is observed
- Discussion of the issue of bullying with bullies, victims, parents, and neutral students (nonparticipants) to clarify school values, expectations, procedures, and consequences (p. 365)

We would add the importance of providing all students with skills for being assertive when confronted with this type of behavior and the value of providing bullies with specific skills for meeting their needs without using aggressive behavior. The situation of bullying is also an excellent example of the value of conducting a functional assessment (see Chapter 10). It is important to know what situations exist that may be causing the problem (are other students victimizing the student, or is the student feeling isolated and rejected?) as well as the function this behavior is serving for the student. Our interventions must deal with both of these issues by providing a more inviting and caring community for the student and providing the student with skills to meet his or her needs without violating the rights of others.

METHODS FOR GROUP PROBLEM SOLVING

Class Meetings

Class meetings allow both teacher and students to resolve problems openly and before they become major issues that negatively affect learning. Whenever people live close together for many hours every day, it is important that time be taken to resolve minor conflicts openly. Like an automobile engine that may appear to run smoothly but will suddenly boil over unless properly lubricated, classrooms require proper maintenance checks and minor tune-ups. When implemented in a positive, supportive atmosphere, class meetings serve as the lubricant for a smoothly running classroom.

Class meetings are an integral part of a program designed to involve students in solving their own problems. Class meetings not only support the use of individual problem-solving conferences but can also provide students with opportunities for improving their social and problem-solving skills.

The use of class meetings will vary with grade level. The ideas presented in the following section are most appropriate for middle school block or elementary classes in which teachers have major responsibility for the social and academic skill development of twenty-five to thirty-five students. Class meetings can also be an important component in other middle school and high school classrooms. Because students at this age spend less time with one group of students, however, and are more sensitive to peer responses, it is generally best to focus on instructional or behavioral matters affecting the entire class, while handling individual student problems in private meetings with the teacher and one or a few students. Class meetings will generally be held less often in secondary school classrooms, and the agenda will usually be presented by the teacher. Students can be encouraged to bring problems to our attention and request that the problem be discussed by the class.

Nevertheless, it is important not to underestimate the value of class meetings in secondary schools. Students have numerous concerns such as the length and timing of homework assignments, the quality of classroom instruction, and relationships in the classroom, which can most effectively be dealt with as a community. A key decision teachers make regarding student behavior is whether issues that affect the group, and are almost always being discussed by members of the group outside of the classroom setting, can be productively discussed and resolved during class time. We believe strongly that it is important to teach students how a group can resolve conflicts or solve problems. Involvement in resolving group concerns enhances students' sense of competence and empowerment and provides important modeling of a lifelong skill.

Although the guidelines presented next apply to elementary or middle school classes, they can be modified for secondary school settings. For example, in most cases secondary teachers will hold meetings when a problem

"This is Wally. He's representing us in our homework negotiations."

arises and will simply work with students to (1) state the problem, (2) brainstorm possible solutions, and (3) select a solution. Recently, a teacher with whom the authors were working decided to bring to her high school class her frustration with the limited space available for group work with thirty-nine students in the class. The students decided they would select a committee to design a classroom arrangement that would facilitate group work and to develop procedures for groups working effectively in a small space. The results were thoughtful, creative, and very useful for the class. Additionally, students were excited about having solved their own problem and were willing to follow the guidelines they had established.

Guidelines for Implementing a Class Meeting

The first step in implementing class meetings is to discuss the concept with students. Students should be informed that class meetings will provide them with an opportunity to discuss things they like about the class as well as things that may need to be changed in order for the class to run more smoothly. Ask students to develop their own list of reasons they think meetings are important. It is important to display enthusiasm and express interest in holding class meetings.

Once students have discussed why class meetings are helpful and are excited about holding their first meeting, present the general guidelines for class meetings. Although we encourage you to create your own guidelines, the authors have found the following guidelines useful for elementary and middle school class meetings:

1. Class meetings will be held in a tight circle with all participants (including the teacher) seated in the circle. The circle must not be too large or it will detract from students' involvement and encourage off-task behavior.

2. All problems relating to the class as a group can be discussed. Problems between two or three individuals, however, will be resolved outside the class meeting unless this problem has an effect on the class.

3. An agenda will be created prior to every class meeting. The agenda is created by students' writing the topic on a clipboard. Students must sign their names behind the agenda item. Students do not list other students' names but merely the issue to be readdressed. (If the children cannot write, they can tell you the item and you can place it on the agenda.) The items will be discussed in the order in which they appear on the board. If an agenda item no longer applies when the meeting is held, however, it will be deleted from the list.

4. Discussions during class meetings are always directed toward arriving at a solution that is not a punishment. The goal of class meetings is to find positive solutions to problems and not to criticize people or occurrences in the classroom.

5. If an individual student's behavior is listed on the agenda, the item will not be discussed without the student's permission. If the student agrees to have a behavior discussed, you should emphasize that the goal of the meeting is to help the student. Be sure that students' statements focus on the youngster's behavior and are presented as I-messages rather than as judgmental statements about the youngster or the behavior. The focus should always be on providing the student with sensitive, thoughtful feedback and positive suggestions for altering behavior.

Students should be informed that several options are available to those who choose not to have their behavior discussed at a class meeting. First, the student may leave the room while the other students attempt to devise an approach for helping the student. You may then wish to tape-record the discussion and share it with the student during an individual conference. Second, the student may choose to discuss the problem with you and a small group of concerned students. With the student's permission, the results of this discussion can be shared with the entire class at the next class meeting. Finally, the student can discuss the problem with you and design a plan for alleviating the problem.

6. Students' responsibilities during class meetings include (a) raising hands and being called on to speak; (b) listening to the speaker and not talking while someone else is speaking; (c) staying on the topic until it has been completed; (d) being involved by sharing ideas that will help the group; and (e) using positive, supportive words to discuss the problem and solutions.

7. The teacher will initially serve as facilitator for the class meetings.

Meeting Frequency and Length

It is best to hold class meetings whenever the agenda indicates that a meeting is necessary. Students should be assisted in listing only issues that are important to the smooth functioning of the classroom. Nevertheless, in an elementary classroom it is possible that a class meeting may be held once or twice a week. Because unresolved issues will only create problems that will significantly detract from students' learning, time spent in class meetings is usually rewarded with increased on-task behavior and the associated academic gains. A class meeting should be held at least once a week regardless of whether an agenda exists. A weekly meeting is necessary to maintain students' interest and skills as well as to reinforce the concept that the group is a valuable source of ideas and solutions. If no agenda exists, you can involve the class in a discussion of the positive aspects of the week. Similarly, you may wish to instigate a positive sharing activity and praise the class for having a positive, problem-free week.

The length of class meetings will vary according to the students' attention spans. Most primary grade teachers find that their meetings can last between ten and twenty minutes, and intermediate grade teachers find thirty minutes optimal. Middle school teachers or specialists in elementary schools who meet with a class five hours or fewer a week often choose to hold class meetings on a biweekly basis or to limit weekly meetings to fifteen minutes so that meetings will not take up a significant portion of instructional time.

Starting Class Meetings

Begin the first class meeting by reviewing the purpose and general guidelines for class meetings. During the initial meetings, it is very important to monitor students' behaviors carefully to ensure that general procedures and responsibilities are followed so that meetings run smoothly and students develop good habits. In order to ensure that initial meetings are viewed as positive and useful, be sure each agenda item is clearly resolved. Do so by asking several students to paraphrase the solution and ask for the group's commitment to carry out any plans that are developed. You may even initially wish to record each decision and post it in a prominent place in the room so that the class is reminded of their decision. A positive feeling can also be enhanced by closing each meeting on a positive note. You can do this by asking each student to state one nice thing that has happened to him or her or that he or she did for someone since the last meeting. Similarly, the group can be asked to say one nice thing about each member of the group.

Reinforce the value of students' solutions by beginning each meeting with a discussion on the results of solutions developed at the previous meeting. Unless students believe that their solutions are useful, they will understandably soon lose interest in class meetings. Furthermore, because class meetings are designed to teach problem-solving skills, it is important to reinforce students' successful efforts, analyze their failures, and help them develop increasingly effective solutions.

Increasing Students' Involvement in Class Meetings

Because a major goal in implementing class meetings is to teach students skills involved in functioning effectively in a problem-solving group, it is desirable to increase gradually their responsibility for facilitating class meetings. This is difficult to do with primary grade children, but third-grade students can be taught to run their own class meetings. The authors have found that these four steps provide a successful approach to having students take over the class meeting:

1. After leading approximately ten class meetings, present students with a handout describing the major functions a leader serves when facilitating a group meeting (Figure 9.9). Discuss each function and behavior with the class and inform them that they will soon be asked to lead their own meetings by having students serve these important functions.

2. Introduce an agenda item or classroom problem. While the class discusses this situation, point out and define each intervention you make. Because you continue to serve all three functions, the discussion will be interrupted on numerous occasions. Students are usually excited about learning the new skills, however, and enjoy your instructional interventions.

3. After running three or four actual class meetings in which you consistently point out the function of each intervention, meet with and teach one student the role of discussion leader. At the next meeting, this student serves as the discussion leader while you maintain the other roles. Prior to the next meeting, you meet with another student who learns the role of task observer. At the following meeting, the student serves this function. After this meeting, you instruct a third student in the role of behavior and feeling observer, and at the following meeting you become a group member who abides by the group responsibilities while the students run the meeting.

4. Students should function in a role for five or six meetings so that they can master the skills associated with the role and effectively model it for other students. If a student has difficulty with a role, take time between meetings to instruct the student in the skills associated with the role. Providing students with this type of experience requires a small amount of time and considerable restraint and patience, but students respond to their new skills by becoming more positive, productive class members. Indeed, behavior-problem children often respond especially well, for they gain self-esteem and peer acceptance when serving as productive participants in class meetings.

FIGURE 9.9
Class Meeting Jobs

Discussion Leader
1. Make sure everyone is comfortable and all distracting things are out of the way.
2. Make sure everyone can see all others in the circle.
3. Give the speaker time to get his or her point across.
4. Give the speaker a nod or a smile.
5. Ask clarifying questions:
   a. Are you saying that . . . ?
   b. Do you feel that . . . ?
6. Summarize:
   a. Is there anything else you would like to say?
   b. Would someone briefly summarize what has been said?

Task Observer
1. Make sure the task gets finished on time.
2. Watch the time.
3. Make suggestions of alternatives to solve the problem.
4. Point out behaviors that do not help in solving a problem.
5. Listen carefully and understand what the discussion leader is doing.
6. Understand the agenda and call out each agenda item.

Behavior and Feeling Observer
1. How did this discussion make you feel?
2. What could we do now? What might help us?
3. Was anything asked that caused you, _____ (name of person), to be concerned?
   Can you tell us what it was and how you felt about it?
4. _____ (person's name), you usually help us out. Do you have any ideas for this problem?
5. Has anyone thought of new ideas for improving our discussions?
6. How many of you feel that the discussion was of value to you? Why?

Case Study: The Bad, the Good, and the Ugly—A Young Teacher's Attempt to Use a Problem-Solving Approach

The following example suggests why even an effectively implemented problem-solving sequence can be undermined if the staff has not decided to consistently support such an approach. This example was presented to one of the authors by a young, very skilled intern who was enrolled in a classroom management course. This is intended to provide an example of how problem solving can both work effectively and be undermined by the lack of an effective schoolwide student management plan. The account is presented exactly as written except the names have been changed.

Ironically enough, I had an opportunity to utilize Glasser's problem-solving approach the day after we had our classroom discussions and role-playing concerning this procedure. On Wednesday morning, I was finishing some math preparation at school while most of the students were gone from the classroom. When the students returned from band, I watched them enter and talked with them in order to see how they were doing. Transition

"How come when you say we have a problem, I'm always the one who has the problem?"

times can sometimes be a problem for them, so, whenever possible, I like to try and get a jump on any grievances. Suddenly Jeremy stormed into the classroom, sat down loudly in his chair, stood up again, and approached Rolando very aggressively. Rolando attempted to retreat, but Jeremy kept following him. At this point, I intercepted the two boys and asked them what the problem was. Jeremy, who has a difficult time controlling his anger, pushed me aside and punched Rolando on the shoulder. I was forced to restrain Jeremy, lest he inflict any more punches on Rolando, but I did tell him that he had chosen this action of mine as a result of his actions. I also told him repeatedly that when he had calmed down I could release him and we could talk about what had happened. A few seconds later, Jeremy was somewhat diffused so I took the two boys down to the office. Using Glasser's method, I talked with Jeremy first since he had been the aggressor within the classroom. Our conversation went something like this:

TEACHER: I'm glad you feel able to talk about what happened and I'm sure we can figure out a plan that will help you. I like having you in class, especially since you have many special interests to share with the class, so I'd like us to try to solve this problem together.

JEREMY: (Nods)

TEACHER: What happened in the classroom? What did you do that is against a school rule?

JEREMY: I hit Rolando, but I was mad because . . . [Since Jeremy infrequently has a voice in these matters, I had him tell me the story of what had led up to the classroom confrontation. Jeremy said that he and Rolando had been playing around, but then Rolando pushed him away and kicked him repeatedly, even after Jeremy told him to stop.]

TEACHER: I'm glad you first told him to stop kicking you. That is a good, nonviolent way to deal with a problem. What happened then?

JEREMY: I was really mad, so I went after Rolando. He tried to get away, but I was really mad, so I hit him.

TEACHER: Yeah, I saw that part. How did hitting Rolando help you solve the problem?

JEREMY: I was mad, so I hit him.

TEACHER: But did that resolve your problem? How did you feel after you hit Rolando?

JEREMY: Not very good. I feel sorry about it. I thought I might have hurt him.

TEACHER: Yeah, I felt that way too. It must feel a little scary to be out of control like that too, huh?

JEREMY: (Nods and starts to cry a little.)

TEACHER: Do you think that hitting Rolando helped him see your point of view?

JEREMY: No. He probably felt scared.

TEACHER: And hitting is against one of our school rules, isn't it?

JEREMY: Yes.

TEACHER: OK. Thanks for being honest about all of that and for telling me about what happened. That helps me to see the whole picture. I also like the way you told Rolando to stop kicking you rather than just hitting him right away. We need to think of a plan for what you can do when it doesn't work to just tell someone to stop.

JEREMY: I could run away and calm down. [Jeremy does this already, but he tends to run away from school, dashing out the door and into the neighborhood during the middle of the school day. I think he feels unwanted and finds the school environment so stressful that he needs to escape.]

TEACHER: That's a good strategy, to just walk away from the situation. But that might be a bit hard to do sometimes. Can you think of another idea, in case you find it hard to just walk away?

JEREMY: I could tell someone about it.

TEACHER: That's a good idea! Who do you think you could talk to?

JEREMY: I don't know. No one really. I could talk to you but you're not always here.

TEACHER: Yeah, that's a hard thing, isn't it? I would be glad to help because I enjoy working with you. Can you think of two other adults you can work with when I'm not here?

JEREMY: I guess I could talk to either the gym teacher or the science teacher.

TEACHER: That sounds like a good plan. What are the strategies we've talked about so far?

JEREMY: Well, first I tell the person to stop. If that doesn't work, then I can walk away or tell you about it.

TEACHER: And what if I'm not here?

JEREMY: Then I tell the science teacher or the gym teacher.

TEACHER: Do you feel that you can agree to this plan?

JEREMY: Yes.

TEACHER: I'm glad to hear that. Thank you very much for being so honest and for helping so much. You are really being responsible for your behavior. Is there anything you need me to do in order to help?

JEREMY: Talk to Rolando, too.

TEACHER: Yes, I have planned to do that. I'll do that right now, and then I'll bring us all together and we can talk about it, OK?

JEREMY: OK.

At this point, I had a similar discussion with Rolando, who provided me with a few more details surrounding the story. Evidently Rolando and another student were having a contest to see who could open their lockers the fastest, and this other student asked Jeremy to hold Rolando. Jeremy obliged, much to Rolando's displeasure, and Rolando told Jeremy to stop. When Jeremy did not, Rolando pushed him away and kicked him a few times. In this case, Rolando's response to the problem warranted a discussion similar to the one I had just completed with Jeremy. Rolando came up with a plan similar to Jeremy's: He would first give a verbal warning, making sure the person heard it (Rolando admitted that it had been loud in the hall, and that Jeremy may not have heard him), and then he would tell a teacher about it.

After this individual conference with Rolando, I brought the two boys together and we talked about what had happened, how they felt about it, and what plans they had developed to prevent future problems. We all agreed that it had been a productive meeting. I told them both that in a few days I would ask them how their plans were proceeding. The two boys shook hands to conclude the meeting.

Throughout this process of problem solving, I had been communicating with the principal in order to make sure I was not overstepping his jurisdiction. He told me to handle the situation as best I could, but when the meeting was over, he wanted to know exactly what I had done. Therefore, after I was finished talking with Jeremy and Rolando, I told the principal how the problem had been solved and how positive I felt about it. At this point, the principal said, "Well, you know they'll have to be punished for their actions." I felt very frustrated by this comment, because it seemed to carry the implicit message: "Well, now that you've done the 'cute' problem-solving stuff, let's get down to the *real* solution." I did not agree with this idea, because I did not feel that a punishment would help them to solve future problems. In talking with the boys, it was obvious to me that both of them needed appropriate strategies and skills for solving their problems, not token punishments. I was not sure how to say this to the principal, however, since his conversational tone left me feeling rather intimidated. He offered a few "acceptable" punishments and left me to choose one for the two boys. I decided to have them stay inside with me during their fifteen-minute lunch recess. Besides being on the principal's "acceptable" list, this would allow us to spend time talking about a variety of topics that would give the boys an opportunity to learn more about each other. In addition, I would have a chance to see how the two would interact together in a more informal setting.

After lunch, I noticed that something was amiss when the principal called me into his office. He stated that he had heard some "new information" pertaining to the altercation between the boys, and he asked me to restate what had happened. After he heard the story from me again, he called the boys down to his office and basically gave them a rather emotional lecture, using sarcastic language and demeaning statements. The principal then said that both boys would be getting referrals, which meant a parent contact for Rolando and an in-school suspension for Jeremy. The principal also told Jeremy, "Now you'll be just one step away from a week-long suspension. Wasn't it just two weeks ago when I had to suspend you from the bus? When are you going to get the message, Jeremy?"

At this point the principal dismissed Rolando back to class and Jeremy to the office chair. He then told me to fill out the two referral forms. He said, "No need to be real extensive about it, just write down what basically happened." I completed the forms and asked if he at least could record that I had held a problem-solving conference with the two boys, during which they had developed thoughtful individual plans for preventing further problems. He agreed.

This example presents not only a situation in which a teacher effectively used problem solving but also an instance in which the lack of a coordinated, congruent approach to assisting students in resolving behavior problems negatively influenced the relationship and sense of empowerment experienced by two students and a teacher. This type of situation can be prevented by staff working collaboratively to develop a schoolwide student management plan.

IMPLEMENTATION ACTIVITIES

Activity 9.1 will enable you to examine whether your responses to student behavior problems assist students in feeling positive about the learning environment and developing new skills.

ACTIVITY 9.1

Examining Your Responses to Unproductive Student Behavior

Take a moment to recall several recent incidents in which students in your classroom, or under your supervision in a common area such as a cafeteria, were involved in inappropriate behavior that violated the rights of other students and that caused you to speak to the students. For these situations answer the following questions:

Did my response model effective adult communication?

Did my response assist the student in feeling valued?

Did my response tend to deescalate the student?

Was my response dignifying to the student?

Did my response provide the student with an opportunity to express his or her thoughts or feelings?

Did my response help the student develop a new skill that could be used should a similar situation arise?

Could I recommend to the student's parent or guardian that they use a response similar to the one I used?

If my administrator needed to talk to me regarding a behavior of mine he or she thought was a concern, would I want this person to use a response similar to the ones I used in responding to my students?

Did the student leave the situation feeling positive about school and prepared to learn?

Did my response provide the student with a model he or she could use as an adult when involved in dealing with a problem in the workplace or home?

As mentioned earlier, one advantage to using a systematic approach to solving problems is that the adults can evaluate their use of the process. Activity 9.2 can help you analyze your effectiveness in employing Glasser's model.

ACTIVITY 9.2

Analyzing
a Glasser
Problem-Solving
Dialogue

Choose a student who is acting inappropriately in the classroom and solve the problem using Glasser's model. Do not choose the most disruptive student, for the model will be learned more effectively if it is initially used to solve less serious problems. At a later time it may be useful to employ this approach with an extremely disruptive youngster and incorporate one or more of the strategies presented in Chapter 10 into the plan.

Analyze your problem-solving interaction by answering the questions listed below. This examination will help clarify exactly how the interchange progressed. Although it will be impossible to report the dialogue verbatim, summarize the essence of each stage as specifically and accurately as possible.

Step 1   What activities or approaches have you used to help the student feel that you care about her?

Step 2   Record the dialogue that occurred as you attempted to help the student describe her behavior. Try to recall accurately the questions you asked and the answers you received.

Step 3   Record the dialogue that occurred as you attempted to help the student make a value judgment.

Step 4   Record the dialogue that took place while you helped the student make a plan, and write the plan that was finally developed.

Step 5   Record the manner in which you asked the student to make a commitment to the plan. Was the student's agreement enthusiastic? Why or why not?

Step 6   How soon after the plan was made did you follow up? Record the interaction that took place during the follow-up.

Step 7   Did you use sarcasm or punish the student? If so, explain the circumstances. If the plan was not effective, record the dialogue that occurred when you confronted the student with the problem. Did you start at Step 1? Were you nonpunitive?

If your intervention was successful, write three reasons you think the model worked for you and the student.

If the use of this method was not effective, carefully examine your analysis of each step. Also, ask yourself these questions:

Do you accept the basic assumptions presented at the beginning of this chapter?
Were you helping the students solve the problem, or were you solving the problem for them?
Was your problem-solving interaction positive and nonpunitive?

Having analyzed the dialogue and answered these questions, list three reasons the approach did not work for you in this case. Do not list factors involving the student; focus on your own behavior.

SUMMARY

The concept of problem solving as a major focus for responding to inappropriate student behavior has existed for more than thirty years. However, experience as well as reviews of the research suggest that it has been systematically implemented into a surprisingly small percentage of teachers' classroom management plans and schoolwide student management systems. This is unfortunate because, when properly applied, problem solving responds to a number of important socioemotional needs of students and helps remediate a wide range of skill deficits experienced by many students who consistently behave unproductively in school.

Fortunately, an increased emphasis on conflict resolution and research supporting its benefits in reducing classroom discipline problems have helped create a positive climate for the use of problem solving. This chapter describes several specific methods for incorporating problem solving into a classroom management plan as well as ideas for using this approach to resolve peer conflicts. The authors' experience indicates that teachers who use these approaches are impressed with the positive student attitudes they generate as well as with their students' abilities to solve problems and take responsibility for their behavior.

RECOMMENDED READING

Girard, K., & Kock, S. (1996). *Conflict resolution in the schools: A manual for educators.* San Francisco, CA: Jossey-Bass.

Glasser, W. (1986). *Control theory in the classroom.* New York: Harper & Row.

Glasser, W. (1990). *The quality school: Managing students without coercion.* New York: Harper & Row.

Hoover, J., & Oliver, R. (1996). *The bullying prevention handbook: A guide for principals, teachers, and counselors.* Bloomington, IN: National Educational Service.

Johnson, D., & Johnson, R. (1991). *Teaching students to be peacemakers.* Edina, MN: Interaction Book Co.

Johnson, D., & Johnson, R. (1995). *Reducing school violence through conflict resolution.* Alexandria, VA: Association for Supervision and Curriculum Development.

Johnson, D., Johnson, R., Dudley, B., & Burnett, R. (1992). Teaching students to be peer mediators. *Educational Leadership, 59*(1), 10–13.

King, R., & Squire, R. (1994). *Face to face: Conflict resolution in school, bullying at school: Strategies for prevention* (videos). Toronto, Canada: King Squire Films Limited, 94 Borden Street, Toronto, Ontario, Canada, M5S 2N1.

Kreidler, W. (1990). *Elementary perspectives #1: Teaching concepts of peace and conflict.* Cambridge, MA: Educators for Social Responsibility.

Long, N., Wood, M., & Fescer, F. (2001). Life space crisis intervention: Talking with children and youth to improve relationships and change behavior (2nd ed.). Austin, TX: Pro-Ed.

Mendler, A. (1992). *What do I do when . . . ? How to achieve discipline with dignity in the classroom.* Bloomington, IN: National Educational Service.

Nelson, R. (1996). Designing schools to meet the needs of students who exhibit disruptive behavior. *Journal of Emotional and Behavioral Disorders, 4,* 147–161.

Nelson, R., Crabtree, M., Marchand-Martella, N., & Martella, R. (1998). Teaching good behavior in the whole school. *Teaching Exceptional Children, 30,* 4–9.

Olweus, D. (1993). *Bullying at school: What we know and what we can do.* Oxford, England: Blackwell.

Rigby, K. (1996). *Bullying and what to do about it.* Melbourne, Australia: The Australian Council for Educational Research.

Schrumph, F., Crawford, D., & Usadel, H. (1991). *Peer mediation: Conflict resolution in schools.* Champaign, IL: Research Press.

Sugai, G., Horner, R., & Gresham, F. (2002). Behaviorally effective school environments. In M. R. Shinn, G. Stoner, & H. M. Walker (Eds.). *Interventions for academic and behavior problems: Preventive and remedial approaches* (pp. 315–350). Silver Springs, MD: National Association of School Psychologists.

10

Developing Individual Behavior Change Plans

Strategies for managing problem behavior in the classroom are increasingly emphasizing directly teaching adaptive behavior patterns. A basic assumption underlying this trend is that many students, particularly at-risk students, have not learned the essential competencies required for school success.

—Hill Walker, Geoff Colvin, and Elizabeth Ramsey (1995)
Antisocial Behavior in School: Strategies and Best Practices

When goals are humane, we must offer the most effective means available to reach them. In many cases, the proven effectiveness of applied behavior analysis procedures makes them the most humane choice.

—Paul Alberto and Anne Troutman (1999)
Applied Behavior Analysis for Teachers

The classical behaviorism of the early 70s, with its emphasis on reinforcers and consequences, has given way to cognitive behaviorism with its focus on self-management and social skills training.

—Vern Jones (1996)
Classroom Management
Handbook of Research on Teacher Education

Students occasionally need highly structured programs to help them change specific behaviors. A few students require our continuing efforts to help them acquire and demonstrate acceptable behavior. Classroom teachers cannot be expected to spend large amounts of time implementing behavior change programs, but to be effective, teachers must be able to incorporate behavior management methods that have proved effective in the classroom. When implemented in classroom settings characterized by supportive interpersonal relationships and instruction matched to students' needs, these methods frequently have dramatic positive effects on students' behaviors.

The increased emphasis on inclusion of students experiencing behavior problems and the increasing number of students living in families that are experiencing serious turmoil or adjustment problems have created a situation in which teachers are asked to work with many children who require considerable help in developing appropriate behaviors. Therefore, teachers need the skills described in this chapter. Teachers should not, however, use these methods unless they have first created a classroom in which all students are accepted by the teacher and their peers, classroom rules and procedures have been agreed on and are consistently monitored, students are involved in interesting work at which they can succeed, and problem solving is taught and consistently used. Employing behavioristic interventions to manipulate students into behaving docilely in an environment that does not meet their personal–psychological and academic needs is unprofessional. Employing individualized behavior change plans to help students adjust to a positive learning environment, however, is an important part of being a competent teacher.

Many educators express concern about using structured procedures to assist students in altering their behaviors. They believe this is not their role or that it is too intrusive to develop a specific intervention to help children change their behavior. This is particularly true when some form of extrinsic reinforcement is used to encourage or motivate the students to alter their behaviors.

> These concerns deserve careful consideration. Yet, they must be weighed against the pressing needs and rights of the young child who is highly aggressive to receive the most effective and timely intervention possible, as well as the equally important needs of classmates to be protected from that child's aggression. (Slaby et al., 1995, p. 83)

Just as we often modify academic work and provide children with special programs and tutors to assist them in the essential skills of reading, writing, and mathematics, we need to use a variety of interventions to assist students in developing the skills needed to become accepted and productive members of the classroom group. When children do not have these skills, they not only are prevented from reaching their academic potential but also they often prevent the teacher and other students from doing their best work. Everyone loses when we fail to develop individual behavior change plans for students whose behavior is disrupting the learning environment.

From 1998 to 2000 the senior author worked in the Vancouver, Washington, school district as resource coordinator for programs serving students with behavior problems. In this capacity he assisted not only teachers in twenty-two classrooms serving students with serious behavior disorders but also worked extensively with principals, teachers, counselors, school psychologists, physicians, and parents to develop individual behavior intervention programs aimed at enabling students to remain in their mainstream classrooms. He was immensely impressed with teachers' desires to assist students and their willingness to modify classroom routines in order to accomplish this. It was also obvious that teachers needed support in developing the intervention plans required to assist these students. The most effective approach to develop these skills was to work with a team of educators who collaborated to develop an individualized intervention plan for a student experiencing serious and ongoing behavior problems.

We are often asked what process to follow when a teacher has concerns regarding a student's behavior. We recommend the following approach:

1. Collect data regarding the behavior. How often does it happen? Under what conditions does it occur? What factors do you think may be influencing the behavior?
2. Meet with the student to conduct a problem-solving session such as that described in Chapter 9. Make sure you and the student have developed a specific plan.
3. Continue to collect data regarding the frequency of the problem behavior.
4. Follow up with the student to discuss how the plan is working.
5. If the behavior is not improving, develop a behavior intervention plan such as those described in this chapter.
6. Continue to collect data.
7. If the behavior still negatively impacts the student's learning or the learning of other students, meet with a team (often several other teachers, a counselor or school psychologist, and an administrator) to discuss the situation and develop a plan.
8. Throughout this process, continue to utilize your classroom management and schoolwide student management plan. Simply because you and the student are involved in problem solving and you have developed a plan to assist the student does not eliminate the student's responsibility for his behavior.

This chapter presents the key ingredients for developing plans for students whose behavior continues to negatively influence their learning and that of other students. It begins with a discussion of the use of behavior change interventions. Next, we discuss the concept of correctly identifying the problem behaviors and analyzing the factors that may be causing the student to use inappropriate behaviors (often termed *functional assessment*). This is followed by a discussion of several cognitive behavioral strategies that can assist students in developing important new social skills. Finally, we discuss the team planning process that can facilitate the development of individualized behavior change intervention plans.

BEHAVIOR MANAGEMENT IN PERSPECTIVE

Behavioristic interventions have, in many ways, been misunderstood by teachers. On the one hand, some teachers have viewed behavioristic methods as a complex, time-consuming approach that nevertheless held the answer to all their discipline problems. On the other hand, many teachers have viewed behaviorism as a manipulative, overly repressive approach to working with students. The answer lies somewhere between these extremes. Behavioristic methods cannot and should not solve all discipline problems. There is no substitute for effective teaching in a caring environment. Behaviorism, though, is also not necessarily a mechanistic, manipulative science. Rather, it can be used to help teachers better understand students' behaviors and improve them by applying consistent positive and logical consequences to students' behaviors. Furthermore, many behavioristic interventions are relatively simple and can be applied quickly and comfortably in a classroom setting.

Most teachers today will be asked to work with a wide range of students with special needs. Whether these students are identified as having fetal alcohol effect, a conduct disorder, attention deficit hyperactivity disorder, or are simply one of millions of students who are in need of some special structure or social skill training, teachers need a repertoire of skills to assist these students. In their thoroughly researched and practical book, *Antisocial Behavior in School: Strategies and Best Practices*, Walker, Colvin, and Ramsey (1995) provide a sound description of both the problem and the multitude of strategies teachers can use to assist those students most in need of their help. Although it may be fashionable or lucrative to criticize behavioral interventions, anyone who has spent years teaching knows that some

"Actually, it's a rather old form of behavior modification therapy."

students desperately need the assistance provided by behavioral interventions thoughtfully applied within the context of a caring classroom community.

As Alberto and Troutman (1999) point out in their book, *Applied Behavior Analysis for Teachers*, the goal of the effective use of behavioral principles is to increase, not decrease, options available to students. Students who are failing their courses have fewer options for attending advanced schooling or obtaining a job. Students who are constantly disruptive and have difficulty focusing on academic tasks may be limiting their options for participating in sports, having free time after school, or developing prosocial behaviors that will help them in the future.

The relationship between behavior and the environment is reciprocal. Students who are involved in behaviors that negatively impact their own learning and violate the rights of others are less likely to be successful learners or to have a wide range of friendship options. Empowering students to develop new skills for managing their behaviors opens rather than closes doors for them. The methods presented in this chapter can and should be implemented in a manner that engages and empowers students while treating them with dignity. These methods also increase students' freedom and positive sense of self.

As discussed throughout this book, a skilled and caring educator provides each student with the assistance she or he needs. This means assessing the student's personal, emotional, and intellectual skills and working with the student, parents, and other educators to provide the best possible educational program. For many students this will include the interventions described in this chapter.

Basic Assumptions Underlying Behavioristic Interventions

Behaviorism is really more a rationale and a methodology than a specific set of procedures. It is based on examining specific data and applying experimentally validated procedures in order to alter behavior. Quite simply, behaviorism is a scientific approach to changing behavior. This approach is based on three major assumptions: (1) behavior is influenced by the antecedents and consequences associated with the behavior; (2) behavior change programs must focus on specific, observable behavior; and (3) data collection is necessary in order to alter behavior thoughtfully and systematically.

Behavior Is Influenced by the Antecedents and Consequences Associated with the Behavior

Behaviorists acknowledge the importance of both antecedents and consequences. Regarding consequences, or events following a behavior, behavioral research has developed three basic rules through careful studies of human behavior: (1) a behavior followed immediately by a reward will occur more frequently, (2) a behavior will be extinguished when it is no longer reinforced, and (3) a behavior followed closely by an undesirable consequence will occur less often. Behaviorists, however, do not ignore antecedent or stimulus conditions. Students cannot be reinforced for producing a behavior unless they possess the ability to emit the behavior. Therefore, we must create positive environments in which students will risk trying new behaviors and must systematically provide children with assistance in gradually developing new skills.

Behavior Change Programs Must Focus on Specific, Observable Behavior

If we wish to help students develop new skills or eliminate undesired behaviors thoughtfully and systematically, we must deal with specific, observable behavior. It is not helpful to either teacher or student to state that the student is disruptive and incorrigible. It is much more helpful if we state that the student will learn more and be better liked by peers if he can reduce the number of times he interrupts the teacher and other students, and can decrease the number of times he hits others. Focusing on observable behavior that can be counted is the first step in developing a program for systematically altering a student's behavior.

Data Collection Is Necessary in Order to Alter Behavior Thoughtfully and Systematically

It is surprising that this basic approach is so often criticized by teachers who state that data collection is too time consuming. Effective teachers base their academic instructional program on assessment activities that indicate the specific skills their students possess. This step is followed by activities specifically designed to develop new skills. Finally, assessment is used to determine how well the skill has been learned and what activities should follow. Collecting data on students' behavior serves a similar purpose. It allows us to determine whether a problem exists, how serious the problem is, and whether the interventions being used are significantly affecting the behavior. When teachers fail to collect some form of data, they often fail to assess a student's behavior accurately. Without data, we cannot objectively determine whether a student's behavior is in reality significantly different from that of her peers, or what behavior most needs changing.

Data collection also allows us to evaluate a treatment designed to change a student's behavior. Unless we collect data, it is easy to become frustrated when a new program or intervention does not bring about an immediate change in the behavior. By collecting data, we can notice small but significant changes in a student's behavior. Because behaviors often change slowly, we may misinterpret the effect of our interventions. An excellent example is found in the criticism trap. Teachers use criticism or reprimands because these cause an immediate, although usually temporary, change in students' behaviors. In the long run, however, the negative behavior often increases because it is reinforced by the teacher's attention. Collecting and analyzing data can prevent teachers from continuing an ineffective behavior change strategy or terminating an approach that is having significant but gradual success.

Advantages of Behavioristic Interventions

There are several advantages to using behavioristic interventions to help students alter their behavior. First, some youngsters need special assistance in developing responsible behavior. Anyone who has worked extensively in special education or child psychotherapy is aware that a few youngsters do not initially respond to the types of interventions that are effective in helping most children change their behaviors. For example, students experiencing fetal alcohol effect or fetal alcohol syndrome are likely to require more structure and will disproportionately benefit from a classroom system that provides clear rewards for productive behavior and consequences for unproductive behavior.

A second advantage of behavioristic interventions is that extensive research clearly demonstrates these interventions can be effective. Research shows that, when systematically applied, the methods presented in this chapter, and other behavioral methods, can assist students in developing more productive behaviors. It is important to note that many of the research projects in which educators have been successful in bringing about dramatic changes in schools have involved some use of rewards or celebrations for improvement (Freiberg, 1996; Sugai, Hoerner, & Gresham, 2002; Wager, 1993).

We need to keep in mind that, although reinforcement needs to be used carefully and thoughtfully, almost all of us do many things because we receive rewards. No matter how committed we are, very few teachers would go to work every day if they were not paid. Children who are taking risks and making significant efforts to attempt new behaviors need to be celebrated for their successes. The issue is not whether we celebrate, but rather how. Reinforcers can be expressions of pride or appreciation from significant others, group celebrations, or written statements of the student's accomplishments. These are indeed extrinsic, but they appear to us to be part of the healthy fabric of our lives, not something to be viewed as negative and undesirable.

Third, although behavioristic intervention requires time and effort, it frequently requires less time than we anticipate and less time than we currently spend attempting to control the student's behavior. Furthermore, the behavioristic intervention may have a positive effect on other students in the classroom, whereas reprimands often create a negative ripple effect that increases classroom disruption.

Teachers who are especially worried about students' self-concepts and peer relationships often state that behavioristic interventions isolate and alienate children. However, research suggests that by helping students improve their behaviors, behavioristic treatment programs may improve students' relationships with their peers.

Disadvantages of Behavioristic Interventions

The major disadvantage associated with behavioristic interventions is that the focus on changing students' behaviors by systematically manipulating consequences, may cause teachers to deemphasize examining their own teaching methods or other classroom factors as possible causes of students' unproductive behaviors.

A second disadvantage to behavioristic strategies for changing students' behaviors is that some behavioristic approaches emphasize external controls. Unless used with caution, this may work in opposition to a child's need for a sense of competence and power and may dramatically conflict with an adolescent's desire to be autonomous. The use of external rewards also tends to reinforce lower levels of moral development. Therefore, overemphasis on behavioristic methods may detract from the important developmental tasks of understanding others' perspectives and learning to make decisions based on the effect one's behavior has both on oneself and on others. Working with youngsters who are experiencing serious behavior problems can be viewed as a reparenting process. These young people may not have learned the social skills or acquired the positive feelings about themselves that enable them to function effectively. Like caring, effective parents, adults who work with these students need to provide them with love and self-respect and with skills in controlling their own environments. Although this may need to be supplemented by behavioristic methods, these interventions should never become the major treatment program. If emphasis on behavioristic interventions sidetracks us from incorporating a wide range of less restrictive, less control oriented treatment interventions that help students to accomplish important developmental tasks, behaviorism can have a negative effect on students' abilities to become competent and positive individuals.

A final disadvantage associated with behavioristic interventions is that they may place a negative connotation on the very goal they are intended to make more desirable. Studies have found that when people are offered an extrinsic reward for performing a task they view as interesting, the task soon becomes perceived as less interesting and on-task behavior and task performance decrease (Ryan & Stiller, 1991). In addition, Kohn (1991) argues that rewards fail to "help children develop a commitment to being generous or respectful" (p. 500), whereas Schwartz (1988) reported that individuals are less likely to be flexible and innovative when they are being rewarded for their efforts. Consequently, whenever possible, we should use the least external control-oriented approach to changing a student's behavior. In the long run, this restraint will encourage a greater sense of personal competence and a more internalized commitment to the values inherent in the desired behaviors.

P A U S E
and Consider   **10.1**

> Stop for a minute and consider the many times you have interacted with young people. Were there instances in which you were frustrated with or concerned about an individual or group's behavior? Did you or another adult working with them ever decide to examine what was occurring prior to and after the behavior of concern to determine whether you could positively influence the behavior? We suggest you write several paragraphs describing one such situation, including the changes you made to assist the individual(s).

CONDUCTING AN ENVIRONMENTAL
ANALYSIS/FUNCTIONAL ASSESSMENT

In his book *What Do I Do When . . . ? How to Achieve Discipline with Dignity*, Mendler (1992) highlighted the importance of examining the environment in order to determine specific interventions for each child when he wrote, "Most discipline programs incorrectly place their emphasis upon strategies and techniques. The latest gimmick is offered to get Johnny to behave. . . . The competent teacher needs to get at the reasons or functions of a given maladaptive behavior to formulate a strategy likely to work" (p. 25).

In recent years several large lawsuits have been brought against school districts for perceived excessive removal of students from the learning environment. In response to such legal action, a number of states now mandate that whenever restrictive interventions are used on a regular basis, it is mandatory that the school staff examine the school environment to determine factors that may be contributing to the student's behavior problems and additionally develop a plan for assisting the student in developing new skills for responding to the antecedents of the acting-out behavior (California, Hughes Bill: A.B. 2586, 1990; Indiana Public Act 89–191: Behavioral Interventions for Students with Disabilities). Recent changes in the Individuals with Disabilities Education Act (IDEA) require school district staff to conduct a functional assessment on or before the tenth day of a suspension or when there is a change to an interim alternative educational placement.

The intent of laws such as those mentioned previously is to ensure that when a student experiences behavior problems, educators carefully examine school and classroom environments to determine factors that may be contributing to the student's anxiety, frustration, and unproductive behavior. Rather than blaming the student, it is critical for educators to consider factors such as instructional strategies, content, classroom peer relationships, and teacher–student relationships. Alfie Kohn (1996) highlighted this concept when he wrote:

> What matters are the reasons and feelings that lie beneath. Discipline programs can (temporarily) change behavior, but they cannot help people to grow. The latter requires a very different orientation in the classroom: looking "through" a given action in order to understand the motives that gave rise to it as well as figuring out how to have some effect on those motives. (p. 69)

Likewise, it is imperative that educators determine any social skills the student may lack that are essential to functioning effectively in the school environment. Perhaps the student would benefit from learning how to make friends or skillfully respond to frustrating events. Again, as educators, we can creatively and effectively address social skill deficits. Instead of throwing up our arms and blaming these children, the skilled educator considers factors that can be addressed in order to increase the likelihood of the student having a successful learning experience.

Considerable research now indicates that functional assessment may be an effective approach to determining interventions for children demonstrating serious or persistent behavior problems. In one of the first studies using a functional assessment methodology to determine causes and suggest interventions for behavior problems of students with serious behavioral and emotional problems, Dunlap and colleagues (1993) wrote that "the empirical demonstration of a functional relationship between classroom variables and an individual student's behavioral challenges allows a teacher and/or consultant to design an intervention logically related to the child's needs" (p. 289). The authors believe this focus provides teachers with an opportunity to make thoughtful, professional decisions regarding interventions that may be most successful in assisting students in modifying their behavior.

Although a great deal has been written about functional assessment, simply stated, a complete functional behavior assessment process involves four components:

1. A functional assessment
2. A positive behavior change plan
3. The implementation of this plan
4. The ongoing monitoring and adjustment of this plan

Furthermore, when a functional behavior assessment has been completed, we will have answers to the following four questions:

1. What are the antecedents and the consequences that cause the behavior to exist?
2. What function(s) does the behavior serve for the student?
3. What environmental changes can be made to change the student's behavior?
4. What behaviors can we teach the student to help him or her act more responsibly and meet his or her needs without using behaviors that violate the rights of others?

Collecting information to determine why the undesirable behavior is occurring is the first step in conducting a functional assessment. A functional assessment can be completed by indirect methods such as interviews with parents, teachers, counselors, administrators, and instructional assistants. It will usually also involve direct observation to collect data regarding events or factors that are associated with the behavior to be changed.

Figure 10.1 is a form that has been used with hundreds of teachers to help them examine their own classroom management and instructional responsibilities as a factor in the unproductive behavior of an individual student or group of students. This form is not intended to be used as an evaluative instrument. Instead, it is to be used by a teacher or a teacher and colleague or consultant to consider whether changes may be warranted in one or more general area(s) related to management and instruction.

P A U S E

and Consider   **10.2**

> If you working in a classroom with a student who is having some ongoing behavior problems (remember that being uninvolved, failing to complete schoolwork, and being isolated are also important behavior concerns), complete Activity 10.1 at the end of the chapter. Because this activity involves assessing the extent to which effective practices have been implemented, this is an activity that you may not want to share initially with the teacher you are observing or with whom you are working. However, if you have a solid professional relationship with this educator, perhaps you could work collaboratively on this activity.

	Yes	Somewhat	No

Level 1: Classroom Management and Instruction

1.1 The teacher interacts positively with the student.

1.2 The teacher communicates high expectations to the student.

1.3 The student is actively involved with peers either through cooperative learning or peer tutoring.

1.4 Classroom procedures are taught to students and this student demonstrates an understanding of the procedures.

1.5 There is a consistent routine in the classroom that is understood by the student.

1.6 The student's instructional program is appropriate to his or her academic needs.

1.7 The student has been involved in some form of academic goal setting and self-recording.

1.8 Rules for managing student behavior are posted in the classroom.

1.9 Rules are appropriate, succinct, stated positively, and all-inclusive.

1.10 Consequences for inappropriate behavior are clear to all students.

1.11 Consequences are appropriate, fair, and implemented consistently.

1.12 The student demonstrates that she or he understands the rules and consequences.

1.13 The teacher has met privately with the student to discuss the problem and jointly develop a plan both parties agree to implement in order to assist the student.

Level 2: Individual Behavior Program

2.1 An academic and/or behavior program has been developed and consistently implemented and corresponding data collected for at least four weeks.

2.2 An alternative program was implemented if the original plan (2.1) proved to be ineffective.

FIGURE 10.1

Interventions before Removing a Student from the Classroom or Referring a Student for Special Education Services

It is important to examine the interventions you have made to modify the learning environment and provide the student with special assistance in meeting the multiple demands of the classroom setting. Figure 10.2 presents a form one of the authors assisted a large K–8 school district in developing in order to help teachers assess their interventions prior to seeking assistance from other teachers or specialists. The purpose of this form is simply to help teachers consider the extent to which they have

FIGURE 10.2
Observation and
Assessment in
the Learning
Environment

Source: Schaumburg
School District 54,
Schaumburg,
Illinois. Reprinted
by permission.

STUDENT: _____ I.D.#: _____ BIRTHDATE: _____

Circle Specific Interventions Utilized	Person Responsible	Specific Interventions and Date Initiated	Outcome and Specify Duration
I. Classroom Environment A. Provide preferred seating (i.e., carrel, dividers, move with peer model/tutor). B. Alter location of school supplies for easy access or to minimize distractions. C. Assign to quiet area in classroom for short periods. D. Post and explain rules and consequences for classroom behavior. E. Increased teacher proximity for targeted student. F. Other:			

II. Instructional Modification
A. Assess student's prerequisite skills.
B. Provide small group and/or one-on-one instruction by:
  1. Teachers
  2. Instructional assistant
  3. Peer tutor
  4. Cross-age tutor
  5. Volunteer
C. Modify materials:
  1. Address only essential skills
  2. Simplify vocabulary of presented materials
  3. Reduce workload
  4. Alter pacing
  5. Use programmed materials (i.e., SRA, computer drill, math kits, etc.)			

FIGURE 10.2
Continued

Circle Specific Interventions Utilized	*Person Responsible*	*Specific Interventions and Date Initiated*	*Outcome and Specify Duration*
6. Repeat and reinforce skills (i.e., tape lesson, games, activity centers)			
7. Change basal text			
8. Provide assignments and tests in segments			
9. Use calculator/ computers			
10. Provide study aids (i.e., highlight main ideas, outlines, study guides, number line, concrete materials, etc.)			
D. Organize materials (i.e., folder, notebook, assignment sheet).			
E. Set time expectations (i.e., use timer, set time allotment, etc.).			
F. Use cues or gestures to indicate appropriate or inappropriate behaviors.			
G. Vary student responses (i.e., writing on chalkboard, art projects, verbal response alone, taping, use manipulatives, etc.).			
H. Modify instructions:			
1. Preview questions/tests			
2. Provide rewards/reinforcers			
3. Ask student to repeat directions and then restate what he's going to do to ensure understanding			
I. Modify grades:			
1. On specific reduced work load			
2. Reflecting performance on essential skills			
3. On report cards			
J. Other:			

(continued)

FIGURE 10.2
Continued

Circle Specific Interventions Utilized	Person Responsible	Specific Interventions and Date Initiated	Outcome and Specify Duration
III. Motivation/Behavior Strategies			
A. Assess appropriateness of task.			
B. Prioritize tasks to be completed.			
C. Privately discuss and explain behavior and resulting consequences.			
D. Use behavior modification techniques (i.e., reinforcing appropriate behaviors, use cueing, gestures, etc.).			
E. Alter frequency of grouping changes to maximize or minimize child's movements.			
F. Change of schedule/group.			
G. Adapt assignments (i.e., reduced work load, verbal responses, etc.).			
H. Refer child to social worker/counselor/ psychologist.			
I. Provide individual assignments/behavior sheets, charts, checklists, etc., monitored by teacher, student, and administrator.			
J. Set up reward/ consequence system: 1. Goal setting—target individual behavior 2. Set up a contract 3. Provide reinforcers chosen from a menu (i.e., social praise, tangible/stickers, activity/free time, games, good news notes)			
K. Daily/weekly progress reports.			

FIGURE 10.2
Continued

Circle Specific Interventions Utilized	Person Responsible	Specific Interventions and Date Initiated	Outcome and Specify Duration
L. Parent/teacher/principal/ child conferences, weekly, bimonthly, etc. M. Other:			
IV. Parent Contact/Support A. Notes sent home (i.e., daily or weekly progress report, good news notes). B. Parent/teacher check in (i.e., mutually signed assignment sheets/notebooks). C. Telephone contact (i.e., weekly, monthly, or as needed). D. Home/school learning/behavior contracts. E. Suggested in-district resources (parent group/TAP). F. Other:			

_____   _____   _____   _____
Date   Signature of Teacher   Date   Signature of Principal, CST
                                                                          Member or Peer Consultant

made reasonable and responsible classroom interventions aimed at assisting the student in having a positive learning experience.

P A U S E
10.3 *and Consider*

For a student with whom you are working or who you are observing (possibly the student you considered when completing Activity 10.1), complete Activity 10.2 (including the form in Figure 10.2). This will allow you to reflect on the types of support that have been provided for a student struggling to be effective in school. Again, if you are working in a classroom under the supervision of a teacher, you will need to be sensitive in determining whether it is best to complete this activity by yourself or working with someone.

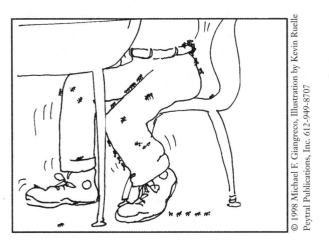

© 1998 Michael F. Giangreco, Illustration by Kevin Ruelle
Peytral Publications, Inc. 612-949-8707

After a hasty special education placement for behavioral problems, school officials were embarrassed to learn that Marty really did have ants in his pants.

In addition to examining your own behavior, it can be extremely valuable to analyze a student's classroom behavior systematically and specifically. Figure 10.3 presents a form the authors have used with hundreds of teachers to assist in determining the factors that may be influencing a student's behavior. Teachers have found this to be extremely helpful and on a number of occasions have adopted it as a model for providing information to colleagues at staffings held to develop intervention plans for students.

You have been introduced to the concepts of antecedents (factors that occur prior to the student behaving irresponsibly—such as the type of work, peer interactions, etc.) and consequences (responses the student receives following an unproductive behavior), and Figure 10.3 introduces another important aspect of a functional assessment. Notice at the bottom of the first page of this form the question, "What function do you think this behavior is serving the student?" This is a key question in conducting a functional behavior assessment. Indeed, this is why the process has been given the term *functional behavior assessment.* This question is based on the belief that all behavior serves a purpose. Although we may not alway be aware of our behaviors or their purposes, virtually everything we do is done because we believe it will provide us with something we want.

PAUSE
and Consider   **10.4**

> Again, consider a student with whom you are working or who you are observing having difficulty behaving in a responsible manner—ideally the same student you considered in Activities 10.1 and 10.2. Complete Activity 10.3 at the end of this chapter with this student in mind.

If you have completed the last three Pause and Consider features, you have completed some aspects of a functional behavior assessment. You have information regarding classroom and school factors that may be influencing the student's behavior as well as interventions that have been attempted to assist this student. You have made some hypotheses regarding the function the behavior serves the student. The next step is to interview individuals who work with the student and discover what factors they believe influence the student's behavior. As the classroom teacher, you have extensive information about the student based on your observations. The next step is to observe the student with these new perceptions in mind to determine whether your hypotheses tend to hold true. For example, if you hypothesized that the student became overly active and noncompliant when faced with work he did not feel confident completing, you could observe him in settings where he is likely to be successful and in a situation

STUDENT NAME _____ BIRTHDATE _____

SCHOOL_____ GRADE LEVEL _____ DATE _____

Describe the problem behavior in specific, observable terms:

_____

_____

_____

_____

How frequently does the problem behavior occur? (i.e., number of times per day/week)

_____

_____

_____

_____

Where does the behavior generally occur? (setting)

☐ Classroom   ☐ Playground

☐ Hallway   ☐ Specific Subjects (specify)

☐ Bus   ☐ Home

☐ Lunchroom   ☐ Other_____

What antecedent seems to precede the problem behavior? (e.g., time of day, type of instructional activity)

_____

_____

_____

_____

What happens as a consequence of the behavior that may be reinforcing and maintaining it?

_____

_____

_____

_____

What function do you think this behavior is serving the student?

_____

_____

_____

_____

FIGURE 10.3
Functional Behavioral Assessment Form

(continued)

FIGURE 10.3
Continued

What interventions have you already attempted to modify this behavior? (be specific; attach copies of interventions and modifications made)

_____

_____

_____

_____

_____

_____

_____

What environmental modifications can be made to reduce the likelihood the student will need to use the problem behavior?

_____

_____

_____

_____

_____

_____

What interventions do you believe would be most helpful in providing the student with an alternative behavior to serve the same function as the problem behavior?

_____

_____

_____

_____

_____

_____

PARTICIPANTS IN STAFFING/PLAN DEVELOPMENT:

_____   _____
Name/Title   Name/Title

_____   _____
Name/Title   Name/Title

_____   _____
Name/Title   Name/Title

in which the work is quite difficult to see if your hypothesis appear valid. If your observations indeed were validated, your next step would be to create a positive behavior change plan (often called a BIP—behavior intervention plan). You could implement changes in the academic work presented to the student, provide a peer tutor, teach the student strategies for working with the materials, and so on.

Before you begin developing such plans, we recommend you read the remainder of the chapter. Later in the chapter we provide a process for developing a positive behavior change plan and you will have an opportunity to develop one or more of these plans. The following pages describe two examples of behavior intervention plans one of the authors developed. These are offered as a schema for what a plan might look like and to provide an introduction to the following sections on strategies you may use when helping students develop more responsible, satisfying behaviors.

Case Studies

The following case studies demonstrate the potential of functional assessment in developing an effective intervention plan for individual students and groups of students experiencing behavior problems in regular education classrooms.

Case Study: Elementary School

Recently the senior author was asked to provide a school staff with assistance in working with a third-grade student who was highly disruptive and was viewed as having both an attention deficit disorder (ADD) and possible serious emotional problems. The boy frequently wandered around the class, disrupted other students, made quacking sounds, and banged his head on the desk. When asked when these behaviors occurred most frequently, the teacher indicated that the wandering and bothering of others occurred primarily in the morning, whereas the more unusual sounds and head banging occurred immediately following lunch. When asked in what activities the student was engaged when these behaviors occurred, the teacher indicated that it was most often during math in the morning and language arts after lunch. The teacher noted that the student, who believed he was very gifted in all academic areas, was very skilled in math but almost equally unskilled in language arts.

The author ate lunch with the student and, given the statement about the boy's potential behavior and possible mental health problems, was somewhat surprised to observe that he demonstrated at least average social skills. Following lunch the author visited the boy's classroom and observed a language arts lesson lasting approximately forty minutes. The student was seated in a row of three students near the back right of the classroom. The students had been given several worksheets with alphabetizing activities, and the student began to complete the task. After less than five minutes the student became agitated and began to make a quacking sound. The author moved over and commented that this seemed like an unusual behavior, especially coming from someone as intelligent as the student had indicated he was. The boy stated that he was bored with the work. It appeared, however, that the student was finding the work rather challenging. He had completed only several lines, whereas most of his classmates had completed a section involving nearly five times the amount of work he had finished. The author noted that it appeared the work was difficult for the student who responded by emphatically repeating that he was smart. The author informed the student that even smart people found some types of work more difficult than others. For example, the author noted that even though he was probably considered by some people to be quite intelligent, he found drawing very difficult. The student asked the author to draw an elephant. The student found the attempt quite amusing and affirmed that the author was indeed not very good at drawing. The author then noted that even smart people needed to improve on some things and asked the student why it might be useful to improve on alphabetizing. The student responded by providing a number of activities that could be enhanced by rapid alphabetizing. The author noted that because this was a useful tool perhaps the student could improve on it even if he was not one of students who found the work quite easy. The student agreed to attempt five problems and signal the author when he was done. In only a few minutes the student signaled. After reinforcing the student's efforts, the author suggested the student set another goal. The student selected two sections and worked until the teacher signaled for attention. As the teacher worked with the class to correct the worksheets, the student raised his hand to answer nine consecutive questions (something the teacher later stated she had not seen all year). When he was not called on to answer the ninth question, the student became agitated and began to make a quacking sound. At this point the author suggested that he and the student be allowed to meet briefly in the counselor's office. During the initial stages of the conference, the student indicated that he found all his schoolwork boring and that this was the reason for the behavior that got him in trouble. As the discussion continued, the student was able to distinguish between academic work that was too difficult and that which was not challenging. He acknowledged that his disruptive behaviors were used to remove him from the work and agreed to use several new strategies.

Figure 10.4 presents the plan or contract developed between the author and this student. Interestingly, the author initially suggested that the student focus on having one morning or afternoon without using one of his disruptive behaviors to respond to his frustration. The student continued to argue that because he was so smart he would go for two weeks. The author finally gave in and allowed what he knew was much too long a time frame to be written into the agreement. The student went eight days without emitting a quacking sound or disturbing another student during math. When he failed to meet his goal the ninth day, the student stated that he would go an additional ten days. Even though he was encouraged to go two days to complete his ten, the student insisted on the higher standard. The student reached his goal and continued for several more weeks.

In most cases a functional assessment will suggest not only social skills needed by the student but also significant modifications in the classroom setting. In this case, an important aspect of the intervention involved providing the student with alternative math work and utilizing goal setting and the use of a computer in language arts. Although the student's behavior was not always what the teacher would have preferred, he did virtually eliminate the two behaviors that were of most concern. As the year progressed, further interventions were needed to assist this student in monitoring other inappropriate behaviors and replacing them with more acceptable options. This involved self-monitoring and some additional social skill training.

Case Study: High School

Several years ago, one of the authors was asked to work with a sophomore who had been referred to the office fifty-one times during the first semester. Late in the semester he had been withdrawn from his first- and second-period classes and assigned to

PLAN FOR _____ **DEVELOPED BY** _____ **AND**

VERN JONES ON _____

FIGURE 10.4
A Contract
to Modify the
Environment

Problem: Sounds and Silly Behavior during Class

Reason for Sounds and Silly Behavior

1) too easy
2) too hard
3) had to sit too long
4) attention from peers

	If work is too easy/boring	If work is too hard	If the student is restless
Plan	1) Finish your work and then get free time 2) Ask for harder work	1) Set a goal and then take a break when goal is reached 2) (stretch, walk to a designated spot) 3) Solution Desk	1) Squeeze your body 2) Stretch your legs but don't bother others 3) Walk to Solution Desk

Why it is a good idea to do the above plan:

1) So I don't bother others or break rules
2) To stay out of trouble
3) So I can learn more and act more mature

Reward:

_____ agrees that if this plan is followed for two weeks, a mechanical pencil and a letter from Vern Jones will be the rewards.

Signatures:

_____	_____
Student	Teacher
_____	_____
Vern Jones	Parent

Remember, _____, even smart people need to learn skills! We all have strengths and weaknesses.

Plan beginning date: _____ Plan ending date: _____

sit in the office. Interestingly, the student was allowed to sit in the most comfortable chair available in the main school office. Additionally, this chair provided him with a wonderful view of the school commons and availability to a wide range of interesting conversations.

When the author asked to see data regarding behavioral patterns, he was informed that the vice principal simply had a list of the number of referrals. No record indicated the time of day, antecedent events, or even a clear statement regarding the type of misbehavior. After interviewing the student and his counselor, it became apparent that the student had considerable difficulty early in the school day. Interestingly, his two most difficult classes were during those periods, and the student frequently arrived at school somewhat agitated by conflicts with his mother. In addition, it became clear the most of the student's discipline referrals were associated with his aggressive responses to teachers correcting his behavior. The pattern that emerged was a student who, when he experienced academic frustration, became active and off-task, was given commands by teachers, and responded to these in what would be termed a rude and sometimes aggressive manner.

The first decision was to modify the student's schedule so that he began the day with a teacher he liked and trusted and in whose subject he experienced moderate success. This was followed by a reading lab and then a subject with which the student had experienced some difficulty. This was followed by a physical education course in which the student was very successful. This pattern continued throughout the day. Next, the student was asked how he would like teachers to make requests that he modify his behavior. He agreed that teachers needed to do this and provided the counselor with several written statements that he felt represented respectful ways of requesting that he alter his behavior. All of the student's teachers attended a brief meeting to practice these less confrontational requests and agreed to use them when addressing the student. Finally, the student was provided with individual social skill training in responding to comments or requests made by teachers.

The results were rewarding. The student had only three office referrals during his spring semester. Although his work continued to be slightly below what appeared to be his potential, he did pass all second-semester courses.

STRATEGIES FOR HELPING STUDENTS DEVELOP NEW BEHAVIORAL SKILLS

Earlier chapters provided you with a wide range of interventions you might use to create a positive, successful experience for a student who demonstrates behavior problems. This section presents several specific methods for helping students become more aware of their behaviors and replacing irresponsible, unproductive behaviors with behaviors more likely to facilitate their learning and be accepted by educators and peers.

Self-Management

As discussed throughout this book, the approach that is most beneficial in helping students change their behaviors is one that provides the greatest amount of student involvement, enhances students' dignity, and helps students develop new skills that can be transferred to other settings. The behavioristic strategies that best fulfill these criteria involve students in monitoring their own behavior. In addition to the problem-solving approaches discussed in Chapter 9, there are three basic approaches to helping students monitor and control behavior. The first method is to help them count and record their own behavior. A second approach is to teach students new social skills for meeting their needs. The third involves working with students to develop some form of agreement or contract to help motivate them to use skills that are in their repertoire but which they are finding difficult to use. This section presents specific procedures for implementing these three strategies.

Self-Monitoring

Students have a basic need to be viewed positively and to demonstrate their competence and power by controlling their own behavior. Often, however, students are not aware of the extent of their unproductive behavior. Some youngsters have difficulty controlling their emotions and behaviors without the assistance of external cues. Self-monitoring involves assisting a student or group of students in establishing a system for monitoring and recording their own behaviors. Involving students in collecting data on their own behaviors can, in some instances, provide enough external structure to produce dramatic improvements in their behaviors. This procedure not only involves students in their own behavior change programs but it also significantly reduces the amount of time spent in collecting data. Furthermore, perhaps because self-monitoring helps create an internalized locus of control, changes in behavior associated with this approach seem more likely to generalize both to other situations and to other behaviors.

Self-monitoring has been reported in the literature for more than thirty years and has been found effective in changing a wide range of specific unproductive behaviors with a diverse population of students (Carr & Punzo, 1993; Smith & Sugai, 2000; Webber, Scheuermann, McCall, & Coleman, 1994). In an early study, McKenzie and Rushall (1974) reported that having youngsters record their behavior on a bulletin board was effective in improving the behaviors of those who were consistently late, absent, or uninvolved in activities at a swim club. Broden, Hall, and Mitts (1971) demonstrated that self-recording attending and nonattending behavior and receiving praise for improvement was an effective intervention with an eighth-grade girl who was failing history. The girl's attending behavior increased from 30 percent to 80 percent under this treatment condition. When developing a self-monitoring plan, we encourage teachers initially to use only social reinforcement to celebrate the student's success. Students can show their data to a predetermined valued other. Our experience suggests that it is seldom necessary to add additional reinforcement. Although self-monitoring can provide excellent results by itself, as noted in later sections of this chapter, it can be effectively combined with strategies for self-instruction, self-evaluation, and self-reinforcement (Cole, 1992; DiGangi & Maag, 1992).

Procedures

When instructing students in counting their own behavior, the first step is to ensure that the students can accurately describe the behavior. You can teach this skill by asking them to demonstrate the desirable and undesirable behaviors. The second step is to develop a method for tallying the data. Especially when working with young children, it is helpful to start by incorporating a visual display of the behavior being counted. A *countoon* can serve this purpose. A countoon includes a picture of the behavior being tallied and a place for the student to mark a tally each time the behavior occurs. Figure 10.5 is an example of a countoon used to help a student become aware of how often he talks out without raising his hand. Older students may not be willing to mark checks on a chart each time they emit inappropriate behaviors. A junior high school counselor we know developed the form shown in Figure 10.6 to help students take more responsibility for their behaviors.

The third step involves implementing the self-monitoring. We suggest you select a relatively short period of time and one that is developmentally appropriate. For

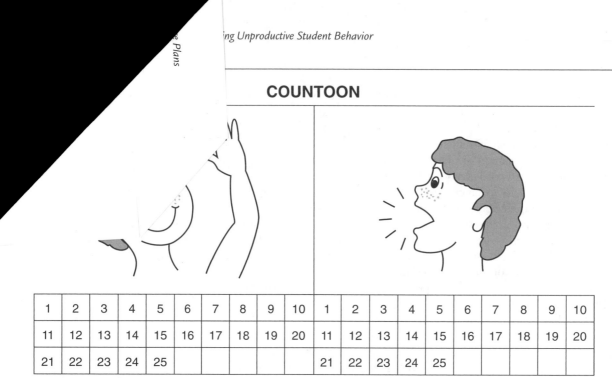

COUNTOON

1	2	3	4	5	6	7	8	9	10
11	12	13	14	15	16	17	18	19	20
21	22	23	24	25					

Count your hand raising

1	2	3	4	5	6	7	8	9	10
11	12	13	14	15	16	17	18	19	20
21	22	23	24	25					

Count your talk outs

FIGURE 10.5
Countoon

example, a second-grade child might monitor talking out for two 10-minute periods, whereas a first-year high school student might monitor this behavior for a class period. The fourth step involves the student meeting with an adult to assess the progress the student is making. This might simply involve meeting for thirty seconds and having the student report the results. It might also include graphing the results so the student can visually see the progress he or she is making.

The fifth step involves providing students with some form of praise. In most cases verbal praise from the teacher will be adequate because students obtain personal satisfaction from the sense of competence and empowerment associated with improving a behavior. In some cases, this verbal praise may need to be expanded to include other significant adults. In other situations, it may be necessary to provide the student with a specific activity to increase the likelihood that the behavior at issue will improve.

We have worked with literally hundreds of teachers and intern teachers to use self-monitoring to assist students in acting more responsibly and being more successful students. Our experience and reading of the research suggests this is an extremely valuable method.

Although most students will accurately monitor their own behavior after these five steps have been accomplished, seriously acting-out students may require more assistance. There are three additional methods you can implement to encourage students to count their own behavior accurately.

Student's name _____

FIGURE 10.6
Student Self-
Monitoring Form

Time	What the Class Is Supposed to Be Doing	What (Student's Name) Is Doing . . . (+ or o)
9:55		
10:05		
10:15		
10:25		
10:35		

Teacher's signature

Start by reinforcing the student for obtaining data that closely match those you or another adult coder obtain. As they learn to record their behavior accurately, reinforcement for accuracy can be replaced by rewarding decreases in the unproductive behavior.

Another procedure involves initially having the student receive reinforcement for improving behaviors that are being recorded by an adult. As the student's behavior improves, she can be allowed to monitor her own behavior and receive designated reinforcements for improved behavior. Finally, the reinforcement is withdrawn and the student simply receives praise for controlling and recording her behavior.

P A U S E

10.5 *and Consider*

Select a student who is behaving in a manner that disrupts his own learning and that of his classmates. Select a specific behavior that it would benefit the student and others to have altered. Collect baseline data on this behavior. Next, develop a format that allows the student to self-monitor this behavior. if possible, meet with the student, discuss the self-monitoring, and have the student self-monitor the behavior for a designated time frame. Finally, meet with the student to discuss the self-monitoring. We strongly encourage you to share your work with several colleagues or classmates. Even if you are not able to actually implement your plan, share your decisions and forms with your peers.

The following case studies provide examples of how an intern and a young teacher implemented these methods in a first- and seventh-grade classroom.

Case Study: Elementary

This study was conducted by a first-grade teacher who was confronted with a particularly difficult class in an inner-city school. Most of her students had been late registrants for kindergarten and, because of overcrowding, had spent their kindergarten experience in an isolated room in the district's administrative office building. Consequently, the children arrived in first grade having had few interactions with older schoolchildren. In addition, their kindergarten class had started nearly a month late, and they had had several teachers during the year. They were also generally a particularly immature, unskilled group, with more than half living in single-parent homes. The following material is taken directly from the teacher's report of her study.

Many distractions within my classroom were caused by students who were not attending to my instructions. My students needed to learn to sit and work without talking, opening and closing their desks, walking to someone else's desk to talk, and so on. I decided to attempt a self-management technique, or a countoon, with my class. This group wanted to please me and be viewed positively by me, but they lacked the inner skills to control their behavior on their own. This technique would let them demonstrate their competence at monitoring and controlling their own behavior. I do not think they were aware of the extent of their off-task behavior. Some children have difficulty controlling their behavior without assistance from an external cue. When children are involved in collecting data on their own behavior, sometimes this act can provide enough external structure to produce dramatic results.

I started my study by collecting baseline data on five children in my group, to determine their off-task frequency. I chose five students who varied greatly in ability, behavior, background, and so forth. I recorded their behavior during seatwork three times at ten-minute intervals, and the results (Figure 10.7) showed that during a ten-minute interval, the frequency of off-task behavior averaged eight per student. I then individually informed the students that I had collected data on them and then I informed the entire group of my results without mentioning the names of the students I had observed. I tried to emphasize to them that I did not think they realized the extent of their off-task behavior. I told them I was going to set up a program whereby they would keep track of their own off-task behavior, with the hope that it would help them to increase their time on task. We then discussed, modeled, and role-played those behaviors which would be considered off-task behaviors. This behavior included talking out loud either to oneself or to a peer; doing any other activity than what I had instructed them to do; getting up from one's desk to wander around the room; or making distracting noises, either by mouth or by opening desks, rolling pencils; and so on. They realized that if they needed assistance from me, they should raise their hand, and because I have a free bathroom-break policy, they could use the bathroom if it was necessary. Students need to be taught how to record their own behavior, and so I spent considerable time in this phase of the project. Also, with students involved in collecting their behavioral data, the time I had to spend on behavior monitoring was lessened. Self-monitoring ideally helps create an internalized source of control, and changes in behavior associated with this approach are expected to be more likely to generalize both to other situations and to other behaviors.

After we had sufficiently practiced and discussed behaviors, I gave each student a countoon. My countoon had a picture of desirable behavior on it, showing an animal deeply involved in doing a worksheet. Originally I had decided to involve only five students in the study, but after a discussion with the class, I decided to give every student a countoon. My results in this study will include only the five students described in the baseline data, but I really felt that it could not hurt to have all the students involved, making them all aware of their talking and behaviors, and keeping track of their off-task times. I then

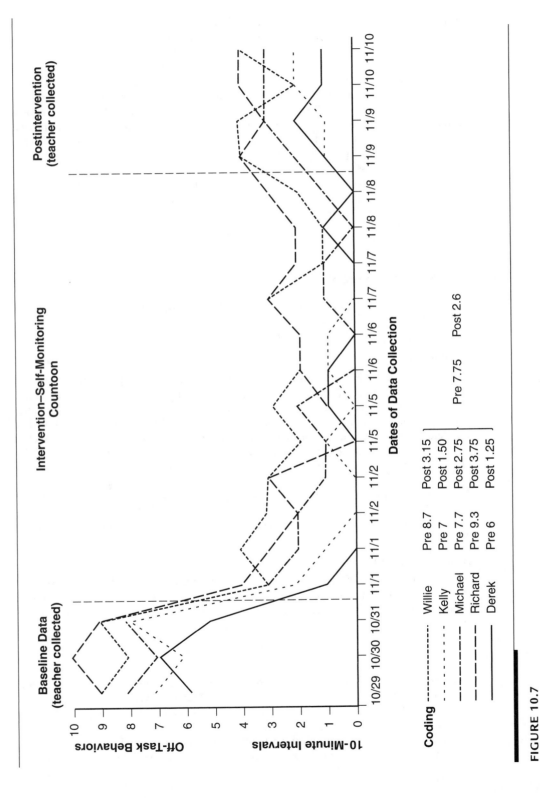

FIGURE 10.7
Elementary Classroom Self-Monitoring Program

instructed the students when to keep track of their behavior. Each box on the countoon was for tallying off-task behavior. After each ten-minute interval, we circled the box with a crayon so that the children could keep track of how many intervals we had done. In that way, if a student had no off-task behavior, the box was still circled to show that we had kept track of that interval. I ran the program for six days, monitoring behavior twice each day for ten minutes each. Generally this monitoring was done during math or science, in which we were working on booklets about baby animals. Several of the children almost completely quit off-task behaviors. They were excited about the program and requested that we keep track of behaviors more often. I think they really did feel they had some control over their situation. Because the results were favorable, they also received praise and points for a class party, and the atmosphere in the room improved significantly during use of the countoons. The five students for whom I had collected baseline data went from an average of eight off-task behaviors to less than three per ten-minute interval during data collection. When I did the followup data collection, without their knowledge, they did regress a little, and were a little more talkative, but overall their off-task behavior was cut in half.

Case Study: Middle School

The following study was implemented by a teacher concerned about the behavior of a student in her last-period study hall. She implemented the study with no assistance and as a project for a course in classroom management.

Background

Samuel (not the student's real name) is a retained seventh grader who has been identified as seriously emotionally disturbed. He has been receiving special education services since the first grade and has attended the same school district since kindergarten. He is functioning in the average range on both the verbal and performance scales of the WISC. His academic achievement does not match his potential. The Woodcock-Johnson Psycho-Educational Battery shows an average knowledge score, low average reading, a mild deficiency in math, and a severe deficiency in written language.

Further testing shows that he has a weakness in visual motor tasks and in visual memory. He gains most of his knowledge auditorily as he has good hearing comprehension. Language is adequate for his age. He expresses his thoughts and ideas appropriately and has good conversational skills. He placed below the fifth percentile on the Piers Harris Children Self-Concept Scale.

Classroom Problem

Samuel is in my ninth-period study hall. He has an extremely high percentage of off-task behavior, which includes talking out, drawing pictures on his assignments, distracting other students, and just generally wasting time. I have tried a variety of interventions through the quarter, including changing his seat, having him stay after school, and glaring at him. The problem continued despite these efforts.

Intervention Plan

For three days I collected baseline data on Samuel and three other students in the same study hall. The results showed that the three control students were off task an average of 6.7 percent during the 40-minute period, whereas Samuel was off task 50 percent during the same period.

I showed the graph to Samuel and told him of my concerns with his off-task behavior. We had a good informative talk, part of which was a pep talk to let him know of his cognitive and academic strengths. I told him about the class I was taking and the project I wanted to involve him in. I showed Samuel the countoon (similar to Figure 10.6) I wanted him to use for the next five days. He was to watch the clock (without having it interfere with his work) and put a plus at the end of each five-minute period that he was on task or a zero if he was off task. I would be doing the same thing, and at the end of the period we would discreetly compare our results. No one in the class would know about our project. This was extremely important to Samuel. The self-monitoring recording sheet was to be kept in his folder each day, and he would stay after school to discuss it.

Results

The first day of self-monitoring Samuel was extremely aware of the clock; it really did distract him. We discussed this after class. The next day was better, and he continued to improve the third day. During the fourth and fifth days, he had only one incident each of off-task behavior. Our comparison data were very similar. A lot of verbal feedback went along with the plan, and Samuel responded well to the praise and individual attention.

The next week Samuel knew I was taking data on him but he was no longer self-monitoring. We discussed his behavior every day and looked at the data. The results (Figure 10.8) were very gratifying to us both. Samuel actually maintained an average of 5 percent of off-task behavior the third week. He was getting an incredible amount of homework done and was receiving positive feedback from his other classroom teachers as well.

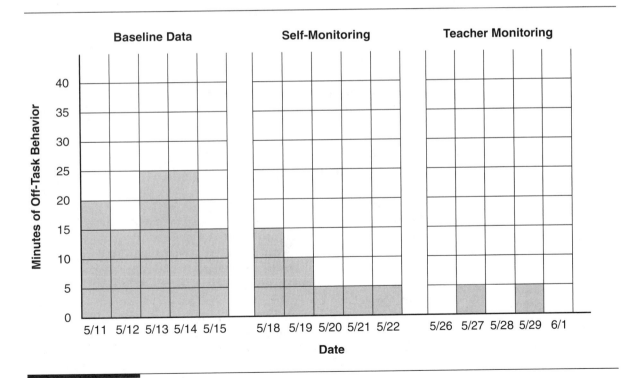

FIGURE 10.8
Self-Monitoring Project with Seventh-Grade Student with Disabilities

Afterthoughts

I am really excited about the results of this project. With it I was able to do in three weeks what I thought was impossible. I thought Samuel was my most difficult student and really did not think I would get dramatic results using this approach.

Self-Instruction

Although self-monitoring can provide excellent results by itself, it is often combined with strategies such as self-instruction, self-evaluation, and self-reinforcement (Di-Gangi & Maag, 1992). Students who consistently act out in a school setting are often characterized by their inability to express or control their emotions productively. Partially because these students have had numerous failure experiences and lack confidence, they frequently respond with intense emotions when confronted by situations their peers handle quite comfortably.

One approach to helping students respond more effectively to frustration and stress is to teach them to give themselves verbal instructions that cue them to behave more appropriately. This approach is based on the concept that students who have attention-deficit hyperactivity disorder (ADHD) or who are labeled *impulsive* are less skilled than normal youngsters in using silent speech to monitor their behavior. When faced with a difficult problem, successful students might say to themselves, "Okay, I'll try it once more and if I can't do it I'll ask the teacher for help." Students with behavior problems may lack the ability to monitor their behavior in this manner and, therefore, respond actively and unproductively when faced with a frustrating task. These students may also use negative silent speech. A student might say to herself, "I'm stupid and I can't do this." This internalized statement compounds the student's problem and intensifies negative emotions.

According to the principles of rational-emotive therapy, students' behaviors can be changed by helping them make positive, thoughtful internalized statements in place of the negative, unproductive statements they often make. Research indicates that this approach can be successful in reducing students' anxiety, improving academic performance of behavior-problem students, reducing rule-breaking behavior, and responding less aggressively to oral taunts from peers.

The basic procedure involves teaching students to use silent statements to control their behavior more effectively. We can do so by providing students with specific statements that they can make when confronted with specific, frustrating situations. Students who become frustrated when attempting to solve math problems can be taught to say, "I can do this if I slow down and relax. What I have to do is first add the two numbers on the right. . . ." Similarly, a student who becomes aggressive when losing a game can be taught to say, "Okay, I didn't win this time, but that's all right. The other students will like me better if I give the ball back and go to the end of the line." We can help students develop these skills by providing them with opportunities to practice self-instruction under our supervision and on tasks they can already perform. While working on fairly simple tasks, students may initially be encouraged to make statements we provide. The students can then be asked to repeat these statements on their own. Next, they can be asked to whisper the words as they complete the task. Finally, they can be encouraged to say the words to themselves. If you are interested in examining these procedures in more detail, you can find additional practical suggestions in Workman's (1995) *Teaching Behavioral Self-Control to Students* and Zirpoli and Melloy's (2001) *Behavior Management Applications for Teachers.*

A similar approach focuses both on self-talk and developing alternative methods for dealing with problem situations. Students can be asked to role-play situations in which they consistently respond in an inappropriate manner. As the role-playing unfolds, students are encouraged to replace unproductive self-talk with statements that help them control their behavior. Likewise, the teacher and other students provide alternative methods of responding. For example, a boy who consistently responds angrily to not being chosen immediately at recess may be asked to replace self-talk such as "Nobody likes me" or "I'm no good" with the statements such as, "I'll be chosen soon. I guess some students are a little better at this game than I am." The student may also be taught how to send an I-message in a class meeting to express his hurt over not being chosen or given help in learning positive social skills that make it more likely that peers will choose him to be on their team.

A final approach to self-instruction involves teaching students skills in self-relaxation. This can be accomplished by the teacher or counselor initially providing direct instruction in how to relax. Students can learn to relax by relaxing and tensing different muscle groups. More simple and less obvious methods involve teaching youngsters yogalike breathing skills or asking them to let their bodies go limp and imagine a warm, relaxing substance flowing through their bodies. After students have learned relaxation methods, they can be encouraged to use these methods when they experience feelings of tension or anxiety. We can assist acting-out students by providing them with cues when it is necessary for them to use relaxation procedures. We can reinforce use of these skills by using them with the entire class before or following tension-producing or exciting activities, such as tests, recesses, or assemblies.

Relaxation can also be used in association with cognitive rehearsal (a strategy similar to self-talk). Before beginning an activity that might evoke anxiety or inappropriate student behavior, we can have students close their eyes and go into a relaxed state. We then describe the upcoming situation and the desired student behavior. Before an assembly, we might have the students envision themselves walking quietly to the gymnasium, sitting quietly during the performance, and applauding at appropriate times. When students visually practice behavior in a relaxed state before performing the activity, their behavior can be significantly improved.

SOCIAL SKILLS TRAINING

Any student who has persistent or serious behavior problems (including such nonaggressive behaviors as infrequent contact with peers and infrequent participation in class discussions) is demonstrating a lack of certain social skills. Therefore, a responsible response to serious and persistent unproductive student behavior will almost always include efforts to assist the student in developing behaviors to replace those that have been the cause of concern.

Social skill training is currently being used in many formats. First, school staff may implement social skill training in all classrooms as part of a schoolwide plan to provide students with prosocial skills. Second, some schools have grade-level teams develop social skills specifically needed by their students. Third, many schools provide small-group social skill instruction for students who appear to be lacking specific social skills. Finally, many school staffs use social skill training to provide individual children with one-on-one assistance in developing skills they will need to more effectively respond to specific situations in which they have experienced serious or persistent behavior problems. Materials at the end of the chapter offer suggestions for the first three types of social skill training. The next section provides the reader with information on effectively developing an individualized approach to teaching social skills. We are focusing on this area because we have found it to be the most effective and because it is almost always needed for students who are having serious behavior problems.

Extensive research supports the benefits of social skill training with students experiencing behavioral difficulties in school settings. In addition, social skill training is increasingly being used in mental health work. In her book *Triumph over Fear*, Jerilyn Ross (1994) examined the benefits of goal setting and practicing for patients with anxiety, panic attacks, and phobias. Similarly, in his book *The Good News about Depression*, Mark Gold (1995) stated that "modern therapy emphasizes practical strategies that apply to daily life here and now. Nonanalytic therapy teaches new patterns, but it does so by directly addressing the person's current thoughts, behavior, and relationships" (p. 306). Finally, in describing the Penn Prevention Program, a program to assist students vulnerable for experiencing depression, Seligman (1995) noted that the two key components of the program are "cognitive skills for kids to fight depression and social skills to ward off the rejections and frustrations of puberty" (p. 24).

Implementing a Social Skills Lesson

The first step in implementing a social skills lesson is to determine what skills the student(s) need to develop. This is best determined by completing a functional assessment. As discussed above, this involves carefully examining the actual situation in which the behavior problems are occurring and determining the specific skills the student(s) failed to demonstrate that led to the problem. For example, a student who becomes angry and hits others when rejected at joining a game may be lacking skill in how to ask to be involved in the game or how to play the game in a way that does not alienate his peers. Similarly, a student who fails to obey reasonable adult requests may lack skills in accepting corrections or directions. As discussed earlier in this chapter, it is imperative to select specific behaviors that can be observed. It is not possible to use social skills training to change a student's bad attitude. The student may, however, be taught more positive and productive methods for responding to corrections from adults.

The remainder of this section provides and discusses a generic lesson outline (Figure 10.9) that can be used with either an individual student or group of students at any age level. As seen in Figure 10.9, the process begins with helping the student to identify the ineffective behavior. This is similar to the second step in problem solving (Figure 9.2). Next, the student is helped to identify the reason for changing the behavior. This is similar to the third step in problem solving, in which the student evaluates the behavior. This is critical because if the student cannot present and accept a reason for changing the behavior, there is almost no possibility that the behavior change will have any long-lasting effect.

The next step is similar to the problem-solving step of making a plan. The difference is that in social skills training, an effort is made to specify in detail the com-

Describe the inappropriate behavior _____

_____

_____

FIGURE 10.9
Social Skills
Lesson Design

Rationale for a new behavior _____

_____

Describe the appropriate behavior _____

_____

_____

Skill Components

1. _____
2. _____
3. _____
4. _____
5. _____
6. _____

Model demonstration example _____

_____

_____

_____

Student practice example _____

_____

_____

_____

Natural setting practice (if different than initial practice) _____

_____

_____

_____

Independent practice assignment _____

_____

_____

Individual or group reinforcement strategy _____

_____

_____

ponents of the new behavior. For example, if the student is going to use positive self-talk or relaxation when confronted by a negative peer comment, the specific steps of these behaviors will need to be described.

After the positive alternative behavior has been identified and broken into its component parts, the next step is for the adult to demonstrate or model the behavior. This can often involve the student playing the role of the other person involved (a teacher, peer, etc.) while the person assisting the student in developing the new skill will role-play the student using the new skill.

The obvious next step is to have the student practice the behavior. This will initially be done in the classroom, office, or wherever the training is taking place. The following step is crucial and is often left out. It is absolutely essential to ensure that the student has an opportunity to practice the new behavior in a setting similar to that in which she will have to use it. For example, if the problem occurs on the playground with peers, the new behavior would need to be practiced on the playground with peers.

The next step is to assign the student the task of attempting the new skill and reporting back to the group or individual adult regarding what happened when he used the new skills. Often, this will involve the student determining a specific situation in which he will attempt to use the new skill. Figure 10.10 provides an example of an independent practice form that might be given to a student.

The final step involves determining whether the student will earn a reward for using the new skills. The authors once worked with a teacher who taught a developmentally delayed first grader a series of new behaviors and had the class mark on the board each time they saw the student using his skill of the week. Initially, when five incidents of use were reported, the entire class was provided with a brief activity reinforcement. Later, this was changed to require ten reports of his using the skill before the class earned its reward.

The authors have used the method outlined in Figure 10.9 to work with students ranging from ADD first graders to high school seniors having difficulty with anger management in interactions with teachers. Literally hundreds of teachers with whom the authors have worked have completed action plans in which they used social skills training to change a student's behavior. The following two case studies exemplify the type of program we have seen teachers, counselors, and principals develop to assist students experiencing serious or persistent behavior problems.

Case Study: A Sixth-Grade Boy Involved in Aggressive Behavior

Several years ago, the senior author was asked to work with a student named Warren (a fictitious name) experiencing rather violent behavior. As part of a functional assessment, the author and Warren's counselor were standing near the edge of the playground observing Warren involved in a game of tag in which players were *safe* as long as they were touching a piece of playground equipment. Warren had cleverly trapped one of the players hanging on the monkey bars and was simply waiting for the student to fall so he could be tagged out. As Warren waited, a student playing another game called Warren's name, and he turned to respond. Unfortunately, it was at this moment that the trapped student's arms gave out and he came crashing down—inadvertently hitting Warren on the side of the head. Warren went into a rage. He pushed the much smaller student to the ground and was preparing to kick him in the stomach when he appeared to

"The apples are from my best students, and the stress ball is from the class clown."

Student: __Todd_____ Date: __October 20_____

Skill: __Asking for help_____

Steps: 1. Ask myself "Can I do this alone?"

2. Raise my hand.

3. Wait, I know I can wait
without talking.

4. Ask in a friendly way.

FIGURE 10.10
Social Skills
Independent
Practice Sheet

Source: From
*Skillstreaming the
Elementary School
Child: A Guide for
Teaching Prosocial Skills*
by E. McGinnis and
A. P. Goldstein, 1984,
Champaign, IL:
Research Press.
Copyright 1984 by the
authors. Reprinted by
permission.

How did I do?

Why did I circle this? __I did all the steps._____

suddenly realize what he was doing and tried to stop. He fell backward, barely grazing the student who was crouched on the ground.

At this point the counselor and author intervened. We checked on the student who had been pushed and then asked Warren to join us in the counselor's office. The author initially helped Warren analyze what had occurred and his involvement in the incident. When asked how else he might have responded when he had become angry, Warren's only response was, "I should not kick him." At this point the author decided to complete a social skill lesson following the outline in Figure 10.9. Warren was assisted in understanding why the behavior was a problem and was involved in generating alternative methods for handling his anger. Then, he was asked to role-play the behavior with the author taking Warren's role. Following this, the situation was repeated with Warren using his new strategies. The next step involved practicing the strategy on the playground and finally practicing it with the student who was pushed and the several other students involved. At this point the principal, who had contacted Warren's mother for permission to have the author work with him, decided not to suspend the student. Her rationale was that no student had been hurt and the work that would need to be accomplished prior to Warren returning to school had been accomplished.

As discussed in Chapters 8 and 9, the authors strongly believe it is critical that, following any violent outburst or major interpersonal conflict, the parties involved work on developing alternative strategies for responding in the situation and negotiate and practice this strategy together. This type of reentry is essential for building social and emotional skills and bridges back to the community of support in which the problem occurred.

Case Study: A Fifth Grader Who Was Running Away from School

The senior author recently worked with a girl named Acasia (a fictitious name) who had a history of becoming upset and leaving the school grounds. School personnel had written several contracts to encourage her to remain at school, but the behavior continued at the same rate. While observing Acasia as part of a functional assessment, the author noticed that when she became upset, two girls in her classroom were quite adept at helping her to calm herself. They provided assistance, made supportive comments, and in one instance even stroked her back. When asked about this, the teacher reported that Acasia frequently responded well to these interventions but that she had more difficulty when not seated by one of these students. When asked why Acasia was not consistently placed by one of these students, the teacher noted that she rotated her cooperative groups. Further assessment indicated no clear pattern regarding events was associated with Acasia becoming so distraught that she left the classroom. It was, therefore, decided to make the environmental modification of having Acasia placed in a group with one of the two students who provided such caring support.

The next step involved providing Acasia with alternative strategies for responding to her anxieties and frustrations. Because Acasia played soccer, it was determined that she and her counselor would develop a yellow and a red card. The yellow card would include a series of strategies Acasia could use if she needed to calm herself and remain in the room. The red card included four options for Acasia on those occasions when she felt she could not remain in the room. These cards were laminated so Acasia could place a check in the box in front of the strategy she was planning to use and later erase it and reuse the card. Acasia was then provided with opportunities to practice each of the strategies and to visit and develop a plan for what she would do in those areas listed on her red card.

The results indicated that while Acasia continued to become upset in class, she frequently used her strategy and did not leave the school grounds for the remainder of the year. Observations and discussions continued in order to determine any causative classroom factors associated with her anxiety and frustration.

We suspect you have observed or worked with many students who have demonstrated a lack of skills in effectively responding in social settings. Social skill training provides you with an opportunity to use your teaching skills to assist students in developing a new repertoire of skills that allow them to become successful in these settings.

Select a student you are teaching or observing who displays difficulties in being successful in a specific social setting. In order to practice how you might work with this student, complete Figure 10.9 for a situation in which you might need to assist this student. Share this with several colleagues or classmates. If you are currently working with this student, meet with him or her and carry out this social skill training lesson. Again, share the results of this work with your colleagues.

Incorporating Social Skill Training into Problem Solving

In many ways, social skill training is simply a more detailed, specific form of implementing problem solving with students. There will be many instances in which you use the problem-solving approach presented in the previous chapter and decide to expand it by actually demonstrating the new behavior (developed as the plan) for the student, having the student role-play the behavior, and giving the student an assignment to use the new behavior and report the results. We have found that many students need this additional structure and teaching in order to understand and feel comfortable attempting the behaviors in their plans.

DEVELOPING CONTRACTS

A behavior contract is an agreement between two or more parties indicating the manner in which one or more of the parties will behave in a given situation. Behavior contracts provide a specific, often written, agreement designating the exact behavior(s) each individual will display. Furthermore, behavior contracts frequently indicate the specific reinforcement or consequence associated with performing or failing to perform the behaviors listed in the contract. Therefore, behavior contracting is a more structured intervention than either problem solving or self-management. Behavior contracting provides students with a structure that encourages them to perform behaviors they have been unable to display consistently without some form of external, concrete payoff or negative consequences.

Because behavior contracts help a student commit to demonstrating a specific behavior, it is important to realize that this behavior must already exist in the student's repertoire. For example, a contract would be unfair and unsuccessful if it asked a student who has not demonstrated skill in walking away or sending an I-message when being taunted to use these skills. It this case, it would first be necessary to assist the student in developing specific skills for responding in these situations before developing a contract to encourage him or her to use these new skills.

Negotiating a Contract

Unless a contract is sensitively and concisely negotiated, you may find that it fails regardless of how effectively it is written. Contracts should ideally result from a teacher–student discussion in which you help the student describe a behavior, decide that it needs to be changed, and suggest a plan for making the change. When students are unable to devise a plan or when previous plans have failed to bring about the desired change, you can help them develop a more structured behavior contract.

An effective behavior contract includes a statement about each of these variables:

1. What is the contract's goal? Why has the contract been developed?
2. What specific behaviors must the student perform in order to receive the rewards or incur the agreed-on consequences?
3. What reinforcers or consequences will be employed?
4. What are the time dimensions?
5. Who will monitor the behavior and how will it be monitored?
6. How often and with whom will the contract be evaluated?

Behavior contracts can be presented to students in many forms. Short-term contracts with elementary school children need not include each of these six components. The important factor is that the child clearly understands the contract. Figure 10.11 is an example of a form you can use to present a contract to a primary grade child, and Figure 10.12 is a form for intermediate grade students. Figure 10.13 is a format we have used successfully with high school students. Though it is not necessary to develop a written contract, putting an agreement in writing tends to clarify each party's responsibilities. Whenever possible, students should be involved in determining the terms of a contract. Teachers should also help students express their feelings about a contract. Finally, once the contract has been negotiated, the student should be able to paraphrase clearly the conditions outlined in the contract.

Selecting Reinforcement Procedures and Consequences

Once you know when a contract should be used and how to negotiate a contract with a student, the next step involves understanding the various types of consequences (positive and negative) that can be incorporated into a behavior contract.

Just as the preventive measures discussed in Parts II and III of this book should precede the corrective measures outlined in Part IV, and problem-solving approaches should be implemented before using behavioristic methods, you should begin your contractual interventions with the least restrictive and most natural types of reinforcers and consequences. Figure 10.14 presents a hierarchic approach to reinforcements and consequences used in behavior contracts. You should start by trying to use contractual agreements based on the types of reinforcers at the bottom of the hierarchy. Only if these fail should you develop a contract based on higher-level reinforcers.

Examining Figure 10.14, notice that teachers should initially use reinforcers that are a normal part of the schoolday and are available to all students. Although token reinforcers may appear to be less natural than curtailment of activity, we constantly provide token reinforcers in the form of grades, points earned on tests, or promises to provide a reward if students behave appropriately for a designated period. Furthermore, we should, whenever possible, focus on positive behavior. Consequences in the form of curtailments of activities should be used only after natural reinforcers have proven ineffective in helping a student change a behavior. Curtailment of activity is listed as more desirable than implementing a response cost (the procedure of taking away points or other rewards when a student misbehaves) primarily because response

I'm Leaping in to Say

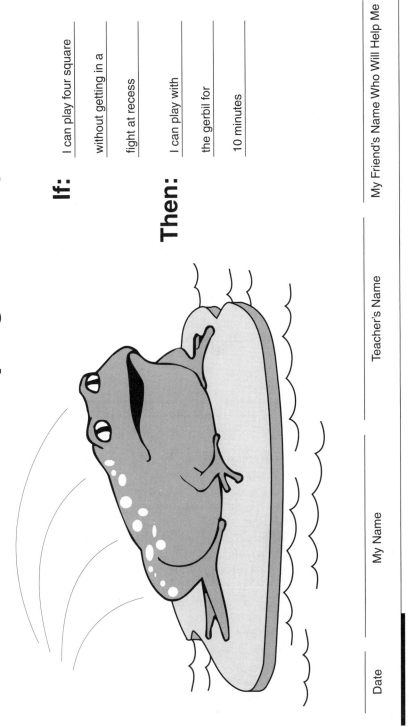

If:

I can play four square

without getting in a

fight at recess

Then:

I can play with

the gerbil for

10 minutes

_____   _____   My Friend's Name Who Will Help Me
Date   My Name

_____
Teacher's Name

FIGURE 10.11
Primary Grade Contract

FIGURE 10.12
Upper Elementary
or Middle School
Contract

I've got the POWER!

Matt
IS GREAT!
NOT LATE!

I WILL be on time to P.E. class, 11:00 a.m. sharp FOR 5 consecutive days . Allan HAS OFFERED TO HELP BY walking to class with Matt . MY TEACHER WILL HELP BY telling me how well I did each day I am on time .
TO CELEBRATE I WILL BE ABLE TO be a student helper in P.E. and referee/umpire activities for 2 days .

_____   _____
DATE   GREAT PERSON

                                        _____
                                        HELPER

                                        _____
                                        TEACHER

cost is a complex intervention and should not be used unless simpler interventions fail. Curtailment of activity is placed lower on the hierarchy than are tangible reinforcers because restricting a student's behavior by requiring the student to stay in from recess in order to practice a behavior is a more logical intervention than is providing the student with candy for completing a task. Furthermore, the use of tangible reinforcements suggests that the desired behavior is not valuable enough to warrant being displayed without a tangible payoff. This statement has subtle but potentially powerful negative consequences for long-term improvement in the student's behavior.

In the next section, procedures for implementing the first four types of consequences listed in Figure 10.14 are presented. Because few teachers use response cost or tangible reinforcers, these consequences are not discussed. If you are interested in these, refer to references at the end of this chapter.

Social Reinforcement
Social reinforcement refers to behaviors of other people that tend to increase the frequency with which a student emits a behavior. If a smile from you is followed by a student's continuing to work on an assignment, the smile may have served as a social

Reason for contract _____

_____

Responsible behavior _____

_____

If I _____ for _____
           (responsible behavior)   (amount of time)

I will _____
                      (positive consequence)

If I do not _____ I will _____
         (responsible behavior)

_____
                (negative consequence)

        Teacher signature _____

        Student signature _____

        Date _____

FIGURE 10.13
High School Contract

Tangible reinforcement
Social, token, and activity reinforcement and response cost
Curtailment of activity
Social, token, and activity reinforcement
Activity reinforcement
Social reinforcement

FIGURE 10.14
Behavior Contract Hierarchy

---

reinforcer. Similarly, if a child consistently returns to a group after having been chased away, the attention inherent in being chased may be viewed as a social reinforcer. Social reinforcement can be used either as a spontaneous teaching strategy for influencing students' behaviors or as a reinforcement in a contract.

When systematically using social reinforcement as a method for improving students' behaviors, you should develop skill in employing a wide range of reinforcers, learn how to give reinforcement, and learn when to use it. Among the many types of social reinforcement, the most obvious involves saying positive things to students. When giving social reinforcement, be careful not to use the same word or phrase constantly. Students appreciate different, creative expressions of encouragement and appreciation. Figure 10.15 lists social reinforcers that can be used at a variety of grade levels.

When using social reinforcement, be especially careful to reinforce specific behaviors. Teachers often use words such as *great, good, nice,* and *super* when referring to students' work or behavior. Unfortunately, this form of reinforcement does not provide the student with specific information on which aspect of behavior is being

FIGURE 10.15
Social Reinforcers

Praising Words and Phrases

Good	That's interesting
That's right	That's really nice
Excellent	Wow
That's clever	Keep up the good work
Good job	Terrific
Good thinking	Beautiful
That shows a great deal of work	I appreciate your help
You really pay attention	Now you've got the hang of it
You should show this to your father	Now you've figured it out
Show Grandma your picture	Very interesting
That was very kind of you	That's an interesting point
Thank you; I'm pleased with that	Nice going
Great	You make it look easy
I like that	What neat work
Exactly	I like the way you got started on your homework

Expressions

Social Contact

Smiling	Walking together
Winking	Sitting together
Nodding head up and down	Eating lunch together
Looking interested	Playing games together
Laughing	Working after school together
	Shaking hands

reinforced. Therefore, it is important to describe the behavior being praised. Rather than saying, "That's nice, Bill," when Bill listens attentively, you might say, "Bill, I appreciate the way you are listening to the discussion. It should help you do well on the assignment."

Although teachers must develop an extensive repertoire of social reinforcers and learn to praise specific behavior, it is perhaps even more important to learn when to reinforce students. The reason social reinforcement is frequently ineffective in changing students' behavior is that it is so often ineffectively used by teachers. Several studies have demonstrated that teachers often dispense social reinforcement at the wrong time. Walker, Hops, and Fiegenbaum (1976) observed the interactions between five acting-out children and their teachers. The results showed that though the five teachers praised the acting-out child's appropriate behavior about once every hour, they attended to inappropriate behavior nine times each hour. Similarly, Walker and Buckley (1973) observed an elementary classroom teacher and found that although 82 percent of the teacher's interactions with successful students followed appropriate behavior, 89 percent of the responses to students with behavior problems followed inappropriate behavior. Taken together, these and other studies suggest that we should attempt to increase our use of positive social reinforcement and make this reinforcement contingent on acceptable student behavior. When a child who demonstrates a high rate of irresponsible behavior demonstrates a positive behavior, we should try to reinforce this behavior immediately.

Social reinforcement is usually viewed as a spontaneous approach to changing students' behaviors, but it can also be incorporated into behavior contracts. Because social reinforcement is inexpensive, readily available, and easy to give, we should attempt to incorporate this type of reinforcement into our initial contracts with a student. There are several approaches to take when using social reinforcement in this manner. A contract can be developed in which a student receives social reinforcement from peers, the teacher, an administrator, or a custodian as a consequence for making a desirable behavior change. We can also involve parents in providing social reinforcement when their child behaves appropriately at school. A contract might indicate that if a student reaches a specified behavioral or academic goal, we will send a note home to the parent and the parents will respond by providing the student with a designated number of specific positive statements.

Activity Reinforcement

Because social reinforcement is not a powerful enough reinforcer to bring about prompt or significant change for all students, we need to use other forms of reinforcers. Involvement in various preferred activities is another natural and easily dispensable reward for desirable behavior.

PROCEDURES. The first step in activity reinforcement is to list activities that students find reinforcing. Students enjoy being involved in this process and often offer creative and surprising ideas. Figure 10.16 lists classroom activity reinforcers. The second step is to develop a contract stipulating what the child must do to obtain the activity reinforcer. Whenever activity reinforcers are used, they should be paired with social reinforcement so that the social reinforcement may gradually acquire some of the reinforcing properties associated with the activity reinforcer.

The problem of delayed gratification (the student becomes frustrated while waiting for the reinforcement) that is frequently associated with activity reinforcers can be dealt with by gradually extending the time a student must wait in order to receive the award. When first implementing a contract, the student can be informed that she can be involved in the activity immediately after performing the desired behavior. As the student's behavior improves, she can be informed that she will have to demonstrate increasingly appropriate behavior as well as wait longer before the reinforcement is provided.

An interesting approach to using activity reinforcers involves allowing students to take home school equipment they find particularly interesting. A student's contract might indicate that he can take a CD or video home for two days if he meets the conditions of the contract. Although this type of reinforcement may at first glance appear to be a tangible reinforcer, the student uses the borrowed item but neither consumes nor acquires permanent possession of the reinforcer. The reinforcer provides the student with an opportunity to reinforce himself by participation in an activity involving school property. In essence the student is involved in the reinforcing event at home rather than at school. Another way to involve the home is to allow the student to select

FIGURE 10.16
Activity Reinforcers

Being group leader
Going first
Running errands
Collecting materials
Helping clean up
Getting to sit where he or she wants to
Taking care of class pets
Leading the flag salute
Telling a joke to the class
Being in a skit
Having a party
Making puppets and a puppet show
Doing artwork related to studies
Spending special time with the teacher
Choosing the game for recess
Earning an extra or longer recess
Choosing songs to sing
Working puzzle
Drawing, painting, coloring, working with
   clay, and so on
Choosing group activity
Taking a good note home to parent
   (arrange a reward with the parent)
Visiting another class
Helping teacher
Taking 10-minute break to choose game
   and play with a friend, QUIETLY
Building with construction materials
Getting time to read aloud
Playing short game: tic-tac-toe, easy
   puzzles, connect the dots
Performing for parents

Taking a class pet home for the
   weekend
Leading the songs
Being team captain
Reading to the principal
Seeing a video
Getting to read a new book
Seeing a movie
Listening to music
Playing games in class
Writing on chalkboard: white or colored
   chalk
Playing with magnet or other science
   equipment
Solving codes and other puzzles
Performing before a group: sing a
   song; tell a poem or riddle; do a
   dance, stunt, or trick
Choosing a book to review for class
Selecting topic for group to discuss
Reading to a friend
Reading with a friend
Receiving the right to tutor a classmate
   who needs help
Getting free time in the library
Being asked what he or she would
   like to do
Listening to CD or radio with earphones
Planning a class trip or project
Working in school office
Working in school library

as an activity reinforcer spending time with someone at home in an activity selected by the student.

Social, Token, and Activity Reinforcement

Token reinforcement refers to a system in which students receive immediate reinforcement in the form of a check, chip, or other tangible item that can be traded in for reinforcement at a future time.

PROCEDURES.   There are five basic steps to implementing a token reinforcement system in the classroom. Before introducing a token system, you should determine specifically how each step will be accomplished.

   1. Determine when and with whom the program should be implemented. You might choose to employ a token system with two children whose behavior during seatwork continues to be extremely disruptive despite your attempts at instigating other types of interventions.

2. Select the specific behaviors to be reinforced. When working with an individual student, you might state that the student will receive a token for every two minutes she is in her seat, not talking to peers, and working on the assignment. When working with several students or the entire class, it is desirable to generate a list of behaviors (the classroom rules may be suitable) that will be reinforced.

3. Decide when tokens will be dispensed. When working with a seriously acting-out student, you will usually have to dispense the tokens whenever the desired behavior occurs. As the student begins to gain control of his behavior, you and the student can tally the occurrence of the desired behaviors (the tallies serve as tokens), and this total can be recorded or actual tokens can be given to the student at the end of a designated time. When employing a token system with an entire class, you may choose to use either a random or a set time frame for reinforcement. In using a random reinforcement system, you move around the room or work with a group, and present tokens to students who are behaving appropriately. Though you must be careful not to overlook students or unfairly focus on some students, a random reinforcement schedule is easy to administer and maintains acceptable behavior at a high rate. If you use a set time frame reinforcement, you simply tell the class that every time they meet the behavior criteria for a designated number of minutes, they will receive a tally. When they reach a certain number of tallies, they will earn a group reinforcement such as five minutes to chat quietly, extra recess time, and so on.

4. Determine how to dispense tokens. There are numerous methods for dispensing tokens. Each student involved in the program can have a card taped on the corner of her or his desk, and you can make a mark on the card each time the student displays the desired behavior. When working with young children, teachers occasionally choose to place a can or box on each participant's desk so that tokens can be dropped into the container when the student behaves appropriately. When working with students who change classes or teachers during the day, a travel card (Figure 10.17) can be used. The desired behaviors are written on the card, and at the end of each period the student receives a check for each desired behavior displayed throughout the period.

5. Select a procedure for recording tokens earned. Because most token systems involve earning tokens over a specified period, it is necessary to devise a system for recording the number of tokens each child has accumulated. Likewise, because children can trade tokens in for preferred activities, a record of tokens spent and remaining must be kept.

Curtailment of Activity

Activity curtailment refers to any situation in which inappropriate student behavior is followed by removal of a desired activity. This method of altering students' behaviors has been used since time began, but it has received considerable attention with formal time-out procedures.

PROCEDURES

1. Students should understand the behaviors that will lead to curtailment of activity, what activities will be curtailed, and how long the restriction will be effective.

FIGURE 10.17
Travel Card

Student _____   Grade _____   Date _____

Desired Behaviors

Period	On Time to Class	Brought Necessary Materials	Handed in Assignment	Obeyed Class Rules	Participated in Class	Teacher's Signature
1						
2						
3						
4						
5						
6						
7						

2. Rules on curtailment of activity should be used consistently and fairly. If fighting on the playground is followed by sitting out the next recess, this restriction should be applied to all students in every instance. You should also consider, however, whether playground facilities and activities support positive play, whether rules are clearly understood, and whether students have been taught methods for resolving inevitable playground conflicts.

3. Be aware of cases in which curtailment of activity provides a more desirable alternative than the activity itself. Students may behave inappropriately in order to receive what appears to you to be a punishment but the student views as a relatively positive consequence. A student may dawdle at work in order to stay in from recess, either because recess is perceived as undesirable or the time in the room is viewed as pleasant. Continuing to use a curtailment of activity in this situation might prevent the child from dealing with important social skill deficits that are causing problems on the playground.

4. Present the negative consequences in a nonpunitive, interested manner. Communicate sincere regret that a punishment is necessary. This attitude helps students accept responsibility for their behavior rather than project the blame onto you. Punishment should never be presented in anger, which only encourages the student to feel persecuted and to transfer the blame to you.

5. When presenting a curtailment of activity to a student, always inform the student which specific behavior(s) were responsible for bringing about the undesirable consequence. The student should also be reminded of the desirable behaviors that could prevent the consequences.

6. When presenting a punishment, inform the student what must be done to terminate the punishment. You might inform a student that he can return to the class activity after quietly completing a problem-solving form.

7. Whenever possible, a curtailment of activity should logically relate to the behavior that necessitated the punishment. If a child could not play on the playground without fighting, it is logical that she should miss recess until she can develop a plan for interacting more appropriately with peers. It is not logical, though, to have children stay after school and write sentences because they fought on the playground.

8. Activity curtailment should, whenever possible, be consolidated with activities aimed at helping the student develop new skills that will prevent repeated performance of the undesirable behavior. Therefore, when being excluded from a desired activity, the student should be involved in examining the problem and developing a plan for solving it.

9. Collect data to help determine whether the curtailment of activity is effective in reducing the undesirable behavior or increasing the desired behavior. Because punishment in any form may have numerous negative side effects, it should be discontinued if data indicate that it is ineffective.

10. Punishment methods of changing students' behaviors should be phased out as soon as possible and replaced by more positive approaches, such as problem solving, self-management, or social or activity reinforcement.

Group Contracts

A group contract involves a situation in which the entire group earns a reward or loses previously awarded points or privileges contingent on the entire group's behaving in a desired manner. Some writers define group contracts as including programs in which an individual student's behavior is reinforced by a desired activity for the entire group, but this technique is more accurately labeled an activity reinforcer.

One approach to devising a group contract is to develop the contract during a class meeting. An excellent example of this method occurred when a graduate student in one of the author's classes expressed concern because students in her eighth-grade math class were averaging nearly ten minutes before they were all seated and ready to begin the day's lesson. The teacher's initial idea was to present the students with an offer to provide the entire class with ice-cream cones on Friday if they could be ready to start class within two minutes after the bell rang for five consecutive days. The author suggested, however, that students would be more likely to accomplish the goal and might need less reinforcement if they solved the problem themselves. The teacher accepted this logic and decided to present the problem to the class along with a large chart indicating the number of minutes it had taken them to settle down during the past ten days.

Because the teacher was well liked by her students and had demonstrated her competence by coming prepared with a data display, the students acknowledged that a problem existed and decided to solve it. The initial solution offered by a student and enthusiastically supported by the class was simply for everyone to be prepared every day when the bell rang. Fortunately, the teacher realized that this was an overly ambitious goal and informed the class that she would be delighted if the class could be prepared to start two minutes after the bell rang. The class then decided to clearly define the term *ready to start* and determined that it meant the entire class (1) being in their seats, (2) having a paper and pencil on their desks, (3) being quiet, and (4) looking at the front of the room. Finally, the class decided to borrow a stopwatch from the physical education department and to allow each member of the class to time the class for one day and mark the results on the large chart the teacher had prepared.

Not surprisingly, the student involvement served as its own reinforcement, and no one suggested any form of extrinsic reward. Results indicated that during the five weeks the class marked the chart, they never required more than one minute and forty-five seconds to become prepared for class. Furthermore, follow-up data collected two weeks after students had ceased to mark the chart indicated that this behavior had been maintained.

The effectiveness of this group contract was based on the fact that the solution responded sensitively to students' needs for competence and power while using a problem-solving approach that incorporated the basic components of a sound behavioristic intervention.

One problem that occasionally arises when implementing a group contract is that one or several students subvert the group's chance for success. When they do so, the teacher might initially implement a Glasser problem-solving discussion in order to help the student acknowledge the situation, decide whether to make a change, and develop a plan. If the student either indicates unwillingness to change or is simply unable to control his behavior adequately in response to a group contract, the student can be placed on an individual contract and the class can be informed that his behavior will not influence the class's chances of earning a reward. Although this intervention may be necessary, it tends to isolate the student. Therefore, the teacher should periodically discuss the situation with the student with the goal of including the student in the group contract.

Case Study: A Contract with a High School Band Class

An excellent example of a group contract was recently presented by a high school band teacher who used a contract to reduce talking during class. In this incident, the students decided that a consequence and reward would help them change their behavior. They agreed to give up one minute of the break following band class for every minute they were off task. They also decided that if they could meet the goal of thirty minutes off task in eight days they would have a pot luck lunch as a reward. Figure 10.18 presents the data associated with this intervention. The data indicate that off-task behavior reduced from 17.2 minutes per class period to 2.88 minutes per period. This teacher also

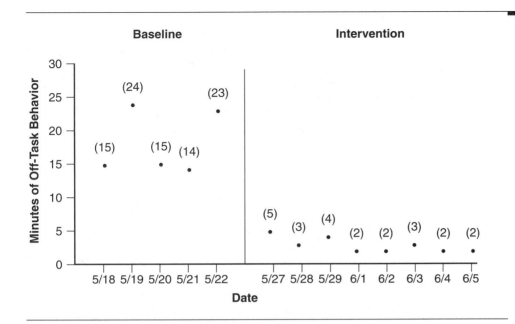

FIGURE 10.18
Group Behavior
Contract

Source: Reprinted
by permission of
Mark R. Gaulke.

found that when students are presented with the data and asked to be involved in determining the solution, dramatic results can often be obtained.

P A U S E

10.7   *and Consider*

> Select a student or class with whom you have worked in developing more responsible behavior but with whom you are not satisfied with the results. For this individual or group, develop a contract to assist them in behaving in a manner that more consistently enhances their learning and that of others. Share this contract with a colleague or classmate and incorporate the feedback prior to implementing it. If you are able to implement the contract, record the data and share this with you colleague(s) or classmate(s).

A TEAM APPROACH TO DEVELOPING A POSITIVE BEHAVIOR CHANGE PLAN

Many teachers have learned to implement the strategies described in this book. However, regardless of one's skill level in creating classroom environments that encourage positive student behavior, some students present challenges that stretch the creativity and patience of even the most talented and dedicated educator. Therefore, it is essential that educators develop structures for working collaboratively to determine what may be causing a student's unproductive behavior and develop a positive behavior change plan to assist the student in having a more positive school experience. As discussed in detail in the section on functional assessment, the development of a plan will be most effective when it is based on a clear understanding of the antecedent conditions, the consequences, and the function these consequences may be serving the student. Team members can be extremely valuable in making hypotheses regarding these important factors. Likewise, team members can be helpful in brainstorming modifications in the environment that may help the student be more successful and strategies for helping the student develop substitute behaviors that enable him or her to meet needs without violating the rights of others. Finally, team members can be helpful in generating, implementing, and assessing interventions aimed at helping the student develop new behavior skills.

Who Should Be on the Team?

There is no one answer to this question. In our combined sixty-four years of work with teacher teams, however, we have found that an effective team often includes two classroom teachers who work with the student, a counselor or school psychologist, an administrator, a parent or guardian, and the student. This team composition provides access to numerous individuals who have firsthand knowledge of the student and the student's behavior as well as individuals with more limited background with the student but who have particular expertise in working with student behavior.

In their book, *A Positive Approach to Understanding and Addressing Challenging Behaviors*, Karen Topper and her colleagues provide a detailed discussion of the composition and functioning of such teams (Topper et al., 1994). While many teams function without family members, these authors strongly support the participation of family members and list the following benefits to family involvement:

- Knowledge of the full history of the student and a total picture of what is going on in the child's life
- In-depth knowledge of the student's strengths, interests and needs, and the skills the student needs to function outside the school settings
- Knowledge and ongoing experience of the most useful strategies for dealing with the student's behavioral challenges
- Knowledge of the key support and resource people in the student's life
- Knowledge of recent or ongoing stressors that may impact the student's functioning at school
- Knowledge of ways to promote prevention, teaching, and response strategies across settings (p. 32)

Although we value the involvement of parents and students, student involvement depends on the age of the student and the severity of the behavior. Parent involvement is also most beneficial and appropriate when the school staff has worked collaboratively and been unable to develop methods that have assisted the student in behaving responsibly. Initially, we believe it is most time efficient and reasonable for the teacher or counselor to meet with the parent and student and for the team to meet without these parties to develop a plan.

Developing a Positive Behavior Change Plan

The team's responsibility is to create a positive behavior change plan that will assist the student in meeting his or her needs without using the behaviors that have been violating others' rights and harming the student's ability to learn. The development of such plans can be expedited by using a structured approach to staffings. An effective process includes these seven steps:

1. Determine the specific student behaviors that need to be changed.
2. Conduct a functional behavior assessment.
3. Determine changes that need to be made in the school environment in order to support the student.
4. Determine the strategies to be used to assist the student in developing new behavioral skills.
5. Assign responsibility to staff for implementing each intervention.
6. Determine the data to be collected for the purpose of assessing the effectiveness of interventions.
7. Set a date to review the program.

It is suggested that you focus on no more than two behaviors and develop no more than three interventions for each behavior.

Figure 10.19 presents the form the authors use to develop a positive behavior change plan. The numbers in parentheses near the top of the form indicate the number

(3) Is Community Interaction Needed?	(7) Behavior to Change	(12) Intervention Plan	(5) Person Responsible	(3) Evaluation Data
	1.	1a. 1b.		
	2.	2a. 2b.		
Roles:	Presenter Recorder Facilitator Timer			

FIGURE 10.19
Developing a Positive Behavior Change Plan

Signed

Teacher	Teacher	Teacher (Monitor)
Teacher	Counselor	Principal

Dated

Monitor agrees to check within seven days to determine how the program is working.

of minutes allocated to that task. The bottom of the sheet lists those individuals who have agreed to be involved in implementing one or more of the interventions, and the mentor is the person who agrees to monitor both the implementation of and the progress achieved in using the plan. Figure 10.20 presents a positive behavior change plan one of the authors helped a staff develop for a fourth-grade boy.

Behavior to Change	Intervention	Person Responsible	Data
Failure to follow reasonable adult requests	1. Role-playing methods for following requests. Do this both with the teacher and with the class. This would include teaching Jason how to remove himself to his seat for quiet work when he cannot handle the large-group work.	Counselor or principal	Tallies of this behavior
	2. Provide Jason with frequent prompts and reinforcements for using his new skills.		
	3. Teach students to ignore him when he is inappropriate.	Classroom teacher	
	4. Countoon with Jason showing improvement to the principal or other valued adult.	Counselor or teacher	
	5. Consistent time-outs when Jason reaches the maximum allowable number of times he fails to follow a request.	Teacher	
Poor peer relationships	1. Class meeting to help students learn how to ignore and reinforce Jason.	Teacher	
	2. Have a peer be his assistant who helps him when he has not heard directions and so on.	Teacher	
	3. Perhaps Jason could tutor in a kindergarten or first-grade classroom so he could be a model rather than needing to obtain attention being inappropriate.	Kindergarten or first-grade teacher and classroom teacher	
	4. Work with Jason and several students from the class on specific activities for recess.	Counselor	

FIGURE 10.20
Positive Behavior Change Plan for Jason

The authors are often asked to discuss the relationship between a teacher assistance team (TAT) and positive behavior change plans. Once teachers have individually implemented effective classroom management methods and considered environmental factors that may be influencing a student's behavior, they are advised to seek assistance. Teacher assistance teams (Chalfant, VanDusgen, Pysh, & Moultrie, 1979; Gilmer, 1985; Hayek, 1987) are comprised of several teachers who meet to provide suggestions for their peers on working with students who are failing to follow school rules or not making satisfactory academic progress. A form used at a TAT team meeting is found in Figure 10.21.

Although strong supporters of the idea of TATs, the authors have also found that most staff attend numerous meetings and also become frustrated when a student is not referred for outside assistance or evaluation after they have met with a team to develop strategies to assist the student. Because the TAT is usually designed to provide teachers with ideas but is not designed to develop a comprehensive plan involving other school personnel, these meetings, although valuable, often fail to provide interventions

---

Name of student _____

Grade _____ Date _____

Referred by _____ Classroom teacher _____

Present _____

Perceived Problem:

Expectations for Change:

Student Strengths: Student Weaknesses:

Prior Strategies:

Brainstorming:

Follow-Up: TAT Coordinator:

FIGURE 10.21
Teacher Assistance Team Worksheet

that alter a student's behavior. Ideally, this would lead to the student being referred to a positive behavior change plan team. Realistically, school staff do not have time or energy for yet another staffing. Therefore, if only one meeting or series of meetings will be held, it is recommended that it be a team that includes a building administrator, two or more teachers, and a specialist whose task is to develop a positive behavior change plan. As previously mentioned, this team is responsible for coordinating the staff resources to develop a plan to involve several adults in assisting the student in improving her or his learning and behavior. Experience indicates that teachers find this type of planning meeting supportive and instructive and that a positive behavior change plan can in many ways eliminate the need for a TAT.

P A U S E
and Consider   10.8

It is extremely important to learn how to work as a team to develop plans for assisting students in making better choices. If you are currently teaching, we encourage you to select a student who needs assistance in behaving responsibly. Create a team comprised of the staff recommended earlier in the chapter, use the format from Figure 10.19, and develop a positive behavior change plan. Implement this plan and meet to review the results.

If you are not able to work with a building team, we encourage you to form a group with your classmates. Select a student one of your group members is observing or working with who engages in a high rate of behaviors that are having a negative influence on his or her learning or that of others. Complete a functional behavior assessment on this student (Figure 10.3) to determine what factors may be influencing behavior. Next, using the format in Figure 10.19 develop a positive behavior change plan that could help this student develop and choose to use more responsible behaviors.

IMPLEMENTATION ACTIVITIES

ACTIVITY 10.1

Assessing Your
Classroom
Management
Behavior

Think of a student whose behavior has created a problem for himself or for the class. With this student in mind, complete the interventions form in Figure 10.1 and then answer the following questions.

1. What changes could you make in your classroom that would create a more clearly structured, inviting environment for this student?
2. What interventions have you already attempted to assist this student in behaving more responsibly?
3. Based on the data you have collected, how effective do you believe you have been in assisting this student?

ACTIVITY 10.2

Assessing Your
Prereferral
Interventions

For the student whose behavior is detrimental to himself or the class, complete the form in Figure 10.2 by (1) circling the interventions you have implemented (or, if you are observing in a class, the interventions you have seen implemented), (2) placing a box around those that you believe would assist the student and you would like to try, and (3) placing an X through the number in front of those interventions that do not seem appropriate or feasible given your teaching situation. After you have completed this, sit down with one or more teachers or students in your college class and share what you have done and the items you selected as possible new interventions.

ACTIVITY 10.3

Completing a
Functional
Assessment

Think of a student whose behavior has created a problem for himself or for the class. With this student in mind, complete the form in Figure 10.3 and then respond to the following items.

1. List as many specific things as possible that you learned about this student's unproductive behavior.
2. Based on these discoveries, what changes could you make in the classroom to assist this student in behaving more responsibly?

The following activities can help you improve your skills in data collection and the use of behavioral interventions.

ACTIVITY 10.4

Clearly Defining
Students' Behavior

For each of the five adjectives listed in the left column, write three specific observable student behaviors that might be displayed by a student described by the adjective.

General Descriptor	Specific Behavioral Descriptor
Angry	1. 2. 3.
Unmotivated	1. 2. 3.
Hyperactive	1. 2. 3.
Uncooperative	1. 2. 3.
Inept	1. 2. 3.

ACTIVITY 10.5	Think of a student who appears to lack skill in one or more social skills such as accepting critical feedback, following directions, or responding to comments from peers. Use Figure 10.9 to develop a social skill lesson for this student.
Developing a Social Skill Lesson	

ACTIVITY 10.6	Think of a student who exhibits a specific behavior that is negatively impacting his learning or the learning of others such as talking out or making unusual sounds. Develop a self-monitoring form that would help this student count his own behavior. Also determine a format for recording the results. Present these to a colleague and have this person provide you with feedback.
Using Self-Monitoring	

ACTIVITY 10.7	Select an individual student's behavior that is detrimental to the student as well as the class. Describe the behavior in behavioral terms, collect baseline data for at least two 30-minute periods, and graph the results.
Implementing and Assessing a Behavioristic Intervention	Next, select one of the procedures for developing a contract described in this chapter and develop a written contract with the student.

Implement the contract for five days. Collect and record data during all times when the contract is in effect.

At the end of five days, discuss the results with the student and determine whether to (1) continue the contract, (2) alter the contract by requiring improved behavior while reducing the reinforcement or employing a reinforcer lower on the hierarchy, or (3) discontinue the contract.

Finally, complete these statements:

The student's behavior . . .
At the end of the five days the student said . . .
I was surprised that . . .
I was pleased that . . .

ACTIVITY 10.8	For the student for whom you completed Figure 10.3, develop a positive behavior change plan and present it using Figure 10.19.
Developing a Positive Behavior Change Plan	

SUMMARY

Even though teachers are not responsible for developing a series of sophisticated behavior change interventions, there are a variety of effective, efficient methods teachers can implement that can dramatically influence student behavior. As teachers work with an increasing number of at-risk students, they will benefit from being able to implement a variety of these methods.

Teachers will increasingly be asked to document both student behavior problems and their interventions aimed at altering student behavior. This chapter provides methods for accomplishing this important task. The chapter describes methods for helping students become involved in data collection and become more aware of and responsible for their own behaviors through self-monitoring. Methods for involving students in setting goals and becoming more aware of the consequences associated with their behavior through the use of contracts have also been explored.

Experience and research with teachers (Jones, 1991) who have implemented these methods show that nearly 80 percent find they can use them in their classrooms and that the methods are effective approximately 80 percent of the time. Although these teachers realize that the quality of their proactive classroom management and instruction are their major responsibilities, they find that using the methods discussed in Chapters 8 through 10 can have a major positive impact on individual students' behaviors. Furthermore, they find that their ability to help these students is professionally rewarding and has a positive impact on the behavior and learning of other students.

RECOMMENDED READING

Alberto, P., & Troutman, A. (1999). *Applied behavior analysis for teachers* (5th ed.). Columbus, OH: Merrill.

Cartledge, G., & Fellows Milburn, J. (1995). *Teaching social skills to children and youth: Innovative approaches.* Boston: Allyn & Bacon.

Fister, S., & Kemp, K. (1995). *The one-minute skill builder: Improving student social skills.* Longmont, CO: Sopris West.

Gable, R. (1995). A critical analysis of functional assessment: Issues for researchers and practitioners. *Behavioral Disorders, 22,* 36–40.

Gable, R., Sugai, G., Lewis, T., Nelson, J., Cheney, D., Safran, S., & Safran, J. (1998). *Individual and systemic approaches to collaboration and consultation.* Reston, VA: Council for Children with Behavioral Disorders.

Goldstein, A., Harootunian, B., & Conoley, J. (1994). *Student aggression: Prevention, management, and replacement.* New York: Guilford Press.

Jones, V., Dohrn, E., & Dunn, C. (2004). *Creating effective programs for students with emotional and behavior disorders: Interdisciplinary approaches for adding meaning and hope to behavior change interventions.* Boston: Allyn & Bacon.

Kaplan, J., & Brainville, B. (1991). *Beyond behavior modification: A cognitive-behavioral approach to behavior management in the school.* Austin, TX: Pro-Ed.

Kauffman, J. (2001). *Characteristics of emotional and behavioral disorders of children and youth* (7th ed.). Upper Saddle River, NJ: Merrill Prentice-Hall.

Kennedy, C. (2000). When reinforcers for problem behavior are not readily apparent: Extending functional assessments to complex problem behaviors. *Journal of Positive Behavior Interventions, 2,* 195–201.

Kerr, M., & Nelson, M. (2002). *Strategies for addressing behavior problems in the classroom.* Upper Saddle River, NJ: Merrill Prentice-Hall.

Knitzer, J., Steinberg, Z., & Fleisch, B. (1990). *At the schoolhouse door: An examination of programs and policies for children with behavioral and emotional problems.* New York: Bank Street College of Education.

Maag, J., & Reid, R. (1994). Attention-deficit hyperactivity disorder: A functional approach to assessment and treatment. *Behavioral Disorders, 20,* 5–23.

Martin, G., & Pear, J. (1996). *Behavior modification: What it is and how to do it.* Upper Saddle River, NJ: Prentice-Hall.

McCarney, S., & Cummins, K. (1993). *The pre-referral intervention manual: The most common learning and behavior problems encountered in the educational environment.* Columbia, MO: Hawthorne Educational Service.

McConnell, K., Patton, J., & Polloway, E. (2000). *Behavioral intervention planning: Completing a functional behavioral assessment and developing a behavioral intervention plan.* Austin, TX: Pro-Ed.

McGinnis, E., & Goldstein, A. (1984). *Skillstreaming the elementary school child: A guide for teaching prosocial skills.* Champaign, IL: Research Press.

McGinnis, E., & Goldstein, A. (1990). *Skillstreaming in early childhood: Teaching prosocial skills to the preschool and kindergarten child.* Champaign, IL: Research Press.

Nichols, P. (1999). *Clear thinking: Talking back to whispering shadows.* Iowa City, IA: River Lights Publishers.

Nichols, P., & Shaw, M. (1999). *Whispering shadows: Think clearly and claim your personal power.* Iowa City, IA: River Lights Publishers.

O'Neill, R., Horner, R., Albin, R., Sprague, J., Storey, K., & Newton, S. (1997). *Functional assessment and program development for problem behavior: A practical handbook* (2nd ed.). Grove, CA: Brooks/Cole.

Quinn, M., Gable, R., Rutherford, R., Nelson, C., & Howell, K. (1998). *Addressing student problem behavior: An IEP team's introduction to functional behavioral assessment and behavior intervention plans.* Washington, DC: Office of Special Education Programs, Center for Effective Collaboration and Practice.

Schrumpf, F., Crawford, D., & Usadel, H. (1991). *Peer mediation: Conflict resolution in schools.* Champaign, IL: Research Press.

Scott, T., & Nelson, M. (1999). Functional behavioral assessment: Implications for training and staff development. *Behavioral Disorders, 24,* 249–252.

Sheridan, S. (1995). *The tough kid social skills book.* Longmont, CO: Sopris West.

Smith, B., & Sugai, G. (2000). A self-management functional assessment-based behavior support plan for a middle school student with EBD. *Journal of Positive Behavioral Support, 2,* 208–217.

Sprick, R., & Howard, L. (1995). *The teacher's encyclopedia of behavior management: 100 problems/500 plans, for grades K–9.* Longmont, CO: Sopris West.

Todd, A., Horner, R., & Sugai, G. (1999). Effects of self-monitoring and self-recruited praise on problem behavior, academic engagement and work completion in a typical classroom. *Journal of Positive Behavior Intervention, 1,* 66–76.

Walker, H. (1995). *The acting-out child: Coping with classroom disruption.* Longmont, CO: Sopris West.

Walker, H., Colvin, G., & Ramsey, E. (1995). *Antisocial behavior in school: Strategies and best practices.* Pacific Grove, CA: Brooks/Cole.

Walker, H., McConnell, S., Holmes, D., Todis, B., Walker, J., & Golden, N. (1987). *The ACCEPTS program: A curriculum for children's effective peer and teacher skills.* Austin, TX: Pro-Ed.

Walker, H., & Sprague, J. (1999). Longitudinal research and functional behavioral assessment issues. *Behavioral Disorders, 24,* 335–337.

Walker, H., Todis, B., Holmes, D., & Horton, G. (1988). *The ACCESS program: Adolescent curriculum for communication and effective social skills.* Austin, TX: Pro-Ed.

Workman, E. (1995). *Teaching behavioral self-control to students* (2nd ed.). Austin, TX: Pro-Ed.

Possible Procedures for Common Areas in an Elementary School

PLAYGROUND

GOAL: Students will play safely in all games and on all equipment.

Responsible Playground Behavior

**1. Rough play is not allowed on the playground.

**2. When the bell rings, students are to stop what they are doing and should line up quickly.

**3. Students will settle differences peacefully using "Stop/Think/Plan" (STP).

4. Students will show respect for others and follow instructions given by staff.

5. Students will stay outside in the morning before school, and during all recesses, unless they have a "pass."

6. Students will stay out of ditches, off hills, and away from puddles and mud.

7. Students will leave rocks, bark, sticks, and other dangerous objects alone.

8. Students will play only on playground areas, not in courtyard, grassy areas, or bushes.

9. Students will show pride in their school by keeping the building and grounds free of litter.

10. Students will take turns on equipment (e.g., 25 swings on swings).

11. Students will not chew gum and candy on playground.

12. Students will leave knives and other unsafe objects at home along with radios, tape players, hard balls, and toys.

13. Students in grades K–3 will stay off monkey bars until the first bell during the lunch hour.

14. Students will leave the playground immediately after school and not return until after 3:00 P.M.

15. During school, students will not leave the playground for any reason without a note signed by their parent and/or their teacher and the principal. The note must be shown to the person on duty.

RESTROOMS

GOAL: The restrooms at Lincoln Elementary will be clean and safe.

Responsible Hallway Behavior

**1. Use restrooms during recess, before the last bell rings.

**2. If restrooms must be used during class, students must have a restroom pass.

**3. Use restrooms appropriately and leave them clean.

4. Put toilet paper in the toilet. Put all other paper in the garbage can.

5. Flush the toilet.

Note: Items marked with ** indicate expectations that students must understand fully and immediately.

Source: Sprick, R. *Responsibility and Discipline Manual: Elementary Sample.* Eugene, OR: Teaching Strategies, Inc. Reprinted by permission.

6. Leave stalls unlocked after use.
7. Wash your hands.

HALLS

GOAL: The halls and breezeways will be a safe and quiet environment where people interact with courtesy and respect.

Responsible Hallway Behavior

**1. Students will move safely through the hallways.

**2. Normal speaking voices will be used in the hallway. (If someone is too far away to hear, move close enough to speak in a normal voice.)

3. During class time, students must have a signed pass to be in the halls.

4. Everyone will be treated with respect.

5. If an adult asks to speak with you, stop and talk with that person.

6. If an adult requests that you correct a behavior, do what the adult asks you to do.

7. No student should be in the halls prior to 8:15 A.M. unless escorted by an adult.

8. Students should go directly home after dismissal from class.

LUNCHROOM

GOAL: The lunch line and lunch area will be a safe and clean environment where people interact with courtesy and respect.

Responsible Cafeteria Behavior

Coming to Lunch and Lunch Line

**1. While in line, students will keep hands, feet, and objects to themselves.

**2. Students will use quiet voices in the lunch line.

3. Students are to be escorted to the lunch area in two lines: "buyers and bringers." Buyers' line is closest to the learning center. Bringers' line is closest to the lunch tables.

4. Monitors will walk quietly and stand in the lunch monitor line.

5. Students will buy lunch, milk, or snacks before they sit down.

Lunch Area Procedures

**1. Students will use quiet voices when talking.

**2. Students will keep hands, feet and objects to themselves.

3. Students will stay in their seats and raise their hands to get help.

4. Students will eat quietly and use good manners.

5. Students will walk in the lunch area.

6. Everyone will treat others with respect.

Dismissal

**1. Students will clean up their own area.

**2. When the bell rings, the supervisor will check each table and dismiss students if the table and floor are reasonably clean.

3. Slow eaters will be reassigned to overflow tables.

4. When dismissed, students will walk quietly to the north door of the cafeteria.

5. Lunch boxes will be left in the playground area where classes line up.

6. Students are to remain on the playground unless they are given a pass to enter the building.

ASSEMBLIES

GOAL: Lincoln students will demonstrate respectful behavior during assemblies by listening, participating, and following directions.

Responsible Assembly Behavior

**1. When the leader goes to the microphone and says, "May I have your attention please," stop talking and look at the person at the microphone.

**2. Listen carefully.

3. Students will follow their teacher's directions regarding where to sit.

4. Everyone will wait quietly for the program to begin. Quiet talking will be allowed until the program is ready to begin.

5. Communicate with the performers with your eyes and ears.

6. Never boo, whistle, yell, or put someone down.

7. At the end of the program, the leader will conclude the assembly by thanking the performers.

8. Students will remain seated until the teacher gives them the signal to stand and follow the teacher from the assembly area.

Agne, K., Greenwood, G., & Miller, L. (1994). Relationships between teacher belief systems and teacher effectiveness. *The Journal of Research and Development in Education, 27,* 141–152.

Alberto, P., & Troutman, A. (1999). *Applied behavior analysis for teachers.* Upper Saddle River, NJ: Merrill.

Aleem, D., & Moles, O. (1993). *Review of research on ways to attain goal six: Creating safe, disciplined, and drug-free schools.* Washington, DC: OERI.

Algozzine, B., Audette, B., Ellis, E., Marr, M., & White, R. (2000). Supporting teachers, principals, and students through unified discipline. *Teaching Exceptional Children, 33,* 42–47.

Allen, T., & Plax, T. (1999). Group communications in the formal educational context. In F. R. Lawrence (Ed.), *The handbook of group communication theory & research* (pp. 493–515). Thousand Oaks, CA: Sage.

American Association of University Women. (1993). *Hostile hallways: The AAUW survey on sexual harassment in America's schools.* Washington, DC: American Association of University Women Foundation.

American Association of University Women Educational Foundation. (1992). *The AAUW report: How schools shortchange girls.* Washington, DC: National Education Association.

America's children: Key national indicators of well-being. (2002). Vienna, VA: Health Resources and Services Administration Information Center.

Anderson, C., & Bushman, B. (2002). The effects of media on violence in society. *Science, 295,* 2377–2378.

Anderson, L., Everston, C., & Brophy, J. (1979). An experimental study of effective teaching in first grade reading groups. *Elementary School Journal, 79,* 193–223.

Antil, L., Jenkins, J., Wayne, S., & Vadasy, P. (1998). Cooperative learning: Prevalence, conceptualizations, and the relation between research and practice. *American Educational Research Journal, 35,* 419–454.

Archer, A., & Gleason, M. (1989). *Skills for school success.* North Billerica, MA: Curriculum Associates.

Archer, A., & Gleason, M. (1994). *Advanced skills for school success.* North Billerica, MA: Curriculum Associates.

August, D., & Hakuta, K. (1997). *Improving schooling for language-minority children: A research agenda.* Washington, DC: National Research Council.

Ballenger, C. (1992). Because you like us: The language of control. *Harvard Educational Review, 62* (2), 199–208.

Banks, J. (1988). *Multiethnic education: Theory and practice.* Boston: Allyn & Bacon.

Banks, J., & McGee Banks, C. (1993). *Multicultural education: Issues and perspectives* (2nd ed.). Boston: Allyn & Bacon.

Barone, F. (1997). Bullying in the classroom: It doesn't have to happen. *Phi Delta Kappan, 79,* 80–82.

Barone, M. (2001). The many faces of America. *U.S. News and World Report,* March 19, 18–20.

Barth, R. (1990). *Improving schools from within.* San Francisco: Jossey-Bass.

Bauer, E. (1973). Personal space: A study of blacks and whites. *Sociometry, 36,* 402–408.

Baumann, J. (1992). Organizing and managing a whole language classroom. *Reading Research and Instruction, 31,* 1–14.

Baumeister, R. (1993). *Self-esteem: The puzzle of low self-regard.* New York: Plenum.

Beane, J. (Ed.). (1995). *Toward a coherent curriculum.* Reston, VA: Association for Supervision and Curriculum Development.

Beane, J. (1997). *Curriculum integration: Designing the core of democratic education.* New York: Teachers College Press.

Becker, W., Engelmann, S., & Thomas, D. (1975). *Teaching 1: Classroom management.* Champaign, IL: Research Press.

Belenky, M., Clinchy, B., Goldberger, N., & Tarule, J. (1986). *Women's ways of knowing: Development of self, body and mind.* New York: Basic Books.

Benson, P., Scales, P., Leffert, N., & Roehlkepartain, E. (1999). *A fragile foundation: The state of developmental assets among American youth.* Minneapolis, MN: Search Institute.

Berliner, D. (1984). The half-full glass: A review of research on teaching. In P. Hosford (Ed.), *Using what we know about teaching.* Alexandria, VA: Association for Supervision and Curriculum Development.

Berry, B. (1995). School restructuring and teacher power: The case of Keels elementary. In A. Lieberman (Ed.), *The work of restructuring schools: Building from the ground up.* New York: Teachers College Press.

Bigelow, B., Christenson, L., Karp, S., Miner, B., & Peterson, B. (1994). *Rethinking our classrooms: Teaching for equity and justice, Volume One.* Milwaukee, WI: Rethinking Schools.

Bigelow, B., Harvey, B., Karp, S., & Miller, L. (2001). *Rethinking our classrooms: Teaching for equity and justice, Volume 2.* Milwaukee, WI: Rethinking Schools.

Binns, K., Steinberg, A., & Amorosi, S. (1997). *The Metropolitan Life Survey of the American Teacher 1998: Building family-school partnerships: Views of teachers and students.* New York: Louis Harris & Associates.

Blackham, G., & Silberman, A. (1975). *Modification of child and adolescent behavior.* Belmont, CA: Wadsworth.

Bloom, B. (Ed.) (1956). *Taxonomy of educational objectives, handbook I: Cognitive domain.* New York: David McKay.

Borba, M. (1989). *Esteem builders: A K–8 curriculum for improving student achievement, behavior and school climate.* Rolling Hills Estates, CA: Jalmer.

Bowers, C., & Flinders, D. (1990). *Responsive teaching.* New York: Teachers College Press.

Bowlby, J. (1982). *Attachment and loss: Vol. 1. Attachment.* New York: Basic Books.

Brendtro, L., Brokenleg, M., & VonBockern, S. (1990). *Reclaiming youth at risk: Our hope for the future.* Bloomington, IN: National Educational Service.

Brendtro, L., & Long, N. (1995). Breaking the cycle of conflict. *Educational Leadership, 52,* 52–56.

Brickhouse, N., & Bodner, G. (1992). The beginning science teacher: Classroom narratives of convictions and constraints. *Journal of Research in Science Teaching, 29,* 471–485.

Broden, M., Hall, R., & Mitts, B. (1971). The effect of self-recording on the classroom behavior of two eighth-grade students. *Journal of Applied Behavior Analysis, 4,* 191–199.

Brophy, J. (1981). Teacher praise: A functional analysis. *Review of Educational Research, 51*, 5–32.

Brophy, J. (1982). Classroom management and learning. *American Education, 18*, 20–23.

Brophy, J. (1983). Research on the self-fulfilling prophecy and teacher expectations. *Journal of Educational Psychology, 75*, 631–661.

Brophy, J. (1986a, April). *Teacher effects research and teacher quality.* Paper presented at the annual meeting of the American Educational Research Association, San Francisco.

Brophy, J. (1986b, April). *Socializing students' motivation to learn.* Paper presented at the annual meeting of the American Educational Research Association, San Francisco.

Brophy, J. (1988). Educating teachers about managing classrooms and students. *Teaching and Teacher Education, 4* (1), 1–18.

Brophy, J., & Evertson, C. (1976). *Learning from teaching: A developmental perspective.* Boston: Allyn & Bacon.

Brophy, J., & Good, T. (1971). Teacher's communication of differential expectations for children's classroom performance: Some behavior data. *Journal of Educational Psychology, 61*, 365–374.

Brophy, J., & Good, T. (1974). *Teacher-student relationships: Causes and consequences.* New York: Holt, Rinehart and Winston.

Brophy, J., & McCaslin, M. (1992). Teachers' reports of how they perceive and cope with problem students. *The Elementary School Journal, 93*, 3–68.

Bruner, J. (1996). *The culture of education.* Cambridge, MA: Harvard University Press.

Butler, J. (1993). *Transforming the curriculum: Teaching about women of color.* In J. Banks & C. McGee Banks (Eds.), *Multicultural education* (pp. 149–167). Boston: Allyn & Bacon.

Butler, R., & Nisan, M. (1986). Effects of no feedback, task-related comments, and grades on intrinsic motivation and performance. *Journal of Educational Psychology, 78*, 210–216.

Campbell, L., Campbell, B., & Dickerson, D. (1999). *Teaching and learning through multiple intelligences* (2nd ed.). Boston: Allyn & Bacon.

Canfield, J., & Siccone, F. (1992). *One hundred ways to develop student self-esteem and responsibility.* Boston: Allyn & Bacon.

Canter, L. (1996, March/April). First, the rapport—then, the rules. *Learning*, 12–14.

Canter, L., & Canter, M. (1976). *Assertive discipline.* Los Angeles: Lee Canter Associates.

Carr, S., & Punzo, R. (1993). The effects of self-monitoring of academic accuracy and productivity on the performance of students with behavioral disorders. *Behavioral Disorders, 18* (4), 241–250.

Carter, K. (1992). Toward a cognitive conception of classroom management: A case of teacher comprehension. In J. Shulman (Ed.), *Case methods in teacher education* (pp. 111–130). New York: Teachers College Press.

Chalfant, J., VanDusgen Pysh, M., & Moultrie, R. (1979). Teacher assistance teams: A model for within-building problem solving. *Learning Disability Quarterly, 2*, 85–96.

Chavkin, N., & Gonzales, D. (1995). *Forging partnerships between Mexican-American parents and the schools.* ERIC Digest, ED 388489. Charleston, WV: ERIC Clearinghouse on Rural Education and Small Schools.

Christenson, S., & Sheridan, S. (2001). *Schools and families: Creating essential connections for learning.* New York: Guilford Press.

Cisneros, S. (1991). *The house on Mango Street.* New York: Vintage Books.

Clandinin, D., & Connelly, F. (1986). Rhythms in teaching: The narrative study of teachers' personal practical knowledge of classrooms. *Teaching and Teacher Education, 2* (4), 377–387.

Cole, C. (1992). Self-management interventions in the schools. *School Psychology Review, 21* (2), 188–192.

Cole, S., Horvath, B., Chapman, C., Deschenes, C., Ebeling, D., & Sprague, J. (2000a). *Adapting curriculum and instruction in inclusive classrooms: A teacher's desk reference* (2nd ed.). Bloomington: Indiana Institute on Disability and Community.

Cole, S., Horvath, B., Chapman, C., Deschenes, C., Ebeling, D., & Sprague, J. (2000b). *Adapting curriculum and instruction in inclusive classrooms: Staff development kit* (2nd ed.). Bloomington: Indiana Institute on Disability and Community.

Collins, M. (1992). Making a difference in the classroom. *Special Report, 65.* Grove City, PA: Public Policy Education Fund.

Combs, A., & Taylor, C. (1952). The effect of the perception of mild degrees of threat on performance. *Journal of Abnormal and Social Psychology, 47*, 420–424.

Cooper, H., & Good, T. (1983). *Pygmalion grows up.* New York: Longman.

Coopersmith, S. (1967). *The antecedents of self-esteem.* San Francisco: W. H. Freeman.

Corbett, D., & Wilson, B. (2002). What urban students say about good teaching. *Educational Leadership, 60*, 18–22.

Costenbader, V., & Markson, S. (1998). School suspension: A study with secondary school students. *Journal of School Psychology, 36*, 59–82.

Cotton, K. (1992). *Schoolwide and classroom discipline. School improvement research series: Close-up #9.* Portland, OR: Northwest Regional Educational Laboratory.

Covaleskie, J. (1992). Discipline and morality: Beyond rules and consequences. *Educational Reform, 56*, 173–183.

Covington, M., & Beery, R. (1976). *Self-worth and school learning.* New York: Holt, Rinehart and Winston.

Craig, W., & Pepler, D. (1996). Understanding bullying at school: What can we do about it? In S. Miller, J. Brodine, & T. Miller (Eds.), *Safe by design* (pp. 247–260). Seattle, WA: Committee for Children.

Crank, J., & Bulgren, J. (1993). Visual depictions as information organizers for enhancing achievement of students with learning disabilities. *Learning Disabilities Research and Practice, 8*, 140–147.

Cummins, J. (1996). *Negotiating identities: Education for empowerment in a diverse society.* Ontario, CA: California Association for Bilingual Education.

Curwin, R., & Fuhrmann, B. (1975). *Discovering your teaching self: Humanistic approaches to effective teaching.* Englewood Cliffs, NJ: Prentice Hall.

Curwin, R., & Mendler, A. (1988). *Discipline with dignity.* Reston, VA: Association for Supervision and Curriculum Development.

Cusick, P. (1994). *The educational system: Its nature and logic.* New York: McGraw-Hill.

Dalton, M., & Zanville, H. (2002). *Oregon research report: Student teacher study—2000–2001 cohort.* Salem: Oregon Quality Assurance in Teaching Project.

Dana, N. (1992, February). *Toward preparing the monocultural teacher for the multicultural classroom.* Paper presented at the 72nd meeting of the Association of Teacher Educators, Orlando, FL.

(ERIC Document Reproduction Service No. ED 350 272)

Darling-Hammond, L. (1997). *The right to learn: A blueprint for creating schools that work.* San Francisco: Jossey-Bass.

Deschenes, C., Ebeling, D., & Sprague, J. (1994). *Adapting curriculum and instruction in inclusive classrooms: A teacher's desk reference.* Bloomington, IN: The Center for School and Community Integration.

DiGangi, S., & Maag, J. (1992). A component analysis of self-management training with behaviorally disordered youth. *Behavioral Disorders, 17,* 281–290.

Dishion, T., French, D., & Patterson, G. (1995). The development and ecology of antisocial behavior. In D. Cicchetti & D. Cohen (Eds.), *Developmental Psychopathology, Volume 2.* New York: Wiley.

Dodge, K., Pettit, G., & Bates, J. (1997). How the experience of early physical abuse leads childen to become chronically aggressive. In C. Cicchetti & S. Toth (Eds.), *Developmental psychopathology: Developmental perspectives on trauma: Vol. 9, Theory, Research, and Intervention* (pp. 263–288). Rochester, NY: University of Rochester Press.

Dorman, G. (1981). *Middle grades assessment program.* Chapel Hill, NC: Center for Early Adolescence.

Doyle, W. (1983). Academic work. *Review of Educational Research, 53,* 159–199.

Doyle, W. (1986). Classroom organization and management. In M. C. Wittrock (Ed.), *Handbook of research on teaching* (3rd ed.). New York: Macmillan.

Dreikurs, R., & Cassel, P. (1972). *Discipline without tears: What to do with children who misbehave.* New York: Hawthorn.

Dreikurs, R., Grunwald, B., & Pepper, F. (1971). *Maintaining sanity in the classroom: Illustrated teaching techniques.* New York: Harper and Row.

Dryfoos, J. (1990). *Adolescents at risk: Prevalence and prevention.* New York: Oxford University Press.

Duke, D., & Trautvetter, S. (2001). *Reducing the negative effects of large schools.* Washington, DC: National Clearing House of Educational Facilities.

Dunlap, G., Kern, L., dePercel, M., Clarke, S., Wilson, D., Childs, K., et al. (1993). Functional analysis of classroom variables for students with emotional and behavioral disorders. *Behavioral Disorders, 18,* 275–291.

Dunn, R. (1983). Learning style and its relation to exceptionality at both ends of the spectrum. *Exceptional Children, 49,* 496–506.

Dunn, R., Beaudry, J., & Klavas, A. (1989). Survey of research on learning styles. *Educational Leadership, 46,* 50–58.

Dunn, R., & DeBello, T. (Eds.). (1999). *Improved test scores, attitudes, and behaviors in American's schools: Supervisor's success stories.* Westport, CT: Bergin Garvery.

Dunn, R., Thies, A., & Honigsfeld, A. (2001). *Synthesis of the Dunn and Dunn learning-style model research: Analysis from a neuropsychological perspective.* Jamaica, NY: St. John's University School of Education and Human Services.

Dunst, C., McWilliams, R., & Holbert, K. (1986). Assessment of preschool classroom environments. *Diagnostique, 11,* 212–232.

Duval, R. (1997). *Building character and community in the classroom.* Cypress, CA: Creative Teaching Press.

Dweck, C. (1975). The role of expectations and attributions in the alleviation of learned helplessness. *Journal of Personality and Social Psychology, 31,* 674–685.

Eccles, J., & Wigfield, A. (1985). Teacher expectations and student motivation. In J. Dusek, V. Hall, & W. Meyer (Eds.), *Teacher expectancies.* Hillsdale, NJ: Erlbaum.

Elam, S., & Rose, L. (1995). Phi Delta Kappan/Gallup Poll of the Public's Attitudes Toward Public Schools. *Phi Delta Kappan, 77,* 41–55.

Elkind, D. (1967). Egocentrism in adolescence. *Child Development, 38,* 1025–1034.

Elkind, D. (1981). *The hurried child: Growing up too fast too soon.* Reading, MA: Addison-Wesley.

Emmer, E. (1994, April). *Teacher emotions and classroom management.* Paper presented at the annual meeting of the American Educational Research Association, New Orleans, LA.

Emmer, E., & Aussiker, A. (1987, April). *School and classroom discipline programs: How well do they work?* Paper presented at the annual meeting of the American Educational Research Association, Washington, DC.

Emmer, E., & Aussiker, A. (1990). School and classroom discipline programs: How well do they work? In O. C. Moles (Ed.), *Student discipline strategies: Research and practice* (pp. 129–165). Albany: State University of New York Press.

Emmer, E., Evertson, C., & Anderson, L. (1980). Effective management at the beginning of the school year. *Elementary School Journal, 80,* 219–231.

Emmer, E., Evertson, C., Sanford, J., Clements, B., & Worsham, M. (1981). *Organizing and managing the junior high school classroom.* Austin, TX: Research and Development Center for Teacher Education.

Englander, M. (1986). *Strategies for classroom discipline.* New York: Praeger.

Epstein, J. (1995). School/family/community partnerships: Caring for the children we share. *Phi Delta Kappan, 76,* 701–712.

Epstein, J., Coates, L., Salinas, K., Sanders, M., & Simon, B. (1997). *School, family, and community partnerships: Your handbook for action.* Thousand Oaks, CA: Sage.

Epstein, J., & Sanders, M. (1998). What we learn from international studies of school-family-community partnerships. *Childhood Education, 74,* 392–394.

Erikson, E. (1963). *Childhood and society* (2nd ed.). New York: Norton.

Erikson, E. (1968). *Identity, youth, and crisis.* New York: Norton.

Evertson, C. (1985). Training teachers in classroom management: An experimental study in secondary school classrooms. *Journal of Educational Research, 79,* 51–58.

Evertson, C., & Emmer, E. (1982a). Effective management at the beginning of the school year in junior high school classes. *Journal of Educational Psychology, 74,* 485–498.

Evertson, C., & Emmer, E. (1982b). Preventive classroom management. In D. Duke (Ed.), *Helping teachers manage classrooms.* Alexandria, VA: Association for Supervision and Curriculum Development.

Evertson, C., Emmer, E., Sanford, J., & Clements, B. (1983). Improving classroom management: An experiment in elementary school classrooms. *Elementary School Journal, 84,* 173–188.

Evertson, C., & Harris, A. (1992). Synthesis of research: What we know about managing classrooms. *Educational Leadership, 49,* 74–78.

Evertson, C., & Randolph, C. (1995). Classroom management in the learning-centered classroom. In A. C. Ornstein (Ed.), *Teaching: Theory and*

Practice (pp. 118–131). Boston: Allyn & Bacon.

Farmer, T., Farmer, E., & Gut, D. (1999). Implications of social development research for school-based interventions for aggressive youth with EBD. *Journal of Emotional and Behavioral Disorders*, 7, 130–136.

Fay, J., & Funk, D. (1995). *Teaching with love and logic*. Golden, CO: The Love and Logic Press.

Feather, N. (Ed.). (1982). *Expectations and actions*. Hillsdale, NJ: Erlbaum.

Feitler, F., & Tokar, E. (1992). Getting a handle on teacher stress: How bad is the problem? *Educational Leadership*, 49, 456–458.

Felsman, J., & Vaillant, G. (1987). Resilient children as adults: A 40-year study. In E. J. Anderson & B. J. Cohler (Eds.), *The Invulnerable Child*. New York: Guilford Press.

Fine, M., & Somerville, J. I. (Eds.). (1998). *Small schools, big imaginations: A creative look at urban public schools*. Chicago: Cross City Campaign for Urban School Reform.

Fisher, C., Berliner, D., Filby, N., Marliave, R., Cahen, L., & Dishaw, M. (1980). Teaching behaviors, academic learning time, and student achievement: An overview. In C. Denham & A. Lieberman (Eds.), *Time to learn* (pp. 7–32). Washington, DC: National Institute of Education.

Fisher, C., Filby, N., Marliave, R., Cahen, L., Dishaw, M., Moore, J., et al. (1978). *Teaching behaviors, academic learning time and student achievement* (Report of Phase III–B, Beginning Teacher Evaluation Study. Tech. Rep. V–1). San Francisco: Far West Laboratory for Educational Research and Development.

Ford, M. (1992). *Motivating humans: Goals, emotions, and personal agency beliefs*. Newbury Park, CA: Sage.

Frankland, C., Edmonson, H., & Turnbull, A. (2001). Positive behavioral support: Family, school, and community partnerships. *Beyond Behavior*, 11, 7–9.

Frericks, A. (1974, March). *Labeling of students by prospective teachers*. Paper presented at the American Educational Research Association Convention, Chicago.

Freeman, D., & Freeman, Y. (2001). *Between worlds: Access to second language acquisition*. Portsmouth, NH: Heinemann.

Freeman, Y., & Freeman, D. (2002). *Closing the achievement gap: How to reach

limited-formal-schooling and long-term English learners*. Portsmouth, NH: Heinemann.

Freiberg, J. (1996). From tourists to citizens in the classroom. *Educational Leadership*, 54, 32–36.

Freiberg, J. (Ed.). (1999). *Beyond behaviorism: Changing the classroom management paradigm*. Boston: Allyn & Bacon.

Freiberg, J., Stein, T., & Huang, S. (1995). Effects of a classroom management intervention on student achievement in inner-city elementary schools. *Educational Research and Evaluation*, 1, 36–66.

Frey, K., Hirschstein, M., & Guzzo, B. (2000). Second step: Preventing aggression by promoting social competence. *Journal of Emotional and Behavioral Disorders*, 8, 102–112.

Garbarino, J. (1999). *Lost boys: Why our sons turn violent and how we can save them*. New York: The Free Press.

Garcia, E. (1999). *Student cultural diversity: Understanding and meeting the challenge* (2nd ed.). Boston: Houghton Mifflin.

Gardner, H. (1999a). *Intelligence reframed: Multiple intelligences for the 21st century*. New York: Basic Books.

Gardner, H. (1999b). *The disciplined mind: What all students should understand*. New York: Simon & Schuster.

Gathercoal, F. (2001). *Judicious discipline* (5th ed.). San Francisco: Caddo Gap Press.

Gay, G. (1993). Ethnic minorities and educational equality. In J. Banks & C. Banks (Eds.), *Multicultural education*. Boston: Allyn & Bacon.

Gersten, R., & Jimenez, R. (1994). A delicate balance: Enhancing literature instruction for students of English as a second language. *The Reading Teacher*, 47, 439–449.

Gibbs, J. (2000). *Tribes: A new way of learning and being together*. Sausalito, CA: Center Source.

Gilmer, J. (1985). *Factors related to the success and failure of teacher assistance teams in elementary schools*. Unpublished doctoral dissertation, University of Arizona, Tucson.

Ginott, H. (1972). *Teacher and child: A book for parents and teachers*. New York: Macmillan.

Glasser, W. (1965). *Reality therapy*. New York: Harper and Row.

Glasser, W. (1986). *Control theory in the classroom*. New York: Harper and Row.

Glasser, W. (1988). On students' needs and team learning: A conversation with William Glasser: R. Brandt (Ed.), *Educational Leadership*, 45, 38–45.

Glasser, W. (1990). *The quality school: Managing students without coercion*. New York: Harper and Row.

Gold, Mark, S. (1995). *The good news about depression: Breakthrough medical treatments that can work for you*. New York: Bantam Books.

Goldstein, A. (1999, December 20). The victims: Never again. *Time*, 154, 53–57.

Goleman, D. (1995). *Emotional intelligence*. New York: Bantam Books.

Golly, A. (1994). The use and effects of alpha and beta commands in elementary classroom settings. Unpublished doctoral dissertation. University of Oregon.

Good, T. (1983). Classroom research: A decade of progress. *Educational Psychologist*, 18, 127–144.

Good, T., & Brophy, J. (1987). *Looking in classrooms* (4th ed.). New York: Harper and Row.

Good, T., & Brophy, J. (1994). *Looking in classrooms* (6th ed.). New York: Harper and Row.

Good, T., & Brophy, J. (2000). *Looking in classrooms* (8th ed.). New York: Longman.

Goodenow, C., & Grady, K. (1993). The relationship of school belonging and friends' values to academic motivation among urban adolescent students. *Journal of Experimental Education*, 62, 60–71.

Goodlad, J. (1983). A study of schooling: Some implications for school improvement. *Phi Delta Kappan*, 64, 552–558.

Goodlad, J. (1984). *A place called school: Prospects for the future*. New York: McGraw-Hill.

Gordon, C., Henry, G., Mashburn, A., & Ponder, B. (2001). *Pre-kindergarten longitudinal study: Findings from the 1999–2000 school year*. Atlanta, GA: Office of School Readiness.

Gordon, T. (1974). *Teacher effectiveness training*. New York: Wyden.

Grant, R. (1993). Strategic training using text headings to improve students' processing of content. *Journal of Reading*, 36, 382–388.

Greenberg, M., Domitrovich, C., & Bumbarger, B. (2001). The prevention of mental disorders in school-aged children: Current state of the field. *Prevention & Treatment*, 4, 1–62.

Greenspan, S. (1997). *The growth of the mind*. Reading, MA: Perseus Books.

Greenspan, S., & Wieder, S. (1998). *The child with special needs*. Reading, MA: Perseus Books.

Gresham, F. (1998). Social skills training: Should we raze, remodel, or rebuild? *Behavioral Disorders, 24,* 19–25.

Grossman, D., Neckermann, H., Koepsell, T., Liu, P., Asher, K., Beland, K., et al. (1997). Effectiveness of a violence prevention curriculum among children in elementary school: A randomized controlled trial. *Journal of the American Medical Association, 277,* 1605–1611.

Hale-Benson, J. (1986). *Black children: Their roots, culture and learning styles* (Rev. ed.). Baltimore: Johns Hopkins University Press.

Haley, P., & Berry, K. (1988). *Home and school as partners: Helping parents help their children.* Andover, MA: Regional Laboratory for Educational Improvement of the Northeast and Islands.

Hamayan, E. (1994). Language development of low-literacy students. In F. Genesee (Ed.), *Educating second language children: The whole child, the whole curriculum, the whole community* (pp. 278–300). New York: Cambridge Press.

Harrington, C., & Boardman, S. (1997). *Paths to success: Beating the odds in American society.* Cambridge, MA: Harvard University Press.

Hattie, J., Biggs, J., & Purdie, N. (1996). Effects of learning skills interventions on student learning: A meta-analysis. *Review of Educational Research, 66,* 99–136.

Hawkins, D., Doueck, H., & Lishner, D. (1988). Changing teaching practices in mainstream classrooms to improve bonding and behavior of low achievers. *American Educational Research Journal, 25,* 31–50.

Hayek, R. (1987). The teacher assistance team: A pre-referral support team. *Focus on Exceptional Children, 20,* 1–7.

Huggins, P., Manion, D., Shakarian, L., & Moen, L. (1997). *Multiple intelligences: Helping kids discover the many ways to be smart.* Longmont, CO: Sopris West.

Hyman, I., & Perone, D. (1998). The other side of school violence: Educator policies and practices that may contribute to student misbehavior. *Journal of School Psychology, 36,* 7–27.

Igoa, C. (1995). *The inner world of the immigrant child.* New York: St. Martin's Press.

Johns, B., & Carr, V. (1995). *Techniques for managing verbally and physically aggressive students.* Denver, CO: Love.

Johns, K., & Espinoza, C. (1996). Management strategies for culturally diverse classroom. Bloomington, IN: Phi Delta Kappa Educational Foundation.

Johnson, D., & Johnson, R. (1975). *Learning together and alone: Group theory and group skills.* Englewood Cliffs, NJ: Prentice-Hall.

Johnson, D., & Johnson, R. (1987). *Learning together and alone: Cooperative, competitive, and individualistic learning* (2nd ed.). Englewood Cliffs, NJ: Prentice Hall.

Johnson, D., & Johnson, R. (1991). *Teaching students to be peacemakers.* Edina, MN: Interaction Book Company.

Johnson, D., Johnson, R., & Holubec, E. (1993). *Cooperation in the classroom.* Edina, MN: Interaction Book Company.

Johnson, R., & Johnson, D. (1985). *Cooperative learning: Warm-ups, grouping strategies and group activities.* Edina, MN: Interaction Book Company.

Jones, F. (1987). *Positive classroom discipline.* New York: McGraw-Hill.

Jones, V. (1980). *Adolescents with behavior problems: Strategies for teaching, counseling, and parent involvement.* Boston: Allyn & Bacon.

Jones, V. (1982). Training teachers to be effective classroom managers. In D. Duke (Ed.), *Helping teachers manage classrooms* (pp. 52–68). Alexandria, VA: Association of Supervision and Curriculum Development.

Jones, V. (1986). Classroom management in the United States: Trends and critical issues. In D. Tattum (Ed.), *Management of disruptive pupil behaviour in schools* (pp. 69–90). Chichester, England: John Wiley & Sons.

Jones, V. (1987). Major components in a comprehensive program for seriously emotionally disturbed children. In R. Rutherford, M. Nelson, & S. Forness (Eds.), *Severe behavior disorders of children and youth* (pp. 94–121). Boston: Little, Brown.

Jones, V. (1991). Experienced teachers' assessment of classroom management skills presented in a summer course. *Journal of Instructional Psychology, 18,* 103–109.

Jones, V. (1996). Classroom management. In J. Silula (Ed.), *Handbook of Research on Teacher Education.* (2nd ed.) (pp. 503–521). New York: Macmillan.

Jones, V. (2002). Creating communities of support: The missing link in dealing with student behavior problems and reducing violence in schools. *Beyond Behavior, 11,* 16–19.

Jones, V. (in press). How do teachers learn to be effective classroom managers? In C. Evertson & C. Weinstein (Eds.), *Handbook for classroom management: Research, practice, and contemporary issues.* Mahwah, NJ: Lawrence Erlbaum.

Jones, V., Dohrn, E., & Dunn, C. (2004). *Creating effective programs for students with emotional and behavior disorders: Interdisciplinary approaches for adding meaning and hope to behavior change interventions.* Boston: Allyn & Bacon.

Jones, V., & Jones, L. (1991). *Responsible school discipline.* Boston: Allyn & Bacon.

Jones, V., & Waksman, S. (1985). *State of Oregon technical assistance paper on the identification and treatment of seriously emotionally disturbed students.* Salem: Oregon State Department of Education.

Justice Policy Institute. (2001). San Francisco, CA: Center on Juvenile and Criminal Justice.

Juvonen, J., & Graham, S. (2001). *Peer harassment in school: The plight of the vulnerable and victimized.* New York: Guilford Press.

Kagan, S. (1989). *Cooperative learning: Resources for teachers.* Laguna Niguel, CA: Resources for Teachers.

Kahle, J. (1990). Why girls don't know. In M. Rowe (Ed.), *What research says to the science teacher: The process of knowing.* Washington, DC: National Science Testing Association.

Kameenui, E., Carnine, D., Dixon, R., Simmons, D., & Coyne, M. (2002). *Effective teaching strategies that accommodate diverse learners* (2nd ed.). Upper Saddle River, NJ: Merrill Prentice Hall.

Kaplan, C. (1992). Teachers' punishment histories and their selection of disciplinary strategies. *Contemporary Psychology, 17* (3), 258–265.

Karr-Morse, R., & Wiley, M. (1997). *Ghosts from the nursery: Tracing the roots of violence.* New York: The Atlantic Monthly Press.

Kauffman, J. (1997). *Characteristics of emotional and behavioral disorders of children and youth* (6th ed.). Upper Saddle River, NJ: Merrill.

Kauffman, J. (2001). *Characteristics of emotional and behavioral disorders of children and youth* (7th ed.). Upper Saddle River, NJ: Merrill Prentice Hall.

Kauffman, J., & Burbach, H. (1997). On creating a climate of classroom civility. *Phi Delta Kappan, 79,* 320–325.

Kaufman, P., Bradby, D., & Owings, J. (1992). *National longitudinal study of 1988: Characteristics of at-risk students in NELS: 88.* Washington, DC: U.S.

Office of Education, Office of Educational Research and Improvement.

Kazdin, A. (1991). Effectiveness of psychotherapy with children and adolescents. *Journal of Consulting and Clinical Psychology, 59*, 785–798.

Kellam, S., Ling, X., Merisca, R., Brown, C., & Ialongo, N. (1998). The effect of level of aggression in the first grade classroom on the course and malleability of aggressive behavior in middle school. *Development and Psychopathology, 10*, 165–185.

Keller, B. (2000). Small schools found to cut price of poverty. *Education Week* (February 9), p. 6.

Kessler, R. (1998, August 13). Cited in M. Elias, "Rich or poor, more kids struggle with symptoms." *USA Today*, p. D1.

Kleinfeld, J. (1972). *Instructional style and the intellectual performance of Indian and Eskimo students.* Project No. I–J–027 (Final Report). Washington, DC: Office of Education, U.S. Department of Health, Education, and Welfare.

Klonsky, M. (1996). *Small schools: The numbers tell a story.* Small Schools Workshop: College of Education, University of Illinois at Chicago.

Kohn, A. (1991). Caring kids: The role of the schools. *Phi Delta Kappan, 72*, 496–506.

Kohn, A. (1993). *Punishment by rewards: The trouble with gold stars, incentive plans, A's, praise, and other bribes.* Boston: Houghton Mifflin.

Kohn, A. (1996). *Beyond discipline: From compliance to community.* Alexandria, VA: Association for Supervision and Curriculum Development.

Kounin, J. (1970). *Discipline and group management in classrooms.* New York: Holt, Rinehart and Winston.

Krathwohl, D., Bloom, B., & Masia, B. (1964). *Taxonomy of educational objectives, handbook II: Affective domain.* New York: David McKay.

Kusche, C., & Greenberg, M. (2000). *PATHS: Promoting alternative thinking strategies: A comprehensive curriculum for preventing bullying and increasing critical-thinking skills in grades K–6.* South Deerfield, MA: Channing Bete Company.

Kuykendall, C. (1992). *From rage to hope: Strategies for reclaiming Black and Hispanic students.* Bloomington, IN: National Education Service.

Kuykendall, C. (2003). *From rage to hope: Strategies for reclaiming Black and Hispanic students* (2nd ed.). Bloomington, IN: National Education Service.

LaBenne, W., & Green, B. (1969). *Educational implications of self-concept theory.* Pacific Palisades, CA: Goodyear.

Ladson-Billings, G. (1994). *The dreamkeepers: Successful teachers of African American children.* San Francisco: Jossey-Bass.

Laird, R., Jordan, K., Dodge, K., Pettit, G., & Bates, J. (2001). Peer rejection in childhood, involvement with antisocial peers in early adolescence, and the development of externalizing behavior problems. *Development and Psychopathology, 13*, 337–354.

Langdon, C. (1999). The fifth Phi Delta Kappan poll of teachers' attitudes toward the public schools. *Phi Delta Kappan, 8*, 611–620.

Lazear, D. (1999). *Eight ways of knowing: Teaching for multiple intelligences* (3rd ed.). Arlington Heights, IL: SkyLight Training and Publishing.

Lee, V. (1991, August). *Sexism in single-sex and co-educational secondary school classrooms.* Paper presented at the annual meeting of the American Sociological Association, Cincinnati, OH.

Lee, V., & Loeb, S. (2000). School size in Chicago elementary schools: Effects on teachers' attitudes and students' achievement. *American Educational Research Journal, 37*, 3–31.

Lewin, T. (1995, December 7). Parents poll shows child abuse to be more common. *New York Times*, p. B16.

Lewis, C., Schaps, E., & Watson, M. (1996). The caring classroom's academic edge. *Educational Leadership, 54*, 16–21.

Lewis, R., & St. John, N. (1974). Contribution of cross-racial friendship to minority group achievement in desegregated classrooms. *Sociometry, 37*, 79–91.

Lewis, T. (2001). Building infrastructure to enhance schoolwide systems of positive behavioral support: Essential features of technical assistance. *Beyond Behavior, 11*, 10–12.

Lewis, T., Sugai, G., & Colvin, G. (1998). Reducing problem behavior through a school-wide system of effective behavioral support: Investigation of a school-wide social skills training program and contextual interventions. *School Psychology Review, 27*, 446–459.

Lightfoot, S. L. (1983). *The good high school.* New York: Basic Books.

Lipsitz, J. (1984). *Successful schools for young adolescents.* New Brunswick, NJ: Transaction Books.

Long, N., & Morse, W. (1996). *Conflict in the classroom: The education of at-risk and troubled students.* Austin, TX: Pro-Ed.

Macias, J. (1987). The hidden curriculum of Papago teachers: American Indian strategies for mitigating cultural discontinuity in early school. In G. Spindler & L. Spindler (Eds.), *Interpretive ethnography of education: At home and abroad* (pp. 363–380). Hillsdale, NJ: Lawrence Erlbaum.

Maher, C. (1987). Involving behaviorally disordered adolescents in instructional planning: Effectiveness of the GOAL procedures. *Journal of Child and Adolescent Psychotherapy, 4*, 204–210.

Maple, F. (1977). *Shared decision making.* Beverly Hills, CA: Sage.

Martin, R., & Lauridsen, D. (1974). *Developing student discipline and motivation.* Champaign, IL: Research Press.

Maslow, A. (1968). *Toward a psychology of being.* New York: D. Van Nostrand.

Masterson, J., & Costello, J. (1980). *From borderline adolescent to functioning adult: The test of time.* New York: Brunner/Mazel.

Mastropieri, M., & Scruggs, T. (1991). *Teaching students ways to remember: Strategies for learning mnemonically.* Cambridge, MA: Brookline.

McCarthy, B. (1987). *The 4-MAT system: Teaching to learning styles with right/left mode techniques.* Barrington, IL: Excel.

McCaslin, M., & Good, T. (1992). Compliant cognition: The misalliance of management and instructional goals in current school reform. *Educational Researcher, 21* (3), 4–17.

McCaslin, M., & Good, T. (1996). *Listening to students.* New York: HarperCollins.

McKenzie, T., & Rushall, B. (1974). Effects of self-recording on attendance and performance in a competitive swimming training program. *Journal of Applied Behavior Analysis, 7*, 199–206.

McLaughlin, H. (1992, April). *Seeking solidarity and responsibility: The classroom contexts of control and negotiation.* Paper presented at the annual meeting of the American Educational Research Association, San Francisco. (ERIC Document Reproduction Service No. ED 349 644)

Meier, D. (1995). *The power of their ideas.* Boston: Beacon Press.

Mendler, A. (1992). *What do I do when . . . ? How to achieve discipline with dignity in the classroom.* Bloomington, IN: National Educational Services.

Morse, W. (1994). The role of caring in teaching children with behavior problems. *Contemporary Education*, *65*, 132–136.

Mortimore, P., & Sammons, P. (1987). New evidence on effective elementary schools. *Educational Leadership*, *45*, 4–8.

Murdick, N., & Gartin, B. (1993). How to handle students exhibiting violent behavior. *The Clearing House*, *66*, 278–280.

Nagel, N. (1996). *Learning through real-world problem solving*. Thousand Oaks, CA: Corwin.

Nagel, N. (2001). Empowering young students to become active citizens through real world problem solving. *Education and Democracy*, *14*, 6–9.

National Association for the Education of Young Children. (1997). *Leadership in early age and education*. Washington, DC: Author.

National Center for Education Statistics. (1996). *How safe are the public schools?* Washington, DC: U.S. Department of Education, Office of Educational Research and Improvement.

National Center for Education Statistics. (1999). *Indicators of school crime and safety, 1998*. Washington, DC: U.S. Department of Education, Office of Educational Research and Improvement.

National Center for Educational Statistics (2001). Indicators of school crime and safety, 2001. Washington, DC: U.S. Department of Education, Office of Educational Research and Improvement.

National Center for Education Statistics. (2002). *Indicators of school crime and safety, 2002*. Washington, DC: U.S. Department of Education, Office of Educational Research and Improvement.

Nelson, J. (1996). Designing schools to meet the needs of students who exhibit disruptive behavior. *Journal of Emotional and Behavioral Disorders*, *4*, 147–161.

Nelson, J., Crabtree, M., Marchand-Martella, N., & Martella, R. (1998). Teaching good behavior in the whole school. *Teaching Exceptional Children*, *30*, 4–9.

Nelson, J., & Roberts, M. (2000). Ongoing reciprocal teacher-student interactions involving disruptive behaviors in general education classrooms. *Journal of Emotional and Behavioral Disorders*, *8*, 27–37, 48.

Nelson, R., Martella, R., & Galand, B. (1998). The effects of teaching school expectations and establishing a consis-

tent consequence on formal office disciplinary actions. *Journal of Emotional and Behavioral Disorders*, *6*, 153–161.

Nichols, P. (1999). *Clear thinking: Talking back to whispering shadows*. Iowa City, IA: River Lights Publishers.

Nichols, P., & Shaw, M. (1999). *Whispering shadows: Think clearly and claim your personal power*. Iowa City, IA: River Lights Publishers.

Nickerson, C., Lollis, C., & Porter, E. (1980). *Miraculous me*. Seattle, WA: Comprehensive Health Education Foundation.

Nielson, G. (1983). *Borderline and acting out adolescents: A developmental approach*. New York: Human Sciences Press.

Nims, D., & Wilson, R. (1998). Violence prevention preparation: A survey of colleges of education and departments of teacher education. (ERIC Document Reproduction Service No. ED 418 052).

Noblit, G. (1993). Power and caring. *American Educational Research Journal*, *30*, 23–38.

Noddings, N. (1984). *Caring, a feminine approach to ethics and moral education*. Berkeley, CA: University of California Press.

Noddings, N. (1992). *The challenge to care in schools: An alternative approach to education*. New York: Teachers College Press.

Noguera, P. (1995). Preventing and producing violence: A critical analysis of responses to school violence. *Harvard Educational Review*, *65*, 189–212.

O'Leary, D., & O'Leary, S. (Eds.). (1977). *Classroom management: The successful use of behavior modification* (2nd ed.). New York: Pergamon Press.

Olsen, L., & Jaramillo, A. (Eds.), (1999). *Turning the tides of exclusion: A guide for educators and advocates for immigrant students*. Oakland, CA: Coast Litho.

O'Neil, J. (1991). A generation adrift? *Educational Leadership*, *49*, 4–10.

O'Neill, B., & Glass, D. (1994). *Kelso's choice: Conflict management for children*. Winchester, OR: Rhinestone Press.

Oregonian. (1996, September 4). Back to School. E1.

Paley, V. (1989). *White teacher*. Cambridge, MA: Harvard University Press.

Peregoy & Boyle (1993). As presented in Grant, R. (1995). Meeting the needs of young second language learners. In E. Garcia & B. McLaughlin (Eds.), *Meeting the challenge of linguistic and cultural diversity in early childhood education* (pp. 1–17). New York: Teachers College Press.

Petersen, R., Pietrzak, D., & Speaker, K. (1998). The enemy within: a national study on school violence and prevention. *Urban Education*, *33*, 331–359.

Phelan, P., Davidson, A., & Cao, H. (1992). Speaking up: Students' perspectives on school. *Phi Delta Kappan*, *73*, 695–704.

Pipher, M. (1994). *Reviving Ophelia: Saving the selves of adolescent girls*. New York: Ballatine Books.

Posthuma, B. (1999). *Small groups in counseling and therapy* (3rd ed.). Boston: Allyn & Bacon.

Postman, M., & Weingartner, D. (1969). *Teaching as a subversive activity*. New York: Delacorte.

Price, G. (1980). Which learning style elements are stable and which tend to change? *Learning Styles Network Newsletter*, *1*, 1.

Purcell-Gates, V. (1995). *Other people's words: The cycle of low literacy*. Cambridge, MA: Harvard University Press.

Purkey, W. (1970). *Self-concept and school achievement*. Englewood Cliffs, NJ: Prentice Hall.

Purkey, W., & Novak, J. (1984). *Inviting school success: A self-concept approach to teaching and learning* (2nd ed.). Belmont, CA: Wadsworth.

Ratzki, A. (1988). The remarkable impact of creating a school community. *American Educator*, *12*, 10–43.

Reiss, A., & Ross, J. (Eds.). (1994). *Understanding and preventing violence, volume 3: Social influences*. Washington, DC: National Academies Press.

Reyes, P., Scribner, J., & Scribner, A. (Eds.). (1999). *Lessons from high-performing Hispanic schools: Creating learning communities*. New York: Teachers College Press.

Rhodes, G., Jenson, W., & Reavis, H. (1993). *The tough kid book*. Longmont, CO: Sopris West.

Rimm-Kaufman, S., Pinata, R., & Cox, M. (2000). Teachers' judgments of problems in the transition to kindergarten. *Early Childhood Research Quarterly*, *15*, 147–167.

Roderick, T. (2001). *A school of our own: Parents, power, and community at the East Harlem block schools*. New York: Teachers College Press.

Roehler, L., Duffy, G., & Meloth, M. (1987). The effects and some distinguishing characteristics of explicit teacher explanation during reading instruction. In J. Niles (Ed.), *Changing perspectives on research in reading/language processing and instruction*.

Rochester, NY: National Reading Conference.

Rosenholtz, S., & Simpson, C. (1984). Classroom organization and student stratification. *Elementary School Journal, 85,* 21–37.

Rosenshine, B. (1980). How time is spent in elementary classrooms. In C. Denham & A. Lieberman (Eds.), *Time to learn.* Washington, DC: National Institute of Education.

Rosenshine, B. (1983). Teaching functions in instructional programs. *Elementary School Journal, 83,* 335–351.

Rosenthal, R., & Jacobson, L. (1968). *Pygmalion in the classroom: Teacher expectation and pupils' intellectual development.* New York: Holt, Rinehart and Winston.

Ross, J. (1994). *Triumph over fear: A book of help and hope for people with anxiety, panic attacks and phobias.* New York: Bantam Books.

Rowe, M. (1986). Wait time: Slowing down may be a way of speeding up! *Journal of Teacher Education, 37,* 43–50.

Roy, P. (1998, June). *Teacher behaviors that affect discipline referrals and off-task behavior.* Paper presented at the meeting of Annual Research Colloquium at the State University of West Georgia, Carrollton.

Rutter, M., Maughan, B., Mortimore, P., Ouston, J., & Smith, A. (1979). *Fifteen thousand hours.* Cambridge, MA: Harvard University Press.

Ryan, R., & Stiller, J. (1991). The social contexts of internalization: Parent and teacher influences on autonomy, motivation and learning. *Advances in Motivation and Achievement, 7,* 114–149.

Sadker, D., & Sadker, M. (1985). Is the o.k. classroom o.k.? *Phi Delta Kappan, 66,* 358–361.

Sandia National Laboratories. (1993). Future requirements: Workforce skills. *Journal of Educational Research, 86* (5), 293–297.

Sanford, J., Emmer, E., & Clements, B. (1983). Improving classroom management. *Educational Leadership, 41,* 56–60.

Schiraldi, V., & Ziedenberg, J. (2001). *Schools and suspensions: Self-reported crime and the growing use of suspension.* Washington, DC: Justice Policy Institute.

Schmuck, R. (1966). Some aspects of classroom social climate. *Psychology in the Schools, 3,* 59–65.

Schmuck, R., & Schmuck, P. (1974). *A humanistic psychology of education. Making the school everybody's house.* Palo Alto, CA: National Press Books.

Schmuck, R., & Schmuck, P. (2001). *Group processes in the classroom* (8th ed.). Boston: McGraw Hill.

Schneider, E. (1996). Giving students a voice in the classroom. *Educational Leadership, 54,* 22–26.

Schunk, D. (1983). Reward contingencies and the development of children's skills and self-efficacy. *Journal of Educational Psychology, 75,* 511–518.

Schwartz, B. (1988). The experimental synthesis of behavior: In G. H. Bower, (Ed.), *The psychology of learning and motivation* (p. 22). San Diego, CA: Academic Press.

Schwartz, D., Pettit, G., Dodge, K., & Bates, J. (2000). Friendship as a moderating factor in the pathway between early harsh home environment and later victimization in the peer group. *Developmental Psychology, 36,* 646–662.

Search Institute. (1998). *Healthy communities.* Minneapolis, MN: Author.

Seligman, M. (1995). *The optimistic child.* Boston: Houghton Mifflin.

Sergiovanni, T. (1994). *Building community in schools.* San Francisco: Jossey-Bass.

Shade, B. (1989). Afro-American cognitive patterns: A review of the research. In B. Shade (Ed.), *Cultural, style, and the educative process.* Springfield, IL: Charles C. Thomas.

Shimahara, N., & Sakai, A. (1995). *Learning to teach in two cultures: Japan and the United States.* New York: Garland.

Shinn, M., Stoner, G., & Walker, H. (Eds.). (2002). *Interventions for academic and behavior problems: Preventive and remedial approaches.* Silver Springs, MD: National Association of School Psychologists.

Shores, R., & Wehby, J. (1999). Analyzing the classroom social behavior of students with EBD. *Journal of Emotional and Behavioral Disorders, 7,* 194–199.

Skiba, R., Peterson, R., & Williams, T. (1997). Office referrals and suspension: Disciplinary intervention in middle schools. *Education and Treatment of Children, 20,* 295–315.

Slaby, R., Roedell, W., Arezzo, D., & Hendrix, K. (1995). *Early violence prevention: Tools for teachers of young children.* Washington, DC: National Association for the Education of Young Children.

Sleeter, C. (Ed.). (1991). *Empowerment through multicultural education.* New York: Albany State University Press.

Smith, B., & Sugai, G. (2000). A self-management functional assessment-based behavior support plan for a middle school student with EBD. *Journal of Positive Behavioral Support, 2,* 208–217.

Smith, G. (2002). Place-based education: Learning where we are. *Phi Delta Kappan, 83,* 584–594.

Smith, W. (1936). *Constructive school discipline.* New York: American Book Company.

Spencer-Hall, D. (1981). Looking behind the teacher's back. *Elementary School Journal, 81,* 281–289.

Stallings, J., & Mohlman, G. (1981). *Principal leadership style, school policy, teacher change and student behavior in eight secondary schools* (Final Report). Washington, DC: National Institute of Education.

Steiner, C. (1977). *The original warm fuzzy tale.* Sacramento, CA: Jalmar Press.

Steiner, C. (1983). *The original warm fuzzy tale.* Sacramento, CA: Jalmar.

Stiggins, R. (2001). Student-involved classroom assessment (3rd ed.). Upper Saddle River, NJ: Merrill Prentice Hall.

Stipek, D. (1988). *Motivation to learn: From theory to practice.* Englewood Cliffs, NJ: Prentice Hall.

Stoiber, K. (1991). The effect of technical and reflective preservice instruction on pedagogical reasoning and problem solving. *Journal of Teacher Education, 42* (2), 131–139.

Sugai, G. (1997). School-wide behavioral systems. *Research Connections in Special Education, 1,* 1–8.

Sugai, G., & Horner, R. (1999). Discipline and behavioral support: Preferred processes and practices. *Preventing School Failure, 43,* 6–13.

Sugai, G., Horner, R., & Gresham, F. (2002). Behaviorally effective school environments. In M. R. Shinn, G. Stoner, & H. M. Walker (Eds.), *Interventions for academic and behavior problems: Preventive and remedial approaches* (pp. 315–350). Silver Springs, MD: National Association of School Psychologists.

Sugai, G., & Horner, R. (2001). Features of an effective behavior support at the school district level. *Beyond Behavior, 11,* 16–19.

Sugai, G., Kameenui, E., & Colvin, G. (1993). *Project PREPARE: Promoting responsible, empirical and proactive alternatives in regular education for students with behavior disorders.* Unpublished data. Eugene: University of Oregon, College of Education.

Sullivan, (1988). Special study groups: Motivating underachievers. *Middle School Journal, 19,* 20–21.

Sylwester, R. (1999). In search of the roots of adolescent aggression. *Educational Leadership, 57,* 65–69.

Sylwester, R. (2000). *A biological brain in a cultural classroom.* Thousand Oaks, CA: Corwin Press.

Testerman, J. (1996). Holding at-risk students: The secret is one-one-one. *Phi Delta Kappan, 77,* 364–366.

Tetreault, M. (1993). Classrooms for diversity: Rethinking curriculum and pedagogy. In J. Banks & C. McGee Banks (Eds.), *Multicultural education.* Boston: Allyn & Bacon.

The 2000 Annual Report on School Safety. (2000). Washington, DC: U.S. Department of Education and U.S. Department of Justice.

Thomas, W., & Collier, V. (1997). *School effectiveness for language minority students.* Washington, DC: National Clearinghouse of Bilingual Education.

Tobin, K. (1987). The role of wait time in higher cognitive level learning. *Review of Educational Research, 57,* 69–95.

Toby, J. (1993, Winter). Everyday school violence: How disorder fuels it. *American Educator,* 46.

Tomal, D. (1998, October). *A five-styles teacher discipline model.* Paper presented at the annual meeting of the Midwestern Educational Research Association, Chicago, IL.

Tomlinson, C. (1999). *The differentiated classroom: Responding to the needs of all learners.* Alexandria, VA: Association for Supervision and Curriculum Development.

Tomlinson, C., & Kalbfleisch, M. (1998). Teach me, teach my brain: A call for differentiated instruction. *Educational Leadership, 56,* 52–55.

Topper, K., Williams, W., Leo, K., Hamilton, R., & Fox, T. (1994). *A positive approach to understanding and addressing challenging behaviors: Supporting educators and families to include students with emotional and behavioral difficulties in regular education.* Burlington, VT: Center for Developmental Disabilities, University of Vermont.

Turnbaugh, A. (1986). A view from the center. *National Center on Effective Secondary Schools Newsletter, 1,* 8–10.

Valdez, G. (2001). *Learning and not learning English: Latino students in American schools.* New York: Teachers College Press.

Vernelle, B. (1994). *Understanding and using groups.* London: Whiting Birch.

Wager, B. R. (1993). No more suspensions: Creating a shared ethical community. *Educational Leadership, 50*(4), 34–37.

Walker, H., & Buckley, N. (1973). Teacher attention to appropriate and inappropriate classroom behavior: An individual case study. *Focus on Exceptional Children, 5,* 5–11.

Walker, H., Colvin, G., & Ramsey, E. (1995). *Antisocial behavior in school: Strategies and best practices.* Pacific Grove, CA: Brooks/Cole.

Walker, H., Hops, H., & Fiegenbaum, E. (1976). Deviant classroom behavior as a function of combinations of social and token reinforcement and cost contingency. *Behavior Therapy, 7,* 76–88.

Walker, H., & Sylwester, R. (1998). Reducing students' refusal and resistance. *Teaching Exceptional Children, 30,* 52–58.

Walqui, A. (2000). *Strategies for success: engaging immigrant students in secondary schools.* ERIC Report EDO-FLO-00-03. Washington, DC: Center for Applied Linguistics.

Wang, M., Haertel, G., & Walberg, H. (1993). Toward a knowledge base for school learning. *Review of Educational Research, 63,* 249–294.

Ward, J. (1995). Cultivating a morality of care in African American adolescents: A culture-based model of violence prevention. *Harvard Educational Review, 65,* 175–188.

Wasley, P., Fine, M., Gladden, M., Holland, N., King, S., Mosak, E., et al. (2000). *Small Schools: Great Strides.* New York: Bank Street College of Education.

Wayson, W., & Pinnell, G. (1982). Creating a living curriculum for teaching self-discipline. In D. Duke (Ed.), *Helping teachers manage classrooms.* Alexandria, VA: Association for Supervision and Curriculum Development.

Webber, J., Scheuermann, B., McCall, C., & Coleman, M. (1994). Research on self-monitoring as a behavior management technique in special education classrooms: A descriptive review. *Remedial and Special Education, 14,* 38–56.

Wehby, J., Symons, F., & Shores, R. (1995). A descriptive analysis of aggressive behavior in classrooms for children with emotional and behavioral disorders. *Behavioral Disorders, 20,* 87–105.

Wehlage, G., Rutter, R., Smith, G., Lesko, N., & Fernandez, R. (1989).

Reducing the risk: Schools as communities of support. Philadelphia: Falmer Press.

Weiner, B. (1979). A theory of motivation for some classroom experiences. *Journal of Educational Psychology, 71,* 3–25.

Weiner, B. (1990). History of motivational research in education. *Journal of Educational Psychology, 82,* 177–188.

Werner, E., & Smith, R. (1992). *Overcoming the odds: High risk children from birth to adulthood.* Ithaca, NY: Cornell University Press.

Williams, D. (1992). Parental involvement teacher preparation: Challenges to teacher education. In L. Kaplan (Ed.), *Education and the family.* Boston: Allyn & Bacon.

Wineburg, S. (1987). The self-fulfilling prophecy. *Educational Researcher, 16,* 28–37.

Winitzky, N. (1992). Structure and process in thinking about classroom management: An exploratory study of prospective teachers. *Teaching and Teacher Education, 8* (1), 1–14.

Wlodkowski, R., & Ginsberg, M. (1995). A framework for culturally responsive teaching. *Educational Leadership, 53,* 17–21.

Wolery, M., Bailey, D., & Sugai, G. (1998). *Effective teaching: Principles and procedures of applied behavior analysis with exceptional students.* Boston: Allyn & Bacon.

Wolery, M., Werts, M., Caldwell, M., Snyder, N., & Lisowski, L. (1995). Experienced teachers' perceptions of resources and supports for inclusion. *Education and Training in Mental Retardation and Developmental Disabilities, 30,* 15–26.

Workman, E. (1995). *Teaching behavioral self-control to students.* Austin, TX: Pro-Ed.

Workplace Essential Skills. (2002). Washington, DC: Employment and Training Administration, Office of Policy and Research, Office of Education Research and Improvement (ED).

Yaffe, E. (1995). Expensive, illegal, and wrong: Sexual harassment in our schools. *Phi Delta Kappan, 77,* 3, K1–K15.

Yoshikawa, H. (1994). Prevention as cumulative protection: Effects of early family support and education on chronic delinquency and its risks. *Psychological Bulletin, 115,* 28–54.

Zirpoli, T., & Melloy, K. (2001). *Behavior management applications for teachers* (3rd ed.). Upper Saddle River, NJ: Merrill Prentice Hall.

NAME INDEX